D'YOUVILLE COLLEGE
LIBRARY

# DOING BUSINESS INTERNATIONALLY
## The Resource Book to Business and Social Etiquette

© TRAINING MANAGEMENT CORPORATION
All rights reserved.

Printed in U.S.A.
by Princeton Training Press
May 1997

ISBN # 1-882390-12-1

## Princeton Training Press

600 Alexander Road, Building 2 ■ Princeton, New Jersey 08540 U.S.A.
Tel: 609-951-9319 ■ Fax: 609-951-0395
Email: ptp@tmcorp.com
Website: http://www.tmcorp.com

# DOING BUSINESS INTERNATIONALLY
## The Resource Book to Business and Social Etiquette

© TRAINING MANAGEMENT CORPORATION
All rights reserved.

Printed in U.S.A.
by Princeton Training Press
May 1997

ISBN # 1-882390-12-1

## Princeton Training Press

600 Alexander Road, Building 2 ■ Princeton, New Jersey 08540 U.S.A.

HF 5389
.D65
1997
c.2

# TABLE OF CONTENTS

JAN 12 1998

# TABLE OF CONTENTS (Cont'd)

## ASIA AND THE PACIFIC continued

## EUROPE

# ADDITIONAL INFORMATION FOR INTERNATIONAL BUSINESS

# SOURCE MATERIALS AND USEFUL INFORMATION

# DOING BUSINESS INTERNATIONALLY SERIES

# Introduction

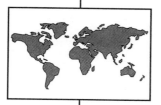

With increasing globalization, people in all levels and functions of organizations are coming into contact with international customers, suppliers, partners and colleagues. On a daily basis, business people working in the United States may find themselves communicating by phone, voicemail, fax or electronic mail, with individuals in Africa, Asia, Europe, the Middle East, Central and South America, Mexico and/or Canada. These same men or women may be interacting in crucial meetings attended by people from around the world or traveling to the site of an international negotiation, conference or global team-building session. Increasingly, business people are being relocated internationally on short- or long-term assignments, managing staff in multiple international locations or becoming involved in joint venture partnerships to gain access to the latest technology or entree to emerging markets. Business trip itineraries can take today's executives from Beijing to Bombay with stops in Hong Kong, Jakarta, Manila, Singapore, Penang, Bangkok and Dhaka along the way. Nine stops with nine distinct cultures, histories and political traditions representing a range of religious and philosophical beliefs.

Confronted with such complexity, the international businessperson may feel overwhelmed. While recognizing the importance of knowing something about the people he or she is doing business with, there simply isn't enough time in the day to become expert in every country or culture. Nor is there enough room in any business traveler's luggage to pack a specific book on each destination. Training Management Corporation's *Doing Business Internationally: The Resource Book to Business and Social Etiquette* was designed with the aforementioned business people in mind. Whether it serves as a handy reference guide for the stay-in-the-office businessperson communicating at a distance with international sites or is taken on the road, this book offers guidance on how to interact with people from over 85 countries around the world.

# INTRODUCTION

Organized by region as well as alphabetized by country, each country section features a historical overview and guidelines on introductions, social tips and conventions, customary business practices, business entertaining, dining out and public customs. These guidelines offer insights into protocol and etiquette, cultural preferences and styles of interaction.

In using a book such as this, there are a number of things to keep in mind. Cultures are made up of individuals. These individuals may be different according to the part of the country they come from, their age, gender, religion, educational level, job function, their exposure to other cultures and/or social class. Depending on the culture, people may behave differently according to the specific situation (planning meetings among peers vs. meetings involving executives and customers), location (hosting a meeting vs. being a guest) or the people involved (depending on such criteria as status, type of relationship or degree of familiarity). Therefore, the guidelines given in this book should be thought of as a starting point for an interaction rather than an absolute set of do's and don'ts.

One strategy for using this resource book is to share it with colleagues and contacts, natives or long-term residents, in the country or culture, and ask for their responses to the information included. Encourage them to offer advice based on the book, suggest priorities or apply the guidelines to specific business situations. Used in this way, the resource book becomes a tool for discussing cultural characteristics and protocol, and provides a vocabulary and format for having such discussions with cultural informants. Since each individual may have a unique understanding of his/her own culture, it is advisable to ask a number of people their perspectives and then build a picture of what is the most appropriate approach for working with people from or in a particular country. Non-natives with extensive experience living and/or working in the country can also offer valuable advice but today's international businessperson should develop a healthy skepticism. The ideal is to balance the advice of natives and non-natives to gain a more well-rounded understanding and not to become blinded by stereotypes and fixed assumptions.

The information contained in this book is most effectively used by individuals who demonstrate curiosity, flexibility, adaptability, receptivity, patience and a nonjudgmental attitude towards people from other cultures. Cultivating an open mind, developing a learning-to-learn attitude, and becoming a keen observer of behavior and communication styles across cultures is more important in cross-cultural interactions than memorizing protocol. Trying to adjust to the expectations of others shows positive intentions and goodwill, but everyone working in the international arena will make mistakes and inadvertently offend others. The key is to learn from mistakes and use them as an opportunity to build relationships and gain enhanced understanding.

When doing business internationally, cultural differences cannot be ignored. Cultural differences can impact every aspect of business from expectations regarding the role of a manager to the strategies used during negotiations. Quite simply, culture can be defined as the dominant set of behaviors, values, beliefs and thinking patterns an individual learns growing up in a culture or social group. While this book does not attempt to list the cultural attributes and values of each country, implicit in the guidelines given are cultural preferences and orientations. By using the cultural orientations model developed by Training Management Corporation, cultures can be analyzed according to their orientations to the ten variables of Environment, Time, Action, Communication, Space, Power, Individualism,

# INTRODUCTION

Competitiveness, Structure and Thinking. The combination of the country-specific information along with an understanding of the ten variables can assist global business people in assessing the obstacles and challenges they may confront in doing business cross-culturally and help determine areas for development and adaptation of business skills and strategies. Again, it is important to remember that while a culture, in general, may prefer one orientation to another, individuals within the culture may not share that value orientation.

On a fundamental level, cultures are slow to change yet business and social customs do evolve over time. In today's fast-paced world with contacts between cultures increasing exponentially, the change process has become accelerated. Particularly in emerging markets and countries moving from communist to capitalist economies, the approach to business is shifting dramatically. In some respects, a book such as this one becomes dated the moment it is printed. Because of this, TMC is committed to periodic updates of this material and we welcome feedback and comments on the contents of this book. Personal experiences and anecdotes, examples of where certain etiquette may be outdated, or specific recommendations on situations when a foreign businessperson needs to adapt to the local customs can be sent to us at:

**Training Management Corporation**
600 Alexander Road, Building 2
Princeton, New Jersey 08540 U.S.A.

or by email at:
info@tmcorp.com

For further information, visit TMC's website at http://www.tmcorp.com
*We look forward to hearing from you.*

### *Acknowledgments*

We wish to thank the following individuals for their contribution to our <u>Doing Business Internationally: The Resource Book to Business and Social Etiquette</u>:

Jane A. Silverman, President
Danielle M. Walker, Executive Vice President
Pamela L. Leri, Vice President, Global Management Development & Training
Richard A. Punzo, Vice President, International Learning Systems
Rose A. Babau, Director, Operations
Gail M. Goldfinger, Manager, Product Development
Laurie A. Quinn, Manager, Design
Melinda S. Hall, Global Programs Coordinator
Louise K. Forman, Manager, Project Management Programs
Jan A. Miller, Freelance Review Editor
Elana Hahn, Research Assistant
Akel Kahera, Research Assistant
Fred Lohr, Research Assistant

For further information, visit IMC's website ... _We look forward to learning from you._

## Acknowledgments

We wish to thank the following individuals for their contribution to our _Doing Business Internationally: The Resource Book to Business and Social Etiquette:_

Jane A. Silverman, President
Danielle M. Walker, Executive Vice President
Pamela L. Lori, Vice President, Global Management Development & Training
Richard A. Punzo, Vice President, International Learning Systems
Rose A. Babau, Director, Operations
Gail M. Goldfinger, Manager, Product Development
Laurie A. Quinn, Manager, Design
Melinda S. Hall, Global Programs Coordinator
Louise K. Forman, Manager, Project Management Programs
Jan A. Miller, Freelance Review Editor
Elana Hahn, Research Assistant
Akel Kahera, Research Assistant
Fred Lohr, Research Assistant

# Country Specific Information

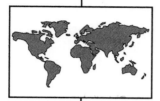

**Minimize Regret:** This principle should act as your guide as you seek to do business with people from another country. A single wrong gesture or remark may not cause you to lose a deal but continual rudeness and a lack of empathy might well do so. Prepare for a cross-cultural encounter with purpose and thoroughness. Take nothing for granted. *Build relationships and your business will build itself.*

| | |
|---|---|

*Throughout this section, we have used the term "host" to refer to either a man or a woman who is hosting a business guest or guests. The exception to the use of "host" in a gender neutral manner is in some Middle Eastern and Asian countries, where the host is almost always a male.*

# ETIQUETTE GUIDELINES

You cannot prepare for every possible *faux pas.* But you can and should keep the following guidelines in mind.

| GUIDELINES | DESCRIPTION |
|---|---|
| Be Formal | • Be more polite and formal in a foreign culture than you would be in your own. Stay formal until you are invited to be more familiar. |
| Communicate Respect | • Take time to learn names and titles and their correct pronunciations.<br>• Learn some of the host country's language.<br>• Don't insult the host by simply talking louder if he or she doesn't appear to understand.<br>• Learn the culture's customs regarding the giving of gifts (also know your company's policy towards gift-giving as well as any legal restrictions of your own or your host's country).<br>• Criticism in public may cause someone to lose face. Know when, where and how to confront.<br>• Handle business cards with care.<br>• Dress somewhat conservatively; better to be safe than sorry. |
| Show Patience | • Don't expect to be received on time wherever you go.<br>• Impatience may cause you and your host stress, destroy the relationship and lose you business. |
| Be Gracious | • Accept and give appropriate hospitality. When entertaining, understand local customs in relation to alcohol and appropriate foods.<br>• You are a representative of your culture and your company twenty-four hours a day. |
| Prepare Well and Seek Confirmation | • Learn about the foreign culture before making your visit. Whenever you can, check your understanding. |

# AFRICA

# THE MIDDLE EAST

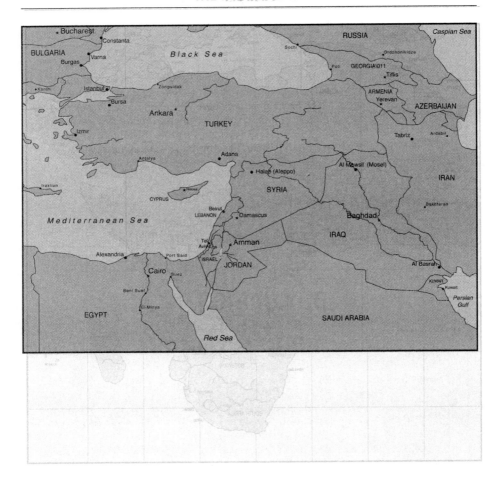

# ALGERIA: HISTORICAL OVERVIEW

- The earliest inhabitants of Algeria were the Berbers, who still account for a significant minority of the population. The region was later controlled successively by the Phoenicians, the Romans and the Vandals.

- The Umayyads (Arabs) invaded the country in 600 A.D. and introduced Islam to the Berbers. The cities of Algiers, Oran, Constantine and Annaba developed during the period of Arab conquest. When the Berbers regained control in the eighth century, they established their own Islamic Empire. Several Berber empires flourished until the 13th century.

- In the 1200s, Bedouins migrated to the area and the local population adopted the Bedouin nomadic lifestyle. From the early 1500s, the area was part of the Ottoman Empire. However, since Algeria was quite far from the center of the empire (Turkey), there was significant local control and relations with European powers developed.

- France invaded in 1830 which resulted in the establishment of Algeria's present borders in 1902. French colonization was widespread, but a fierce independence movement developed and open warfare eventually broke out in 1954. Finally, Algeria became an independent state in 1962. When the French army withdrew, nearly one million European colonists evacuated.

- Following an eight-year conflict with Arab nationalists (from 1954-1962), Algeria received independence from France. The new government was led by Ahmed Ben Bella, a member of the *National Liberation Front* (*FLN*). A leftist, Ben Bella nevertheless outlawed the communist party and shortly thereafter was elected president. He undertook a number of reforms, including the redistribution of land.

- Conflict within the *FLN* led to the removal of Ben Bella in 1965. He was replaced by Colonel Houari Boumedienne, who promptly dissolved the National Assembly and suspended the constitution. Boumedienne established a 26-man Revolutionary Council to assist him. He managed to avert a 1967 attempted coup and a 1968 plot to assassinate him.

- Boumedienne died in December 1978 and was succeeded by Colonel Chadli Bendjedid, who became not only president but also Secretary General of the *FLN*.

- In early 1980, Algeria endured riots by Muslim fundamentalists. The *FLN* was squandering earnings from oil, failing to invest in the future. Unemployment climbed to 30% and corruption in the government was widespread. Many people turned to Islamic fundamentalism.

- The Muslims increased the frequency of their violence and terror, much of it directed against women. Muslims, split into many factions, contributed to the victory of the military's candidate, General Liamine Zeroual, in the 1995 presidential election.

- President Zeroual attempted to reach out to the Muslims and achieve a national reconciliation, but this was a hugely difficult task. The political crises had a devastating effect on the Algerian economy, which in 1996 was in a downslide of 5%-7%.

# ALGERIA

## INTRODUCTIONS

A warm and firm handshake is the most common greeting. However, you should keep in mind that religious men never shake hands with women. A handshake is sometimes accompanied by an embrace.

Close friends of the same sex often kiss each other when greeting.

When addressing someone, one should use the last name preceded by the English title "Mr.," "Mrs." or "Miss." It is also a good idea to use professional titles, such as "Doctor," "Professor," "Engineer," "Architect" or "Attorney," when appropriate. One may also use the French titles *"Monsieur"* ("Mr."), *"Madame"* ("Mrs."), *"Mademoiselle"* ("Miss"), *"Docteur"* ("Doctor"), *"Professeur"* ("Professor"), *"Avocat"* ("Lawyer"), etc.

If one uses an Arabic title, the title should be used with the first name. Arabic titles include *"Say-yeéd"* ("Mr."), *"Zów-gah"* ("Mrs."), *"Oo-stéz"* or *"Pro-fes-sór"* ("Professor"), *"Doctór"* ("Doctor") or *"Moo-háhn-dis"* ("Engineer," "Architect" or "Attorney"). There is no Arabic equivalent for "Miss." Instead, simply use the French title *"Mademoiselle."*

In small gatherings, it is polite to greet each individual. Elders are greeted first.

## SOCIAL TIPS AND CONVENTIONS

Algeria is not only the largest country in the *Maghreb* (Algeria, Morocco and Tunisia), but it is also the most conservative. The population is almost entirely Muslim. The three main languages are Arabic (the official language), French (the language of the administrative and intellectual elite) and Berber. People often mix these languages when speaking.

Algerians are formal and traditional. They are also quite expressive and individualistic. Expressiveness, courtesy, individualism and formality are all key attributes of the Algerian character.

The society is male dominated and sex roles are clearly defined. Only about 10% of the labor force is female. Nevertheless, some women do fill important positions in public and private professions.

One should not discuss a person's family or members of the opposite sex unless the host suggests this topic. Instead of discussing personal issues, focus on the country as a whole or the area in which one is located. Algerians will appreciate comments on the beauties of the country or the quality of the food. Algerians will also appreciate hearing interesting stories about life in your country. Considerable time is usually spent discussing weather, health or the latest news. Soccer is a favorite sport in Algeria; discussing it is a good way of starting a conversation.

Avoid bringing up anything that has to do with France since most Algerians are sensitive about their colonial past. Also avoid mentioning religion or any Middle East situation.

Because Algeria is predominantly Muslim, remember to use only the right hand to touch food or people or to pass objects. The left hand is reserved for personal hygiene. The right hand or both hands together may be used when passing or receiving objects.

Algerians are hospitable to foreigners, due to a blend of warm Arabic and Gallic customs.

# ALGERIA (Cont'd)

## CUSTOMARY BUSINESS PRACTICES

You should be prepared to make several trips to Algeria to accomplish your goal. Almost all business dealings involve Algerian government organizations, which can be very bureaucratic. Both the State Planning Secretariat and the Ministry of Finance must approve all contracts with foreign companies. Approval, above all, requires some Algerian investment (100% foreign-owned companies will not meet with much success).

It is advisable to have contacts in Algeria for making introductions to Algerian companies. The Commercial Section of the U.S. embassy in Algeria, the National U.S.-Arab Chamber of Commerce and the Algerian Mission at the United Nations can be helpful for establishing contacts.

Try to make appointments well in advance (one or two months), even if your Algerian colleagues resist making such a commitment. Be aware that most Algerian businesses use telexes instead of fax machines. Most hotels, however, offer fax machine service.

It is advisable to try to arrange appointments between 9:00 a.m. and noon. Even though Algerian businesspeople tend to be late for appointments, you should be punctual. This will impress your colleagues, and it is especially important when dealing with top-level executives.

The first business meeting will usually begin with a general discussion about your respective companies, rather than moving directly to the business at hand. You should express interest in the Algerian company and be prepared to talk about your own. You should emphasize your company's accomplishments and completed projects as well as the benefits that Algeria will realize by working with your company.

Algerian contracts will be written in great detail. Performance requirements, deadline dates and other obligations will be included. To protect yourself, it is advisable to pay a good deal of attention to the details of the contract and to allow twice as much time for a project as you would in the U.S. or Europe. It is common for a contract to require a foreign company to pay a penalty if obligations are not fulfilled. This is true even if it is because the Algerian company has not fulfilled its own obligations to the foreign company.

While traditional attitudes toward women may prevail in Algeria, businesswomen should expect to be accepted and treated with respect in Algiers.

You should have your business cards translated into either French or Arabic. Also, have any materials you plan to use in presentations translated into French.

It is advisable to hire an interpreter if you are not fluent in French and your counterparts are not fluent in English.

Business attire for men is a suit and tie. Women should wear a simple but elegant suit and comfortable shoes (not high heels).

During the winter, business hours are Saturday to Thursday, 8:00 a.m. to noon and 2:00 to 5:30 p.m. During the summer, business hours are 8:00 a.m. to noon and 3:00 to 5:30 p.m. During *Ramadan*, hours are 9:00 a.m. to 4:00 p.m.

# ALGERIA (Cont'd)

## BUSINESS ENTERTAINING

Business dinners are more popular than lunches because of the intense heat in the middle of the day. Customarily, the person who issues an invitation to a restaurant pays for everything. There are a variety of restaurants in Algeria, including those that serve French and Algerian cuisine as well as others that serve Thai, Chinese and Vietnamese food. To entertain a businessman, it is best to take him to a restaurant in one of the best hotels or to a seafood restaurant near the beach.

If you are a businessman traveling with your wife, feel free to ask an Algerian businessman if he would like his wife to join both of you for dinner. If he is conservative, he will probably refuse, but he won't be offended that you asked.

In Algiers, there are a lot of French-style cafés. Women may go into these cafés either alone or with friends. However, in other towns, women should not go into cafés even with friends.

Be aware that alcohol, including Algerian wine, is available only in international hotels. If you are in a restaurant with an Algerian with whom you are negotiating and you are not sure if the person drinks alcohol, refrain from ordering an alcoholic beverage. Such a *faux pas* could cause you to lose the deal.

Do not be surprised if you are invited to stay with your Algerian colleague's family once your contract is signed. However, he will not issue such an invitation before negotiations are complete, so as not to show favoritism during the negotiating process.

If you are invited to dinner in a home by members of the older generation, it is recommended that you bring pastries such as *napoleons* or *millefeuilles*. But if the invitation is from young people, it is appropriate to bring flowers. Good choices are pink or red roses or tulips. You should not bring violets since they are associated with sadness.

Appreciated gifts from abroad include cameras, instant coffee, jeans, good quality sunglasses, T-shirts, running shoes, good quality chocolates, whiskey (if you know the person drinks alcohol) or cigarettes.

For a meal at a home or a party, men should wear suits and ties. Women should wear dinner or cocktail dresses that fall below the knee. Women should remember not to wear anything revealing.

## DINING OUT

Since the state owns most restaurants, the quality of service can vary.

You can call the waiter by saying *"Garçon."*

At restaurants, a 15% service charge is normally included in the bill. Any extra tip is optional.

# ALGERIA (Cont'd)

## DINING OUT (Cont'd)

Breakfast, served between 7:00 and 8:00 a.m., consists of *baguettes*, *galettes* (a thick Syrian bread), *croissants* or *brioches* with butter or jam. The usual drink is *café au lait* with strong Turkish coffee and boiled milk. Lunch, the main meal of the day, is served between noon and 2:00 p.m. Usually the meal includes soup, salad, *couscous*, fruit and coffee. On special occasions a pastry will be served for dessert. People usually drink soda or water with the meal.

Dinner is normally served at about 7:00 p.m. in the winter (December to February) and 8:00 or 8:30 p.m. in the summer (June to August). Dinner is a light meal, which usually consists of *couscous* with various sauces, *makatafa* (a soup made of lamb, tomatoes and herbs) and *torta* (turnovers filled with ground lamb, cheese and parsley). Oranges, melons and grapes are popular fruits, which are served with meals. Typically, *baguettes* (long French loaves) are also served.

People usually drink water, milk or a kind of buttermilk called *l'ben*. If you want Algerian bottled spring water, you should ask for *saida* (pronounced "sye-dah"). Algerian beer, which comes in unmarked bottles is very weak and watery. In Algeria, you should only drink bottled water and similarly should not use ice cubes or eat raw fruit or vegetables which cannot be peeled.

There is a great variety of Algerian food, which has a strong Gallic flavor. Lamb, chicken, stews and pastas are popular. The most popular Algerian dish is *couscous*, a pasta-like semolina cooked with lamb or chicken and vegetables. Muslims do not eat pork.

Appetizers and drinks are very rarely served before a meal. Also, when guests are present at a meal, men and women will dine apart. Do not expect a special seat, even if you are the guest of honor.

Different styles of eating are used in Algeria. Some people sit on low couches with a big table in the middle; some sit on mats on the floor around a low table; still others sit on chairs around a standard dining table.

Some people eat with cutlery, while others use the right hand. The use of utensils usually depends on the dish being served. *Couscous* is always eaten with a large spoon. Steak is eaten with a fork and knife. Stew is eaten with a fork while the sauce is scooped up with bread.

It is impolite to refuse food or refreshments. If a guest is unable to eat what is offered, he/she may ask for a substitute.

Algerians are complimented when a guest leaves a little food on his/her plate, as this is a sign of the host's ability to more than adequately provide for his guests.

Normally, guests do not leave immediately after dinner. They usually remain up to two hours after the meal.

*Doing Business Internationally*

# ALGERIA (Cont'd)

## PUBLIC CUSTOMS

While Western-style clothing is common, especially in urban areas, traditional North African Muslim clothing is also prominent. In public, it is proper for all people to dress conservatively and modestly. For casual dress in public, women should not wear jeans, shorts or slacks. Instead, it is advisable for them to wear skirts and tops with sleeves. In some areas, women are veiled. Also, men should not wear shorts.

Men and women are separated at public and private gatherings. Women should never go to the beach or to sporting events alone. Even if a woman is escorted to a sporting event, she may feel conspicuous since Algerian women are rarely in attendance.

Women should be aware that young men often verbally harass Algerian women. As a foreigner, a woman can deal with similar harassment by saying, "*Sib-nee fi-hah-lee*," which means "Leave me alone." Women are less likely to encounter harassment away from the main tourist areas. However, farther away from tourist areas they are more likely to be treated as inferiors.

Bargaining is acceptable and even expected everywhere except in grocery stores.

Ask for permission before photographing people. Many Algerians are very sensitive about having their pictures taken. Also be aware that there are certain areas (such as defense zones) where taking pictures is forbidden.

If you are in Algeria during the Muslim holiday *Ramadan*, you should know that many restaurants remain open for non-Muslims even though Muslims are fasting. However, during this holiday, you may want to avoid eating in public since this might offend others.

It is acceptable for non-Muslims to visit mosques, but not during prayer time or during *Ramadan*.

Using the fingers to point at objects or people is considered impolite. Also, care is usually taken not to let the sole of the foot point toward another person.

# BAHRAIN: HISTORICAL OVERVIEW

- Bahrain has attracted the attention of traders and invaders over the years. The Romans, Greeks, Portuguese and British have all tried to conquer or trade with the island.

- In 1521, the Portuguese captured Bahrain and ruled until 1602. After they were pushed out of the region, the Islands were alternately controlled by Arab and Persian groups. In 1783, the Arab Utub tribe expelled the Persians. The Al Khalifa family (part of the Utub tribe) took control of Bahrain. This family has maintained control ever since.

- Beginning in the early 1800s, the Al Khalifa family periodically turned to Great Britain for aid against local threats. In 1816, Bahrain became a British Protected State and the ruling sheikh shared control with a British adviser. The British also established a shipping and trading outpost in Bahrain, which was to remain until 1971.

- After a series of territorial disputes, Persia (now Iran) made a claim to Bahrain in 1928.

- In 1968, the British announced their intention to withdraw their military forces by 1971. That same year, Bahrain joined the states of Qatar and the Trucial States (now the United Arab Emirates), which were also under British protection, to form the Federation of Arab Emirates. However, the interests of Bahrain and Qatar soon proved to be incompatible with the other parties and both of these countries withdrew from the federation.

- In 1971, Bahrain became a fully independent state headed by Emir Shaikh Issa bin Salman Al Khalifa. At the time of independence, the country signed a treaty of friendship with the United Kingdom. The Emir had been the Bahraini monarch since 1961, and he became the full sovereign leader at the time of independence.

- The territorial dispute with Iran subsided in 1970, when Iran accepted a report commissioned by the United Nations which showed that the citizens of Bahrain overwhelmingly favored complete independence over union with Iran.

- Bahrain is pro-Western in foreign affairs and it gained international approval when it signed the Nuclear Nonproliferation Agreement in 1988. It has also become increasingly allied with Saudi Arabia, especially since the 1986 opening of the causeway linking the two countries.

- The introduction of representative democracy has begun in small steps. In 1993, a *shura* council was formed by the Emir and the Prime Minister. It is composed of citizen members appointed by the country's leaders. While the council does not criticize the Al Khalifa government directly, it has increased democratic opportunities for the people.

- Present-day Iran still maintains a claim to Bahrain and has renewed that claim as recently as 1993.

# BAHRAIN

## INTRODUCTIONS

The most common greeting in Bahrain is *"Assalam alikum"* ("the peace of Allah be upon you"). The correct reply is *"Alikum essalam,"* meaning virtually the same thing.

Handshakes are common in Bahrain and may last the length of the conversation. This exemplifies friendliness, as does a hand lightly grasping the person's arm. Good friends of the same sex may kiss a number of times on both cheeks.

Women, especially those from traditional rural families, generally look down in the presence of men. Therefore, a man should not greet a woman unless the greeting is part of business protocol.

It is customary to use the title *"Shaikh"* (for a man) or *"Shaikha"* (for a woman) in front of the name of a member of the royal family. *"Bin"* in the middle of a name means "son of."

Formal and informal nicknames are common. Among formal nicknames, you will find *"Abu,"* which means "father of" when used before the given name of the oldest son, such as "Abu Mohammed" (father of Mohammed). Similarly, *"Ibn"* means "son of," as in "Ibn Rashid" (son of Rashid).

Do not address a Bahraini by his first name until he addresses you by your first name.

Arabic is the official language of Bahrain. English is also widely used, especially for business. It is common for people in Bahrain to speak two or more languages.

## SOCIAL TIPS AND CONVENTIONS

The majority of people living in Bahrain are Muslims. About 75% are Shi'a Muslims. The others, including the royal family, are Sunni Muslims. Bahrain, Iraq and Iran are the only three Gulf region countries with Shi'a majorities.

Religion plays a central role in Bahraini culture. Work often stops during prayer. Bahrain's citizens are among the best educated in the Gulf region. Bahrainis deal with people from many foreign cultures because their country is a key trading and banking center.

In villages, dress is traditional. Men wear long robes and their heads are covered by a light cloth headdress kept in place by a heavy cloth ring. Women wear long black robes; many cover their hair and much of their faces. In urban areas, there is usually a combination of traditional and western dress.

Extended family ties are strong in Bahrain. The father is the ultimate authority in the home. The elderly are given respectful and loving treatment.

Do not admire a possession of your host to excess; he/she may insist upon giving it to you.

You may see men holding loops of beads called "worry beads." They serve as tension relievers, and have no religious significance.

## CUSTOMARY BUSINESS PRACTICES

Business is generally conducted from Saturday through Thursday. Friday is the Muslim Sabbath.

Try to make appointments well in advance of your arrival.

Before conducting business or shopping, it is usual to spend time on greetings and light conversation. Serious business may not even be discussed during the first couple of meetings. Coffee is generally served at business meetings, although sometimes tea or soft drinks are also offered.

Arrive for business and social appointments on time, although your host may be late. Your meeting may be interrupted several times.

The phrase, *"Insha'allah"* meaning "Allah (God) willing" is often used.

Shake hands at the beginning as well as at the end of a meeting.

In business settings, men should wear suits and women should wear modest dresses (nothing sleeveless).

Business cards should be printed with English on one side and Arabic on the other. Present the card with the Arabic side facing up.

## BUSINESS ENTERTAINING

At a party, expect to be introduced to each person individually. Shake hands with each one.

Do not ask for an alcoholic drink unless it is offered.

When invited to a Bahraini home, do not bring a gift for the hostess or ask about her. You may, however, bring a small gift for the host, such as chocolates, flowers or Arab sweets. You may also bring a gift for the children of the host.

Bahrainis like to feed their guests well, so be prepared to eat large amounts. It is polite to leave a small amount of food on your plate.

Don't invite a businessman to a meal unless he has already offered you an invitation.

Don't offer to entertain an Arab at a nightclub or a bar. Instead, suggest a hotel restaurant.

## DINING OUT

Eating with the right hand is most common; do not use the left.

Traditionally, people eat while seated on an Arabian sofa that rests on the floor. Everyone eats out of communal dishes using their hands.

Pork is not eaten by Muslims.

# BAHRAIN (Cont'd)

## DINING OUT (Cont'd)

Popular dishes include *beryani* (rice with meat), *machbous* (rice, meat, tomatoes and lentils) and *saloneh* (mixed vegetables). Fish and seafood are also staples. *Halwa* (a starch pudding mixed with crushed cardamom seeds, saffron sugar and fat) is a traditional dessert. Dates are served with meals.

## PUBLIC CUSTOMS

Sit so that the soles of your shoes are not showing.

Public displays of affection are frowned upon.

# COTE D'IVOIRE (IVORY COAST): HISTORICAL OVERVIEW

- The early history of Cote d'Ivoire is virtually unknown. France made its initial contact with Cote d'Ivoire in 1637 when missionaries landed near the Ghana border.

- In the 18th century, the country was invaded by two related ethnic groups – the Agnis, who occupied the southeast, and the Baoules, who settled in the central section.

- During 1843-1844, Adm. Bouet-Williaumez signed treaties with the kings of the Grand Bassam and Assinie regions, placing their territories under a French protectorate. French explorers, missionaries, trading companies and soldiers gradually extended the area under French control inland from the lagoon region.

- The Mandingo people, led by Samory Toure, resisted French expansion in the region. The French, while able to sign treaties with coastal chieftains, also met fierce resistance from the warlike Ashanti people in the west. Eventually, however, the French prevailed, and Cote d'Ivoire was completely conquered by 1915.

- The country suffered through the Depression, as the price of its agricultural exports dropped. During World War II, Cote d'Ivoire was under control of the pro-German administration that had been established in France.

- After the war, colonial rule continued, but there was a rapid rise in nationalism among natives in Cote d'Ivoire. Faced with rebellion in Vietnam and Algeria, France was in no position to oppose the nationalist demands, and in 1956, passed the Overseas Reform Act which gave the African colonies internal autonomy.

- Full independence was gained on August 7, 1960, and Felix Houphouet-Boigny became the first president. Houphouet-Boigny was a shrewd, idealistic leader who built the backward French colony into an industrious, comparatively wealthy republic. One key to his success was that unlike many newly-independent African nations, he was successful at avoiding tribalism.

- For virtually all of Houphouet-Boigny's rule, the *Cote d'Ivoire Democratic Party (PDCI)* was the sole political party. Though multi-party elections were held in the early 1990s, the *PDCI* remains dominant.

- In December 1993, Houphouet-Boigny died, and the constitutional successor to the presidency, Henri Konan Bedie, assumed office.

- Although Cote d'Ivoire has a solid agricultural base, a continuing worldwide coffee surplus as well as the epidemic of AIDS is slowing economic growth.

# COTE D'IVOIRE (IVORY COAST)

## INTRODUCTIONS

A handshake is customary when meeting for the first time. If meeting more than one individual, make sure to give your name and your company name to each.

Ivorian businessmen will greet you at the airport and drive you to your hotel. A handshake and a formal greeting of either *"Comment allez-vous?"* (French) or *"E-kah kay nay wah?"* (local tribal language) meaning, "How are you?" is customary.

You should refer to your host as *"Monsieur"* or "Mr.," or *"Madame"* or "Mrs." Some Ivorian names are long and complicated. Seek advice on individual pronunciation.

Once you get to know your host personally, you can expect to be greeted with a hug and what seems like a kiss, but is more a touch on the cheeks, first the left, then the right, then left again.

## SOCIAL TIPS AND CONVENTIONS

Ivorians, as well as many other Africans, are very sensitive about "Westernized superior attitudes." Be careful so as not to be offensive. Make sure to recognize past achievements and economic developments. Discuss the culture and the country. A genuine interest in local food, music, art and customs is always welcome.

If you do not speak French, you will need an interpreter, although some Ivorian businessmen do speak English (usually with difficulty). Almost all high-level businessmen speak English.

Be punctual for meetings. Meetings may begin with non-business-related conversation as a way of getting acquainted.

Ivorians are extremely cordial and may spend a lot of time becoming better acquainted with you.

Ivorians are impressed with French culture and customs. They strongly believe that the best clothing, for example, bears a "made in France" label.

Gift-giving is common, and gifts are usually presented to the family as a whole. Never present a gift to the wife only. Chocolates, electronic gadgets or a small memento of your country are always welcome.

## CUSTOMARY BUSINESS PRACTICES

It is best to send letters of introduction through a courier or parcel service that specializes in service to West Africa. Usually, a third party should provide an introduction, but local firms for the most part are receptive to unsolicited business proposals.

Be sure to confirm your appointment by letter or fax. Reconfirm the appointment by phone.

Weekday business hours are between 8:00 a.m. and noon, and from 2:30 to 6:00 p.m. On Saturday, hours are from 8:00 a.m. to noon.

It is not uncommon for African businessmen to have sunrise meetings over breakfast and coffee.

## COTE D'IVOIRE (Cont'd)

### CUSTOMARY BUSINESS PRACTICES (Cont'd)

A local agent or representative is essential to conducting business successfully, although the law does not require one to be appointed.

There are two types of Ivorian executives, French nationals and Ivorian nationals – many of whom have been educated in France. Both tend to be formal in their approach toward business.

Personal relationships will be the foundation of any business agreement. Ivorians rarely do business with a person who is not within the extended family or a friend.

The personal relationship will develop through a series of invitations to eat together or to visit your host's home, or maybe through a trip to the Ivorian countryside.

Business cards are important.

### BUSINESS ENTERTAINING

Ivorians are not flamboyant, but they do have the French flair for enjoying the finer things in life. Most likely, they don't drink wine without food or eat a meal without wine.

Entertaining is a way of promoting the friendship necessary for a good business relationship.

Most western food is imported and therefore expensive, so business entertainment may not include Western cuisine.

When meal invitations are extended, acceptance is expected.

If invited to your host's home, expect dinner to be informal. It is appropriate to bring flowers or a gift.

Ivorians enjoy dancing after dinner at a local nightclub. Nightlife usually begins around 10:30 p.m. and lasts until 3:00 or 4:00 a.m.

### DINING OUT

If your host takes you to a restaurant, it will most probably be one that offers either French cuisine or hot and spicy Ivorian specialties.

The traditional Ivorian restaurant for lunch or dinner, a *maquis,* is popular. Your host will invite you to sample a favorite Ivorian specialty, Ivorian rice with sauce.

Ivorians love fish – the spicier the recipe, the better. Fish dishes are served with a variety of sauces – coconut and cream or hot and spicy with chili and peppers.

Braised chicken and fish smothered in onions and tomatoes, served with *attieke* (the national dish of the Ivory Coast – you may think it is *couscous,* but it is in fact grated *manioc*) are popular meals. Some Ivorians also favor beef *brochettes* and Chicken *Redjenou* (the local specialty).

# COTE D'IVOIRE (Cont'd)

## DINING OUT (Cont'd)

To hurry through a meal or to show signs of gluttony is considered vulgar.

To ask for a second helping of food is considered impolite.

## PUBLIC CUSTOMS

Criticism of the President, colonialism, government and politics in general should be avoided.

Because of the extreme climate (warm and humid), lightweight and linen suits with a tie are required for men. For women, cotton or light knit dresses or suits are appropriate.

Do not expect favors in return to those given. All personal actions are taken as an investment in friendship.

# EGYPT: HISTORICAL OVERVIEW

- Egypt has endured as a unified state for more than 5,000 years. The earliest recorded Egyptian dynasty united the two kingdoms of Upper Egypt and Lower Egypt around 3100 B.C. Egypt was ruled by Pharaohs for many centuries. Egypt's ancient history is divided into the Old and Middle Kingdoms and the New Empire.

- Egypt came under Persian control in 525 B.C. and was then conquered by Alexander the Great in 332 B.C., bringing Egypt under Greek rule. The Roman emperor Augustus established direct Roman control over Egypt after Queen Cleopatra's death, initiating almost seven centuries of Roman and Byzantine rule.

- Egypt was one of the first countries to adopt Christianity. Egyptians followed their own Coptic patriarch and eventually were subjected to religious persecution by the Byzantines. As a consequence, Egyptians welcomed the Muslim invasion that began in 642 A.D. By the eighth century, Egypt had become mainly Muslim.

- For centuries Egypt was ruled by Islamic dynasties, including the Ottoman Turks in the 16th century. Egypt was associated with the Ottoman Empire until World War I.

- Napoleon Bonaparte of France arrived in Egypt in 1798. The three-year sojourn of Napoleon's army and French scientists opened Egypt to direct Western influence. Throughout the 19th century, France and Britain vied for influence over Egypt.

- After the completion of the Suez Canal in 1869, France and Britain exerted increasing control. Britain made Egypt a protectorate in 1914.

- Egypt was given independence in 1922, but Egyptians regard 1952 as the beginning of real independence. In that year, a revolution overthrew the British-supported monarchy.

- Gamal Abdel Nasser ousted the first president of Egypt in 1954 and became an influential leader. He governed until his death in 1970. During Nasser's reign, Egypt fought two wars that involved Israel (1956 and 1967). They lost the Sinai Peninsula to Israel in 1967.

- Nasser was succeeded by his vice president, Anwar el-Sadat. His government led a war with Israel in which they regained a foothold in the Sinai. Sadat signed a peace treaty with Israel in 1979 that returned the Sinai to Egypt. He was assassinated in 1981 by fundamentalists who disagreed with his policies.

- Sadat's vice president, Hosni Mubarak succeeded him and has become an important leader of moderate Arab nations.

- The late 1980s saw several serious problems emerge: falling oil revenues, lowered receipts from canal revenues and a drop in tourism. This drop was due to the rise of fundamentalist violence. Mubarak widened a campaign to end the terrorism.

EGYPT

## INTRODUCTIONS

Greetings in Egypt are often elaborate and warm. Friends of the same sex usually shake hands and kiss on both cheeks. If the friends have not seen each other for a long time, they may repeat the kisses and add a kiss to the forehead.

A man will shake hands with a woman only if the woman extends her hand first. Otherwise, he will greet her verbally only.

Titles are important. Do not use first names unless invited to do so. Good friends use first names in social settings, but may add an honorific title to the first name in more formal settings.

## SOCIAL TIPS AND CONVENTIONS

One of the most important pastimes in Egypt is visiting others because personal relationships with friends and relatives are paramount.

Married children often visit parents on Fridays (the Islamic day of rest and worship) and holidays.

Egyptians like to relax and enjoy life. Their phrase *"Ma'alesh"* can be translated as "Don't worry" or "Never mind."

Over 90% of the country belongs to the Sunni sect of Islam. Egyptian life is therefore thoroughly infused with Islamic philosophy, which has an impact upon the country's laws, business relations and social customs.

The concept of *"Insha'allah"* or "Allah (God) willing" dominates all aspects of Muslim life. This utilizes a lot of patience, as Egyptians view events in an extended time frame.

Egyptians are known for their sense of humor, especially their love of riddles, jokes, sarcasm and wordplay.

One should dress conservatively in Egypt. Many women cover their hair and bodies completely, except for their faces and hands. Men wear modest clothing and skullcaps. A beard can be a sign of religious faith, but it can also signify membership in certain political organizations. In large cities, Western-style clothing is popular as long as it is modest. Business representatives generally wear business suits.

Avoid discussing the politics of the Middle East region.

Appropriate conversation topics include Egyptian advancement and achievement, Egyptian cotton and Egypt's ancient civilization.

# EGYPT (Cont'd)

## CUSTOMARY BUSINESS PRACTICES

The usual work week is from Saturday through Thursday. Business visits usually begin with light conversation and coffee or tea.

Arabic is the official language in Egypt, although English and French are widely used in business and in education. Bilingual business cards are helpful.

Shake hands with everyone when arriving as well as when departing.

It is not unusual for a meeting to be interrupted frequently with telephone calls, visitors and many cups of tea or coffee.

Many offices close for a long lunch break and stay open until 7:00 p.m. or later.

Egypt is famous for its abundant "red tape." You need to be patient, as things move very slowly, especially when the government is involved.

Appointments are always necessary.

## BUSINESS ENTERTAINING

Egyptians prepare elaborate meals when they entertain guests.

To refuse anything is an insult to the host.

When eating a meal, do not feel you have to finish everything on your plate; leftover food is a symbol of abundance and a compliment to the host for providing so well.

Lunch is the main meal and is usually served from 2:00 to 4:00 p.m. Dinner may not be served until 10:30 p.m. or even later.

When invited to dine at someone's house, bring a gift of flowers or chocolates. Do not bring alcohol.

During the month of *Ramadan* (which occurs at different times each year due to the lunar calendar), Muslims will not eat or drink between sunrise and sunset.

## DINING OUT

Finger food is eaten with the right hand only. When Western utensils are used, they are used in the continental style, with the fork in the left hand and the knife remaining in the right hand.

The *Qur'an* (the holy scriptures of Islam) prohibits eating pork and drinking alcohol.

# EGYPT (Cont'd)

## DINING OUT (Cont'd)

The staples of the Egyptian diet have changed little over the centuries. The walls of tombs show paintings of garlic, beans, leeks and rice. These remain the basics for Egyptians today.

Traditional foods include flat Egyptian bread, skewered meats and fava beans. *Tahina* (sesame seed paste), tomatoes, yogurt and cucumbers are often eaten with meals.

The national dish is *molochaia* ("green herb" cooked with chicken broth, tomatoes and garlic).

## PUBLIC CUSTOMS

Avoid showing the sole of your shoe or inadvertently pointing it at someone. The sole of the shoe is considered the dirtiest and lowest part of the body.

Pointing at a person is considered impolite.

You may see men fingering loops of beads that are similar to a Catholic rosary. These are tension relievers called "worry beads" and have little or no religious significance.

Smoking in public places is very common.

The distance between men while conversing is much closer than in the U.S., but it is much further apart for members of the opposite sex.

Remove your shoes when entering a mosque. Don't plan to visit mosques between noon and 1:00 p.m. on Fridays. At this time, mosques may be restricted to Muslims and you won't be allowed to enter.

Two gestures to know: (1) The right hand held up with the palm facing away from the body and the fingers waving up and down means "Come here;" (2) The hand and palm facing toward you with all fingertips touching and the hand moving up and down can mean, "Wait a minute," "Shut up!" or "Take it easy!"

When you enter an elevator, always greet the people in it.

# GHANA: HISTORICAL OVERVIEW

- Ghana, formerly the Colony of the Gold Coast, was the primary source of gold for the large West African inland trading empires that flourished from the 4th to the 11th centuries A.D.

- In 1487, the Portuguese established a fort at Elmina as their headquarters for the gold trade. Competition among the European powers for gold and slaves led to the establishment of numerous bases on the Gulf of Guinea coast. In 1874, control of the Gold Coast was taken by Great Britain. After several years of battles with the Asante tribe, the British gained control of present-day Ghana in 1901.

- Opposition to British control increased after World War II. Dr. Kwame Nkrumah led the independence movement. The Colony of the Gold Coast, along with British Togoland, became Ghana and was granted independence in 1957.

- Three years later, the country became a republic with Nkrumah as its president. In 1962, he was made president-for-life, but was deposed by a military coup in February 1966.

- Ghana gradually returned to civilian rule. A second military coup occurred in January 1972, deposing Prime Minister Kofi Busia. The regime of Lt. Col. Ignatius Kutu Acheampong abolished the presidency and dissolved the National Assembly. He was, in turn, ousted in 1978.

- In June 1979, Flight Lt. Jerry Rawlings led a successful revolt against the military government. Rawlings turned power over to newly elected president Dr. Hilla Limann and the new National Assembly, but was not satisfied with their performance and again seized power in December 1981. The constitution was again suspended and the National Assembly dissolved. Rawlings appointed a seven-member Provisional National Defense Council (PNDC).

- In 1988, a new national assembly was established, but members could not belong to political parties. Ghana returned to democratic rule with national elections in 1992. Rawlings was elected President. Ghana is now officially a multiparty democracy.

- In the early 1990s, Ghana was economically depressed. The banking system was nearing mass failure, the currency had been greatly devalued, and the inflation rate was in excess of 80% annually. The bloated government bureaucracy employs 400,000 people whose salaries make up 43% of state spending.

- Rawlings tried a program of privatization, and economic progress occurred. Germany and Libya made large concessions on debts owed them by Ghana, and diamond, gold and agricultural production greatly increased.

# GHANA

## INTRODUCTIONS

Ghana has many different ethnic groups, each having its own distinct language, culture and customs. Because of these pronounced differences, there is no one greeting or introduction that is a standard all over the country.

English greetings and handshakes are common due to the country's long colonial affiliation with the British Empire.

A handshake is common with most people and happens naturally before beginning a conversation.

Several greetings are recognized for getting someone's attention so that they continue to listen to what is said after one says such things as "Good morning" or "Good evening."

Titles and family names are used to address new acquaintances.

Friends and family members often use given names.

Children refer to any adult who is well known to the family as "Aunt" or "Uncle," even when they are not related.

## SOCIAL TIPS AND CONVENTIONS

The most popular day for visiting is Sunday and many people like to dress up for the occasion.

Visitors are usually welcome to stay as long as they wish. It is polite to avoid visiting during mealtime, but an unexpected guest would be invited to share the meal.

When the visit is over, guests are accompanied to or given transportation to their home. It is impolite to let them leave on their own.

Ghanaians are proud of their status as the first sub-Saharan colony to gain independence from a European power.

The Ghanaian people generally have a relaxed disposition.

Western visitors need to pay special attention so as to avoid acting superior because they are from an industrialized nation.

## CUSTOMARY BUSINESS PRACTICES

Most businesses are open Monday through Friday from 8:00 a.m. to noon and from 2:00 to 4:30 p.m. Some are open on Saturday morning.

Business dress is conservative.

# GHANA (Cont'd)

## CUSTOMARY BUSINESS PRACTICES (Cont'd)

Tipping for personal services is an opportunity to extend *dash* (from the Portuguese *das* meaning "give"). Ghanaian compensation may be in the form of money, goods or favors for personal services performed.

Although the system of *dash* is discouraged by the government, it is widely practiced and includes anything from watching a car to expediting the movement of goods in and out of the country. Except in restaurants and hotels, *dash* is usually paid before the service is given.

## BUSINESS ENTERTAINING

Casual dress is the rule in most circumstances. A shirt, tie and suit or a dress, however, is required for formal occasions.

Hospitality is important, and Ghanaians work hard to please their guests. Most visits occur in the home and it is polite to bring at least a small gift for the children. Be aware that some hosts prefer that guests remove their shoes when entering the home.

Guests are nearly always served refreshments. It is considered impolite to refuse these offers.

## DINING OUT

Western etiquette is practiced when eating with most Ghanaians.

The diet consists mainly of yams, cassava (a starchy root), maize, plantains and rice.

Ghanaians enjoy hot and spicy food and most of their meals are accompanied by a pepper sauce made with meat, fish or chicken. Foreigners generally require some time to become accustomed to the spicy food.

Specialty dishes include *fufu* (a dough-like combination of plantain and cassava), *ampesi* (a green vegetable dish) and palm or peanut oil soups and sauces.

Most larger restaurants serve Western food as well as native Ghanaian food. A tip is usually included in the bill; however, it is polite to leave an additional small gratuity as well.

## PUBLIC CUSTOMS

Ghanaians consider it impolite to gesture with the left hand. You should not pass or receive items with your left hand.

It is important to cover your mouth when yawning or using a toothpick.

The sole of your foot should not point at another person. It is impolite to place your feet on chairs, desks or tables.

It is considered impolite and an act of defiance for children to have direct eye contact with adults.

# ISRAEL: HISTORICAL OVERVIEW

- A Hebrew Kingdom, ruled by King David, was established in the Holy Land from the 12 tribes of Israel that came out of Egypt with Moses about 3000 years ago. After the reign of Solomon, David's son, the kingdom was split into two states – Israel and Judah. The states of Israel and Judah were destroyed by Assyria and Babylonia in the eighth and sixth centuries B.C. and, as a result, the populations were dispersed or taken captive. However, after the Persians conquered the Middle East, many Jews were allowed to return to the Holy Land to establish a nation and build a temple. The land subsequently fell to the Greeks and later to the Romans, who named it Palestine. During the Byzantine era (313-636 A.D.), the Jewish population dropped sharply because of persecutions. In the 600s, the area was conquered by the Muslims, who ruled for the next 1000 years.

- From the 16th century until World War I, the Ottoman Turks controlled Palestine. In 1890, Theodor Herzl established Zionism as an international movement to restore Palestine to the Jews. When the British took over Palestine after the First World War, various plans were put forth for partitioning the area, but none were ever implemented.

- During World War II, Jewish people began to immigrate to Israel in large numbers trying to escape the Holocaust. The British were unable to stop the Jews from returning to what they considered to be their homeland. In 1947, the United Nations voted to divide the area into two states – one Arab and one Jewish. In 1948, Israel proclaimed its independence as a state and the British withdrew. Following independence, neighboring Arab nations opposed to a Jewish state attacked, and wars were fought in 1956, 1967 and 1973. In 1979, Egypt and Israel signed a peace treaty, as Egypt became the first Arab nation to recognize Israel's right to exist. Throughout the 1980s, Arab terrorism and border wars with Lebanon were serious problems. The conflicts focused on the status of territories occupied by Israel since the 1967 war.

- In 1987, the Palestine Liberation Organization (PLO) renounced terrorism and accepted Israel's right to exist. At the same time, the PLO declared an independent Palestinian state in the occupied West Bank and Gaza. The declaration was rejected by Israel and violence persisted. Due to continued violence and recognition of the need for change, Israel agreed to discuss plans for peace with Arab neighbors and the Middle East peace process began in 1991. Peace talks frequently broke down, as internal dissent and violence on both sides broke out until secret talks in Norway between Israeli Prime Minister Yitzhak Rabin and PLO leader Yasser Arafat led to a breakthrough in 1993. The agreement involved limited autonomy in parts of the occupied territories and by mid-1994, Gaza and Jericho (in the West Bank) had achieved autonomy. While resistance on both sides has led to continued violence, Israel and the PLO have continued to discuss complex plans for peace and autonomy. The *Knesset* (Israeli parliament) elected Ezer Weizman as the nation's seventh president in 1993.

- In November 1995, Rabin was assassinated by an Orthodox Jew who believed that Rabin had negotiated away Israel's land and was endangering settlers. Rabin's partner in the peace process, Shimon Peres, became Acting Prime Minister. As he formed a new cabinet, the policy of peace through negotiation became popular among Israelis. A series of suicide attacks in early 1996 by Islamic terrorists changed the minds of many Israelis, and support increased for Benjamin Netanyahu and his *Likud Party*. Netanyahu became Prime Minister in the May 1996 election. Later in 1996, violence erupted on a large scale as Palestinian police battled Israeli soldiers in what began as a conflict over a newly discovered ancient tunnel. Netanyahu met with Arafat in Washington in an attempt to prevent more bloodshed.

# ISRAEL

## INTRODUCTIONS

Hebrew is the official language of Israel. Arabic is also an official language and is taught in the schools. English is used frequently in business and is spoken by most Israelis.

The usual greeting is *"Shalom,"* which means "Peace." *"Shalom"* is said upon departing as well. Israelis also use the term when answering the phone.

Greetings are informal and handshakes are common.

Some men who are good friends may pat each other on the back or shoulder when greeting each other.

First names are commonly used once someone has been introduced. Titles are not necessary, and even military officers are referred to by their first names.

## SOCIAL TIPS AND CONVENTIONS

Punctuality is expected for important occasions. For informal events, it is permissible to arrive 15 minutes late.

Visits to see a friend may be made without an invitation. Israelis often stop by a friend's home for conversation.

Israelis are very civic-minded and involved in their community.

They are inquisitive and avid readers who enjoy frank discussions.

Israelis are devoted to their culture and their nation. Jewish immigration from around the world is encouraged.

Except among Orthodox Jews and traditional Muslims, western-style clothing is worn, and dress is casual. Men wear shirts unbuttoned at the neck. Ties and suits are worn only for formal occasions.

Orthodox Jews observe the Jewish Sabbath – from sundown Friday to sundown Saturday.

Holidays are important in Israel. Businesses close and public transportation stops. The Jewish calendar is based on the lunar cycle, so dates for holidays vary yearly.

The family is central to Israelis. Family ties remain strong as the children grow into adulthood. Married children are expected to live near their parents or other family members and they are also expected to care for their elderly parents.

## CUSTOMARY BUSINESS PRACTICES

General business days are Sunday through Thursday.

Business procedures are similar to those in the U.S. and the pace is quite fast.

# ISRAEL (Cont'd)

## CUSTOMARY BUSINESS PRACTICES (Cont'd)

You should make appointments prior to your arrival in Israel.

When bargaining or negotiating, Israelis often start off with an extreme position and gradually work toward a compromise.

## BUSINESS ENTERTAINING

Israelis are very friendly and informal, and they often invite new friends to their homes. A gift is not necessary, but it is appreciated (books, candy or flowers are appropriate).

You will more likely be invited to a business lunch than to a business dinner.

## DINING OUT

Eating habits vary as Israelis have a diverse cultural heritage.

Generally continental manners are used, with the knife kept in the right hand and the fork in the left. Some foods are eaten by hand.

Your host or the oldest person will generally begin the meal.

The main meal of the day is eaten in the early afternoon. Evening meals are generally light.

Israeli food specialties include *falafel* (pita bread filled with balls of fried chick-pea batter), vegetable salads, *kebabs* (skewered meats) and other foods that reflect the heritage of the various countries of the ancestors of today's Israelis.

Many people observe the traditional *Kosher* dietary laws that prohibit milk and meat from being eaten during the same meal. Under these laws, pork and shellfish are also forbidden at any time.

Restaurants may add a service charge to the bill. It is suggested that you leave something extra for the waiter if service was good.

Israeli wines are of high quality.

## PUBLIC CUSTOMS

Hands are often used in conversation to emphasize a point.

Pointing at someone with the index finger is considered rude.

Women should not wear shorts in areas populated with Arabs or religious Jews. In addition to being stared at, they may be reprimanded and will not be admitted to any of the holy places.

Soccer and basketball are the favorite sports in Israel.

# JORDAN: HISTORICAL OVERVIEW

- Since Jordan is part of the "Fertile Crescent" of the Middle East, it has been settled and conquered by a number of peoples. The early settlers of the area included the Amorites, Edomites, Moabites and Ammonites. Later, the land was conquered by the Hittites, Egyptians, Israelites, Assyrians, Babylonians, Persians, Greeks and Romans.

- In the seventh century, the Arabs invaded the area, and while Christian crusaders ruled for a time, the region has been essentially Muslim since the Arab invasion.

- The Ottoman Turks ruled for many years, until the Great Arab Revolt of 1916, in which the Arabs were supported by the British. In 1922, after the Turks were defeated, the British created the Emirate of Transjordan, a semiautonomous region ruled by the Hashemite Prince Abdullah.

- The British slowly turned control of the region over to local Arab officials, and Transjordan became independent in 1946. In 1950, the name of the country was shortened to "Jordan," and it included the territory now known as the West Bank. In 1951, Abdullah was assassinated and his son Talal was proclaimed king, but because of poor health, he was deposed by government officials. Talal's 17-year old son, Hussein, became the new Jordanian monarch.

- During the 1967 War, Jordan lost the West Bank to Israel, and many Palestinian refugees fled to Jordan. This sudden influx of immigrants caused unrest and violence. Members of the Palestinian resistance (*fedayeen*) were expelled from Jordan after an assassination attempt was made against King Hussein.

- After the War of 1967, Jordan considered the people of the West Bank part of its population and provided for Palestinian representatives in the Jordanian parliament. However, in 1988, King Hussein announced that Jordan no longer would claim the West Bank as its territory. As a result, strains between the Jordanian government and the Palestinian Liberation Organization (PLO) relaxed. It also caused the dissolution of Parliament since many of its members represented the West Bank.

- Elections for the new parliament took place in 1989, and a new legislature was convened. In 1991, King Hussein restored multiparty democracy. He also lifted a number of martial law provisions that had existed since 1967.

- Full multiparty elections were held in 1993, with 534 candidates competing for 80 seats. A strong voter turnout elected a centrist group of leaders for the new parliament, confirming support for King Hussein's policies.

- Since 1991, King Hussein has been working in the peace process toward settling issues with Israel and the Palestinians related to secure borders, water, refugees, arms and the environment. Jordan signed an economic accord with the PLO in 1994.

- Abdul Karim Kabariti was elected Prime Minister in 1996, and his energetic, pragmatic approach won support, even among some of the opposition Islamic parties.

# JORDAN

## INTRODUCTIONS

Greetings are important, and Jordanians greet each other as well as strangers warmly.

A handshake is the most common greeting. It is usually accompanied by verbal greetings and inquiries about each person's health.

Friends of the same sex often exchange a kiss on either cheek.

A common term for "Hello" is *"Mar-haba."*

A term used to welcome someone is *"Ahlan wa sahalan." "Ahlein mar-haba"* might also be used as a welcome greeting.

When entering or leaving a room, it is customary to shake hands with each person (except, of course, at large gatherings).

Remember that first names are not used between strangers when greeting.

## SOCIAL TIPS AND CONVENTIONS

Arabic is the official and most commonly used language in Jordan. However, English is widely spoken among the educated.

Except for small minorities of Circassians (1%) and Armenians (1%), all citizens of Jordan are Arabs.

About 90% of the people are Sunni Muslims. Islamic values and laws are an integral part of the society.

Each religious community has the right to regulate personal matters such as marriage, divorce and inheritance according to religious traditions.

Jordanians are good-natured, friendly and hospitable.

They place great worth on the family and traditions, but are also very modern.

Time is not as important in Jordan as in the West. Jordanians believe that people are more important than schedules. Thus patience is a valuable asset.

Although many Palestinians residing in Jordan hold Jordanian citizenship, they consider themselves Palestinians first. Some don't consider themselves Jordanians at all and resent being called Jordanians. These people strongly support the establishment of a Palestinian homeland. Visitors should be aware of their views.

## CUSTOMARY BUSINESS PRACTICES

Women comprise only about 10% of the work force.

Government offices are usually open from 9:00 a.m. to 2:00 p.m., Saturday through Thursday.

Businesses are open from 8:00 a.m. to about 2:00 p.m. and from 4:00 to 7:00 p.m.

Most businesses close on Friday, the day of worship for Muslims.

Christian businesses close on Sunday as well.

Employers look after the interests of their employees and are responsible for a wider area of concerns than in the West. In many cases, an employer is regarded more like an uncle or a father than a boss.

The currency is the Jordanian *dinar* (JD).

## BUSINESS ENTERTAINING

Visiting (and entertaining) plays a fundamental role in Jordanian society.

Guests are greeted by both husband and wife.

Invited visitors may bring gifts of flowers or sweets, but never alcohol.

Coffee or tea is almost always offered to guests, no matter how short the visit.

It is customary for a person who has had enough to drink to shake the empty cup back and forth.

Coffee is generally served shortly before guests are expected to leave; it is considered impolite for a person to leave before the coffee is served.

Guests not originally invited for a meal may be expected to remain. It is polite to decline the offer initially before accepting. However, it is impolite not to accept the offer, although some guests will refuse the invitation up to three times before accepting it.

A Jordanian will entertain in his/her home more often than at restaurants because it is a greater honor for a guest to be invited to a home.

Visitors should avoid excessive admiration of any object owned by the hosts because the hosts may feel obligated to offer it to them. In most cases, it is wise to remember that the offer is made only to demonstrate the host's generosity. It is therefore expected that the admirer will decline the item. If the host insists several times, the guest must accept it or risk embarrassing the hosts.

# JORDAN (Cont'd)

## BUSINESS ENTERTAINING (Cont'd)

In any situation where gifts are given, the recipients should not immediately accept them.

Excessive praise of children is considered bad luck for the family.

When Jordanians have guests, the host provides a large assortment of food.

When invited to a home for a meal, it is polite to leave a little food on the plate. This tells the host that the guest has eaten well, and that the host has been generous.

## DINING OUT

Keep in mind that Islamic law prohibits the consumption of pork and alcohol, and most Muslims are careful to obey these restrictions.

Most meals include meat and bread, along with vegetables and fruits that are in season.

There are many types of bread, the most common of which is flat, round bread. A variation of this bread is known in the West as pita.

The national dish of Jordan is *mansaf*, a large tray of rice covered with chunks of stewed lamb (including the head) and *jameed* (yogurt sauce). It is eaten by hand from the serving tray.

Other popular dishes include *mahshi* (stuffed vegetables), *musakhan* (chicken with onions, olive oil, pine seeds and seasonings) and *meshwi* or *shish kebab*.

Lamb and chicken are the most common meats.

Tomatoes, onions, eggplant, cabbage and other vegetables are also eaten regularly.

Coffee is important at all meals. *Qahwah Saadah* (Bedouin coffee) is sipped slowly from small cups. Arabic or Turkish coffee is sweeter. It is deliberately not stirred so as to keep the thick coffee grains at the bottom of the cup.

## PUBLIC CUSTOMS

Most men wear Western-style clothing, often accompanied by the traditional white or red-checkered headdress.

Women also wear Western clothing, but many continue to wear traditional Islamic floor-length dresses, head scarves and veils. Either way, clothing is always conservative and never revealing.

Visitors should dress conservatively; cotton clothing is most comfortable.

Shorts are not worn by adults or teenagers, except during athletic events.

Jewelry is an important part of a woman's wardrobe.

# JORDAN (Cont'd)

## PUBLIC CUSTOMS (Cont'd)

It is improper to pass or accept objects or eat with the left hand; the right hand or both hands should be used. The left hand is traditionally reserved for personal hygiene purposes.

It is impolite to point the sole of one's foot or shoe at another person. For this reason, crossing one's legs is generally avoided.

Good posture is important, especially at social events.

It is improper to be affectionate in public.

Hand gestures are used a great deal in conversation and for everyday communication.

Arabs love children; they lavish a great deal of time and attention on them. Likewise, the elderly are greatly respected and cared for by their children.

To be able to help another member of the family is considered a great honor as well as a duty.

Gender roles in the family follow mostly traditional lines. The mother is expected to take care of the children and household. The father is considered the head of the family as well as the financial provider.

National holidays follow the Western (Gregorian) calendar and fall on fixed dates. They include Labor Day (May 1), Independence Day (May 25), Arab Revolt and Army Day (June 10), King Hussein's Accession to the Throne (August 11) and King Hussein's Birthday (November 14).

Christians celebrate Easter and Christmas, but they are not national holidays.

Islamic religious holy days follow the lunar calendar, which is a few days shorter than the Western calendar. One important holiday is *'Eid al-Fitr*, a three-day feast at the end of the month of *Ramadan*. During *Ramadan*, Muslims do not eat or drink from dawn to dusk; in the evenings, they eat with family and visit friends and relatives.

*'Eid al-Adha* is known as the Feast of Sacrifice and comes after the pilgrimage to Mecca. The birth of the prophet *Moulid al-Nebi* (Muhammad) is also celebrated.

Jordan has a good system of transportation. Roads are generally in good condition, and they connect with all major cities. In cities, taxis are available, but expensive.

Service taxis, which travel fixed routes and carry a small number of passengers, are less expensive and widely used. Buses are also common.

Water is not potable. Remember that boiled water must be used for brushing teeth, in ice cubes and so forth.

Do not take pictures of people praying; ask permission before taking a picture of anyone.

# KENYA: HISTORICAL OVERVIEW

- More than 50% of Kenya's current ethnic groups have origins in the Bantu peoples, who migrated many centuries ago from western Africa. Other groups from Arabia and North Africa also settled in this area and mixed with the original inhabitants. From these mixed peoples, the Kiswahili language emerged.

- Portuguese explorers, led by Vasco de Gama, arrived in 1498 and established trading posts. They were driven out by the Arabs in 1729.

- After 1740, Arabs ruled the Kenyan coast from their capital on the island of Zanzibar.

- In 1887, the British East Africa Company leased the Kenyan coast from the Sultan of Zanzibar. Kenya became a British protectorate in 1895 and was organized as a British Crown Colony in 1920.

- Great Britain granted Kenya its independence in 1963 after a period of violent uprisings called the Mau-Mau Rebellion. It has remained in the Commonwealth as a sovereign republic.

- Jomo Kenyatta was the leader of the independence movement and became Kenya's first president. He remained in power until his death in 1978 and was succeeded by Daniel T. arap Moi.

- Kenyatta had formed a strong central government under one political party, the *Kenya African National Union (KANU)*.

- In 1982, *KANU* was proclaimed the only legal political party. Free elections were still held, but all candidates had to register with *KANU*.

- Protests and pressure from other countries eventually led Moi to change this policy. In 1991, he rescinded the constitutional provision that gave *KANU* its dominance.

- Dozens of political parties formed in anticipation of national elections to be held in December 1992. Moi exploited the differences among the various parties so as to prevent a united opposition. He also had his supporters in the legislature push through a constitutional amendment that changed the election laws and made it virtually impossible for him to lose. In the legislature, the opposition did make gains, but Moi dissolved the legislature after riots broke out on the opening day.

- Moi's reign increased terror and oppression and his corrupt government accumulated a large foreign debt.

# KENYA

## INTRODUCTIONS

Kenyans are friendly and greet people with warmth. Politeness is important in greetings.

In Kenya, physical contact is important. Handshakes are used often and are considered a gesture of trust and peace. They are common and an important part of a greeting throughout the country.

Because most people speak Swahili, the term, *"Hujambo, habari?,"* meaning *"Greetings! How are you?"* is often used. English greetings are also acceptable.

Greeting customs may differ between ethnic groups since Kenya is inhabited by more than 30 different ethnic groups.

Kenyans will introduce themselves with their surname first and given name last. Since English is the principle business language, a Kenyan man is addressed as "Mr.," a married woman by "Mrs." and a single woman by "Miss."

## SOCIAL TIPS AND CONVENTIONS

Because of strong family ties and friendships, visiting is a common activity among Kenyans. Sunday is the most popular day for visiting relatives and friends.

The Catholic Church is a very strong entity, and morality is high among the Kenyan people. This is due to the powerful influence of the missionary work exerted during the last century.

Kenyans are extremely proud of their country, and it is not wise to offer gratuitous or condescending criticism or advice about national or local affairs.

It is best to speak in a low-toned and mild-mannered voice. It's considered an insult to shout at anyone, even with words of praise.

Never use the word "Blacks" when describing Kenyans.

Conservative lightweight business suits for men and cotton or linen dresses for women are the usual attire because of the year-round warm climate. Women are advised never to wear dresses above the knee.

Kenyans place great importance on keeping in touch with visitors and friends. Sending birthday and holiday cards will be remembered for years.

## CUSTOMARY BUSINESS PRACTICES

Business correspondence, catalogs and advertising material prepared in English are readily understood by most potential buyers.

Punctuality is important to Kenyan businesspeople.

# KENYA (Cont'd)

## CUSTOMARY BUSINESS PRACTICES (Cont'd)

Personal visits are warmly welcomed and are generally regarded as the most efficient method of establishing new trade contracts.

Correspondence and personal calls play a significant role in conducting business in Kenya. Therefore, expeditious handling of correspondence is expected and greatly appreciated.

Business cards are both presented and received with your right hand. The left hand is considered unclean and unlucky; therefore, using it would be impolite.

When receiving a business card, it is considered appropriate to pause and read it thoroughly before putting it away.

Meetings are generally informal. Kenyans are well known for being casual, humorous and seemingly carefree. Business procedures may vary according to race, tribe and religion, but the strong British influence is noticeable in formality and manners.

Plan to arrive in Kenya a day before your first meeting and reconfirm your appointments when you arrive.

Kenya is dominated by a society of upper class and wealthy families. Long-established families control much of the business in the country.

Business hours are from 8:00 a.m. to 5:00 p.m. Monday through Friday, and from 8:30 a.m. to 3:00 p.m. on Saturday.

## BUSINESS ENTERTAINING

Since Kenyans are very hospitable, be prepared for many business and social gatherings to center around meals.

If you are a first-time visitor, you will most likely be taken to a restaurant by your Kenyan host. It is recommended that you reciprocate soon after by taking your host to your hotel's restaurant.

Lunch and dinner are both appropriate for business meals. Your spouse is not generally welcome, but, with advance notice, plans can be arranged to include him/her.

It is best to give gifts to your host at dinner or if you are invited to a Kenyan's home. Flowers and candy are suitable for Kenyan women; toys and Western music for children.

Breakfast is usually served between 7:00 and 8:30 a.m., lunch between noon and 2:00 p.m. and dinner between 7:00 and 9:00 p.m.

# KENYA (Cont'd)

## DINING OUT

Kenyan cuisine is a cross between Indian, European and various tribal influences. It is interesting to discover the cooking of the various tribal groups, particularly that of the Abaluhya and the Kikuyu.

The staples of Kenyan cooking are meat (goat, beef and mutton) and starches (potatoes, rice or *ugali*, a cornmeal cooked like porridge).

The Abaluhya menu might consist of groundnut soup, *ugali*, *m'baazi* (pea beans), *Ndizi* (bananas steamed in leaves) or *M'chuzi Wa Kulu* (chicken in a coconut dish).

The Kikuyu's menu is different because the meal centers around the *irio*, which is a seasoned puree of corn, peas and potatoes. *Irio* is used with steak and sauce dishes of salad relish and the popular *pilli-pilli* (a small red hot pepper).

Desserts are mostly made from fruit with an abundance of papaya, oranges and mangoes. The most popular after dinner drink is *Mazuva Ya Kuganda*, a sour skimmed milk served cold. Coffee and tea are also available.

Kenya is well known for its lively brewing industry, and beer is consumed in great amounts.

One Kenyan wine to avoid is the ubiquitous papaya wine, which may seem foul to the taste and smell of Westerners.

## PUBLIC CUSTOMS

Patriotism is evident in people's respect for the national flag. Whenever the flag is raised or lowered, Kenyans stop to observe the short ceremony.

Public displays of affection are not acceptable in most areas, although they are becoming increasingly common in the capital city of Nairobi.

It is common for men to hold hands while walking in public, although a man and a woman would not do so.

Eye contact is important to Kenyans as it instills a sense of trust.

Kenyan society has a great deal of respect and appreciation for age. Thus older family members carry the most status.

# KUWAIT: HISTORICAL OVERVIEW

- Kuwait's history began relatively recently, in the 18th century, when a nomadic tribe wandering north from the area of Qatar established a settlement in the region now known as Kuwait. The name "Kuwait" is an Arabic word, meaning "fortress built near water."

- The Kuwaitis came under the rule of the Al Sabah family in 1751, and in about 1775, they established a relationship with the British. The Kuwaitis looked to the British for support in maintaining their autonomy. The relationship between Kuwait and the British was formalized by a treaty in 1899, which established a protectorate that lasted until 1961.

- Although oil was discovered in 1937, its exploration had to be delayed until the end of World War II. After exploration started, Kuwait flourished economically. In 1976, the Kuwaiti government nationalized oil operations that were originally granted jointly to British Petroleum and Gulf Oil. Since then, Kuwait has expanded its oil producing, processing and marketing role.

- When Great Britain withdrew in 1961, Kuwait was immediately threatened by Iraq, which claimed that before the arrival of the British, the territory had been part of the Ottoman Empire administered from Baghdad. This threat resulted in the immediate return of British forces to the region.

- While Kuwait managed to maintain a delicate diplomatic balance in the Middle Eastern turmoil, it was affected by local conflicts, especially the Iranian revolution and the Iran-Iraq War. Although it remained nonbelligerent, Kuwait provided support for Iraq in its war with Iran, since the most severe threat came from Iran and its sympathizers.

- In 1983, Shi'ite terrorists based in Iran bombed the U.S. and French embassies in Kuwait City. Several subsequent international hijackings and hostage situations in Lebanon had the announced purpose of forcing the release of the convicted terrorists from Kuwaiti prisons. The government consistently refused to yield to the pressure, and in 1986, there was a car bomb attack on the Emir as well as a series of refinery bombings. When it was found that native Shi'ites were responsible, a Sunni backlash removed Shi'ites from sensitive positions in the oil industry, army and police.

- As Kuwait came increasingly under attack from Iran, it appealed for help to the five permanent members of the U.N. Security Council. The Soviet Union, Great Britain, France and the U.S. sent ships to the area, and in 1987, the U.S. began escorting Kuwaiti tankers, leading to armed clashes with both Iran and Iraq.

- In 1990, Iraq invaded Kuwait. This invasion triggered the Gulf War, which involved the U.S. and other powers. This war wrought destruction in the small country, especially when the Iraqi forces lit oil fires upon their retreat in 1991. These fires burned out of control for the greater part of the year. Kuwait spent the next few years rebuilding from the destruction wrought by the war. The country made extraordinary progress in rebuilding after the conflict; however, the cost of rebuilding put a strain on the economy. Kuwait also worked more closely with the U.S. after the war because the U.S. role in liberating Kuwait generated goodwill.

# KUWAIT

## INTRODUCTIONS

The most common form of greeting is a handshake, especially in business. Foreign business-women should wait for a Kuwaiti businessman to offer his hand. Similarly, a foreign businessman should wait for a Kuwaiti businesswoman to offer her hand.

Kuwaitis may also greet you with a short, quick bow. In a more traditional form of greeting, Kuwaitis may extend one hand to a visitor's shoulder, grasp the visitor's hand with the other, kiss both cheeks and then hold the visitor's hand for a moment before releasing it.

It is very important to use titles in Kuwait. If someone has a doctorate, you should address them as "Doctor," followed by the last name, unless otherwise requested. If you are addressing a government official that has a title, you should use the title, followed by a last name. *"Sheiks"* (pronounced, "shake") should be addressed as "Your Excellency" or as *"Sheik,"* followed by the given name.

If the person you are addressing does not have a title, you should use "Mr.," "Mrs." or "Miss," followed by a last name. First names should not be used unless your host requests that you use it and a closer relationship has been established.

In general, Arabic names are written in the same order as English names – title, given name, middle name (patronymic) and surname (see examples below). A Kuwaiti's second name is his father's name. If an Arab's grandfather was (or is) a famous person, he may sometimes add his grandfather's name after his father's name and before his surname. Women in Kuwait adopt their husband's name after marriage. The terms *"al"* and *"bin"* literally mean "from" and, in practice, can mean either "son of…" or "from the town of…" The female form of *"bin"* is *"bint."* For example the name "Dr. Mahmoud bin Sultan bin Hamad al-Muqrin" means "Dr. Mahmoud, son of Sultan, grandson of Hamad, of the house (family) of Muqrin." Similarly, "Princess Fatima bint Ibrahim al-Saud" means "Princess Fatima, daughter of Ibrahim, of the house of Saud."

## SOCIAL TIPS AND CONVENTIONS

While Kuwait has been successfully modernized and urbanized, it still preserves Islamic traditions, heritage and faith. The customs of Islam dominate all aspects of daily life. Nevertheless, Kuwaitis are more open to the outside world, are more tolerant of others and are more progressive in comparison to other Islamic countries.

Kuwaitis are generous and amiable. They communicate with a modest demeanor rather than with a pragmatic and outgoing manner.

Good topics of conversation include sports, technology and travel. Soccer, horse and camel racing and hunting are popular sports. Kuwaitis also enjoy hearing praise of their country and its accomplishments.

To avoid topics which Kuwaitis find too personal, follow the lead of your host. While you should not specifically ask or talk about a man's wife or daughters, you may inquire about the family or children in general.

Avoid discussing Middle Eastern politics or Israel.

# KUWAIT (Cont'd)

## SOCIAL TIPS AND CONVENTIONS (Cont'd)

Kuwaitis do not speak loudly, and they tend to stand close together when conversing. A calm demeanor is taken as a sign of intelligence. Maintaining eye contact is also very important. If you shift eye contact away from your host, it may be interpreted as a sign that you are not trustworthy.

Since maintaining personal honor is very important, one should avoid embarrassing or criticizing anyone. Compromises may sometimes be necessary simply in order to maintain someone's sense of honor.

Be aware that Kuwaitis demonstrate trust and comfort with small gestures, such as tapping the shoulder or back. It is appropriate to smile and nod your head approvingly as a response. Similarly, it is quite common for men to hold hands. You should not be taken aback or embarrassed if your Kuwaiti colleague grasps your hand.

The left hand is considered unclean; only use the right hand for passing objects or for touching food or people.

## CUSTOMARY BUSINESS PRACTICES

Avoid arranging business travel during the period of *Ramadan*, since most businesses close during the day at this time so Kuwaitis may fast and pray. Since the exact time of *Ramadan* changes every year, check if any festivals or religious holidays are coming up before arranging your visit.

In order to conduct business in Kuwait, foreign firms must appoint a Kuwaiti representative or agent. The agent introduces the foreign business to potential markets and government officials and helps facilitate the slow process of establishing business operations in Kuwait. The appointment of an agent can be arranged through the Kuwait Chamber of Commerce or through international banks.

Letters of introduction should be forwarded by a third party – the Kuwaiti Chamber of Commerce, a banker or your agent – accompanied by a letter from a senior official from your firm.

Setting firm appointments is extremely important. "Dropping by" unannounced at an office makes a very poor impression.

While your counterparts may arrive late or a meeting may be delayed, it is very important to arrive on time in order to make a good impression.

Business may proceed at quite a slow pace in Kuwait since negotiations can be slow and a great deal of time is spent on reinforcing personal relationships.

Very often, the first meeting (or first few meetings) will simply be spent on polite small talk. While they may seem banal, these preliminary meetings should be taken seriously. During this time, your Kuwaiti counterpart will be trying to evaluate subjectively whether or not business should take place in the future. Often, after an initial talk, your counterpart will end the meeting and will invite you to come to another meeting where the actual business discussions will be conducted. The Kuwaiti executives will indicate when they are ready to start discussing business.

# KUWAIT (Cont'd)

## CUSTOMARY BUSINESS PRACTICES (Cont'd)

Establishing a personal relationship of depth and trust is one of the most important elements of conducting business in Kuwait. You should allow plenty of time for conducting transactions in Kuwait. At times, several days may pass between meetings and it is not acceptable to close deals by phone or fax communication.

Rank and status are very important in conducting business in Kuwait. Subordinates are expected to defer to senior management. The use of titles is also very important. People of high rank will amply display their wealth with lavish offices and expensive cars. Personal relations and strong (often family) connections play an important role within the small Kuwaiti business community.

Don't be surprised if your Kuwaiti counterparts take time to pray during a meeting. Praying five times a day is the Islamic practice. It is out of place to ask a Muslim to interfere with this practice; one should simply be patient. The period of prayer usually lasts only about 20 minutes and the flow of conversation is readily picked up when the prayer has concluded.

Visual aids make a good impression. Presentations should be concise and direct, particularly when you are dealing with senior executives. More lengthy presentations are customary when junior level executives take over to discuss technical details.

In negotiating, a calm but firm, sincere and personal approach works best. Kuwaiti business people do not appreciate a "hard-sell" approach or being hurried; instead, lengthy haggling almost always occurs.

You should be aware that Kuwaitis do not like dealing with lower level executives in negotiating, since decisions are made only at the top levels of Kuwaiti firms. While lower-level management may be involved in some parts of the negotiating process, the senior executive is expected to make final decisions. The decision maker in a Kuwaiti firm may speak very little and, instead, quietly observe the negotiations in order to make a decision.

It is unwise to bring lawyers during initial meetings since this will be interpreted as a sign of distrust. However, it is appropriate to include lawyers in the final stages of negotiation. Contracts should be simple and concise and should be translated into Arabic. It is advisable to hire a Kuwaiti lawyer who is familiar with local laws and with the subtleties of the Arabic language.

Business meetings are rarely private. It is important to be patient since there are often numerous interruptions for phone calls and visitors. Since people wander in and out of meetings, you may be asked to deliver a presentation a number of times.

Since Arabic is a language of hyperbole, a "yes" very often means "maybe."

More so than in other Islamic countries, women occupy positions in both business and government. At the same time, foreign businesswomen may encounter some initial disrespect, since Kuwaiti businessmen are not accustomed to dealing with female executives who are decision makers. Nevertheless, these traditional beliefs are gradually changing as more and more women are breaking into high-level management and decision-making positions in Kuwait.

# KUWAIT (Cont'd)

## CUSTOMARY BUSINESS PRACTICES (Cont'd)

Business cards are very important since it is standard practice for people to have unlisted phone numbers in Kuwait. The card is also used as a tool of presentation: it should look conservative and professional (with no color unless there is color in your company's logo). If you have a university degree above a bachelor's degree, it should be included on your card. Your position or title within your firm should also be printed. Business cards should be printed in both English and in Arabic and should be presented with the Arabic side up, using the right hand. When receiving a card, it is considered polite to read it thoughtfully and then to nod at your counterpart before putting it away.

In the summer (April to September), Kuwaiti businessmen usually wear lightweight suits (linen or cotton). The winter months are cooler and rainy, but not cold. Business attire during this time is generally conservative – a dark suit and tie with a white shirt for men and a dark suit or skirt with a white blouse for women. Suits should be cut conservatively and jewelry (e.g., cufflinks, watch, ring, etc.) which should be kept to a minimum, should be gold.

Businesses are usually open from 8:30 a.m. until 12:30 p.m. and then from 4:30 until 8:30 p.m., Saturday through Thursday. Businesses are closed on Fridays because it is a religious day.

## BUSINESS ENTERTAINING

Lunch, the largest meal of the day, is the most common business meal in Kuwait and is usually taken between 12:30 and 2:00 p.m. Business dinners, which are less common and tend to be lighter meals, usually take place between 8:00 or 9:00 p.m. Business is usually not discussed during the first meal together or during dinners. Business meals are perceived as a social opportunity to establish trust and personal rapport between the executives working together on a transaction.

Even when the meal takes place in a home, spouses are rarely included in business entertainment. It will be specified if they are; if you are unsure, check in advance.

If you invite your counterparts to a meal, it is appropriate to dine in your hotel restaurant or to ask them to choose a restaurant for you. If possible, pay the bill in advance. Keep in mind that it is inappropriate to take your Kuwaiti guests to a bar or nightclub.

It is considered an honor to be invited to a Kuwaiti's home and it is considered very rude to decline such an invitation.

Gift-giving is not an important part of doing business in Kuwait and it can be wrongly perceived since laws against bribery are seriously enforced. Expensive gifts should never be given during negotiations or when bidding on contracts if there is any chance that they may be misinterpreted as a bribe.

Gifts that have the company logo on them are the most appropriate, since it is unlikely that they would be interpreted as bribes. Avoid presenting gifts to your host when you are alone. If you give gifts to a group of businesspeople, be mindful that each gift matches the status of each individual within the team.

## BUSINESS ENTERTAINING (Cont'd)

To congratulate your Kuwaiti business counterpart or when visiting a home, flowers are the most appropriate gift. It is also appropriate to have any kind of flowers sent to the home before a dinner party. If you are invited to a home for a meal, be aware that your host will be insulted if you bring food or drink as a gift (which would be taken to imply that you think your host is not generous). Also, avoid giving a gift soley to your host's wife. It will seem too personal. Also, do not bring alcohol (which is prohibited in Muslim countries).

Any kind of book or gift for your host's children is considered appropriate. Gold pens, finely-made compasses (so that your host will always know where the Mecca is), business-card cases and cigarette lighters make appropriate business gifts.

Avoid gifts that portray people or animals. Images of the human body are frowned upon according to Islamic custom and certain animals are considered unclean or are symbols of negative characteristics.

Generosity is considered one of the highest values in Kuwait. The greatest compliment you can pay your host is to acknowledge his generosity. Similarly, when you are offered a gift by a Kuwaiti, it is impolite to refuse.

Avoid admiring an object or any other possession to an excess, or your host may feel obliged to give it to you. It would then be impolite to refuse.

Even if your Kuwaiti host encourages you to drink alcohol, it is advisable not to do so. While a host may feel obligated to offer you alcohol, he may also feel offended if you do not respect local custom (which prohibits the consumption of alcohol).

When entering a house or tent, keep in mind that you may be asked to remove your shoes.

## DINING OUT

Rice is a basic element of the Kuwaiti diet. When it is mixed with onions, it is called *mashkoul*; when it is mixed with lentils it is called *muaddas*. *Cous-cous* (a grain-like pasta) is also popular. The main spices of Kuwaiti cuisine are turmeric, ginger, cardamom, nutmeg, parsley, rosewater, pepper, saffron and ground citrus fruits. Ground limes are used in many dishes and are called *loomi*. Cucumber, tomatoes, chick-peas, eggplant, onions and olives often accompany many dishes. Broiled lamb, barbecued fish, chicken and prawns are also common.

Kuwaiti cuisine includes Middle Eastern and European dishes, along with traditional Kuwaiti ones. For example, *samouli* is a white bread, which is similar to the French baguette. Popular dishes include *kabab maswiis* (ground beef or lamb served on Arabic bread with yogurt-cucumber sauce), *lahm bil bayd* (a deep-fried dish made with ground beef and boiled eggs), *machbous* (a spicy lamb dish served with rice) and *basal mahshi* (onions stuffed with rice and either beef or lamb).

Desserts are usually made with a light, flaky dough, stuffed with raisins, nuts and honey. The dough is then baked or fried. Some popular desserts include *sabb al-gafsha* (a gooey, fried sweet pastry puff with honey syrup), *samboosa halwa* (deep-fried triangles of dough and nuts) and *ghi raybah* (shortbread balls with powdered ginger exteriors). Sweet drinks made from yogurt and fruit juices also make popular desserts. Arabic coffee is served in very small cups. You are expected to drink two or three cupfuls.

# KUWAIT (Cont'd)

## DINING OUT (Cont'd)

Appetizers are not customarily served, but exceptions may be made when a foreign guest is invited to a meal.

It is polite both to sample all the dishes offered and to consume large amounts of food. This will be understood as a compliment to local cuisine and to your hostess. It is also appropriate and even appreciated if you ask your host to describe certain unfamiliar foods to you.

Dining style varies depending on the particular home. In some homes, guests may be seated Western-style (on chairs around a table). Otherwise, guests may be seated on the floor next to a low table. Food may be eaten with utensils or with the right hand only, using Arabic bread to pick up food or move it on the plate. Sometimes a jug full of water is passed around to each diner before a meal, so that each person may wash his/her hands.

It is polite to wait for your host to seat you. It is likely that you will be seated to the right of your host or at the head of the table. All dishes are usually served at the same time and guests help themselves to the food, which is presented on communal trays.

Kuwaitis may toast with fruit juice, mineral water or iced tea. The host may say *"Mah-bruk!"* ("Congratulations!") or *"Sahatak!"* ("To your health!"), depending on what is appropriate.

During meals, conversation is usually minimal. After the meal, guests usually gather in a smoking room to smoke from a water pipe, to have coffee or mint tea and to converse. When you leave, your host may say, *"Al-lah is-ah-mahk,"* which means, "May God keep you in peace."

## PUBLIC CUSTOMS

While appropriate women's clothing styles are more relaxed in Kuwait than in other Muslim countries, women should still avoid wearing revealing garments and should keep makeup and jewelry to a minimum. Knee length or longer skirts with at least elbow-length sleeves are acceptable, and women should always cover their shoulders. Shirts should be buttoned up to the neck. Neither men nor women should wear shorts in public. As a foreign visitor, you may offend some Kuwaitis if you wear traditional Kuwaiti clothing.

Good posture is expected when you are sitting. You should be especially careful not to point the sole of your shoe towards anybody, especially if you cross your legs. Generally, it is best to keep both feet flat on the ground.

It is not appropriate to get too physically comfortable with those around you. You should not rest your arm on someone else's chair, pat someone on the back, gesticulate or touch people (other than a hand shake).

Avoid coughing, sneezing or clearing your throat in public. If it cannot be avoided, you should try to muffle it.

It is considered impolite to point at another person.

The "thumbs up" gesture is considered to be very rude.

# MOROCCO: HISTORICAL OVERVIEW

- The earliest settlers of Morocco were the Berbers.

- Morocco's history, due to its location on the Mediterranean, is filled with foreign invasions from the Phoenicians as well as the Carthaginians, Romans, Vandals, Visigoths and Greeks. Ancient Morocco was called Mauretania.

- The Arabs invaded in the seventh century A.D. and introduced Islam to Morocco. The Berbers fought off direct Arab rule and established an independent kingdom in the eighth century. Morocco was ruled by several Berber dynasties until the 13th century. Moroccan territory included much of Spain and North Africa.

- The Alawi dynasty, which claims descent from the Prophet Mohammed, took control in the 17th century.

- In 1787, Morocco became one of the first nations to sign a peace and friendship treaty with the U.S.

- European nations became involved in Morocco in the 19th century, particularly after France conquered Algeria in 1830. France made the country a protectorate in 1912.

- The French ruled until 1956, when Morocco was granted its independence.

- Morocco is ruled by a constitutional monarchy. The current king, in power since 1961, is Hassan II. He is a direct descendent of kings of the Alawi dynasty, which began in 1660.

- A new constitution, adopted in 1972, increased the size of the Chamber of Representatives, giving it more legislative power.

- In 1975, Morocco reclaimed the Spanish Sahara (now the Western Sahara) as its territory. Spain was forced to withdraw its troops. Neighboring countries, especially Algeria, objected to Morocco's development of the area and fighting ensued. A cease-fire went into effect in September 1991, ending 15 years of civil war. A referendum to choose independence or annexation by Morocco, sponsored by the U.N., has been postponed due to a disagreement over who is qualified to vote.

- The increasing mechanization of agriculture has allowed for the export of large quantities of produce and citrus to Europe each year. Also, increasing privatization has attracted over two billion dollars in foreign investment since 1992. The growth of the fishing industry is now being emphasized.

- The regime of Hassan II has become less strict, but direct criticism of the king is prohibited and may still result in a prison sentence.

# MOROCCO

## INTRODUCTIONS

The practice of shaking hands when greeting or when introduced in Morocco is widely accepted. Handshakes are made with the right hand only.

It is common for women or good friends – both male and female – to greet each other by kissing each other on each cheek.

Less than fervent greetings are considered rude.

Whether in conversation or when greeting, women should never make eye contact with men who are strangers (as it may be construed as an invitation).

Placing your hand over your heart signifies personal warmth or pleasure in seeing the person being greeted. Older people usually partake in this custom.

Titles are always used in formal situations as well as when introduced to acquaintances. When meeting anyone for the first time, use French titles – *"Monsieur," "Madame," "Mademoiselle."* You should greet doctors and professors (M.D. or Ph.D.) by their title, followed by their last name.

Be advised that there are two titles of importance – *"Haj"* (masculine) and *"Haja"* (feminine) – which signify that the individual has been to Mecca. However, as a Westerner, it is suggested that you do not use this title when addressing someone.

At a party or group gathering, expect to be introduced individually. Make sure that you shake hands with each person.

## SOCIAL TIPS AND CONVENTIONS

Most Moroccans are bilingual, speaking both Arabic (Moroccan dialect) and French. Spanish is also spoken in the north. English is widely studied and is gaining popularity.

Moroccans value family, honor, dignity, generosity and hospitality. Moroccan culture is rooted in the Islamic sense of fatalism, the doctrine which states that all events are predetermined by fate and therefore cannot be changed by human beings. This may affect individual attitudes in business.

When meeting someone, remember to ask about that person's family. If the person is a man, do not ask about his wife. Other good subjects to ask about are soccer, track, golf, basketball, Moroccan history, culture and architecture.

Avoid talking about religion, Mid-East tension or Israel. Don't be surprised if people ask about your view on Islam. It's best to say that Islam has some beautiful customs, but that you are of another religion.

Expect Moroccans to be very formal. Behavior should conform to the social situation, not to a specific individual. French culture is regarded as the ideal and anything French is considered superior.

## SOCIAL TIPS AND CONVENTIONS (Cont'd)

It is considered impolite to say "no" directly. Expect Moroccans to say "yes" even when they do not mean it.

Be careful about admiring objects to an excess. Otherwise your host may feel obligated to give it to you as a gift.

Items are passed with the right hand or with both hands, but never with the left hand.

It is impolite to point at people or to show the bottom of one's foot. It is also generally considered improper to cross one's legs.

A businesswoman traveling alone should be prepared to be asked frequently if she is married. If she is not married, she will be confronted with further inquiry.

## CUSTOMARY BUSINESS PRACTICES

The Moroccan business atmosphere tends to combine Middle Eastern and French styles. Both styles tend to be very formal.

It is acceptable to contact Moroccan firms directly by forwarding several letters before your arrival, stating your purpose along with company history and the scope of business at hand.

Bring business cards printed both in English and in Arabic.

Moroccans place a lot of emphasis on the importance of strong relationships in business. Successful business in Morocco requires at least one or two visits by a senior executive. Sending a few executives on the trip indicates the seriousness of your proposal.

Make appointments well in advance, when possible. Your host may not arrive on time for a meeting, but you are expected to be punctual.

Be aware that business discussions may occur in hotels and restaurants, but final deals are always made in an office.

The business organization structure is very precise, centralized and structured, so there is little room for mistakes. Prior to your appointment, inquire as to who the top level negotiator is as well as who will be making final decisions.

It is important to be conservatively well-dressed in order to gain respect. Businesswomen should avoid low necklines, bare shoulders, short skirts and short sleeves. It also suggested that women wear long sleeves for business entertaining. Women with long hair should wear their hair up.

In Tangier, business operates Monday through Friday, 9:00 a.m. to noon and 4:00 to 8:00 p.m. In Casablanca and in the rest of the country, business hours are 9:00 a.m. to noon and 3:00 to 6:00 p.m.

# MOROCCO (Cont'd)

## CUSTOMARY BUSINESS PRACTICES (Cont'd)

To contact people, it is best to go to an office directly since it can take up to an hour for a telephone call to go from place to place within the same city.

## BUSINESS ENTERTAINING

Moroccans are very polite and they should be approached with gestures of courtesy.

Be prepared to participate in the customary drinking of tea, without which business is never done.

Do not give a gift to someone when you first meet. It may be interpreted as a bribe. Also, be especially careful about giving alcohol as a gift since consumption of liquor is prohibited in the Muslim religion.

The giving of gifts is not taken lightly in Morocco. Moroccans place more emphasis on respect for tradition and manners. Do not expect a gift to be accepted with profuse thank-you's – Moroccans do not like to appear materialistic.

When invited to a meal by a family living in the city, gifts are not expected. However, if you do bring gifts, bring nuts, dates, candy, flowers or small toys for children. Appropriate gifts from abroad for children and teenagers include solar calculators, cassettes of popular U.S. music, clothing and Frisbees or T-shirts with a city's or university's insignia.

It is impolite to refuse offered refreshments (even if a token refusal is made before accepting the offer.)

Only men often socialize in public coffee houses, especially on weekends or in the evenings. As a businesswoman, you should not go into a coffeehouse unless you see other women inside.

It is common for Moroccan businessmen to invite colleagues to their homes for huge feasts. However, you will rarely meet their wives.

You should offer to remove your shoes before entering a Moroccan home. Enter a home with your right foot first.

If you eat at someone's house, you will please your host by complimenting the home.

In restaurants or cafes, snapping one's fingers is used to call a waiter/waitress.

In restaurants, a service charge is usually included in the check, which is paid for by the host. If the service charge is not included, leave a gratuity of about ten percent.

## DINING OUT

Moroccans prefer to eat at home. However, if they do dine out, they favor French and Italian restaurants.

Breakfast is served between 7:00 and 8:00 a.m. and usually consists of mint tea or French-roast coffee and bread with honey.

# MOROCCO (Cont'd)

## DINING OUT (Cont'd)

Lunch is served around 2:00 p.m. and is the main meal of the day. It's also the preferred business meal.

Dinner is eaten between 8:00 and 11:00 p.m. and is usually a light meal with the exception of special business meals. Dinner is typically a snack of cheese and bread or pasta and salad.

It is common for a meal to be eaten with the fingers (of the right hand only) from a communal dish. You should eat from the section of the dish directly in front of you. Never reach beyond the closest area, and do not touch the meat until your host pushes it toward you.

A basin of water is usually available in the eating area. Each person washes his/her hands before and after eating. It is important to wash your hands in front of everybody.

Moroccans dine while sitting on low banquette seats (large overstuffed pillows).

Cumin is the main spice in Morocco. Two versatile staples are *cous-cous* (a grain-like pasta and the national dish of Morocco) usually accompanied by chicken, lamb and vegetables, and fish such as tuna, whiting, red mullet and perch. Fruits and soups are also popular in Moroccan cuisine.

*Bstilla* (a traditional Moroccan delicacy) is a flaky pastry filled with pigeon meat and spices, sprinkled with cinnamon and sugar. *Merguez,* another delicacy, are flavorful, spicy beef or lamb sausages served with a powerful "tongue-numbing" pepper called *harissa.*

The serving of tea requires a particular ceremony in Morocco. When women are serving, they must pour in a manner that produces a ring of bubbles (called a *fez*) around the inside rim of the glass. If you are asked to pour tea, you may want to decline unless you feel that you have the necessary skills to produce *fez.*

Men and women usually eat separately. The number of tablecloths on the serving table will indicate how many courses a Moroccan meal will contain.

Remember to use only your right hand for handling food. The left hand is to be kept in your lap while eating.

In homes, it is generally considered impolite for the guests to finish eating before the host, as this can imply that the food did not taste good. Licking your fingers is a sign that you are finished.

## PUBLIC CUSTOMS

If you want to use a gesture to say "come here," use the Western good-bye wave.

Don't be surprised to see men and men or women and women holding hands. This simply signifies warmth and friendship.

Western-style clothing is becoming more popular in Morocco. However, short pants and casual attire are not worn in public. Shorts are only worn on the beach.

# MOROCCO (Cont'd)

## PUBLIC CUSTOMS (Cont'd)

When one visits a mosque, clothing that covers the entire body (except the head and hands) should be worn and shoes should be removed. However, foreigners usually are not allowed in mosques.

Each year Muslims observe *Ramadan*, a month of fasting and prayer. (Because Muslims use a lunar calendar, the dates change every year.) During this time, no eating or drinking is permitted between dawn and sunset. Visitors are exempt from the fast. However, at this time, foreign visitors should exercise discretion when eating in public during the day.

It is considered improper for a woman to travel alone at night. If a woman does travel alone at night, it is likely that she will be harassed.

Bargaining is widely practiced and is expected, except in restaurants.

# MOZAMBIQUE: HISTORICAL OVERVIEW

- Arab traders are believed to have set up outposts in Mozambique as early as the eighth century A.D. They traded in ivory, gold and slaves.

- A distinct Islamic culture was in place by the time of the first Portuguese settlement in 1505. The Islamic tradition is still strong in coastal areas.

- Portugal found the colony to be a plentiful source of slave labor, particularly for trade. In addition to the slave trade, Portugal found the area to be good for agriculture and as a transport corridor for other states. The Portuguese did little to develop industries other than transportation and agriculture.

- The Portuguese ruled from the early 1500s to 1975. The struggle for independence began in 1962, when the *Front for the Liberation of Mozambique (FRELIMO)* was formed. Two years later it started a guerilla movement against the Portuguese rulers. In 1974, following a change of government in Portugal, a cease-fire was declared and independence was soon granted.

- *FRELIMO* ruled the newly independent nation. It instituted a rigid socialist economy and supported the struggle for independence in neighboring Rhodesia.

- Opposition to *FRELIMO*'s control of the economy, especially the establishment of state-run agriculture, gave rise to a dissident movement (called *RENAMO*, the *Mozambique National Resistance*). The ongoing civil war devastated Mozambique's economy and much of the transportation system was destroyed.

- By 1987, *RENAMO* had control over most of Mozambique. They destroyed 50% of the crops before harvest and a terrible drought finished off what was left.

- The U.S. was shocked when it learned that the Soviet Union, which had always had an interest in Mozambique, had been supplying clandestine military aid to the *FRELIMO* government since 1982.

- With the demise of the Soviet Union, communism became irrelevant in Mozambique. The fighting became no more than a rivalry between the leader of *FRELIMO*, President Joaquim Chissano, and the *RENAMO* leader, Afonso Dhlakama. Conditions worsened in 1990. It was not until 1992 that a cease-fire was signed and since that time, *RENAMO*'s power has been in decline.

- Power struggles are largely settled, but the people are resentful of President Chissano and the toll that his years of communist-style government have exacted. Foreign aid has helped the economy along in the last two years and will be necessary in the future for Mozambique's survival.

# MOZAMBIQUE

## INTRODUCTIONS

A handshake is the proper greeting in Mozambique.

The handshake, however, is a three-step process. The two people grasp each other's hands, rotate the wrist up then resume back to a normal handshake.

First names are rarely used and professional titles should be used as much as possible.

## SOCIAL TIPS AND CONVENTIONS

Be advised that there is a strong affiliation among tribes in Mozambique. As in most African countries, families are very close and the people are friendly.

Good topics of discussion include history and culture. Avoid discussing politics and regional disputes.

## CUSTOMARY BUSINESS PRACTICES

Business cards are used widely in Mozambique.

It is best to confirm your meeting on the day it is scheduled. Be advised that you may be kept waiting in an office for awhile – the higher the management level of the individual, the longer your wait may be.

Mozambique has a strong Portuguese influence and has adopted many of Portugal's practices and procedures. You will most likely find that business agreements require a "stamp of approval" from many different officers and that decision making will take a long time.

It is best to try to understand the many different power circles involved in the decision-making process in Mozambique. Be more sensitive and adjust your expectations accordingly to a slower pace.

Women are accepted in the business world very well in Mozambique, as opposed to some other traditional African nations. It is quite common to have women in the family become involved in business matters.

## BUSINESS ENTERTAINING

Lunch and dinner appointments at local restaurants are appropriate for business meetings. It is uncommon, however, to invite spouses.

Avoid lavish gifts (over $10). Mozambique is one of the poorest countries in the world (minimum wage is $13/month) and you may offend people if you present them with expensive gifts. It is also wise not to bring or wear expensive jewelry. They may take offense at any hint of pretentiousness.

# MOZAMBIQUE (Cont'd)

## DINING OUT

The most popular food in Mozambique is chicken. There are many restaurants which can capture the spicy tastes of the local cuisines.

A specialty in Mozambique is tiger prawns, which are shrimp from 10-12 inches in length.

# NIGERIA: HISTORICAL OVERVIEW

- Nigeria has a diverse history that stretches back to at least 500 B.C. when the Nok people lived in the area.

- Various empires flourished for centuries in different regions of what is now Nigeria.

- The Hausa peoples, who inhabit northern Nigeria, converted to Islam in the 13th century and established a feudal system.

- The Fulani built a great empire in the 1800s.

- In the southwest, the Yoruba established the Kingdom of Oyo and extended its influence as far as modern Togo.

- The Ibo, in the southeast, remained isolated.

- European explorers and traders made contact with the Yoruba and the Benin peoples at the end of the 15th century. They began a profitable slave trade.

- British influence increased until 1861, when Britain declared the area around the city of Lagos a Crown Colony. By 1914, the entire area had become the Colony and Protectorate of Nigeria.

- Nigeria became independent in 1960, and became a republic in 1963. Tensions mounted among the various ethnic groups. Following two coups, the Ibo-dominated eastern region attempted to secede and establish the Republic of Biafra. Civil war followed from 1967-1970 and the Ibos were forced back into the republic.

- In 1979, under a new constitution, national elections were held. This civilian government headed by President Shehu Shagari lasted only until late 1983. A military coup placed power in the hands of General Mohammed Buhari who banned political parties.

- Another coup followed in 1985, resulting in Major General Ibrahim Babangida becoming the nation's new military leader.

- A commission was established in 1986 with the goal of organizing a peaceful transition from military to civilian rule by 1992. However, elections scheduled for 1989 were never held. Free national elections, scheduled for 1992, were not held until June 1993. Babangida promised to turn power over to the winner of the election, but he refused to accept the final election results. He appointed Ernest Shonekan as the civilian government leader, however, he was deposed after only three months.

- Nigeria's latest military ruler, General Sani Abacha, abolished all democratic institutions, with promises to let new political parties form after a "national constitutional conference" which has not yet occurred.

- The social and economic disorganization is ongoing. These factors, as well as the high inflation rate, have made trade with Nigeria increasingly difficult.

# NIGERIA

## INTRODUCTIONS

Nigerians place great value on properly greeting someone and handshaking is customary. Upon meeting a Nigerian business associate, the greeting is Westernized but formal.

Learning local greetings is very much appreciated by prospective business partners (for example, always shake hands when greeting someone, no matter how busy he/she is). A few words, even phrased imperfectly, show a willingness to adapt as well as an appreciation for local customs.

Although there is a great diversity of customs, cultures and dialects in Nigeria, be aware that English is widely used when exchanging greetings.

## SOCIAL TIPS AND CONVENTIONS

When conversing, members of the same sex stand much closer to each other than do people in North America.

Good conversation topics include modern and future aspects of the country. Nigerians are proud and self-confident and part of this confidence comes from the belief that their country is in many ways a leader in Africa.

Friendship is a valued commodity among most Nigerians. Hospitality is abundant and generous. Also, relationships develop quickly and tend to be long-lasting.

Family ties are very strong in Nigeria. Family members remain close to each other throughout their entire lives. It is not unusual for family members to expect a relative to either find or create a job for them once this relative is employed.

## CUSTOMARY BUSINESS PRACTICES

After greeting your Nigerian counterparts, take some time to converse socially before commencing business; better yet, let them first broach the subject. Small talk is considered part of the greeting process.

Business cards are sometimes called the "compliment card." They often say "with the compliments of " and are given with more meaning than as just a handy reference. You are expected to have a card if you want your business initiatives to be taken seriously.

Age is highly respected and associated with wisdom. To increase your chances of success, it is recommended that an older person be sent to meet with prospective business partners. Sending a younger executive may suggest to Nigerians that their business is not worthy of the attention of the elders who are presumed to head an organization.

Business hours are weekdays from 8:30 a.m. to 5:00 p.m. In the Muslim areas, business in not done on Fridays or Saturdays for religious reasons.

# NIGERIA (Cont'd)

## CUSTOMARY BUSINESS PRACTICES (Cont'd)

Almost half of all Nigerians are Muslims and they dominate the northern part of the country. The area where you are conducting business will greatly determine the type of business environment you will encounter.

Foreign executives should avoid lumping vaguely related cultures together in the same general groupings. The culture of the Ibos in the largely Christian south and the Hausas in the mainly Muslim north are different and so are the respective deal-making and business styles of these two ethnic groups. The Ibo people adapted well to Westernization during British colonial rule. The Hausas, however, are more formal and conservative in their business approach.

In Nigeria, any significant business transaction is always conducted in person. Any attempts to conduct business by telephone or by mail is interpreted as unimportant or trivial. Nigerians tend to schedule business appointments well in advance and prefer face-to-face meetings.

It is best to schedule no more than two appointments a day and to allow plenty of time in between. Nigerians do not have a rigid sense of time and punctuality is not very prevalent. Your 8:00 a.m. appointment may not show up until 4:00 p.m. or not at all.

## BUSINESS ENTERTAINING

Most entertaining, especially in Lagos, is conducted in clubs, hotels or elegant, expensive restaurants. Food and customs in these establishments are very much in the style of the British.

Breakfast meetings are very popular as Nigerians start their day early. Discussing business during breakfast is often very productive.

It is common to continue business over lunch. It is unlikely that you will be invited out for a social evening until a friendly relationship has been established or you are close to closing a business deal.

If you are invited to a Nigerian home for a social evening, remember to always bring gifts. Perfume and makeup are acceptable for a woman. Your Nigerian host would enjoy customized stationery or Western-style clothing.

The most interesting part of Nigerian entertaining is the music and dancing. Lagos has more nightclubs with live music than most of Africa combined, and one can expect to be shown to his host's favorite discos during a night out. *Juju*, a local style of pop music with strong local flavor and rhythms, dominates many clubs.

# NIGERIA (Cont'd)

## DINING OUT

Nigerian cooking is often very spicy. Specialties include dried fish and herbs, *Alapa* (smothered red snapper), *frejon* (smothered catfish in bean sauce), chicken and beef loaf, *chicken imoyo* (chicken and okra), *o jo jo* (meatballs), *akara* (bean balls), *puff-puff* (fried bread), *fetri detsi* (spicy chili chicken) and *moyinmoyin* (steamed dumplings stuffed with shrimp).

In Yoruba country as well as other areas of Nigeria, stews are made with *Egunsi* – melon or gourd seeds – that are boiled and then soaked several days until fermented.

Many herbs used as condiments by Nigerians in food preparation have medicinal properties.

Nigeria has long been a fertile producer of cocoa, palm oil, *cocyams*, tubers, sorghum millet, rice and other agricultural bounties.

Breakfast is usually eaten between 7:00 and 9:00 a.m. and consists of hot porridge or rice, bread and English tea. Lunch is served from 1:30 to 3:30 p.m., often with a siesta around the same time. Dinner typically begins around 8:30 p.m. and may end around 11:00 p.m. or later.

Nigerians often have their meals at home, although small, cozy restaurants featuring traditional foods are also popular settings for eating.

A real treat is a traditional Nigerian buffet, where a savory array is offered for large gatherings. This array includes the local cuisine, with the centerpiece consisting of bananas, surrounded by coconuts, avocados, mangoes, fresh pineapple slices, cucumbers, eggplants and peanuts.

## PUBLIC CUSTOMS

As in many other cultures, the left hand is considered unclean in Nigeria. It is extremely impolite to extend the left hand to others or to eat with it, even if a person is left-handed.

Although women in the cities and young girls often wear Western dress, most women wear traditional long wraparound skirts, short-sleeved tops and head scarves. Traditional Nigerian men's dress is loose and comfortable.

# SAUDI ARABIA: HISTORICAL OVERVIEW

- Saudi Arabia's modern history began in the seventh century, when the prophet Muhammad began proclaiming the message of Islam from the (now Saudi Arabian) cities of Makkah and Medina, uniting the country for the first time. As Islam spread from the peninsula to parts of Asia, Northern Africa and other regions of the world, the Arab Empire flourished.

- The Arab Empire expanded and became a great power. During its period of grandeur, the Arabs developed an advanced society and culture, they excelled in the sciences and invented algebra. At the same time, the peninsula was inhabited by a number of nomadic tribes, which were often at war with one another, especially as the Empire started to decline in the 13th century.

- Fighting between different factions was particularly heavy in the last 30 years of the 19th century. Then, in 1902, the present state of Saudi Arabia was founded. The House of Saud, a leading family in the region, recaptured its ancestral home in Riyadh. The House of Saud united the major factions of the country, seized power in the central area of Arabia and Abdul Aziz Al-Saud declared himself king. Four of King Abdul's sons have succeeded him in the monarchy beginning with Saud, Faisal, Khalid and then King Fahd bin Abdul Aziz, who ruled as an absolute monarch. Another brother, Abdullah, was the crown prince. Abdullah was named as the successor to the King.

- During World War I, King Abdul extended rule over the Western province along the Red Sea, largely at the expense of the crumbling Ottoman Empire. In 1925, the kingdom was officially established by the son of King Abdul, King Ibn Saud. He united the warring tribes of the region and the country was named in his honor as founder of the royal dynasty. In 1932, the country received the official name of the Kingdom of Saudi Arabia.

- In the 1970s, Saudi Arabia was transformed into a modern state, when what Saudi Arabians call *Al Tafra* ("The Eruption") occurred. Oil prices rose to unforeseen levels and Saudi Arabia became a major economic force with the U.S. becoming a close ally. This boom was short-lived. Falling oil prices in the 1980s put the country into a recession from which it is still recovering.

- Saudi Arabia supported Iraq in the Iran-Iraq War in the 1980s. Since the late 1980s, when the country severed relations with Iran, King Fahd has been a positive influence on peace and stability in the Middle East. When Iraq invaded Kuwait in 1990 and threatened Saudi Arabia, the Saudis hosted the international coalition that liberated Kuwait and protected Saudi Arabia.

- After the 1991 Gulf War, the issue of political and social liberalization was raised and while Saudi Arabia has remained determined to retain conservative customs, in 1992, some political changes were announced. A number of social welfare programs have been introduced. While politics have been stable, the conflict between "traditionalists" and "modernizers" continues.

- Competition from non-OPEC countries is likely to continue into the future which will further drive down the price of crude oil. Another problem facing the King and the government is the resurgence of Islamic fundamentalists.

# SAUDI ARABIA

## INTRODUCTIONS

In Saudi Arabia, it is customary to shake hands lightly, but sincerely, with everyone in an office when meeting and when departing. The handshake is long and often continues through the entire greeting.

It is likely that you will shake hands frequently, possibly several times a day with the same person. For example, whenever someone enters the room, you should shake hands.

Men who know each other quite well often embrace each other and kiss each other once on each cheek when greeting.

It is extremely unlikely for foreign businessmen to come in contact with Saudi women.

When addressing people, use the titles "Mister," "Mrs.," "Doctor" (for both M.D. and Ph.D.), *Sheik* (pronounced "Shake," if you *know* that the person is a *sheik*), "Your Excellency" (for government ministers) or "Your Highness" (for members of the royal family), followed by the last name. Find out which ministers are royal (since there are thousands of them) and these ministers should be addressed as "Your Royal Highness," rather than as "Your Excellency."

At a party, expect to be introduced to each person individually. Even if you are not, you should act as if you have been and shake each person's hand.

It is polite to accompany a visitor to the street when the visitor leaves. Your host may also hold your hand in his as you leave, as a sign of friendship.

## SOCIAL TIPS AND CONVENTIONS

Saudis tend to stand very close and make direct eye contact when talking to others. This is a sign of courtesy and respect. They may also touch often, in order to heighten communication.

Saudi customs regarding women differ substantially from many other cultures. It is *not* acceptable to inquire about the adult women (more than 12 years old) in a Saudi man's family. However, it *is* acceptable to inquire about a colleague's family in general or about his children. A businesswoman traveling in Saudi Arabia will have to accept the role assigned to women by a very strict Muslim society, including rules about visiting certain places and being in the company of men.

Saudi women dress very modestly and foreign women should respect this custom. Women should always completely cover their arms, legs and hair (wear a long skirt, down to the ankles, and a long-sleeved blouse) and dress so as not to attract attention to their bodies. Businesswomen should never wear pantsuits.

A Saudi appreciates admiring comments about his country, his city, his office or his taste in art. However, avoid admiring an individual possession to an excess or he will feel obligated to give it to you.

Politics, religion and topics with sexual content or those which are detrimental to Islam or the royal family are best avoided in conversation. Also, if you mention what is usually called the "Persian Gulf," you should refer to it as the "Arabian Gulf."

# SAUDI ARABIA (Cont'd)

## SOCIAL TIPS AND CONVENTIONS (Cont'd)

Avoid criticizing anyone (Saudi or non-Saudi) publicly. Saudis find this kind of behavior intolerable because it causes a loss of dignity.

## CUSTOMARY BUSINESS PRACTICES

Keep in mind that Arabic is the country's only language and that European languages are not as widely used as in other Middle Eastern countries. Bring business cards printed in English on one side and in Arabic on the other.

Be aware that people sometimes remove their shoes before entering an office. Check if there is a pile of shoes by the door and then proceed accordingly.

It is not unusual to arrive for a business meeting and find another meeting already underway. It is also common practice for other people to interrupt or to walk in on your meeting and for the meeting to be reconvened several times. Although this may test your patience, the Saudis have a more relaxed attitude toward appointments. It will be necessary to tolerate frequent diversions and waiting. It may, in fact, be impossible to conduct a private meeting.

A business meeting customarily begins with social conversation. Accept endless cups of coffee or tea.

Negotiation and bargaining is a traditional Saudi ritual. It generally begins with inflated proposals, proceeding through a series of concessions. The price should be discussed as a matter between friends, establishing trust as you proceed. Take your time and be prepared to discuss many unresolved issues simultaneously.

It is best to allow time for your Saudi business counterparts to deliberate. Do not press for immediate answers or a direct "Yes" or "No."

To facilitate communication, eye contact and gestures of openness are important.

You may find it difficult to arrive at a final agreement and you should not confuse politeness with a decision. Although it is wise to get a written contract, do not be surprised if the deal is renegotiated later. Nothing is final.

Working with a Saudi agent is a good idea. Once contact is established, the agent may prefer to work directly with you and avoid middlemen. Make frequent visits to solidify the business relationship.

It is recommended that business not be conducted by telephone or by mail. It is not improper, just futile. Business is best conducted face to face. Saudis like to develop long, close business relationships.

## BUSINESS ENTERTAINING

Be aware that Saudi Arabian men do not typically socialize with other men outside of the family. Women do not attend social gatherings. However, from working with Westernized companies over the past 15 years, the Saudis have adapted to the practice of business entertaining.

# SAUDI ARABIA (Cont'd)

## BUSINESS ENTERTAINING (Cont'd)

A Saudi wife should never be included in an invitation to a business meal.

Business entertaining is generally conducted during lunch at a hotel or restaurant. Lunch is usually the largest meal of the day and takes place after the noon prayer.

Do not expect to find traditional Saudi restaurants. Rather, the restaurants in Saudi Arabia are predominantly Chinese, Korean, Indian, Pakistani or Ethiopian.

No alcohol is served in Saudi Arabia.

If you are invited to a restaurant, you should not argue when the bill arrives and your host pays or your host will be insulted. Reciprocating invitations is not expected, but is appreciated.

Women should not go into restaurants alone, unless accompanied by a couple or a male relative. Most hotels have two restaurants – one for men and one for families. Foreign women should always eat in a family restaurant.

Waiters should be tipped about 15%. Be sure to check the bill because the tip is sometimes included.

If invited to a house, it is suggested that you bring small gifts for the children, but do not bring anything for the wife, who is never seen. When invited to a meal, you can bring pastries or imported candies in a box.

After meeting someone two or three times, you may want to present him with a modest gift. It should not advertise anything and should not be very valuable (e.g., desk accessories, electrical gadgets).

## DINING OUT

If invited to a Saudi home, expect to have tea in a sitting room and then be accompanied to another room for the main meal. In fact, if you are invited for dinner for a specific time, the meal may not actually be served until several hours later. It is common to play cards or listen to music before the meal.

At meals in homes, people traditionally sit in a circle on the floor in front of a large mat with food on it. There are no individual plates. When sitting on the floor, sit cross-legged or kneel on one knee. Make sure that your feet are not touching the food mat and that your soles are not facing anybody.

Men and women always eat separately.

Before the meal, a basin of water may be passed around for each person to wash his hands.

Handle food with the right hand only. If you are dining at a restaurant, cutlery will probably be available. As a foreign guest, you may be offered a bowl along with a fork and a spoon.

# SAUDI ARABIA (Cont'd)

## DINING OUT (Cont'd)

At lunch or dinner, fruit, rice, salads, chicken or fish is usually served. However, when there are guests present, camel, sheep or goat is served because chicken or fish are not considered festive enough. Lamb and chicken are the most popular meats. Dairy products from sheep, goats and camels are also very common in Saudi cooking.

Water and fruit juices are usually served with the meal, while tea, coffee, goat and camel's milk may be served afterward. Desserts (generally fruits and pastries covered with honey) are usually served with tea after the meal.

A formal meal may include *khouzi* (stuffed mutton garnished with almonds and eggs), fried shrimp, ragout of okra, *kabsah (kebabs* of lamb with vegetables and rice). Your host will be delighted to explain the ingredients as well as the preparation of the different dishes.

At the end of the meal, you should say *Bismillah* (which means "Thanks to God") or simply "Thank you."

## PUBLIC CUSTOMS

Remember to always use the right hand for passing objects, touching food or touching other people.

Remove your shoes when entering a home.

In Saudi Arabia, "Yes" may be indicated by swiveling the head from side to side and "No" by tilting the head backwards and clicking the tongue.

Appropriate dress for men is conservative, preferably lightweight, suits. In general, people tend to cover themselves, no matter how hot the weather. Shorts should not be worn in public.

You should be aware that Saudis pray five times a day – between 4:30 and 5:00 a.m., around noon, some time between 2:00 and 4:00 p.m., at sunset and one hour after sunset (never later than 9:00 p.m.). This schedule varies according to the time of year and the part of the country. At prayer times, everything stops so you may want to make plans around the prayer schedule.

Be extremely careful taking photographs. The Koran prohibits the depiction of the human form by graven images. Since Saudi Arabia is the strictest Muslim country, your film may be confiscated or you may be arrested for taking a photograph that includes human figures. You should definitely not photograph women or religious processions.

If your passport contains a "religion" category, it should not read "none."

*Never* swear or use obscenities in Saudi Arabia.

Foreigners may not enter mosques in Saudi Arabia.

# SENEGAL: HISTORICAL OVERVIEW

- Great empires and independent kingdoms flourished in modern-day Senegal from 300 A.D. to the 19th century.

- Islamic traders from North Africa introduced Islam in the 10th century. Today nearly all Senegalese are Muslims.

- In the 13th and 14th centuries the area came under the influence of the Mandingo empires to the east.

- Portuguese sailors first traded with the people in this area in the mid-1400s. They were replaced by the French, English and Dutch in the 1500s. The slave trade was then established and peanuts became an export crop.

- France became dominant in the area by the 1800s. They conquered several kingdoms and established one of several colonies in its federation of French West Africa. Slavery was abolished in 1848. French economic, educational, political and judicial systems remained in place. Dakar was the capital of all of French West Africa after 1902.

- After World War II the movement for independence gathered steam. The colony gained its independence in 1960, beginning as a member of the Mali Federation. The federation broke up that same year.

- After several famines in the 1970s, Senegal created a loose federation with Gambia, known as Senegambia. The two nations retained full sovereignty but shared military and economic systems. This alliance was dissolved in 1989.

- Senegal's constitution was amended to eliminate restrictions on various political parties in 1981. It has been a multi-party democracy ever since. The president serves as chief of state and the prime minister is the head of government. Habib Thiam was elected prime minister in 1991 and reelected in 1993. Abdou Diouf was first elected president in 1981 and has been reelected twice.

- In 1989, Senegal barely avoided war with Mauritania, when the latter's Islamic government expelled over 1,000 people southward into Senegal. An additional problem has been an ongoing separatist revolt in the Casamance province.

- Senegal's economy has, for the past three decades, been based on the production of peanuts, but the country has begun to diversify.

- The government was able to maintain its strong control in 1995, due to shifting political alliances. Much of the power in Senegal, however, resides with its conservative Islamic societies, which greatly influence the political, commercial and social life.

# SENEGAL

## INTRODUCTIONS

Senegalese greetings vary depending on circumstances and how well people know each other. Shaking hands and kissing alternate cheeks three times is common.

Traditionally, men would not shake hands with women, but this custom is changing. Whatever greeting was used when meeting is also used when parting.

## SOCIAL TIPS AND CONVENTIONS

In general, the family and its history are a source of strength and pride for Senegalese. In most rural areas and among traditional urban families, extended families live together in family compounds.

Senegalese enjoy visiting one another often in the home. Because most people do not own telephones, dropping by uninvited is acceptable.

Senegalese are hospitable and can make a guest feel comfortable without expecting anything in return.

Foreign visitors should remember not to drink water unless it is bottled. To decline a drink, it is polite to say that one has just finished drinking.

Avoid cigarette smoking in traditional Muslim homes. It is considered especially rude for women to smoke.

Asking personal questions is impolite; it is considered bad luck to ask specific questions about children, such as when a baby is due, how many children one has or their ages.

## CUSTOMARY BUSINESS PRACTICES

Muslims do not schedule business meetings during prayer times, which take place five times each day. If a meeting runs into prayer time, it might be stopped depending on the area (whether it is traditional or Westernized).

Meetings are formal and people do not roll up their sleeves or remove their jackets.

Business hours are from 9:00 a.m. to 1:00 p.m. and from 4:00 to 7:00 p.m., Monday through Saturday. Offices close at midday because of the heat.

## BUSINESS ENTERTAINING

Generally, breakfast is eaten between 6:00 and 9:00 a.m., lunch from noon to 1:30 p.m. and dinner from 8:00 to 9:30 p.m. In traditional homes, the sexes and different age groups eat separately.

Traditionally, the main dish is usually served in large bowls placed on mats on the floor or the ground or on coffee tables. Several people eat from the same bowl using their fingers or a spoon. Clean hands, eating only from the portion of the communal dish directly in front of a person and avoiding eye contact with persons still eating are important.

# SENEGAL (Cont'd)

## BUSINESS ENTERTAINING (Cont'd)

Only the right hand is used when eating. The left can be used only when eating foods difficult to handle such as fruit or meat with bones.

When hosting Western visitors, Senegalese will eat at tables from individual plates with utensils.

## DINING OUT

Preparing and presenting food are skills that all Senegalese women learn at an early age. Each ethnic group prepares its own traditional dishes and some urban women cook French cuisine as well.

Meals usually consist of one main dish of rice, millet or corn over which a sauce of vegetables, meat (traditional Muslims do not eat pork), poultry, fish, beans or milk and sugar is added.

One popular dish is *yassa* (rice and chicken covered with a sauce of onions and spices). Another is *thiebou dien*, a meal of fish and rice that is popular for lunch.

A traditional Wolof dish is *mbaxal-u-Saloum* (a sauce of ground peanuts, dried fish, meat, tomatoes and spices served with rice).

## PUBLIC CUSTOMS

Men do not go out in public without a shirt and few women wear pants or shorts (only urban youths).

In general, Senegalese receive and give objects with their right hand or with both hands.

Scratching in public is impolite, as are public displays of affection.

Eye contact is avoided with a person considered to be a superior (in age or status) or with someone of the opposite sex.

# SOUTH AFRICA: HISTORICAL OVERVIEW

- Little is known of the history of the native tribes of modern South Africa. The largest African ethnic groups in South Africa today are the Zulu and the Xhosa.

- In 1652, the Dutch established a provisions station at Cape Town. French Huguenot refugees joined the Dutch colony in 1688 and Germans arrived later. The colonists became known as Boers (farmers).

- Britain gained formal possession of the Cape Colony in 1814, following the Napoleonic Wars. Many Boers, unhappy with British rule, migrated to the interior between 1835 and 1848. This migration, known as the Great Trek, led to war with the indigenous Zulus and other tribes. The Boers defeated the Zulus in a series of battles, including the 1838 Battle of Blood River.

- Britain annexed parts of the Boer territories in the late 19th century after gold and diamonds were discovered there. Tensions between these two groups erupted into the Boer War (1899-1902), in which the Boers were defeated.

- In 1910, Britain combined the two British colonies, Cape and Natal, with the Boer republics of the Orange Free State and Transvaal to create the Union of South Africa.

- In 1948, South Africa's *National Party* came to power. It began building the apartheid system that separated blacks from whites.

- In 1961, the country gained independence from Great Britain and became a republic. It withdrew from the British Commonwealth because of criticism of its racial policies.

- Since the 1960s South Africa has been torn by violence. In 1960, the *African National Congress (ANC)* formed in 1912 to fight for black rights, was banned. The *ANC*, in conjunction with other political organizations, launched a guerilla campaign against the government. Many *ANC* leaders were jailed, including Nelson Mandela. In the 1970s, the U.N. took various actions against South Africa in condemnation of apartheid. In the 1980s, a multinational boycott of South African products damaged its economy. In 1986, the government declared a state of emergency that gave police broad powers.

- President F.W. de Klerk, elected in 1989, began implementing a series of reforms, including the freeing of political prisoners, desegregating public facilities, lifting the state of emergency and giving the ANC legal status. De Klerk also began talks with Mandela and other black leaders. Many nations lifted their trade bans in 1991, when nearly all apartheid provisions were abolished. There are disagreements, not only between the government and the ANC, but between the ANC and other black groups, such as the *Inkhatha Freedom Party*, led by Zulu leader Mangosuthu Buthelezi.

- Elections, in which all races were free to vote, were held in April 1994, and gave the presidency to Nelson Mandela. Mandela has not been able to deliver on the unrealistic promises made during the 1994 campaign. The economic condition of blacks has not changed, and a high crime rate, illegal strikes and corruption continue in the black communities. Mandela has declared that he will not run in 1999. Opportunistic radicals, such as Mandela's ex-wife, Winnie, could come to power and lead the country into greater trouble.

# SOUTH AFRICA

## INTRODUCTIONS

Shake hands at the beginning and at the end of business encounters. Shaking hands is more common among whites, but is also a greeting used by other ethnic and tribal groups.

Good friends in some black tribal groups greet with an intricate triple handshake.

Because of the ethnic and cultural diversity in South Africa, many different greetings are used. They range from English greetings such as "Hello" and "Good morning," to Afrikaans (a derivation of Dutch) phrases like *"Goeie more,"* ("Good morning") in addition to the Zulu *"Sawubona,"* ("Hello"). The Xhosa *"Molo"* and the Sotho or Tswana *"Dumela"* are similar to "Good morning" and "Hello" as well.

Address people as "Mr.," "Mrs." or "Miss" until you are invited to use first names. Titles are valued.

English and Afrikaans are the official languages. More than 80% of white South Africans are bilingual.

## SOCIAL TIPS AND CONVENTIONS

South African society is undergoing rapid changes and attitudes throughout the country are changing as well. Afrikaners (whites) consider themselves sturdy and independent. English-speaking whites value their British heritage and their role in South Africa.

You may not be able to avoid a discussion of local politics, particularly the policy of apartheid.

Popular conversation might center on South African taste in art, music, movies and literature, which is eclectic. It ranges from popular western to traditional Asian and African cultures.

Whites are descendents of both the English-speaking English, Irish and Scottish settlers and the Afrikaans-speaking Dutch, German and French settlers.

Conservative business clothes are appropriate, including vested suits for men.

South African men may wear shorts with knee socks instead of pants. Women generally wear comfortable dresses or pants. Indian women often wear the traditional *sari.* Some rural blacks wear traditional clothing for special purposes as well as for everyday wear.

Soccer, rugby, surfing, swimming and boating are all popular sports. Many people also participate in cricket, squash, lawn bowling, golf, field hockey and tennis. Horse and car racing draw large audiences as well.

# SOUTH AFRICA (Cont'd)

## CUSTOMARY BUSINESS PRACTICES

Appointments are required for business and government meetings and punctuality is very important.

South Africans value status and education. Within companies, merit is usually more important than family connections.

Be prepared for bureaucratic delays and red tape.

Both Afrikaners and South Africans of British descent tend to be rather reserved, disliking loud and boisterous behavior.

Many foreign firms print all promotional literature in both Afrikaans and English.

Business and government offices are usually open from 8:30 a.m. to 5:00 p.m.

The nature and size of the business being conducted will dictate whether junior, middle or senior management will attend initial meetings. Women have made significant inroads in the business community and are achieving top-level positions with firms, as are the nations' blacks. Therefore, foreign firms should not hesitate to send either women or blacks to conduct business in the country.

## BUSINESS ENTERTAINING

Entertaining is generally done in the home and in private clubs. South Africans are very hospitable to guests and they enjoy conversing and socializing. Guests are usually served refreshments.

In an Indian home, it is not polite to refuse refreshments and it is appropriate to accept second helpings when eating a meal.

Business dinners are more common than business lunches. Barbecues, known as *braaivleis* or *brais*, are also common.

Dinner may be served as early as 5:00 p.m. Be prepared to stay for several hours after the meal.

Dinner guests are not expected to bring a gift, but guests often bring something to drink, such as juice or wine.

Etiquette in the home varies between different ethnic and tribal groups. However, the continental style of eating, with the fork held in the left hand and the knife in the right, is generally used in South Africa.

After socializing, hosts will usually accompany their guests outside to the gate, car or street when they leave.

# SOUTH AFRICA (Cont'd)

## DINING OUT

South Africa's restaurants serve cuisine similar to North America and Europe. Tipping is at the customer's discretion.

Among the national specialties are *sosaties* (kebab), *bobotie* (minced curried lamb), *bredies* (vegetable and meat casseroles) and South African rock lobster. The Indian population has contributed to the local cuisine with a variety of curries and chutneys.

South Africa produces many fine wines.

## PUBLIC CUSTOMS

Other than eating ice cream or standing at a vendor's stand, South Africans generally do not eat on the street.

Cover the mouth when yawning or coughing.

Among some ethnic and tribal groups, it is not polite to gesture with the left hand, while in others it is polite to receive something with both hands cupped together.

It is considered rude to point at someone using the index finger or to have a conversation with your hands in your pockets.

# UNITED ARAB EMIRATES: HISTORICAL OVERVIEW

- The region now known as the United Arab Emirates (UAE) began in ancient times as tribally-organized sheikdoms along the southern coast of the Persian Gulf and the northwestern Gulf of Oman. The region was embroiled in dynastic disputes for centuries. It was converted to Islam in the seventh century.

- Between the 17th and the 19th centuries the area became known as the "Pirate Coast," since raiders based there harassed foreign ships. Raids occurred intermittently until 1835, when, according to various treaties with European powers, the sheiks finally agreed not to engage in hostilities at sea.

- Prior to independence, the UAE was known as Trucial Oman, or the Trucial Sheikdoms (a federation made up of seven sheikdoms). Mainly in reaction to the ambitions of other European powers, the United Kingdom and the Trucial Sheikdoms established a closer bond in an 1892 treaty. The sheiks ceded some control of foreign affairs and, in return, the British promised to provide protection for the Trucial Coast.

- In 1952, a local body called the Trucial Council, comprised of the rulers of the seven sheikdoms, was established. The Council was to encourage the adoption of common policies in administrative matters among the component states. In 1955, the UAE entered a dispute with Saudi Arabia about territory along its southern border. This issue, as well as the border with Oman, remains unsettled even today. Petroleum was first discovered in the area in 1958.

- In 1968, the United Kingdom announced that it would end the treaty relationships with the seven Trucial Sheikdoms as well as with Bahrain and Qatar. The nine regions attempted to form a union of Arab emirates, however, they were unable to agree on terms. Bahrain and Qatar declared independence. At the end of 1971, when the treaty with the British expired, the Trucial Sheikdoms became fully independent and six of them entered into a union called the United Arab Emirates. A seventh emirate, Ras al-Khaimah, joined in early 1972. While there is a federal government, each of the Emirates – Abu Dhabi, Dubai, Sharjah, Ras Al Khaimah, Fujairah, Umm Al Quwain and Ajman – retains considerable autonomy over local affairs.

- Since the 1973 Arab-Israeli War which strongly supported the Arab cause, the UAE has contributed large sums of money to Arab countries. In 1981, the UAE was a founder of the Cooperation Council for the Arab States of the Gulf. This Council seeks to achieve greater political and economic integration between Gulf countries.

- In the 1990 Gulf War, together with most Arab states, the UAE supported resistance to Iraqi aggression. Since the beginning of the Middle East Peace Process, the UAE has provided financial assistance to the Palestinians. In 1992, conflict arose between the UAE and Iran concerning the sovereignty of Abu Musa, an island situated in the Persian Gulf between the two states. While tensions have eased, this issue has remained unresolved.

- The current leader, Sheikh Zayid, is aging and a new generation of rulers will soon take power. The concentration of oil wealth will provide for continued economic development in a country where 75% of the population consists of expatriates.

# UNITED ARAB EMIRATES

## INTRODUCTIONS

*"Sabaah al-khayr yaa"* ("Good morning"), *"Massa a al-khayr yaa"* ("Good afternoon") and *"Massa a al-khayr yaa"* ("Good evening") are the usual greetings.

## SOCIAL TIPS AND CONVENTIONS

Arabic is the official language. Farsi and Urdu are spoken by many in the expatriate population. English is widely spoken and understood, especially in business.

Standard Arabic is generally understood everywhere and the effort of a visitor to use even a few basic words and phrases, no matter how inexpertly pronounced, is appreciated.

Do not inquire about family members. Public mention of wives and children is regarded as an invasion of privacy.

Politics are best left undiscussed.

## CUSTOMARY BUSINESS PRACTICES

As throughout the Islamic world, Friday is the day of rest.

Workday hours vary from summer to winter and among the Emirates.

Government hours are 7:00 or 8:00 a.m. to 1:00 or 2:00 p.m., Saturday through Wednesday and 7:00 or 8:00 a.m. to 11:00 or noon on Thursday.

Business hours are from 7:00 or 8:00 a.m. to 1:00 p.m. and 4:00 to 7:00 or 7:30 p.m., Saturday through Wednesday and 7:00 or 8:00 a.m. to 11:00 or noon on Thursday.

Banks are open from 8:00 a.m. until noon, Saturday through Thursday.

Business appointments must be made in advance and the visitor should be punctual even if the host is late.

Bilingual business cards are recommended.

The unit of currency is the *dirham* (UD or Dh).

## BUSINESS ENTERTAINING

During *Ramadan*, Muslims refrain from eating, consuming beverages and even smoking from sunrise to sunset.

Non-Muslims are expected to refrain from eating, consuming beverages or smoking in public during *Ramadan*, although some restaurants stay open for foreigners, and, of course, hotels serve meals.

It is impolite to refuse coffee or other refreshments offered at meetings.

## UNITED ARAB EMIRATES (Cont'd)

### BUSINESS ENTERTAINING (Cont'd)

Keep in mind that a 10% service charge is usually included in hotel bills.

In restaurants, if the service charge is not added, the recommended tip is roughly 10% to 15% of the bill.

For porters, two *dirhams* per piece of baggage is the suggested amount.

It is not necessary to tip taxi drivers.

### DINING OUT

Dining in restaurants tends to be expensive.

Most of the good restaurants in Abu Dhabi are located in the hotels, where alcohol may be served to non-Muslims.

Cuisines available range from the indigenous to French *haute* and Tex-Mex.

Although there are some good, independent restaurants, Dubai dining is hotel-oriented for the convenience of businesspeople.

Dubai is considered a livelier city than Abu Dhabi and it offers more night life. All major hotels have clubs or discos that are open until 2:00 or 3:00 a.m. They also serve alcohol.

### PUBLIC CUSTOMS

Summer clothing, especially lightweight cottons, is worn most of the year. Synthetic fabrics which hold heat should be avoided. Heavier clothing (sweaters, jackets) is needed for the winter months, particularly in the evenings.

Religious dates vary according to the lunar calendar while national holidays are fixed dates. These include The Birthday of the Prophet, National Day (December 2), New Year's Day (January 1), National Day (February 13), *Isra' al' Mi' Raj* (Anniversary of the Night Journey), Labor Day (May 1), *Ramadan, Lailatul-Qadr, Idul Fitr, Idul-Adha*, Accession of the Ruler, Islamic New Year, *Ashura*.

Avoid sitting with the soles of your feet facing anyone.

Do not shake hands, eat food or pass objects with the left hand.

Do not smoke unless the host does so.

Do not excessively admire a host's possessions. It will be taken as a request that he make a gift of the object of attention to you.

# UNITED ARAB EMIRATES (Cont'd)

## PUBLIC CUSTOMS (Cont'd)

The overall pace is slower than Westerners may be accustomed to, but any show of impatience or a hurried attitude is considered bad manners.

Although tap water in Dubai is considered safe, keep in mind that both water and sewage problems do exist.

Water at top hotels is treated; but elsewhere, it should be filtered and boiled.

Bottled mineral water is available.

Women should not go to public beaches alone and they may be excluded from other local events.

Both men and women are permitted to drive in the UAE, although few Arab women drive.

# ZIMBABWE: HISTORICAL OVERVIEW

- Bantu migration into the area comprising present-day Zimbabwe began perhaps as early as the fourth century A.D. The Zimbabwe ruins, the only remnants of pre-European architecture found in sub-Saharan Africa, are dated sometime between the sixth and 13th centuries A.D. The buildings were constructed by the Mashona people.

- Zimbabwe was abandoned in the early 19th century when the Mashona were attacked by migrating Zulus.

- The British commissioned the British South Africa Company in 1889. Led by Cecil Rhodes, the British founded the town of Salisbury in what was then known as Mashonaland, which was inhabited by Bantus.

- The settlement of Rhodesia (the name given by white settlers to the area) was slow, because it was believed that diamonds and gold were to be found only in South Africa. In 1923, the white government was granted independence from Britain and became an autonomous commonwealth. White control was further strengthened by the passage of the Land Apportionment Act of 1931, which gave one-half of the best land to the 150,000 whites and relegated the three million blacks to the other half.

- By the end of World War II, Salisbury had become a cosmopolitan city which attracted a large number of white Europeans.

- In 1953, Rhodesia joined into a loose federation with present-day Zambia and Malawi. The African people, who had been restricted to poorer lands during the development of Rhodesia, began to rise in protest during the 1950s. In the early 1960s the nationalist movements in Malawi (then Nyasaland) and Zambia (then Northern Rhodesia) succeeded in convincing the British to grant them their independence.

- The nationalist movement in Rhodesia was led by the *Zimbabwe African People's Union (ZAPU)* and the *Zimbabwe African National Union (ZANU)*. The two groups led minor rebellions in the late 1960s. A third group, the *United African National Council*, led by Bishop Abel Muzorewa, was less radical and more interested in developing a relationship between blacks and whites for the future.

- In a 1979 referendum, white voters approved a new constitution which granted majority rule, but would also protect their interests during the transition period. Bishop Muzorewa's party won the elections in that year. The rebels, however, would not accept the new government and warfare erupted, with an average of 100 lives lost each day. The *ZANU* and the *ZAPU* entered into an alliance and pressed for new elections in 1980. The *ZANU* captured a majority in the new parliament and installed marxist Robert Mugabe as Prime Minister. The country, which had recently been renamed, was officially recognized as an independent nation on April 18, 1980.

- The post-election calm soon vanished as the *ZANU* forces went to war against the disgruntled *ZAPU*. White-owned newspapers were taken over by the government and whites started to leave the country in great numbers. Through the 1980s, Mugabe's government engaged in the systematic persecution of members of *ZAPU* and its principal supporters, the Matebele people.

# ZIMBABWE

## INTRODUCTIONS

A handshake is common when greeting. "Good morning, how are you?" and "Hello" are the usual greetings and are understood by all language groups.

Three-part handshakes are often used. First, the two people shake hands in a standard fashion, then the fingers are bent and linked, with the up-pointing thumbs touching, finally another standard handshake is given.

Common *Shona* (a native language) greetings include *"Manguanani"* ("Good morning"), *"Masikati"* ("Good day") and *"Maneru"* ("Good evening").

Greetings among friends may include lengthy inquiries about one's family. A person claps hands when asking how things are. Traditionally, passing a stranger without a word is considered bad manners; however, in cities it is now acceptable to do so.

Zimbabweans do not commonly address each other by title, except in urban areas where people often follow English customs.

## SOCIAL TIPS AND CONVENTIONS

Zimbabweans are generally friendly, cheerful, optimistic and courteous. While open and enthusiastic among friends, they are more cautious and reserved with strangers.

In urban areas, private cars are relatively common and are often used for taxi service (although this practice is illegal). People rely heavily on the rail system when traveling from one city to another.

English is the official language in Zimbabwe and is spoken by most educated people. In rural areas, people speak in their native language.

Many people speak more than one language and mix parts of other native languages together while conversing.

Zimbabweans are sensitive to racism and to discrimination, due to years of colonial rule.

The concept of a nursing home is highly offensive. The elderly are considered a family treasure and there is always room for them. Children are expected to obey without question.

Urban families often have electricity and running water. However, some rural families continue to live a more traditional life in thatched-roof homes without modern conveniences.

Sports are very important to Zimbabweans. Among the most popular are soccer, cricket, polo, bowling, field hockey, squash, golf and horse racing. People also enjoy watching television and going to the movies.

# ZIMBABWE (Cont'd)

## CUSTOMARY BUSINESS PRACTICES

In cities, businesses, government offices and shops are open Monday through Friday from 8:00 or 8:30 a.m. to 5:00 or 5:30 p.m. Banks close at 2:00 p.m. most days and at noon on Wednesdays.

Men prefer to wear suits while conducting business and women generally wear long or short cotton dresses in either modern or traditional styles. It is not uncommon for a woman to wear a scarf on her head.

Dressing neatly in clean clothes is important. Zimbabweans wear Western-style clothing, as traditional African dress is reserved for special occasions.

Traditionally, one gives and accepts items with both hands.

Government officials should be dealt with pragmatically, as they have the potential to become a serious bother if they are treated poorly.

## BUSINESS ENTERTAINING

Patience and politeness are important assets in relationships with Zimbabweans.

When guests are entertained, the host usually serves each plate and it is polite to leave a little food behind to show that one is not greedy.

Guests are expected to arrive on time.

Tea is popular with meals as well as in the office.

In rural areas, unannounced visits are common and schedules are flexible.

A person asks permission of others to leave the table when he/she is finished eating.

## DINING OUT

In cities, people tend to follow a more Western diet, including meat and potatoes or rice.

People eat breakfast before beginning work, eat a light lunch during the day, and eat the main meal after work.

Guests wait for an invitation from the host before being seated. In villages, people may seat themselves without waiting for an invitation.

*Sadza,* a stiff porridge made from *maize* (cornmeal), is the staple of most Zimbabweans and is served at nearly every meal. Various local vegetables are served as a garnish and meat is eaten when it is available.

While many people use utensils, in rural areas it is also common to eat with the fingers.

When in someone's home, water or beer is often served in a communal cup.

# ZIMBABWE (Cont'd)

## PUBLIC CUSTOMS

Direct eye contact during conversation is considered rude, principally in rural areas, because it shows a lack of respect.

A person may clap hands as a gesture of gratitude or politeness. Women and girls, especially in rural areas, often curtsy as a gesture of politeness.

It is rude to decline a gift.

For minor things, such as a store clerk giving you change, you can show thanks by receiving with the right hand while touching the left hand to the right elbow. Spoken thanks are uncommon, and if you use them often you will be thought of as odd.

Regardless of how people eat, they first wash their hands. Rural families may eat from a communal dish, depending on the food served.

The national holidays in Zimbabwe include New Year's Day, Easter (Good Friday and Easter Monday), Independence Day (18th April), Workers Day (1st May) and Christmas.

# THE AMERICAS

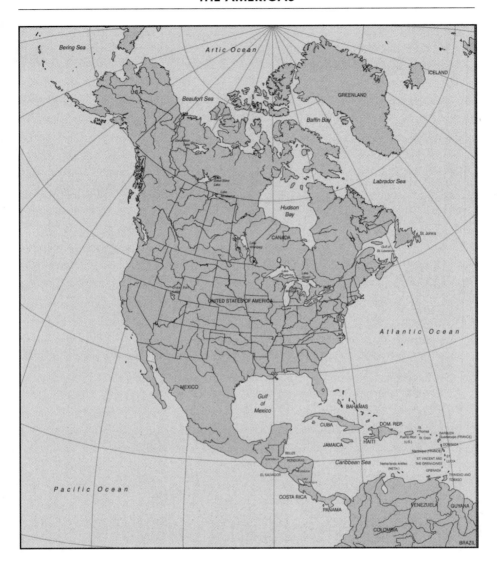

# ARGENTINA: HISTORICAL OVERVIEW

- Before the Spanish colonized Argentina in the 1500s, the country was populated by various indigenous groups. Colonization first started slowly, as it was met by strong local resistance. However, the momentum of colonization increased later in the 1700s.

- The British were defeated when they tried to capture Buenos Aires in 1806. At that time, the colony included present-day Argentina as well as Paraguay and Uruguay.

- A revolt, which started in 1810, resulted in a declaration of independence in 1816. The declaration became reality under the leadership of José de San Martin, who marched an army across the Andes to free Chile. He also led his forces to capture the city of Lima, the first step in the liberation of Peru. When San Martin later returned to Argentina, he found a country divided as a conflict was raging between the central government and the provinces regarding how Argentina should be governed. These internal conflicts lasted for years; however, Argentina was finally unified in 1862.

- Industrialization came to Argentina in the latter half of the 19th century, largely due to British investment. Labor unions also formed during this period, and these unions began to challenge the historic domination of the ruling elite. In 1912, the unions were successful in bringing about a democratization of the electoral laws.

- In 1916, the new laws paved the way for a *Radical Party* (*RP*) victory over the large landowners and industrialists. The *RP* ruled for 15 years, but its programs fell short of expectations, and in 1930, the *Conservative Power* was restored.

- A group of pseudofascist army officers seized power suddenly in 1943, but they were unorganized, and political confusion ensued. Out of the turmoil emerged Colonel Juan Domingo Perón. He, along with his glamorous wife Maria Eva Duarte, who became popularly known as "Evita," united the country and implemented some significant social reform.

- Gradually, however, economic problems began to mount. In 1955, a military insurrection ended Perón's rule. The military then ruled until 1973 (ending an 18-year period in which Argentina often bordered on anarchy), when Perón returned to power in a landslide victory. Upon regaining power, he immediately began a program of leftist foreign policy and conservative domestic policy. He died in 1974, however, and was succeeded by his second wife, Isabel. She was inept and was ousted in a 1976 military coup.

- The military momentarily resurrected the economy, but by 1982, the country was gripped by recession. To deflect attention and increase its popularity, the military seized the *Malvinas* (Falkland Islands) in April. The British, who also claimed the islands, defeated the Argentine army handily. In 1983 with the military having lost its credibility, democratic elections were held in which the *Radical Civil Union* was victorious. Quickly the economic picture darkened, and in 1988, the *Peronísta Movement* nominated Carlos Saúl Menem for president. Menem won and once in office began a program of privatization which helped turn the economy around.

- Menem, despite having lost support because of some austere economic measures, was reelected in 1995. Inflation has been way down, and both the economic and political futures are bright for Argentina.

# ARGENTINA

## INTRODUCTIONS

When introduced, men shake hands with other men. If men and women are introduced by a woman friend, they sometimes kiss, but usually they shake hands. Women usually kiss other women on the cheek when they're introduced.

When greeting, close male friends hug one another in an *abrazo* (a brief hug). This may include a few hearty pats on the back.

Women who are friends shake hands with both hands and kiss one another on both cheeks. Men and women friends usually kiss.

Use titles with last names, as they are important to Argentines. Examples are "Doctor," "Professor," "Architect," "Lawyer" or "Engineer."

At large parties, introduce yourself. At small parties, you will be introduced by the host or hostess. Shake hands and say "Good-bye" to each person when you leave.

## SOCIAL TIPS AND CONVENTIONS

Argentines pride themselves on their European heritage (mainly Italian, British, Spanish and German). There is a tendency to look down upon the native Indians.

Spanish is the official language. Italian and German are spoken as second and third languages. Argentine Spanish contains many distinct phrases and terms not used in other Spanish-speaking countries.

Among good topics of conversation are sports (especially soccer), opera, culture, home and children. Conversation topics to be avoided include religion and politics especially the Peron years and the *Malvinas* (Falkland Islands) conflict. Be aware that Argentines use and prefer the Argentine name *Malvinas* to refer to the Falkland Islands.

When talking to one another, Argentines generally stand closer together than do Europeans or North Americans. Additionally, an Argentine man may touch another's arm, shoulder or lapel of the man with whom he is speaking.

Do not sit down until invited to do so.

Argentines are fashion-conscious. They like to keep up with fashion trends, especially those from Europe.

Women may be asked personal questions such as: "Do you have children?;" if not, "Why not?"

Do not take offense if someone makes critical comments about someone's physical appearance in front of others (such as, "Are you going to lose weight?"). It is considered friendly banter and not meant as an insult.

A head tap generally means "I'm thinking" or "Think."

# ARGENTINA (Cont'd)

## SOCIAL TIPS AND CONVENTIONS (Cont'd)

Never discuss politics or government when first meeting someone. Passions run high about Argentina's recent past, especially the Peron years. After you have known someone for a while you may be asked your opinion of Argentine politics. Read up on Argentine history, especially recent history and current events, before arrival.

## CUSTOMARY BUSINESS PRACTICES

Contacts are extremely important when dealing with both government and with private business.

Always make appointments well in advance. However, many people don't keep appointments or may keep you waiting for a long time.

Conservative business clothing is appropriate, although dress may vary from region to region.

Avoid personal conversations until they are initiated by your Argentine counterpart. Don't ask if the other person is married or has children at your first business meeting.

Avoid the two weeks before and after Christmas and Easter for a business trip. In addition, be aware that the summer vacation period is January to March.

You will generally be offered espresso or tea at a business meeting.

Do not expect to complete your business in a single meeting; it is important to have patience.

Argentine women do not work outside the home in great numbers (about 30%). Foreign businesswomen, however, should not experience problems, assuming they are professional in manner and dress.

Appointments may begin around 9:30 a.m., but don't be surprised if your Argentine colleague arrives late. Allow extra time before another appointment.

An Argentine may be quite willing to meet with you in his office as late as 7:00 or 8:00 p.m.

Be prepared for the business day to extend until 10:00 p.m.

Although most businesses are open from 9:00 a.m. to 7:00 p.m., some government offices are open only in the morning; some are open only in the afternoon. Be sure to check the hours of the office you wish to visit.

Most business is done face-to-face, rather than over the telephone.

Have your business cards and documents translated into Spanish.

Women should avoid giving gifts to male colleagues; even the most innocuous present might be misconstrued as a personal overture. Gifts for children from both men and women are welcomed.

# ARGENTINA (Cont'd)

## CUSTOMARY BUSINESS PRACTICES (Cont'd)

Business gifts should not be given until a friendly relationship has been established. If you plan a return visit, ask your colleague if he/she would like you to bring something particular from your home country.

Avoid giving 13 of anything (considered bad luck), anything in black or purple (a reminder of the solemn Lent season), knives of any kind (which cut off a relationship) or handkerchiefs (associated with tears).

## BUSINESS ENTERTAINING

Business lunches are important, although more for introductory purposes than for getting business arrangements accomplished. Argentines do not generally like to talk business during a meal.

There is no such thing as a breakfast meeting in Argentina. Argentines keep late hours and do not conduct business early in the morning.

Dinner is served about 10:00 p.m., and later on weekends.

Argentines will rarely invite you to their homes, unless you are a relative or a very close friend. If invited to a meal in a home, men should wear jackets and ties and women a skirt and blouse or a dress. To an *asado* (an outdoor barbecue), men and women should wear nice casual clothes. Casual wear for men is a sweater, shirt and pants, or just a shirt and pants. For women, casual wear is a top with very chic pants or a skirt.

If you are invited to dinner in a city, drinks may be served in the living room before dinner, but in rural areas guests generally go directly to the meal.

Do not admire a possession of your host to excess; he may insist on giving it to you and you must accept.

Expect to spend a long time at meals. Some observers say that "Argentines live to eat."

Formal wear for men is a tuxedo and for women, mid-calf dresses. Formal wear is for special events like an opera or theater opening, or a political inauguration.

Dinner guests should bring a small gift such as flowers, candy or pastries. Bird of Paradise flowers are considered particularly elegant. Do not bring wine, as it is common, but you may bring French champagne or a bottle of high quality Scotch.

## DINING OUT

When dining in a formal restaurant, men should wear a jacket and tie and women should wear a dress or a skirt and blouse.

Argentines use the continental style of eating, with the knife in the right hand and the fork in the left. To cut meat, they hold it with the fork and cut the meat through the prongs of the fork.

# ARGENTINA (Cont'd)

## DINING OUT (Cont'd)

Hands, but not elbows, should always be above the table, not in the lap.

Using a toothpick in public is considered bad manners. So is blowing one's nose or clearing one's throat at the table.

Restaurant waiters are summoned by raising the hand with the index finger extended. Tipping is not required, but is becoming customary in many restaurants.

Eating in the street or on public transportation is considered inappropriate.

Argentines are a meat-loving people. They consume more beef per capita than any other people including those of the U.S.

Among the national dishes are *churrasco* (a thick grilled steak) and *parrilada mixta* (a mixed grill). *Arroz con pollo* (chicken with rice), *puchero de gallina* (chicken, sausage, corn, potatoes and squash, all cooked together), *milanesa* (breaded and fried beef or chicken), *empanada* (a meat pie) and pasta dishes are other popular items.

Argentines are proud of their fine wines, particularly reds. Argentines often add soda or mineral water to their wine, particularly in the summer. Never pour wine backhanded or with the left hand, as it is considered rude.

When toasts are made, raise your glass to those around you and say *"Salud"* ("To your health").

Breakfast is usually a *medialuna* (croissant-like pastry), or *pan de leche* (a muffin with cream on top), served with coffee, milk or *maté* (Argentina's national drink).

*Maté* is a type of tea made from the young leaves of an evergreen tree of the holly family. The dry tea is called *yerba maté*. *Maté* is generally served in homes and not in restaurants. It is frequently sipped through a silver straw from a gourd, and is passed from one person to another. People often drink it instead of coffee; it contains a good deal of caffeine. *Maté* is served in a number of ways: with sugar, anise seeds, orange peel or milk. It is enjoyed all over Argentina, but particularly in the interior, reflecting the *gaucho* (cowboy) heritage.

Do not include an Argentine wife in an invitation to a meal in a restaurant unless you have met her.

To show that you have finished eating, place your knife and fork on the plate, crossed, with the tines of the fork facing down.

## PUBLIC CUSTOMS

It is improper for a man and a woman to show affection in public.

Avoid yawning without covering the mouth. Also avoid placing one's hands on one's hips.

Remove hats in buildings, houses, elevators and in the presence of women.

Argentines consider eye contact important during conversation.

# ARGENTINA (Cont'd)

## PUBLIC CUSTOMS (Cont'd)

It is customary to show respect to the elderly and to women, following the traditions of Spain and Italy.

Men frequently cross their legs knee-over-knee; women do not.

There is a strong Italian heritage in Argentina, therefore many gestures from that country are known and used.

# BAHAMAS: HISTORICAL OVERVIEW

- The Bahama Islands were originally inhabited by the Lucayan Indians. The first contact by the European powers occurred in 1492, when Columbus landed at San Salvador on his journey west from Spain. Nevertheless, since the Spanish chose to settle instead in Cuba and Hispaniola, the islands of the Bahamas remained relatively obscure until the 17th century.

- In 1648, a group of Eleutheran adventurers migrated from Bermuda in search of religious freedom. Then, in 1660, the British colonized New Providence Island (the site of the present-day capital of the Bahamas). Through colonization, the British hoped to establish trade with the American colonies. They granted the area to the six Lord Proprietors of Carolina in 1670.

- The Lord Proprietors took little interest in establishing civil order in the islands, and the Bahamas entered a half-century of piracy and anarchy. The Bahamas were free of piracy only after Woodes Roger's arrived in 1718 and remained there until his death in 1732. During that 14-year span, he had followed a motto of "Pirates Expelled, Commerce Restored." After his death, illegal trade and piracy returned and flourished until the American Revolution.

- During the American Revolution, British loyalists came to the island with their slaves to establish cotton plantations. The islands were prosperous until 1838 when slavery was abolished and insects destroyed the cotton crop. A period of economic depression followed these events.

- When the American Civil War began, the islands again prospered. They participated in illegal gunrunning for the Confederacy. The Bahamas received another economic boost from illegal activity during Prohibition (1919 until 1933) by producing and trading rum. Most recently, the Bahamian economy has been affected by illegal drug traffic.

- During World War II, the Bahamas served as a flight training center for both the U.S. and the British Royal Air Forces.

- In the postwar period, wealthy investors recognized the great potential of the Bahamas as a tourist destination. Since then, tourism has played a vital role in the economic development of the Bahamas. It now accounts for about 70% of the Gross National Product and is expected to continue to grow.

- In 1973, the Bahamas became an independent and sovereign nation and a member of the British Commonwealth of Nations.

- Citrus groves have replaced dairy farming as the most important sector of agriculture with much of the fruit being shipped to the U.S. Other major exports are rum and salt.

- In the 1980s, the *Progressive Liberal Party* dominated under the leadership of Prime Minister Lynden O. Pindling. In 1992, the opposition *Free National Movement* prevailed in elections, resulting in the installment of the Prime Minister, Hubert A. Ingraham.

# BAHAMAS

## INTRODUCTIONS

Basic pleasantries are expected when meeting. Handshakes are appropriate between two men as well as between men and women, but not usually between two women.

Surnames with the appropriate forms of address are used. Due to the large number of North Americans in the country, there is a tendency in some areas to use first names, especially among senior managers.

## SOCIAL TIPS AND CONVENTIONS

Bahamians are open and good-natured when conversing, and gestures and close contact are common.

Religion is taken very seriously. In most cases, it may be preferable to avoid discussion of this topic.

English is spoken with an accent.

## CUSTOMARY BUSINESS PRACTICES

The Bahamian tax system attracts the presence of many North American and European firms. Accordingly, Bahamian business practices have been influenced by the presence of these companies.

There is a more stringent adherence to schedules than found in other parts of the Caribbean.

U.S. banks are highly visible and provide useful contacts.

Conservative dress is required for business meetings. Men should wear suits, and women should wear suits or dresses.

## BUSINESS ENTERTAINING

Business entertaining is frequently done in the home. Luncheons and banquets in restaurants and hotels are also popular.

A gift, such as fruit or flowers, is appropriate for the host and his/her family.

## DINING OUT

Continental manners (the fork held in the left hand and the knife in the right) are most commonly used. Good table manners are considered a product of "good breeding."

Conversation is lengthy at the table, and it usually covers a wide area of subjects.

## PUBLIC CUSTOMS

People are fashion conscious and dress in western-style clothing, jewelry and makeup.

Dress in tourist resorts is informal.

# BELIZE: HISTORICAL OVERVIEW

- Between the third and the ninth centuries A.D., Belize was part of the Mayan empire, which included Guatemala, Honduras, Mexico and El Salvador.

- Little is known about the period after the decline of the Mayan empire until the arrival of the first Europeans in the 16th century.

- During the 16th century, the Spanish came to the area looking for gold, but had little interest in Belize when they did not find any there.

- In the 17th century, British pirates lived and flourished along the Belizean coast. Shortly after their arrival, British woodcutters followed bringing slaves to help in logging the forests. Some pirates also turned to woodcutting. The mahogany trade flourished for these British who became known as the "Baymen."

- Spain, and later Guatemala, continued to lay claim to the region, even though they had never settled it. The Spanish repeatedly tried to expel the British settlers. In 1798, the "Baymen" fought back Spanish invaders. The "Baymen" then asked Great Britain for protection and Belize became a colony subordinate to Jamaica in 1862. In 1884, Belize was made a separate crown colony.

- In 1964, the British granted Belize self-government. Nevertheless, the country was called "British Honduras" until 1973.

- In 1981, through an independence movement and the support of the United Nations, Belize became a sovereign country within the Commonwealth of Nations.

- Although Belize became a sovereign nation, British troops remained in the country to protect its borders. However, after Guatemala relinquished its claim to Belize in a 1991 agreement, Great Britain withdrew its troops in 1993.

- Belize's relationship with Guatemala has remained tenuous. Basing its campaign largely on opposition to Guatemala, the *United Democratic Party* took control in 1993 and continues to rule under the leadership of Prime Minister Manuel Esquivel.

- Drug trafficking from Colombia to the U.S. via Belize was a problem in the early 1990s. However, this problem has largely disappeared. The people seek to preserve the relative peace and stability which has dominated the country for several decades.

- For many years, forestry was the most important aspect of the economy, but because of dwindling timber supplies, sugar cane-growing became more significant and is now the leading industry.

- Currently, there is an emphasis on tourism and on the settlement of wealthy people in retirement homes. Land is relatively affordable in Belize because of its low population density.

# BELIZE

## INTRODUCTIONS

Men shake hands when they are introduced. Although women don't usually shake hands with other women, men and women sometimes shake hands. A man should wait for a woman to offer her hand first.

Close friends and relatives of both sexes hug each other when greeting. Older women sometimes give others a one-armed hug and a pat on the back. Friends sometimes shake by clasping the palms and locking thumbs, by locking all fingers or just pressing fists together.

The use of titles is very important, reflecting earlier British influence. "Doctor" is used for a Ph.D., a lawyer or a medical doctor; "Professor" is also used when appropriate. First names are usually used in informal settings.

With a group of 10 or fewer, you should expect to be introduced to each person by your host. You should shake hands with each. With a larger group, you will probably be introduced to the group as a whole.

## SOCIAL TIPS AND CONVENTIONS

English is the official language of Belize. A Belizean Creole dialect of English is widely spoken. Spanish is common in the north.

Although Belize is located in Central America, its citizens claim the country as part of the Caribbean, as the culture is more closely linked to those customs than to Central America's heritage.

One attitude, however, that Belize shares with its Central American neighbors is *machismo* (the general habit of men to demonstrate or claim their manliness through macho acts or sexually-oriented language). Women in Belize generally ignore this behavior and accept it as part of everyday life.

The people of Belize take great pride in their country. It is greatly appreciated when foreigners demonstrate their knowledge of or take an interest in Belize. Compliments on the country as a whole or favorable comments regarding the specific area visited are also welcomed.

Avoid discussing politics, race or religion or asking personal questions.

People in Belize are nonconfrontational. The people are generally fun-loving, happy and relaxed. Equality and coexistence are important concepts. While prejudices exist in the multicultural country, they do not exist on the level of hatred.

Belizeans are generally very animated in conversation. Nonverbal communication plays a vital role; hand and facial gestures are varied and sometimes complicated.

It is a good idea to have a contact in Belize to ensure success in business. The Belize Chamber of Commerce can be helpful in obtaining contacts.

# BELIZE (Cont'd)

## CUSTOMARY BUSINESS PRACTICES

Appointments should be made from abroad at least one week in advance.

Punctuality is expected, but may not always be practiced. The pace of life is regulated by people and events, rather than by the clock.

Keep in mind that business decisions are made by only a few top people in any company.

Time estimates for completing projects are usually not very reliable.

Suits and ties are appropriate for businessmen and dresses are appropriate for business-women. Some Belizean men wear *guayaberas* (untucked cotton shirts that are sometimes embroidered).

Businesses are usually open from 8:00 or 9:00 a.m. to 5:00 p.m., Monday through Friday.

## BUSINESS ENTERTAINING

Belizeans are very hospitable. Socializing (often unannounced) usually takes place in the home. It is considered impolite for the host not to offer refreshments or for the guest not to accept.

When invited to a meal in a home, it is appropriate to bring wine or a dessert. Although gifts are not expected, they are appreciated.

It is only necessary to include the people with whom you are negotiating when entertaining business associates.

Good gifts from abroad include crystal vases or ashtrays, French perfumes and cosmetics, pocket calculators, blank videocassettes, cassettes of Western-style music, Scotch or a liqueur.

If you suggest dining in a restaurant, be prepared to pay for the meal. If a group informally decides to go out to lunch, each person may pay individually.

Women are not allowed to pay for men. A foreign businesswoman who wants to pay for the meal may want to entertain in her hotel restaurant so she can make arrangements to have the meal paid for in advance by the company.

In the north and west, restaurants serve mainly local dishes such as *tortillas* (thin, round unleavened bread made from cornmeal or wheat flour), black beans and charcoal-grilled beef. There are numerous Chinese restaurants.

Belizeans do not dine out often so restaurant meals may not be very creative. In small restaurants, you should not expect a wide variety of dishes.

# BELIZE (Cont'd)

## BUSINESS ENTERTAINING (Cont'd)

For more formal occasions, men should wear a dark suit and women should wear a dress. Strictly formal clothing (e.g., a tuxedo) is rarely worn.

To call the waiter, say "Miss" or "Mister" while raising your hand. Never shout loudly.

At a restaurant, it is customary to leave a 10-15% tip.

## DINING OUT

For breakfast, people usually eat eggs or beans, tortillas made of corn flour and thin oatmeal made like a drink. Occasionally there is ham or sausage and "fried jack" (fried dough). In the cities, people often eat bread with coffee or tea for breakfast.

Lunch, usually called "dinner," is served at about noon. It typically consists of rice or beans (cooked with coconut milk – the national dish) with chicken, meat or fish. There may also be soup with tortillas. Accompanying the meal, there are often fried plantains as well as a salad of shredded cabbage and carrots with vinegar dressing.

The evening meal, called "supper" or "tea," is served between 6:00 and 8:00 p.m. It is usually a lighter meal than lunch when it is eaten at home. There is usually rice and beans or soup and a little meat served with coffee or tea. Dinner is also sometimes referred to as "drinking tea."

At a dinner party in the city, cocktails and appetizers are sometimes served. "Rum and Coke" is a popular before-dinner drink. Dessert or coffee is generally not served after a meal. Common beverages served with meals are soft drinks, juice and water.

Seafood and fish are abundant and inexpensive. Local Belizean specialties include a number of creole dishes: conch fritters, stewed turtle, "Johnnycakes" (flour, shortening and coconut cream mixed and then baked), conch soup with okra, creole bread, stewed chicken or iguana (which is only served in homes and tastes like chicken). Sometimes, there may be a "boil up" (yams, plantains, cabbage, pickled pig tails, boiled conch and steamed fish all served on a single plate and covered with a sauce made of fried onions, tomatoes and coconut oil). Creole desserts include bread pudding, sweet potato pudding, lemon meringue pie, rice pudding and coconut pies.

Other local specialties include *tamales* (chicken or pork rolled in cornmeal dough and wrapped in banana leaves or aluminum foil), *panades* (ground corn filled with fish or refried beans and then shaped into half-moons), *gornachas* (fried tortillas spread with refried beans, onions and Edam cheese) and *relleno* (a thick soup made of boiled chicken and vegetables).

The most common staple is white rice and kidney beans. Fruits (bananas, oranges, mangoes, papayas, limes, etc.) are abundant and are part of the daily diet, while vegetables are more limited and often imported.

# BELIZE (Cont'd)

## DINING OUT (Cont'd)

Although cutlery is used for most dishes, a number of foods may be eaten with the hands. It is common to tear up your tortilla and pick up food with the pieces.

It is considered impolite to refuse any food or drink offered to you. Also, make an effort to finish everything on your plate.

To indicate that you are finished, push your plate forward with the silverware on it.

If you are at a dinner party in someone's home, leave about 30 minutes to an hour after the meal if conversation is the only after-dinner activity. If your hosts expect you to stay longer, they will suggest playing games, watching a video or looking at photographs.

## PUBLIC CUSTOMS

Western-style and casual clothing is worn. Jeans and other less formal wear are acceptable for both men and women. Belizeans consider the way a person is dressed as an indication of taste and status. Provocative clothing is not acceptable (this generally means that women should avoid shorts or revealing dresses).

It is polite to ask permission before you photograph people. Do not be surprised if some people request a fee. Also, you should not photograph airports since army troops often use them for maneuvers.

Bargaining is common in markets; however, you should expect to pay set prices in stores.

Women will usually not be harassed when walking alone. It is also safe for them to take taxis alone. However, it is unwise for women to hitchhike or to walk alone after dark.

It is considered impolite to not greet even slight acquaintances or to return a greeting, even when passing on the street. When entering places of business, it is appropriate to greet the clerk or receptionist.

When passing on the street, a simple nod of the head or a wave is acceptable for strangers, and it might be accompanied with "Hey, how?" or "Y'aright?" for acquaintances.

Staring or pointing at someone is rude. Belizeans might indicate a person or direction with the head or lips.

Sucking air through one's teeth can mean "Give me a break."

People might hiss to get someone's attention. This is considered offensive, especially by women.

# BOLIVIA: HISTORICAL OVERVIEW

- In the 1400s, the Aymara and other Indian tribes were conquered by the Incan armies, bringing the area of present-day Bolivia into the Inca empire. The Incans introduced the language of Quechua as well as a new social system.

- The Spanish began their conquest of the country in 1532. By 1538, all of Bolivia was under their control. At that time it was known as Upper Peru.

- Bolivia was one of the first colonies to rebel. Political uprisings occurred frequently in the 18th century, but they were always quelled.

- After a War of Independence that lasted for 16 years, the area gained independence in 1825 and was named after its liberator, Simón Bolívar.

- Bolivia's first president was ousted and decades of factional strife, revolutions and military dictatorships followed.

- Portions of its original territory were lost in wars with Chile, Brazil and Paraguay. As a result of the War of the Pacific (1879-1884), Bolivia lost its ocean access to Chile. This has had wide repercussions for Bolivia's economy.

- After 15 years of disorder, Victor Paz Estenssoro was elected President in 1951. A military junta intervened, but a popular revolution overthrew it, and Paz Estenssoro returned as president until 1956. He was reelected in 1960, but was overthrown in 1964 shortly after beginning a third term.

- In 1971, power was seized by General Hugo Banzer Suárez, who ruled for seven years.

- In 1982, Hernán Siles Zuazo assumed the Presidency in a coalition government. Inflation spiraled out of control under his leadership.

- Victor Paz Estenssoro was reelected as President in 1985, and he imposed a stabilization program for the economy. His term ended peacefully in 1989 when Jaime Paz Zamora was elected as his successor.

- In 1993, Gonzalo Sánchez de Lozada, who received the largest percentage of votes in the presidential election, was named president by Congress after no candidate received a majority of the votes cast.

- For more than 400 years, Bolivia's economy has been based on its mineral resources, especially tin, but mismanagement and the decline of world demands for its minerals have crippled the economy.

- Corruption of national and local officials is widespread, and though its manufacture is technically illegal, the export of coca paste sales, chiefly to the Cali cartel in Colombia, accounts for about 25% of the gross domestic product.

# BOLIVIA

## INTRODUCTIONS

Greetings are usually accompanied by a handshake.

The title of *"Señor"* ("Mr."), *"Señora"* ("Mrs.") or *"Señorita"* ("Miss") is added for first-time introductions or when greeting strangers, such as a store owner. *"Señorita"* is used for any woman, unless she is older or the speaker knows she is married.

The *abrazo* is a hug, a handshake, two or three pats on the shoulder and another handshake. It is used frequently by close friends and relatives.

Women friends often embrace and kiss each other on the cheek.

Professional titles are important, such as *"Doctor"* (used for Ph.D.'s as well as medical doctors), *"Arquitecto"* ("Architect"), *"Ingeniero"* ("Engineer") and *"Abogado"* ("Lawyer").

Common greetings include *"Buenos días"* ("Good morning"), *"Buenas tardes"* ("Good afternoon") and *"Buenas noches"* ("Good evening"). Less formal greetings, such as *"Cómo estás?"* ("How are you?") and *"Hola"* ("Hi") are also common.

Common phrases for farewells are *"Hasta luego"* ("Until later") and *"Hasta mañana"* ("Until tomorrow"). Friends may use the more casual *"Chau."* *"Adíos"* generally implies a longer separation. It might be used when seeing someone off on a trip.

Spanish, Quechua and Aymara are all official languages. Spanish is used in government, education and business.

Always present a business card printed in Spanish.

At large parties, you should expect to introduce yourself.

## SOCIAL TIPS AND CONVENTIONS

Bolivians stand close to one another during conversation. They often use hands, eyes and facial expressions to communicate.

Always make eye contact when conversing; avoiding another's eyes may be interpreted as showing suspicion or lack of trust as well as shyness.

Bolivians enjoy visiting one another and often drop by unannounced.

Avoid using "America" when you mean "The United States."

Good topics of conversation include Bolivian culture, families, soccer, car races and food. Avoid praising Chile while in Bolivia. The two countries have had a dispute over borders for more than a century.

# BOLIVIA (Cont'd)

## SOCIAL TIPS AND CONVENTIONS (Cont'd)

People wear different kinds of clothing depending on where they live and their social class. People in urban areas generally wear western-style clothes. However, women in these areas may wear a *pollera* (a colorful full skirt). Rural women wear a *pollera* with a *manta* (shawl). Bowler hats are very common, and styles may differ from area to area. Indian men wear shin-length pants, a shirt and a thick leather belt, often with a *poncho* and a hat.

## CUSTOMARY BUSINESS PRACTICES

Business hours are usually Monday through Friday, from 9:00 a.m. to noon and 3:00 to 7:00 p.m. Government offices are also open on Saturday from 9:00 a.m. to noon.

Make appointments two to three weeks before your arrival. Arrive a day or two before your first appointment as one may need to become acclimated to the altitude.

Visitors should be punctual, even if your Bolivian contact is late.

Many businesspeople vacation sometime during the months of January through March. Avoid business trips during *Carnival* (a week of feasting and celebration preceding Lent), which begins the Saturday before Ash Wednesday. Another time to avoid a business trip is early August as Bolivian Independence Day is celebrated on August 6.

Business clothing varies with the city. In La Paz, men wear three-piece dark business suits. In Santa Cruz, a lightweight suit or a *guayabera* (a dressy shirt) is worn; in Cochabamba, a two-piece business suit is customary.

Women may wear a suit, dress or skirt and blouse for business. Be sure to wear stockings. Miniskirts and revealing dresses are not advisable.

Tea will be served in offices promptly at 4:00 p.m.

## BUSINESS ENTERTAINING

Businesspeople are most often entertained in a restaurant for lunch or dinner. Spouses are not usually invited.

It is recommended that one bring flowers or a small gift for the hostess when visiting a home. Avoid yellow flowers, which signify contempt, or purple flowers, which are associated with funerals. Gifts will not be opened in your presence.

Visitors may also be presented with a gift; do not open it in the presence of the giver.

Visitors are usually offered a drink or light refreshment upon arrival. It is impolite to refuse.

One should avoid starting a conversation on the doorstep.

# BOLIVIA (Cont'd)

## BUSINESS ENTERTAINING (Cont'd)

If invited to dinner at someone's home, it is suggested that you arrive 15 to 30 minutes late.

If you are a special guest, you will be served first. Otherwise, the father of the family is served first.

When invited to dinner, a guest is expected to try all the dishes offered. Compliments on the food are appreciated. If you give a compliment during the meal, you should expect a second helping. However, do not ask for one. Wait until you are offered more food. Also, don't accept the first time you are offered more food; wait until your host or hostess insists.

It is courteous to stay about 30 minutes after the meal is finished.

Guests should address their hosts by the honorific *"Don"* (for men) or *"Doña"* (for women) followed by their first name (for example, "Don Pedro" or "Doña Maria").

## DINING OUT

Always use utensils, not your hands when dining. Use a fruit knife and fork to eat fruit, even bananas.

Keep your hands above the table, resting the wrists lightly on the edge of the table.

Summon a waiter by raising your hand, clapping two or three times or snapping your fingers softly.

Do not pour wine with the left hand or "backhanded" (turning the hand so that the palm faces upward).

The host will usually insist upon paying for the meal.

Restaurants generally include a service charge in the bill, but it is recommended that a small amount extra be given to the waiter.

Lunch is usually the main meal of the day. Water is generally served with meals. On special occasions, beer or wine is served. Coffee is served after the meal.

Around 4:00 p.m. women often invite other women for tea, coffee, pastries and bread with *dulce de leche* (a sweet made with condensed milk). Many families don't have dinner, but repeat the 4:00 p.m. tea at about 9:00 p.m.

A formal dinner will offer several courses.

# BOLIVIA (Cont'd)

## DINING OUT (Cont'd)

Potatoes, rice, soups and fruits are staples of the Bolivian diet. Many foods are fried and are usually very spicy. Potatoes come in hundreds of varieties, and are prepared many different ways.

Local specialties include *sopa de maní* (roasted peanut soup), *empanada salteña* (meat turnovers), *silpancho* (very thin breaded steak served with rice, fried potatoes, fried egg and tomato), *picante de pollo* (a spicy chicken dish) and *fricassé* (pork cooked in a hot sauce with potatoes and white corn).

## PUBLIC CUSTOMS

Women friends frequently walk arm in arm.

It is considered bad manners to eat on the streets.

Do not bargain in stores with fixed prices; however, in open markets, people love to haggle over cost.

A common gesture is the raised hand, palm outward and fingers extended, twisting quickly from side to side. This is a way of saying "no," sometimes used by taxi drivers to indicate that their vehicles are full or by vendors in a marketplace to indicate that certain items have been sold out.

Always cover your mouth when you yawn or cough.

Indian women do not like being photographed; they think the camera will capture their souls. Indian men usually don't mind, but they will sometimes ask for payment.

Do not whisper to anyone when you are in a group.

Friday night in the city is called *viernes de soltero* (bachelor Friday). Men go out drinking with male friends. Women never accompany them.

Both men and women can wear jeans for casual wear, but not shorts. You may not be allowed into churches and official buildings if you are wearing shorts.

# BRAZIL: HISTORICAL OVERVIEW

- Brazil was first colonized by Portugal. Both France and the Netherlands tried to establish colonies, but were driven out.

- Colonization took a number of decades, and expansion did not really begin until the latter half of the 17th century.

- Napoleon captured Lisbon, Portugal in 1808, and the royal family fled to Brazil. They established Rio de Janeiro as the seat of the Portuguese Empire. This made Brazil a part of the Kingdom of Portugal and Brazil.

- King João VI returned to Lisbon in 1821 leaving his son, Dom Pedro I, to govern Brazil. He declared Brazil's independence in 1822 and was crowned emperor. His son, Dom Pedro II followed him and ruled for almost 50 years. He was deposed in 1889 by a military coup, following the abolition of slavery in Brazil.

- The period of the "Old Republic" (1889-1930) was a time of expansion and increasing prosperity.

- Since that first military coup, the military has seized control five times, generally with little violence. A dictator, Getúlio Vargas, ruled from 1930 to 1945. After him, elected presidents governed.

- A coup in 1964 gave the military control once again.

- Brazil's relatively honest, non-political military government imposed austere economic measures in order to control inflation. The government was interested in industrial development. Social programs and the upholding of human rights were low priorities.

- A civilian president was appointed by an electoral college in 1985. A new constitution was ratified in 1988.

- Elections in 1989 brought Fernando Collor de Mello to power as the first directly elected president in 29 years. Collor began an austerity campaign to revive Brazil's economy. Collor resigned in 1992 before he was to be impeached on corruption charges. This event marked the first time in Brazil's history that a leader was removed from office by legal, constitutional means.

- Ittmar Franco, Collor's vice president, assumed the presidency and he was widely regarded as ineffectual and unintelligent. His dynamic finance minister, however, Fernando Henrique Cardoso, developed a sweeping economic program which managed to drastically reduce inflation. Cardoso subsequently ran for president and won in the election of 1994. He has gone forward with an aggressive program of privatization and productivity in Brazil has risen dramatically.

# BRAZIL

## INTRODUCTIONS

Handshakes are the usual greeting, although they tend to be less firm than U.S. handshakes.

When visiting an office or business establishment, shake hands with everyone present. People also customarily shake hands all around when parting from a small group. Men who know each other well may add a pat on the back or shoulder to the handshake.

Women customarily greet each other with a kiss on both cheeks (actually they put their cheeks together and kiss the air). Good friends often embrace when they meet.

Brazil is the only country in Latin America in which Portuguese, not Spanish, is spoken. English, German and French are also spoken by many Brazilians. Spanish is understood by Portuguese speakers, but they may be offended if you deliberately speak to them in Spanish. A visitor should try to learn and speak some Portuguese.

Business cards are a necessity in Brazil, since surnames are extremely varied and often difficult to pronounce. Always offer a business card when first meeting. It should be printed in both English and Portuguese.

Unlike the Spanish-speaking countries, the father's name appears as the last name in Portuguese, and is the surname. Many people refer to each other by a title and a first name, such as *"Senhor Antônio"* ("Mister Anthony") or *"Doutor Paulo"* ("Doctor Paul"). Women, for example, are referred to as *"Dona Regina"* ("Mrs. Regina").

Brazilian informality makes it appropriate to call colleagues either by their first names or their surnames but only after you have gotten to know them.

## SOCIAL TIPS AND CONVENTIONS

The vast majority of Brazilians are Roman Catholic. However, Protestant churches are rapidly gaining in membership.

When beginning a business conversation, it is customary to discuss the weather, local sights or light conversational topics for 15–30 minutes. Do not include personal topics, such as questions about age or salary, but you may ask if your host has any children as Brazilians are very proud of their sons and daughters. Expect to keep constant eye contact during a conversation.

Brazilians tend to be blunt about personal characteristics, such as whether you are fat or thin. These comments are meant as observations and are not intended as insults.

Brazilians are fashion-conscious. They prefer European fashions, especially in the city.

Brazilians have a relaxed attitude toward time, although less so in São Paulo.

Family ties are very strong in Brazil, and their obligations can affect many aspects of business.

# BRAZIL (Cont'd)

## SOCIAL TIPS AND CONVENTIONS (Cont'd)

Brazilians tend to stand closer to each other than do North Americans when talking or standing in line.

Brazilians tend to express their opinions forcefully. This should not be misinterpreted as anger.

## CUSTOMARY BUSINESS PRACTICES

When visiting a Brazilian office, expect to be offered a small cup of coffee, "cafézinho." It is to be drunk black with sugar or sweetener. It is polite to accept even if you do not drink the entire cupful. You may also be offered tea, soft drinks, freshly squeezed juices or bottled water.

Presenting a gift, such as liquor, to your Brazilian business contact is an excellent way of beginning a meeting.

Executives traditionally wear three-piece suits, while office workers dress in two-piece suits. Men should always wear long-sleeved shirts. Businesswomen should wear elegant suits or dresses. Short-sleeved blouses are acceptable. Many women also wear dressy pants suits in the office. This attire is for professional women; women in lesser positions will wear more casual clothing.

Be aware that frequent interruptions may occur during the course of a business meeting.

Be prepared to make several trips to Brazil when negotiating a business deal. Make appointments at least two weeks in advance of your trip. The best times for appointments are mid-morning and mid- to late afternoon. Do not schedule too many appointments in one day, as Brazilians do not keep strict schedules. Brazilians may be at least 30 minutes late for an appointment.

## BUSINESS ENTERTAINING

Business entertaining often occurs at very high-quality restaurants. These are only moderately expensive. São Paulo is cosmopolitan and has numerous restaurants specializing in international cuisine.

If you are invited to a private home, it is customary to send your hostess flowers the following day. Do not include purple flowers; they are associated with death. Alternatively, you can bring candy or a bottle of liquor or wine. Guests normally arrive 10–15 minutes late and stay at least two hours. Dinner parties may not begin until 10:00 p.m. with drinks and appetizers. The main meal may not be served until midnight.

It is customary for the guest of honor to sit at the head of the table. The host and hostess sit on one side of the table.

# BRAZIL (Cont'd)

## DINING OUT

Brazilians eat continental style, holding the knife in the right hand and the fork in the left. They wipe their mouths each time before drinking. Do not use your hands to pick up food. If you must pick up food (such as a sandwich) with your hands, use a napkin.

Never use the side of your fork to cut food, even soft food. Always use a knife.

Both hands should be kept above the table at all times. Elbows should never rest on the table.

Before passing the salt shaker to someone else, tap it on the table.

Place your utensils horizontally across your plate to indicate that you are done.

At a restaurant, the waiter is beckoned by holding up the index finger or by saying *"garçon"* (pronounced "garsohn"). The check is requested by saying *"conta, por favor"* (pronounced "kohn-tuh, por fah-vor").

Dress for dinner should be casually formal even though during summer months (November through March) a tropical jacket may be too warm. Men usually wear earth tone colors and keep their shoes well polished.

Breakfast is usually bread, cheese or marmalade and butter, accompanied by *café com leite* (coffee with milk).

Lunch and dinner are the main meals of the day. These meals may include beans, rice, meat, salad, fruit, potatoes and bread. A common dish is *bife* (or *frango*) *com arroz e feijão* (steak or chicken with rice and black beans). Each region has its own food specialties. The national dish is *feijoada* (a black bean stew) made with various meats and served with *arroz* (white rice), *couve* (kale), *farofa* (fried manioc flour), *vinagrette* (vinaigrette made with chopped tomatoes, onions and green peppers), and *laranja* (sliced oranges to cleanse the palate). A southern speciality is *churrasco*, a barbecue with a variety of meats.

*Dendê* oil is a palm oil frequently used in the cuisine of Bahia. It gives the food a yellow-orange color. Another seasoning used frequently is the *malagueta* pepper, which is very hot and spicy.

Water, carbonated beverages, fruit punch or beer is served with meals. Beverages are always drunk from a glass, never from the bottle or can.

A popular drink, other than coffee, is *mate* (an herbal tea). The national drink is *caipirinha* made from *cachaça*, a Brazilian rum, with fresh lime juice, sugar and crushed ice.

Fruit is often served after lunch and dinner. It should be peeled, sliced and eaten with a fork and knife.

Brazilians generally wait to smoke until the meal is finished.

# BRAZIL (Cont'd)

## PUBLIC CUSTOMS

Brazilians tend to dress casually, except for such formal events as attending the opera. Invitations for lunch during the weekend are very informal, and jackets and ties are rarely worn.

It is common for men to stare at women or make comments as they walk by. It is best for women to ignore this behavior.

A first-time visitor to Brazil should not rely on any taxi driver to find an address. Obtain directions from the hotel concierge or porter, who will usually give the taxi driver directions on how to find the destination.

It is considered obscene to make the U.S. "okay" sign, where the forefinger and thumb touch and the other fingers are extended. Punching your fist into a cupped hand is also a rude gesture.

Brazilians use the "thumbs up" gesture to show approval.

A Brazilian may pinch his earlobe between his thumb and forefinger to indicate appreciation, such as after enjoying a meal.

Do not chew gum or eat while walking on the street.

Brazilians are passionate about *futebol* (soccer). Brazil's soccer teams are among the finest in the world. Some businesses and schools close during the World Cup tournament or important national competitions.

*Carnaval* (a week of feasting and celebration preceding Lent). It is the most famous holiday in Brazil, marked by street parades, dancing, parties, drinking and costumes.

A symbol of "good luck" is a fist with the thumb sticking out between the second and third fingers. Amulets and charms are sold depicting this gesture.

Be sure to ask permission before photographing anyone.

Shorts may be worn along the beach, not in the city.

# CANADA: HISTORICAL OVERVIEW

- Canada's first inhabitants were the Inuit Indians and other Native Americans. A few explorers from Iceland and Greenland had landed in Labrador and Newfoundland, but they failed to establish viable communities.

- In 1497, French explorer Jean Cabot discovered Newfoundland. In the 1530s, Jacques Cartier sailed into the Gulf of St. Lawrence and sailed up the St. Lawrence River as far as modern-day Montreal. In 1610, Henry Hudson of England discovered the Hudson and James Bays.

- The first permanent European settlers were French. The French settlers established a huge fur trading network throughout the Great Lakes region and down the Mississippi Valley. The region became known as New France.

- The British and French fought often for control of this region throughout the 1600s.

- The French were dominant until 1760, when the French in North America were conquered by the English. In the Treaty of Paris, France lost to Great Britain all their North American holdings east of the Mississippi, except for two small islands off the coast of Newfoundland. They also relinquished to Spain all their holdings west of the Mississippi, which eventually became part of the U.S. via the Louisiana Purchase.

- In its peace treaty of 1783, Great Britain retained its holdings north of the Thirteen Colonies, which were to become the United States. English "Loyalists" fled north and settled in Canada.

- In 1867, the British North America Act created the Dominion of Canada from Nova Scotia, New Brunswick, Québec and Ontario. Much of the west was purchased by Canada in 1870, out of which the provinces of the prairies were formed. British Columbia joined in 1871 and Prince Edward Island in 1873. Newfoundland remained a separate colony until 1949.

- In 1931, Great Britain relinquished its formal authority over Canadian affairs with the Statute of Westminster, retaining only the right to have the last word on constitutional matters. In 1982, it gave up that right and Canada's constitution was changed to reflect its full sovereignty.

- Canada still considers Britain's Queen Elizabeth II as the official head of state, but Canada operates independently from the British government. The Queen is represented in Canada by a Governor General.

- In 1991, the Canadian government announced plans to grant the native Inuit tribe control of 772,000 square miles in the north. The measure was approved by voters in the Northwest Territory in 1992, splitting that territory into east and west. The eastern portion is now called Nanavut. The two areas will eventually become two separate provinces.

# CANADA

## INTRODUCTIONS

Throughout Canada, people usually shake hands when meeting and when departing. A nod of the head may take the place of a handshake in an informal situation. Men should shake hands with women if they offer their hand.

Introductions vary from region to region, depending upon the person's cultural background.

In Québec and other French-speaking areas, the traditional French greeting *"Bonjour"* ("Good day") and a firm handshake are the usual introduction. Use the polite *vous* (you) pronoun rather than *tu*, which is generally reserved for family and very close friends. Among close friends, both men and women greet each other by exchanging kisses on both cheeks, although close women friends may embrace.

When first introduced to Canadians, it is proper to use surnames. First names should only be used after being invited to do so. Titles are used with new acquaintances and on formal occasions.

## SOCIAL TIPS AND CONVENTIONS

Canada has a strong identity, which is quite different from that of the United States, although many people in the U.S. tend to emphasize the similarities between the two countries and overlook the differences. Canadians resent these exaggerated comparisons. They have their own heritage and culture and are not U.S.-type people who happen to live in Canada. Canadians value the preservation of their culture, especially against undue influence from the United States.

Canadians take great pride in their country as a whole as well as in the individual provinces. They welcome favorable comments about their country and people.

The majority of Canadians have a British, French or other European heritage, but there are many other ethnic groups as well. The population of Vancouver, for example, is 15% Chinese, most of whom have emigrated from Hong Kong. Native Inuit groups live mainly in the more northern areas of the country.

English and French are both official languages in Canada. French is a key language in the provinces of Québec and New Brunswick. However, barely 15% of the population actually speaks both languages. Most government employees are bilingual.

In the province of Québec, where the official language is French, most people are not fluent in English. If you are traveling to Québec, a working knowledge of French is essential. In the province of New Brunswick, about a third of the population speaks French as their first language.

Canadian English differs somewhat from the U.S. English. The British spelling, such as *theatre* rather than *theater is* used.

# CANADA (Cont'd)

## SOCIAL TIPS AND CONVENTIONS (Cont'd)

Three facts about Canada should be kept in mind. It is the second largest country in the world and it is the largest trading partner of the United States. In addition, more than 75% of Canadians live within 100 miles of the U.S. border.

Sports are a good topic for conversation. Ice hockey is very popular all over Canada, as are many other winter sports. Boating, fishing, swimming, soccer, baseball, rugby, tennis, golf and lacrosse are also popular.

The topic of partition (separation into French-speaking and English-speaking states) should be treated delicately. Avoid taking sides on this issue.

Because of strong cultural ties to Europe (particularly France and England), traditional European business styles prevail. In general, conservative behavior is preferred. Punctuality is expected in most of Canada.

## CUSTOMARY BUSINESS PRACTICES

Business is conducted in a direct, forthright and concise manner. The Canadian business community values clarity and thoroughness in the exchange of information. Business communications tend to be more formal in Ontario and Atlantic Canada than in Québec and the West.

By law, all writing on packaging must be printed in both French and English. It is also best to prepare advertising and promotional materials in both languages.

Refreshments are generally offered, but it is not considered impolite to refuse them.

## BUSINESS ENTERTAINING

Business entertaining is usually conducted in restaurants and clubs.

The dinner hour varies. It may be served as early as 5:00 p.m. or as late as 7:00 p.m., and it usually lasts for two to three hours.

Continental dining style is used in Canada, with the fork held in the left hand and the knife in the right. Some people, however, use the style common in the U.S. where the fork is transferred back and forth between the two hands.

Traditionally, the host will indicate where dinner guests should sit.

At a formal meal, it is considered impolite to reach across the table. Instead, ask that items be passed to you.

In French-speaking areas, one should keep both hands above the table during a meal. Women rest their wrists on the table, men their forearms. Elbows can be placed on the table after the meal is finished. Proper etiquette is to wipe the mouth before drinking.

# CANADA (Cont'd)

## BUSINESS ENTERTAINING (Cont'd)

At the end of the meal, guests should place utensils on their plate.

There is a wide variety of foods and eating habits throughout Canada, especially in the largest cities. This is due to Canada's many ethnic groups. Seafood (such as Pacific salmon) is most popular on the coasts. Food in Québec has a definite French influence.

To beckon a waiter, raise your hand at or above head level. In Québec, beckon a waiter by nodding the head backward slightly or raise your hand discreetly. To signal that you would like the check, make a motion with your hands as if you were signing a piece of paper.

A holiday unique to Québec is the two-week *Carnaval de Québec*, usually held in February.

If you are entertained in a private home, it is courteous and recommended to bring or send flowers to your hostess and follow-up with a thank-you note. Avoid sending white lilies since they are associated with funerals. An alternative is to bring candy or wine.

Canadians usually dress formally for social occasions. If attending dinner at a restaurant or a colleague's home, men should wear suits or jackets and ties, and women should wear dresses. On less formal occasions, Canadians dress casually.

In general, dress habits are similar to those in the U.S., but a bit more conservative and formal.

## PUBLIC CUSTOMS

Two important forms of communication, eye contact and smiles, are always welcome.

In social situations, men will usually rise when a woman enters a room.

The U.S. sign of thumbs-down (meaning *no*) is an offensive gesture in Québec and should be avoided. It is also considered offensive to belch in public, even if one excuses oneself.

English-speaking Canadians from Ontario tend to be more reserved than both French Canadians and English-speaking Canadians from the western provinces. They do not welcome body contact or gestures in greeting or in conversation. Generally, people with a French heritage are often more outgoing and open than those of British descent.

Etiquette and politeness are valued by both French- and English-speaking Canadians. It is accepted practice for a man to open a door or give up his seat for a woman.

In Québec, it is improper to eat on the streets unless you are sitting at an outdoor cafe or standing outside of a food stand.

# CHILE: HISTORICAL OVERVIEW

- Ferdinand Magellan was the first European to sight the Chilean shore after he successfully navigated around the southern tip of South America in 1520.

- In its attempts to conquer the area, Spain was met by strong local resistance.

- Chile formed part of the Viceroyalty of Peru and was controlled from Lima.

- Chile began a fight for independence from Spain in 1810. In 1817, Spain was defeated with the help of armies under the leadership of José de San Martín of Argentina. One of the heroes of the revolution, Bernardo O'Higgins, became the new country's leader.

- The policies of O'Higgins' government were not popular with the landed aristocracy, and he left the country in 1823. A period of anarchy followed.

- After 1830, stability allowed Chile to create a new constitution.

- From 1879 to 1884, Chile fought the War of the Pacific against Peru and Bolivia. Chile was victorious and annexed the provinces of Arica and Antofagasta in the north.

- A civil war in the 1880s was followed by unstable governments and military interventions until elections were held in 1932.

- Many years of growth and peace followed in the middle of this century, although economic inequalities grew as well. President Eduardo Frei, 1964-1970, tried his hand at reform, but could not meet raised expectations.

- Salvador Allende was elected in 1970, becoming the first freely elected Marxist president in South America. By the end of 1972, however, the country faced economic disaster. General Augusto Pinochet Ugarte led a military coup in 1973 that ended Allende's socialist government.

- Pinochet ruled by decree. In 1980, a new constitution gave Pinochet the right to rule until 1988. In 1988, Pinochet held a plebiscite (a direct vote by the people) to determine if he should continue to rule or to allow free elections. He lost the plebiscite and called for elections in December 1989.

- Patricio Aylwin became the first elected president since 1970, although Pinochet retained his position as head of the army. President Aylwin has been succeeded by Eduardo Frei, elected in December 1993. Frei is the son of the president of Chile from 1964 to 1970 of the same name.

- Chile has prospered due to free trade and foreign investment and the economy is still growing at an average of 10% per year. The country has also managed to all but wipe out corruption in the government, in contrast to almost all of the other countries in Latin America.

# CHILE

## INTRODUCTIONS

Men shake hands with other men when they are introduced. After they know each other well, they also pat one another on the back. An *abrazo* (an embrace) is also common.

Women kiss one another on one cheek when they know each other well. Men and women who know each other well will also do this.

Men should stand when a woman enters a room. Be prepared to shake her hand if she offers it. A seated woman, however, is not obliged to rise or offer her hand when a man enters.

At a small party, greet each person individually. At a large party, saying "Hello" to the whole group is acceptable.

Professional titles used regularly include "Doctor" (for a medical doctor) and *"Profesor"* ("Professor").

People use either their full name (including both the father's family name and the mother's family name) or their father's family name, which is the official surname. An example would be Eduardo Jose Peres Garcia; he would be known as "Señor Peres" or "Don Eduardo."

## SOCIAL TIPS AND CONVENTIONS

Light conversation is customary before business discussions.

Avoid talking about local politics and religion. Good topics include family, children, Easter Island and history.

People tend to stand closer together than they do in North America.

Good eye contact and good posture are important during conversations. Respect and courtesy are quite important in general.

Neatness and cleanliness are important to Chileans, and this is reflected in how they dress. European fashions are followed.

Men generally wear suits and ties for business and social events, not sports jackets. Do not wear anything in the lapel. Women should wear a suit and heels for business and a dress for dinner.

Nearly 30% of the labor force is female. Many women have important political and business positions.

Formal dress is rare, even for weddings.

About 75% of Chile's population are of *mestizo* (mixed white and native Indian) origin.

# CHILE (Cont'd)

## SOCIAL TIPS AND CONVENTIONS (Cont'd)

*Futbol* (soccer) is very popular, as is skiing, swimming and fishing. Theater, music and movies are also popular.

In areas where cattle have been important, rodeo is very popular. Chilean rodeo is very different from the version enjoyed in the U.S.

## CUSTOMARY BUSINESS PRACTICES

Spanish, called *Castellano*, is the official language. However, some terms common to Chile will not have the same meaning in other Spanish-speaking countries. Often, the final syllables are eliminated.

It is important to use Spanish in all business documents and trade literature. Business cards should be bilingual.

Business hours are generally from 9:00 a.m. to 6:00 p.m. In many areas, a midday *siesta* (a rest after the midday meal) is still common, when offices and shops close.

Vacations are generally taken in January and February, the Chilean summer.

Business dress is conservative.

Prior appointments are a necessity, preferably at least two weeks in advance.

Chileans respect punctuality.

Your first meeting will, for the most part, be an introduction to discuss your company and your position. Much of the time will be spent on conversation other than business.

Business decisions are usually made by a few people at the top of an organization.

Avoid impatience regarding the time needed for decision making and delays.

Promptly answer all correspondence, preferably in Spanish.

Women should avoid giving gifts to male colleagues. Even the most innocuous present might be misconstrued as a personal overture. Gifts for children from both men and women are welcomed.

Business gifts should not be given until a friendly relationship has been established. If you plan a return visit, ask your colleague if he would like you to bring something particular from your home country.

Avoid giving 13 of anything (considered bad luck), black or purple (a reminder of the solemn Lent season), knives (which, symbolically, cut off a relationship) and handkerchiefs (associated with tears).

# CHILE (Cont'd)

## BUSINESS ENTERTAINING

Business entertaining is generally done at major hotels and restaurants.

If you are invited to a meal by a Chilean businessperson, he/she will pay. If you issue the invitation, you will pay. Splitting the check, even in a group, is unusual, and is called "American treat."

The main meal of the day is generally lunch. A lighter meal is eaten between 8:00 and 10:00 p.m. Teatime, called *onces*, usually consists of small sandwiches, beverages and cookies or cakes.

Do not expect spouses to be included in a business lunch. For business dinners that are primarily social, it is appropriate to include spouses.

When visiting a home, wait outside the door until invited inside.

When invited to dinner at someone's home, arrive 15 minutes late. If invited to a party, arrive 30 minutes late.

Greet the head of the family first.

Bring a gift, such as flowers or chocolates, for the host.

Do not admire a possession of your host to excess. He/she may insist on giving it to you, and you must accept.

Compliment the host on the meal.

It is considered impolite to ask for second helpings. Even if second helpings are offered, guests are expected to decline. Take more food only if the host insists.

It is impolite to leave immediately after eating. You should plan to stay for conversation.

If you invite Chileans to a business lunch, ask them to suggest a restaurant. For dinner, entertain at your hotel's restaurant.

## DINING OUT

Chileans seldom eat anything with their fingers.

The continental style of eating is used, with the fork in the left hand and the knife in the right.

Both hands are kept above the table.

Chileans are very proud of their local wines, especially white wines. When toasts are made, raise your glass, look at your host and others present and say *"Salud"* ("To your health"). Never pour wine with the left hand.

# CHILE (Cont'd)

## DINING OUT (Cont'd)

National dishes include *cazuela de ave* (a stew of chicken, potatoes, rice and green peppers), *empanadas de horno* (turnovers filled with raisins, olives, meat, hard-boiled eggs and onions), *empanada frita* (a fried meat pastry) and *pastel de choclo* (a casserole of meat, onions, and olives, topped with cornmeal and baked). There are many local seafood dishes, especially conger eel, *paila chochi* (a kind of bouillabaisse) and *parrillada de mariscos* (grilled mixed seafood).

Except for ice cream, it is not polite to eat while walking in public.

*Café con leche* is made by pouring hot milk into a cup that has a single spoonful of coffee in it. *Té con leche* is a small amount of tea with hot milk.

## PUBLIC CUSTOMS

Yawns should be stifled or covered with your hand.

Only a waiter should be beckoned with hand gestures.

Making a fist and slapping it up into the palm of the other hand is a rude gesture.

Holding the palm upward and then spreading the fingers means that someone is stupid.

## COLOMBIA: HISTORICAL OVERVIEW

- The first permanent Spanish settlement was made at Santa Marta on the Caribbean coast in 1525. Cartagena was founded in 1533. In the western section, inland from the Pacific Ocean, Cali was founded in 1536. Bogotá was also founded during this period in 1538.

- In 1564, the area was set up as the Presidency of the Kingdom of Nueva Granada and this plan controlled the whole country plus present-day Panama, Ecuador and Venezuela. The Presidency was replaced in 1718 by a viceroyalty at Bogotá which included present-day Venezuela. It was then independent of the viceroyalty of Peru to which the area had been subject previously.

- In 1794, Antonio Nariño translated into Spanish the French Declaration of the Rights of Man and set in motion the movement toward independence from Spain.

- In 1808, when Napoleon replaced Ferdinand VII of Spain with his own brother, Joseph, there were several revolts. After Napoleon's fall in 1815, Spain attempted to reassert its authority over Nueva Granada. Simon Bolívar assembled an army and defeated the Spanish troops in 1819.

- On December 17, 1819, the revolutionary congress proclaimed the Republic of Gran Colombia. Venezuela broke away in 1829, and Ecuador followed in 1830. The remaining provinces were then named Nueva Granada. Not until 1863 was the name Colombia restored.

- A liberal revolt in 1899 turned into a civil war, The War of the Thousand Days. The Liberals were defeated in 1902 after much loss of life.

- In 1903, Panama declared its independence from Colombia.

- The strife between the Conservatives and the Liberals was again ignited in another civil war known as *La Violencia* from 1948 to 1957. This conflict ended by a political truce, which required the presidency to alternate between the liberal and conservative political parties until 1974. Since then, elections have been held regularly.

- Guerilla movements and drug cartels caused unrest and violence throughout the 1980s. During the 1990 presidential election, the candidates of the *Liberal Party* and the *Unión Patriótica* were assassinated. César Gaviria Trujillo was elected President.

- A new constitution took effect in July 1991. This constitution encourages political pluralism, the rule of law and special rights for the local indigenous peoples.

- In 1994, Ernesto Samper of the *Liberal Party* was elected president. Evidence shows that his campaign was substantially financed by the Cali drug lords. President Clinton placed Colombia on a list of countries failing to adequately combat drug traffic, and this move severely hurt Colombia's economy.

# COLOMBIA

## INTRODUCTIONS

A handshake is the common way of greeting. Men often shake hands with everyone when entering a home, greeting a group or leaving.

Women who are acquainted often kiss each other on the cheek, otherwise they offer a verbal greeting. Sometimes they will grasp each other's forearms instead of shaking hands.

Young people will also kiss on the cheek if they are good friends.

The *abrazo* (hug) is common between close friends and relatives.

Titles are important during introductions. People who have a university degree should be addressed as *"Doctor."* Be sure your business cards include your title on them.

The official language is Spanish.

It is customary for a child to bear two family names. The last name is the mother's family name and the next-to-last name is the father's family name. People use either their full names or go by their father's family name, which is the official surname. Someone named Jorge Lopez Muñoz would be called "Señor Lopez."

At parties, the host will introduce you individually to the others present. When leaving, say good-bye to each guest.

## SOCIAL TIPS AND CONVENTIONS

Politeness and etiquette are important in Colombia.

Colombians will seldom turn down an invitation directly, although they may plan not to attend. They will say something like "I'll try to come." You will have to learn how to pick up their cues.

Colombians often judge people by how they look and dress. The proper dress for each occasion is essential.

Men wear suits, white shirts and ties in urban areas. Women wear comfortable dresses. Indians often wear traditional clothing, which may include wraparound dresses, bowler hats and *ponchos.*

Friends often drop in on each other unannounced.

The family is an important part of Colombian society.

Good conversational topics include sports, especially *fútbol* (soccer), art, Colombian coffee and the scenic countryside. Bullfighting is popular in Colombia. Do not make adverse comments about it.

Women should be especially careful not to make any glance or gesture that could be considered flirtatious or provocative.

# COLOMBIA (Cont'd)

## CUSTOMARY BUSINESS PRACTICES

Business hours are Monday through Friday, 7:00 a.m. to 6:00 p.m. There is a break for lunch between noon and 2:00 p.m. Shops generally close at midday.

Businesspeople usually vacation in December and January. In Barranquilla, they also vacation during June and July. Avoid visiting the week before and after Easter and during the two weeks before and after Christmas.

Make business appointments at least a week in advance. Arrive a day or two before your appointment in Bogotá. The altitude may affect you, and you will need time to get acclimated.

Be punctual for appointments, but do not expect Colombians to be on time.

You will most likely be offered coffee when you arrive for a meeting. Be sure to accept it.

Expect not to discuss business directly during your first or perhaps even your second appointment. Don't begin to discuss business until your Colombian counterpart initiates the conversation.

No matter how hot it is, men should wear a jacket to a business meeting. They will probably be invited to remove it.

If you meet workers in a factory, shake hands with those nearest you when you are introduced and when you leave. Do not participate in any manual labor as status is very important in Colombia.

## BUSINESS ENTERTAINING

You may be invited to a business associate's home. Colombians like you to meet their spouses and families. If time permits, send a gift of fruit, flowers or chocolates before you arrive. If not, send a gift afterwards along with a note of appreciation.

When invited to dinner at someone's home, a man should wear a suit and tie; a woman, a skirt and blouse or dress.

You will probably be offered a before-dinner drink, such as Scotch, vodka, gin, etc. Wine may be served with the meal as a dinner for guests is a special occasion. If you don't drink, ask for soda water. Hors d'oeuvres will be served with before-dinner drinks.

It is considered polite to leave a small amount of food on your plate to indicate that the host has provided abundantly for his/her guests.

Reciprocate an invitation to someone's home by hosting a dinner in a restaurant.

The major occasions for formal wear are weddings and graduation parties. An invitation will specify formal dress.

# COLOMBIA (Cont'd)

## DINING OUT

Lunch is frequently the main meal of the day. When possible, the family gathers for this meal. In urban areas, there is a trend toward having the main meal in the evening.

Colombians use the continental style of dining, with the knife held in the right hand and the fork in the left.

To give a toast, raise your glass, look at the people around you and say *"Salud"* ("To your health").

To show that you have finished eating, place the knife and fork horizontally across your plate.

Soup, rice, meat, potatoes, salad and beans are staples. *Arroz con pollo* (chicken with rice) and *sancocho* (stew with meat and vegetables) are popular national dishes. *Arepas* (cornmeal pancakes) are popular at breakfast. Other specialties include *hallacas* (meat stuffed into ground corn dough and wrapped in banana leaves) and *pabellón criollo* (shredded beef with rice, black beans and plantains).

Colombian coffee is the favorite beverage. Black coffee is called *tinto*. Coffee with milk is called *café perico*. A cup of milk with a little coffee added is called *café con leche*.

Popular desserts include guava paste with milk and *manjar blanco* (soft toffee made with milk, sugar and spices).

## PUBLIC CUSTOMS

Do not yawn in public or eat on the streets.

Beckon someone by extending the arm palm down and moving the fingers in a scratching motion.

Colombians do not usually wait politely in line (for example, when waiting for a bus).

When you visit a church, do not use flash photography.

Do not wear shorts when visiting churches or while walking on the street. Jeans should be stylish and clean.

In open markets you may bargain, but not in stores.

In Colombia, there are particular gestures for showing the size of things. To show how tall an animal is, the flat palm is held downward. To show the height of a person, the flat palm is held sideways with the thumb on top. To show the length of something, hold the right arm out, the palm flat with thumb on top and use the left hand to mark off the length along the right hand, wrist or forearm. You would offend Colombians by holding out your two hands and pointing with the two index fingers to indicate the distance between the two fingers as the indicated length.

# COSTA RICA: HISTORICAL OVERVIEW

- A variety of native peoples lived in present-day Costa Rica before Columbus arrived in 1502. In the north, indigenous populations were influenced by Mayan civilization and, in the south, they were influenced by other South American groups.

- Beginning in 1522, Spain colonized the Costa Rican area along with most of Central America. The Spanish intermarried with the native peoples, who were assimilated into the Spanish culture. Nevertheless, because minerals were scarce in Costa Rica, the area was relatively ignored by the Spanish crown and remained quite isolated.

- In 1821, Costa Rica joined other Central American countries in declaring independence from Spain during a nonviolent revolution.

- In 1824, Costa Rica became a state of the Federal Republic of Central America. Costa Rica fell victim to the civil wars that followed the separation of the Central American republics from the short-lived Mexican empire. Nevertheless, remoteness from the center of the quarrels minimized the effects of war on Costa Rica. After the Republic collapsed in 1838, Costa Rica became a sovereign nation.

- Costa Rica has one of the most stable governments in Central America. It only had one major experience with dictatorial government when Tomás Guardia came to power in 1870 and led the country until 1882. However, Costa Rican political freedom was recovered in elections of 1889. Only three subsequent attempts were made to seize government. These occurred in 1917, 1932 and 1948.

- The 1948 attempt to seize the government was the last instance of political unrest. In that year, a civil war erupted for six weeks after a dispute over elections. José Figueres Ferrer led an interim government until 1949 when the election dispute was settled. Figueres, who was elected president in 1948 and again in 1970, abolished the army in 1948 and established a civil guard. A new constitution was introduced in 1949, and Costa Rica has enjoyed peace and democracy ever since.

- In the 1980s, Costa Rica faced severe economic problems and communist infiltration of the labor party from within. Additionally the country found itself surrounded by armed conflict in both Nicaragua and El Salvador. Oscar Arias Sánchez was voted president in the 1986 elections. Arias (who left office in 1990) was a creator of the Central American Peace Plan. Arias won the Nobel Peace Prize for his efforts to bring peace to the region, despite the number of adversities that existed at the time.

- Since Arias was not legally eligible for another term in office, Rafael Calderón Fournier was elected president in 1990. He implemented measures to modernize the economy and reduce the size of government. When his successor, José Maria Figueres Olsen, was elected in 1994, it marked the 11th peaceful transfer of power since 1948.

# COSTA RICA

## INTRODUCTIONS

A strong but friendly handshake is appropriate each time you meet acquaintances or friends, especially when arriving or leaving a meeting place.

Among Costa Ricans, first names are used quickly, usually after the first meeting but only among equals of similar status and age. Foreigners should wait for a signal from their counterparts before using first names. Usually, business acquaintances are addressed by the first name with the prefix *"Don"* or *"Doña"* (which denotes respect) or with the term *"licenciado"* (which refers to a college degree or doctorate) before the last name.

Among women, a full embrace and pats on the back are very common. Kisses on the cheek are customary among female friends.

Costa Ricans, popularly known as *"ticos,"* follow the Spanish tradition of full names (first name, middle name, father's last name and mother's last name, in that order).

## SOCIAL TIPS AND CONVENTIONS

After you have come to know a Costa Rican, any topic is appropriate for conversation (except taboo subjects such as sex or very personal matters).

People stand no more than two feet apart when speaking.

English is accepted and widely spoken among business executives.

## CUSTOMARY BUSINESS PRACTICES

Appointments should be arranged well in advance. Government officials can be as much as a half an hour late for meetings. However, businesspeople from the private sector are usually very punctual with their appointments.

For the new or infrequent business visitor, a good lawyer is a prerequisite for conducting business.

It is customary to engage in informal conversation before discussing business matters. Coffee is offered in most meetings.

Business lunches can last up to three hours. It is recommended to leave any business until the end of the meal.

Dress for business meetings is formal. Ties and jackets should be worn. Women should wear conservative dresses. (Note: women have a better chance to succeed in Costa Rica than in other Latin American countries.)

Have any sales literature printed in both Spanish and English.

## COSTA RICA (Cont'd)

### BUSINESS ENTERTAINING

It is customary to invite visitors to restaurants. Costa Ricans are very private with their families. However, Costa Ricans may occasionally invite business acquaintances to their homes. When invited to a private home, it is customary to arrive half an hour late and to bring a gift for the host. Flowers are an appropriate gift.

It is wise for ladies to accept only business lunch invitations from a gentleman. Invitations to dinner should be accepted only if the occasion will be attended by a group of people.

Invite spouses, both foreign and Costa Rican, to business dinners.

### DINING OUT

The preferred style of eating is U.S.-style (knife in the right hand and fork in the left when cutting, then switching the fork to the right hand for eating), not continental.

It is considered polite to linger for about an hour after the meal is finished before leaving.

### PUBLIC CUSTOMS

Dressing is usually informal, especially in hot weather. Men can wear short sleeved shirts and do not need to wear ties, unless it is a formal occasion. Jackets are not usually worn. However, if worn, it is best to wait for a sign from the host before removing it.

Men usually give their seats to women in crowded waiting areas and public places.

## DOMINICAN REPUBLIC: HISTORICAL OVERVIEW

- In pre-Columbian times, the indigenous Arawaks and Tainos occupied the island now comprising the Dominican Republic and Haiti. After the arrival of Columbus in 1492, Christianity, colonization, slavery and disease were brought to the island. Diseases and Spanish brutality decimated the native population by 1520. As the indigenous labor force was destroyed, West Africans were imported to provide cheap labor for the mines, sugar plantations and cattle farms.

- The first permanent European settlement in the New World, Santo Domingo, was established by Columbus' brother, Diego, in 1496. Spain planned to conquer the Americas, maintaining the center of power in this settlement. However, the importance of the island declined in the 16th and 17th centuries. In 1697, the western third of the island of Hispaniola (now known as Haiti) was given to France, and in 1795, the rest of the island was ceded to France.

- During the end of the 18th century and the beginning of the 19th, the island was fought over by the French, Spanish, Haitians and Dominicans. In 1801, rebellious slaves seized Santo Domingo and established Haiti as the first independent country in Latin America. The Haitians dominated the Dominicans from 1822 until 1844. This domination left a legacy of mistrust and strained relations that still endures.

- In 1844, the Dominicans declared independence, although Spanish rule returned intermittently during the 19th century. Convinced that the republic could not survive without outside support, the Dominicans negotiated a treaty providing for U.S. annexation in 1869. Although the Dominican electorate supported the treaty, the U.S. Senate refused to ratify it. After a series of corrupt and inept governments, the country fell deeply in debt to the U.S. In 1905, the U.S. assumed control of Dominican customs and a U.S. military government was established in 1916. Only after occupation by U.S. Marines, between 1918 and 1924, was a constitutional government established.

- Beginning in 1930, the country was controlled by a military dictatorship under the elected President Rafael Leonidas Trujillo. Under Trujillo, the country achieved some economic progress and was politically stable, but at the cost of brutal repression. The dictatorship was brought to an end when Trujillo was assassinated. His death resulted in a division of the army, civil unrest and political revolt. Trujillo's handpicked successor, Joaquin Balanguer, was appointed president. In 1965, U.S. Marines and other peace-keeping forces supported by Latin American countries entered the country in an effort to quell the unrest. In 1966, stability was restored, elections were held, and the constitutional government was reestablished.

- Since 1966, the constitutional government has been maintained. The Dominican Republic is the largest and most populous democracy in the Caribbean region. Never-theless, violence and repeated coup attempts from both the left and the right have continued to characterize Dominican politics. For most of the past three decades, power has rested either in the hands of Balanguer or in those of his rival, Juan Bosch. Only in the 1994 elections did the two face a serious challenge from another candidate. Nevertheless, Balanguer narrowly won elections for a seventh term.

# DOMINICAN REPUBLIC

## INTRODUCTIONS

Spanish is the official language of the Dominican Republic and is spoken by virtually all of the population.

## SOCIAL TIPS AND CONVENTIONS

Avoid business travel during the Christmas season. Festivities start early in December and continue until January 6 (Epiphany).

## CUSTOMARY BUSINESS PRACTICES

The usual work week is from Monday through Friday. Offices open and business is conducted early so as to avoid the oppressive heat during the day. Appointments may begin as early as 7:30 a.m. with the last meeting of the day beginning about 4:00 p.m.

Contacts are extremely important for conducting business with the government and with private companies. It is recommended that you use your bank or embassy if introductions are needed.

Always make appointments in advance and confirm them upon arrival in the country. Dominicans can be informal and might assume that appointments made some time ago are no longer valid.

There is usually some light social conversation before business is discussed.

Do not expect to complete your business in one meeting. Patience is required.

Men wear business suits. Women may wear tailored suits or dresses.

## BUSINESS ENTERTAINING

Business lunches are important, although more for getting acquainted than for actual detailed negotiations.

Exchanging gifts and favors is common in Spanish-speaking America (this is one way to get things done). Never go to someone's home empty handed.

Women should avoid giving gifts to male colleagues. This might be misconstrued as a personal overture.

Do not bring a business gift until a friendly relationship has been established.

Gift-giving should follow business. A less formal setting, such as lunch is more appropriate.

Gifts for children, from both men and women, are appreciated.

# DOMINICAN REPUBLIC (Cont'd)

## BUSINESS ENTERTAINING (Cont'd)

If you are planning a return visit, it is polite to ask your Dominican colleagues if they would like you to bring them something from your home country.

Avoid giving 13 of anything (bad luck); an item or items which contain the color black or purple (associated with Lent, a somber season); knives (they cut off relationships); or handkerchiefs (associated with tears).

Do not admire any particular item owned by your host to excess. He will insist on presenting it to you.

## DINING OUT

Restaurants generally include a service charge on bills; however, it is customary to leave an extra 10% tip.

The Dominican national dish is *sancocho* (a stew of beef, chicken, pork, root vegetables and herbs). Other favorites include *chicharrones de pollo* (pieces of fried chicken) and *pastelitos* (meat pies).

*Arroz con habichuelas* (rice and beans), is a frequent part of the Dominican diet.

Dominican coffee is of very high quality. Be sure to order some with your dessert.

Local beers are also very popular.

# ECUADOR: HISTORICAL OVERVIEW

- The area of Ecuador was already densely inhabited by indigenous populations, when the territory was conquered in the late 1400s by Incas from the south. The Incan empire ruled Ecuador until dynastic rivalry led to the downfall of the Incas, and the Spanish conquered the region in 1534. After the collapse of Incan control, a period of virtual anarchy ensued as the conquerors searched madly for gold and fought among themselves. During the Spanish conquest, Spaniards took control of large tracts of land and large numbers of indigenous people. However, Ecuador remained relatively peaceful under Spanish control until the 19th century.

- Ecuador's independence was imposed by self-styled liberators. In the early 1800s, Antonio Jose de Sucre led a campaign against the Spaniards. The country, along with Colombia and Venezuela, gained its independence in 1822 and became part of "Gran Colombia," a federation that was dissolved only a few years later. Ecuador declared itself a republic in 1830.

- In 1941, Peru invaded Ecuador in the southern Amazon region. Global politics and World War II forced Ecuador to sign a treaty that gave Peru half of its territory (almost all of it Amazon jungle). Ecuador still claims this ceded territory, and the issue has caused violence to erupt between the two nations. For example, international maps show the territory as part of Peru, while maps in Ecuador reflect pre-1941 boundaries. Negotiations to resolve the dispute and to restore friendly relations between the two countries have been unsuccessful.

- Ecuador's history has been marked by political instability. For the 19th and most of the 20th centuries, Ecuador has been ruled by a series of authoritarian governments, with leadership drawn almost exclusively from the white elite. In addition, the significant differences and intense rivalry between the *Costa* (the Coast) and the *Sierra* (the mountainous inland region) have prevented the formation of real political parties since no politician has been able to consolidate power in both regions. Between 1830 and 1948, Ecuador had 62 presidents, dictators and military juntas.

- In 1948, President Galo Plaza Lasso became the first freely-elected president to serve a full term. Although his presidency was followed by two other peaceful administrations, military rule followed again in 1963. Military and civilian governments alternated until 1979, when a new constitution allowed for the first freely-elected president in a decade.

- Elected President Jaime Reynolds died in a plane crash in 1981 and was succeeded by his vice president. Since the Reynolds administration, Ecuador has had stable political leadership even though democracy and constitutional process remain fragile. Nevertheless, the elections of 1992, in which Sixto Durán Bellén was elected president, marked the fourth consecutive peaceful transition of power and emphasized Ecuador's commitment to democracy and civilian rule.

- The economy became better organized under Durán, but poor people were largely ignored.

# ECUADOR

## INTRODUCTIONS

It is customary to shake hands when making someone's acquaintance for the first time.

Close friends appear to kiss each other on the cheek. They are in fact "kissing the air" while brushing or touching cheeks.

If men know each other well they will often embrace.

It is considered proper to address people by a title (*"Señor," "Señora," "Doctor," "Doctora,"* etc.) upon introduction.

Among friends, the title *"Doñ"* or *"Doña,"* followed by the first name, is a common greeting that indicates respect and friendship.

*"Buenos dias"* ("Good day") or *"Como esta?"* ("How are you?") are common greetings.

## SOCIAL TIPS AND CONVENTIONS

Ecuadorians are proud of their country and their history. Ecuador is still a developing country, the people do not appreciate being thought of as inefficient or inferior.

The *Serranos* (people from mountainous areas) are more formal, conservative and reserved than the *Costeños* (people in the coastal regions). The *Costeños* are cosmopolitan, open and liberal (most of the businesspeople of Ecuador are *Costeños*). These two groups are distrustful of each other and are political rivals.

Indigenous people (Indian groups from the Sierra, Coastal and Amazon areas) prefer to remain in their own communities and retain their own traditions.

Food and eating habits are an important part of Ecuadorian culture. Holidays are associated with certain kinds of food and each town has a specialty dish.

Both social as well as business conversation is appropriate at meals.

Family is important in society and the elderly are well-respected. Many families live modestly in small homes or apartments, and several generations may reside together.

## BUSINESS ENTERTAINING

If you invite a guest to a restaurant, you are expected to pay the bill. Young people will often split the bill. Splitting the bill is referred to as "doing as the North Americans."

When a guest is invited to visit someone's home, the arrival time is stated. However, it is considered bad taste to specify an ending time. Guests are not expected to arrive on time and can be anywhere from 10 minutes to an hour late.

# ECUADOR (Cont'd)

## BUSINESS ENTERTAINING (Cont'd)

Evening socials sometimes end after midnight, especially on the coast. The evening will consist of eating, drinking and dancing. The meal is usually served later in the evening, after which some guests leave while others stay.

At smaller gatherings, it is customary for arriving guests to say "Hello" to each person they know. The host will then introduce them to the rest of the guests. Guests who do not say "Hello" to those they know are considered not to be placing enough worth on their relationships.

## DINING OUT

There are three daily meals. The midday meal is by far the most important.

The *Serranos* favor corn and potatoes, while the *Costeños* favor rice, beans and bananas.

Fresh fruits are abundant and fish is a staple. Soup is almost always served at both the midday and evening meals. A popular afternoon snack is hot bread.

Some favored dishes include *arroz con pollo* (fried chicken with rice), *locro* (soup made with potatoes, cheese, meat and avocados), *llapingachos* (cheese and potato cakes), *ceviche* (raw seafood marinated in lime and served with onions, tomatoes and spices), *fritada* (fried pork) and *empanadas* (pastries filled with meat or cheese).

## PUBLIC CUSTOMS

One common custom is that when a family opens its doors to a guest, the door is always open.

Yawning in public, whistling for someone's attention or pointing with the index finger are considered impolite gestures. They display a lack of respect for others.

Ecuadorians might point by puckering their lips, and by lifting or lowering their chin.

Hand gestures are used to emphasize verbal communication. Touching is important and shows friendly concern.

To indicate "Sorry, the bus is full" or "Sorry, we're out of tomatoes," or something similar, stick out your hand, as if to shake hands, and move it in a manner similar to waving.

# EL SALVADOR: HISTORICAL OVERVIEW

- In 1524, Pedro de Alvarado, a Spaniard, led a group of Mexican soldiers in the conquest of El Salvador. He then united the region with the colonial territory of Guatemala. The Spanish settlers intermarried with the native Indians and established agricultural estates in the fertile valleys of the volcanic uplands.

- On September 15, 1821, El Salvador declared its independence from Spain along with the other countries of Central America. In a short-lived federation of these nations, liberal republicanism flourished in El Salvador. During this period (until the breakup of the federation in 1838), El Salvador sought admission to the U.S. while making attempts to unify with Honduras and Nicaragua. After a period of relative peace, El Salvador fell into virtual anarchy in 1925. The chaotic state lasted until 1931, when Hernández Martínez seized absolute power. A year later, his regime brutally suppressed a peasant uprising, leaving 20,000 people dead. Martínez remained in power until 1944.

- A military-civilian *junta*, or council, took power in 1960 and promised to reform the political structure and hold elections. A new constitution was adopted in 1962 and presidential elections were held that same year. The only candidate, Adalberto Rivera of the *Partido de Conciliación Nacional (PCN)*, proved a capable administrator, encouraging the development of light industry and supporting participation in the Central American Common Market.

- In the 1972 elections, José Napoleón Duarte, of the *Christian Democratic Party*, apparently defeated *PCN* candidate Colonel Arturo Armando Molina. The "official" government count gave Molina the victory; however, Congress confirmed that the *PCN* actually held a two-thirds majority. The military tried to rig the 1977 elections. The *PCN* candidate, General Carlos Humberto Romero, was declared the winner by a two-to-one margin. Riots broke out in response to the results, which prompted the imposition of martial law. In 1979, with El Salvador descending into chaos, a group of liberal army officers led by Colonel Adolfo Arnoldo Majano ousted Romero.

- President Carter of the U.S. supported the reforms of the new government with economic and military assistance. Right-wing violence escalated prompting Carter to cut off aid in late 1980. This led to a political crisis, out of which emerged a new four-member *junta* led by José Napoléon Duarte of the *Christian Democratic Party*.

- President Reagan of the U.S. issued a report claiming that the Soviet Union was behind the Salvadoran guerrilla front. The U.S. consequently resumed military and economic assistance to El Salvador.

- Duarte held elections in 1982 for a new Constituent Assembly and arch conservatives, led by Roberto D'Aubuisson, won a majority. The new Assembly excluded the Christian Democrats from power and elected a new president, Alvaro Alfredo Magaña. Assembly President D'Aubuisson soon began an attempt to wipe out the guerrilla movement. In response, the nation's five Marxist groups became coordinated under a single organization, the *Farabundo Marti National Liberation Front (FMLN)*. A civil war ensued that would persist through the 1980s.

- By 1991, the *FMLN* had been greatly weakened and peace negotiations had begun. The cease-fire was prepared by "neutrals" from other countries who called for a purge of the military. The U.S. endorsed this purge which angered and confused the military. In 1994, *National Republican Alliance (ARENA)* candidate Armando Calderón Sol was victorious. The fighters of the *FMLN* were promised jobs and stipends, but this has not materialized and the former revolutionaries have split into numerous factions, all of which engage in thievery, kidnapping and extortion throughout the countryside.

# EL SALVADOR

## INTRODUCTIONS

A handshake is the customary greeting. However, a slight nod of the head is sometimes used instead of or along with the handshake. Salvadoran handshakes may last longer and be less firm than U.S. handshakes. You should adjust your grip accordingly.

Women often pat each other on the right forearm instead of shaking hands. Women may also hug each other, especially if they have not seen each other in a long time or if they are good friends.

Salvadoran men normally will only shake hands with a woman if she extends her hand first. Foreign men should also wait for a Salvadoran woman to initiate the handshake.

Titles should be used to show respect, particularly when greeting older people. The first name or family name alone is all that is used among close friends. Professional titles, used alone, are the most appropriate forms of address. A Ph.D. or a physician is addressed as *"Doctor,"* teachers use the title *"Profesor,"* engineers go by the title *"Ingenerio,"* architects go by the title *"Arquitectô"* and lawyers are addressed as *"Abogado."* If a person does not have a professional title or if you are not sure of it, you may use *"Señor"* ("Mr."), *"Señora"* ("Mrs.") or *"Señorita"* ("Miss").

Most Salvadorans have two surnames, one from their father (listed first) and one from their mother. Normally, the father's name is used when addressing someone. For example, Señor Hernan Antonio Martinez Garcia is addressed as "Señor Martinez" and Señorita María Elisa Gutierrez Herrera is addressed as "Señorita Gutierrez." When a woman marries, she usually adds her husband's surname and goes by that surname. For example, if the two people in the above example married, the woman would be known as "Señora María Elisa Gutierrez Herrera de Martinez." She would be addressed as "Señora de Martinez" or, more informally, "Señora Martinez."

Common greetings include *"¡Buenos días!"* ("Good day" or "Good morning"), *"¡Buenas tardes!"* ("Good afternoon") and *"¡Buenas noches!"* ("Good evening").

It is appropriate to stand when meeting others and when being introduced.

At parties, it is customary to greet and shake hands with each person in the room.

## SOCIAL TIPS AND CONVENTIONS

Spanish is the official language, although English is widely spoken in big cities, tourist centers and among well-educated members of the population.

The country as a whole or the area you are currently visiting make good conversation topics. Salvadorans love their country and are proud of its accomplishments. Now that the 12-year civil war has ended, people are optimistic about the future of their country and of achieving a democracy.

Family and work are other good conversation topics as is sports, especially soccer. Some consider El Salvador as the sports capital of Central America, since Salvadorans excel in a number of sports, and most towns have a gym and an athletic field.

Avoid discussing political unrest, violence, religion and U.S. intervention in Latin America.

# EL SALVADOR (Cont'd)

## SOCIAL TIPS AND CONVENTIONS (Cont'd)

Salvadorans are hearty people. They are hard-working, warm and very hospitable. Visitors are expected to display warmth and friendship as well as dignity and general courtesy.

While women may be able to work side by side with men, any semblance of equality may be forgotten at home. Visitors may have to deal with macho behavior or comments. This behavior is usually ignored as machismo and is an accepted part of life.

You should be careful not to refer to U.S. citizens as "Americans." Latin Americans also consider themselves to be Americans and are very sensitive to the use of this term.

Personal honor is very important to Salvadorans. Avoid criticizing or embarrassing someone or pulling rank in public.

Friends and acquaintances usually stand very close to each other when conversing. You might offend a Salvadoran if you step back. It is considered poor manners to use excessive hand gestures in conversation or in expressing feelings. Also, Salvadorans tend to speak softly. Try to match the volume level of the people with whom you are speaking.

## CUSTOMARY BUSINESS PRACTICES

Although Salvadorans do not strictly adhere to timetables, they appreciate and expect punctuality from foreign visitors.

Appointments should be made well in advance (at least a month). The best time to make appointments is between February and June or between September and November, thus avoiding peak vacation times.

It is important to establish a relationship with your Salvadoran counterparts before commencing business discussions. In fact, before you travel to the country, it is very helpful to have a Salvadoran contact (through an embassy, bank, etc.) who can arrange introductions.

Business generally takes place at a slower pace than in the U.S. Delays are fairly common and several trips to El Salvador may be necessary to complete a transaction.

When negotiating, you should keep in mind that Salvadorans can be subjective and associative in dealing with issues and facts. They may place greater weight on personal perspective (including faith or political ideology) than on universal rules or facts. They may also be skeptical about information provided by outsiders or by those who support the opposite side of an issue. At the same time, many businesspeople have been educated in the U.S., and these people may tend to be more objective and abstract than their El Salvador-educated counterparts.

You may find that while Salvadoran businesspeople assume individual responsibility and initiative, the best interests of the group (i.e., the organization, business team, nation, etc.) may be considered to be of greatest importance. Salvadorans are very collectivistic and base self-identity on relationships within social groups. Expertise is less important than the ability to fit into the group.

Most businessmen wear conservative, lightweight suits and ties, and businesswomen wear blouses and skirts or dresses.

# EL SALVADOR (Cont'd)

## CUSTOMARY BUSINESS PRACTICES (Cont'd)

It is quite unusual to find women in upper levels of business although this is gradually changing. Visiting businesswomen should act very professionally and should emphasize that they are representing their company, rather than speaking for themselves.

Businesses are usually open from 9:00 a.m. to noon and then from 2:00 to 6:00 p.m., Monday through Friday. They are often open from 8:00 a.m. to noon on Saturday.

## BUSINESS ENTERTAINING

It is appropriate, but not necessary, for small gifts to be exchanged with first-time visitors. Good gifts include books about your country, crafts from your area, nice pens and pocket calculators.

Business may be discussed during a meal. However, it is not discussed in the home or around family. If you are invited to a home, the visit is strictly for socializing.

If you are invited to a meal at someone's home, it is appropriate to bring a gift of candy or flowers. You should avoid bringing white flowers, since they are associated with funerals.

Salvadorans appreciate sincere compliments about their homes, children or gardens when a guest pays a visit. Similarly, if you are invited to a meal in a home, complimenting the host or hostess on the meal is also appreciated. This is understood as a sign that the guest feels welcome.

## DINING OUT

Salvadoran food is less spicy than that of many other Latin American countries. Basic foods of the diet include *frijoles* (black beans), refried beans, thick tortillas (thin, round unleavened bread made from cornmeal or wheat flour), rice, eggs, meat and fruit.

The main meal of the day is at noon. This meal usually includes black beans or meat with tortillas and fruit or vegetables.

If you are invited to a meal in a home, each person usually serves himself/herself. It is polite for guests to try some of every dish served. You may want to be discretionary in selecting food since it is considered rude to take food and leave it untouched on your plate. At the same time, leaving a little food on your plate is considered good manners.

Men should stand when a woman leaves the table.

## PUBLIC CUSTOMS

Because of the warm climate, light summer clothing is appropriate year round. People take care to have a neat and clean appearance in public. For both men and women, short pants or jeans are not appropriate attire. Women usually wear skirts and blouses; they very rarely wear pants. Revealing clothing may offend some people.

General courtesy is expected in El Salvador. For example, it is appropriate to stand when a woman enters the room. If a yawn cannot be suppressed, cover your mouth with your hand.

It is not appropriate to point feet or fingers at anyone. Only close friends are beckoned with a hand wave (wiggling the fingers with the palm down).

# GUATEMALA: HISTORICAL OVERVIEW

- The Mayan empire flourished in the region now known as Guatemala for more than 1000 years until it began to decline in the 1100s.

- The Spanish ruled Central America, including Guatemala, from 1524 to 1821. After gaining independence in 1821, Guatemala was annexed by Mexico and then very soon became a member of the Central American Federation. This federation was dissolved in 1838.

- Between 1838 and 1944, Guatemala was under the control of military dictatorships. Finally, in 1944, a revolution took place which overthrew the government. However, even after the revolution, democracy did not flourish. While leaders tried to address some of the country's social ills, violence and rebel activity were common.

- In 1954, after an elected president was overthrown by a U.S.-backed military coup, rebels began a civil war. Repeated coups and outbreaks of civil war made political stability impossible until 1984. In that year, a constituent assembly was elected to write a new constitution.

- In 1986, civilian rule returned in Guatemala under Marco Vinicio Cerezo Arévalo, who withstood two military coups. During the 1980s and early 1990s, the military continued to have more control over some regions than civilian authorities, which presented serious problems for political and economic progress.

- The first peaceful transfer of power from one elected official to another took place in the 1990 elections. Elected President Jorge Serrano Elías began peace talks with the rebels in 1991 and, by 1993, the country seemed to have made significant steps toward the end of civil war.

- Unfortunately, peace talks ended during a 1993 political crisis when Serrano dissolved the Congress and the Supreme Court, and suspended the Constitution. The President announced emergency rule, supported by the army. This event triggered civilian protest. Eventually, the military withdrew its support and Serrano was forced to leave Guatemala.

- After Serrano left the country, military leaders recalled the Congress, which chose a popular human rights activist, Ramiro de León Carpio, to finish Serrano's term of office. This action raised the hope of the possibility of peace and democracy in the future.

- In 1994, talks with rebels opened again and the two sides agreed to develop a broad-based assembly to recommend and discuss solutions to the country's political and social problems.

- The years since 1994 have been turbulent. Torture and murder are still common, and violence by rural people against tourists has occurred. In the hotly contested 1995 elections, moderate-conservative Alvaro Arzu won by a narrow margin. Arzu is known for honesty and integrity, and he appears more interested in securing agricultural rather than military aid.

# GUATEMALA

## INTRODUCTIONS

Always offer a handshake when you are introduced to either a man or a woman. Women often pat each other on the right forearm rather than shaking hands. Don't expect – or give – a firm handshake. Such handshakes are for those who are from urban areas or those that are familiar with the U.S.

Men who are good friends give each other an *abrazo* (an embrace with a pat on the back).

Titles are very important. *"Licenciado"* is anyone with a college degree (e.g., B.A.). Other titles include *"Arquitecto"* (architect), *"Ingeniero"* (engineer), *"Doctor"* (medical doctor or lawyer) and *"Profesor"* (professor).

## SOCIAL TIPS AND CONVENTIONS

Learn a little about Guatemala before you visit the country so that you can show an interest in the history and culture.

Talk about children, your interests and your job. Don't be surprised if people ask about your job and marital status after a very short acquaintance.

Avoid discussing politics or "the violence" of which Guatemala has suffered a great deal since 1978.

Another good subject for conversation is travel, both within Guatemala and abroad. But do not compare Guatemala to other Central American countries or other regions.

## CUSTOMARY BUSINESS PRACTICES

It may be necessary to make several trips to Guatemala to complete your business. You must establish a personal relationship with a Guatemalan businessperson before discussing business. A mutual contact can help move the business process along.

Make appointments at least two weeks in advance if you are coming from outside Guatemala. While in the country, a few days notice is usually sufficient.

Guatemalans are usually punctual for business appointments. But you may experience unforeseen delays that are often caused by the country's power shortages.

Ask questions quietly, be patient and never raise your voice or insult anyone.

It is not necessary to translate business cards into Spanish. However, manuals and sales materials should be translated.

Don't bring gifts on your first business trip to the country, but for subsequent trips, it is polite to ask people what they would like from abroad.

Men should wear a lightweight suit, and women should wear dresses or suits, never pants.

# GUATEMALA (Cont'd)

## BUSINESS ENTERTAINING

If a colleague invites you to his/her home for a meal, do not discuss business. If your spouse is accompanying you on the business trip, invite your Guatemalan counterpart and his/her spouse to a social dinner in a restaurant.

There are no set rules or customs regarding whether one person pays for the group or whether each person pays individually. Offer to pay, but if one person absolutely insists on paying, let him/her follow through and then reciprocate the gesture at the next meal. If a group goes for drinks and not a meal, most often each person will buy a "round."

In Guatemala, business lunches are more popular than dinners. Do not discuss business until you have first spent time addressing non-business topics.

## DINING OUT

After a meal, expect everyone to say *"Muchas gracias"* ("Thank you"). *"Buen provecho"* is often said before a meal (roughly translated, this means "May it do you good").

## PUBLIC CUSTOMS

Do not wear shorts in the cities or in the highlands. Do not wear jeans in cities. Men should wear pants and a shirt, and women should wear a skirt and a blouse. Indians may be offended to see a woman wearing pants.

# HONDURAS: HISTORICAL OVERVIEW

- The Mayan Empire flourished in the region now known as Honduras until about 800 A.D., when the Mayan population in the area declined. A number of small empires then controlled the region until the arrival of Spanish explorers.

- In 1502, Columbus arrived and named the region *"Honduras"* ("depths") because of the deep waters off the north coast. The indigenous people living there at the time fought against Spanish occupation until 1539. In that year, the last of the indigenous chiefs was killed, and the Spanish settled a city at Comayagua. Honduras was incorporated into Spain's Captaincy General (colony) of Guatemala. After settlement, the Spanish population began to grow, especially after silver was discovered in the area in the 1570s.

- At the request of the Mosquito Indians, the British occupied the Mosquititia region of the country beginning near the end of the 16th century, withdrawing only in 1859.

- In 1821, Honduras and four other Central American provinces declared independence and joined together as a federation under the Mexican Empire. The period under this new empire was short-lived, however. In 1838, complete independence was declared, and the republic of Honduras was established.

- During its first 161 years of independence, Honduras witnessed 385 armed rebellions, 126 governments and 16 constitutions. By the end of the 19th century, due to internal instability, the country came under Nicaraguan influence.

- Internal political instability continued in Honduras until Tiburcio Carías Andino took power in 1932. He made no pretense of democratic rule, governing instead as a benevolent despot. Carías did more to advance the social and economic well-being of the country than any of his predecessors. However, he maintained his power only by jailing or exiling his critics. Carías' military rule lasted until 1948, when he peacefully surrendered power following elections. Nevertheless, even once Carías stepped down, military leaders continued to exercise control. Military rule, a number of coups and corruption marked the period between the 1950s and 1980s.

- Finally, in 1981, elections restored civilian rule. Free elections and civilian rule continued, and the elections of 1989 marked the third free election in a decade as well as the first peaceful transfer of power to a political opposition party in half a century. The military, however, continues to exercise a great deal of power and influence throughout the country. Also, many people feel that there is too little popular participation in the political process, which is confined to a two-party system between liberal and conservative factions of the elite.

- Carlos Roberto Reina, who was elected and took office in 1994, promised to attack corruption and to reduce the military's budget. The issues of land reform, unemployment, military control as well as disputes with neighboring Guatemala, El Salvador and Nicaragua have all left their mark on 20th century Honduran politics.

# HONDURAS

## INTRODUCTIONS

A handshake is the most common form of greeting for both men and women. Women sometimes pat each other on the arm or shoulder instead of shaking hands. Be aware that handshakes are not as firm as those given in the U.S., and you should adjust your grip accordingly.

Middle and upper class women kiss male and female friends on the cheek. The *abrazo* is a warm embrace shared by close friends and relatives.

When people meet for the first time, a person's official title should be used. Professional titles used alone are the preferred forms of address. People who do not have professional titles, should be addressed as *"Señor"* ("Mr."), *"Señora"* ("Mrs.") or *"Señorita"* ("Mrs."), followed by the surname. People also use *"Usted"* (the formal form of "you"), when meeting someone for the first time.

Most Hispanics have two surnames, one from their father (listed first) and one from their mother. Normally, the father's name is used when addressing someone. For example, Señor Hernan Antonio Martinez Garcia is addressed as "Señor Martinez" and Señorita María Elisa Gutierrez Herrera is addressed as "Señorita Gutierrez." When a woman marries, she usually adds her husband's surname and goes by that surname. For example, if the two people in the above example married, the woman would be known as "Señora María Elisa Gutierrez Herrera de Martinez." She would be addressed as "Señora de Martinez" or, more informally, "Señora Martinez."

When you meet a small group of people, you should greet and say good-bye to each person individually.

## SOCIAL TIPS AND CONVENTIONS

Spanish is the official and dominant language. However, English is widely understood in urban and tourist centers and in business circles.

In Honduras, as in many other Latin American countries, the social philosophies of fatalism, machismo and *hora latina* play a role in daily life. Machismo reflects the fact that Honduran society is male-dominated and that there are clear and classic role differences between the sexes. *Hora Latina* refers to a concept of time, in which individuals are considered to be more important than schedules. Being late for appointments is very common.

Christian beliefs as well as environmental values (ties to the land and agriculture) are very important to Hondurans. You should be careful not to offend these values.

Maintaining dignity, regardless of social class, is very important in Honduran culture. You should avoid openly criticizing or embarrassing someone or pulling rank.

Good topics of conversation include Honduran tourist sites, your family and your job. You should avoid talking about local politics or the unrest in Central America.

Sports, which are extremely popular in Honduras, make good topics of conversation. *Fútbol* (soccer) is the national sport. Also, wealthier Hondurans enjoy cycling, baseball, golf, tennis and swimming.

# HONDURAS (Cont'd)

## SOCIAL TIPS AND CONVENTIONS (Cont'd)

Be careful about in referring to U.S. citizens as "Americans." Hondurans also consider themselves to be Americans and are sensitive to the use of this term.

People stand close together when conversing. Stepping away will offend the person with whom you are speaking. Hand and body language are very important forms of communication. Clasping both hands indicates strong approval. Waving the index finger is often used to say "No."

## CUSTOMARY BUSINESS PRACTICES

The best time for business travel is between February and June, since the rainy season lasts from May to November and December and August are popular vacation times.

Punctuality is generally not considered to be important in Honduran society. However, people in the city as well as in business settings, tend to be more punctual out of the need to accomplish their business goals. Nevertheless, scheduled appointments may be delayed. Punctuality is, however, expected of foreign visitors.

Personal relationships are very important when conducting business in Honduras. It is important to develop a relationship(s) before starting on business discussions. Also, it is important to make contacts through the appropriate intermediaries. While doing business, you should try to establish a long-term relationship based on mutual trust and reliability. If several trips are made, it is important that the same person be involved each time.

Extensive negotiations may be necessary to complete your transaction. Subjective feelings, enhanced by cultural heritage or religious faith, are the primary source of decisions. Universal laws and objective facts are rarely used in making decisions, and Hondurans tend to get personally involved with all problems. An emotional approach, emphasizing trust, mutual compatibility, the benefits to a person's pride, etc., will be more effective than the logical bottom line of a proposal.

Hondurans place great importance on the collective group and their role within the social system. The decision-making process is strongly affected by the need to maintain group harmony. Harmony is often considered to be more important than innovation or showing initiative or expertise.

While Hondurans work hard, business may progress at a slower pace than in the U.S. Speed of progress is not a major goal, and Honduran businesspeople tend to exhibit a somewhat laid-back behavior. This is true even in high-paced situations, partly to reduce anxiety.

Try not to direct "yes/no" questions in discussions with your Honduran counterparts because they may try to answer a question according to what they believe you want to hear, regardless of whether the information is accurate. It is better to phrase questions in such a way that they will require more detailed responses than a simple "Yes" or "No." It is important to get all agreements in writing, since a verbal "Yes" may be considered simply polite, rather than binding.

# HONDURAS (Cont'd)

## CUSTOMARY BUSINESS PRACTICES (Cont'd)

void saying "No" in Honduras. This might embarrass the person with whom you are speaking. Instead, milder responses, such as "Maybe" or "We'll see," will be understood as a "No." Similarly, remember that if your Honduran counterpart seems particularly hesitant or noncommittal in response to a question or request, this may indicate a "No."

If there is a disagreement, be aware that a compromise may be difficult to reach, as this will be seen as weakness.

Using graphs and other visual aids in presentations makes a very good impression.

It is rare for women to occupy top positions in Honduran companies. A foreign businesswoman may also face an initial lack of respect. She should respond to this by acting extremely professionally and by emphasizing her role as a representative of her company.

Hondurans are very status-conscious. It is therefore a good idea if at least one member of the foreign negotiating team is from a higher level of management.

Have your business cards printed in both English and Spanish and present the card to Hondurans with the Spanish side up.

Businessmen generally wear a conservative suit or a *guayabera* (a decorative shirt worn rather than a shirt and tie). Businesswomen generally wear a skirt and blouse or a dress.

Business hours are usually from 7:30 a.m. to 4:30 p.m., although some offices close for the *siesta* (a rest after the midday meal). Businesses are often open on Saturdays from 8:00 a.m. until between noon and 2:00 p.m.

## BUSINESS ENTERTAINING

It is very common for business meetings to take place over breakfast, lunch or dinner. It is best to let your Honduran counterpart suggest the time for a business meeting over a meal.

Foreign businesswomen should never invite a Honduran businessman to a dinner unless spouses also attend. If a businesswoman invites a Honduran businessman to lunch, the man will not let her pay. If she wishes to pay, it is a good idea for her to invite him to eat at her hotel and arrange to have the bill added to her hotel tab in advance.

Hondurans are courteous and generous to guests in their homes, even when guests arrive unannounced. Refreshments are almost always offered. Even if a guest does not feel like eating, the host may wrap up a little food to send home with the visitor.

If you are invited to a home or if a spouse is included in an invitation, you should not expect to discuss business. The engagement will be purely social.

While social events may have official starting times, it should be understood by both hosts and guests that this time is flexible. It is not uncommon for people to be up to an hour late for a social engagement. In fact, it is generally considered polite to arrive about 30 minutes late for social engagements.

# HONDURAS (Cont'd)

## BUSINESS ENTERTAINING (Cont'd)

When in someone's home, you should be careful not to admire the person's belongings too much, or they may feel obligated to give them to you.

When leaving a home, guests should be especially respectful of the head of the household and should say good-bye to each person.

## DINING OUT

At more formal restaurants, a 10-15% tip is appropriate. Tips are not usually expected in less formal restaurants.

Breakfast is served between 6:00 and 8:30 a.m. The main meal of the day begins around noon. A light evening meal is eaten between 6:00 and 8:00 p.m. Dinners with guests tend to be larger and will be served at about 8:30 or 9:00 p.m.

Beans, corn, *tortillas* (thin, round unleavened bread made from cornmeal or wheat flour) and rice are staples. The most common fruits and vegetables are bananas, pineapples, mangos, citrus fruits, coconuts, melons, avocados, potatoes and yams.

Special dishes include *tapado* (a stew of beef, vegetables and coconut milk), *mandago* (tripe and beef knuckles), *nacatamales* (pork tamales) and *torrejas* (a dish similar to French toast served at Christmas). *Topogios* or *charramuscas* (frozen fruit juice in a plastic bag) are popular during the summer months. Coffee (often with milk) is a common drink, which is usually served with the main meal of the day.

Pizza, hamburgers and other North American dishes are served in some restaurants in big cities.

Both hands, but not elbows, should be kept above the table when seated for a meal.

Continental manners, with the fork in the right hand and the knife remaining in the left, are the most commonly used. However, pieces of *tortilla* may also be used to move or pick up food.

At the table before a meal, one always says "*Buen provecho*" ("Enjoy your meal"). In a restaurant, a person approaching or passing a table also says "*Buen provecho*" to the people at the table.

## PUBLIC CUSTOMS

Western-style clothing is very common and wealthy people follow trends in Western fashion very closely. Urban women are especially stylish with regard to clothing, hair and makeup.

It is considered inappropriate for men or women to wear shorts in public, except in coastal areas where it is hot and humid. It is considered inappropriate for women to wear revealing clothing, and a woman may even offend some people by wearing pants. Men can often be seen wearing a *guayabera*.

# HONDURAS (Cont'd)

## PUBLIC CUSTOMS (Cont'd)

It is customary to give a general greeting when entering a room.

When you pass someone in the street, you should say *"Adios"* ("Good-bye") which is used as a general greeting in this situation.

Placing the finger below the eye is used as a warning for caution.

A hand placed under the elbow usually means that someone is thought to be stingy.

To express enthusiasm, Hondurans place their middle finger and thumb together and shake their hand, producing a snapping noise.

It is rude to beckon someone with the index finger. Beckoning is done by waving the hand with the palm facing down.

Bartering is common in marketplaces and shops where prices are not posted. Otherwise, prices are fixed.

Older people are given preference. For example, if you are standing in line do not be surprised if an elderly person is served before you.

Honduran men are very warm and friendly with each other. They often touch shoulders or arms. When other men withdraw from such contact it is considered insulting.

# JAMAICA: HISTORICAL OVERVIEW

- Jamaica's original inhabitants were the Arawak Indians, who called the island *Xaymaca*, meaning "land of wood and rivers." In 1494, Columbus landed on the island, and Spanish colonization followed. The Arawaks were virtually wiped out within 50 years of Spanish occupation due to the harsh treatment they received as slaves as well as the many diseases brought from Europe.

- The English captured Jamaica from the Spanish in 1655 and began colonizing it. They hoped to use the island as a base for the conquest of Central and South America. Most of the Spaniards fled to Cuba or Hispaniola (now known as the Dominican Republic), while others fled to the hills to wage guerilla warfare. By the end of the 17th century, the British had established sugarcane plantations on the island and were importing large numbers of Africans to be slaves.

- Under British rule, buccaneers turned Jamaican ports into the richest and most active ports in the Caribbean. With the pirates' help, the new colony flourished. The British government supported the pirates, knighting their leader, Henry Morgan, and appointing him lieutenant governor of the island.

- Jamaica reached its greatest prosperity in the 1700s, based on the sugar and slave trades. However, slavery was abolished in Jamaica in 1838. The Spaniards who had stayed in Jamaica after the British conquest mixed with the African people. Today, the descendants of these unions, a small group called the Maroons, have some political autonomy within Jamaica.

- Beginning in the 1860s, Jamaica gained the status of a British Crown Colony (as opposed to being a simple colonial possession).

- In the 1930s, Jamaicans began to call for self-determination. In 1938, serious social unrest erupted because of long-standing injustices and labor problems. Alexander Bustamante and his aide, Norman Manley, led the workers and brought about important social change. These two men also formed today's key political parties.

- In 1944, a new constitution was written, providing for adult suffrage, and rule by the British Crown Colony government was ended. Nevertheless, Jamaica remained under nominal British rule until it gained full independence in 1962.

- Jamaica was run by a socialist government during the 1970s. It was then replaced by a conservative government in the 1980s.

- In 1989, by promising to reduce the national debt, the socialists again took control through national elections.

- In 1993, P.J. Patterson, the head of the People's National Party, ran an openly racist campaign. He appealed to the 75% black population, which resulted in his landslide victory.

- Jamaica's economy improved, but the picture was still bleak, with the external debt exceeding the annual gross national product.

# JAMAICA

## INTRODUCTIONS

Greetings range from a nod or bow to a handshake or a slap on the back to a kiss, all depending on the people involved and the occasion.

When people are introduced, however, a handshake is customary.

Jamaicans are formal in their introductions, using titles and surnames.

Children generally refer to adults other than family as "Sir" or "Miss."

## SOCIAL TIPS AND CONVENTIONS

Jamaicans are lively in public, friendly and hospitable. They may, however, be more reserved when first meeting strangers.

Informal visitors are greeted at the gate of the house. People don't approach the house door until greeted and invited past the gate.

Surprise guests are almost always welcome. Unannounced visits are common since many rural Jamaicans do not have telephones.

Attitudes toward time vary according to lifestyle. It is not uncommon for events and appointments to start later than arranged.

Their good-natured answer to challenges is "No problem, man."

Jamaicans do not appreciate being asked personal questions.

Jamaicans are fashion conscious and like to wear jewelry. Western-style clothing is most frequently worn, but traditional clothing is also worn.

## CUSTOMARY BUSINESS PRACTICES

Business hours are generally 8:30 a.m. to 4:30 p.m., Monday through Friday. Government offices stay open until 5:00 p.m.

## BUSINESS ENTERTAINING

Visitors in homes are usually offered a drink and sometimes a meal. Guests often bring a small gift for the host or hostess. Appropriate gifts include fresh produce, flowers or a bottle of wine.

## DINING OUT

Meals are relaxed, social occasions, even when formal.

Buffet meals are popular.

# JAMAICA (Cont'd)

## DINING OUT (Cont'd)

It is common to be invited to breakfast or brunch.

Eating outdoors is popular, especially in gardens and on patios.

Continental manners are used, with the knife kept in the right hand and the fork in the left.

Street vendors selling food are plentiful and relatively inexpensive. Food may be eaten on the spot.

Restaurants generally add a service charge to the bill.

Many Jamaicans say grace before or after a meal.

Jamaican food is usually quite spicy.

*Ackee* and salt fish, the national dish, is usually eaten for breakfast. Fish and various curries are popular. Another favorite food is *jerk*, spicy barbecued pork or chicken, often served with a hard-dough bread.

Coffee and tea are popular drinks, and it is common for all hot drinks to be called "tea" (i.e., coffee, cocoa, etc.).

Women usually do not drink alcohol in public.

*Bammy* (cassava/manioc bread) is a standard food still prepared in the style of the Arawak Indians. *Bammy* with fried fish is a common combination.

## PUBLIC CUSTOMS

Beckoning is done by clapping the hands or by making a "pssst" sound.

Jamaicans use an abundance of hand gestures, and their voices may be loud and excited during discussions.

Cricket and football (soccer) are the most popular sports in Jamaica.

# MEXICO: HISTORICAL OVERVIEW

- The early history of Mexico includes a long line of advanced Indian civilizations whose accomplishments rival those of the Egyptians and the early Europeans. The Olmecs are thought to have been among the area's earliest inhabitants at around 2000 B.C.

- The Mayans built amazing cities throughout North and Central America; their civilization fell in the 12th century because of internal rivalry and warfare.

- The Aztecs were the last great empire, but they were conquered by the Spanish in 1519. The Spanish, who ruled until the 19th century, virtually destroyed the Aztec culture.

- The movement for independence from Spain began in 1810, led by Miguel Hidalgo, a Mexican priest. Independence was achieved in 1821. The country then included parts of the present-day western U.S. A constitution was adopted in 1824, and a republic was established.

- In 1833, Antonio López de Santa Ana took power and ruled as a dictator until 1855. During his regime, Texas seceded and became part of the U.S. Also during this period, Mexico fought a war with the U.S. (1846-1848) in which it lost more territory. Benito Juárez became president upon Santa Ana's resignation in 1855.

- In 1861, French troops invaded Mexico City and named Archduke Maximilian of Austria the emperor of Mexico. Mexican forces under Juárez overthrew Maximilian in 1867.

- Another dictator, Porfirio Díaz, took power in 1877 and was overthrown in 1910. A period of internal political unrest and violence followed.

- The *Institutional Revolutionary Party (PRI)* emerged in 1929 to lead the nation. The *PRI* has ruled the nation as a single party for many years.

- Mexico's economy experienced a period of steady growth following World War II, however, in the early 1970s foreign debt rose and farm output failed to keep pace with population growth. In the 1980s, Mexico was gripped by an international oil glut during which inflation soared.

- In 1993, the U.S. surprisingly passed legislation ratifying the North American Free Trade Agreement (NAFTA) with Mexico, which in effect created a common market.

- In December 1988, amid cries by the opposition of election fraud, *PRI* candidate Carlos Salinas de Gortari was inaugurated president. He was succeeded by the Zedillo Ponce de Leon who won amid rumors of irregularities and fraud. Foreign investment, however, increased until the catastrophic devaluation of the peso in 1994.

- The *PRI* has been losing governorship races and will no longer be able to function in its traditional style. Poverty is a terrible problem and has contributed to a soaring crime rate.

# MEXICO

## INTRODUCTIONS

When introduced to business colleagues or friends, it is customary to shake hands. People usually shake hands each time they meet. People often shake hands both on arrival and on departure. Men should let the woman make the first move toward handshaking.

Women often greet each other with a kiss on the cheek.

For closer acquaintances, an *abrazo* (a full embrace with a pat on the back) is common between men. After two or three meetings with your Mexican colleagues, you might be greeted this way. However, this does not mean that you may call your colleague by his first name; wait until he invites you to do so.

When addressing someone, use their surname unless you know the person well. *"Señor"* ("Mr.") is used when speaking with a man and *"Señora"* ("Mrs.") or *"Señorita"* ("Miss") should precede the surname of a married or unmarried woman, respectively. *"Doña"* is a term of respect used before a first name, somewhat like *"Dame"* in Britain. Also, always refer to a female secretary as *"Señorita,"* regardless of her age or marital status.

Titles are considered to be an important part of business protocol. Common titles are *"Doctor," "Professor," "Químico"* (chemist), *"Ingeniero"* (engineer), *"Arquitecto"* (architect). Lic., following a person's name in writing, means that he or she has a bachelor's degree.

Spanish names usually include the mother's family name after, not before, the father's family name, although the father's family name is considered the surname. For instance, a man named José Rodriquez Ortega would be called "Señor Rodriquez." A married woman or widow usually uses her maiden name in the middle position.

Initial contact with a Mexican firm should be between the top managers from both the foreign and Mexican companies. The foreign manager should make the initial trip to Mexico (accompanied by members of the firm's staff).

## SOCIAL TIPS AND CONVENTIONS

Spanish is the national language of Mexico. Amerindian languages are also spoken in some regions. The English language is widely studied in Mexico and, therefore, is quite widely understood and spoken. English is spoken by most members of the business community and in larger cities. (Many Mexicans at the managerial level also speak French.) However, Mexicans appreciate visitors' efforts to speak Spanish.

Mexicans are very proud of their country and appreciate it when visitors compliment Mexico's progress and achievements. They take these to be accomplishments on their own initiative. Avoid comparisons with the U.S.

Mexicans are generally open and expressive people.

Good topics of discussion are Mexican culture, history, art, museums, fashion and travel.

# MEXICO (Cont'd)

## SOCIAL TIPS AND CONVENTIONS (Cont'd)

Sports such as soccer, bullfighting, *jai alai* (type of handball), *charreada* (Mexican type of rodeo), baseball, tennis and volleyball are popular.

Avoid discussing religious or political subjects, earthquakes or poverty. Also, jokes about "Montezuma's revenge" (diarrhea and/or upset stomach) are inappropriate.

Patience is considered important and you should avoid showing anger (for example, when you encounter delays or interruptions).

Mexicans refer to people from the U.S. as North Americans and call them *Americanos*. They also like to remind U.S. citizens that they are not the only Americans and that Mexicans are also North Americans.

## CUSTOMARY BUSINESS PRACTICES

In Mexico, the business atmosphere is friendly, gracious and easygoing.

It is helpful to have either a contact in Mexico or a letter of introduction. The contact letter should be written in Spanish and you should indicate in the letter whether or not you speak Spanish.

It is a good idea to have your business cards printed in both English and Spanish. Make sure that your university degree and your title follow your name.

Mexicans will appreciate if your presentation materials have been translated into Spanish prior to your meeting. Also, they will be impressed with scientific displays (e.g., charts, graphs, three-dimensional models).

Mexicans have a relaxed attitude toward time and do not place a high premium on punctuality. It is not unusual for a colleague to arrive half an hour late for a business meeting. However, you should always be on time for meetings and should not complain about tardiness.

Business is often conducted during the long midday break and many appointments are set between 10:00 a.m. and 1:00 p.m. However, meetings can also be scheduled at uncommon hours – for example, at 8:30 p.m.

You should make appointments at least two weeks in advance. However, it is common for government officials to reschedule at the last minute.

People are considered to be more important than schedules. In Mexico, it is considered appropriate to meet with an unexpected business visitor first, even when a scheduled visitor has arrived first. Be prepared for interruptions. Also, if a visitor drops in, you should give him/her your full attention.

# MEXICO (Cont'd)

## CUSTOMARY BUSINESS PRACTICES (Cont'd)

Mexicans do not appreciate hasty decision making. Be prepared to have social discussions before commencing business transactions. Also, you should remain flexible regarding deadlines.

Businesses are open five days a week, generally from 9:00 a.m. until 6:00 p.m. However, there is an extended lunch break from about 1:00 to 4:00 p.m. Banks are open from 9:00 a.m. to 1:30 p.m. and the official working hours for government offices are from 8:30 a.m. to 2:30 p.m.

Women in business may not be accorded the same respect as men. In fact, it is very rare to find a woman in a top business position. A businesswoman should strive to be extremely professional.

Lightweight business suits are generally advisable, although winter weight suits may be worn in the evening or during colder times of the year.

For dinner, a dark suit is appropriate.

Never wear shorts or tank tops when visiting churches or religious sites.

## BUSINESS ENTERTAINING

Mexicans are warm and friendly. They view entertaining as an important and enjoyable part of business. Mutual invitations are essential and one should always reciprocate.

In Mexico, entertaining in the home is reserved for closer acquaintances.

Gifts are not expected but they are appreciated. Gifts should be wrapped and presented. For ladies, popular brands of perfume or personal accessories are appropriate. For men, popular brands of personal or office accessories (e.g., books, calculators, clocks, etc.) are appropriate. It is customary to present all secretaries and support staff involved in a business transaction with small gifts. Unique items related to the art or history of your homeland are appreciated.

If you are invited to a private home, flowers or wine are appropriate gifts. Also, if you know that the family has children, bring small gifts for them. If you do bring flowers, remember that, according to popular beliefs, purple and yellow flowers connote death (also, avoid purple clothing or gifts in which purple is the primary color), red flowers cast spells and white ones lift spells. Avoid red roses.

Many business meetings are held during breakfast or luncheons. Business lunches are often quite lengthy and are held between 2:00 and 4:00 p.m. These are actually social meetings for the most part and business is conducted only in the last few minutes.

The midday meal, eaten from about 1:00 to 4:00 p.m., is the main meal of the day.

# MEXICO (Cont'd)

## BUSINESS ENTERTAINING (Cont'd)

Business is rarely conducted at dinner. (Most restaurants don't serve dinner until 9:00 or 9:30 p.m.) However, younger executives may suggest meeting at 7:00 p.m. for snacks and drinks.

On a business trip, try to stay in the best possible hotel or entertain in the best possible restaurants. Also, make a point of dressing neatly and elegantly. These are important elements in enhancing your prestige in the eyes of Mexicans.

Popular drinks are tequila (the maguey worm in some brands of tequila is considered a delicacy), beers and margueritas. Wines are not popular because vineyards do not thrive in Mexico, so all good wines must be imported. Mexicans appreciate Scotch, both when abroad and when given as a gift.

A foreign businesswoman should never make dinner appointments with Mexican male colleagues unless they are accompanied by their spouses.

If a businesswoman entertains a Mexican businessman at lunch, she should arrange to have the lunch in her hotel's restaurant so she can have the check added to her bill in advance. If the check is presented at the table, a man will not allow her to pay.

Restaurant bills usually include a service charge. It is customary to contribute an additional 5% tip.

During the meal, both hands should be kept above the table.

Guests do not usually leave immediately after a meal.

Toasts are common. Allow the host to toast first.

Even at finer hotels or in restaurants, people often order mineral water because it is not advisable to drink the tap water. Many better restaurants, however, serve purified iced water.

There are two common ways of getting the attention of a waiter/waitress. You can make a "psst-psst" sound or make a kissing sound with pursed lips. However, keep in mind that, even though these signals are common, they are considered slightly impolite.

## DINING OUT

Bread and rice are eaten with spicy foods or with a pinch of salt to relieve the burning sensation. Very spicy food is called *picante*, while hot, temperate food is called *caliente*.

Some foods are eaten with utensils, others with the hand. *Tortillas* (thin, round unleavened bread made from cornmeal or wheat flour) are often used as scoops for sauces. Observe your host or others dining with you for guidelines.

# MEXICO (Cont'd)

## PUBLIC CUSTOMS

Mexican people typically stand close to each other while they talk. Also, many Mexicans are "touch-oriented," meaning that they will linger over a handshake, casually touch the forearm, elbow or lapel of the other person's suit. These touches signify a willingness to be friendly. If you withdraw, Mexicans may take offense and you will be establishing an emotional distance.

Refrain from placing your hands in your pockets while conversing, as it is considered impolite.

To beckon someone, extend the arm, palm down and make a scratching motion.

When passing an object, hand it to the other person; never toss it. Similarly, when paying for a purchase, place the money in the cashier's hand, not on the counter.

A distinctive, very rude gesture in Mexico is a "V" made with the index and middle fingers and placed under the nose with your palm against your face.

Hand and arm gestures are often used in conversation.

Many gestures commonly used in North America are understood and even used in Mexico (i.e., the "thumbs up" gesture can be used to show approval).

A sweeping or grabbing motion toward your body means that someone is "stealing" or "getting away with something."

Other than verbally, "no" can be indicated by shaking the head from side to side and extending the index finger with the palm outward.

Placing your hands on yours hips can suggest aggressiveness.

# NICARAGUA: HISTORICAL OVERVIEW

- Columbus was the first European to visit Nicaragua, landing in 1502. He was followed by Spanish conquistadores, who explored the region. Indigenous groups resisted the Spanish until they were finally conquered in 1522.

- British settlements were established along the Caribbean coast in the 17th century, leading Britain to claim sovereignty over the coast in 1740. However, despite the British claim, Spain ruled Nicaragua until 1821, when it declared independence. Upon independence, the country became a member of the United Provinces of Central America, but it chose to become an independent republic in 1838.

- After Nicaragua became a republic, political clashes between liberals and conservatives often led to violence. Internal chaos and U.S. economic interests led to the intervention of the U.S. Marines at various intervals, beginning in 1909. During the 1920s and 1930s, guerillas led by Augusto Cesar Sandino fought the U.S. occupation. Sandino was assassinated in 1934 and General Anastasio Somoza García seized the presidency in 1936.

- General Somoza ruled as a dictator until he was assassinated in 1956. After his death, Somoza's family continued to rule until the 1970s. In 1962, a revolutionary group called the *Sandinistas* was formed with the goal of overthrowing the Somozas. They carried out unsuccessful terrorist attacks for 15 years on Somoza's National Guard which was armed by the U.S.

- After the assassination of a prominent anti-Somoza newspaper editor in 1978, riots broke out, the *Sandinistas* stormed the national palace and civil war ensued. Fifty-thousand people were killed in the war. In 1979, the Somozas were forced to flee and the *Sandinistas* took control.

- The new Marxist government seized the Somoza fortune, redistributed their lands to the peasants, suspended the constitution and tightened controls, suspending elections until 1984. Anti-*Sandinista* activity on the part of the *Contras* began in 1980. Concerned that the *Sandinistas* were aiding Marxist rebels in El Salvador, the U.S. suspended economic aid to Nicaragua in 1981. However, during the 1980s, the *Contras* were aided by U.S. funds.

- *Sandinista* leader Daniel Ortega Saaverda was elected to power in the 1984 general elections. As a result, the U.S. imposed a trade embargo on the nation and continued funding the *Contras*. A peace plan proposed by the Costa Rican President in 1987 led to negotiations between the *Contras* and *Sandinistas* and, while fighting continued, free elections were ensured for 1990.

- In the 1990 elections, Violeta Barrios de Chamorro, the widow of an assassinated newspaper editor, defeated Ortega. The U.S. backed her candidacy and pledged to end trade restrictions. The *Contras* began to disband in 1990. However, since then, unfortunately, severe economic difficulties have contributed to increasing tensions. In 1992, *Sandinista* soldiers and *Contras* began to rearm. Since 1993, with dwindling support for the government and *Sandinistas* still controlling the army, many people have begun to have doubts about the future of democracy in Nicaragua.

# NICARAGUA

## INTRODUCTIONS

When meeting someone for the first time, Nicaraguans smile, shake hands heartily and say either *"Mucho gusto de conocerle"* ("Glad to meet you") or *"¿Cómo está usted?"* ("How are you?"). Complete attention is given to the person being greeted; eye contact and smiles are very important.

Close friends hug and pat each other on the back. Close male friends may greet each other with an *abrazo*, a brief hug. Women usually kiss each other on the cheek and give each other a gentle hug in greeting.

Titles should be used when addressing the Nicaraguans that you meet. First names are used only with close friends, family or children. It is preferable to use a professional title, such as *"Doctor"* (used for a Ph.D. or physician), *"Profesor"* (used for a teacher), *"Ingeniero"* ("Engineer"), *"Arquitecto"* ("Architect") or *"Abogado"* ("Lawyer"). If the person does not have a professional title or you are not sure of it, you may use the titles *"Señor"* ("Mr."), *"Señora"* ("Mrs.") or *"Señorita"* ("Miss"), followed by a last name. The titles *"Don"* and *"Doña"* are used with men's and women's first names, respectively, to indicate special respect and familiarity or affection.

Most Nicaraguans have two surnames, one from their father (listed first) and one from their mother. Normally, the father's name is used when addressing someone. For example, Señor Hernan Antonio Martinez Garcia is addressed as "Señor Martinez" and Señorita María Elisa Gutierrez Herrera is addressed as "Señorita Gutierrez." When a woman marries, she usually adds her husband's surname and is addressed by that surname. For example, if the two people in the above example married, the woman would be known as "Señora María Elisa Gutierrez Herrera de Martinez." She would be addressed as "Señora de Martinez" or, more informally, "Señora Martinez."

Common terms of greeting include *"¡Buenos días!"* ("Good morning"), *"¡Buenas tardes!"* ("Good afternoon") and *"¡Buenas noches!"* ("Good evening"). A casual greeting, especially among the youth is *"¡Hola!"* ("Hi").

If you are at a small party, it is polite to greet and shake hands with each person individually.

## SOCIAL TIPS AND CONVENTIONS

Spanish is the official and predominant language. Nicaraguan Spanish has several unique words and is known for its forcefulness. Words considered profane in neighboring Costa Rica are used daily in Nicaragua. Small groups that live along the Caribbean coast speak English and other ethnic languages. English is understood by some in the capital city.

Nicaraguans enjoy being with others and are very warm and sociable. They are particularly hospitable to foreign visitors. They enjoy hearing stories about life in your country and also enjoy being asked about the Nicaraguan tourist sites and culture.

Traditional values support social hierarchy and *machismo* (the concept that men are superior to women). Because it is traditionally considered that only the opinions of those holding power are important, power is highly valued and often sought. Nevertheless, people living in urban areas tend to be less traditional. They will accept modern values and will tend to be less influenced by tradition.

# NICARAGUA (Cont'd)

## SOCIAL TIPS AND CONVENTIONS (Cont'd)

Personal honor is considered very important and will be defended verbally or even physically. Be careful not to embarrass or criticize someone or attempt to pull rank.

Expressing admiration for material objects is not as important as complimenting others on their good personality traits.

Good topics of conversation include jobs, history, culture and family. Inquiring about the health of family members demonstrates friendliness between acquaintances. Avoid discussing poverty, politics and religion. Be somewhat diplomatic when discussing U.S. involvement in Nicaragua, since some Nicaraguans love and respect the U.S., but others see it as their enemy.

Sports also makes a good topic of conversation. Baseball is the national sport; people also enjoy soccer, boxing, basketball and volleyball.

## CUSTOMARY BUSINESS PRACTICES

The best time to arrange a trip to Nicaragua is between February and July or between September and November, when people are not on vacation.

It is important to make appointments well in advance (at least one month) from your country, either by telephone or fax.

Since establishing a personal relationship is so important in negotiating in Nicaragua, contacts are very important. It is important to try to establish them before you visit and to have them arrange introductions with major clients. You can establish *enchufados* (contacts) through embassies, banks, etc.

Because people are considered to be more important than schedules, punctuality is often not observed. However, it is admired and appreciated and is expected of foreigners.

Expect business to be conducted at a slower pace in Nicaragua. A good deal of time will be spent on establishing personal relationships and delays in the schedule are quite common.

In negotiating, be aware that Nicaraguans may be suspicious of information provided by outsiders. Also, they tend to look at problems and situations from a subjective, personal perspective. They seldom rely solely on abstract rules and hard facts in making decisions. Similarly, they will seldom use objective facts to prove a point. An emotional appeal (to pride, trust, mutual compatibility, etc.) is generally more common and more successful in negotiating than an appeal to reason.

Individuals tend to be group oriented. Self-identity is based on an individual's position and performance in the group. Individual expertise and initiative tend to be subordinated to personal connections and the individual's ability to be part of the group. Appeals highlighting the benefits of a particular business deal for the group (for example, the company, the negotiating team or the country) tend to be most successful.

# NICARAGUA (Cont'd)

## CUSTOMARY BUSINESS PRACTICES (Cont'd)

Because *machismo* is quite strong in Nicaragua and because there are very few women at top positions in Nicaraguan firms, foreign businesswomen may encounter an initial lack of respect. Foreign businesswomen should act very professional and should emphasize that they are representing their firms and not themselves.

Businessmen customarily wear conservative dark suits and ties. However, in the hottest summer months, they will seldom wear jackets. Businesswomen normally wear a dress or a skirt and blouse.

Businesses are open from 8:00 a.m. until 6:00 p.m., Monday through Friday and from 8:00 a.m. until noon on Saturday. There is usually a two-hour *siesta* (a rest after the midday meal) break for lunch and resting, between noon and 2:00 p.m.

## BUSINESS ENTERTAINING

Business breakfasts or lunches are preferred to dinners. If you are invited to a meal in a home or if spouses are included at a meal, it is a purely social engagement. Nicaraguans do not discuss business at home or around family members.

Business gifts are usually not given on the first trip to Nicaragua. It is more appropriate, at the end of your visit, to ask your Nicaraguan counterparts if there is anything you can bring them from your country on your next visit.

It is usually a good idea to bring a gift for the secretaries and receptionists, who can be very influential. Perfume or scarves make appropriate gifts.

If you are invited to a home, it is appropriate to bring a small gift of candy or flowers. Do not bring white flowers, which are normally reserved for funerals.

Punctuality is not strictly observed for social engagements. In fact, it is polite to arrive a few minutes late.

## DINING OUT

The main meal of the day is at 12:00 noon. This meal traditionally includes black beans, *tortillas* (thin, round unleavened bread made from cornmeal or wheat flour) or meat and fruit and vegetables. It is usually followed by a *siesta*, which corresponds to the hottest time of the day when it is difficult to work.

Beans, rice and corn are the basic elements of the Nicaraguan diet. Typical dishes include *tortillas*, *enchiladas* (a tortilla rolled and stuffed with meat and/or vegetables served with chili sauce), *nacatamales* (meat and vegetables with spices), *mondongo* (tripe and beef knuckles) and *baho* (meat, vegetables and plantain). Tropical fruits and fried bananas (*plátanos*) are popular. A typical vegetable dish is called *vigorón*.

Meals tend to last longer since eating is accompanied by pleasant conversation. People avoid bringing up controversial topics during meals.

# NICARAGUA (Cont'd)

## DINING OUT (Cont'd)

Both hands but not elbows should remain above the table at all times.

## PUBLIC CUSTOMS

Due to the year-round warm climate, cool, lightweight clothes are most commonly worn. Women generally wear cotton dresses or skirts and blouses. In some areas, a woman may offend others by wearing pants. In cities and rural areas, shorts and jeans are inappropriate for both men and women. Also, a woman should avoid wearing revealing clothes, which might offend some people. Men sometimes wear the traditional *guayabera*, a lightweight shirt, which is sometimes embroidered and worn without being tucked in the pants.

Most gestures that are used in the U.S. are also common in Nicaragua. However, making a fist with the thumb positioned between the index and middle fingers (the "fig" gesture) is vulgar.

To beckon someone, make a scooping gesture with the fingers with the palm facing down.

When Nicaraguans wave good-bye, they sometimes wave with their hand facing out. They also sometimes wave with the palm facing inwards, as if they were fanning themselves.

Be careful when taking photographs, especially of individuals and religious ceremonies. Some people object to having their pictures taken. Also, avoid photographing transportation depots and bridges which may have military significance.

Deference is shown to older people. It is appropriate to stand when they enter or leave a room and give your seat to them when on public transportation. Don't be surprised if an older person is served before you when you are standing in line.

# PANAMA: HISTORICAL OVERVIEW

- The history of Panama has been greatly affected by its geographic location.

- Originally, Columbus claimed the area for Spain in 1502. It was considered part of what is now Colombia.

- Spanish rule was eventually overthrown in 1821, and Panama became a province of Colombia.

- During the 1880s, France tried to build a canal across Panama, but yellow fever claimed many lives. Subsequently, the canal rights were sold to the U.S.

- In 1902, Panama declared its independence from Colombia, and the U.S. sent troops to support the new government.

- Construction of the Panama canal began in 1907 under U.S. supervision. It was completed in seven years and was under U.S. control.

- In 1968, Arnulfo Arias, a fiery nationalist, was elected president. He served only eleven days before he was ousted by the National Guard, whose leader, Omar Torrijos Herrera, subsequently assumed dictatorial power. He turned power over to a civilian, Aristedes Royo, in 1978.

- In 1978, the U.S. signed a treaty calling for the return of the canal to Panama.

- A succession of civilian presidents followed, with the first popular election in 12 years taking place in 1980.

- Manuel Antonio Noriega, the chief of defense, ousted Eric Arturo Delvalle Henríquez in 1988 after Noriega's rule had been challenged in 1987; he suspended the constitution and civil rights, banned freedom of the press and declared a state of emergency. The U.S. invaded Panama in December 1989. Noriega was eventually taken prisoner and extradited to the U.S. to stand trial for drug-related charges.

- In 1992, the new government, under elected President Guillermo Endara began the task of rebuilding the nation.

- Endara, however, was not up to the task, and chronic unemployment and rampant corruption persisted. In 1994, Ernesto Perez Balladares, a former Citibank official with a U.S. education, was elected President.

- As 1999 draws near, it is becoming clear that Panama is ill-prepared for the withdrawal of U.S. troops. Both the canal and the parallel railroad are in poor shape, and if the tariffs are raised too high, tonnage will either cross the U.S. by land or go around the South American continent. The government is preparing to renegotiate the treaty so that some U.S. troops remain, and efforts will also be made to obtain financial assistance from the U.S.

# PANAMA

## INTRODUCTIONS

A handshake is the appropriate greeting between new acquaintances or business associates.

The most common forms of greeting among male friends is a nod and an *abrazo* (a brief hug). Women friends usually embrace and make a kissing motion on one cheek. These gestures are generally repeated upon departure.

Panama's official language is Spanish, although English is widely spoken.

At large parties, your host will not introduce you. You will need to introduce yourself to each person.

Professional titles are important when addressing someone.

## SOCIAL TIPS AND CONVENTIONS

In the interior of the country, gift-giving among friends is common, but only inexpensive items such as food or seedlings. This is not the case in the urban areas, however.

In Panama, the ideal man is a *macho* man of action, forceful, daring and virile. The ideal woman is expected to be well-bred, understanding and feminine. However, people in large urban areas are more cosmopolitan and are less likely to still feel this way.

Nationalism is very strong in Panama. Although relations with the U.S. are generally good, it is best to avoid conversation about the issues of U.S. financial aid and the 1989 invasion as well as the continued presence of the U.S. in the canal zone.

Good subjects for conversation include family, common friends or acquaintances, hobbies and sports such as baseball and basketball.

## CUSTOMARY BUSINESS PRACTICES

Business executives wear dark suits and ties. Women in Panama dress similarly to women in the U.S. Most other urban male workers wear open-necked shirts (*camisillas* or *panabrisas*).

The business day starts early, in some cases as early as 7:00 a.m. and ends early, usually between 3:30 and 4:00 p.m. Most businesses are also open on Saturday. Government offices are closed on Saturday and Sunday.

Make business appointments at least two weeks before arriving in Panama.

Panamanian businesspeople want to get to know you before talking about business.

## BUSINESS ENTERTAINING

Panamanians are proud of their tradition of hospitality. They are informal, open and generous with their guests.

Ending times for visits are not generally given so as to avoid having a guest feel unwelcome after a designated time.

## BUSINESS ENTERTAINING (Cont'd)

When invited to a party, you may arrive up to two hours late. For a large dinner party, you may arrive an hour late. If you (or you and your spouse) are the only guests, appear no more than 30 minutes late.

Gifts are not usually given when you are entertained in someone's home. Panamanians harbor the feeling that the favor will be reciprocated, so nothing extra is required.

In families, the father sits at the head of the table. The guest of honor usually sits at the other end of the table.

You will please your host by eating everything on your plate, but you will not offend him/her if you leave an item that you really don't enjoy.

## DINING OUT

Table manners vary from family to family and between urban and rural areas. Generally, hands should be kept above the table.

Restaurants usually do not include a service charge. A 10% tip to the waiter is customary.

The person who does the inviting generally pays for the meal.

Staples in the Panamanian diet include kidney beans, rice, plantains, corn and chicken. Omelettes and *tortillas* (thin, round unleavened bread made from cornmeal or wheat flour) are popular national foods.

Other popular items are *ceviche* (marinated raw fish); *carimañola* (boiled, mashed yucca wrapped around ground beef and fried); *ropa vieja* (shredded beef, green pepper, and spices served with plantains and rice); *empanadas* (fried meat pies); *sancocho* (a stew of chicken, yucca, onions, potatoes and corn).

Place your knife and fork vertically and parallel on your plate to signal that you have finished.

Use the term *"Mozo" or "Señor"* to summon a waiter; use *"Señorita"* for a waitress.

The most common dessert is fruit. A specialty is *buñuelos de viento* (fritters served with syrup). Coffee, usually espresso, is served after dinner.

## PUBLIC CUSTOMS

Nonverbal communication is used more by people outside of urban areas. "No" is indicated by wagging the index finger from side to side. To express "over there" or "time to go," people pucker their lips to point.

Eye contact is important in conversation.

Cover your mouth when you yawn or cough.

# PANAMA (Cont'd)

## PUBLIC CUSTOMS (Cont'd)

Most Panamanians do not wear shorts in public. In general, women should avoid revealing clothing.

Baseball is the most popular sport in Panama. Other favorites include boxing, basketball and soccer.

Ask permission before photographing a Panamanian.

# PARAGUAY: HISTORICAL OVERVIEW

- Spanish explorers first came to Paraguay in 1524 and established Asunción in 1537.

- Spanish colonial rule lasted until the 19th century. Paraguay peacefully gained independence in 1811, and José Gaspar Rodríguez Francia became its first leader. Until 1840, Rodríguez ruled as a dictator and closed the country to the outside world.

- In 1865, Francisco Solano López brought Paraguay into the War of the Triple Alliance against Brazil, Argentina and Uruguay. Eventually this war was lost, along with 55,000 square miles of territory and 500,000 lives. As a result of the war, foreign troops stayed until 1876, and Paraguay remained politically unstable for another generation.

- Paraguay fought Bolivia in the Chaco War, a territorial dispute, from 1932 to 1935. This war was successful in terms of regaining territory, but the victory cost a large number of lives and did not stabilize the nation politically.

- The country continued to be marked by political instability and dictatorships. Various dictators and one elected president ruled until 1954, when General Alfredo Stroessner, commander of the army, took control of the Paraguayan government and established a dictatorship. While this period of dictatorship brought about economic development, it was also marked by human rights violations, corruption and oppression.

- A 1989 coup ousted Stroessner, who now lives in Brazil. General Andrés Rodríguez Pedotti led the coup, and was subsequently elected as the country's president. General Rodriguez restored civil rights, legalized political parties and promised not to serve past 1993. He was the first leader in Paraguay's history to implement democratic reforms. Under his leadership, a new constitution was ratified in June 1992, and Paraguay emerged from its isolation to join regional and international organizations.

- As he had promised, General Rodríguez ended his term in 1993, and national elections were then held. Juan Carlos Wasmosy was elected President.

- Wasmosy tried, unsuccessfully, in 1993 to exclude the military from membership in the main political parties. In 1995, however, Wasmosy told the military commander, General Lino Oviedo, that he must resign, offering him in exchange the office of Secretary of Defense. Popular demonstration against Oviedo convinced him to decline the offer. Thus, Paraguay became a civilian-ruled nation for the first time in 165 years.

- Paraguay has become a major banking center in recent years. It is considered a good credit risk and a good place for investment due in part to lower inflation. Human rights violations are far less frequent than in the 1980s, though the problem of bureaucratic corruption has yet to be dealt with adequately.

# PARAGUAY

## INTRODUCTIONS

Men and women always shake hands either when being introduced or when greeting.

Close male friends may either shake hands or embrace each other when greeting. When women greet each other or when a woman greets a man, they will kiss one another on each cheek as well as shake hands. Some women will greet others with a pat on the arm or a brief hug.

Since most businesspeople speak Spanish, it is appropriate to use Spanish greetings and titles. The Spanish greeting *"¡Mucho gusto!"* ("Pleased to meet you") is often used with strangers or in somewhat formal situations. Acquaintances use less formal Spanish phrases and greet each other by saying *"¡Hola! ¿Cómo estás?"* ("Hi, How are you?"). Friends and family most commonly speak in Guaraní (Paraguay's common language) when greeting.

Only close friends, family members and children address each other using first names. Professional titles, followed by the last name, should normally be used to show respect. Anyone who graduated from a university can be addressed as a *"Licenciado"* (pronounced, "lee-sehn-SYAH-doh"); a physician or a Ph.D. may be addressed as *"Doctor;"* teachers should be addressed as *"Profes¡or;"* engineers are called *"Ingeniero;"* and architects should be addressed as *"Arquitecto."* If the person does not have a professional title, use the titles *"Señor"* ("Mr."), *"Señora"* ("Mrs.") or *"Señorita"* ("Miss"), followed by the last name. Also, remember that urban men are customarily addressed as *"Don,"* followed by the last name, while women are addressed as *"Doña,"* followed by a first name.

Most people in Paraguay have two surnames, one from the father (listed first) and one from the mother. Normally, the father's name is used when addressing someone. For example, Señor Hernan Antonio Martinez Garcia is addressed as "Señor Martinez" and Señorita María Elisa Gutierrez Herrera is addressed as "Señorita Gutierrez." When a woman marries, she usually adds her husband's surname and goes by that surname. For example, if the two people in the above example married, the woman would be known as "Señora María Elisa Gutierrez Herrera de Martinez." She would be addressed as "Señora de Martinez" or, more informally, "Señora Martinez."

At a party, it is important to shake hands with each person individually, both when arriving and when leaving.

## SOCIAL TIPS AND CONVENTIONS

In Paraguay, Spanish is the language used by people in government, urban commerce and school. Guaraní, however, is the official language. Also, Portuguese is spoken along the Brazilian border.

If you plan to speak Spanish while in Paraguay, be aware that Paraguay's Spanish is called *Castellano* (Castillian) rather than *Español*. Thus many words are different than those used in other Spanish-speaking countries, in part because a number of Guaraní words are mixed with Paraguayan Spanish. Also, Paraguayans use the informal *tú* (you) form of address more rarely than in other Spanish-speaking countries.

# PARAGUAY (Cont'd)

## SOCIAL TIPS AND CONVENTIONS (Cont'd)

Paraguayans are very proud of their country and cultural heritage and they enjoy being asked about the beautiful sights as well as their customs. They enjoy defining themselves by exhibiting the unique elements of the country's culture (for example, by speaking Guaraní). Paraguayans say that Spanish is the language of the head and Guaraní, the language of the heart.

Be aware that Paraguay is a traditional society whose people place a great value on large families, property, beauty, virility, money and status. The ultimate goal is harmony and lack of problems, or *tranquilo* (tranquility). Deviations from or criticisms of these values are not appreciated.

Avoid making negative comparisons between Paraguay and other countries. Paraguayans do not appreciate stereotypes about poverty and inferiority in developing nations. In addition, many Paraguayans are of the belief that other nations take advantage of their country.

Paraguayans are not very tolerant of divergent political views. Avoid offering any political opinions. Instead, wait until your Paraguayan counterpart has voiced his/her opinion and then choose a position that does not disagree.

Sports make a good topic of conversation. *Fútbol* (soccer) is the most popular spectator sport, while volleyball is the most popular participatory sport. U.S. football (*fútbol americano*), basketball and horse-racing are also popular.

Avoid referring to U.S. citizens as "Americans" since Paraguayans consider themselves to be (South) Americans and are very sensitive to the use of the term. They prefer to refer to U.S. residents as *"Norteamericano"* (for men) or *"Norteamericana"* (for women) meaning, "North American."

Loud or disruptive behavior is inappropriate.

Paraguayans tend to stand quite close together when speaking. If you step away, you may offend the person to whom you are speaking.

## CUSTOMARY BUSINESS PRACTICES

The best time to arrange business trips to Paraguay is between June and October, when people are not on vacation or celebrating holidays.

Many business executives speak English. However, it is wise to check before your visit and to arrange for an interpreter if necessary.

Arrange appointments well in advance. The morning is the best time to schedule appointments (between 8:00 a.m. and noon).

Punctuality is not considered particularly important by Paraguayans. However, although business meetings rarely start on time, a foreigner (especially a North American) is still expected to be punctual.

# PARAGUAY (Cont'd)

## CUSTOMARY BUSINESS PRACTICES (Cont'd)

In Paraguay, the pace of business is generally slow. Delays are common, Paraguayans maintain a relaxed attitude even in fast-paced situations, and a considerable amount of time is spent on establishing personal relationships before transacting business.

Accomplishing a business transaction may require several trips to Paraguay. It is a good idea for the same individual(s) to be sent each time because the development of the relationship is important. If your company's representative changes, it will be like starting from scratch – a new relationship will have to be built before business can proceed.

Contracts are rarely agreed upon in sections. Until the entire contract is signed, each section is considered to be renegotiable.

When negotiating, be aware that Paraguayans tend to look at problems and situations from a subjective, personal perspective. They seldom rely solely on abstract rules and hard facts in making decisions. Similarly, they will seldom use objective facts to prove a point. An emotional appeal (to pride, trust, mutual compatibility, etc.) is generally more common and more successful in negotiating than an appeal to reason. Also, a Paraguayan's sense of what is the truth and what constitutes a solution to a problem may be guided by faith in the ideologies of nationalism and religion.

When doing business in Paraguay, be aware that individuals tend to be group oriented. Self-identity is based on an individual's position and performance in the group. Individual expertise and initiative tend to be subordinated to personal connections and the individual's ability to be part of the group. Appeals to the good of a business deal for the group (for example, the company, the negotiating team or the country) tend to be most successful.

Since Paraguay is a traditional society with clearly defined hierarchical gender-based and social roles, decision making is usually based on perceptions of power and hierarchy within the negotiating teams.

Because *machismo* is quite strong in Paraguay and because there are very few women in top positions in Paraguayan firms, foreign businesswomen may encounter an initial lack of respect. Foreign businesswomen should act very professional and should emphasize that they are representing their firms and not themselves.

On the other hand, since Paraguayan men dislike confronting or offending women, it can be useful to include a female business representative on a negotiating team.

While it is not necessary to translate materials into the Guaraní language, business cards and all presentation materials and brochures should be translated into Spanish.

Business dress is conservative. Men wear dark suits and ties. Women wear white blouses and dark suits or skirts. Women do not usually wear nylons in the summer and sometimes jackets and ties are removed, due to the hot climate. Foreign businesspeople should follow the example of their Paraguayan counterparts.

# PARAGUAY (Cont'd)

## CUSTOMARY BUSINESS PRACTICES (Cont'd)

Urban businesses are usually open from 7:00 a.m. until noon and then from 3:00 until 6:00 p.m., Monday through Friday. There is a *siesta* (a rest after the midday meal) between noon and 3:00 p.m., during which people eat their midday meal and rest or sleep. Some businesses are open on Saturday mornings as well.

## BUSINESS ENTERTAINING

Paraguayans are very hospitable. They enjoy entertaining guests, even those who drop by unexpectedly. Refreshments are offered at most visits.

Gift-giving can be a sensitive area in Paraguay since corruption and bribery was widespread during the former regime. Any gift should be of high quality. If the gift has a corporate name or logo on it, the name or logo should be printed discreetly. Also, avoid giving knives which are taken to symbolize the severing of a relationship.

Business lunches are quite rare since most people go home for the midday *siesta*. However, as Paraguayan businesspeople are becoming more influenced by North American practices, they may work through the afternoon and attend business lunches.

Most business entertaining is done during dinner, which is usually served late, around 9:00 or 10:00 p.m. In fact, many restaurants do not serve dinner before 9:00 p.m. and stay open until midnight. At the same time, most dinners are considered to be social occasions and one should not try to discuss business unless the host first broaches the subject.

Urban residents enjoy inviting guests to their homes for a meal, while more rural people tend to extend such invitations only for special occasions.

Punctuality is not expected in social occasions. In fact, it is considered polite and people will be more comfortable if you arrive up to 30 minutes late.

If you are invited to a home for a meal, it is not expected but is appropriate to bring a small gift, such as flowers, wine or chocolates.

The custom in Paraguay is that food and drink should be shared. For example, it is unusual to order oneself a drink; instead, a larger pitcher should be ordered for everyone at the table. Additional rounds are usually ordered by the other diners.

If you are meeting business associates in a casual situation, it is recommended that men wear slacks (avoid jeans) and a blazer. Women may wear pants as casual wear, but should avoid shorts.

In restaurants, service is included in the check and an additional tip is not expected.

## PARAGUAY (Cont'd)

### DINING OUT

Mealtimes and eating habits vary according to the region and the family. In cities, families usually eat their main meal of the day together. When guests are invited, children might eat before the guests arrive or before they are served.

Breakfast usually consists of *cocido* (*yerba* tea, cooked sugar, milk) or coffee, bread and butter, rolls or pastries. Lunch is usually the main meal of the day. Dinner is normally eaten at the end of the work day.

Some Paraguayans define themselves not only by speaking Guaraní, but also by drinking *yerba* tea and eating *mandioca* (cassava). *Mandioca* is a staple food, which is served at almost every meal. *Yerba* leaves are made into a mildly stimulating tea, which is either served cold (called *tereré*) or, less commonly, hot (called *maté*). Paraguayans drink these teas very often as they have been part of the culture for hundreds of years.

The most important staples include *mandioca*, *sopa Paraguaya* (cornbread baked with cheese, onions and sometimes meat), *chipa* (hard cheese bread), *tortillas* (thin, round unleavened bread made from cornmeal or wheat flour) and *empanadas* (deep-fried meat or vegetable pockets). Beef is the most common meat. Chicken and pork dishes are also popular.

Guests are usually served full plates of food. Additional portions can be taken from serving dishes placed on the table.

In formal situations, certain rules of etiquette are followed. The hands, but not elbows, should be kept above the table. Also, guests should first wait for the host to begin eating.

The *asado* (barbecue) is a popular family gathering in many places.

*Tereré* is often consumed from a common *guampa* (container, usually made of wood, cattle horns or gourds) through a *bombilla* (metal straw). The host passes the *guampa* to one person, who drinks and returns his/her container to the host, who then makes another portion for the next person. The drinking of the *yerba* tea is a social custom, which is enjoyed along with conversation and relaxation.

Paraguayans normally do not drink during the meal, but wait until they are finished eating.

Leaving food on your plate is considered an insult to the cook. In addition, hosts usually insist that their guests take several servings.

Meals can be quite extended. Guests are normally expected to stay after a meal for conversation and tea.

# PARAGUAY (Cont'd)

## PUBLIC CUSTOMS

Western-style clothing is commonly worn throughout Paraguay and the youth, in particular, wear North American fashions. A clean and neat appearance is emphasized and lightweight, natural fabrics are usually worn because of the hot climate. Adults do not wear shorts in public and men rarely wear sandals. Regardless of economic conditions, women, in particular, pay attention to their appearance. Society considers it important for women to be beautiful; thus styled hair, makeup, jewelry and manicured nails are all considered important.

The most common gesture used in Paraguay is the "thumbs up" sign, which expresses anything positive or encouraging. It is commonly used when a person is answering a question.

Wagging the index finger means "No" or "I don't think so."

The North American "Okay" sign, with the tip of the thumb and the tip of the index finger touching to form a circle, is an offensive gesture in Paraguay.

Tapping one's chin with the top of the index finger means "I don't know." A backwards tilt of the head means "I forgot."

Be aware that winking is not used as a casual gesture in Paraguay. It has romantic, even sexual, connotations.

Since loud behavior is inappropriate, Paraguayans will not shout to get someone's attention. Making a "tsst-tsst" sound is the most common way to get a person's attention. If this does not work, a Paraguayan might whistle or run after the person.

On public transportation, Paraguayan men usually give up their seats to older or pregnant women or women with children. Also, seated passengers will often offer to hold children or packages for standing passengers.

It is acceptable and common for people to eat in public as street vendors sell a variety of food on urban streets.

Whenever you have a snack or small meal, it is polite to offer some of the food to whomever is around. If you are offered food by someone, it is polite to decline.

It is common for close friends of either sex to walk arm-in-arm.

Proper posture is important when sitting. It is considered rude to slump or to sit on a ledge, box or table. Also, it is very impolite to put your feet up on a table.

# PERU: HISTORICAL OVERVIEW

- A number of indigenous groups populated the area now known as Peru before the arrival of European settlers. The last of these groups were the Incas.

- In 1532, the Spanish invaded Peru under the leadership of Francisco Pizarro and conquered the Incan Empire by 1533. Because of its location and its abundance of minerals, Peru soon became the richest and most powerful Spanish colony in America.

- Peru declared independence in 1821 under the leadership of the South American liberator, José de San Martín. A war ensued which lasted until 1826, when independence became complete.

- Although the 1933 Peruvian constitution provided for democratic leadership, military leaders and dictators dominated Peruvian politics starting in the 1930s. Political instability and a chain of dictatorships created more economic problems in Peru.

- In 1980, the *Sendero Luminoso* ("Shining Path"), a Maoist group, began a decade of violent warfare against the government. They consolidated power in the Upper Huallaga Valley, where drug traffickers paid them for protection and the right to operate in the region.

- A semblance of democratic rule began in the late 1970s when free elections were held. However, political instability and economic problems continued. During Alan García's presidency (1985-1990), key industries were nationalized, the foreign debt crisis deepened and relations with the U.S. dwindled. Nevertheless, in 1990, plans for major military cooperation between Peru and the U.S. to fight drug trafficking were implemented.

- Despite instability, economic problems and terrorist attacks, free elections were held in 1990. Alberto Fujimori, a son of Japanese immigrants, was elected as García's successor. He vowed to reinstate civil rights and democracy and to improve the economy by imposing austerity measures.

- Fujimori suspended the constitution in April 1992 and dissolved congress, citing Shining Path insurgency, government corruption and legislative inefficiency. In trying to defeat the Shining Path and to reform the government, he took emergency powers and restricted civil liberties. While some people supported the move, domestic and international pressure soon mounted, and Fujimori announced a quick return to democracy.

- In 1992, the Shining Path leader was captured and sentenced to life in prison. Within a year of imprisonment, the Shining Path leader began encouraging former followers to make peace with the government and desertions from the organization were, subsequently, high in 1993.

- Also in 1992, a new constitution, which enshrined the principles of a free market economy and a democratic system, was drafted and was put into effect after the 1995 elections. The document was approved in a 1993 national referendum. Fujimori ran in the 1995 elections and won a second term as President.

# PERU

## INTRODUCTIONS

Both men and women shake hands when greeting and when departing. Sometimes when men and women or two women are introduced, they may kiss one another.

Men who are close friends may embrace each other or pat each other on the back. Women who are close friends may kiss one another on the cheek.

Officials or elders should be greeted with their last name, preceded by a title. Common titles are *"Doctor," "Profesor," "Architecto"* (architect) or *"Ingenerio"* (engineer). First names are only used among friends.

## SOCIAL TIPS AND CONVENTIONS

Spanish is Peru's first official language. Quechua, the language of the Incas, is the other official language.

Peruvians are a strong-willed and nationalistic people. They have a good sense of humor, are accommodating and are easy to please. At the same time, they can be sensitive about certain things. Jokes about their lifestyle, especially coming from foreigners, are considered offensive. Personal criticism, if necessary, is expressed in a positive manner.

Peruvians welcome foreigners very warmly. Do not be surprised if people discuss family and occupation as soon as they meet you. Peruvians may ask you a lot of questions about your country's government as well as technology, so you may want to organize your thoughts on these subjects in advance. However, people generally avoid discussing salary or how much something costs.

Avoid discussing Peruvian government and politics. Even if you hear complaints and criticisms about Peru's government, refrain from making remarks. Also, don't ask Peruvians about their ancestors since they feel more comfortable being associated with their Spanish colonial heritage than with their Indian heritage.

It is appreciated if you ask questions about the area in which you are visiting or for advice about sights to see or places to eat. Soccer and other sports also make good topics of conversation.

In Peru, people stand close to each other when conversing. If you back away, you may offend those with whom you are speaking.

## CUSTOMARY BUSINESS PRACTICES

Avoid planning business trips during the January to March period, when most business people are on vacation.

It is important to have contacts in Peru. Contacts in the diplomatic world are especially valuable.

# PERU (Cont'd)

## CUSTOMARY BUSINESS PRACTICES (Cont'd)

Business appointments should be made from abroad at least two weeks in advance. You will have more success in scheduling business meetings in the morning rather than in the afternoon. Most businesspeople take lunch breaks from 1:00 until 3:00 p.m. Also, be aware that morning appointments usually lead to lunch invitations. Therefore, avoid scheduling two consecutive morning appointments.

Foreigners are expected to be punctual for business engagements, although Peruvians do not adhere to strict timetables.

Including charts or visual aids in your presentations will impress Peruvian businesspeople.

Carry business cards printed in both English and Spanish.

Business may proceed very quickly since foreign investment is welcomed.

You should proceed subtly, as Peruvians do, when negotiating. Avoid confronting people directly by asking questions that require a "yes" or "no" response. Most Peruvians will tell you what they think you want to hear rather than what they really believe.

It is very difficult for foreign businesswomen to succeed in Peru as traditional roles are ascribed to women. For example, a married woman needs her husband's consent in order to open a bank account.

In winter, businessmen wear dark wool suits and, in summer, they wear dark lightweight suits or blazers and slacks. Businesswomen should wear a dress or a skirt, blouse and a jacket.

Businesses are generally open from 8:30 a.m. to 12:30 p.m. and then from 3:00 to 6:30 p.m., from Monday to Friday.

## BUSINESS ENTERTAINING

When invited to a dinner at a home, men should wear a sports jacket and a tie; women should wear a dress or skirt and blouse. If the occasion is a party at a home, men should wear a suit and tie and women a dress or skirt and blouse. If an invitation says that dress is formal, men should wear tuxedos and women should wear cocktail dresses.

Lunches are more appropriate for discussing business, while dinners tend to be more social affairs.

If you are invited to a meal, it is appropriate to arrive 30 minutes late. Most dinner invitations are scheduled for 9:00 p.m., although dinner often is not served until 10:30 p.m.

The person who issues the invitation to a meal at a restaurant should pay for the meal.

# PERU (Cont'd)

## BUSINESS ENTERTAINING (Cont'd)

If you are entertaining for a business discussion, it is appropriate to invite only those with whom you have been negotiating directly. However, when the deal is completed, feel free to invite everyone who has been involved in a project to a meal.

Peruvian businesspeople like to be entertained at luxurious restaurants. They will be particularly impressed if you invite them to a restaurant that caters to luxury dining. It is recommended that you ask someone in the firm or call the tourist office to get the names of appropriate restaurants.

When invited to a meal at a Peruvian's home, it is recommended that you bring wine, liquor or chocolates as a gift. Your host will not expect anything, but any gift will be appreciated. If you bring or send flowers, choose roses. In Peru, other flowers are so inexpensive that they don't seem like a gift.

Other good gift items include perfume, scarves, elegant neckties or costume jewelry. Avoid giving people synthetic clothing since Peruvians prefer natural fabrics. Also, inexpensive cameras, calculators or good pens make excellent business gifts.

When dining in a home or at a restaurant, refrain from drinking the tap water. Also avoid eating raw shellfish or raw fruits or vegetables that cannot be peeled. When ordering a drink, order it without ice by saying *"Sin Hielo"* (pronounced, "seen yeh-loh"). Be cautious with lemonade since many people make it with unboiled water.

In a restaurant, the waiter is summoned by waving.

Restaurants usually add a 10% service charge to the bill. If the service is outstanding, you may add another 5% or leave the equivalent of 25 or 50¢ extra.

## DINING OUT

Breakfast is a simple meal of rolls with ham, cheese or jam and *café con leche* (coffee with milk). Lunch, served from 12:30 or 1:00 to 3:00 p.m., usually consists of a pasta course followed by steak, chops, chicken or fish with salad and rice. Finally fruit and demitasse are served. Herbal teas (e.g., *yerba Luisa*) are more popular than coffee. Wine, lemonade or soft drinks are usually served with the meal. Many people also mix wine with water. At 6:00 p.m., people routinely have cake and cookies with tea. At 8:30 or 9:00 p.m., dinner is served, which includes soup with noodles and *guiso* (vegetables pureed with spices) served with rice. The meal ends with coffee or an herb tea.

Popular drinks before dinner are *pisco* (grape brandy) or a *pisco* sour (grape brandy, lemon, sugar and beaten egg whites), Campari and whiskey. With meals, Peruvians usually drink beer, wine, fruit juices, lemonade, Coke, Inca Cola (a yellow carbonated soft drink that tastes like bubble gum) and *agua mineral* (bottled, carbonated mineral water).

The main staples in the Peruvian diet are rice, beans, fish and a variety of tropical fruits. Corn, native to Peru, is also popular. *Cebiche* (raw fish seasoned with lemon and vinegar) is popular on the coast. Potatoes, onions and garlic are frequent ingredients for dishes in the highlands. Fresh vegetables are eaten in season.

# PERU (Cont'd)

## DINING OUT (Cont'd)

The host and hostess usually sit next to one another. A male guest of honor sits to the right of the hostess and a female guest of honor to the right of the host.

The continental style of eating is used, with the fork held in the left hand and the knife remaining in the right. If fish is served, you should use the fish knife and fork provided.

Keep your hands (but not your elbows) above the table during a meal.

In Peru, people normally eat enormous quantities of food. Your host may press you to eat a lot, but you should not feel obligated. Similarly, you should not feel obliged to finish everything on your plate – in fact, it is polite to leave a little food (indicating that you are satisfied).

To indicate that you have finished eating, place your utensils either diagonally or vertically across the plate.

You should stay only about 30 minutes after the meal ends. Even if your host urges you to stay, he/she is usually just being polite and you should leave anyway.

## PUBLIC CUSTOMS

Western-style clothing is worn regularly in most urban areas, although more traditional clothing may also be worn. For casual attire, men should wear slacks and an elegant shirt. Women should wear a skirt or pants and a blouse.

It is common for people of the same sex to walk arm-in-arm, as a sign of warmth and friendship. Do not be surprised if someone takes your arm when you are walking with them.

Always offer cigarettes to the people around you if you light one for yourself.

To beckon someone, wave your hand back and forth while holding it vertically, palm facing out.

Women should cross their legs at the knee, while men should cross their legs by placing one ankle on the knee of the other leg.

Be discreet when taking pictures of Indians; some object to having their pictures taken and others might become angry if they are not offered a tip. Similarly, you should not photograph airports, military installations or industrial plants.

# PUERTO RICO: HISTORICAL OVERVIEW

- In 1493, Columbus arrived in the region now known as Puerto Rico and claimed the island for Spain, calling it San Juan Bautista. In 1508, Spanish settlers began colonizing the island, and they began importing African slaves in 1513. During this period of colonization, the indigenous Taino tribe was virtually wiped out.

- In 1873, slavery was abolished on the island. In 1897, self-government was granted to Puerto Rico, which became a dominion under Spain. The first leader under dominion status was Luis Muñoz Rivera, who had been instrumental in winning this status for the island.

- In 1898, during the Spanish-American War, the United States invaded the island of Puerto Rico and defeated the Spaniards. Spain ceded the island to the U.S. in that year. Puerto Rico became the first colony of the United States.

- In 1917, Puerto Rico became a U.S. territory, and its people were granted citizenship.

- Puerto Rico was hit hard by the Great Depression in the 1930s, which caused 60% unemployment and great suffering.

- The first island-born governor, Jesus Toribio Pinero, was appointed by U.S. President Truman in 1946.

- In 1952, Puerto Ricans voted to establish the self-governing Commonwealth of Puerto Rico, with its own constitution. The status of commonwealth has meant that a resident high commissioner represents the country in the U.S. House of Representatives, citizens do not vote in national elections, and they do not pay federal income taxes. However, they are subject to the draft, they receive partial welfare benefits and they elect their own officials. Also, Puerto Ricans are restricted by federal controls in managing their territory.

- The issue of commonwealth status has been volatile and has sometimes caused violence to erupt. In 1954, militants from Puerto Rico shot several congressmen in Washington during a session of the House of Representatives. Today, Puerto Ricans continue to be divided over the issue of whether to request statehood or remain a commonwealth.

- In 1993, a referendum regarding Puerto Rico's status took place; however, it did not seem to resolve the issue since the decision to remain a commonwealth passed by only a slim margin. Many people feel that the 1993 referendum reflected changes in attitudes since referendums in 1967 and 1981 passed the commonwealth status by a greater margin.

- The Puerto Rican economy is in fairly good shape, but agriculture and tourism have suffered, mainly due to an increase in crime associated with a burgeoning drug traffic. Another factor that hurts the economy is the large bureaucracy: 28% of the populace works for the government.

- Pedro Rosello was elected governor in late 1996 and carried the pro-statehood *New Progressive Party* to victory.

# PUERTO RICO

## INTRODUCTIONS

People generally shake hands when they meet. Close friends often embrace and women may grasp each other's shoulders and kiss each other's cheek when greeting. Also, people stand very close while conversing.

Puerto Ricans often use titles such as *"Doctor," "Profesor," "Ingeniero," "Abogado,"* etc. Always use a title or *"Señor," "Señora"* or *"Señorita."* Sometimes the informal custom of using first names is borrowed from the mainland, but don't call your client or counterpart by his/her first name until invited to do so. Sometimes a single last name is used in business. A business card may simply read "Jose Castillo," instead of the traditional custom of including both matronymic and patronymic names as is often seen in Latin America (where the card would read "Jose Castillo Contreras" and he would still be called "Jose Castillo.") However, don't be surprised to see both names on the card as he may want to be addressed by both names. In any case, inquire as to his preference.

## SOCIAL TIPS AND CONVENTIONS

Puerto Ricans object to open criticism, "pushiness" and greed. They would rather discuss their cultural heritage and the rapid economic growth of Puerto Rico. Statehood with the U.S. is a hotly debated and divisive issue and may be best left untouched. Politics and religious topics should be avoided in conversation and in public addresses. Puerto Ricans are not disturbed by interruptions while conversing and they may do so freely. Also, commenting quietly while others are talking is not generally considered offensive.

Puerto Ricans seem to have the ability to tune out background noise. They can transact business, listen to one another and carry on a meaningful conversation in spite of surrounding noises.

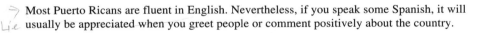

Most Puerto Ricans are fluent in English. Nevertheless, if you speak some Spanish, it will usually be appreciated when you greet people or comment positively about the country.

## CUSTOMARY BUSINESS PRACTICES

Puerto Ricans are spontaneous and warm in their relationships and this sentiment carries over into business meetings. You may spend time socializing before your business begins. This usually involves discussing family which is one of the most important factors in Puerto Ricans' lives.

Personal and interpersonal relationships have a great impact on business. A task may be very important and it will get accomplished; however, people are considered much more important than any task.

Business is conducted more slowly in Puerto Rico than on the mainland and it is critical that the process not get rushed along. Meetings will begin or close at the appointed time, but as Puerto Ricans have a more relaxed lifestyle, lateness should not be chastised.

Dress codes are similar to those on the mainland, although it is not unusual to see an older gentlemen wearing the traditional *guayabera* (a decorative shirt worn rather than a shirt and tie) during the summer. Women dress professionally in lightweight suits or dresses.

# PUERTO RICO (Cont'd)

## BUSINESS ENTERTAINING

After a meeting, it is customary to invite the client for a drink or to dinner. Business should not be discussed during dinner as this occasion is considered a time to become better acquainted. The pace of dinner is usually relaxed and includes good-natured joking. It is not considered polite to eat and run and it is customary to linger over coffee.

It should be noted that outside San Juan, the pace of business as well as entertainment is slower.

## DINING OUT

Both the continental and the U.S. styles of eating are acceptable. An offer of a toast to the health of all and success in all endeavors is appreciated.

You will sometimes hear a hissing sound in a restaurant. This sound is used to call a waiter. Do not comment on its strangeness.

## PUBLIC CUSTOMS

Businesspeople should not wear shorts or bathing suits outside the confines of their hotel pool/recreation area.

# UNITED STATES OF AMERICA: HISTORICAL OVERVIEW

- While North America's history before the Europeans arrived is incomplete, it is clear that indigenous populations had advanced civilizations. In the 17th century, European settlers started displacing Native Americans.

- The first permanent settlement was in Jamestown, Virginia (1607). However, the "Pilgrim Fathers," the group of Puritans from England and Holland who landed at Plymouth, Massachusetts in 1620, are widely regarded as the true founders of the U.S. During the 17th and 18th centuries, the British established the Thirteen Colonies on the east coast of North America.

- The American Revolution in 1776 led to independence from Britain and a loose confederation of states. The U.S. Constitution of 1787 established the basic government as it exists today. The U.S. has had free elections to determine its leadership since its creation and considers itself a guardian of democracy and freedom.

- After independence, explorers and pioneers headed west and settled large areas of land. The U.S. acquired territory from France, Mexico and Spain throughout the 19th century. By the 20th century, the U.S. had expanded its borders from the Atlantic to the Pacific Oceans.

- In 1861, civil war broke out between the Union states in the North and the Confederate states in the South over the issues of slavery and secession as well as economic differences. Union forces, under President Abraham Lincoln, defeated the Confederates in 1865 and reunited the country. As a result of the Civil War, the slaves were liberated, however, they were not integrated into the general society.

- During the remaining years of the 19th century, the first transcontinental railway was completed and settlement of the West developed rapidly. The nation maintained a traditional isolationist policy toward the rest of the world.

- U.S. troops were involved only in the last year of World War I. However, the country was a major combatant in World War II, from which it emerged as the strongest economic and military power in the world. The U.S. financed the postwar recovery of much of the world, including the rehabilitation of Japan as well as the Marshall Plan for Europe. The country assisted developing nations economically and technologically and spread U.S. values and ideals (which were not always welcome) throughout the world.

- In the 1970s, after the U.S. withdrawal from the Vietnam War (1973), U.S. prominence declined. However, this trend seemed to reverse in the 1990s, as the U.S. participated in the 1991 Gulf War, invaded Somalia in 1992, signed the North American Free Trade Agreement (NAFTA) and signed the Start II Treaty (Strategic Nuclear Arms Reduction) in 1993. In addition, since 1991 the U.S. has been a key sponsor of the Middle East Peace Conference.

# UNITED STATES OF AMERICA

## INTRODUCTIONS

Greetings in the U.S. are brief and uncomplicated. Firm handshakes accompanied by a smile and direct eye contact are typical, both as a greeting and as a farewell among men and women.

U.S. women usually expect the man to let them take the initiative in shaking hands. Women may shake hands less often in social situations. However, in business, women will almost always offer a hand. It is considered rude not to shake hands when the woman offers it.

As an alternative to the handshake, good friends and family members may embrace when they meet. In casual situations, a wave may be used instead of a handshake. Bowing or hand-kissing is rare.

When people in the U.S. greet someone they will often say "Pleased to meet you" or will ask "How are you?" The visitor should note that the expected response to this question is a perfunctory "Fine, thank you," not a detailed description of the state of one's health. A simple "Hello" or "Hi" are other forms of address. There are also regional variations, such as "Aloha" in Hawaii or "Howdy" in parts of the West.

A standard opening line in the U.S. when people meet socially is "What do you do?" While in many other countries this question is insulting, it is asked frequently in the U.S. as a topic of conversation.

Combining a title ("Miss," "Mrs.," "Dr.," etc.) with a surname shows respect. Regarding the correct way of addressing the U.S. woman executive – usually Ms. (pronounced "Mizz") and then the last name will do, unless the woman indicates a preference for another form of address.

Once acquainted, people address each other by their given names. No ritual precedes the switch to first name usage. This informality is a sign of friendliness and reduces communication barriers.

## SOCIAL TIPS AND CONVENTIONS

Gift-giving is not common. The U.S. has bribery laws that restrict the value of gifts that can be given.

Permission should be asked before smoking whether at a place of business or a home.

The design of most offices encourages peer/colleague interaction, but people in the U.S. tend to avoid close personal relationships in business. They can become territorial when under much stress and uncertainty.

Touching is tolerated socially, but could be construed as sexual harassment in the workplace.

People in the U.S. tend to stand an arm's length away from each other while conversing.

People in the U.S. generally respect queues or lines. To shove or push one's way into a line will often result in anger and verbal complaint.

## UNITED STATES OF AMERICA (Cont'd)

### SOCIAL TIPS AND CONVENTIONS (Cont'd)

Appearance, in general, is important to the individual in the U.S. Formal clothing is worn for certain social occasions. However, clothing habits are generally a matter of personal preference. Clothing is often used to make a personal or social statement. Although people in the U.S. emphasize cleanliness, people may purposely wear tattered or casual attire in public.

### CUSTOMARY BUSINESS PRACTICES

Most U.S. businesspeople carry business cards. However, they are not always exchanged automatically on meeting but usually only if there is some reason you want to get in touch later.

If there is no one to introduce you at a business meeting, it is acceptable to introduce yourself and to present your business card.

It is a good idea for a visitor to present a business card early. However, the visitor should not be offended if he/she is not given a business card in return.

Direct eye contact is very important in business. Not making eye contact implies boredom, dishonesty, lack of confidence or disinterest.

Displays of emotion are best avoided, although some embellishments and boasting of accomplishments can occur.

The U.S. is not particularly rank and status conscious. Titles are not used when addressing executives. People in the U.S. usually like to use first names soon after meeting. Informality tends to be equated with equality.

Business meetings usually start with a formal agenda, outlining the tasks to be accomplished. There is very little small talk. Participants are expected to express their ideas openly; disagreements are common.

Always make a point to be punctual as businesspeople in the U.S. can be very time conscious. However, arriving a few minutes late (depending on the circumstances) for a business meeting is usually not frowned upon. People in the U.S. also tend to conduct business at a fast pace and make quick decisions although the decisions may not be final. Decisions can be changed quickly if it appears things are not working. Keep in mind that people in the U.S. want to accomplish the job with a minimum expenditure of time and effort.

Most people in the U.S. like to do one thing at a time; they don't like interruptions and have a strong need to complete their assignments or projects.

Most people in the U.S. can have a tendency to see things as "white" or "black," "right" or "wrong;" and, therefore, are either "for" or "against" something, often without fully examining the alternatives. They can appear to oversimplify and look for instant solutions.

A dark suit with a tie is always acceptable business dress for men. Businesswomen typically wear a business suit or dress.

# UNITED STATES OF AMERICA (Cont'd)

## CUSTOMARY BUSINESS PRACTICES (Cont'd)

People in the U.S. value and expect punctuality.

As with business meetings, punctuality is expected for social engagements, especially if a meal is being served.

Firm appointments should be arranged well in advance. Such appointments are easy to make by mail. A letter is an acceptable substitute for personal contact in the U.S. and if it contains a clear message, it will reach the appropriate person in the target organization. Whether by telephone or by mail, the visitor should be fully prepared to explain clearly the purpose of his/her visit.

## BUSINESS ENTERTAINING

In an office, accepting or rejecting offers of coffee is perfectly proper. To most international visitors, the coffee served in the U.S. is a disappointing beverage.

People in the U.S. frequently use meal times for business purposes. Business discussions will often take place during lunch or dinner. Business lunches, which are the most common form of business entertainment, take place from about 12:30 to 2:00 p.m. Lunch is usually not a heavy meal, since the regular workday continues immediately afterwards. Dinner is the main meal of the day and when you are invited to a dinner, it will usually begin between 7:00 and 9:00 p.m. Also, breakfast invitations (at about 7:30 a.m.) are becoming increasingly common. Business luncheon meetings and dinners in restaurants generally require a suit.

People in the U.S. enjoy socializing in small or large groups for almost any occasion. They enjoy talking, watching television or a movie, eating and relaxing together. Hospitality takes several forms. You may be invited to a restaurant for a meal or you may be invited to a home for a formal dinner, an outdoor barbecue or even a visit where refreshments may or may not be served. Most events are casual as guests are expected to feel comfortable, to sit where they like and to enjoy themselves. If an international visitor receives an invitation to the home of his/her U.S. counterpart, he/she would be wise to ask about the manner of dress. Most businesspeople, when home, change into less formal clothes.

An invitation to a U.S. home is relatively rare. Home invitations are an honor – a sign of friendship and approval. Such encounters typically include spouses. U.S. businesspeople will suggest entertainment in clubs or theaters only after a lengthy, good relationship has developed.

In restaurants, you may signal to the waiter/waitress that you want the check by making a writing motion in the air. A service charge is generally not included in the bill. A tip of at least 15% is recommended.

Lighting a cigarette without asking if anyone objects is rude. Saying frankly that one does object is not rude. In some states, smoking in offices is unlawful.

Generally, people in the U.S. eat with the fork in the hand with which they write. When the knife is not being used for cutting or spreading, it is laid on the plate or the table. When the knife is used, the fork is switched to the other hand. Bread is often used to push food onto the fork. Some foods, such as french fries, hamburgers, pizza and tacos are eaten with the hands.

## UNITED STATES OF AMERICA (Cont'd)

### BUSINESS ENTERTAINING (Cont'd)

Table manners are informal and speeches do not usually occur at the table. Generally, napkins are placed on the lap and it is considered rude to rest elbows on the table. Also, the left hand often rests in the lap during a meal. Toasting is casual and rare, but is appreciated.

Drinks may be served before or during a meal. Dessert, coffee and other after-dinner refreshments are often served away from the table. Guests are expected to stay for a moderate period of time after the meal to visit with the host.

Conducting business meetings during a meal (usually breakfast or lunch) has become a well-accepted ritual. However, suggesting special appointments during the weekend is inappropriate. Reconfirming an appointment on the day preceding the meeting is wise and proper.

Opening conversation might best center on persons, not on issues or business. Thanking the person for his/her time and interest is appropriate. The visitor might also relate a brief, perhaps humorous, personal experience about his/her travel to and in the U.S. A little humor will help open the door to more useful topics.

In many countries, appropriate business behavior involves presenting gifts at different parts of business negotiations. However, even a modest present may embarrass the U.S. businessperson. If a gift is given, it should be given either at arrival or after negotiations are completed. A token from your home (a book about your country, a handicraft, a national beverage, etc.) is the most appropriate type of gift. People in the U.S. may not reciprocate immediately or at all.

Gifts are not expected when visiting a home. However, small token gifts such as wine, flowers, candies or a handicraft are appreciated. The most appropriate gesture of gratitude is to send a short, informal note to the hostess after the event.

Eating styles and habits vary between people in the U.S. of different backgrounds. The best guideline is to imitate the behavior of the people with whom you are dining. Due to the variety of backgrounds of people in the U.S., it is difficult to name a national food. There are many types of restaurants throughout the U.S. In big cities, Italian, Mexican, Chinese, Korean, Japanese and French food are quite popular. Generally, people in the U.S. will readily try any food and the culture easily adapts to new tastes.

### DINING OUT

People in the U.S. generally eat large amounts of beef, pork, chicken and other fowl, compared to the amounts eaten in other parts of the world. However, eating habits are changing with health concerns. Fresh vegetables and fruits are available year-round.

There is an abundance of fast-food restaurants in the United States and these foods are popular among most segments of the population. The popularity of fast-food reflects a lifestyle as much as a preference.

# UNITED STATES OF AMERICA (Cont'd)

## PUBLIC CUSTOMS

Beckoning is done by raising the index finger and curling it in and out, or by raising the hand and curling the fingers back toward the body.

Using the hand and index finger to point at objects or to point out directions is a common gesture. Pointing (it is acceptable to extend the index finger) and beckoning is done by waving all fingers (or the index finger) with the palm facing upwards. To wish someone "good luck," cross the middle finger over the forefinger.

"No" is signaled by waving the forearm and hand (palm out) in front of and across the upper body, back and forth.

Very little that one says or does in innocence is taboo in the U.S. The country's broad mixture of people and culture has precluded traditional prohibitions.

It is common for members of the opposite sex to hold hands or show affection in public.

The gestures of "thumbs up" or of joining the thumb and forefinger to make a circle (which means "okay" in the U.S.) are acceptable gestures. These gestures do not have the negative connotations that they have in other cultures. Also the "V-for-victory" sign does not have the negative connotations that it has in Britain.

In the U.S., slapping someone's back is a common gesture of friendliness and good humor. However, many people dislike this gesture or consider it rude, so it is best to avoid it.

A U.S. male might be seen idly swinging his arms and slapping the fist of one hand into the palm of the other. While this gesture might be considered rude in other cultures, it is acceptable in the U.S.

Looking into the face or eyes of the U.S. businessperson you are visiting is proper. Frequent eye contact is essential during conversation since it signals straightforwardness, honesty, strength and personal warmth.

People in the U.S. are very casual when sitting and often will prop their feet up on chairs or place the ankle of one leg on the knee of the other. Crossing legs at the knee is just as common as sitting with legs spread apart. Poor posture in sitting and standing is not appropriate or polite. However, it is quite common.

# U.S. VIRGIN ISLANDS: HISTORICAL OVERVIEW

- The U.S. Virgin Islands were originally inhabited by Carib and Arawak Indians. In 1493, the islands were claimed for Spain by Columbus. In 1555, Spanish forces defeated the Carib Indians and, by 1596, the indigenous populations were wiped out.

- The islands were then settled by English and Dutch planters. The islands of St. Thomas and St. John were colonized by the Danish. The first permanent settlement was established in 1672 by the Danes.

- In the mid-17th century, the islands were invaded by the French. Between two periods of French rule, the island of St. Croix was held by the Knights of Malta. France abandoned the region by 1700, leaving it under Danish influence.

- The Danish purchased the island of St. Croix from the French in 1733. The islands of St. Croix, St. Thomas and St. John, all together, then became known as the Dutch West Indies.

- In 1917, the Virgin Islands were purchased by the United States from Denmark for $25 million in a treaty ratified by both nations. This purchase was prompted by the islands' strategic importance, as they command the Anegada Passage from the Atlantic Ocean to the Caribbean Sea and the approach to the Panama Canal.

- In 1927, the Virgin Islands' inhabitants became U.S. citizens, although the islands are, constitutionally, an "unincorporated territory."

- The Islands were given a measure of self-government by the 1954 Organic Act, which created an elected 15-member Senate. Since 1970, executive authority has been vested in the elected Governor and Lieutenant-Governor. Since 1973, the U.S. Virgin Islands has been represented in the U.S. House of Representatives by one popularly-elected Delegate, who is permitted to vote only in committees of the House.

- Since 1954, there have been five attempts to redraft the Constitution to give the U.S. Virgin Islands greater autonomy. However, each draft has been rejected by a referendum. The U.S. has stated that it will welcome reform as long as it is economically feasible and does not affect U.S. national security.

- According to the most recent referendum, which took place in 1993, 80% of the inhabitants voted in favor of retaining the islands' existing status. However, the results of this referendum were invalidated by low turnout, since only 27.4% of registered voters took part (50% participation is required for a referendum to be valid).

- Tourism is the mainstay of this economy, which has a 5% unemployment rate – very low by Caribbean standards.

- Roy L. Schneider was elected governor of the Virgin Islands in November 1994, succeeding Alexander A. Farrelly, who had served since 1986.

# U.S. VIRGIN ISLANDS

## INTRODUCTIONS

In the U.S. Virgin Islands, greetings extend beyond a mere "Hello." Basic pleasantries are expected upon introductions.

Handshakes are appropriate between two men, between men and women but not usually between two women. When friendships develop, men will offer each other a slap on the back while women and men will usually hug one another.

Surnames with the appropriate titles are used, although, due to the large number of U.S. citizens in the Virgin Islands, there is a tendency to use first names especially among senior managers.

## SOCIAL TIPS AND CONVENTIONS

Islanders tend to be gracious but somewhat conservative and undemonstrative.

While English is the prevailing language, Spanish, French, Dutch and several dialects are also spoken. English is spoken with an accent.

Privacy is cherished.

In the Caribbean, conversations are held in close proximity especially between friends. One's personal space is not generally held in high regard.

While it is acceptable to discuss the economy, the tourist business and the weather, it is advisable to avoid discussing local politics, religion and controversial subjects, particularly race.

## CUSTOMARY BUSINESS PRACTICES

Appointments are advisable.

Business meetings, like most other engagements, begin later than scheduled. However, mainland U.S. businesses in the Virgin Islands usually adhere to schedules.

Developing a personal understanding and a relationship with business associates is helpful. Islanders tend to be cautious of mainland U.S. citizens because of the transiency of many of their businesses.

Businesspeople in the Virgin Islands practice business at a relaxed pace. Business often begins with extended social conversation.

Conservative dress is required for business meetings. Men should wear suits; women should wear suits or dresses.

Visiting businesspeople should bring an ample supply of business cards printed in English. Business cards are important and used extensively.

## U.S. VIRGIN ISLANDS (Cont'd)

### BUSINESS ENTERTAINING

Business luncheons are popular; however, entertaining in the home is common and not much encouragement is required to have a party.

Exchanging of gifts is not required or customary. However, if you are invited to a home, a gift such as fruit or flowers is appropriate for the host and his/her family.

### DINING OUT

The preferred style of eating is continental with the fork held in the left hand and the knife in the right.

The main meal of the day is generally the midday meal.

Conversation at the table is acceptable and may include a number of topics from business to religion.

Table manners are very informal.

### PUBLIC CUSTOMS

Casual warm-weather clothing is acceptable in most areas. It is inappropriate for women and men to dress scantily.

Civility is an important part of interaction. Politeness and patience are expected.

# URUGUAY: HISTORICAL OVERVIEW

- The original inhabitants of the region now known as Uruguay were a group of small, native tribes called the Charúas.

- In 1516, Spanish explorers came to the area and established their first settlement in 1624 at Soriano. The Portuguese had a presence in the area from 1680 until they were driven out by the Spanish in 1726. The Spanish pursued colonization aggressively and the native population was almost completely wiped out.

- In 1811, in conjunction with a general uprising throughout South America, a war of independence began. Uruguay was unsuccessful in breaking from Spain despite five years of fighting as well as the efforts of José Gervasio Artigas, the leader of the revolt. However, even though the revolt failed, Artigas is considered to be the "Father of Uruguay."

- Despite the failure of this first revolt, Spanish rule ended in 1820 when the Portuguese from Brazil invaded and overtook the area. Artigas' efforts then inspired another uprising in 1825 when a group of patriots known as the "Thirty-Three Immortals" declared Uruguay an independent republic. Independence from Brazil was granted in 1828.

- A civil war (1839-1851) followed independence. From 1865 until 1870 Uruguay was at war with Paraguay, after which a dictatorship was implemented and presidential elections were not held until 1903. José Batlle y Ordóñez won this election and served two terms. He then changed the constitution to allow himself to govern until 1929.

- In the first part of the 20th century, the government of Uruguay implemented socialism. It was the first South American government to grant women the right to vote and was among the first to legalize divorce. It was also the first South American country to recognize the rights of trade unions.

- In 1976, terrorist violence and unrest due to economic problems led the government to turn to the military and to ban all political activities in an attempt to regain control. A new President, Aparicio Méndez, was installed.

- In 1980, elections were held to decide if the military should retain control of the government. However, the vote went against the military and it then simply nullified the results and appointed General Gregorio Alvarez as President in 1981. Reforms during Alvarez's tenure paved the way for general elections in 1984.

- The military stepped down in 1985 and President-elect Julio Maria Sanguinetti was sworn into office. Basic human rights were restored. In 1989, Luis Alberto Lacalle Herrera was elected President and power was transferred democratically for the first time since 1971. Lacalle encouraged market-oriented solutions to Uruguayan economic problems. A persistently high inflation rate in 1993-1994 led to Julio Sanguinetti's election and return to the presidency. The legislature is in perpetual gridlock and Sanguinetti is not the charismatic, altruistic figure needed to bring Uruguay through its economic troubles.

# URUGUAY

## INTRODUCTIONS

The most common way to greet others is with a warm, firm handshake.

Women appear to kiss each other when meeting. They are actually just brushing cheeks and "kissing the air." Men sometimes greet good friends or acquaintances with an *abrazo*, a warm hug.

Verbal greetings depend on the time of the day or the specific situation. A common casual greeting is *"¡Hola!"* ("Hi") and a slightly more formal greeting is *"¡Buen día!"* ("Good day").

Only close friends, family members and children address each other using first names. Professional titles, followed by the last name, should normally be used to show respect. Anyone who graduated from a university at any level as well as physicians, may be addressed as *"Doctor;"* teachers should be addressed as *"Professor;"* engineers go by *"Ingeniero."* If the person does not have a professional title, use the titles *"Señor"* ("Mr."), *"Señora"* ("Mrs.") or *"Señorita"* ("Miss") followed by the last name.

Most Uruguayans have two surnames, one from the father (listed first) and one from the mother. Normally, the father's name is used when addressing someone. For example, Señor Hernan Antonio Martinez Garcia is addressed as "Señor Martinez" and Señorita María Elisa Gutierrez Herrera is addressed as "Señorita Gutierrez." When a woman marries, she usually adds her husband's surname and goes by that surname. For example, if the two people in the above example married, the woman would be known as "Señora María Elisa Gutierrez Herrera de Martinez." She would be addressed as "Señora de Martinez" or, more informally, "Señora Martinez."

At a small social function, it is appropriate to greet and shake hands with each person individually. When leaving, also say farewell to each person individually. Group greetings and farewells are considered impolite.

## SOCIAL TIPS AND CONVENTIONS

While Italian and other languages are spoken by small minorities, Spanish is the official language and is spoken by most of the population.

Uruguayans are very proud of their country and they enjoy talking about its history, beautiful sights and culture. Avoid praising other countries over Uruguay because Uruguayans do not like being treated as inferior.

While Uruguayans can be individualistic, pessimistic and opinionated, they do not like aggressiveness. They are tolerant of other people and other social groups.

Sports make a good topic of conversation. *Fútbol* (soccer) is the national sport and basketball, volleyball and swimming are also very popular.

Avoid asking questions about family unless you are prompted by your Uruguayan counterpart, since some family members may have been victims of the military dictatorship that ruled the country for 14 years. Also, it is best to avoid talking about politics and communism.

# URUGUAY (Cont'd)

## SOCIAL TIPS AND CONVENTIONS (Cont'd)

If you graduated from the University of Chicago, you should avoid making this fact known. During Uruguay's military rule, the generals took their economic policy from the "Chicago boys" – free market economic advisors trained by Milton Friedman at the University of Chicago. Many Uruguayans are resentful of this group of advisors and what they view as having been an economics experiment.

Hand gestures are used a great deal in conversation. Do not hide your hands or fidget with them while conversing because you could inadvertently convey unintended messages.

Most Latin Americans stand close to each other when conversing.

## CUSTOMARY BUSINESS PRACTICES

Many executives speak English. However, it is best to check in advance to verify if there could be any communication obstacles. Arrange for an interpreter, if necessary.

The best time to arrange business meetings is between May and November, when people are not on vacation or celebrating holidays.

While punctuality is not always practiced by Uruguayans, it is appreciated and is expected of foreigners. The more formal a meeting is, the more important it is to be on time. However, even if you are on time, do not be surprised if a meeting starts late.

Business is generally conducted at a relaxed pace in Uruguay.

Business meetings tend to be conducted quite formally.

When negotiating, be aware that Uruguayans have a spirit of moderation and compromise. They take a pragmatic and materialistic approach to life. At the same time, they extol humanistic and spiritual values and subjective feelings often have an effect on decision making.

While Uruguayans have a strong sense of individualism and individual responsibility, self-identity is determined by one's role in the social system or the group. Expertise is considered to be of less importance than fitting into the group and personal relationships play a major role in business transactions.

Do not be surprised if you find highly competent Uruguayan executives working at lower levels than you would expect (e.g., a 40-year-old junior executive). This is likely the result of exile, imprisonment or "political unreliability" during the 14-year military dictatorship. Avoid asking questions or initiating any discussion of this subject.

Have your business cards and all presentation materials and brochures translated into Spanish.

Business attire in Uruguay tends to be conservative. Men wear dark suits and ties; women wear white blouses and dark suits or skirts. Normally, women do not wear panty hose in the summer and men may remove their jackets or loosen their ties. Foreign businesspeople should follow the example of their Uruguayan counterparts in terms of warm-weather dressing.

# URUGUAY (Cont'd)

## CUSTOMARY BUSINESS PRACTICES (Cont'd)

Businesses are usually open from 9:00 a.m. to noon and then from 2:30 to 7:00 p.m., Monday through Friday.

## BUSINESS ENTERTAINING

Uruguayans are very hospitable and will always offer refreshments to guests. It is considered impolite to visit unannounced. Since Uruguayans are concerned with appearance and they prefer to have advance notice of a visit so that the house can be cleaned and refreshments can be prepared.

Business is commonly discussed during lunch. However, if you are invited to a dinner, it is a social occasion. Avoid discussing business on this occasion unless your host brings it up first, since this might make him/her feel uncomfortable.

It is common for Uruguayan businesspeople to invite their colleagues home for coffee after a dinner. While it is polite to accept, it is best not to stay late if the next day is a business day.

There are many casinos in Uruguay and it is quite common for Uruguayan businesspeople to invite colleagues out to see them.

The person who extends an invitation will pay for the meal in full. If you are invited to a meal and would like to reciprocate or split the cost, it is best to simply extend an invitation to your Uruguayan counterpart. It is particularly appreciated if you invite your counterpart to a good-quality French or Chinese restaurant or to a restaurant in an international hotel.

Uruguayans are very sensitive to the actions of others. Courtesy is expected and appreciated on the part of guests.

Gift-giving is not a common part of doing business in Uruguay.

If you are invited to a Uruguayan home, you are not expected to bring a gift. However, bringing or sending (in advance) a small gift of flowers or chocolates is appreciated. Roses are the most appreciated type of flower.

If you are meeting business associates in a casual situation, avoid dressing in jeans. Instead, wear a jacket or blazer and dress slacks. Women should not wear shorts.

To signal a waiter, simply raise your hand. Some Uruguayans make a hissing sound, but it is considered rude.

## DINING OUT

Although meal habits are changing in the cities due to fast-paced business schedules, the main meal is usually eaten at midday. Some people may even go home for lunch. In the morning, a small breakfast is eaten and only a light dinner is served late in the evening (at 9:00 or 10:00 p.m.). Sometimes a snack is eaten at 5:00 p.m.

# URUGUAY (Cont'd)

## DINING OUT (Cont'd)

Roasts, stews and meat pies are popular dishes. Since Uruguay is a cattle producer, some of the best beef in the world is served there.

Uruguayans use the continental style of eating, with the fork held in the left hand and the knife in the right.

Hands, but not elbows, should be kept above the table at all times.

It is polite to take second helpings to show that you like the food.

It is common for people to wipe the plate clean with bread when finishing. Dinner guests remain at the table until everyone is finished eating.

To indicate that you have finished eating, place your utensils side by side on your plate. It is impolite to use a toothpick in public.

## PUBLIC CUSTOMS

While Western-style clothing is worn, clothes tend to be more conservative and well-tailored in Uruguay. Women often wear dresses. Uruguayans also favor subtle colors more so than people in other Latin American countries.

To beckon someone, it is common to snap the fingers and make a "ch-ch" sound. This gesture and sound can also be used to get someone's attention.

The hand gesture made by joining the tips of the thumb and index finger together to form a "zero," which means "okay" in North America, is extremely rude in Uruguay. Instead, the "thumbs up" gesture is commonly used to show approval.

Brushing the back of the hand under the chin means "I don't know." Raising one's shoulders quickly can mean "What's up?" Curling the fingers around so that they touch the thumb (usually on the right hand) indicates doubt.

Proper posture is considered important. It is rude to rest your feet on a chair, table or any other object. Also, it is improper to sit on anything other than a chair (i.e., a table or a ledge).

Yawning in public is usually avoided. It will be taken to mean that you are bored or not enjoying your company.

The elderly are respected and deferred to in Uruguayan society. Also, men usually allow women to enter through doorways first and give up their seats to women on public transportation.

# VENEZUELA: HISTORICAL OVERVIEW

- Before the arrival of Columbus in 1498, Venezuela was inhabited by warlike tribes of Carib and Arawak Indians who offered brave but ineffective resistance to the invaders.

- The first settlement was established at Cumaná in 1520 and Caracas, the capital of Venezuela, was founded in 1567.

- In 1564, the area was set up as the Presidency of the Kingdom of Nueva Granada, which controlled present-day Colombia, Panama, Ecuador and Venezuela. The presidency was replaced in 1718 by a viceroyalty at Bogotá, which included present-day Venezuela. This gave the area its independence from the viceroyalty of Peru.

- In 1794, Antonio Nariño translated into Spanish the French Declaration of the Rights of Man and set in motion the movement toward independence from Spain.

- In 1808 when Napoleon replaced Ferdinand VII of Spain with his own brother, Joseph, there were several revolts. After Napoleon's fall in 1815, Spain attempted to reassert its authority over Nueva Granada. The Spanish were finally expelled and on December 17, 1819, the country achieved full independence, becoming a part of the Republic of Gran Colombia led by President Simón Bolívar. In 1821, the forces of Bolívar won a victory at the Battle of Carabobo.

- Venezuela broke away in 1829, as did Ecuador in 1830, to form independent republics.

- The early 20th century saw Venezuela under the rule of dictator Cipriano Castro, who was, in turn, deposed by Juan Vicente Gómez, whose brutal rule lasted from 1909 to 1935.

- A freely elected president, Rómulo Gallegos, came to power in 1958. He moved too fast on reform, however, and was ousted in a military coup within three months. The new dictator was Marcos Pérez Jiménez, who unleashed a reign of terror. Mercifully, it was short, and he was forced out in 1958 when a combined military and civilian committee took over the government. Three enlightened presidencies followed and Venezuela grew rich from its oil revenue. In 1973, Carlos Andrés Péres won the presidential race in a landslide. He quickly launched ambitious agricultural and educational reforms.

- In 1976, Venezuela joined OPEC in raising oil prices by more than 400%, which led to windfall profits. This, in turn, caused inflation, but the government was able to channel money overseas and the huge income greatly increased Venezuelan influence in South America. However, the new wealth was in the hands of a few and the poor continued to suffer. An oil glut in the 1980s hit the country hard, which led the new government to institute austerity measures in 1984.

- Two attempted coups occurred in 1992 and Pérez, who had returned to the presidency in 1988, was accused of stealing $17 million in public funds. He was impeached and ordered to step down in 1994. Venezuelans then elected Rafael Caldera to the presidency and he faced an economy in dire straits, with the national debt at more than half the annual GNP.

# VENEZUELA

## INTRODUCTIONS

Shake hands when either being introduced to someone or when departing. Venezuelan men greet each other with an *abrazo* (hug); women greet one another with an embrace and a kiss on the cheek. Always accept or return whatever greeting is offered.

Use titles such as "Doctor," "Profesor," "Lawyer," "Architect" or "Engineer." Titles are considered important to Venezuelans.

At large parties, introduce yourself. At smaller gatherings, expect your host to introduce you. Shake hands and say "Good-bye" to each person when you meet or depart.

## SOCIAL TIPS AND CONVENTIONS

Venezuelans, especially younger people, are quite fashion-conscious. The latest European fashions are popular. Prepare to find people dressed rather formally in cities.

Shorts and beachwear are only worn at beaches or recreational spots, not in the cities.

People stand very close to each other when having a conversation, so it is best not to back away.

Good topics for conversations include people's jobs, local sights, art and literature. Venezuelans are very interested in visitors' views of their country and may ask them questions.

Don't discuss politics or tell political jokes.

It is advisable not to ask personal questions such as whether someone is married or has a family until you know the person fairly well.

## CUSTOMARY BUSINESS PRACTICES

The language of business is Spanish. Although many executives speak English, do not expect this convenience. Have business cards printed in English on one side and Spanish on the other.

Lightweight, conservative business clothing is required. Men should wear a suit and tie. Women may wear a suit, a dress or a skirt and a blouse. Venezuelan women rarely wear stockings, but visiting women should wear them when trying to make a good impression.

Appointments are always necessary. It is preferable to give advance notice of your arrival in the country.

Don't try to rush a deal or show impatience if your colleague indicates that some time and thought might be necessary. Any show of irritation is considered rude.

Be aware that you may need to exhibit additional patience when dealing with government officials or offices, due to possible unavoidable bureaucracy.

Latin Americans appreciate the feelings of mutual respect and cordiality known as *simpatica*. Being domineering, overly friendly or too high pressure will be resented.

# VENEZUELA (Cont'd)

## CUSTOMARY BUSINESS PRACTICES (Cont'd)

Businesspeople are well educated and sophisticated.

Avoid doing business during the two weeks before and after Christmas, *Carnival* (a week of feasting and celebration preceding Lent) and Easter. At Christmas time, some companies close entirely for a few days and government offices are open only for limited hours.

Don't suggest a business meeting after 4:00 p.m. on a Friday.

Try to make your initial contacts with the top people in a Venezuelan firm. Decisions are made by individuals, not by teams.

Try to be punctual. If late, a good excuse at any hour is to say that you were stuck in traffic.

Venezuelans don't spend a long time socializing before beginning business discussions.

Expect Venezuelans to be direct without subtlety. When they say "No," they mean "No." Be direct in your responses as well.

Translate any materials and specifications you'll be using in a presentation into Spanish.

If you have a morning appointment, don't make plans for lunch. You may be invited to lunch, but may not be asked until you arrive for your appointment.

Expect to be offered a cup of coffee or tea at a meeting. It is wise to accept even if you only sip a little bit.

## BUSINESS ENTERTAINING

Business is sometimes discussed during a meal, but usually after working hours; the business lunch is not common.

Venezuelans generally invite only special, close friends to their homes, but you may be invited out to dinner at a restaurant or club.

If invited to someone's home, never go empty-handed. Flowers, including an orchid (the national flower), are appreciated.

Don't admire a possession of your host to excess; they will insist upon giving the item to you and you must accept it.

If the occasion arises for gift-giving, good quality items are preferable. White and purple orchids, the national flower, are appropriate for a hostess.

Do not bring a business gift for a Venezuelan executive until a friendly relationship has been established. Gift-giving should follow business, when the setting has become relaxed and less formal. Lunch is usually a good time.

Tailor your gift to the recipient's needs and tastes. If you plan a return trip, ask your Venezuelan colleagues if there is something that they would like you to bring them from your home country.

# VENEZUELA (Cont'd)

## BUSINESS ENTERTAINING (Cont'd)

Avoid giving 13 of anything (considered bad luck), black or purple items (a reminder of Lent, a somber season), knives (cut off a relationship) and handkerchiefs (associated with tears).

Women should avoid giving gifts to male colleagues; it could be misconstrued as a personal overture.

Gifts for children from men and women are greatly appreciated.

## DINING OUT

Venezuelans dine late, starting at 9:00 p.m. or later. This is usually a lighter meal than lunch. Some dinner parties don't begin until 11:00 p.m.

The person who suggests the meal is the one who pays. Splitting the bill ("Dutch treat") is simply not done. If a man and woman go out, the man always pays.

Most women in Venezuela don't drink beer or strong liquor.

Coffee is available in a variety of ways. These include *guayoyo,* mild black coffee; *negro,* strong black coffee; and *marron,* strong coffee with a little milk. Another popular beverage is hot chocolate which people sometimes drink at breakfast or in the evening.

In elegant restaurants, men must wear a jacket and tie. Women may wear fancy cocktail dresses. Many theaters also require men to wear jackets and ties in the evening.

The seats at the head and foot of the table are generally reserved for the mother and father of a family. Wait for your host to seat you.

Always wait until everyone at the table has been served before starting to eat.

Don't feel obligated to finish everything on your plate. In addition, your host will not push you to have extra helpings.

A Venezuelan specialty is *sancocho* (a stew of vegetables, especially yuca, with meat, chicken or fish). Also try *arepas* (a white corn bread); *cachapas* (a corn pancake wrapped around white cheese); *pabellon* (made of shredded meat, beans, rice and fried plantains); and *empanadas* (corn-flour pies filled with cheese, meat or fish). Two popular desserts are *quesillo* (a flan that is steamed); and *bien-me-sabe de coco* (a cake topped with muscatel wine and coconut cream).

## PUBLIC CUSTOMS

Baseball is the major spectator sport. The playing season is from October through February. Some U.S. major leaguers play "winter ball" in Venezuela. Other popular spectator sports are boxing, horse racing and bullfighting.

Most Venezuelans are not terribly concerned with privacy and won't mind being photographed.

When entering a shop or an office, always say *"Buenos dias."* Say *"Adios"* when leaving.

# ASIA

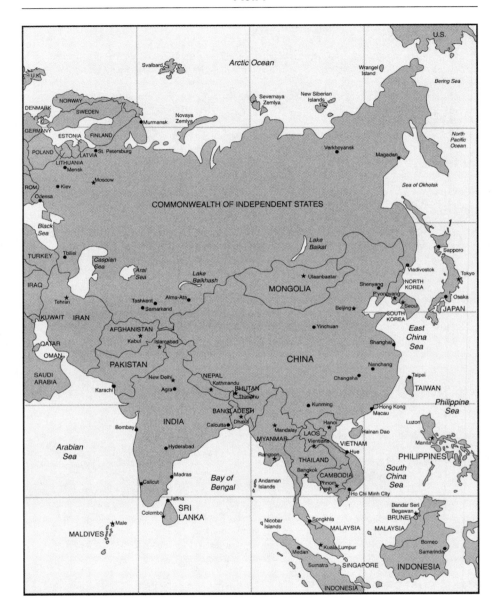

# THE PACIFIC

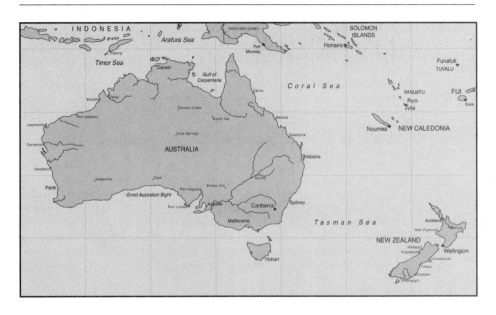

# AFGHANISTAN: HISTORICAL OVERVIEW

- Islamic religion and its culture first appeared in the seventh century and was dominant by the 10th century. The Mongols swept through the land in the 14th century, followed by the hordes of Timur Lane in the 15th century.

- In the early 16th century, Babur, a Turkish chief, conquered the southern part of the country toward the Indus and Ganges Valleys, founding the Mogul Empire. In the eastern region of present-day Afghanistan, the Safavid Empire ruled.

- The Afghans of Kandahar revolted against the Safavids in the 18th century. The Afghans were then soon expelled in 1738 by Nadir Khan, a conqueror who built pyramids out of his enemies' skulls. His assassination in 1747 created a chance for the founding of an Afghan nation. Ahmad Khan, an Afghan subordinate of Nadir Khan, proclaimed himself king and gaining the title of *Shah*, and seized control of the eastern part of the former empire. Tribal struggles ensued for several decades following Ahmad Shah's death in 1773. In 1820, the Mohammedzais family consolidated their rule over principal centers in Afghanistan. The Mohammedzais concentrated on controlling a smaller territory rather than overextending themselves as the previous dynasty had done. In 1863, they drove the Persian forces out of Herat.

- Until 1919, British Indian officials periodically intervened in Afghanistan affairs, supporting the tribal leaders who were most agreeable to British policy. The British also wished to stop Russian influence in the region. Amanullah succeeded his father, Habibullah, as Amir in 1919 and in 1928, announced a plan of social and educational modernization. This caused tribal revolt enabling another branch of the Mohammedzai family to take power. Its leader was Mohammed Nadir, who introduced some modern organization. In the 1940s and 1950s, members of the royal family dominated the highest posts in the government.

- The king granted a new constitution for Afghanistan in 1964, providing for a legal system that would not be based solely on Islamic law. He also provided for the elections for representatives to a legislative body.

- On July 17, 1973, the army seized power. The general leading the coup was Mohammed Daud Khan, who also proclaimed himself President and Prime Minister. Daud's dictatorship proved unpopular and in a day-long battle in Kabul in 1978, he and many of his ministers perished at the hands of Soviet trained, communist members of the Afghan army. The new communist government, led by Nur Mohammed Taraki, adopted sweeping reform which naturally aroused opposition from a sect of rebels called the *Mujahidin*. In 1979, a Soviet invasion force seized control of the country to avert a likely defeat of communism. A bloody conflict began between the Soviets and the *Mujahidin*. By 1986, the Soviets decided to loosen their grip on the government. The rebels eventually took power in April 1992, but civil war ensued, and changes in leadership occurred one after another.

- As anarchy threatened in 1994, a group of religious scholars, the *Taliban*, formed a protest movement espousing Islamic laws. They were successful, soon controlling half the country including the capital, Kabul, by late 1995. As the war continued, the secular *Mujahidin* scored major victories against the *Taliban*.

# AFGHANISTAN

## INTRODUCTIONS

Men and women greet each other with, *"Assalaamu alaikum"* ("Peace be upon you"); the appropriate response is *"Waalaikum assalaam"* ("And peace be upon you also"). This greeting is accompanied by a handshake and a pat on the back.

Afghans also greet each other with the Dari (a form of Persian) phrase *"Khubus ti"* ("How are you?") or the Pashto (one of Afghanistan's major languages) equivalent of "Good-bye" *"Sanga ye? Khoda hafiz."*

Greetings may vary by region or by ethnic group; however, *"Assalaamu alaikum"* is universally accepted. Women and men do not shake hands or touch in public, although a man may greet a woman verbally or in an indirect way. Women greet each other by shaking hands, embracing and giving a kiss on alternating cheeks three times.

Special titles are used when formally greeting and are reserved for academics or profession-als. A person who has made the pilgrimage to Mecca is referred to as *Haji* (pilgrim), e.g., *Haji Khan. Haji* or *Khan* (sir) is also used based on a person's social and economic status.

Titles are often combined with names, for example *"Umm* (mother of) *Muhammed"* or *"Abu* (father of) *Alam."* First names or nicknames are used to address a friend.

## SOCIAL TIPS AND CONVENTIONS

The official language of Afghanistan is Persian, which is similar to Farsi (spoken in Iran). The second language, Pashto, is also widely used.

The Afghan people have very strong family ties. The elderly are cared for at home and are highly respected by all.

Afghans participate in a variety of sports. The national sport, *buzkashi,* is a game played by two teams on horse back that compete by carrying the headless carcass of a calf the distance of one-half circle to a spot, then returning it to the circle. Afghans also enjoy wrestling, soccer and volleyball.

Private cars are rarely used because of the high cost of fuel. Villagers either walk or ride donkeys, horses or horse-drawn carts. There are no railroads; however, buses run between major cities.

Urban areas have networks of telephones, but they are largely unreliable. Public phones are widely used. Most people have televisions and radios, but newspapers and television broadcasts must be received from neighboring countries. The BBC is listened to regularly.

Community life in rural areas centers on daily prayers at the mosque. Local celebrations, festivals and religious activities also take place there.

Afghan people are generally friendly, hospitable and courteous. They place high value on piety, loyalty and identity with the family, kin group, clan and tribe.

Strict and inflexible codes are common within a group to ensure responsibility and roles. Disputes are not easily resolved because of the need to protect a group's strict codes of honor.

# AFGHANISTAN

## SOCIAL TIPS AND CONVENTIONS (Cont'd)

Land ownership and the size of one's herd defines a rural person's wealth, but urban residents view wealth in terms of money or possessions, which they consider equal to education in status.

Although Islam dominates the life of virtually every Afghan, the religion has not overcome ethnic differences. The belief in fatalism helps people to accept and deal with their harsh lives.

It is considered impolite to pass an item with the left hand since it is reserved for personal hygiene purposes.

Major industries include agriculture, pastoralism and mining.

## CUSTOMARY BUSINESS PRACTICES

Offices and banks are open from 8:00 a.m. to 5:00 p.m. Food stores are open from 7:00 a.m. to 8:00 p.m. from March through October, and from 9:00 a.m. to 3.30 p.m. throughout the rest of the year.

During *Ramadan* (the holy month of fasting), offices close at 2:00 p.m. daily.

Traditionally, you must be accepted as a friend before any business will be transacted. Keep in mind that business in Afghanistan must be done in person.

Large shops and *bazaars* (markets) are divided into many smaller shops and are grouped together by the products they sell.

## BUSINESS ENTERTAINING

The Afghan people are known for their hospitality, and generosity is considered a sign of social status. Hosts serve guests food as well as tea depending on the time of the day. Business discussions begin after refreshments.

Guests are expected to drink at least three cups of tea and are not expected to bring gifts.

Men and women are segregated when visiting or when entertaining, as this is a social custom in the country.

Afghans speak 32 languages and dialects, including Dari, Pashto, Uzbeki and Turkoman. There is no official language.

Some Afghans only eat at home, while others choose to occasionally dine in restaurants. Some restaurants have booths for families or separate dining areas for women.

## DINING OUT

Afghans are, for the most, part Sunni Muslim and are forbidden by religious dogma to drink alcohol and eat pork.

Belching after a meal is considered a sign of satisfaction.

# AFGHANISTAN

## DINING OUT (Cont'd)

Afghans in rural areas eat breakfast and dinner and occasionally a light lunch. Families generally eat together, except when entertaining a non-family member.

The left hand is never used to eat or to pass food; instead, the fingers of the right hand are used to serve oneself.

Regardless of how people eat, they first wash their hands. Everyone eats from a common plate located in the center of the floor or table. Rural families may eat from a communal dish, without eating utensils.

Afghan dishes are influenced by the foods of South and Central Asia, China and Iran. The cuisine consists of *pilau* (rice mixed with meat and/or vegetables), *qorma* (vegetable sauce), *kebab* (skewed meat), *ashak* or *mantu* (pasta dishes) and *nahn* (flat bread). *Chai* (green or black tea) is served in *piallas* (bowls) with every meal.

Afghans consume a variety of meats including beef, chicken and mutton. Vegetables (such as tomatoes, spinach, carrots, cucumbers, eggplants and peas), a variety of fruits (fresh and dried) and nuts are also popular.

## PUBLIC CUSTOMS

Afghan men wear a *Perahan tunban* (a knee length shirt) over baggy trousers.

Common footwear includes sandals, sneakers and boots, all of which are removed for prayers.

The *kolah,* or turban cap, is worn on the head as a means of protection from the harsh winter weather.

Another form of headdress is the *qarakuli* (cap) made from the skin of the *karakul* (sheep).

Women rarely appear in public, but when they do, they usually wear a *chadiri* (head-to-toe covering) or a *chador* (shawl-veil). Women may also wear a short jacket, a long coat or a shawl.

Silver and gold jewelry, often made with local semi-precious stones such as lapis lazuli and garnet, is worn. A *tawiz* (white amulet) is worn on the arm by many people because it is believed that white brings protection against evil and misfortune.

The gesture of pointing the palm downward is used to call someone. Afghans *du'a* (supplicate) before a meal, a trip or any transaction. To *du'a*, the palms of both hands are held up to chest level and opened like a book.

Afghans very seldom use their hands while speaking; instead, men handle *tasbe* (prayer beads) during a conversation.

The national holidays include *Id al-Fitr* (the feast at the end of Ramadan), *Ashura* (the martyrdom of Imam Husayn), *Roza-Maulud* (the Prophet Mohammed's birthday), *Nooruz* (New Year's Day), Muslim National Day (April 28), Day of Remembrance (May 4), and Independence Day (August 18).

# AUSTRALIA: HISTORICAL OVERVIEW

- The Aborigines were the only inhabitants of Australia until the Dutch began exploring parts of the continent in the 1620s.

- In 1770, Captain James Cook took formal possession of the coast for Britain. Starting in 1788, the British founded penal colonies in Australia, mainly in the areas of the present-day cities of Sydney, Hobart and Brisbane. As a result, many of the early settlers of Australia were prisoners or soldiers.

- Free settlements were established in Melbourne, Adelaide and Perth. The number of people immigrating to Australia increased rapidly after gold was discovered there in 1851. The successful breeding of sheep, which created an export product (wool) for Australia, also attracted immigrants. In 1850, the Australian Colonies' Government Act extended a large degree of self-government to the colonies. In 1868, the transportation of convicts to Australia ended, and convicts were declared free. By that time, six colonies had been established: New South Wales (N.S.W.), Tasmania, Western Australia, South Australia, Victoria and Queensland. While the colonies shared a common language (English) and common customs, each one developed differently according to different local laws.

- In 1901, the six colonies became states, as they agreed to join together as the Federal Commonwealth of Australia. A government was created with a constitution that, as in the U.S., defines the powers of the central government and reserves other powers to the states. Western Australia's attempts to secede from the Commonwealth in the 1930s failed. Complete autonomy from Great Britain was established in 1942 by the passage of the Statute of Westminster Adoption Act. This legislation simply formalized the country's autonomy that had, in practice, existed since 1900.

- The country has been stable and has grown throughout the 20th century. During World War II, it established close ties with the U.S. and since then, it has been active in global politics. After the war, there was a substantial number of immigrants who came to Australia. Most were Caucasian, due to discriminatory immigration policy. This policy was altered in 1966. In the 1970s, however, the overall immigration rate was reduced.

- During the period between 1949 and 1972, the country was governed by a coalition of the *Liberal Party* and the *Country Party*, which, for 17 years, was under the leadership of the colorful Sir Robert Menzies. The *Labour Party* came to power in 1972, but the economy did badly under its leadership, and the *Liberal Party* took control in 1975 and ruled until 1983. In that year, the *Australian Labour Party* dominated elections and ruled with the leadership of Prime Minister Robert Hawke until 1991.

- In the 1990s, the *Australian Labour Party* lost support, and in March 1996, a coalition of the *Liberal Party* and the *National Party* won a landslide victory, giving the new government a 40-seat margin in Parliament.

- Currently, Australia faces no immediate external threats. Although unemployment and the deficit are concerns, the economy is growing due to increasing trade with Japan, China and Vietnam.

# AUSTRALIA

## INTRODUCTIONS

First names are widely and quickly used in Australia. However, it is wise to wait to use first names until invited to do so. Many visitors have found themselves surprised by the speed with which Australians adopt the first name as the way of addressing their visitors. This should not be mistaken as a sign of real friendship – it only indicates Aussie friendly informality. Australians are generally quite informal. Don't be too stiff or overly tactful.

People shake hands upon introduction as well as at the beginning and end of meetings. The handshake should be firm and friendly.

When addressing business colleagues, even senior managers, the business title is generally not used. Australians tend to quickly switch to first or given names.

Australia has its share of British titles and honors, as a member of the Commonwealth. As is the case in the United Kingdom, holders of such titles in Australia may or may not use them. In case of doubt, the general term "*Sir*" may be used to address anyone with respect and formality.

## SOCIAL TIPS AND CONVENTIONS

Australians are direct, like people from the U.S.

There are many unique words and phrases in Australian English.

Introductory conversation unrelated to business should be short. The spectacular Australian architecture, local cultural events as well as leisure and outdoor activities are useful conversation topics.

It is best to avoid making comparisons between the United States and Australia. People from England should also not make comparisons to their country.

Don't give unsolicited advice or comments and avoid any affectation of "airs." Australians are suspicious of pretension and status-conscious behavior. They are critical of affectation. It is very difficult to impress an Australian.

Men are fairly quick to call another man "*mate*" if they take a liking to him.

The Australians have a healthy sense of humor. Often their barbs may be directed at the visitor in a good-natured way. The international visitor should not take such teasing lying down. In a self-confident manner and with frank and friendly demeanor, he or she can reply with good humor and become respected by the hosts. Australians frequently use humor when they are under stress.

Australians enjoy controversy and love to discuss subjects about which they disagree. Fairness is an important principle in Australian life.

Australians do not give praise easily. When they do, it is often done in a sarcastic, joking manner.

# AUSTRALIA (Cont'd)

## CUSTOMARY BUSINESS PRACTICES

Australians are motivated to work hard by affiliation and quality of life. This may be a stark contrast to other countries, where status and money are viewed as key incentives.

Punctuality is highly regarded. Appointments are necessary, preferably one month in advance. Always arrive on time for an appointment, and handle correspondence as promptly as possible. Use business cards.

Business is often conducted during drinks. Buy only when it is your turn, as it is considered rude to buy out of order.

With regard to manner, Melbournians are slightly more conservative than their peers elsewhere in the country.

Customary business dress is similar to that in North America and the United Kingdom. For both men and women, a suit is necessary in Sydney and Melbourne. In Brisbane, the dress is more casual. A lightweight suit is appropriate for visitors at a first meeting; thereafter, men may wear a shirt, tie and shorts. Melbourne is more formal than either Sydney or Perth.

Because of the great distances, it is important to have representation within Australia. There is an Australian version of the *"Old Boy"* network among senior industrial executives, and it does help to have connections and introductions from one of these key people.

At meetings, preliminary comments (sports, cultural events, Australian sights) should be brief. Get down to business quickly. Presentations should be complete, while not concealing problem areas. Communicate directly and respond to Australian pointedness with confidence and good humor.

The vast majority of Australians speak English only. Visitors who have difficulty with English will find interpreters easy to engage, but hosts do not routinely provide this service.

Australians are, first and foremost, pragmatic. Time has value and they will not waste it. Delays are viewed as inefficient.

Decision making in Australia still tends to be concentrated at the top echelon of the company. Sometimes the need to get attention and approval at higher company levels causes delays. It is important not to press public officials or employees for answers faster than they can be generated through normal channels.

Informality reigns in matters of etiquette. People are seated in random fashion, generally with no special seat of honor. Seniors in company status may receive certain gestures of respect, but such a show is a formality only. Australians do not practice deference. Their overall sense of equality is well ingrained.

# AUSTRALIA (Cont'd)

## BUSINESS ENTERTAINING

Business lunches are a popular and acceptable way of both initiating and doing business. However, business and pleasure do not mix in Australia. Do not use social occasions, besides lunches, as an opportunity to talk business.

Once a social relationship has been established, a businessperson may invite his/her contact to lunch.

Dinner is usually about 6:00 p.m. Come a half-hour early or be on time, but never be late. Guests sometimes bring flowers or wine, not gifts. A "thank you" upon leaving is all that is expected.

More formal evening entertaining is in order when the visitor is dealing with upper managerial levels or once a business relationship has been established.

Formal occasions, especially if the Australians host them, are likely to take place in a club. Clubs are often formed around athletic events, but may also be professional or social status oriented.

Invitations to an Australian's home are not common and must be considered special. Since this kind of entertaining could be formal or utterly informal, it is best to ask the host about appropriate dress. Often such visits will center around a casual outdoor barbecue and will include all family members. A modest gift for the host's home on such occasions would be unexpected but appreciated. Otherwise, the practice of giving gifts is unwelcome in Australia; it might even be considered taboo.

The business visitor should not propose entertainment events over the weekend period. Australians treasure their free time.

## DINING OUT

The main meal of the day is eaten in the evening. It is usually called dinner, but may be called tea if it is a smaller meal.

Table manners are European, but viewed with informality and flexibility. While it is considered proper to use the fork with the left hand, other styles of using table utensils are tolerated.

When eating soup, do so by moving the spoon away from you, not toward you.

Salads are generally served with the main course.

Indicate that you have finished eating by laying your knife and fork parallel on your plate.

At a restaurant, use a simple hand gesture to get the waiter's attention.

Beer is the most popular national drink.

# AUSTRALIA (Cont'd)

## PUBLIC CUSTOMS

Australians deny the existence of any taboos. However, they may have a double standard about the use of their favorite expletives. While they may use strong language at times, they do not appreciate it when an international visitor does likewise.

Winking at women is considered inappropriate, as are public displays of affection. When yawning, you should cover your mouth and then excuse yourself.

The "thumbs up" gesture is considered rude in Australia.

Sports are very important to Australians. Among the most popular are Australian football, soccer, rugby, cricket, basketball, cycling, hiking (or bush walking) and tennis. Good sportsmanship is very important in Australia.

# AZERBAIJAN: HISTORICAL OVERVIEW

- In ancient times, two countries – Atrapatakan and Caucasian Albania (unrelated to present-day Albania) – occupied the territory of contemporary Azerbaijan. Both countries had their own languages and well-developed economies.

- Beginning in the 7th century, the area was dominated by Arabs who introduced Islam, which soon became the dominant religion. The Arabic language was introduced, and Arabic script was used for the Azeri language until 1924. The Azeris then switched to Latin script and then to Russian script. They switched back to Latin script upon the dissolution of the Soviet Union.

- For most of its history, the country was dominated by either Turkey or Iran (Persia). It has also been ruled by the Mongols and most recently, by the Russians. According to an 1828 treaty between Russia and Iran, northern Azerbaijan became part of Russia and the southern part was allocated to Iran. This division profoundly affected the region. During the Soviet era, it was difficult for relatives to visit each other across the border. Present-day Iran has a larger Azeri population than that of Azerbaijan.

- While Azerbaijan attempted to declare itself independent in 1918, its efforts were suppressed by the Red Army. In 1920, the country was made part of the Soviet Union and in 1922, it was joined with Georgia and Armenia to form the Transcaucasian Soviet Socialist Republic. In 1936 under Stalin's new constitution, this republic was dissolved, and the Azerbaijan Soviet Socialist Republic reemerged.

- The new Azerbaijani leaders favored a policy of edging out non-Azerbaijanis and replacing them with Azerbaijanis. This sentiment targeted Armenians and led to the request of the Armenians of the Nagorno-Karabakh Autonomous Republic that they be transferred to Armenian jurisdiction in February 1988. The Armenian Republic supported the move, and these events led to spontaneous riots in the Azerbaijani city of Sumgait, which turned into a slaughter of Armenians. Retaliatory moves against Azerbaijanis living in Armenia followed. Gorbachev dismissed the secretaries of the Azerbaijani and Armenian Communist Parties in May for losing control of the situation. He also suspended Azerbaijani control over Nagorno-Karabakh. These moves inspired anti-communist, nationalist feelings in Azerbaijan. The *Azerbaijan Popular Front* organized a road and railroad blockade of Armenia. Gorbachev sent in Soviet troops to restore order and installed Ayaz Mutalibov as head of state. Mutalibov resigned as head of the party in 1990, but retained control after winning popular elections. Growing political opposition, however, forced Mutalibov to agree to the creation of a National Council and the establishment of an Azerbaijani army.

- On October 18, 1991, the Supreme Soviet passed a law reestablishing Azerbaijan's independence. Soon thereafter, war broke out between Azerbaijan and Nagorno-Karabakh. The Azerbaijanis were unsuccessful in taking the area, and the next development occurred in June 1992, when Abulfaz Elchibey was elected President. Elchibey had to answer for a series of humiliating defeats by the Armenians. He was also challenged by his own forces when a regional commander rebelled. Elchibey was forced to flee, leaving a political vacuum in the capital of Baku.

- In new elections, Eidar Aliyev was elected President. He has been unable to end the war, but he has welcomed Russian mediation, and Azerbaijan has rejoined the Commonwealth of Independent States.

# AZERBAIJAN

## INTRODUCTIONS

When greeting each other, men shake hands and say *"Salem"* ("Peace"). Women also say *"Salem,"* but they do not shake hands.

Female friends or relatives might hug and kiss.

Another common greeting is *"Sagh ol"* ("Be well"), which is also used at parting.

If people are acquainted, the greeting is followed by *"Nejasiniz?"* ("How are you?"). One also often asks about the health of the other's family.

People of the same age call each other by first names.

It is common to use *"Hanum"* ("Miss" or "Mrs.") or *"Hala"* ("Aunt") after the given name of a woman, and *"Ami"* or *"Dayi"* ("Uncle") after a man's given name. *"Bey"* ("Mr.") is also used after a man's given name at social gatherings or at work. Its use was banned in 1920 when Russia invaded Azerbaijan, but it is again becoming a preferred way to address men.

## SOCIAL TIPS AND CONVENTIONS

Men and women generally wear Western clothing.

It is common during social gatherings to recite poems of native poets.

It is impolite to speak loudly to one's colleagues.

Azeris recognize various Muslim holidays, the most important being the feast to end the month of *Ramadan*. During that month, Muslims fast from sunrise to sunset and eat only in the evenings. Forty days later, *Kurban Bairami*, the holiday of sacrifice, commemorates the pilgrimage season.

## CUSTOMARY BUSINESS PRACTICES

Offices are open weekdays from 8:00 or 9:00 a.m. to 5:00 or 6:00 p.m. Stores and shops are also open on Saturday, but they often close an hour each afternoon for dinner.

Azeri is the official language. Many Azeris can speak Russian and many of the country's publications are in Russian.

## BUSINESS ENTERTAINING

Eating at restaurants is not common; it is generally reserved for special occasions and the host pays the entire bill and tip.

At meals, the fork is held in the left hand and the knife in the right.

Guests do not serve themselves; they are served by others.

Visitors, especially those who have adopted Russian customs, often take gifts to their hosts, such as flowers, candy or pastries. A wrapped present is not opened in the presence of the giver.

# AZERBAIJAN (Cont'd)

## DINING OUT

Guests are often invited for a meal or for "tea," which is a mid-afternoon affair that includes pastries, fruit preserves (not jam), fruit, candy and tea. At other times, guests may be offered tea and sweets. Tea is served in *armudi stakan* (small, pear-shaped glasses).

In the summer, it is best to drink boiled or bottled water.

The most popular dish, *pilau*, is made of steamed rice topped by a variety of foods. *Kebab* is grilled pieces of meat or fish (lamb, chicken or sturgeon) on a stick. *Piti* is a lamb broth with potatoes and peas cooked in clay pots in the oven. *Dovga* consists of yogurt, rice and herbs, and is served after the main meal at celebrations.

Popular spices in foods include cilantro, dill, mint, saffron, ginger, garlic, cinnamon and pepper. Azeris refer to their cuisine as "French Cuisine of the East."

## PUBLIC CUSTOMS

It is impolite to cross one's legs, smoke or chew gum in the presence of elders.

The right hand is used in handshakes and other interactions; it is rude to use the left hand unless the right hand is occupied.

One may point at objects but not people with the index finger. Shaking the index finger while it is vertical is used to reprimand or warn someone. The index finger is also used to attract a listener's attention.

Shoes are removed before entering mosques.

When an older person or a woman enters a room, those present stand to greet him or her.

The "thumbs up" gesture is used for "fine" or "okay." Rounding the finger to touch the thumb tip and form a circle (the traditional U.S. gesture for "okay") is obscene.

Since hospitality is part of the culture, visiting relatives or friends is popular and often occurs without prior notice.

Azeris value family over the individual and family needs come first. Men are protective of women in the family. An Azeri would commonly swear by his mother, because she is the most valuable person on earth.

# BRUNEI: HISTORICAL OVERVIEW

- From the 14th century to the 16th century, Brunei was the cornerstone of a Muslim empire which included most of northern Borneo and the Philippines. By the early 17th century, the empire had been seriously weakened, and the Sultan of Brunei's rule was confined to an area today formed by Sarawak and part of Sabah.

- In the mid-1800s, Brunei came under attack from South China Sea pirates, and in a desperate bid to secure military help, the ruling Sultan ceded the entire region of Sarawak to English adventurer Sir James Brooke. The Englishman appointed himself Rajah, or "king", of the region and was succeeded by his nephew and the latter's son until 1946.

- The Sultan attempted to enter into a trade agreement with the U.S. in 1865, but the venture was soon abandoned by the U.S. The British set up the *North Borneo Company*, which acquired the assets of the U.S. firm and forced more land concessions from the Sultan. In 1881, Brunei was reduced to its present size.

- Brunei continued to depend on British protection and in 1906 permitted a British commissioner to reside in the country. The commissioner's job was to advise the Sultan in all matters involving defense and foreign affairs.

- In the 1910s, the economy began to grow largely due to the cultivation of rubber. In the 1920s, huge oil reserves and natural gas were discovered in the western part of the nation, thus changing the economic picture in a drastic way. Offshore deposits were discovered in the 1960s, paving the way for enormous wealth.

- A 1962 rebellion, led by a pro-Indonesian leftist, prompted the government to declare a state of emergency in which political parties were banned, and the government could detain people without trial. The latter condition remains in practice today. In 1963, the Federation of Malaysia was established, as a bulwark against Indonesian imperialism and the possibility of a Communist takeover in Singapore. The Sultan rejected the plan in fear that his power and his country's wealth would be diminished.

- *Brunei Darussalam* regained its full independence on January 1, 1984. Brunei became a member of the British Commonwealth and has also joined the United Nations (U.N.) and the Association of Southeast Asian Nations (ASEAN).

- The present Sultan took over after his father's abdication in 1968. He has invested funds in many different countries in an effort to diversify the economy. In the past few years the Philippines have claimed nearby Sabah, but this has never been seriously pursued. There is little political activity, which the government credits to the widespread distribution of wealth among the people. Lifetime health service is free, and the government will pay for an overseas flight for any citizen needing medical attention unavailable in Brunei.

- Environmental problems are growing and have yet to be adequately addressed. The other issue of concern is the multi-ethnic nature of the society which has caused some domestic tension.

# BRUNEI

## INTRODUCTIONS

Full names are used in Brunei, and titles are considered very important.

The title *"Haji"* (for men) and *"Hajjah"* (for women) are given to those who have completed the pilgrimage to Mecca.

## SOCIAL TIPS AND CONVENTIONS

Ethnically, over 60% of the people are Malay. Many cultural and linguistic differences make Brunei Malays distinct from the larger Malay populations in Malaysia and Indonesia. There is a sizable minority of ethnic Chinese.

The official language is Malay, although English is widely understood and is used in business. Chinese and Iban are spoken as well.

Islam is the official religion. Although freedom of religion exists, Brunei has in the past several years moved closer toward Islamic fundamentalism. Alcohol was banned in 1991, and stricter dress codes are enforced.

Roads are poor in Brunei, so rivers are the main means of transport. Public transportation is infrequent and unreliable.

Approximately half of Brunei's 90,000 jobs are held by foreign expatriates.

## BUSINESS ENTERTAINING

Night life is almost nonexistent, therefore expatriates produce their own entertainment like *karaoke* (singing along to background music using special audio/visual equipment) or home video viewing.

## DINING OUT

Bruneians customarily eat with their fingers rather than with spoons and forks. You should always eat with your right hand, because the left hand is considered unclean.

It is polite to accept food and drink when it is offered, even if only a little. When refusing anything offered, it is polite to touch the plate lightly with your right hand.

Brunei caters to international tastes. A favorite local dish is a Malay-style *satay* with tangy peanut sauce. *Rendang*, a beef in coconut milk and local spices, is also popular.

## PUBLIC CUSTOMS

Giving and receiving should be done with the right hand.

Many Malay women wear a *tudong* (a traditional head covering). Men who have completed the *Haj*, the pilgrimage to Mecca, wear a white *songkok* (a sheet-like covering for the body).

# BRUNEI (Cont'd)

## PUBLIC CUSTOMS (Cont'd)

Bruneians generally sit on the floor, especially when there is a large gathering of people. Women typically sit with their legs tucked to one side, while men often sit with their legs folded and crossed at the ankles. It is considered rude to sit with one's legs stretched out in front, especially if someone is sitting there.

It is considered rude to eat or drink while walking in public, or in the presence of Muslims during *Ramadan*, the month of fasting.

Islamic doctrine dictates strict legislation which prohibits a non-Muslim from being in the secluded company of a Muslim of the opposite sex. Even in an open setting, casual contact with the opposite sex will make Muslims uncomfortable. Bruneians are also prohibited from singing or dancing in public.

When walking toward someone, especially an elder or one higher in rank or status, it is respectful to bend down slightly to the side in the direction of the person that one is passing. At the same time, one of your arms should be kept straight down along the side of your body.

Several gestures that are acceptable in the West are considered offensive in Brunei. For example, leaning on a table or a chair where someone is seated, especially if one is visiting an official or a colleague, is rude. So is resting one's feet on a table or a chair.

Touching or patting someone on the head, including a child, is regarded as disrespectful.

Do not motion to someone with the index finger. The polite way to beckon is to use all four fingers of the right hand, with the palm down, and motion them toward yourself.

National Day is celebrated on February 23.

# CAMBODIA: HISTORICAL OVERVIEW

- The Khmer people, from whom the modern Cambodians (Kampucheans) descend, first organized themselves in a state known as Funan in about 500 A.D. in southern Cambodia.

- By the early 10th century, the powerful Khmer Empire had come into power, and it was to dominate much of southeast Asia until its eventual demise at the end of the 15th century. For the next three and one-half centuries, Cambodia was alternately ruled by the Thai and the Annamese of Central Vietnam.

- In the mid-18th century, France began to take an interest in Cambodia and in 1863, the French established a protectorate over the country. The French did not dethrone the royal family, however, and the relationship between the two countries was harmonious.

- Japan swiftly overran Cambodia in 1941 and, as a favor to its Thai allies, the Japanese gave them two Cambodian border provinces.

- Appointed king by the French in 1941, Prince Norodom Sihanouk ruled in the postwar years. He abdicated the throne in 1955 in order to become premier and to play a more active role in politics. Through the 1960s, Sihanouk managed to remain neutral in the Cold War while skillfully averting the threat of the North Vietnamese by allying himself with the People's Republic of China.

- In 1970, displeased by the rise of communist revolts on the borders of Thailand and Laos, anti-communist Cambodians held major demonstrations in the capital, Phnom Penh, which resulted in the ouster of Sihanouk. The new government, however, led by Lon Nol was unable to stop the inroads of the communist rebels, known as the *Khmer Rouge.*

- The *Khmer Rouge* finally took Phnom Penh and control of the government in 1975. Sihanouk returned, but the government was run by a shadowy leadership of the *Cambodian Communist Party* known as the *Angka*, of which Pol Pot was Secretary General. Thus began a period of horrendous brutality in which more than 3.4 million Cambodians were killed by the regime.

- During the 1980s, Pol Pot was faced with the incursion of Vietnamese forces in the west. The Vietnamese were successful in taking Phnom Penh and established their own very repressive government. An anti-Vietnamese coalition, led by Sihanouk, was unable to compel the Vietnamese to leave, but in 1988, the Vietnamese, with their own economy in dismal shape, voluntarily began its withdrawal.

- A four-party coalition governed. This included the *Khmer Rouge* which threatened to take total control. In the late 1980s, a flurry of diplomatic activity took place, as various countries in the region and around the world tried to negotiate peace between the *Khmer Rouge*, which was now loosely allied with Sihanouk, and the pro-Vietnamese faction in Phnom Penh.

- A new parliamentary-style government has emerged through the efforts of the four-party coalition, but little progress towards real democracy has been made, and the *Khmer Rouge* is still strong along the Thai border.

# CAMBODIA

## INTRODUCTIONS

When greeting someone, the hands should be placed together in a prayer position at chest level, without touching the body, never higher than the level of the nose. The higher the hands, the greater the sign of respect. The hand gesture is accompanied with a slight bow when greeting persons of higher status or age.

When carrying something in one's hands, simply bow the head slightly. Shaking hands is uncommon and is considered embarrassing for women.

## SOCIAL TIPS AND CONVENTIONS

Khmers comprise almost 95% of the population, making Cambodia the most ethnically homogenous country in Southeast Asia.

Many gestures, greetings and eating habits are influenced by Buddhism. For example, people remove their shoes when entering a home or a pagoda. Cambodians follow the religious practices of the Theravada Buddhists (except for the Cham minority who are Muslim).

The culture and traditions of the Chinese and the Khmer (the terms Khmer and Cambodian are often used interchangeably) dictate the customs, lifestyle and language of the country.

Angor Wat is a favorite tourist attraction as well as being a symbol of Khmer culture.

In the 1980s, most outdoor recreation areas fell into disrepair, were destroyed by Pol Pot, or were banned. Therefore, there are not many entertainment activities available to visitors.

Small village theaters are created by the use of video machines, but people also enjoy dancing, singing, playing music, soccer, table tennis, volleyball and badminton.

During weddings and religious festivals people have the opportunity to relax, have picnics, play cards and ride bicycles or motorcycles.

The Khmer tradition allows a man to marry more than one woman at a time, including widows. Women who do not find spouses tend to gather together in small clans with their children for mutual aid, because so many men were killed during the civil war.

The Khmer do not intermarry with other ethnic groups.

Guests are given the best place to sit and the biggest portion of food when dining.

## CUSTOMARY BUSINESS PRACTICES

During the U.N. mission to Cambodia, Phnom Penh, the capital, was a booming business center. Business was enhanced by the presence of bustling shopping streets, plentiful food and a good climate.

# CAMBODIA (Cont'd)

## CUSTOMARY BUSINESS PRACTICES (Cont'd)

Agriculture employs 90% of the population with food processing, forestry, logging and rubber being key sectors. Timber is the major industry, and mining is also conducted for precious stones and rubber. In addition, fish, rice and pepper are exported.

Wages are low and many people take extra jobs in towns or work on roads to make a living.

Business hours are from 8:00 a.m. to 1:00 p.m. and then from 3:00 to 6:00 p.m. or dusk.

Communist regulations require that all workers spend at least one day a week doing manual labor. White collar workers can, therefore, be observed in fields making half-hearted attempts to break the soil.

Foreigners need a valid passport to enter Cambodia and should be prepared to pay cash in all or most transactions.

## BUSINESS ENTERTAINING

Frequent and unannounced visits are common among relatives and friends. Cambodians are cautious about inviting strangers into their homes, but are, in general, hospitable and friendly.

Very few hotels have running water.

## DINING OUT

Cambodian dishes are influenced by Indian, Chinese and European cuisine; however, they are not as spicy as those from neighboring countries.

More types of seafood and gravies are served here than in neighboring countries, such as Thailand. Rice is eaten at every meal and is prepared in several ways depending on the region it is from.

Soup and rice are the two staples and may be prepared with any combination of fish, eggs, vegetables, meat and spicy broth.

Cambodians enjoy a wide variety of fruit and vegetables with their meals.

Cambodians eat with spoons, chopsticks or their fingers, depending on family customs and the type of food prepared.

It is acceptable to clean one's teeth with a toothpick after the meal; however, be sure to use your free hand to cover your mouth when doing so.

# CAMBODIA (Cont'd)

## PUBLIC CUSTOMS

It is improper to embarrass another person in public. Waving your hand is considered a friendly gesture, as is good eye contact or a smile. It is important to distinguish whether a person understands what you are saying when he/she says "Yes."

Getting angry is impolite and lowers one's status in the eyes of others.

To beckon someone, make a motion toward yourself with your hand palm down. Also, pointing is considered offensive.

While sitting, do not point your feet toward another person or toward a Buddha image.

The head is considered to be the most sacred part of one's body, therefore it should not be touched (this includes children's heads as well). Standing or sitting at a higher level than an older person should be avoided.

Traditional as well as Western-style clothing is worn in Phnom Penh. Women wear large rectangular pieces of traditional cloth wrapped around their hips like a skirt or a kilt down to the ankles. The women's wrap is known as a *sampot* or *sarong* and the men's as a *sarong soet*.

Small yellow, red and pink hats are worn by young women. A *krama* (large scarf) can also be used as a hat, a small blanket or a baby carrier.

The national holidays include Liberation Day (January 7), The Chinese New Year (in February), The Buddhist New Year (in April), Revolution Day (April 17), *Chun Ben* (in September), King Sihanouk's Birthday (October 31), Independence Day (November 9) and The Front Day (December 2).

# CHINA (PEOPLE'S REPUBLIC OF): HISTORICAL OVERVIEW

- China is one of the world's oldest continuous civilizations. Throughout most of its history, China was ruled by a series of dynasties.

- The Shang Dynasty was founded around 1550 B.C. and was followed by the Zhou Dynasty, whose capital remained the ritual center of a number of feudal states for almost 1,000 years.

- The Han Dynasty (206 B.C.-220 A.D.) adopted the teachings of Confucius as official ideology.

- The Chinese empire reached its zenith under the Tang Dynasty (629-907 A.D.). Its military strength and its culture transformed the societies of present-day Japan, Korea and Vietnam.

- The Song Dynasty (960-1279 A.D.) was marked by rapid economic and commercial development, but fell to the Mongols under Genghis Khan and his grandson Kublai. The Mongols built their capital at Beijing.

- Chinese rule was restored by the Ming Dynasty in 1386, who were later ousted in 1644 by the Manchurians (thus beginning the Qing Dynasty).

- China suffered defeat at the hands of the British in the Opium War (1841-1842). The British won Hong Kong Island at this time.

- A revolution inspired by Sun Yat-Sen overthrew the Qing Dynasty in 1911.

- Sun Yat-Sen established the *Kuomintang (KMT)* Political Party in an effort to unify China, which was being fragmented by opposing warlords, during the 1920s.

- Chiang Kai-shek took control of the *KMT* in 1927 and ousted the once-allied *Communist Party (CCP)*.

- Japan seized Manchuria in 1931.

- Mao Zedong led the Communists on their "Long March" across China to regroup and fight the *KMT* for control of China.

- After World War II, with the defeat of the Japanese, civil war continued and Mao's forces gained control. Chiang's army fled to Taiwan.

- The People's Republic of China was proclaimed on October 1, 1949. Mao Zedong ruled China from 1949 to 1976.

- Deng Xiaoping and his allies legitimized free market forces and opened the country to Western investment and cultural influences.

# CHINA (PEOPLE'S REPUBLIC OF)

## INTRODUCTIONS

In China's larger cities such as Beijing or Shanghai and in business situations, the customary greeting is a handshake. You should first wait for a Chinese person to extend a hand, since not everyone uses this greeting. The handshake is usually light, but may last several seconds. Throughout the rest of China, the most common greeting is a nod or slight bow.

If you bow, never do so with a hand or hands in your pockets.

Business cards in Chinese and English are essential. Present your card with both hands after the handshake. Receive your counterpart's card with both hands and take a moment to examine the card and what it says, even if it is printed only in Chinese characters.

In Chinese names, the family name always comes *first* (for example, in the name Chen Wu, *Chen* is the family name and *Wu* is the given name). He should be addressed as Mr. Chen. Only family members or close friends use first names.

Chinese people often will not look you straight in the eye when greeting you. They sometimes lower their eyes slightly as a sign of respect. Looking directly into a Chinese person's eyes may make them uncomfortable and make you seem rude.

## SOCIAL TIPS AND CONVENTIONS

The Chinese are known for their good manners, hospitality and reserve.

Confucianism has had a great influence on attitudes and actions. The basic tenets of Confucian thought are: obedience to and respect for superiors and parents, duty to family, loyalty to friends, humility, sincerity and courtesy.

Respect and status increase with age. Older foreign businesspeople will likely be received with greater respect and will be regarded more seriously than will younger businesspeople.

Good conversation topics include personal questions, sights, Chinese culture, shopping and life in Western countries. Topics to avoid include government, politics and Taiwan. You may be asked how much money something costs or how much you earn. If this seems awkward, you may wish to explain that things cost a lot more in your country so that your purchasing power is not as high as it may seem.

China should be referred to as the "People's Republic of China" (PRC). Among the mainland Chinese, Taiwan is called the "Province of Taiwan," *never* the "Republic of China."

Chinese businesspeople will usually not come out directly and say "No" to a proposal. They will find many indirect ways to reply.

Periods of silence during business or dinner is a sign of politeness and of thought. Do not be quick to fill the silence with words. Also, be careful not to interrupt during a conversation.

# CHINA (Cont'd)

## SOCIAL TIPS AND CONVENTIONS (Cont'd)

The concept of "face" is important in understanding the Chinese people. Be careful to avoid causing someone to "lose face" by insulting, criticizing or embarrassing him/her in front of others, or by treating the person with less than the proper respect due his/her status in the organization.

Chinese people generally stand closer to each other than do Europeans and North Americans.

When nervous or embarrassed, Chinese people may smile or laugh and cover their mouths with their hands.

You may be greeted by a group of people with applause, such as when touring a factory. Returning the applause is the proper response.

## CUSTOMARY BUSINESS PRACTICES

Several trips to China will probably be necessary before business arrangements are finalized. With this in mind, keep your return plans flexible in case negotiations do not proceed according to schedule.

A network of personal connections is very important. This is called *guanxi*. Little or no distinction is made between business and personal relationships. To succeed in China, you must establish close personal ties with your Chinese business colleagues. Respect and trust must be earned before Chinese people will do business with you.

Business appointments are necessary and punctuality is important.

When entering a business meeting as a group, the highest ranked person should lead the group. Conventionally, the senior members of the Chinese and foreign teams head the discussion. It is not usually expected for junior members of your group to interject.

The hierarchy within a Chinese organization is complicated. It is often difficult to identify who makes the final decision. Thus, treat everybody with equal respect and be prepared to present your material to many different people at varying levels of authority.

Avoid using maps showing a British Hong Kong or an independent Taiwan.

Part of Chinese negotiating strategy involves being an excellent host. You should *not* misinterpret this as an indication of their attitude toward you or your project.

Formal dress for men is a suit and tie. Pantsuits are appropriate for businesswomen, since Chinese women often wear pants. Dress styles are changing rapidly in China. You should dress fashionably, but be conservative in all your accessories. Do not wear very short skirts or low necklines. For business meetings or dining out, women should wear a suit or a dress and as little makeup as possible. Jewelry should be modest and of excellent quality.

# CHINA (Cont'd)

## BUSINESS ENTERTAINING

Keep track of all favors done for you, small gifts received, etc. You will be expected to reciprocate in the future.

As a foreign businessperson, you will be treated to an evening banquet. You should reciprocate the invitation as soon as possible, preferably on the same trip. When you are in China, it is polite to allow the Chinese person to issue the first invitation.

Your delegation should all arrive for a banquet at the same time. Be punctual.

In making the invitation list for your banquet, include everybody with whom you have interacted because it is often difficult to discern who is the person with the ultimate authority. Do not risk excluding the most important person. If your spouse co-hosts a banquet, be sure to include the spouse of the principal guest in your invitation.

An invitation to a Chinese home is rare. If you are invited to someone's home, bring a small gift with you, such as a fruit basket or flowers. A memento from your home country is also appreciated. Gifts for the children are welcomed, as is perfume for the wife.

Business is generally not discussed during meals, although indirect references to business are common practice.

Seating arrangements are important, whether for business meetings or for dining. The principal guest sits next to the host when dining. Guests will be shown where to sit. At meetings, the main guest is seated facing the door and the host with his back to the door.

It is considered inappropriate to give an individual a business gift. It would be more appropriate to present a *modest* gift from your company division to the Chinese unit with which you are dealing. It should be presented to the most senior person in the Chinese unit. Gifts might include books about your country, records, a magazine subscription, pens, notepads or calendars. If suitable, wrap the gift in red, which is considered a lucky color, and present it at a banquet. It is common for the Chinese to refuse a gift or other offering two or three times, before accepting it. It is not necessary for foreigners to go through the same ritual.

Tipping is officially illegal in China. Some people, however, will accept tips in private.

## DINING OUT

A wide variety of cuisines is represented in the different regions of China.

If you are invited to a restaurant, dinner will be served at a round table with dishes in the center. The table will probably be set with a soup bowl, several pairs of chopsticks (to take food from serving plates to individual bowls), a wine cup, a rice dish and a dish for shells and bones.

Banquets may consist of 10-12 courses, so eat only a small portion of each.

Begin eating only after your host picks up his/her chopsticks.

## DINING OUT (Cont'd)

The host may serve you. Otherwise chopsticks should be used for reaching the food rather than passing around the serving dishes. If there is more than one pair of chopsticks at your place setting, use a different pair of chopsticks from the one you are putting in your mouth. Otherwise, use the other end of the chopsticks. It is considered polite to take what is close to you in the serving dish. Do not to pick through items.

Eat one dish at a time using the chopsticks. Never touch food with your fingers.

Refusing food may be considered rude. If you don't want to eat a particular item, just move it to the side of your dish.

Meat dishes may have small bones. Remove the bones from your mouth using your chopsticks. It is rude to use your hands.

To eat rice, bring the bowl to your mouth, and shovel the rice into your mouth with your chopsticks. Do not stick your chopsticks upright in your rice. Some Chinese people have a superstition that this could bring bad luck.

Chinese people generally do not drink alone. They propose a toast so that others will join them.

Indicate that you have finished eating by placing your chopsticks parallel across your plate. Don't worry about leaving a little food on your plate. It is polite to leave some food to show that you have eaten your fill, and that the host has provided more than you can eat.

Tea is much more common than coffee. At a meal, if you do not want more tea, leave some in your cup.

Soup is sometimes one of the last courses served. The serving of fruit signals the end of the meal. Your host will probably rise to show that the banquet has ended. If not, wait 10 minutes after tea is served and hot towels have been distributed before leaving.

## PUBLIC CUSTOMS

It is rude to put your hands in your mouth. As a result, you should refrain from biting your fingernails or using your nails to remove food from your teeth. It will disgust the Chinese.

Public displays of affection are rare. Chinese people do not touch each other much in public.

Good friends of the same sex may walk hand in hand (a sign of friendship).

Direct eye contact or staring in public places is not common in large cities. In smaller towns, a Westerner may be greeted with curiosity and stares.

Good posture is important. Do not put your feet on a desk or a chair. Do not use your feet to point at something or to move objects.

# CHINA (Cont'd)

## PUBLIC CUSTOMS (Cont'd)

Always ask permission before taking photographs of anyone.

Pointing is done with an open hand, not with one finger. The gesture for beckoning someone is done with the palm facing down and the fingers moving in a scratching motion.

# HONG KONG: HISTORICAL OVERVIEW

- The British East India Trading Company began using Hong Kong harbor for trade with China as early as 1699.

- Hong Kong was acquired by Great Britain from China in three stages: Hong Kong Island in 1842; the Kowloon Peninsula in 1860; and the New Territories in 1898, under a 99-year lease.

- Hong Kong was occupied by Japan from 1941-1945.

- The population greatly increased following victory of the Communists in China in 1949. Over one million refugees arrived immediately following China's civil war.

- Hong Kong's importance as a free port grew after World War II, when it became a leading commercial port and tourist center.

- During the 1980s, Hong Kong became a destination for Vietnamese refugees.

- Under the Sino-British Joint Declaration, issued on December 19, 1984, Hong Kong reverts to China on July 1, 1997. It becomes a Special Administrative Region.

- Chris Patten, a conservative, was appointed by the British as Governor of Hong Kong in 1992. He took steps to strengthen the democratic process in an attempt to determine the future of the prosperous region.

- There are several indications of what might happen when China takes control of Hong Kong. The Chinese parliament, the National People's Congress, has passed a resolution saying that it will do away with all legislative structures created under Governor Patten's reforms. All judges will have to be reappointed. The Bill of Rights, which among other things allows citizens to sue the government for violations of civil rights, will be scrapped.

# HONG KONG

## INTRODUCTIONS

Hong Kong has two official languages: Chinese (Cantonese) and English. Although dialects from all parts of China are heard, the Cantonese dialect is predominant and is officially recognized. Street signs, telephone directories and government documents are written in both languages.

Both English and Chinese greetings are common in Hong Kong. Therefore, shaking hands when meeting is appropriate and acceptable, and should be done when leaving as well. A handshake is usually quite light and may last as long as 10 seconds.

Business cards are essential and they should be printed with English on one side and Chinese on the other. Present and receive business cards with both hands, then take a few moments to look over the business cards you receive.

The Chinese do not look people directly in the eye when they greet someone. Sometimes, they lower their eyes as a sign of deference and respect.

Following introductions, polite conversation will include inquiries about one's health, business affairs or school activities.

Make a special effort to greet and show respect to older people.

In Chinese names, the family name precedes the given name. In Hong Kong, some Chinese people adapt Western first names for use in international business settings.

## SOCIAL TIPS AND CONVENTIONS

The Chinese people are reserved and show modesty when dealing with others. Humility or self-demeaning comments are generally used to describe oneself or one's accomplishments. They will usually deny praise, although sincere compliments are given and appreciated.

Strong elements of Taoism, Confucianism and Buddhism, form part of the religious background of many Hong Kong residents.

The Confucian ethics of proper social and family relationships form the foundation of Chinese society.

The Chinese are very conscious of social position. Anything you can do to enhance their opinion of your social position is worthwhile, as long as you do not appear arrogant or haughty.

A person's actions reflect on the entire family. To "save face" or avoid embarrassment, shame or dishonor, is very important. Never do or say anything which could cause someone to "lose face."

Expect to be asked personal questions, especially about your family, how much you earn, how much your watch cost or what type of car you drive. It is not necessary to answer such questions if you do not feel comfortable.

# HONG KONG (Cont'd)

## SOCIAL TIPS AND CONVENTIONS (Cont'd)

The Chinese prefer to be indirect when they need to say "No." They may say something is inconvenient or difficult or that it is under consideration.

Laughing or smiling may indicate embarrassment.

## CUSTOMARY BUSINESS PRACTICES

Although the influence of the British over the last century has left its mark, you should expect to experience many familiar Chinese customs.

All styles of clothing are worn in Hong Kong, from traditional to modern. Men wear Western-style suits for business and women wear suits or dresses.

Businesspeople are generally punctual for appointments.

Personal connections are indispensable to doing business in Hong Kong. Little distinction is made between business and personal relationships.

The people of Hong Kong place great value on reliability and trustworthiness. Permanence of a relationship is very important, and therefore the emphasis in doing business is on promoting long-term mutual benefits.

Business transactions are seldom made in a hurry in Hong Kong, although the pace of life is fast.

Tea may be served during business meetings; if so, do not drink until your host does. If your host leaves his or her tea untouched for a lengthy period of time, it may indicate that the meeting is over.

Gifts are often given to individuals in Hong Kong. A good gift would be something not available in Hong Kong, such as an item made in your home area or town. If gifts are given to a number of people, make sure that they are of roughly the same value but the chief executive's gift should be of greater value.

## BUSINESS ENTERTAINING

Business is often conducted during lunch or dinner. Guests are expected to arrive on time.

Lavish restaurant meals are traditional for special events among people in the Chinese community. Additionally, those of European heritage may hold dinner parties at their homes.

At a restaurant, the guest of honor usually rises at the end of the meal and thanks the host on behalf of the entire group.

If you are invited to someone's home, take along a small gift of fruit or candy. A picture book about your home area is a welcome item, as is perfume for the hostess and toys for the family's children.

# HONG KONG (Cont'd)

## BUSINESS ENTERTAINING (Cont'd)

Red and gold are considered lucky colors and gifts are often wrapped in paper of these colors. Avoid using black or white wrapping paper, as these are considered mourning colors.

As with business cards, present and receive a gift with both hands.

Unwrapping a gift in front of the giver is not done unless the giver encourages it.

Be aware that a Chinese person may refuse a gift two or three times before finally accepting it. It is not necessary, however, for a foreigner to go through the same ritual.

Shoes are not generally removed when entering a home, although the custom is widespread in other parts of Asia.

Visitors should sit when invited to do so and maintain good posture.

## DINING OUT

Rice is the main staple. Chinese dishes are often prepared with fish, pork, chicken and vegetables.

In the home, chopsticks are used for eating most meals. Dishes are usually placed in the center of the table. Everyone helps themselves to a portion of food from the main platter with chopsticks and places it in their own personal bowl of rice. In some families, it is acceptable to use the same chopsticks for serving and eating.

The proper way to eat is to hold the rice bowl close to your mouth.

Your host will offer to refill your bowl with more rice and other food until you politely refuse.

You may find both chopsticks and western utensils at a meal, which is a reflection of Hong Kong's heritage as a British Crown Colony. When using a knife and fork, the continental style is followed, keeping the knife in the right hand and the fork in the left.

When somebody pours you tea at a meal, indicate "thank you" by lightly tapping your fingertips on the table.

Always leave some food in your dish to indicate that your host has provided more food than you could possibly eat.

In restaurants, a service charge is often included in the bill; however, it is customary to leave an additional tip.

Signal a waiter that you want the check by making a writing motion with your hands.

Reciprocate a toast made by your host. A common time for toasts in a multi-course meal is when the shark's fin soup is served (often considered the highlight of the meal). Toasts can also be made when a new dish is served and before people start eating that dish.

# HONG KONG (Cont'd)

## PUBLIC CUSTOMS

When sitting, place your hands in your lap and keep your feet on the floor. Traditional Chinese do not cross their legs, but it is all right for women to do so.

Winking at someone is considered impolite.

An open hand, not just the index finger, is used for pointing. Beckon someone with the palm down and all fingers waving.

Eating on the streets is considered inappropriate.

The Chinese do not usually show affection in public, although this is changing somewhat with younger people.

Friends of the same sex may walk hand-in-hand.

*Mah-jong*, a traditional game played with tiles, is a popular pastime.

Favorite sports include ping pong, soccer, squash, tennis, swimming and boating.

Holidays are based on the lunar calendar and may fall on different days each year. The Chinese New Year is often in February and is the most important holiday.

# INDIA: HISTORICAL OVERVIEW

- The Indian subcontinent was the site of the Indus Valley civilization more than 5,000 years ago. Around 1500 B.C., Aryans arrived from Central Asia. They gradually pushed the native Dravidians to the south. The Aryans gave to India many of its basic institutions and cultural habits, such as the caste system.

- Alexander the Great invaded India in 327 B.C., but his influence was short-lived. The first great Indian empire was the Maurya, established shortly after Alexander's invasion. It was this empire that unified the entire north and spread Buddhism throughout the region. The influence of Buddhism later waned, and Hinduism became more dominant. Hindu philosophy and legal codes were developed under the Mauryas and succeeding dynasties.

- The fourth to sixth centuries A.D. are considered a golden age of science, literature and the arts in the northern Gupta Kingdom. There were also several great empires in southern India, which developed separately. They established a maritime trade that spread throughout the East.

- Arab, Turk and Afghan Muslims ruled successively in various parts of the Indian subcontinent from the 8th to the 18th centuries. This provided some basis for the historical animosity between Hindus and Muslims. Most notable among the Muslim rulers were the Moguls, who founded their empire in 1526.

- Portuguese, Dutch, French and British traders established bases in India, starting with the landing of Vasco da Gama in 1498. The British eventually assumed political control of the area in 1858.

- After World War I, Mahatma Gandhi led a continuing nationalist movement advocating civil disobedience and passive resistance to British rule. India gained independence from Great Britain in 1947.

- Pakistan was established as a separate Muslim country due to religious rivalry and violence. Bangladesh broke away from Pakistan in 1971.

- Violence has marked Indian politics, including the assassinations of Mahatma Gandhi (1948), Indira Gandhi (1984) and Rajiv Gandhi (1991). Religious strife has continually cropped up in various areas around the country.

- In 1991, the *Congress Party* – in power since 1947 – lost much of its support to the *Bharatiya Janata Party* and the *Janta Dal Party*.

- India has massive poverty problems due to insufficient domestic economic growth, rapid population growth and insufficient harvest size.

- In 1993, the Indian economy began to improve with lower inflation, lower tax rates and increased foreign investment. India has six operational nuclear facilities, several car manufacturing and industrial plants and huge mineral deposits.

- In June 1996, Hardanally Doddegowda was elected Prime Minister.

# INDIA

## INTRODUCTIONS

The proper form of greeting is important. The traditional Indian greeting is called *namaste* – a ritual where one presses the palms together (fingers up) below the chin and inclines the head slightly, while saying the word *"Namaste."* Do not bow. Greet the oldest person in the group first, not the host. When greeting a man, shake hands. When greeting a woman, make a *namaste*. Indians usually won't shake hands with a woman. If meeting a man and woman together, make a *namaste*.

Don't use first names unless you know someone well. Use "Mr.," "Mrs." or "Miss." Use titles such as "Professor" and "Doctor," and use "Sir" with a superior.

You may have a garland of flowers placed around your neck as a sign of affection and respect. Accept it and remove it immediately to show humility.

## SOCIAL TIPS AND CONVENTIONS

Indian people are very family oriented with strong religious and spiritual ties. Physical and spiritual purity are highly valued, and humility and self-denial are respected. Fatalism is widespread and a component of the major religion (83% are Hindu). Indians are very proud of being the world's most populous democracy.

British manners prevail. Be subdued. Self-control is favored over impulsiveness. A quietly self-confident aura breeds trust and respect. However, one should be friendly and communicative.

Maintain a distance of about an arm's length with members of the opposite sex.

Public displays of affection, even among married couples, is not considered proper.

Hindu culture and heritage (which is very rich and of which Indians are proud) are good topics of conversation, except with individuals from a Christian, Moslem or Sikh background. In general, Indians enjoy talking about their rich artistic and architectural heritage as well as life in other countries. Ask about India's thriving motion picture industry. Bombay, known as "Bollywood," has the largest movie industry in the world. Soccer, cricket and hockey are popular sports, as well as good conversation topics.

Avoid discussing sex, salaries, poverty, beggars, famines, snake charmers and widow-burning. Other sensitive topics to avoid discussing are India-Pakistan relations, the weather, (which is often incredibly hot and humid), politics and comparisons of Hinduism and Islam with Christianity.

Be prepared to answer personal questions. You will often be asked about yourself, your family, your hobbies and whether you like sports. You should show curiosity about your host's family and bring pictures of your own family.

Don't be surprised if the Indians you meet, even very casually, ask for your home address. They don't want the address to come visit you. They want simply to be accepted as a friend.

# INDIA (Cont'd)

## SOCIAL TIPS AND CONVENTIONS (Cont'd)

Be sure not to touch the head of an Indian, as it is considered a sacred part of the body.

When accepting anything, including food, or when eating, always use your right hand. In India, the left hand is used for personal hygiene purposes.

Expect to be overwhelmed with hospitality. Never refuse an invitation, but don't make an explicit commitment unless you are genuinely sure that you can keep it.

Don't thank someone repetitively as this is considered superficial.

Indians use "Thank you" to signify the end of a transaction or relationship, such as purchasing an item in the market.

Women should dress conservatively, covering up as much of the body as comfort permits. Indian women usually wear a *sari* (a long, colorful wraparound dress). Both single and married women may wear a *bindi* (a dot) on their foreheads.

Compliments to women from men who are not close relatives are considered inappropriate.

## CUSTOMARY BUSINESS PRACTICES

Your Indian colleagues will speak perfect English. Although Hindi is the predominant language, English is the language of commerce and administration. Most government publications are printed in both languages. Be aware, though, that 24 languages with a million or more speakers of each, also exist. Dialects and language vary widely among India's regions.

Though Indians are impressed by punctuality, they are often late themselves. Try to keep a flexible schedule to accommodate these delays. Don't be surprised if Indian businesspeople are somewhat vague about a commitment since they don't like to be pressed for exact times.

Generally, business is conducted at a slow pace. Be prepared for a good deal of discussion, followed by a long wait for a final decision. Be patient and enjoy the pleasantries and conversation that are typical during business transactions.

Contracts and other documentation related to business arrangements will usually be scrutinized very carefully, sometimes taking weeks or months.

Make appointments at least 30 days in advance. Most Indian executives prefer their meetings in the late morning or early afternoon. Construct your schedule with enough flexibility to accommodate extra days in India for unforeseen meetings.

Decisions are made by top executives. Try to make contacts at the highest levels and provide incentives for middle managers and assistants to help nudge your concerns or proposals upward.

## CUSTOMARY BUSINESS PRACTICES (Cont'd)

Business cards may be in English. However, promotional and sales materials should be printed in Hindi to reach wide markets.

You may add your academic credentials to your business card, identifying degrees and the disciplines they are in, even the name of the institution if it is particularly distinguished.

Phrase questions carefully. Indian responses can be ambiguous so as to avoid upsetting a person.

Indians are tolerant of others. However, be cautious in giving criticism, as Indians easily take offense.

Most Indian businessmen are Westernized, but many have fairly old-fashioned ideas regarding the status of women. It is best that a Western woman not initiate a handshake with a man. Most Indian women, however, will shake hands with other women, but not with men.

Men should wear a suit on the first business visit and for all government visits; afterwards, you may follow the lead of your host. Men usually wear slacks and short-sleeved sports shirts to the office. Similarly, women should wear a suit for the first visit. Women generally wear casual dresses or pants outfits for daytime, and cocktail dresses, suits or long dresses to evening receptions and to more formal restaurants.

Be aware that Indian businessmen may graciously pat or slap you on the back. This signifies cordiality and friendship.

Be deferential when dealing with bureaucrats.

## BUSINESS ENTERTAINING

Indian businesspeople are generally very gracious, informal hosts.

The prelude to most business meetings is a cup of tea.

Business can be discussed during meals, but let your host initiate the discussion. Business meals usually take place in the evening. The traffic and humidity limit luncheon meetings.

When offered refreshments or snacks in or out of the home, it is polite to initially refuse and then to accept. If it is not to your taste, simply leave it.

Food and religion are interwoven to Indians. The giving of food is considered a spiritual act as their religion states that food comes from the gods.

Most Hindus and all orthodox Moslems abstain from alcoholic drinks.

To thank an Indian host after a meal is considered an insult because Indians take it as a payment. Instead, you should reciprocate with an invitation.

# INDIA (Cont'd)

## BUSINESS ENTERTAINING (Cont'd)

When invited to dine at an Indian home, do not arrive early. It is wise to have a snack before you arrive, because dinner may not be served for quite some time. Leave immediately after dinner has concluded.

Bring a gift of sweets and pastry or fruit and flowers. Avoid frangipani flowers which are used for funerals.

The religion of your hosts will determine the menu. Muslims eat beef, but not pork or shellfish. Many Hindus are vegetarians. Those who are not, will never eat or serve beef since the cow is considered sacred.

In rural homes, women may be seated separately. Even when the guests are mixed, the sexes usually talk only to each other.

In traditional homes, you may sit cross-legged on floor mats at low tables. Expect to be seated first, but there is no particular place of honor.

Always wash your hands before and after meals. In Hindu homes, you will be expected to wash your mouth as well. If so, swirl some water around in your mouth and then spit it into the sink.

Do not serve yourself; always wait to be served. Guests and men will be served first.

## DINING OUT

Indians are fastidious about cleanliness. It is advised never touch a common dish or serving with your fingers or with a utensil that you have used. Always use serving spoons.

Unless you are offered a fork, eat with your hands just as the Indians do.

The Continental style of eating, with the fork held in the left hand and the knife held in the right, is used in most Westernized restaurants or settings.

Your Indian host will likely entertain you at a private club, a prestigious hotel or in a restaurant, rather than at home. Wives are generally invited, except for Muslim wives, who are kept from public view.

The guest of honor should be seated to the right of the host. Otherwise, there are no seating formalities.

Indians rarely split the bill for a meal. The party that issued the invitation will pay.

The tip for meals is usually 10% of the bill.

# INDIA (Cont'd)

## DINING OUT (Cont'd)

If you are not sure of the meaning of a menu item, do not hesitate to ask as Indian cuisine is complex and varied. There is no such spice as "curry," as the word simply means "dish" or culinary preparation. In northern Indian cuisine, there are a variety of interesting breads such as *chapatti, nan* and *paratha.* Southern cuisine is accompanied by rice. Some specialties include *tandoori* chicken (marinated and then cooked in a clay oven) and *samosas* (fried pastry triangles with a meat or vegetable filling). A large variety of vegetarian dishes are also popular.

Indians in the south drink coffee and those in the north drink tea, but they both usually drink water or buttermilk with a meal.

After eating, it is customary to consume *pan,* a mixture of spices rolled in a betel leaf, as a digestive.

Do not offer anyone food from your plate, even a member of your family. It is considered socially offensive. Hindus do not let anyone outside their caste or religion touch their food.

## PUBLIC CUSTOMS

Before entering a home, ask if you should remove your shoes.

Whistling is considered very impolite.

One's feet or shoes should not touch another person. If they do, an immediate apology is necessary. Keep feet flat on the floor.

Beckon with the palm turned down, flexing fingers rapidly a few times.

In the south, tossing the head from side to side means "yes."

Bargaining is employed only in certain shopping districts and is totally unknown in others.

When visiting a mosque, temple, Sikh *gurdwara* or other religious place, be sure to cover your arms and legs and women should cover their heads. Normally shoes are removed outside of a place of worship. Be aware that some shrines do not permit foreigners. Additionally, photography is sometimes forbidden at religious sites.

# INDONESIA: HISTORICAL OVERVIEW

- Indonesia is made up of 13,760 islands that stretch 3,200 miles; only 6,000 of the islands are inhabited.

- Early Indonesian culture was influenced by India. The Hindu and Buddhist kingdoms on Sumatra and Java from the 7th through the 14th centuries succumbed to the advance of Islam.

- Islam was introduced through traders in the 15th century and is the predominant religion today.

- Indonesia has more than 60 ethnic groups, each with its own customs, culture and language. The Javanese people form the largest group.

- Europeans, led by the Portuguese, arrived in the 16th century. They built fortresses to protect their spice trade.

- Indonesia became a Dutch colony in 1816 and remained under Dutch rule until the 1940s.

- Japan occupied the islands during World War II.

- Independence from the Netherlands was proclaimed in August 1945. A republic was formed under President Sukarno.

- Sukarno created external problems to cover up the wretched state of the Indonesian economy. In the 1950s, emboldened by his popularity, he seized control of foreign investments and then, with Soviet aid, forced the Dutch to surrender West Irian, the western portion of New Guinea, in 1962. His next target was Malaysia, but the British, who controlled the area, were ready to fight for it.

- At the same time, Sukarno devised a coup against the army leadership. General Soeharto crushed the rebellion and long-grown resentment led to the slaughter of thousands of communists. Sukarno was stripped of his power. Soeharto had no interest in Malaysia and instead took on Indonesia's massive economic problems.

- Throughout the 1970s and the early 1980s, Indonesia was overcome by food shortages, government corruption and many other problems. Soeharto, who is still in power, has been a heavy-handed ruler who controls monopolies that are profitable, but detrimental to the economy. There was tampering in the election of 1987, enabling Soeharto's party, the *Golkar* of Java, to win 73% of the popular vote.

- In the past several years, there has been some liberalization of Soeharto's authoritarian political system. These charges are partly due to the impact of democratic developments in the Philippines and South Korea. Nevertheless, severe political repression continues in East Timor. In 1991, a pro-independence demonstration in East Timor was violently suppressed by the army.

# INDONESIA

## INTRODUCTIONS

Indonesian culture is based on honor and respect for the individual. Respect should always be shown when greeting others.

Elders are introduced before younger people and women before men.

People usually shake hands only when introduced for the first time or when congratulating someone. On other occasions, it isn't customary to shake hands. Shake hands lightly and state your name when first meeting someone. If someone touches her/his heart while shaking hands, that means that the greeting is very heartfelt and that the person being greeted is very special. It is appropriate to bow slightly when greeting an older person. Women usually do not shake hands.

Except for hand shaking, physical contact is usually avoided in greetings. Smiling, bowing or nodding is considered more gracious.

Bring business cards. They should be exchanged at the first meeting. The flashier the card, the better. Use the acronyms for whatever degrees you hold.

If a person has a title, use it in greeting and in general conversation. A man may be referred to as *"Bapak"* ("Father") either instead of or in addition to his name. Similarly, a woman may be referred to as *"Ibu"* ("Mother") in the same fashion.

Many Indonesians have only one name.

Guests are welcomed warmly. At a party, expect to be introduced individually. Don't be surprised if your host and other guests make welcoming speeches and call upon you to give a speech as well. Simply acknowledge that you are happy to be at the party and to have met everyone; thank the host for the invitation.

## SOCIAL TIPS AND CONVENTIONS

Families are a major source of conversation topics. Personal questions are often asked, even on short acquaintance. Good topics of conversation might include food and the beauties of Indonesia.

In Java, avoid personal questions about such subjects as job, age, salary, prices and religion. Also avoid any discussion of material goods.

Nearly 90% of Indonesians are Muslim, which represents the largest population of Muslims in the world. Be aware of when the holy month of *Ramadan* occurs each year (the dates are based on the lunar calendar). At that time, Muslims do not eat or drink from sunrise to sundown. The people of Bali are mostly Hindu.

Indonesians greatly value a quiet voice, an unassuming attitude and agreement by consensus. Disagreement and criticism should be handled privately, as it is a great insult to embarrass someone. Confrontation and disharmony are to be avoided.

Indonesians often laugh to cover their anger, shock or embarrassment.

# INDONESIA (Cont'd)

## SOCIAL TIPS AND CONVENTIONS (Cont'd)

Unannounced visits are common in Indonesia. Visitors wait to be invited to sit, and stand when their host/hostess enters the room. Drinks may be served; however, visitors should wait to drink until invited to do so. If hors d'oevres are offered, eat a little bit to avoid insulting your hosts.

## CUSTOMARY BUSINESS PRACTICES

Punctuality is important, but is not emphasized over personal relations. Indonesians tend to arrive late. Keep mentioning the time of an appointment, or arrange it for about a half an hour earlier than when you want it to start. Foreigners are expected to be punctual.

An Indonesian virtue is to not speak directly. "Yes" does not necessarily mean "Yes." Indonesians use the indirect approach, often taking their time before getting to the point. The word "No" is rarely used. They will say *"Belum"* ("Not yet") instead.

For a business meeting, men should wear a white shirt, tie and slacks. A safari suit, common throughout Asia, is also acceptable. Jackets aren't necessary except for meetings with government officials. Women should wear a dress or a skirt with a blouse.

Do not schedule business trips to Indonesia during July or August since most businessmen take their vacations at this time. Check the dates of holidays before planning your trip, as most vary from year to year.

Indonesians do not conduct business transactions or make decisions in a direct fashion. Businesspeople should be prepared to spend a good deal of time with clients before getting to the business at hand. Patience is the key. Never lose your temper or show strong emotions. Consensus, rather than confrontation, is necessary for successful negotiation.

Plan to spend a minimum of a week negotiating the simplest agreement. Business dealings tend to be slow and may cause frustration to people accustomed to a faster pace.

The atmosphere of most business meetings may be informal. Do not voice criticism at a meeting. It is always given in private.

Most Indonesian businesses close for two to three hours in the middle of the day. Business and government offices close at midday on Friday for worship.

After returning home, follow up with business contacts by fax, then be prepared for a long response time – or no response at all. Indonesians can have difficulty in communicating from a long distance. Generally they communicate much better face-to-face.

Generally, be prepared to be frustrated by a lack of long-distance communication, even though some Indonesian managers insist employees answer faxes within 24 hours.

Indonesians do business with "friends." Developing a rapport and a friendship is crucial. While quality and price are important, they remain secondary to the personal interaction of the business partners. There are no sales without face-to-face negotiation.

# INDONESIA (Cont'd)

## CUSTOMARY BUSINESS PRACTICES (Cont'd)

Be prepared to encounter managers and business owners from the People's Republic of China or of Chinese descent in Indonesia.

## BUSINESS ENTERTAINING

Expect to be entertained by Indonesian business counterparts. Be sure to reciprocate on the same trip.

If a businesswoman wishes to entertain, she should say, "It would give me great pleasure to invite you to dinner," and then arrange payment beforehand by giving the maitre d' her credit card.

In Java, you, as a foreigner, are expected to be punctual. Many, but not all, government and business representatives are used to dealing with foreigners.

In Java, business lunches are more popular than business dinners. A man should not invite a Javanese businessman's wife to attend a meal unless his own wife will be present. A businesswoman, however, should include a Javanese man's wife in the invitation.

Gifts are not expected by traditional Indonesians. More Westernized Indonesians will appreciate flowers or candy brought by dinner guests. Any gift you give will be accepted graciously since it is considered impolite to refuse anything. The gift will not be opened in the presence of the giver with the exception of "official" gifts such as those given at the end of a lecture or official visit.

## DINING OUT

In Muslim homes, neither alcohol nor pork is served. Indonesians, however, tend not to be as strict as other Muslim societies, such as those in the Middle East. Drinking alcohol in front of your host does not usually present a problem.

Many Westernized Indonesians use a fork and a spoon to eat, but more traditional families eat with their hands. If using a fork and spoon, hold the fork in the left hand, hold the spoon in the right and eat from the spoon.

Keep both hands above the table while eating.

Rice is the main staple. Vegetables, fish and spicy sauces are often served with rice. The national dish is *nasi goreng*, which is fried rice with egg, spices and vegetables.

Many Indonesian dishes are highly spiced. One spicy dish, containing coconut milk, is known as *padang*. It was named after the city on Sumatra where it originated. Other popular dishes are *satay* (grilled skewered meat with a spicy peanut sauce) and *gado gado* (a salad with a peanut sauce).

Tea and coffee are the most common drinks.

By finishing a drink, you are sending a signal for the glass to be refilled. Similarly, leave some food on your plate or people will think you want more.

# INDONESIA (Cont'd)

## DINING OUT (Cont'd)

Bread with butter and sugar on it is served as a dessert. Fresh fruit is also often served as dessert.

Beckon a waiter by raising your hand. To ask for the check, make a writing motion with both hands.

Tipping is not common. At restaurants, a service charge is usually included in the bill.

Guests should wait for the host to invite them to begin eating. During the meal, don't worry if there is not much conversation. Indonesians like to concentrate on eating their meals.

## PUBLIC CUSTOMS

Indonesians dress modestly whether they are dressed in Western styles or traditional clothing. The traditional dress for women is called a *sarong,* which is a long wraparound dress with an intricate *batik* pattern. *Batik* is a traditional handicraft using molten wax to create designs on cloth. *Batik* clothing may be worn by both men and women for formal situations.

It is disrespectful to be affectionate with members of the opposite sex in public.

Don't beckon with a single finger. Signal with the whole hand down, palm open, waving your fingers toward you.

Pointing is done with the thumb in Indonesia.

Never use your left hand to touch others, take or give money, signal a waiter or pass food. The left hand is reserved for personal hygiene purposes.

Don't touch anyone's head. It is the seat of the soul and is sacred.

Shoes are removed when entering carpeted rooms and holy places, especially mosques.

Avoid standing with your hands in your pockets or on your hips. It is felt to be a sign of defiance or arrogance.

Indonesians do not usually cross their legs. If you do, one knee should be over the other or you may cross your ankles. Never cross your legs by placing one ankle on the other knee. Also avoid having your foot or the sole of your shoe face another person.

It is considered inappropriate to eat while walking on the street.

Sports, especially soccer, are very popular. Badminton, volleyball and tennis are also enjoyed.

# JAPAN: HISTORICAL OVERVIEW

- Japan has been ruled by emperors for over 2,000 years. According to legend, the first Emperor was Jimmu in 600 B.C.

- Japan came under the cultural influence of China in the sixth century A.D. with the import of Buddhism and the Chinese writing system. It modeled its governmental and cultural institutions on the Chinese Tang Dynasty.

- *Shoguns* (feudal lords) held political control from the 12th century A.D. until the late 19th century. Portuguese traders and missionaries arrived in the 16th century, followed by the Dutch and the British. The *shoguns* expelled all foreigners in the 17th century with the exception of a few on Deshima (an island off the coast of Nagasaki).

- In 1853, Matthew Perry (U.S. Navy) renewed Western contact with the Japanese.

- The *shoguns* lost power in the 1860s, and the emperor again took control.

- In 1895, the Japanese defeated China. The Japanese then gained the influence that China had held in Korea.

- Japan was also victorious in the Russo-Japanese War in 1905, which led to its recognition as a military power.

- Involvement in World War I brought Japan increased global influence. At Versailles, Japan was one of the "big five" (one of the five nations to have representatives on the Council of Ten) which negotiated the terms of peace.

- Japan invaded Manchuria and much of China in the 1930s.

- On December 7, 1941, Japan launched an air attack on U.S. naval forces at Pearl Harbor in Hawaii.

- After its defeat in World War II, Japan was occupied by military forces (mainly from the U.S.), from 1945 to 1952.

- In 1947, a new constitution was adopted that declared Japan a democracy.

- From the end of World War II until the early 1990s, the Liberal Democratic Party (LDP) controlled politics in Japan.

- The current emperor, Akihito, ascended to the throne in 1989. He is the head of state, but has no governing power.

- In January 1996, Ryutaro Hashimoto became Japan's Prime Minister. This was the fourth change in government since 1993, and it returned the LDP to power. Throughout the political instability of the early 1990s, the fundamental problems of Japanese politics such as factionalism, corruption, the dominance of big business and "money politics" continued to exist.

# JAPAN

## INTRODUCTIONS

Japanese people tend to be more restrained than people from the West, and customarily adhere to traditional rituals. When formally introduced, it is proper to bow, although recently the combination of a bow and a handshake has become more widespread. The depth and length of your bow indicates the degree of respect.

*Meishi koukan* (business card exchange) is an important aspect of business etiquette. Present your card with both hands and bow slightly. Receive business cards with both hands and take a moment to study it before bowing or shaking hands. Place the card in front of you on a table or desk for reference and as an additional sign of respect. Do not quickly stuff it into a pocket or wallet. Do not write on business cards you receive. Print your business card in your own language and in Japanese with one language on each side of the card. When written in Japanese, the surname comes before the given name(s).

When addressing people, always use "Mr.," "Ms.," "Mrs.," "Miss" or the Japanese suffix *"san."* Mr. Hanafusa, for example, would become "Hanafusa-san." The Japanese often address someone by using their title, for example Ogushi plus the Japanese word for manager ("Ogushi-*bucho"*).

Be aware that Japanese people refrain from any physical contact when greeting others in public, no matter how close the relationship. Younger people often shake hands with Westerners, while more cosmopolitan Japanese men and women may combine a bow with a handshake. Take your cue from the Japanese person with whom you are meeting as to whether you should bow or shake hands.

When meeting someone, a Japanese person will lower his/her eyes out of politeness and respect. He/she will not make the same degree of direct eye contact as would a Westerner.

Spoken Japanese is not closely related to the spoken Chinese language, but written Japanese is based on Chinese ideographs (characters). The Japanese also use two phonetic alphabets simplified from the ideographs. A third phonetic alphabet uses Roman letters.

## SOCIAL TIPS AND CONVENTIONS

Japanese people enjoy social conversations, especially those that express a healthy curiosity about their culture and country. Suggested topics for conversation include your reactions to Japan (of great interest to the Japanese), Japanese food, sports (especially baseball and golf), other countries you have visited and questions you have about Japan.

To demonstrate politeness and other-centeredness, ask other people their opinion before expressing your own.

Although Japanese people study English while in school, their knowledge of the language is often more academic than conversational. If you are having trouble communicating, you may find that it is helpful to write down your questions, since it is often easier for people to understand written rather than spoken English.

# JAPAN (Cont'd)

## SOCIAL TIPS AND CONVENTIONS (Cont'd)

Age and tradition are highly honored in Japan. Show respect for age, rank and status.

*Wa* (harmony) and politeness are very important to the Japanese; they avoid saying "No" directly. They may instead say something like "I will think about it" or "It may be difficult." "Yes" may only mean "Yes, I'm listening."

Know that harmony and politeness do not pertain in crowded public situations, such as those encountered on the subway, where pushing and shoving is common.

Japanese society is very group-oriented. Loyalty to the group and to your superiors takes precedence over personal feelings. A popular proverb in Japan that illustrates this point is "The nail that sticks up gets hammered down."

The concept of "face" is also extremely important. Never do anything to embarrass, criticize or question the knowledge of a Japanese person in front of others.

In Japan, laughter or a smile does not necessarily signify joy or amusement. Instead, it can be a sign of embarrassment or distress.

Outward style is very important in Japan. For example, gifts are carefully wrapped, food is displayed artfully, etc.

Traditionally, most Japanese people have practiced a combination of Buddhist and Shinto religions. Shintoism as well as Confucian thought have been important in forming Japanese social values.

## CUSTOMARY BUSINESS PRACTICES

The only acceptable way to approach a Japanese firm is through an introduction by a third party, preferably someone who knows you, your background, your company and the Japanese company with which you want to transact business. This introduction could be made either by letter or in person.

Always dress in conservative business suits and ties. Businesswomen should use makeup, perfume and jewelry sparingly. Make sure your shoes are polished. Slip-on shoes are generally more convenient than lace-up shoes since you may need to remove them in certain places. You may be provided with slippers to use indoors except in rooms in which the floors are covered in straw *tatami* mats, where you are expected to walk in your stocking feet. Always remove your overcoat in the hall before entering an office.

In Japan, a business relationship is based more on personal relations than on the cost of the product. The Japanese first want to become acquainted and familiar with you, learning vital facts including your age, the university you attended and details about your firm. Business comes later. Your Japanese counterparts will appreciate you showing the same interest in their backgrounds.

# JAPAN (Cont'd)

## CUSTOMARY BUSINESS PRACTICES (Cont'd)

Although it has been customary and, indeed, very common for a Japanese person to be employed by one company throughout his/her working life, you should be aware that recent changes in Japanese attitudes toward employment now include more job flexibility.

Japanese people don't like surprises. It is necessary to prepare them for upcoming presentations or discussions by sending them written material well in advance. Arrange for several copies to be printed – translated into Japanese – of any written material you plan to use. This will allow each member of the team to have a copy, which will in turn, speed the decision-making process.

If possible, prepare visual aids such as charts, drawings, samples, slides and films for use in your presentation.

Make business appointments as far in advance as possible. Punctuality is very important in Japan. Be sure to allow ample time between appointments.

At meetings, the most senior person will usually sit furthest from the door and the most junior person nearest the door. Wait until you have been shown where to sit before sitting down.

The decision-making process can be very slow in Japan. Input from workers at all levels of a company is considered. The process involves many face-to-face discussions, and the contract must be approved at each level of the company. Patience is considered a virtue. Once a decision is made, however, implementation is immediate.

Be prepared for periods of silence during a business meeting. Silence may indicate that the Japanese businesspeople have not come to a decision and are thinking. It may also mean that something has been done to displease them. Be patient and allow your Japanese counterparts to speak first.

A Japanese person may show concentration by closing his/her eyes and slightly nodding the head up and down.

Be very careful not to interrupt when a Japanese person is speaking. Westerners do have a tendency to interrupt, and this is not received well in Japan.

Many Japanese businesspeople work late into the evening. They rarely take work home, however. After work, executives frequently go to bars for drinking and informal business discussions. It is seen as an extension of the regular work day.

The most popular vacation periods are mid-December to mid-January (especially near the New Year) as well as in July and August. Many offices also close during "Golden Week," which extends from late April into the first week of May.

# JAPAN (Cont'd)

## BUSINESS ENTERTAINING

When you begin a business relationship with a Japanese firm, you will be given a gift. After receiving it, present your Japanese associations with a group gift, such as an item that represents your company, fine wine, rare Scotch, golf balls, books about your area of the country or a subscription to a magazine. Avoid garish wrapping paper, bows and ribbons. A safe route is to have the present wrapped by someone at the store from which it was purchased.

Remember to receive or give a gift with both hands and bow slightly. The recipient of a gift is not expected to open it immediately. Avoid giving an even number of something, especially four. (The word for "four" sounds like the Japanese word for "death.") An exception to the rule of preferring odd numbers is the number nine. The word for "nine" sounds like the Japanese word for "suffering," therefore, avoid giving nine of anything.

Business deals are sealed with dinner in a restaurant or a drinking session at a bar. In Japan, the lengthy business lunch is rare and lunchtime drinking is unusual. After business has concluded, allow the Japanese executive(s) to issue the first invitation to a dinner. As at meetings, the seat of honor in a restaurant is usually furthest from the door. Wait to sit until you have been shown where to be seated.

Always reciprocate hospitality by inviting the most important members of the Japanese team to dinner. It is best to invite your Japanese business colleagues to a Chinese or Western-style restaurant, preferably in a large hotel. It is suggested that Westerners not entertain their guests in a Japanese restaurant because they don't understand the subtleties of Japanese dining well enough to act as hosts. Wives rarely accompany their husbands on business-oriented social occasions.

Prepare to be taken to a nightclub called a *karaoke* (singing along to background music using special audio/visual equipment) bar. The standard drink offered is called a *mizuwari* (Scotch and water). If you don't wish to drink much, leave your glass half full and then act tipsy when offered more to drink. One way of avoiding a refill is to cover your glass with your hand when others are trying to pour you another drink.

After being invited to a *karaoke* bar, reciprocate by inviting your Japanese colleagues to a restaurant. Japanese businesspeople, however, don't expect you to take them to *karaoke* bars.

It is an honor to be invited to play golf with your Japanese hosts.

If you are invited to a Japanese home, bring a gift of fruit or cake to the host/hostess. Since Japanese rarely entertain in their homes, it is a great honor to be invited to an individual's home.

# JAPAN (Cont'd)

## DINING OUT

The traditional Japanese diet consists largely of rice, fresh vegetables, seafood, fruit and small portions of meat. Rice and tea are part of nearly every meal.

When dining either at someone's home or in a restaurant, you will receive a set of disposable chopsticks in a paper wrapper. Western utensils are generally used only when eating Western foods.

Traditional etiquette among the Japanese people emphasizes humility. If you are offered tea or fruit, before accepting you should express a slight hesitation. It is also courteous to deny compliments graciously and to avoid extending excessive compliments on the decor. Understated compliments are more appropriate.

Japanese culture is steeped in tradition, a part of which applies to dining. Japanese people generally consume food in a certain order. For example, first a chopstickful of rice is eaten, then one of the side dishes and then more rice. It is considered rude to eat just one dish at a time.

After being seated, you will be given an *oshibori* (damp cloth) for cleaning your hands. Remember not to use this on your face, neck or arms. Put it back on the tray from which it was served when you are done. Handkerchieves are often used in place of napkins during a meal.

You may want to consider having your Japanese host order for you.

Japanese food is frequently served to individuals on square or rectangular trays containing food in dishes or compartments.

When eating all dishes except rice, use chopsticks to bring the food to your mouth. If you do not know how to use chopsticks, your Japanese hosts will enjoy showing you how. Do not use your chopsticks for pointing.

For rice dishes, it is proper to bring the dish up toward your mouth, rather than bending over it. Do not mix sauces or other foods with the rice.

Wait until your host/hostess picks up his/her chopsticks before you touch yours, but do not wait until he/she starts eating. The highest ranking guest is the one who should start eating first. The custom is for the host to bow to the guest and for the guest to say "*Itadakimasu*," which means literally "I receive this feast." A variation is for your host to bow and say this; you should then reply with the same word and start eating.

Soup is usually served before the main course and is consumed quietly straight from the bowl. Pieces of tofu or fish that are in the soup should be picked out using chopsticks. During the meal, try tasting the various dishes one at a time, alternating each bite with some rice. Pickles should be eaten only after you have finished the other food.

# JAPAN (Cont'd)

## DINING OUT (Cont'd)

If you want more rice, leave a few grains of rice in your bowl and the waiter or waitress will refill it. If you do not want any more, be sure not to leave any grains of rice in the bowl. Generally, only second helpings of rice are offered, and it is considered impolite to ask for more food.

When you have finished, leave the chopsticks on the chopsticks rest. Never leave them standing in a bowl of rice or other food. When taking food from a communal serving bowl, reverse your chopsticks and use the blunt ends to be polite. It is rude to directly transfer a piece of food from your chopsticks to another person's chopsticks.

Drinks are refilled by your host or other guests. Never refill your own glass. When someone pours a drink for you, reciprocate by filling his/her glass. When a drink is being poured into your glass, hold your glass up off the table.

A traditional breakfast might include *miso* soup, raw eggs, grilled fish, pickles and tea.

Green tea is the most popular drink in Japan, although coffee has become more common in recent years. Western-style soft drinks are also popular.

*Sake*, a traditional drink in Japan, is made from rice. It is served slightly warmed in tiny cups. A *sake* cup should be held with one hand underneath the cup and the other around it.

Japan produces excellent beer.

Toasting is common. To toast someone, raise your glass and say *kanpai* (which literally means "drain the cup").

If you are sitting at a meal and have to blow your nose, it is polite to get up, excuse yourself and leave the table. Use a paper tissue to blow your nose, not a handkerchief. A handkerchief is used for wiping the fingers, the brow or as a napkin during a meal.

The main meal of the day is eaten in the evening. Popular Japanese specialties include *miso* (bean paste) soup, various kinds of noodles (*ramen*, *udon* and *soba*), *sashimi* (uncooked fish), *tofu* (soybean curd) and pork dishes. *Sushi* is a combination of fish (cooked or raw) and rice with vinegar. *Sukiyaki* is thinly-sliced beef cooked with vegetables in soy sauce and *sake*. *Tempura* is fish or vegetables dipped in batter and deep-fried.

Be aware that Japanese people generally do not eat desserts, except for fresh fruit.

To beckon a waiter/waitress, catch his/her eye and then nod your head downward.

At many restaurants, it is customary for men to sit cross-legged on the floor. Women sit either on their legs or they tuck their legs to one side.

Conversation at meals can be intermittent and there may be periods of complete silence, but don't be surprised if the atmosphere suddenly becomes lively. Do not rush to fill the silences.

# JAPAN (Cont'd)

## PUBLIC CUSTOMS

Showing an open mouth is considered impolite. Therefore, cover your mouth if you must cough or yawn. This belief is why many Japanese people cover their mouths when they laugh.

Do not stand with your hands in your pockets, especially if you are speaking to someone, as it is considered rude.

Pointing is done with the entire hand, palm down. Beckoning is done in the same way, but with wiggling all the fingers.

It is not proper to chew gum in public. Although many young people eat while walking in public, it is also considered bad manners. If you purchase food or drink at a street stand, eat or drink it at the stand.

Good posture is important, especially while seated. Sit up straight in a chair with both feet on the floor. You may cross your legs at the knee or at the ankles, but do not place an ankle over a knee.

Public displays of affection are frowned upon, although some young people disregard this sentiment. Foreigners create a bad impression when they engage in this type of behavior.

Shoes are removed before entering a Japanese home. Place them together, pointing away from the house.

Men and women do not wear shorts, except at resorts or while jogging.

Traditional sports include *sumo* wrestling, *judo*, *kendo* (fencing with bamboo poles) and *karate*. Baseball has been played in Japan since the 1870s and is considered the national sport.

Tipping is virtually nonexistent in Japan, and a tip may very well be refused. At hotels and restaurants, be prepared to have a service charge added to your bill.

# KOREA (REPUBLIC OF): HISTORICAL OVERVIEW

- Shilla kings united three warring kingdoms in 668 A.D., and they began to develop a Buddhist culture.

- A new kingdom, Koryo, came into power on the peninsula by 935. The name Korea comes from the original name of this kingdom.

- In 1392, Koryo fell to the Choson (or Yi) Dynasty, which ruled for more than 500 years.

- In the later period of Yi rule, China and Japan sought control of Korea, which Japan eventually attained. Japan annexed Korea in 1910.

- At the end of World War II, the peninsula was divided at the 38th parallel into two administrative zones, with the Soviet Union in charge in the North and the U.S. in charge in the South.

- In 1948, after attempts at holding nationwide elections failed, a pro-Western government was established in the South with Syngman Rhee becoming president. Kim Il Sung became head of North Korea.

- In June 1950, war broke out between the two newly created states, which lasted for three years. The U.S. and the United Nations sent troops to support South Korea. China sent troops to aid North Korea. A peace treaty has still not been signed, and violent border incidents have occurred over the years.

- Rhee resigned from office in 1960 under charges of political corruption. South Korea, subsequently, changed its form of government from a presidential to a cabinet system.

- John Chang was elected prime minister, but his government was ousted by a military coup, led by General Park Chung Kee, in 1961. Park ruled South Korea until October 1979 when he was assassinated. A military coup followed, and Chun Doo Hwan eventually emerged as president.

- A constitution adopted in 1987 established direct presidential elections and protection of human rights. Roh Tae Woo was elected president in that year.

- In 1990, peace talks were held between the prime ministers of both North and South Korea, the first since the 1950s. Talks continued despite tensions over North Korea's possession of nuclear weapons.

- In 1992, Kim Young Sam was elected as the first civilian to occupy the office of president in more than 30 years.

- South Korea endured major shockwaves in 1995 when two of its former presidents were convicted on corruption charges. Though this indicated the extent of political corruption in the past, the convictions gave hope that the rule of law and democratic principles was emerging in South Korea.

# KOREA

## INTRODUCTIONS

How Koreans greet you depends on your age and social status, relative to the greeter. A bow, usually accompanied by a handshake, is the traditional greeting. During a handshake, the left hand supporting the right arm is a sign of respect. The senior person offers to shake hands first, but the junior person bows first. Men always shake hands; however, women only sometimes do. A U.S. businesswoman should extend her hand first to Korean men and women.

When addressing a Korean, use "Mr.," "Miss," "Ms." or "Mrs." and the family name. In business situations, family names are customarily used. Only the closest friends in the same peer group are on a first name basis.

Koreans usually address each other by family name or full name followed by the honorific term *"songsaengnim"* (song-sang-nim), which means "respected person." Feel free to use this title, even when addressing someone in English.

Remember that Koreans have three names – first the family name, then the clan name and finally the given name. Some Koreans put their family names last when writing in the Roman alphabet.

A common greeting is *"Annyong haseyo?,"* meaning "Are you at peace?" To express great respect, the honorific form *"Annyong hashimnikka?"* is used.

Bring plenty of business cards printed in English on one side and Korean on the other. Business cards are exchanged (accepted and presented) with both hands, when professionals meet for the first time. When you receive a business card, keep it on the table in front of you or examine it carefully, then put it in a pocket above the waist as a sign of respect.

## SOCIAL TIPS AND CONVENTIONS

According to the Confucian ethic, status, dignity, courtesy and formality regulate social behavior. Hard work, piety and extreme modesty are valued. In business, the boss is all-powerful.

Since Koreans place great importance on family, especially sons, the family is an excellent topic of conversation. You may want to ask a Korean man if he is the eldest son in his family. If he is, he will be very proud of that prestigious role.

Public displays of anger are unacceptable in Korea. It is considered better to accept an injustice quietly in order to keep harmony. Criticism and public disagreements are avoided. Koreans may withhold bad news or disagreement or express them indirectly.

Koreans can be very direct, depending on their status and the person with whom they are communicating, yet they are also polite and proper. As a result, they sometimes agree with each other simply to preserve harmony. Emotional control and patience are vital.

# KOREA (Cont'd)

## SOCIAL TIPS AND CONVENTIONS (Cont'd)

Korea is a very interesting and beautiful country. This makes for good conversation topics, as does the country's rapid growth during the past 20 years, Korean food and the 1988 Seoul Olympics. Another good topic of discussion is sports. Soccer is popular in Korea, as is baseball, boxing, basketball, volleyball, tennis and swimming. *Taekwondo* (a form of martial arts) comes from Korea and a type of wrestling called *sirum* (where contestants are tied together during their match) is unique to Korea. You might want to avoid discussing socialism, communism or Korea's internal politics.

It is common to discuss personal subjects when first meeting. You may be asked "How old are you?," "What degree(s) do you have?," "Are you married?" or "How many children do you have?" People ask your age to fit you into a social hierarchy; the older you are, the higher your rank.

Koreans are quite friendly and proud of their personal achievements.

Because of their respect for humility, if you offer a compliment to a Korean, expect it to be graciously denied.

Friendship is highly valued and Koreans are quick to make friends. In fact, success depends greatly on social contacts.

## CUSTOMARY BUSINESS PRACTICES

Korean businesspeople maintain tight cultural ties. The best way to introduce yourself prior to traveling to Korea is by making contact with a Korean in your country who can serve as a reference for you. It would then be appropriate to send a letter of introduction.

Personal relationships are more important than contracts. Therefore, it is vital to have a long-term perspective in business, with your goal being to maintain and nurture personal contacts.

English is widely spoken in Korean business circles and most correspondence is in English. Catalogs and promotional materials written in English are acceptable.

Koreans expect people to be punctual for appointments, although many Koreans may not be punctual themselves.

Koreans will appreciate it if you show respect by using their business titles, e.g., Manager Kim, Director Lee. It will also help you to remember people, since over 50% of Korea's population is named Park, Lee or Kim.

Questions should be phrased carefully. Koreans tend to answer "Yes," frequently, because they place great importance on being polite. For example, instead of saying "Can the shipment be ready in four weeks?" ask "When can this shipment be ready?"

Interrupting someone is considered a desirable sign of eagerness among Koreans. Therefore, don't be insulted if you are interrupted by a Korean colleague.

# KOREA (Cont'd)

## CUSTOMARY BUSINESS PRACTICES (Cont'd)

It is common to give gifts in order to obtain favors, especially in the workplace. When you accept a gift you must reciprocate.

Conservative, Western-style dresses and business suits are the normal attire (fine fabrics, dark colors and white shirts or blouses). Conservative fashion is especially important for foreign businesswomen (hemlines, necklines, sleeves and makeup). Women should remember to avoid pantsuits. If your Korean counterpart removes his/her jacket, feel free to do so as well.

Businesses are generally open from 8:30 a.m. to 7:00 p.m., six days a week. Banks and government offices close earlier. The average work week for Koreans is 50 hours, one of the longest in the world.

## BUSINESS ENTERTAINING

It is customary in Korea to exchange business gifts on your first visit. You should wait for Koreans to give you your gift first. Open it only after you have left the group. It is a good idea to bring a gift made in your country, preferably something with your company's emblem, or bring a bottle of Scotch.

Most business entertaining in Korea is done in restaurants, rather than in private homes.

Women should wear loose skirts or dressy pants when going out with Koreans in the evening. The occasion may include an invitation to a restaurant or coffee shop where guests will be seated on cushions on the floor, and women won't be comfortable in a tight skirt.

Tipping is not expected, as a service charge is usually included in the bill.

Guests invited to a home should remove their shoes before entering. Visitors are seated on cushions on the *ondol* floors (floors that are heated from below). The guest receives the warmest or best position.

Guests customarily bring a small gift of something that can be served at the gathering. Wrapped gifts are not opened in front of the giver.

The host accompanies a guest to the door or outside of the house at the end of a visit.

## DINING OUT

The evening meal usually begins with appetizers. Cocktails are served with food and will not be offered before dinner. *Soju* and *magulli* are common alcoholic drinks to serve to guests before the main meal.

Each diner sits on an individual cushion which is placed on a floor mat under a separate low table. Do not sit with your feet straight out in front of you under the table. Men sit cross-legged and women tuck their legs to one side beside them.

# KOREA (Cont'd)

## DINING OUT (Cont'd)

Korean food is generally hot and spicy. Ginger, chilies and garlic are popular. Koreans appreciate it when Westerners try their food, although they are not offended if visitors are unable to eat it.

Rice and *kimch'i* (a spicy pickled cabbage) are staples at almost every meal. Rice is often combined with other ingredients, such as red beans or vegetables. Soups and fish are common. *Bulkogi*, strips of marinated and barbecued beef, is a common delicacy. Barley tea is served with most meals and fruit is a popular dessert.

Chopsticks and spoons are the most common eating utensils.

When you are offered more food, it is customary to decline politely twice and then accept. If you are entertaining Koreans, be sure to offer more food three times.

People in Korea pour drinks for one another, they never do so for themselves. If you pour a drink for your Korean friend, he/she will do the same for you. When someone is pouring your drink, lift up your glass. The junior person always pours for the senior (usually age is a mark of senior position). Formerly, drinking alcoholic beverages was only permissible for men, but this tradition is changing in large cities. Women may pour drinks for men, but don't typically pour for other women.

Loud talking and laughter is permissible during business entertaining, although it is generally not permissible at other times. After dinner there may be singing and laughter. If there is singing after dinner, try to go along with the fun – no matter how poorly you sing!

During dinner, a small communal cup may be passed around. One should drink from the cup and pass it along. Also, it is polite to fill one's neighbor's small soy sauce dish.

## PUBLIC CUSTOMS

Good posture is considered to be very important. Avoid slouching or putting your feet up on a table or chair.

Keep in mind that emotional control is considered to be very important. As a result, laughter is used to disguise many emotions, such as embarrassment, anger, frustration and even fear.

Older people are treated with the utmost respect in Korea. You should stand when an elderly person enters the room and greet him/her with a slight bow. However, don't remain standing too long, causing you to look down on them. Keep a respectable distance from an older person when you are seated and never tap them on the shoulder or touch them on the head.

It is not uncommon to see Korean men (usually younger) hold hands or walk with a hand on the other's shoulder as an expression of friendship. However, it is not appropriate to touch older people or members of the opposite sex.

Korean society is male-dominated. Men generally have priority. They go through doors first, women may help them on with their coats, etc.

# KOREA (Cont'd)

## PUBLIC CUSTOMS (Cont'd)

When handing an object to someone or receiving one, you should use both hands (or the right hand grasped at the wrist or the forearm by the left).

Koreans beckon by extending the arm, palm down, and making a scratching motion. Beckoning with the index finger is considered very rude.

Facial expressions are even more important than body language. Therefore, eye contact is very important.

In general, people do not wait in line for things. Pushing and crowding is common and not considered to be impolite.

Eating while walking on the street is considered inappropriate for adults.

# KYRGYZSTAN: HISTORICAL OVERVIEW

- The Republic of Kyrgyzstan is located on a western spur of the Tien Shan Mountains. The Kyrgyz people have dwelled in the area since at least the 16th century and have, until recently, lived a nomadic life.

- The Kyrgyz people came under the nominal control of the Kokand Khanate in the 18th century. This lasted until the 1850s, when Russia began to colonize the region. The Kyrgyz people then revolted against the colonists in 1916, but the revolt was put down with great force.

- Following the Russian Revolution, this area became part of Soviet Turkistan. After several changes in classification, it was finally recognized in 1936 as a constituent republic, the Kirgiz Soviet Socialist Republic.

- During the Soviet years, nomadic life ended as the people settled on collective and state farms. Industrialization and mining increased the number of urban jobs, although these were mostly occupied by non-Kyrgyz residents. The Kyrgyz people generally preferred to remain in farming or stock raising.

- *Perestroika* did not affect Kyrgyzstan until 1990, when ethnic riots broke out along the border with Uzbekistan. The riots damaged the standing of Absamat Masaliev, the *Kyrgyz Communist Party* leader. The opposition organized itself into a new party, *Democratic Kyrgyzstan*, led by Askar Akayev, who in the 1991 elections defeated Masaliev and became President.

- In August 1991, as part of the attempted coup against Gorbachev, the local communists tried to depose President Akayev but were unsuccessful. Akayev subsequently banned the *Communist Party* from government offices.

- Despite the drop in the standard of living since the breakup of the Soviet Union, Akayev remained very popular. He pushed democratic reforms and tried to create a market economy, though he was frustrated by the legislature in these efforts.

- Akayev dismissed the old Supreme Soviet and proposed a new legislature. The proposal was passed by referendum, and in 1995, elections were held with about 80% of the candidates running as independents.

- Over the past two years, thousands of Russians have left Kyrgyzstan to return to Russia, leaving many technical jobs unfilled. As a gesture to help stem this tide of emigration, Akayev has proposed restoring Russian as a second national language with the first remaining Kyrgyz.

- Because of its democratic reforms, Kyrgyzstan received more per capita U.S. aid than any of the other ex-Soviet republics. Additionally, it has received $240 million from the World Bank.

# KYRGYZSTAN

## INTRODUCTIONS

The Kyrgyz greet each other with the standard greeting of *"Salamatsyzby"* ("Hello") and a handshake. Adult men greet each other with *"Assalamu alikum"* ("Peace be upon you"); the correct response is *"Waalaikum assalaam"* ("And peace be upon you also").

Women in business greet each other with a handshake, while older women embrace each other and kiss children. A Kyrgyz woman bows to an older man, particularly a relative of her husband.

When addressing an older person by his/her first name, you should add the patronymic (fathers first name with the suffix *"-ovich"* for son or *"-ovna"* for daughter).

Another custom is to greet a person by his/her father's first name followed by *"uulu"* (son) or *"kyzy"* (daughter) along with the person's own given name, for example, *Kadyrbek uulu Ulan* (Kadyrbek's son, Ulan).

Special titles such as *"Agai"* or *"Baikay"* (older brother) or *"Ejay"* (older sister) are used with the title being placed at the end (i.e., *Salamatsyzby, Gulsara Ejay*).

*"Kosh"* ("Good-bye") or *"Rakhmat"* ("Thank you") are customarily said when departing.

## SOCIAL TIPS AND CONVENTIONS

Kyrgyz is the official language and two major dialects are spoken (northern and southern). There are also various regional dialects spoken among the Kyrgyz. The language has been replaced and reestablished many times. It was based on Arabic in 1924, Latin script in 1928 and Cryllic symbols in 1941. Russian is also spoken widely in urban areas.

The Kyrgyz are generally tolerant, soft-spoken, exceptionally hospitable and courteous people.

The Kyrgyz business, social and political network is structured along extended family lines. The family network structure is often referred to as "tribalism" and is gradually changing to include non-family members.

The Kyrgyz socialize at home or in the office, but never in a restaurant. There are several types of homes ranging from modest single-family dwellings or apartments, to *bohzooi* or *yurtas* (round tents).

Community life in rural areas centers on daily prayers at the mosque where local celebrations, festivals and religious activities take place.

The Kyrgyz have very strong family ties. The nuclear family consists of the husband and wife, brothers and sisters, children and grandparents. The elderly are cared for at home and all the generations show much respect to the elderly.

The Kyrgyz enjoy a variety of sports. They engage in *Aht Chabysh* (long distance races), *Dzhorgosalysh* (betting races), *Oodarysh* (wrestling on horseback), *Tyin Enmei* (falconry on horseback) and *Kyz dzharysh* (girls races).

# KYRGYZSTAN (Cont'd)

## SOCIAL TIPS AND CONVENTIONS (Cont'd)

The Kyrgyz also enjoy outdoor activities such as fishing, hunting, picnicking, skiing and hiking in the mountains and on Lake Issyk-kul. Most families have mountain *dachas* (cottages). The Kyrgyzstan people are fond of ballet, drama, concerts, movies, the circus, art galleries and museums. Urban Kyrgyz often gather to eat, drink and talk.

Most people who live in rural areas do not own cars because of the expense of the fuel. Villagers walk or ride donkeys, horses or horse drawn carts. Buses run between major cities and many areas are connected by train. In urban areas commuters use electric trolleys, buses, taxis and minibuses.

Urban areas have networks of telephones but they are largely unreliable. Most people own a television and a radio; however newspapers and television broadcasts are received from neighboring countries.

Two major industries are agriculture (cotton and tobacco) and mining (gold, antimony, uranium, coal and natural gas). The country is in the midst of a transition to a market economy.

## CUSTOMARY BUSINESS PRACTICES

Traditionally, people have been considered to be more important than time schedules. However, this attitude is changing as the new generation of bankers, students and merchants become more concerned with the value of time.

Business offices are open from 8:00 a.m. to 5:00 p.m. and food stores are open from 7:00 a.m. to 8:00 p.m.

Tours of facilities and factories are common at initial meetings.

Usually, all officials who are involved in your business negotiations will attend one large meeting rather than having many separate meetings. Often, however, only the senior person will speak.

Fruit, alcohol, books, candy or items with your company's logo are all appropriate business gifts.

Business cards are exchanged, and it is advisable to have cards printed in Russian on one side and in English on the other.

## BUSINESS ENTERTAINING

The Kyrgyz are, for the most part, Sunni Muslim and the consumption of alcohol and pork is strictly prohibited by their religion. However, although alcohol is forbidden, most Kyrgyz families drink anyway.

The Kyrgyz are known for their hospitality. A guest is given *tapochki* (slippers) upon removing his/her shoes.

Kyrgyz culture places a high value on establishing social relationships during business negotiations. Casual and extended conversation with tea or a long dinner is of considerable value.

# KYRGYZSTAN (Cont'd)

## BUSINESS ENTERTAINING (Cont'd)

Business meetings often lead to invitations to meals. These meals can last many hours, and include countless courses and countless toasts.

## DINING OUT

When invited to someone's home, it is advisable not to arrive before noon.

Kyrgyz families eat three meals a day together, as their schedule allows. The farthest seat facing the entrance is reserved for the most honored individual. Women sit with their legs tucked under themselves, or to the side covered by a skirt.

Regardless of how people eat, they first wash their hands. Everyone eats from a common plate located in the center of the floor or the table. Rural families may eat from a communal dish *pa kirghizi* (without utensils).

Breakfast typically consists of tea, honey and bread with butter or *varynya* (preserves).

Many popular Kyrgyz dishes consist of *nahn* (flat bread) served with lamb, carrots, onions and garlic. Other popular foods include: vegetables such as potatoes, tomatoes, cucumbers, carrots, peppers and squash; fruits such as grapes, melons and apples; starches such as breads, rice and noodles; and meats including beef, mutton and chicken. *Chai* (tea) is served in *piallas* (bowls) with every meal.

## PUBLIC CUSTOMS

Pointing with one's finger is considered impolite. Gestures are made with the entire hand to call someone, to point or to beckon.

Blowing one's nose in public, chewing gum, yelling and yawning are all considered impolite.

Men wear western-style clothing, but they also wear a *kolpak* (a traditional white wool pointed hat) which protects the head of the wearer, and stands for the national sign of patriotism as well. The high point of the *kolpak* represents the mountains.

During the winter, men generally wear a *tumak* (Russian fur hat). A *tebetei* (fur hat decorated with fox a tail) was once commonly worn, but this style has become expensive, although it is very popular.

Traditional Kyrgyz clothing (colorful silk dresses and head scarves) is worn by women in rural areas. Silver jewelry is preferred over gold because it is closer in color to white, and it is believed that the color white brings good luck. The Kyrgyz also believe that silver protects against misfortune.

The national holidays include New Year's Day (January 1), *Orozo Ait* (feast at the end of Ramadan), International Women's Day (March 8), Victory Day (May 9, for the ending of World War II), *Kurban Ait* (Day of Remembrance), Independence Day (September 9), Constitution Day (May 5), Christmas (January 7) and Easter.

# MALAYSIA: HISTORICAL OVERVIEW

- Malaysia received centuries of cultural influence from India and China.

- Portuguese traders arrived in 1511 and captured Malacca.

- The Dutch followed the Portuguese in 1641, and were, in turn, followed by the British, who acquired the island of Penang in 1786. By 1795, the British had taken over most of the Malay peninsula's west coast. By the early 20th century, Britain had gained control of all the Malay states including those on Borneo as colonies or protectorates.

- The British introduced Chinese and Indian labor as well as the rubber industry to the region.

- The Japanese occupied Malaysia during World War II, which spurred nationalist sentiment.

- The period after World War II was marked by a 12-year Communist insurrection, which led to Great Britain granting independence to Malaysia in 1957. The nation was then called the Federation of Malaya.

- Six years later the Federation of Malaya and the former British colonies of Singapore, Sarawak and North Borneo (Sabah) united to become Malaysia. Tension between the Malay-dominated government in Malaya and the Chinese-dominated government in Singapore led to the creation of an independent Singapore in 1965.

- Following the 1969 widespread racial rioting, the government changed the constitution in 1971 to give Malays more rights. A quota system was established that required Malay participation and representation at specified levels in government, business and education.

- Malaysia has two different and distinct land regions: the Malaysia Peninsula and East Malaysia, which is located on the island of Borneo.

- Elections in 1974 resulted in victory for the *National Front*. This party continued to rule in the 1980s although it experienced internal leadership struggles. Another problem during this time was the rise of Islamic militancy.

- In 1989, the Malaysian government had two big successes. It agreed to buy $1.7 billion worth of arms from the United Kingdom, and it secured the surrender of communist insurgency leaders.

- Prime Minister Mahathir Mohamed, a talented and shrewd politician, is interested in speeding up the development of this already strong economy. Ethnic tensions are fading, but the challenges posed by radical Islam remain.

# MALAYSIA

*There are three distinct cultures in Malaysia – Malay (53%), Chinese (32%) and Indian (15%). The official religion is Islam. However, the Chinese people are mostly Buddhist and the Indians are mostly Hindu. Each culture has its own social, business and greeting customs. As a result, the best guideline is to follow the example of your host and others around you.*

## INTRODUCTIONS

Generally, a simple, not overly firm handshake is the customary greeting. A lengthy greeting is a sign of an old friendship.

Women should be greeted with a nod and a smile. Chinese people of both sexes will shake hands, but Malays and Indians will not. If a Chinese woman wishes to shake hands, she will extend her hand first. Handshakes between men and women are particularly rare among members of the older generation. Generally, if you are a businessman, avoid initiating contact with Malaysian businesswomen, but you may shake a woman's hand if she offers it. If you are a businesswoman, nod and smile.

Malays will often bow slightly when greeting others. Men may engage in a *salaam* ritual, in which they offer both hands outstretched, touch each other's hands and then bring them back to touch their own chests.

Indians may greet you with the *namaste* (placing the hands in a prayer-like position, chest high and bowing slightly).

Using "Mr." and "Mrs." is appropriate in addressing others. Titles are often used, as in the case of the Prime Minister, who presents himself as "Dr. Mahathir Mohamad," but is referred to as "Mr. Prime Minister."

In traditional Malaysian names, the family name comes first. For example, *"Osman bin Mohamad"* would be called *"Mr. Osman."*

You can address a Moslem man as *"Encik"* or a woman as *"Cik,"* followed by the individual's name to show respect.

A common greeting is *"Salamut pagi"* ("Good morning"); a more casual greeting is *"Halo"* ("Hello").

At the first business meeting, it is customary to present business cards. Remember that visitors should handle or receive papers, cards and samples with the right hand only.

## SOCIAL TIPS AND CONVENTIONS

The Malay people are very friendly. English is commonly spoken, but is second to Malaysian.

Many Malaysians are fatalistic. In addition, a person's ancestral background is often considered to be important to social status and to future opportunities.

It is important to note that Indians indicate agreement by moving their head quickly from side to side (many Westerners misread this gesture as meaning "no").

# MALAYSIA (Cont'd)

## SOCIAL TIPS AND CONVENTIONS (Cont'd)

Small talk and the exchange of personal information will most likely dominate the conversations of the first meeting. Don't be surprised if you are questioned about your health, family or children. Wives, however, are not an acceptable conversation topic.

The Malays are proud of their people and culture. They appreciate comments about their country, city or enterprise. Family, sports, food and travel are also good conversation topics. Your host's business or social achievements are excellent topics of discussion.

Avoid discussing matters that are religious, political or racial in nature. Also, don't compare standards of living in Malaysia with those in the West.

As in other Muslim cultures, the left hand is reserved for personal hygiene and is therefore considered "unclean." It should not be used for touching others, for eating or for passing along gifts or other objects.

If you see a small rug that is either silk or wool and has a decorative design of floral patterns in a Muslim's office or home, be certain not to stand on it or touch it with your feet, as it is most likely a prayer rug.

To cover up their feelings of embarrassment, people in Malaysia may smile or laugh at someone else's discomfort or misfortune.

## CUSTOMARY BUSINESS PRACTICES

Malaysia is a multi-ethnic country: the Chinese people are the predominant residents in urban areas as well as in business, and Malays (mostly Muslim) predominantly live in rural areas.

Business activities and attitudes toward work are often affected by folk beliefs, customs and the belief in fate.

Respect is extremely important among Malaysians. Malays recognize rank and status when dealing with each other. In their own language, they carefully differentiate importance by using special terminology or honorific terms. Visitors are expected to show respect, if not outright humility, toward the host.

Be careful not to appear condescending to your Malaysian business counterparts. Also, never underestimate their knowledge of any topic.

The overall atmosphere of the first business meeting is likely to be informal, warm and friendly. When a Malaysian smiles, it indicates a desire to please and demonstrates respect and consideration for the visitor. It is best to go out of your way to be approachable, personal and friendly in return.

In Malaysian business negotiations, a relationship factor is integrated into the bargaining process and it weighs heavily in business transactions. When Malays field a team of negotiators, they enjoy the cooperative effort involved, which can overshadow their competitive interests or their desire for economic gain.

# MALAYSIA (Cont'd)

## CUSTOMARY BUSINESS PRACTICES (Cont'd)

Negotiations are conducted in a spirit of friendship, civility and pleasantry. Mutual respect is emphasized. Be aware, however, that Malays can appear manipulative. Yet they will take offense at the slightest loss of self-esteem, which can present a challenging situation for the visitor. It is more important to be "nice" than to be effective.

During business conversations, the host may serve nonalcoholic beverages. It is best to accept this sign of hospitality by drinking at least some of the beverage offered.

It is also quite acceptable to weave business and personal topics together which may project a favorable image.

Business is conducted at a slower pace in Malaysia and is never completed in the first meeting. You should plan to leave after an hour or so, but not before arranging a follow-up meeting. Expect that the second meeting may well include a business lunch.

Be prepared for frequent interruptions during a business meeting. Some of these interruptions may even include calling participants out of the meeting to see superiors or to answer the phone. It is important to maintain a good sense of humor throughout the process.

Deadlines are often extended in Malaysia. If you have critical timelines, it is a good idea to remind the Malays regularly of your deadlines.

Decisions take place at the top. Middle management either acts in a consultative role or executes directives from higher up. Authority receives unquestioned loyalty.

You will discover that a consensus has been reached by the enthusiastic response among lower level negotiators. Actual notification will come from the decision maker at a higher level. Either party may propose drafting a written agreement. The deal is firm when both sides sign the contract.

Malay businesspeople are most likely to be impressed with projects that build their company's image or are proven concepts.

Presentations should be complete. Take nothing for granted. An audio/visual presentation will be impressive to your Malaysian counterparts. After you establish a mutual trust, it will become possible to get rid of some of the details.

Appropriate business dress is a jacket, a long-sleeved shirt, a tie and trousers for men. Light fabrics will add to your comfort. Because of the climate, jackets are not necessary, except for meetings with high government officials or receptions. Women wear modest light short-sleeved dresses. Women should not wear slacks, shorts or sleeveless dresses and should avoid loud or garish colors or patterns.

Businesses are generally open from 8:30 a.m. to 5:00 p.m., Monday through Friday. Some businesses are open on Saturday. In many cases, businesses close for one hour at lunch.

The best time to schedule appointments is usually after 2:30 p.m.

# MALAYSIA (Cont'd)

## CUSTOMARY BUSINESS PRACTICES (Cont'd)

Strict punctuality is not valued by Malaysians. You may find yourself waiting, perhaps for as long as half an hour for your appointment. Therefore, it is important to be patient. However, punctuality is expected and scheduling appointments is advisable. It is best to arrive on time as a sign of reliability and practicality.

## BUSINESS ENTERTAINING

Malays appreciate entertainment which they believe enhances personal relationships. Therefore, entertainment is an important part of business arrangements. In fact, important meetings should be followed by a dinner or a lunch.

It is rare to be entertained in someone's home. Business entertainment usually takes place at a restaurant.

Business lunches are quite common, although it is not considered polite to discuss business during the meal. Eating is considered private and will be accompanied by very light conversation. Speeches are sometimes expected at dinner.

Dinners are usually for larger groups and will not include women. Business is not discussed. You should reciprocate by hosting events such as lunches or dinners.

Spouses are rarely included in business entertaining.

Visitors should demonstrate a restraint by avoiding broad gestures, loud outbursts or a show of emotion.

It is not common to present gifts, but most Malaysians would appreciate receiving an item from your company or country. Gifts should not be presented on the first visit and alcohol as well as inexpensive mementos should be avoided altogether. Never present the gift to the wife of your Malay host.

It is a good idea to send a thank-you note or flowers following a meal.

## DINING OUT

When seating guests at a Malay table, the seat of honor is to the right of the host. If seated on the floor, men should sit cross-legged and women should sit with their legs tucked under themselves.

Do not begin eating until invited by the host to do so.

In Malaysia, cuisines vary. Hindus and some Buddhists do not eat beef. Muslims do not eat pork. Alcoholic beverages are forbidden to Muslims and are generally not offered to guests, although it is not necessary that you abstain.

When toasting or when handing a dish to another person, use the left hand to support the right arm as a sign of respect.

# MALAYSIA (Cont'd)

## DINING OUT (Cont'd)

Follow the lead of the host in deciding which hand to use to eat food. Malays use only their right hand and spoons. You may use a fork in the left hand to push food onto a spoon held in the right hand. Indians use the fingers of the right hand (never soiling their fingers above the first knuckle). Guests will usually be provided with a fork and spoon. Using the left hand to eat is acceptable among Chinese people. When in doubt, use only your right hand.

When dining among the Chinese people, be aware that placing your chopsticks across your plate indicates that you are still hungry. (To indicate you have had enough to eat, place them on the small stand instead.) Also, waving chopsticks in the air to gesture is considered to be rude and sticking a chopstick upright in a bowl of rice is considered to be a bad omen. Slurping soup and belching during a meal are acceptable.

It is considered rude to blow your nose or clear your throat at the dinner table or in public.

Leave food on your plate to indicate that you are full or you will be given more.

To get a waiter's attention, raise your hand. Avoid shouting or pointing.

## PUBLIC CUSTOMS

If you are invited to someone's home, be aware that it is proper etiquette to remove your shoes and sunglasses before entering the house. Shoes are also removed before entering a mosque.

The Malay culture is predominantly and officially Muslim. Women are treated with deference and should dress modestly.

Elderly people are given great respect. One should open doors for them, give up a seat for them, etc.

Casual touching between men and women should be avoided.

People do not line up for things (buses, etc.). Instead, pushing and crowding is both common and acceptable.

Avoid touching the head of a Malay or Indian person. That is where they believe the spirit or soul resides.

Pointing the sole of the shoe at someone is considered rude. Therefore, try to keep your feet flat on the ground and avoid using your feet for moving objects.

Malays consider it a sign of anger if a person stands with their hands on their hips.

Do not smack your closed fist into the palm of the other hand. It is considered a rude gesture.

Malays consider it rude to point with the forefinger. Instead, point with the thumb with the other four fingers curled into the palm.

# MYANMAR (BURMA): HISTORICAL OVERVIEW

- The Burmans were a powerful force in this fertile coastal region by the mid-11th century. Under the leadership of King Anawrata, they established a national capital in the central city of Pagan.

- The dominance of the Burmans was resented by the Shan people of northeastern Burma, who, in the late 13th century, enlisted the aid of the Mongols. Sent by Khubilai Khan, a force of Mongol cavalrymen invaded and destroyed the Burman kingdom.

- The Mongols turned rule over to the Shan, who tried repeatedly to establish a permanent state. From the 13th through the mid-18th century, Burma endured repeated civil wars between the Shans, Burmans and Mons, with no group emerging victorious.

- In 1753, a warlike Burman kingdom held power. The kingdom invaded Thailand and, in the early 1800s, also invaded Assam to the west. The British East India Company, which controlled Assam at the time, sent British troops to push the Burmans out of the region. The British were successful in this First Burmese War, and the Burmans surrendered some coastal land and permitted the establishment of a British minister in the capital of Ava.

- The Burmans treated the British with contempt and interfered with colonial commerce, which led to the Second Burmese War in 1852. These same problems led to the Third Burmese War in 1885-1886, which ended Burman rule. The country was governed as a province of British India until 1937, when it became a Crown Colony.

- The Japanese invaded Burma in 1942 and set up an oppressive administration. The Allies eventually liberated the country in mid-1945, and, after the war, the British tried for a brief time to resume control before agreeing to give Burma its independence in 1947.

- Power was in the hands of the *Anti-Fascist People's Freedom League (AFPFL)*, a left-wing nationalist group. Strife within the party, however, enabled the military, commanded by Ne Win, to take control of the country in 1958. In a few years, Ne Win had abolished existing political parties, imprisoned several communist leaders and announced that he would make Burma a socialist – although not a communist – state.

- Ne Win was able to withstand the Chinese-supported rebels, and his repressive, unpopular, inept government ruled through the 1960s, 1970s and early 1980s. Ethnic insurgents, students and urban residents began to press for an end to the dictatorship, and, in 1988, a long series of massive demonstrations occurred.

- Finally, in 1990, the military agreed to free elections, but when the opposition party, the *National League for Democracy*, won 80% of the vote, the army refused to surrender power and kept the opposition leader, Aung San Suu Kyi, under house arrest.

- The military has since been strengthened by arms purchases from China, and the State Law and Order Restoration Council (SLORC) has neutralized various rebel groups by signing individual ceasefire agreements.

# MYANMAR (BURMA)

## INTRODUCTIONS

Do not shake hands with a woman unless she initiates the handshake.

Verbal greetings usually take the form of rhetorical questions about one's health and mood. Smiling in return is the accepted response.

Burmans are generally curious and will not hesitate to ask personal questions immediately after meeting someone.

## SOCIAL TIPS AND CONVENTIONS

Burmese is the official language and English is a second language but has recently declined in usage.

Burmans are very kind to foreigners, especially if one attempts to speak their language.

Burmans are proud of their history, which does not include many scientific advances.

Theravada Buddhism is the principal religion and has a profound effect on Burmese life. An important concept is that of *kan* or *kharma*, which holds that actions in past lives affect the present life. Therefore, one should behave according to Buddhist precepts so that future lives will be blessed. *Kan*, though, allows people to attribute shortcomings to powers beyond their control.

Buddhist monks are the exemplars for society and are treated with great respect. They are not allowed to touch females. Nearly all Burmese men spend some time in a monastery.

Women normally dress in a *sarong* (a wrap-around skirt) with a short blouse on top. Men also wear *sarong* tied in front, often with a Western-style shirt.

Burmans tend to be more emotional than rational. Alhough they are open and carefree, they are also very proud and are easily insulted.

Public transportation is unsafe and unreliable. Mini-pickups are used as taxis and are generally uncomfortable and in bad condition. Travel by train and river steamboat is also difficult and unreliable.

## CUSTOMARY BUSINESS PRACTICES

The work week is Monday through Friday, typically from 9:00 a.m. to 4:30 p.m. Westerners may be unhappy with the productivity of workers, although in general their performance is improving. The literacy rate has risen to 82% in the past two decades.

Traditionally-oriented Burmans are uncomfortable on committees, preferring governance by seniority or hierarchy. Egalitarianism is perceived as a threat to harmony.

## CUSTOMARY BUSINESS PRACTICES (Cont'd)

The word *anade* describes the behavioral pattern of withdrawal when faced with the embarrassment of a direct affront. Burmans are also embarrassed by compliments. Direct praise and criticism, therefore, can create discomfort and lead to problems. It may be difficult to realize when you have made an error because Burmans tend to smile when they are embarrassed.

The initial meeting is a time to start building a trusting relationship and often, little or no business is discussed.

Strong relationships are necessary to accomplish business goals in Burma. If someone does a favor for you, it is expected that you will return the favor without needing to be asked.

Buddhist tradition considers discussing money tasteless and the result is that services and goods are sometimes given for free.

Burmans prefer to do all business face-to-face rather than over the phone.

It is important to get names and rank correct when speaking with government officials, which you will almost surely have to do when conducting business in Myanmar.

The exchange of business cards is standard practice.

Neatness is key for business attire. Men should wear a tie and a long-sleeved shirt and women should wear suits.

Burmans are quite superstitious and astrological calculations are sometimes made prior to business negotiations.

## BUSINESS ENTERTAINING

Business entertaining is usually done in hotels and restaurants. You may, however, be invited to a large feast in someone's private home.

Gifts are expected only on special occasions, such as someone's retirement.

## DINING OUT

Some popular foods are oil-based curries, salted fish, salad and rice. Burmans are not heavy drinkers.

When entering someone's home, take off your shoes at the entrance. An offer to help with the dishes will be appreciated, although it will probably not be accepted. The host will admire any efforts you make to play with and to entertain the children.

Seating arrangements are not important and you will usually seat yourself.

# MYANMAR (BURMA) (Cont'd)

## PUBLIC CUSTOMS

Burmans will lose respect for you if you show too much emotion. Both anger and affection must not be overtly displayed.

Be careful not to point your feet at someone as it is considered rude.

Loud, boastful body language is offensive as is hugging or kissing in public.

Teasing is common among friends and is a sign of intimacy.

Staring is accepted and is common and is sure to be encountered by a Westerner, especially Caucasians.

Be sure to show respect for Buddhist images. Posing for pictures in front of them or climbing such images is considered highly offensive.

Women should never ride on the roofs of boats or other vehicles as this is a sign of looseness or coarseness.

Spitting is the ultimate gesture of contempt.

Independence Day is celebrated on January 4.

# NEW ZEALAND: HISTORICAL OVERVIEW

- The first phase of New Zealand's history is the Maori phase, before the arrival of the Europeans. The Maori, the first settlers, arrived in a series of migrations from the vicinity of Tahiti about 1,000 years ago. The period of the so-called "Great Migration" of the Maoris took place during the 13th and 14th centuries. Maori culture developed mainly on the warmer North Island with little outside interference.

- In 1642, the Dutch explorer Abel Tasman discovered New Zealand, but he did not go ashore. He called the islands *Staten Landt*. The name was later changed by Dutch geographers to the Dutch term for New Zealand (*Nieuw Zeeland*), after the Dutch province of Zeeland.

- The next contact that New Zealand had with Europe was when Captain James Cook of England arrived in 1769. However, sealers and whalers were the first to settle in the area. As a result of disease as well as the introduction of firearms into Maori warfare, the Maori population began to decline dramatically. At the same time, European settlers began to demand that the British protect them from the Maoris.

- In 1840, the Maoris ceded sovereignty to the British in return for legal protection and rights to perpetual ownership of Maori lands (only the Crown could buy land from the Maoris, while an individual settler could not). According to the agreement, the British were supposed to mediate disputes between the settlers and the Maoris. However, they did not do so and skirmishes broke out, further reducing the Maori population and weakening the Maoris influence in local affairs.

- British colonization proceeded rapidly and by 1852, internal self-government was granted and provincial parliaments governed the area. The discovery of gold in 1861 brought new waves of settlers. In 1877, a central administration was established and in 1907, New Zealand became an independent dominion within the British Commonwealth.

- New Zealand was one of the most progressive countries at the end of the last century, introducing old-age pensions, a minimum wage, arbitration courts, child health care services as well as giving women the right to vote in 1893.

- New Zealand fought with distinction in both world wars. New Zealand's troops also fought with the allies in Korea and alongside the U.S. in Vietnam. Involvement in Vietnam triggered a national debate on foreign policy and forces were withdrawn in 1971. Shortly thereafter, New Zealand also withdrew from the Southeast Asia Treaty Organization.

- In recent years, New Zealand has taken a strong antinuclear stand, refusing entry to U.S. nuclear-powered ships and condemning French nuclear testing in the Pacific. As a result, the U.S. dropped New Zealand from the ANZUS treaty agreements and French agents sank a vessel belonging to an antinuclear group in Auckland's harbor.

- In March 1995, Prime Minister Bolger met with President Clinton and overall relations appear to have mended.

# NEW ZEALAND

## INTRODUCTIONS

While a handshake is the standard greeting, be aware that styles of greeting can be quite unpredictable in New Zealand. The manner of greeting can vary from U.S.-style openness and Maori graciousness to British reserve. The style of greeting usually depends on the individuals involved and the circumstances. Generally, New Zealanders wait to be approached, but are very friendly once they are greeted.

In formal situations such as a business meeting or dinner party, a man usually waits for a woman to offer her hand.

The somewhat formal greeting, "How do you do?," is often used when people first meet. General verbal greetings include "Good day" (pronounced "Gidday") or a simple "Hello" or "Hi."

Titles such as "Mr.," "Mrs." or "Miss" or a professional title followed by the last name should be used at first meetings. Most people use first names after an initial introduction.

Among the Maori, people sometimes greet each other with a hug or the traditional *hongi* – pressing the noses together with the eyes closed and making a low "mm-mm" sound. The *hongi* is not used with non-Maoris.

## SOCIAL TIPS AND CONVENTIONS

English and Maori are the official languages of New Zealand, although Maori is used primarily for Maori ceremonies and other special occasions.

The English language is spoken in New Zealand includes several distinctive expressions. Also, some Maori words have been adopted into English. For example, a *Kiwi* is a New Zealander and a white person is a *Pakeha*.

There are words or phrases that are not commonly used in the U.S., such as "over the road" ("across the street"), "pop downtown" ("go downtown"), "go to the loo" ("go to the bathroom") and "come around" ("come over"). The hood of a car is called a "bonnet," a "lift" is an elevator, a "bathroom" is a place to take a bath and "petrol" is gasoline. If someone says that you are a "mate" or a "hard case," consider it a compliment because he/she means that you are a "friend" or a "funny person."

New Zealanders are open, friendly and hospitable, and their attitude toward life is relaxed and informal. A New Zealander is more likely to discuss leisure activities and family interests rather than occupations, incomes or career objectives.

New Zealanders are very proud of their country as well as their values of self-reliance and practicality. The country, the culture and the area in which you are staying make good topics for conversation.

While many Maoris have been integrated into mainstream society, they retain roots to their land and ethnic group. The Maoris are proud of their Polynesian culture, which emphasizes humility, truth and a strong sense of community.

# NEW ZEALAND (Cont'd)

## SOCIAL TIPS AND CONVENTIONS (Cont'd)

Good conversation topics also include sports and politics. Many New Zealanders participate in outdoor, non-competitive sports such as hiking, fishing or sailing. New Zealanders appreciate lively political discussions, especially with those who maintain strong beliefs or convictions. Hold up your end of the debate without becoming personal or insulting.

Avoid bringing up racial topics or the treatment of the Maori as well as religion, personal questions or nuclear energy. Also, be aware that New Zealanders try to establish a distinct identity from Australia and that there exists a strong rivalry between the two countries (therefore, make a point to never confuse them). Finally, avoid any praise of Australia or Australians.

New Zealanders do not like to stand too close to others or to touch during conversation. Also, New Zealanders speak softly and do not open their mouths wide when speaking. They maintain more of the traditional British reserve than their Australian counterparts do.

## CUSTOMARY BUSINESS PRACTICES

It is advisable not to try and organize a business trip during the months of December and January, when most people are on vacation (these are the summer months).

Appointments should be arranged in advance. Punctuality is important. In fact, it is advisable for foreign visitors to arrive a few minutes early for any engagement.

In New Zealand, the pace of business is generally slower than that found in the U.S., but faster than in Australia.

Be aware that the accumulation of objective facts is the most important element of negotiating and little importance is given to subjective feelings. New Zealanders are direct but friendly when negotiating and will not hesitate to say "no."

There is a lot of individualism in decision making and individual initiative and achievement are emphasized. At the same time, the individual will follow company policy, so that dealing with different executives at different times will not disrupt business.

Rank is minimized in business and equality is emphasized.

Business dress is somewhat formal and conservative. Most businessmen wear a dark suit and tie and businesswomen wear a dark skirt suit with a white blouse.

Usually, business hours are from 9:00 a.m. until 5:30 p.m., Monday to Friday and then from 9:00 a.m. until 12:30 p.m. on Saturday.

## NEW ZEALAND (Cont'd)

### BUSINESS ENTERTAINING

Introductory meetings usually take place in an office but, after that, you may suggest meeting over lunch at a restaurant or in a hotel. Lunch appointments are usually for conducting business, while dinner engagements are more relaxed occasions for socializing. Spouses are normally included in invitations.

Entertaining in the home is popular and common, even more so than in the U.S. New Zealanders enjoy cooking and, therefore, will often invite guests for dinner.

Summer barbecues (called "barbies") are very popular and are usually held on weekends. Inviting people for "afternoon tea," at about 3:00 p.m., is also popular. Even if not invited for afternoon tea or a meal, guests will always be offered refreshments.

Dinner guests almost always bring a gift. Acceptable gifts include wine, flowers, a potted plant or a box of chocolates. Gifts should be simple since ostentation usually meets with disapproval.

In restaurants, waiters will not hurry unless asked to do so since they consider it their job to let diners take their time.

People avoid talking loudly in restaurants. In fact, little conversation takes place during the meal. Instead, there is conversation afterwards.

### DINING OUT

A service charge is generally not included in the restaurant bill and tipping is not expected.

Dinner, called "tea," is the main meal of the day. In homes, "tea" is served around 6:00 or 7:00 p.m., although when eating out the meal takes place closer to 8:00 p.m. (Note the difference between "tea" and "afternoon tea," which is served at 3:00 or 4:00 p.m.) Sometimes, a light "supper" is served in the late evening.

The New Zealand diet has traditionally been based upon the British style, with hearty and heavy meals of meat and potatoes. Recently, however, the diet has been changing to reflect a more health-conscious population. Seafood, fresh fruits and vegetables are now eaten more often. Portions are generally smaller and less red meat is eaten. Beef, pork and mutton are still common as are meat pies and sausage rolls, while fish and poultry are gaining popularity. Also, New Zealand specializes in dairy products. A unique New Zealand food is *vegemite* (a yeast extract) which is used as a spread for bread.

New Zealanders eat in the continental style, with the fork in the left hand and the knife remaining in the right.

You should be aware that "napkins" are called "serviettes" in New Zealand. The word "napkin" is used to designate a diaper. In restaurants, "appetizers" are referred to as "entrees."

# NEW ZEALAND (Cont'd)

## DINING OUT (Cont'd)

It is best to keep your hands but not your elbows above the table.

To indicate that you have finished eating, place your utensils parallel on your plate. If they are not parallel, it will indicate that you have not finished.

## PUBLIC CUSTOMS

Western-style clothing is the standard, although the Maoris wear a variety of traditional clothing for cultural events. A neat, clean appearance is important in public. Warm clothes and rain gear are common due to New Zealand's temperate climate.

Most offensive gestures used in the U.S. are also offensive in New Zealand. Also, the "V-for-victory" sign is considered obscene, especially when done with the palm facing inwards.

The mouth is covered if a yawn or a cough cannot be suppressed. Similarly, chewing gum or using a toothpick in public are considered offensive.

# PAKISTAN: HISTORICAL OVERVIEW

- In the eighth century, Arab traders introduced Islam to Pakistan. In the 10th century, Muslim warriors conquered most of the area, and their power grew until it reached its apex in the 16th century under the Moghul Dynasty.

- By the 19th century, the British East India Trading Company exerted great influence in the area and the British gained dominance in the region. The last Moghul emperor was deposed in 1858.

- After World War I, British control of India, Pakistan and present-day Bangladesh was contested by various independence movements. A number of independence movements united for a time under Mahatma Gandhi. At the same time in 1940, Mohammed Ali Jinnah, leader of the Muslim League, began advocating separate Muslim and Hindu nations.

- Finally, in 1947, Britain granted independence to the entire area. Fearing that Hindus (the majority) would control the entire new country, Muslim leaders pressed for separation of the Hindu and Muslim nations. As a result, each region ruled by a native prince was given a choice to join either India (Hindu control) or Pakistan (Muslim control). The areas that chose Pakistan became East and West Pakistan, separated by 1,000 miles of India. The people of Kashmir (northern India) chose Pakistan, but their Hindu Prince chose India. As a result, the area remains in dispute even today.

- When East Pakistan (inhabited by Bengalis) declared independence in 1971, civil war erupted. Pakistani troops, which were sent to quell the movement, were defeated and East Pakistan became Bangladesh, under Bengali rule.

- Following the creation of Bangladesh, Zulkafir Ali Bhutto was elected leader of Pakistan. However, during the 1977 period of civil unrest, General Mohammed Zia ul-Haq seized control of the government and jailed Bhutto, who was eventually hanged in 1979. Zia established *Shari'a* (Islamic law) in the country and suspended civil rights.

- In 1988, Zia was killed in a plane crash and, subsequently, free elections were held. Bhutto's daughter, Benazir Bhutto, was elected Prime Minister, becoming the first female leader of an Islamic country. Civil rights were restored and reforms were implemented, and Bhutto was ousted by the opposition in 1990.

- Nawaz Sharif was elected Prime Minister in 1990, and he began to liberalize the economy and to reform the bureaucracy. In 1993, the President attempted to dismiss Sharif, but this attempt was overruled by the Supreme Court, and Sharif remained in office. In the 1993 elections, Benazir Bhutto returned to the office of Prime Minister. On the basis of her regained political strength, her choice for President, Farooq Leghari, was elected by both houses of parliament and four provincial legislatures.

- Corruption has discredited officials and politicians, while at the same time it has strengthened the appeal of Islamic fundamentalists, who promise a moral society. Another major issue has been human rights. Eight to ten million children are presently employed in factories, domestic service and agriculture. There has also been severe violence and rioting caused by ethnic rivalry, primarily in the Sindhi cities of Karachi and Hyderabad.

# PAKISTAN

## INTRODUCTIONS

A handshake is the most common greeting, although close friends may embrace if meeting after a long time.

Women may also greet each other with a handshake or a hug.

It is not appropriate for a man to shake hands with a woman or to touch her in public, but he may greet another man's wife verbally without looking directly at her.

Verbal greetings often include inquiries about one's health and family. Answering these inquiries may take some time.

In Pakistan, the most common greeting is *"Assalaam alaikum"* ("May peace be upon you"). The reply is *"Waalaikum assalaam"* ("And peace also upon you").

The Pakistani phrase for good-bye is *"Khodha Haafis."*

Titles and last names are used when addressing someone.

In small groups, each person is greeted individually.

## SOCIAL TIPS AND CONVENTIONS

Pakistan's population is divided into five major ethnic groups. The Punjabi is the largest group, comprising about 65%. The other four groups are the Sindhi, the Baluchi, the Pashtuns and the Muhajir.

The Pashtuns have been referred to as Pathans in the past, but today some consider that name derogatory.

The Muhajir ethnic group is made up of immigrants from India and their descendants.

Pakistan is also home to more than three million Afghan refugees who fled civil war in Afghanistan and lived in camps maintained by Pakistan's government.

Due to the diversity of ethnic groups and the great difference between dialects in a single language, many languages are spoken in Pakistan. English is an official language and is used by the government and educated elite. It is also taught in school. But the other official language, Urdu, is being encouraged as a replacement for English in these cases; it is also the nation's unifying language. While only 7% of the people speak Urdu as a native tongue, most people in the country speak it in addition to their own language.

The force uniting the diverse peoples of Pakistan is Islam. About 97% of the people are Muslims. Most of these (77%) are Sunni Muslims, while the remainder are *Shi'a* (Shi'ite) Muslims. The rest of the people are either Christian or Hindu, or belong to other religions. Freedom of worship is guaranteed.

Visiting between friends and relatives is a very important social custom and occurs as often as possible.

# PAKISTAN (Cont'd)

## SOCIAL TIPS AND CONVENTIONS (Cont'd)

*"Insha'allah"* ("God willing") is a term commonly employed to express hope for success on a project, for one's family or for a positive outcome to events.

Hospitality is important and guests are made to feel welcome.

Islamic law permits a man to have up to four wives if he can care for each equally, but very few actually have more than one.

Local transportation consists of donkeys and horse-drawn carts in rural areas. In cities, buses, minibuses and motorized rickshaws are available.

Although 40% of the roads are paved, many are in poor condition. Roads in rural areas are not paved and many areas are not accessible by car.

Following the British tradition, traffic moves on the left side of the road.

Most people do not own telephones.

Water is not safe for drinking in most areas.

## CUSTOMARY BUSINESS PRACTICES

Because about half of the population is engaged in agriculture, most work schedules are determined by the seasons and by the crops.

In urban areas, business hours extend from 8:00 a.m. to 4:00 p.m., Sunday through Thursday. In the summer, this is extended by 30 to 40 minutes.

## BUSINESS ENTERTAINING

Visitors are often treated to coffee, tea or soft drinks and may be invited to eat a meal. Visitors should accept this hospitality, although refusing politely with good reason is appropriate.

Guests often bring gifts if well acquainted with the host or if the occasion calls for a present. Gifts might include something for the children, a decoration for the home, fruit or sweets. Above all, gifts should not be too expensive because that could embarrass the host.

It is customary to socialize before a meal and then to leave soon after the meal is finished.

In traditional homes, men and women do not socialize together. Rather, men receive their male guests in a special room to enjoy conversation and refreshments.

In urban areas, people may eat with utensils or the hand.

Whenever possible, the whole family eats together, usually sharing the same platter and eating the portion directly in front of him/her.

## BUSINESS ENTERTAINING (Cont'd)

In large groups, men and women eat in separate areas.

During the month of *Ramadan*, Muslims do not eat or drink from sunrise to sundown each day. They eat together in the evenings, which are also occasions to visit or offer prayers.

During *Ramadan*, it is impolite for non-Muslims to eat or drink in front of Muslims during daylight hours.

## DINING OUT

The mainstay of the Pakistani diet is *chapati* or *roti*, an unleavened bread similar to pita bread. *Chapati* is used to scoop up food.

Pakistani food is generally hot and spicy as curry is one of the most popular spices.

Islamic law forbids the consumption of pork and alcohol, and there are strict civil laws regarding the sale and consumption of alcoholic beverages.

Yogurt is a common ingredient in meals.

Rice is part of most meals and desserts. Two customary dishes include *pillau* (lightly fried rice with vegetables) and *biryani* (rice with meat and spices). *Kheer* is a type of rice pudding.

The most common meats are lamb, beef and chicken. Fish is also popular.

There are significant regional differences in cuisine. For example, while cooking with curries and heavy spices prevail in the south, barbecuing is more common in the north. *Kebab*, strips or chunks of meat barbecued over an open grill on a skewer, is cooked with or without spices and is prepared in various ways.

Pakistanis consume large amounts of vegetables and fruits.

Tea is the most popular drink.

## PUBLIC CUSTOMS

Although Western-style clothing is worn in Pakistan, the national dress, the *shalwar-qameez* (two-piece pantsuit) is more common in both rural and urban areas. Made of cotton, the *shalwar-qameez* differs for men and women. Men wear solid, plain colors and add a vest or coat for formal occasions. For women, the colors are brighter and patterns bolder, and the tailoring is more precise.

Women wear a *dupatta* (scarf) around their heads and sometimes another long scarf around their shoulders.

Men usually wear some kind of headdress and it is often possible to determine a man's ethnic group from his headwear. Some wear turbans, others pillbox-type hats, and still others wear *karakuli* (fez-type) hats.

# PAKISTAN (Cont'd)

## PUBLIC CUSTOMS (Cont'd)

It is important to dress conservatively.

Despite the heat, Pakistanis cover their legs, arms and heads in public.

Men wear shorts only for athletic events. Women never wear shorts.

If sitting on the floor or if crossing the legs, remember to position your feet so as not to point them directly at another person.

Items are preferably passed with the right hand or both hands.

To beckon, all fingers of the hand are waved, with the palm facing down.

Using individual fingers to make gestures is very impolite.

Male friends may walk hand in hand or with their arms over each other's shoulders, but it is inappropriate for members of the opposite sex to touch in public.

Secular holidays include Pakistan Day (March 23); Labor Day (May 1); Independence Day (August 14); Defense of Pakistan Day (September 6); the Anniversary of the Death of Quaid-e-Azam, or Mohammad Ali Jinnah, the nation's founder (September 11); Allama Iqbal Day (November 9); and the Birth of Quaid-e-Azam (December 25). Bank holidays fall in December and July.

Islamic holidays are regulated by the lunar calendar and fall on different days each year. The most important ones include *Eid-ul-Fitr*, the three-day feast at the end of the month of *Ramadan*; *Eid-ul-Azha* (Feast of the Sacrifice), which commemorates Abraham's willingness to sacrifice his son, as well as the *haj* (pilgrimage) to Mecca; and *Eid-i-Milad-un-Nabi*, the birth of the Prophet Muhammad.

# THE PHILIPPINES: HISTORICAL OVERVIEW

- The Philippines is a collection of 7,107 islands. Many of these islands are uninhabited. Most of the population is on 11 main islands, of which Luzon and Mindanao are the largest.

- Magellan made the first Western contact with the Philippines in 1521 and claimed the area for Spain. Spain maintained control for almost 400 years, fending off attempts by China, Japan and other countries to conquer the Philippines.

- José Rizal, a writer and a patriot, inspired a revolt against Spain in 1896. At the same time, Spain and the U.S. were engaged in war. When Spain lost the war, they handed over the Philippines to the U.S.

- Japan occupied the Philippines during World War II.

- On July 4, 1946, the Philippines became an independent republic with a constitution based on the U.S. model.

- Throughout the 1950s and 1960s, social unrest over inequalities threatened the stability of the government. In 1972, President Ferdinand Marcos declared martial law. He ruled by decree until 1986.

- In February 1986, Marcos lost the presidential elections, but declared himself the winner anyway. His opponent was Corazon Aquino, widow of political rival Benigno S. Aquino, Jr. who was assassinated in 1983. Corazon Aquino led a peaceful "People's Power Revolution" that eventually led to Marcos's downfall. Marcos fled the country. Aquino chose not to run for reelection in 1992.

- Aquino's successor was Fidel V. Ramos.

- Ramos was faced with opposition from several different groups, including the *National Democratic Front*, the *Muslim National Liberation Front*, the *Muslim Islamic Liberation Front* and the old political elite. To its credit, Ramos's government reached agreement with the *Muslim National Liberation Front* and foiled an attempt to assassinate Pope John Paul II during his visit to Manila. However, the *Muslim Islamic Liberation Front* became an increased threat. Its members attacked the town of Appall in April 1996, killing 57 people.

- There was substantial economic growth in the early 1990s, especially in agriculture. Another encouraging note was that the Ramos administration already turned over more land to the peasants from 1992 to 1996 than was turned over in the past 20 years.

- In January of 1997, Ramos was in failing health. Two possibilities for successors include Defense Secretary Ronato de Villa and Vice President Joseph "Erap" Estrada.

# THE PHILIPPINES

## INTRODUCTIONS

On first and subsequent meetings, the appropriate greeting is a handshake – for men and men, women and men or women and women. Foreign men should wait for Filipino women to extend their hands.

The eldest person should be greeted first as a sign of respect. To show special honor when greeting older persons, especially relatives, the terms *"lolo"* and *"lola"* are used.

At a party, expect to be introduced to each guest individually. Shake hands with each person as you are introduced.

Address business superiors as "Sir" or "Ma'am" or by their title or profession (e.g., "Congressman," "Attorney"). Use "Mr.," "Mrs." and "Miss" with business peers.

Don't be surprised to see Filipinos greet each other by making eye contact and then raising and lowering their eyebrows.

## SOCIAL TIPS AND CONVENTIONS

In the Philippines, 80 different languages are used, including some Spanish. While Tagalog (or Pilipino) has been declared the official language, it has failed to replace English as the country's unifying language. English is widely spoken and is the *de facto* national language in law, commerce, government and popular entertainment.

Filipino culture has been influenced by the Chinese, Malayan, Spanish and U.S. cultures. Many aspects of these different cultures can be identified, i.e., while Filipinos are fun-loving and casual, they can also be very sensitive and conscious of maintaining appearances.

A sense of propriety, a need to maintain social harmony and consciousness of indebtedness are central to Filipino culture.

Filipinos tend to be very sensitive to others and also to how one presents oneself. As a result, confrontation is avoided. When in the Philippines, strive to be sensitive and tactful.

Great importance is placed on the role of the family, relationships to authority and harmony in relationships. Appearances and a sense of dignity within the community are of great importance. Also, Filipinos have a strong sensitivity to matters of authority.

Younger people defer to older people in the family, in daily social life and at work.

Good topics of discussion include culture, history, business, the place you are from, your job or your family. Filipinos are very family-oriented, so children are a good topic of discussion. In fact, expect to be asked many personal questions, even on first meetings.

Avoid discussing politics, corruption, foreign aid and religion. Even as a joke, don't criticize a person, his or her family or an established institution.

Filipinos prefer a quiet, listening, unassuming attitude and a cheerful disposition.

# THE PHILIPPINES (Cont'd)

## CUSTOMARY BUSINESS PRACTICES

Be aware that English is the usual language of commercial correspondence. Many leading businessmen have traveled to the West.

In the Philippines, business dress is not formal. However, because of strong values relating to status and authority, conservative, appropriate and neat business dress is very important. Men should wear a jacket and tie. Women should wear a dress or a skirt and blouse and, despite the heat, stockings. People are very fashion-conscious; to make a good impression, dress well.

After repeated visits to a firm, feel free to wear a *barong*, the national dress shirt (a white or pastel-colored embroidered shirt that is worn hanging over pants). However, men should remember to wear a coat and tie for business meetings.

In the Philippines, the presentation of business cards is quite important. As a foreign visitor, you should present your card first.

If your company isn't well known, bring letters of introduction from mutual friends or business associates.

Make business appointments about a month in advance. Schedule appointments for the morning or late afternoon, since there is a midday siesta break. While punctuality is not always observed in the Philippines for social occasions, punctuality is expected for business meetings.

Realize that you will almost certainly have to make more than one trip to conclude a business deal in the Philippines.

Business is conducted very slowly in the Philippines. This is usually because Filipino businesspeople are just as concerned with maintaining group harmony as with accomplishing business objectives. You will only make a bad impression if you try to rush things.

When doing business in the Philippines, be aware that Filipinos often react to decisions, rather than participating in making them. Filipino businesspeople often will not want to disagree or present a problem or request directly. Blunt and emphatic words are avoided and, at the extreme, true meanings may have to be guessed, based on hints. It can be difficult to participate in open discussions with Filipino businesspeople.

Filipinos dislike saying "no" because they believe that this undermines good personal relations. Therefore, at each stage of your negotiations, you may want to try to get a written agreement. Filipino businesspeople may say "yes" to save face but may not really mean it, so it is important to have commitments in writing.

When conducting business in the Philippines, do not show impatience or act condescendingly. Filipinos do not react well to pushiness.

# THE PHILIPPINES (Cont'd)

## CUSTOMARY BUSINESS PRACTICES (Cont'd)

Don't be surprised when Filipino businesspeople laugh at a crucial point in the meeting. In Filipino culture, people tend to laugh at tense moments, to release tension without confrontation.

Businesswomen should behave in a highly professional manner, without being overly aggressive or impolite.

## BUSINESS ENTERTAINING

In the Philippines, business entertaining is very important since business relationships are often highly personalized. It is appreciated if you show genuine interest in Filipino culture and make an effort to interact with your Filipino colleagues. Filipinos entertain with ease, warmth and joy.

U.S. practices tend to prevail in business entertaining (style of eating, customs, etc.).

In the Philippines, when food, drink or cigarettes are *first* offered, you should refuse. You can accept the item the second time, if you wish.

In public and when dining at someone's house, usually only men drink alcohol (principally beer and wine). Women are usually offered soft drinks such as Coca-Cola, orange juice or *calamansi* (a native drink made of a citrus fruit similar to lemon). However, it is becoming more common for women to drink wine.

While taking part in business entertainment, you may be asked to engage in solo or group singing. It is appreciated if you join in, no matter how poorly you sing.

A service fee is usually included in a restaurant bill. However, if this fee is not included, a 10% tip should be left for the waiter/waitress.

People in restaurants may hiss to gain the waiter's/waitress's attention. It is more polite to beckon with your hand (palm facing downwards).

If you are invited to someone's home, keep in mind that, at some homes, you should remove your shoes before entering. Follow the example of your host.

## DINING OUT

Remember that Filipinos almost never cook anything by itself, except for fish, which is broiled or grilled. Chicken, fish, vegetables and noodles are all combined in soups and stews and then served with rice. The rice and food are mixed together on the plate and *bagoong* or *patis* are added. *Bagoong* is a pungent fish or shrimp paste; *patis* is an amber-colored liquid fish seasoning. In homes, there will be bottles of these two condiments on the table, while in restaurants they are added to the food in the cooking. Filipino food tends to be sweet or salty, rather than bland or intensely spiced.

# THE PHILIPPINES (Cont'd)

## DINING OUT (Cont'd)

French, Italian, U.S., Chinese and Middle Eastern foods are commonly eaten in the Philippines, especially in restaurants in big cities.

Don't expect drinks to be served before dinner.

At your place setting, look for a fork and a spoon. In some homes, knives are placed on the table. Take the spoon in your right hand and the fork in your left. Push food onto the spoon with the fork.

Try a small amount of every type of food offered and leave a little of each item on your plate to show that your host has prepared enough and that you are satisfied.

To indicate that you are finished, place utensils horizontally on your plate.

If invited to a home for a meal, you may bring a gift such as flowers, which should be given upon arrival. Thank-you notes are also appreciated. You may even send a small thank-you gift to a host, following a dinner.

## PUBLIC CUSTOMS

Note that someone may touch you lightly on the elbow to gain your attention.

Do not use your finger to beckon someone. Rather, with your hand palm down, move your four fingers toward you.

Don't be surprised to see men or boys holding hands with one another (or women and women). The gesture has no sexual implications. In contrast, physical contact with members of the opposite sex in public should be avoided.

Remember that in the Philippines, raising the eyebrows means "No."

Instead of pointing to an object, Filipinos will shift their eyes towards it, purse their lips and point with the mouth.

Don't be surprised if a Filipino smiles when upset or embarrassed. This is the Filipino way of changing the atmoshere during a difficult moment or situation.

Never show anger in public. Also, placing your hands on your hips is interpreted as a sign of anger or confrontation.

Filipinos are very respectful of women and elders and tend to be very reserved in mixed company.

Be aware that customs related to food are extremely important. If a clerk in a store you are visiting is having a snack or a coffee break, prepare to wait a long time for service. If you eat in front of others, it is advisable to offer them some food.

# THE PHILIPPINES (Cont'd)

## PUBLIC CUSTOMS (Cont'd)

Although Filipino women seldom smoke or drink in public, it is acceptable for foreign women to do so.

Before taking a picture, look for any signs indicating that photography is forbidden. Feel free to photograph people, although it is courteous to ask permission first.

People seldom form orderly lines and crowding is both acceptable and expected.

# SINGAPORE: HISTORICAL OVERVIEW

- Singapore is an island nation located off the tip of the Malaysian peninsula. Singapore is actually a city-state without any truly rural areas.

- Three major cultures (Chinese, Malay and Indian) are all represented in Singapore. About 75% of the population has a Chinese heritage.

- Singapore's strategic location and natural deep-water ports attracted the British in the early 19th century. In 1819, Sir Stamford Raffles established a British trading post on the island. Britain acquired it as a possession in 1824.

- Singapore fell to the Japanese in 1942.

- Singapore became a British Crown Colony in 1948. Internal self rule was granted in 1959. It became part of Malaysia in 1963. But this caused domestic political problems and the island became independent in 1965.

- Lee Kuan Yew led Singapore for 31 years. Lee resigned in 1990 in favor of a younger man, Goh Chok Tong, who continued Lee's policies.

- In 1993, Singapore revamped and enhanced the office of the president, to which Ong Teng Cheong was elected later that year. He and Prime Minister Goh have maintained a hard line against anyone critical of Singapore or its government. They believe that authoritarian means are justifiable when the ends are economic prosperity and a safe, clean environment.

- Two events occurred in 1994 which raised questions about authoritarian rule. The first involved the charges of criminal defamation leveled against a U.S. academic in Singapore who wrote an article critical of intolerant Asian regimes. The government later assured the people that free expression would be expanded, but slowly, over the next two decades. The other event was the sentence of U.S. citizen Michael Fay to 40 lashes of the cane for vandalizing cars. While the U.S. Trade Representative was critical of the punishment, most U.S. citizens were ambivalent or supportive of it.

- Singapore has enjoyed steady economic growth for the past decade. Foreign trade and investment have increased, as has industrial development. The standard of living is very high, however, overcrowding has resulted in a very tight housing market.

- The *People's Action Party*, which has dominated the politics of Singapore since its independence, is expected to face stronger opposition in the next few years.

# SINGAPORE

*Singapore is a multicultural (approximately 70% Chinese, 15% Malay and 15% Indian) and cosmopolitan society. As a result, social customs and etiquette vary according to the specific situation and the people with whom you are dealing.*

## INTRODUCTIONS

In Singapore, greetings vary depending on the age and nationality of the people involved. However, most commonly, people shake hands when meeting. Men shake hands with both men and women. While women also shake hands, close women friends hold both hands.

Especially when greeting older or Chinese people, a slight bow may be added to the handshake. In fact, bowing slightly when you enter or leave a room or pass a group shows courtesy.

When being introduced, use the titles "Mr." or "Mrs." ("Ms." is not common) followed by the family name for Chinese and followed by the given name for Indians or Malays. Chinese put their last name first, middle name next and given name last. For example, a Chinese man, Lee Kuan Hock is "Mr. Lee." Malay names are complex. They often attach their father's name after their own. For example, a Malaysian man, Hassan Ahmed is "Mr. Hassan." Most Indians do not have surnames but may use the initial of their father's name in front of their given names.

While various languages are used when greeting, English is acceptable and common.

Business and government officials exchange business cards when greeting each other. The cards should be presented respectfully using both hands.

## SOCIAL TIPS AND CONVENTIONS

While it is common for people in Singapore to ask personal questions, it is best if a visitor refrains from asking about family or personal life.

Some good topics of conversation include sports and travel. Singaporeans enjoy water sports, soccer, badminton, tennis, golf and basketball. Martial arts (such as *tae kwon do*) and *taijiquan* (shadow boxing) and the French game of *petanque* are also popular.

Additional conversation topics include your host's success in business and in social activities, Singapore's future plans and its economic advances. Movies and books are also good subjects of conversation.

It is best to refrain from discussing religion, politics or the government even if coaxed. You should also avoid referring to the small size of the country or making comparisons between Western standards and those of Singapore. Avoid making jokes until you know someone quite well.

It is acceptable for visitors to ask for recommendations when looking for places to eat.

The English language is widely spoken and studied throughout Singapore.

# SINGAPORE (Cont'd)

## SOCIAL TIPS AND CONVENTIONS (Cont'd)

Older people as well as those with seniority are treated with respect in Singapore. Show deference to elders and those senior in rank in the Asian group by allowing them to go through doors and be seated first.

Singaporean society is very disciplined. Singaporeans avoid showing emotions in public or expressing individualism. The individual defers to authority and to the collective good. Also, importance is placed on status, which may be indicated by fashionable clothing and lavish entertainment.

## CUSTOMARY BUSINESS PRACTICES

The business community in Singapore is primarily Chinese. Most of the urban Chinese are Buddhist or Christian. People of Malay heritage are Muslims.

It is prudent to arrange for a letter of introduction before you arrive. You can contact the trade office in your country for help in finding contacts.

It is a good practice to send your proposal before making your business trip. This way, your colleague will be very familiar with it when you meet and will want to discuss it in great detail.

For best results, have your company's delegation headed by someone around the age of 50. Singaporean businesspeople are impressed by older, experienced people.

Singaporeans value practicality. Negotiations are usually direct and quick. At the same time, Singaporeans sometimes consider aggressive negotiating methods to be excessively pushy.

Although Western business practices have been adopted, Confucianism still dominates management and business practices in Singapore. Businesses are run like families and harmony and paternalism are the most important concepts used in running them. Human relations are very important and business will be conducted on the basis of trust. The individual defers to the group and to authority.

About one third of the Singaporean labor force is female. Generally, women are treated as equals in business. However, because of local religious beliefs, foreign businesswomen must be very careful not to offend others by their manner of dress. It is best to dress modestly and conservatively. Do not wear short skirts or sleeveless dresses or blouses.

Punctuality is valued in Singapore. Visitors are expected to be punctual for business meetings and for business entertainment. It is a good idea to make appointments.

Most businesses are open from 8:30 a.m. to 4:30 p.m., Monday through Friday and sometimes from 8:30 a.m. to 12:30 p.m. on Saturday. If a business is open on Sunday, it is required by law to be closed on another day.

# SINGAPORE (Cont'd)

## BUSINESS ENTERTAINING

Business entertaining usually takes place in a restaurant for lunch or dinner. Business lunches can be long and informal and business can be discussed during the meal. You should wait until you have met someone several times to invite that person to a meal. Also, be aware that public officials are not allowed to accept invitations.

If you are entertained in someone's home, regardless of their cultural heritage, be aware that shoes should be removed before entering the house.

Gift-giving among business relations is fairly uncommon in Singapore. A gift could be offensive, as it could be taken as an indication of bribery (especially by government officials). Therefore, remain cautious when giving gifts and only give gifts to individuals you know quite well. Avoid expensive gifts.

When invited to someone's home for a meal, it is appropriate to bring chocolates, flowers or pastries. Be aware that Singaporeans will not open gifts in the presence of the giver. Do not be offended if the gift is not opened in front of you.

When choosing a gift for your host, be aware that T-shirts from your home country make good gifts. Gifts should always be given in even pairs, which is a sign of happiness and good luck.

In restaurants, a service charge is usually included in the bill. Even if a service charge is not included, tips are not necessary and may even be discouraged.

## DINING OUT

Since Singapore has become quite Westernized, eating customs and dining etiquette vary according to the type of food being eaten and the culture of the people eating it.

In Singapore, a wide variety of foods are available including spicy Malaysian foods, Indian curries, Chinese dishes and a number of European foods. Rice and seafood are very popular. Pineapple, papayas, bananas and mangoes are commonly served.

In Singapore, it is customary for the host to be modest and humble. Compliments are appreciated, even though they will be denied for the sake of modesty. Your host will probably apologize for the inferior quality of the food. You should simply reply by saying that the food is good.

While chopsticks are the most popular eating utensil in Singapore, Western-style utensils are usually available.

It is considered impolite to refuse food that is offered to you or not to finish the food on your plate. At the same time, you will usually be served very generously. It is polite to finish at least one serving of each food. Then, to indicate that you are finished, place your chopsticks across your dish. Leaving food in your dish – even a small amount – politely indicates that your host was so generous that you could not possibly finish.

# SINGAPORE (Cont'd)

## DINING OUT (Cont'd)

Among the Chinese, the host and hostess sit opposite one another. Most guests sit facing the front entrance, with guests of honor to the left of the host and hostess.

Before the meal, the host will invite the guests to drink wine. It is polite to take a sip or at least pretend to, even if you don't wish to drink. Raise your glass with both hands, holding it in your right hand and keeping your left hand under the glass.

Between courses, chopsticks should be laid on the chopstick rest, the soy sauce dish or the bone plate. It is improper to rest them on your dinner plate or on the rice bowl. It is an especially bad omen to place your chopsticks upright in your rice bowl.

Soup should be eaten using the porcelain spoon for the liquid and the chopsticks for the chunks of food. Tilt the soup bowl toward you while eating. Feel free to slurp your soup if you like.

Remove bones from your mouth with the chopsticks, not with your fingers. If there is a bone plate, use it. If one has not been provided, put the bones on your own plate.

The second-to-last dish at a Chinese meal is usually plain, boiled rice. Follow the example of the host. He or she may decline or eat only a little bit. This shows that you have had plenty to eat and are no longer hungry.

When among the Indians, always go to the washroom to wash your hands before eating.

Indians do not always use cutlery. If none has been provided, use your right hand to eat. Never touch food with your left hand.

Although Indian women don't usually drink alcoholic beverages, Western women should feel free to accept drinks if they are offered.

Among the Malays, it is customary to entertain at home rather than in restaurants.

The guest of honor is usually seated at the head of the table or to the right of the host.

Hands are washed before the meal at the table. Your host will offer you a small bowl and a towel. It is best to eat and pass food with your right hand only.

Your Malaysian host will be insulted if you refuse any food or drink, whether it is offered during a meal or as a snack. Therefore, take at least a little of what is offered even if only for a taste. To be considered well-mannered, however, you should finish everything on your plate. If you must refuse it, give a specific reason.

# SINGAPORE (Cont'd)

## PUBLIC CUSTOMS

Remove your shoes when visiting religious buildings.

It is impolite to cross your legs in front of elders or to put your feet on a chair. Sit in such a way that your legs don't show prominently and be especially careful that the soles of your feet/shoes are not showing. If you do cross your legs, make sure that one knee rests over the other (rather than only placing the ankle of one leg over the knee of the other).

It is considered extremely impolite to touch someone's head.

It is impolite to use your foot to move objects or to have the bottom of your foot pointing at someone.

Finger gestures (e.g., pointing or making the "okay" sign) are considered extremely rude. Also, beckoning with one finger is considered to be an offensive gesture. When gesturing toward a person, use your whole right hand with the palm facing upward. To summon a person, keep the palm of your hand turned down and wave your hand downward.

The gesture of hitting the fist into a cupped hand is considered impolite.

Singaporeans tend to laugh when embarrassed or when in a highly emotional situation. Be careful not to misinterpret this behavior.

For your general comfort, it is advisable to wear clothes made from natural fabrics such as cotton, linen or silk in the heat and humidity of Singapore. Synthetic fabrics tend to be uncomfortable.

Be aware that Singapore has very strictly enforced laws regarding minor offenses (such as littering, jaywalking, etc.) and antisocial behavior (wearing hair too long, chewing gum, etc.)

# SRI LANKA: HISTORICAL OVERVIEW

- The first inhabitants of Sri Lanka were the Veddahs. Around 500 B.C., an Indo-Aryan group, led by Prince Vijaya, migrated to Sri Lanka and formed a small kingdom. The present-day Sinhalese are descendants of this group. Around 300 B.C., the Indian Prince Mahinda introduced Buddhism to the Sinhalese population and Sri Lanka became its stronghold in South Asia. Another ethnic group, the Tamils, came to the area at an early date, and again in the 19th century, when they were brought by the British from India to work on the plantations.

- Sri Lanka was dominated by European powers for centuries. The Portuguese dominated the region in the 16th century, followed by the Dutch in the 17th century and the British in the 18th and 19th centuries.

- In 1948, the island was granted independence from Britain. The nation has had free elections since its creation and its politics have been stable, except in 1959 and 1971. In 1959, the Prime Minister was assassinated. In 1971, a Maoist group led an uprising of unemployed people and the government declared a state of emergency to suppress the violence by force. In 1972, a new constitution was approved, the name of the country was changed from Ceylon to Sri Lanka (which means "resplendent island") and the government began to socialize the economy.

- In 1978, a new constitution was approved that established a democratic, socialist republic and a strong presidency. In the early 1980s, Tamil groups seeking an independent Tamil state (called *Tamil Eelam*) became violent and began leading insurgencies against the government. When violence between the Sinhalese and the Tamils peaked in 1987, the Sri Lankan government implemented reforms to give the Tamils some measure of autonomy. Although the separatists had originally promised to stop fighting in exchange for autonomy, they backed out of this agreement and began fighting the Indian forces that had been sent to quell the violence. Conflict continued throughout the 1980s, until the Sinhalese joined the Tamils in protesting the presence of Indian troops.

- The last Indian troops left Sri Lanka in March 1990 after negotiations with the Sri Lankan President. The President's action brought about the cooperation of Tamil guerillas, who halted their militancy and participated in national elections, winning several seats in parliament. However, fighting broke out again in 1990 and continued until 1991. Many people were killed and the *Liberation Tigers of Tamil Eelam* had taken control of northern parts of the island. In 1993, President Premadas was killed at a political rally and his Prime Minister, Dingiri Bandaas, was sworn in as Interim President until elections were held in 1994.

- Following the 1994 elections, a leftist government, led by Chanrika Kumaratunga, came to power and negotiated a cease fire with the *Liberation Tigers*. However, the cease fire broke down and the civil war resumed in April 1995. The government's highest priorities continue to be improving the economy and ending the war. President Kumaratunga has extended greater autonomy to the Tamils. She has also increased privatization and strengthened the military. In January 1997, 23 government soldiers were killed in an attack by the Tamils. A new offensive against the Tamils was undertaken in February 1997. Despite the demands of the Sinhalese nationalists and the Tamils, President Kumaratunga claims peace is possible.

# SRI LANKA

## INTRODUCTIONS

While greetings can vary between different ethnic groups, placing one's palms under the chin and bowing the head slightly is the most common. Foreigners are not expected to initiate this gesture but it is appreciated if they return it.

Because of Great Britain's influence on Sri Lanka, the handshake is an acceptable form of greeting for both sexes especially in business.

Common verbal greetings are *"Ayubowan"* (pronounced "ah-you-byu-one") in Sinhalese or *"Vannakkhan"* ("one-eh-come") in Tamil. Both expressions mean "May you be blessed with the gift of a long life." Also, if you bow, the bow may be accompanied by *"Aaibowan"* (in Sinhalese) or *"Namaste"* (in Tamil), which means "I salute the god-like qualities within you."

Since titles are important to Sri Lankans, it is advisable to use them when addressing acquaintances. English titles, such as "Mr.," "Mrs.," "Miss" are acceptable. It is customary to address a Sinhalese person as *"Mahattaya"* ("Sir") or *"Nona"* ("Madam") following his/her last names or simply by this title alone. Tamils, on the other hand, generally do not use titles. Instead, they use *"Aiyaa"* ("father") or *"Ammaa"* ("mother") when addressing an older person to show respect.

At a party, make a point to greet and shake hands with each person in the room.

Business cards are usually exchanged at first meetings. It is appreciated if you have the card printed in English and the local language. However, this is only a good idea if you can distinguish between Tamil and Sinhalese. Otherwise, having the card printed only in English is advisable and perfectly acceptable.

## SOCIAL TIPS AND CONVENTIONS

Be aware that Sri Lanka is correctly pronounced "SHREE-lanka."

Both Sinhala (an Indo-European language with roots in Sanskrit and Pali) and Tamil (in the Dravidian group of languages) are official languages in Sri Lanka. About 10% of the population speaks English although its use is declining. Most businesspeople and government officials, however, speak English fluently.

Ethnic, religious and social divisions run deep in Sri Lanka. This is in part due to a historic division of society by caste (although the importance of the caste system is declining). Generally, Sri Lankans are very friendly and have relatively open attitudes. While some groups may wish to secede from the country, people generally seek peace, unity and economic development for the entire nation. However, it is best to avoid discussing ethnic or religious issues. Also avoid pressuring Sri Lankans to violate their beliefs in the caste system, which is accepted as a part of daily life.

Sports make a good topic of conversation. Sri Lankans enjoy a number of sports introduced by the British, including soccer, rugby, cricket, tennis and horse racing. Other good topics include hobbies, culture, family, schools, your own country and the sights of Sri Lanka.

### SOCIAL TIPS AND CONVENTIONS (Cont'd)

Avoid discussing the ethnic struggle between the Tamils and Sinhalese, the caste system, relations with India and the topic of sex.

The left hand is reserved for hygienic purposes and should not be used for touching people or food or for passing objects. Objects are passed with the right hand only or with both hands.

Nonverbal signals for agreement are reversed from those in Western countries. A nod of the head means "no" and shaking your head from side to side indicates "yes."

### CUSTOMARY BUSINESS PRACTICES

It is recommended that you make appointments at least a week in advance. It is advisable to reconfirm those appointments a day or two before the meeting.

Punctuality is valued and expected from Westerners even though Sri Lankans are rarely on time for business appointments. Since Sri Lanka has very heavy traffic, it is advisable to allocate ample time between appointments.

Business does not move very quickly in Sri Lanka. Delays are common and several trips may be necessary to finalize a deal. Establishing rapport and a relationship of trust is very important, and negotiations are always preceded by socializing.

For Sri Lankan businesspeople, interpersonal relationships, dictated by tradition and the situation of the moment, are more important than abstract rules and facts.

Both Sinhalese (Buddhists) and Tamils (Hindus) use traditional and religious beliefs, in combination with their personal feelings, as a foundation for truth and decision making. Don't be surprised if your counterparts consult an astrologer before making significant business commitments.

When making important business decisions, the Sinhalese are concerned with responsibility to the self and to interpersonal relationships. Tamils concern themselves with the individual's responsibility to the group – the family, social group and religion. Thus, Sri Lankan businesspeople tend to place importance on the group and on an individual's position and rank within the group.

It is quite rare to find women in top business positions in Sri Lanka. However, it is not as unusual in neighboring India or Pakistan. Expect foreign businesswomen to be treated with respect.

Conservative, but lightweight clothing is worn because of the climate. Businessmen rarely wear jackets and ties and businesswomen simply wear a modest, light blouse and skirt.

Business hours are generally from 8:30 a.m. to 4:30 or 5:00 p.m., Monday through Friday. Be aware that, even if people are seated at their desks, business is not conducted during the morning and afternoon tea break.

# SRI LANKA (Cont'd)

## BUSINESS ENTERTAINING

Many introductory meetings are held during meals. Lunch in a restaurant is the most common; however, it is also common to be invited to a Sri Lankan home for either lunch or dinner. Unannounced visits are also acceptable and commonly take place between 4:00 and 7:00 p.m.

The person who initiates an invitation to a restaurant is expected to pay for the entire meal.

Sri Lankans are very hospitable and will always offer refreshments at the beginning of a meeting. This is meant as a sign of good will and it is impolite to refuse. Compliments on the refreshments are welcomed and always appreciated.

If you are invited to a home for a visit or a meal, it is polite to reciprocate by inviting your host(s) to a meal in your hotel's restaurant.

If invited to a home for a meal, a gift is not expected but is appreciated. Good gifts include fruit, expensive chocolates and crafts from your country. It is best to avoid bringing liquor, unless you know that your host drinks alcohol. If you do bring alcohol, imported whiskey is a good choice.

Be aware that there may be as much as two or three hours of socializing before the meal begins in a Sri Lankan home.

In some homes, it is appropriate to remove your shoes before entering. Follow the example of your host or of other guests.

## DINING OUT

Breakfast is served between 7:00 and 8:00 a.m. and lunch is served between noon and 2:00 p.m. Dinner is served late, usually between 7:00 and 10:00 p.m.

Since Sri Lankans of all religious types (Buddhist, Hindu, Islamic or Christian) seek to avoid foods that cause spiritual pollution, what is and is not eaten is determined by the region of the country. Those that adhere strictly to Buddhism do not eat meat of any kind, although some Buddhists will eat fish or eggs. Hindus do not eat beef or pork, and Muslims do not eat pork.

While each ethnic group is known for its own dishes, Sri Lankan cuisine, in general, is a combination of all the different types. Rice is the basic food at all meals in the Sri Lankan diet. A variety of curries (from the Sinhalese) are popular, from mild to very spicy. While Sri Lankans typically consume very little meat due to religious restrictions, they eat large amounts of peas, beans and nuts. Tamil cuisine, in particular, includes a lot of beans and peas. The Birghers, an ethnic group in Sri Lanka, are known for cakes and sweetmeats (another important part of the Sri Lankan diet consisting of candy and crystallized fruit). Tea is the most common beverage served either with meals or as a refreshment.

## DINING OUT (Cont'd)

At a meal, communal dishes are usually placed in the center of the table and each person serves himself or herself. Remember not to use your left hand when serving food. Also, it is best not to allow the serving utensils to touch your plate.

Food is eaten with the right hand. Bread and rice balls are used to scoop up curries and vegetables. Sometimes a plantain leaf is used as a plate (this should not be eaten!).

It will be complimentary to your host if you eat a few servings of food. Therefore, it is advisable to take only small portions at first. However, if you are full, you may politely refuse additional servings.

## PUBLIC CUSTOMS

While Western-style clothing is worn, especially in the cities and among the youth, traditional forms of dress also remain popular. Neat, cool clothing is appropriate for casual attire. Shorts and sleeveless, low-cut or revealing clothing and bathing suits are inappropriate for women except at the beach or in resort areas.

As in many other Asian cultures, the head is considered the most sacred part of the body. Be careful not to touch another person's head.

Don't point the sole of one's foot at anyone or use the foot to move an object or point at something. Avoid propping your feet up on furniture.

Using the index finger to point or to beckon someone is considered impolite. To beckon someone, wave all fingers with the palm facing down.

A smile is sometimes used instead of saying "Thank you." However, women should also be aware that smiling can be considered a flirtatious gesture in Sri Lanka.

According to religious beliefs, women are forbidden to touch a Buddhist monk. Also, a monk is forbidden to touch money. Remember to use both hands when giving anything else to a monk.

Remove your shoes and hat before entering a Buddhist temple. An image of Buddha is considered sacred so never touch, lean or sit on one.

# TAIWAN: HISTORICAL OVERVIEW

- Chinese immigration to the island of Taiwan began as early as the Tang Dynasty (618-907 A.D.).

- The Dutch took control of the island in 1628. The Manchus of mainland China conquered the island in 1683 and made it a province of China.

- China ceded the island to Japan following the Sino-Japanese War (1895) and it remained under Japanese control until 1945.

- During the period of Japanese rule of Taiwan, forces on mainland China battled for governmental control. Chiang Kai-shek's *Kuomintang (KMT)* forces battled Mao Zedong's Communist forces, lost and were forced to flee. They established the Republic of China (ROC) on Taiwan after Japan's defeat in World War II. Chiang's government declared itself the legitimate government of all of China and established a policy to eventually reunite with the mainland.

- In 1950, the U.S. signed an agreement to protect Taiwan in case of an attack from the PRC.

- In 1971, the People's Republic of China was admitted to the United Nations. In 1979, the U.S. normalized diplomatic relations with the PRC and broke them with the ROC. Relations between the U.S. and Taiwan continue on an unofficial basis.

- After Chiang Kai-shek died in 1975, his son Chiang Ching-kuo replaced him as premier.

- The *KMT* ruled Taiwan as a one-party state under martial law until 1987. Political reforms allowed a multiparty democracy to start emerging in 1989.

- National elections, held in 1989, elected Lee Teng-hui as president.

- A national assembly was elected in 1991 to revise the constitution and legislative elections were held in 1992.

- Legislative elections in 1993 pitted President Lee's *KMT*, which favored a centrist approach, against the *Democratic Progressive Party (DPP)*, which was outspoken in support of independence for Taiwan. Neither party did as well as they had hoped and Taiwan remained a two-party system.

- Taiwan's first presidential elections were held in March 1996. The incumbent, President Lee, won with 54% of the vote. Lee has skillfully raised the international profile of Taiwan. The political future of Taiwan is uncertain, as the PRC seeks reunification of Taiwan with China and some people in Taiwan advocate Taiwan independence.

- Taiwan's economy grew 6.4% in 1995, slightly less than expected. The infrastructure is weak, and domestic investment is needed. Though birth rates are down, population growth remains an issue.

# TAIWAN

## INTRODUCTIONS

A smile, with a nod of the head, is both customary and sufficient when greeting someone in Taiwan. However, the handshake is also very common, especially in business circles. Make a point to greet older people first, adding a small bow as a sign of respect.

Stand when a guest, elderly person or a person higher in rank, station or authority enters the room.

First names are rarely used alone. It is more appropriate to address people by a title with the last name.

For Chinese names, the family name comes first. For example, Chiang Ching-kuo is "Mr. Chiang." It is common to have both an English and a Chinese first name (e.g., Michael Wang Kuo-ching). Since there are many Lis, Wangs, Chiangs and Kuos, many people use their initials placed in front of their last name, according to Western customs (e.g., Mr. C.K. Chiang). Remember the initials, especially when you are transacting business with a large family firm in which there are a number of senior people with the same surname.

Common greetings are *"Ni hao ma?"* ("How are you?") and *"Qing dzwo"* ("Please sit").

Exchanging business cards, respectfully using both hands, is an important part of introductions among businesspeople.

## SOCIAL TIPS AND CONVENTIONS

Polite inquiries about health are considered appropriate. Also, show an appreciation for the significant economic gains that Taiwan has achieved.

Movies, music, baseball and hiking are popular pastimes. Taiwan's Little League champions consistently do well in the Little League World Series (they were the champs in 1991).

Loud behavior is inappropriate and considered poor taste.

Although it is a controversial, open topic among the people of Taiwan, discussions regarding mainland China or reunification with mainland China should be avoided. The issue of Chinese reunification has great emotional importance.

When conversing with people from Taiwan, the country of "Taiwan" should be referred to by its official name "The Republic of China" (as opposed to mainland China, which is "The People's Republic of China").

Politically, there is still a substantial gap between Chinese mainlanders and native Taiwanese. To an outsider, the cultural gap is usually virtually imperceptible – Taiwan society is an authentic Chinese society.

# TAIWAN (Cont'd)

## SOCIAL TIPS AND CONVENTIONS (Cont'd)

Many elements of Taiwan culture are based on Confucian principles. According to Confucianism, great importance is placed on the family. Also, according to Chinese styles of thinking, the people of Taiwan can be quite superstitious and fatalistic. Confucianism discourages a sense of individuality and fosters acceptance of the status quo. At the same time, it also instills a sense of honor and humanitarianism.

As in China, the people of Taiwan place great importance on status and maintaining harmony and appearances. Emotions such as anger, annoyance or embarrassment are not shown in public.

## CUSTOMARY BUSINESS PRACTICES

While both Mandarin Chinese and Tainanese (a southern Fujian dialect) are spoken in Taiwan, English is also widely used by members of the business community.

Taiwan has a very active, fast-paced business community that devotes a great deal of energy to surpassing the competition and meeting deadlines on a tight schedule. The people of Taiwan view business as essential to growth and stability.

The people of Taiwan, particularly the older generation, value hard work as a virtue. This attitude dominates the business community. People often work 10 hours or more per day. Businesspeople of Taiwan are also noted for practicality, simplicity and shrewdness when negotiating.

Foreign businesspeople should be thoroughly prepared, take copious notes at meetings and pay close attention to detail during negotiations since they will be fast-paced.

While negotiating, be aware that, according to the Confucian principle of maintaining harmony, the people of Taiwan are reluctant to say anything that may be construed as negative. Instead of refusing a request, a businessperson from Taiwan might suggest alternatives or say that something is inconvenient. In such cases, pressing the issue will only cause embarrassment.

Other influences of Confucianism on business culture include fostering family networks and connections, fostering small "family-size" businesses and maintaining a slow-paced development of business relationships through the cultivation of personal relationships.

Establishing a business relationship may involve a number of "courtesy calls" on the part of your Taiwan colleagues. These meetings will involve formality, polite small-talk and even commemorative photographs (even if the meeting is unproductive or banal).

Doing business with a Taiwan-based firm may be time-consuming and may require patience on the part of foreign businesspeople. After initial contact, there is a considerable period during which the business relationship will be strengthened through visits, dinners, gift-giving and small favors. While this process may seem costly, it is vital. Declining gifts or favors is taken as an insult. Also, you should be aware that if you accept, you will be expected to reciprocate at some point in the future.

## CUSTOMARY BUSINESS PRACTICES (Cont'd)

It is a good idea for a foreign firm to designate one individual to represent the firm on a long-term basis since executives from Taiwan treat every business interaction as personal.

Although composing a detailed contract is important, personal commitments may be considered more important than written contracts by the business community in Taiwan.

Businesses are open from about 9:00 a.m. to 5:30 p.m. although many businesspeople work longer hours. Try to set appointments in the morning or after 2:00 p.m., since business lunches usually take place between 12:30 and 2:00 p.m.

It is usually a good idea to make the initial contact with a Taiwan-based firm through a third party in your home country since business in Taiwan relies on personal contacts and trust.

If you arrange appointments yourself, you should make arrangements in advance and then confirm them upon your arrival in Taiwan.

Meetings are usually short and directly to the point although they may involve customary courtesies (serving of tea or coffee). Accept the beverage and begin talking about business only after finishing your drink.

Meetings are usually short at the beginning of the negotiating process. Once a business relationship is established, you may be expected to sacrifice your personal life to make the deal work. It is not unusual to receive phone calls at home at late hours.

Bring plenty of business cards, printed in both Chinese and English. Many members of the business community carry two sets of cards – one printed in English and one printed in Chinese – or bilingual business cards. (There are numerous printers in Taiwan who can fill such an order in two or three days. Try to use a printer from Taiwan since there are differences between the PRC and Taiwan writing systems, and some businesspeople in Taiwan may consider it tactless to use a PRC-printed card.)

Men are expected to wear a jacket and tie to meetings, even in hot weather. Women are expected to wear suits or dresses.

## BUSINESS ENTERTAINING

The banquet is an important part of the negotiation. Negotiators from Taiwan – particularly the men – like to entertain during the evening in Chinese restaurants. You are not expected to reciprocate. If you *do* reciprocate, it is most appropriate to invite your guest(s) to a Western-style restaurant or to a good Chinese restaurant, which knows how to prepare a banquet. The best time to reciprocate is at the conclusion of your business or the evening before you leave Taiwan.

*Karaoke* (singing along to background music using special audio/visual equipment) clubs are also popular places for business entertainment.

# TAIWAN (Cont'd)

## BUSINESS ENTERTAINING (Cont'd)

It is very unusual to be invited to a home in Taiwan for business entertainment. If you are invited to a home, remember to remove your shoes before entering the house.

Dinner usually begins about 6:00 to 7:00 p.m., and can easily continue for two or more hours as your host orders several courses of Chinese food. Ordering is done by the host only.

Business is not usually discussed during meals. If it is, let your host bring up the subject first. Conversation during meals often centers on the meal itself (the ingredients and how the meal was prepared).

Bring a small gift to your business counterpart. Business-related gifts are appropriate (e.g., a pen, etc.). If you are invited to a home in Taiwan, appropriate gifts include a basket of fruit, tea, flowers, foreign liquor, toys for children, perfume for a wife or a memento from your home country.

Be aware that it is polite for the recipient to refuse the gift two or three times before accepting it. It is not necessary for a foreigner to adopt this practice when offered a gift. Also, if the gift is wrapped, your host will refrain from opening it in front of you.

In most restaurants, tipping is not necessary. A 10% service charge is usually added to the bill. It is appropriate, however, to leave an additional gratuity on the table when you pay the bill.

Never attempt to split the bill with Chinese people.

## DINING OUT

Banquets have their own rules of etiquette. For example, you will be escorted into the dining room only when the entire delegation has arrived. The head of the delegation enters first. Do not be surprised if you are greeted by applause. You will be seated according to a seating arrangement based on rank.

The people of Taiwan usually drink tea or soft drinks. Occasionally and usually at banquets, they will drink beer, brandy or cognac. Hard alcohol is reserved for toasts.

Your Taiwan hosts may drink a toast to you and then pass you the empty glass. It will then be filled by one of the hosts. You are then expected to toast your hosts and drink the whiskey or wine. The drinking sessions can carry on for many hours. It is recommended that you pace yourself.

Food is placed in the center of the table. For a formal banquet, it is the host's responsibility to serve the guests. For a family-type (or home) banquet, each person is given a personal bowl of rice in addition to the food. The rice bowl is held near the mouth and chopsticks are used to eat the food. Do not begin to eat until the host urges you to start.

# TAIWAN (Cont'd)

## DINING OUT (Cont'd)

Eat sparingly; there are many courses. Leave a small amount of rice at the bottom of your bowl when you are finished so that your bowl won't be refilled. An empty bowl signals the desire for more rice.

Rice is eaten with nearly every meal. Soup, seafood, pork, chicken, vegetables and fruit are also commonly served. Many foods are stir-fried. Local Taiwanese dishes as well as Peking, Cantonese, Sichuan and other cuisines are available.

## PUBLIC CUSTOMS

To beckon someone, extend your hand and make a waving motion with your fingers with your palm facing downwards.

Pointing at a person is considered very rude or even hostile. Similarly, winking is very rude.

Note that Taiwan people may cover their faces with their hands when they are embarrassed.

It is impolite to use your feet to move an object or to point at something. In particular, it is very rude if your foot is pointing at a person.

The people of Taiwan rarely hug or display emotion through physical contact. However, friends of the same sex may hold hands or put their arms around each other's shoulders when walking down the street.

In Taiwan, a smile does not only signify happiness or amusement. A smile can also signify embarrassment, annoyance or lack of agreement. Since it is inappropriate to show negative or strong emotions, a smile is used to try to suppress any display of these feelings.

# TAJIKISTAN: HISTORICAL OVERVIEW

- The Tajiks are descendants of Iranian-speaking people who entered Central Asia as early as 2000 B.C. They were incorporated into the Persian Empire and later the Empire of Alexander the Great.

- The people of Central Asia were overrun in the 10th century by an invasion of Turkic-speaking people. Many Tajiks were assimilated at this time, with Tajik culture surviving primarily in the mountains. The Tajiks were later brought under the rule of the Emirate of Bukhara.

- In the 18th century, Afghanistan extended its control over the area. In the 1860s the Russian Empire gained control over the region, and established Bukhara as a Russian protectorate.

- Following the Russian Revolution, part of the area of the Tajik people was incorporated into the Turkistan Autonomous Soviet Socialist Republic. The Red Army took over Bukhara in 1920 and claimed most of modern Tajikistan.

- The area was soon after put under the jurisdiction of the Tadzhik SSR. It was governed during most of the Soviet era, by officials sent from Moscow, and even as late as 1990, Tajiks were a minority in the *Tajik Communist Party. Glasnost* and *perestoika* changed this, and the Tajik Supreme Soviet asserted Tajikistan sovereignty in 1990. Kakhar Makhkamov, who had supported the failed coup against Gorbachev, resigned as party leader in 1991 and was replaced by Kadriddin Aslonov, who issued a decree banning the *Communist Party of the Soviet Union* on Tajik territory.

- The communists, however, were still strong, and they ousted Aslonov. In November 1991, the Supreme Soviet created a popularly elected presidency. This election was won by Rakhman Nabiyev. He soon encountered demonstrations by the Islamic-led opposition. Nabiyev called a state of emergency and ruled by decree. In 1992, the opposition seized control of Dushanbe, the capital, forcing Nabiyev to agree to form a "government of national reconciliation."

- The compromise did not last. The Islamic-democratic coalition rebelled again and this time forced Nabiyev out. Meanwhile, the northern and most developed part of the country was controlled by ex-communists. The situation in Dushanbe remained very unstable. Forces loyal to the former president took the city in December, placing Imamali Rakhmonov in power. As the civil war continued, the Takik Government received aid and troops from Russia, whose fear was that Islamic forces would seize control and create a militant Islamic regime.

- In 1996, Rakhmonov was faced with opposition from within his government. Another civil war with the rebels also loomed and the Russian Government had said that this time it would not intervene. So Rakhmonov negotiated with the rebels and agreed to dismiss several top officials.

- Rakhmonov is not interested in economic reform, which Tajikistan definitely requires. The political situation remains unstable and thousands of Tajikistan citizens are still living in Afghanistan as refugees.

# TAJIKISTAN

## INTRODUCTIONS

To pass a stranger without greeting him/her is considered bad manners. Friends commonly use nicknames and given names when greeting each other. Men greet each other with a handshake while saying *"Assalamu alikum"* ("Peace be upon you"); the correct response is *"Waalaikum assalaam"* ("And peace be upon you also").

Urban men greet women with a handshake, while rural men and women greet verbally only. Women embrace each other or shake hands. Upon parting Tajiks say *"Khair!"* ("Good-bye") or *"To didana"* ("See you later").

Between close friends, the expression *"Salom"* (Tajik for "Peace") is used. Greetings such as *"Chee khet shoomo?"* ("How are you?"), the Uzbek equivalent *"Yakhshi me seez,"* or the Russian greeting, *"Kak dela"* ("How are things?") are also exchanged.

Greetings among friends may involve the ritual of putting the right hand over the heart before, during or after a handshake and embracing and kissing each other three times on the cheeks. Close acquaintances make lengthy inquiries about one's family.

## SOCIAL TIPS AND CONVENTIONS

Community life in rural areas centers around daily prayers at the mosque, where local celebrations, festivals and religious activities take place.

Tajiks have very strong family ties. The *oilai kalon* (extended family) is the center of Tajik society. Families may have several generations who all show much respect to the elderly. Each family lives in a *havli* (a compound).

The family structure is patriarchal. Older men spend much time at the mosque and at tea houses. Although women are the main disciplinarians for their children, men take the action when severe punishment is needed.

Tajiks are fond of dancing, on special occasions men dance with men or women.

Private cars are uncommon in rural areas. Instead, people walk, or ride donkeys, tractors or horses. Buses run between major towns and many areas are connected by train. In urban areas commuters use electric trolleys, buses, taxis and minibuses.

Urban areas have large networks of telephones, but they are largely unreliable. Most people own a television and a radio. Newspapers are printed in Russian, Tajik and Uzbek and broadcasts are made in these languages as well.

Tajik industries include the agriculture of fruits and vegetables; cotton and silk; and mining (gold, iron, lead, mercury, bauxite, tin). The economy is enhanced by the use of hydro-electric power from the mountains.

Tajiks participate in a variety of sports. The most popular include soccer, basketball, tennis and volleyball.

# TAJIKISTAN (Cont'd)

## SOCIAL TIPS AND CONVENTIONS (Cont'd)

Tajiks are generally friendly, cheerful, optimistic and courteous. While open and enthusiastic among friends, they are more cautious and reserved with strangers.

## CUSTOMARY BUSINESS PRACTICES

Russia is a key trading partner, but the government is making efforts to increase trade with other countries as well.

Offices are open from 9:00 a.m. to 5:00 p.m., with an hour for lunch.

Urban men wear Western-style clothing for conducting business, women generally wear *curta* (long, colorful dresses) with *aezor* or *pajomah* (long pants) underneath. Scarves are commonly worn by women on the head.

Traditional Tajik clothing includes a *faranji* (a veil to cover the head and/or face), which is worn by women when men approach. Men in rural areas wear a *joma* or a *chapan* (long coat) and a *toqi* or a *tupi* (a distinctly colored four-corned hat).

In 1989, *Tajoki* (Tajik) replaced Russian as the official language. It is similar to the south west Iranian group of languages and is also closely related to Farsi or Persian. There are various regional dialects spoken as well.

Uzbek is also spoken by many people. Both languages were originally written in Arabic script, but since 1940 it is written in Cyrillic. Russian is still taught in many schools.

## BUSINESS ENTERTAINING

Tajiks are known for their hospitality and their willingness to share with friends and family. They help others and care for those who are alone.

When entertaining guests, food is served on a platter and each person prepares his/her own plate.

Regardless of how people eat, they first wash their hands. Rural families may eat from a communal dish, depending on the food served.

## DINING OUT

Never arrive empty-handed at someone's house. A gift for the house or for the table is appropriate. Don't be surprised if you are not thanked for the gift. Tajiks consider a gift a sign of God's generosity, rather than that of the giver.

Take your shoes off at the door of someone's home, and never put your feet on a table.

Blowing one's nose should be done very discreetly, and should not be done at the table, as it is considered disgusting.

# TAJIKISTAN (Cont'd)

## DINING OUT (Cont'd)

Islam places great emphasis on treating guests well, so be careful not to take advantage of the selflessness which will likely be shown toward you.

Bread is served at all meals and *nahn* (unleavened bread) is the most common type served. Eating with the fingers is common.

The Tajiks are, for the most part, Sunni Muslim therefore the consumption of alcohol and pork is restricted by religious belief.

The Tajik diet consists of *nahn* served with vegetables (such as potatoes, tomatoes, cucumbers, carrots, peppers and squash), fruits (such as grapes, melons and apples) and meat (such as beef, mutton and chicken).

*Palav* (carrots) and rice mixed with meat is a popular dish. Other favorite dishes are *mantu* (pasta filled with various meats or squash), and *shashlik* (skewered meat). Pudding, pies, yogurt, nuts and dried fruits (raisins and apricots) as well as *halvo* (sweet dishes) are often served.

Tea is popular with meals. Black or green tea may be served after meals as well.

## PUBLIC CUSTOMS

The right hand is used to pass items, while the left hand is held on the heart or is used to support the right hand.

In rural homes, people sit on the floor with their legs crossed, but it is improper to point the bottom of one's foot or shoe at another person.

The entire hand is used to point or to call someone. Using one finger to point or to beckon is considered rude.

To celebrate a circumcision or a birth, men play *buzkashi*, a rough polo-type game played between teams of horsemen who try to carry a goat from one spot through a set of poles and back again.

The national holidays include New Year's Day, *Id -i-Ramazon* (feast at the end of Ramadan), International Women's Day (March 8), *Id-i-Navruz* (Islamic New Year), Victory Day (May 9, for the ending of World War II), *Id-i-Qurban* (feast of sacrifice), Independence Day (September 9), and Constitution Day (November 6).

# THAILAND: HISTORICAL OVERVIEW

- Thailand's early history is linked with that of southern China. The Thai nation was founded in the 13th century and Buddhism was introduced in the 14th century.

- After a struggle with the Burmese in the 18th century, Rama I founded the Chakri Dynasty and established Bangkok as the capital. The country was then known as Siam. As Siam, the country was ruled by a king and his court, until 1932 when King Rama VII accepted a change to a constitutional monarchy. The country was renamed Thailand in 1939.

- Thailand never came under colonial rule, unlike many other countries in southeast Asia.

- Japan occupied Thailand for a short time during World War II. After the war, Thailand increased its ties with the U.S. and helped to halt the spread of Communism during the 1960s and 1970s.

- Until the 1970s, the Thai army, having been strengthened in response to numerous threats in the 1940s and 1950s, had a virtual monopoly on political power. This gave way, however, to an informal sharing arrangement between the army and civilian politicians and officials. Much of the army leadership has not been willing to cooperate, and power has shifted between civilian and military-dominated governments. No matter who has been in power, corruption has been a widespread problem.

- A number of military dictators have ruled Thailand over the last few decades. A popular revolt in 1973 overthrew Field Marshal Thanom Kittikachorn and Prapas Charusathiara, who had annulled the constitution and declared martial law two years earlier. A civilian-led government lasted only three years.

- Since 1975, Thailand has been a key destination for many Indochinese refugees.

- In 1976, the military installed General Kriangsak Chomanan as premier. General Prem Tinsulanond succeeded Kriangsak in 1980 and began a slow return to democratic principles. In 1988, Chatichai Choonhavan was elected, but his government was overthrown by a bloodless military coup in 1991, having been discredited by corruption. General Suchinda Kraprayoon became premier after the coup.

- King Rama IX, who has ruled since 1946, forced General Suchinda Kraprayoon's resignation and popular elections returned a nonmilitary government in September 1992. From 1992 to 1995, the government was ruled by a five-party coalition, which made it difficult to proceed on legislative reform. The current government is led by Prime Minister Banharn Silpa-Archa of the *Chart Thai* party. Banharn was plagued by allegations of corruption and a new Prime Minister, Chavalit Yongchaiyudh, took office in December 1996.

- Although the gap between the rich and the poor is large, the Thai economy is one of the fastest growing in East Asia. The government has taken on environmental problems and infrastructure development is moving ahead. It remains to be seen whether the military can be kept out of politics, and whether a stable democracy will emerge. Another major issue is AIDS, as Thailand has the fastest growing infected population in Asia.

# THAILAND

### INTRODUCTIONS

The traditional and most common greeting in Thailand is called the *wai*. A person places the palms of the hands together with fingers extended at chest level and bows slightly. Women curtsy. The higher the hands are placed, the more respect is shown, but the tips of the fingers should not be above eye level. Among adults, it is considered an insult not to return the *wai*. As with the bow in Japan, the *wai* can mean not only "Hello," but also "Thank you" and "I'm sorry."

Westerners are greeted with handshakes.

Address people as "Mr.," "Mrs." or "Miss," along with the last name. Thais address each other by their first names, preceded by *"Khun"* (for example, "Khun Sariya"), and reserve surnames for formal occasions.

The Thai given name comes first followed by the family name.

Often, *"Khun"* or "Mr.," "Mrs." or "Miss" are substituted by organizational, professional, occupational, military or noble titles.

Many of the top people in Thailand are relatives of the royal family. A visitor should note certain abbreviations: P.O.C. means the grandchild of a king; M.C. stands for the great-grandchild of a king; and M.R. indicates the great-great-grandchild of a king.

### SOCIAL TIPS AND CONVENTIONS

Buddhism deeply affects the daily lives of the Thai people. Thailand is the only country on the Pacific Rim that is overwhelmingly Buddhist which makes the country a unique realm. Most Thais live by the Buddhist principle of following a middle path, avoiding extremes and seeing one's well-being as ultimately more important than material things and career achievement.

Guests may offer compliments on the home or the children, but should avoid admiring any specific object to an excess because the host may feel obligated to present the item as a gift.

Thais are very reserved and usually consider criticism of others to be in poor taste.

A sense of humor, laughter and a pleasant, smiling attitude are highly regarded.

In Thailand, smiling is a way of life. The smile says "hello," "thank you," "yes," "never mind" and "excuse me." It also covers embarrassment. More importantly, a smile forestalls and defuses conflict.

Thais love talking about their cultural heritage. Thailand's King and Queen, Buddhism, iconography, Thai food and Thai classical dance are good conversational topics.

Thais are proud of their cultural heritage and are often offended by those who see "development" as a need to Westernize and change traditional religious and cultural habits.

# THAILAND (Cont'd)

## SOCIAL TIPS AND CONVENTIONS (Cont'd)

The King and Queen are the most respected and honored persons in Thailand, and a Thai would be offended by any joke or ill reference to them. There are very strict laws governing the way people may refer to royalty.

Avoid talking about religion or politics. Also, Western humor and sarcasm can be misunderstood.

A good way to start a conversation is to ask a male Thai whether he underwent *phansa*, the three-month monkhood that half of all Thai males undergo early in their careers. Most Thai men, especially harried officials and businessmen, covet fond memories of their *phansa* experience, and enjoy reliving it through detailed conversation.

Traditionally, success was measured by a person's religious and nationalistic attitudes. The trend is now toward wealth and education.

The Thais have great respect for those who unselfishly help others and who lead virtuous lives. Thais are very tolerant, sociable and free of prejudice. They value these qualities in others.

Avoid discussions of the AIDS epidemic in Thailand, drug trafficking or regional politics.

Eye contact is not only acceptable but is very important in establishing relationships.

Thais view speaking loudly or showing anger in public as offensive and may cause loss of respect.

Thai families are very close, and several generations may live in the same household. The oldest male is customarily the patriarch of the family. Members of the family (even adults) are usually expected to abide by the advice of their elders, although this is becoming less true with time and modernization.

Only pass or touch objects, food or people with the right hand.

## CUSTOMARY BUSINESS PRACTICES

English is usually spoken by people in top management in most businesses. However, when dealing with a smaller company or one outside of Bangkok, you may need to hire an interpreter.

The best months for business travel to Thailand are November through March as most business vacations take place during April and May. Also avoid the week before and after Christmas.

Arrange for a letter of introduction. It is best to try and have an acquaintance, albeit through a third party, with a potential business connection before your arrival. Some small companies, however, will accept visits without appointments.

Be sure to be on time for appointments, but don't be surprised if your Thai counterparts are late.

When scheduling appointments from abroad, it is recommended that you give your Thai business counterpart notice of at least two to three weeks.

# THAILAND (Cont'd)

## CUSTOMARY BUSINESS PRACTICES (Cont'd)

The foreign visitor must strive to match the hierarchical status of business contacts. For example, a senior vice president – not a sales manager – should meet with the president of a Thai firm.

The visitor should not schedule very early or very late business appointments especially in Bangkok. Thai managers often want the freedom to arrive at their desks without having to wrestle with Bangkok's rush-hour traffic.

Meetings generally open with small talk. Discussing business matters without becoming personally acquainted is considered impolite.

Expect frequent interruptions in meetings (i.e., messengers carrying papers in and out, secretaries coming in to consult with their employers, etc.).

During negotiations, be aware that, because Thais try to avoid conflict, they will typically avoid saying anything negative, even in response to a request or when questioned about their understanding of an issue. In fact, there isn't a word for "no" in Thai. However, a Thai "yes" can indicate varying degrees of firmness. Quizzical expressions, suggestions of alternatives by the Thai associates or an indication that something is inconvenient may indicate a lack of understanding or a problem with the request. Also be aware that pressing the issues could lead to embarrassment.

Thais have an expression *"Mai Pen Rai"* ("Never Mind"). This characterizes their general feeling toward life that it is to be enjoyed, that problems and setbacks should not be taken too seriously. This attitude influences Thai behavior in business. While Thais are by no means lazy or unproductive, they are generally happy with the status quo and will rarely engage in radical change or be seriously affected by a setback.

Business tends to be quite slow-paced in Thailand. Thai businessmen usually take a long time to reach a decision. Never show anger or impatience in business negotiations.

Business cards should be printed in Thai on one side and in English on the other.

For businessmen, a long-sleeved white shirt, tie, slacks and closed shoes are acceptable. A synthetic-blend suit or a light, wrinkle-resistant jacket adds status. Senior executives generally come to work in lightweight suits. The senior executive may invite the visitor to shed his jacket during a meeting.

Women's clothing should be modest. Skirts are traditional in Thailand, but slacks are acceptable. Women should not wear shorts in public and should avoid sheer dresses or miniskirts, all of which offend Thailand's Buddhist code of modesty.

A work week can be as short as 35 hours or as long as 48 hours depending on the occupation. Businesses are normally open from 8:00 a.m. to 5:00 p.m., Monday to Friday and sometimes for a half-day on Saturday. It is inappropriate to try to make appointments outside of these hours.

# THAILAND (Cont'd)

## BUSINESS ENTERTAINING

Entertainment is essential to business life. Lunches, dinners and evening entertainment serve to establish a good social relationship and are an important part of doing business in Thailand.

Let your host bring up the subject of business during a meal.

Home entertaining is rare. However, if you are invited to a social/business occasion at a Thai home, remember to remove your shoes before entering. Dinner at a Thai home will usually be served buffet-style when entertaining guests. Also, be prepared to sit on the floor to eat. Do not stretch out your feet in front of you during the meal. Women generally tuck their legs to the side and behind them. Men sit cross-legged.

Gifts are not necessary when visiting, but it is not uncommon for guests on extended stays to present their hosts with a gift of appreciation.

The rite of gift-giving in Thailand is quite Westernized and free of many of the formalities found elsewhere in Asia such as Japan and Korea.

In general, Westerners should bring gifts to everyone who is a consistent contact. Gifts can be small – souvenirs, flowers, books, food baskets, calendars, pens, calculators, etc. Gifts should be wrapped.

Look for symbolic gifts – white elephants symbolize royalty in Thailand, as do umbrellas (nobles were once sheltered by them). Pewter elephants and nice umbrellas make fine gifts.

Gifts are exchanged in offices, between businesspeople and at the celebration of the Thai New Year in mid-April.

## DINING OUT

Usually, various dishes are placed at the center of the table at dinner, from which you then choose the different foods to eat with rice.

Thais generally use forks and spoons. Chopsticks are used in Chinese homes and restaurants. Hold the spoon in the right hand. Use the fork to push food onto the spoon, and then carry it to the rice bowl, where it can be mixed with rice. Serve yourself more rice from the bowl on the table or request an additional portion from a server. Bones and other such items are placed on your plate. When finished, the utensils are placed together on your plate.

Rice is the staple in Thailand. It is usually served with very spicy dishes that consist of meat, vegetables, fish, eggs and fruits. Curries and pepper sauces are popular.

When dining out, foreign men may wear a nice shirt without a tie; a crisp new *batik* (a dyed print) shirt, especially for a home visit, is appropriate.

In restaurants, tips are not usually necessary, but some people give a small amount (5-10%) to the waiter or waitress for special service.

# THAILAND (Cont'd)

## PUBLIC CUSTOMS

A person's head is considered sacred, and one should neither touch another's head nor pass an object over it.

The bottoms of your feet are considered the least sacred part of your body. Do not cross your legs when sitting, stamp your feet or use them to move or point at objects or other people. When sitting, try to ensure that the sole of your foot is not conspicuous.

Waving at or patting people on the back is unacceptable, particularly in public and especially if the person involved is not of the same gender.

Throwing objects or pointing at someone or something is offensive. To beckon someone, wave your fingers with your palm facing downwards.

Placing one's arm over the back of the chair in which another person is sitting is offensive.

Compared to most other Asian countries, there tends to be a lot of touching in Thailand in public. However, while good friends of the same sex may hold hands, men and women generally do not touch each other or show affection in public.

Visitors should avoid stepping on the doorsill of a building because Thai tradition says that a soul resides there.

According to religious traditions, women must never touch or offer to shake hands with a Buddhist monk.

All religious monuments and shrines are sacred and should not be defiled or treated disrespectfully.

It is customary to remove one's shoes when entering a Buddhist temple or a private home.

Bring an envelope containing 100-200 *baht* (Thai currency) when attending a religious ceremony of any kind in Thailand. The gift is for the host at the ceremony to "make merit" with the spirits.

Western clothing is very common in most areas especially in Bangkok. Men and women frequently wear straw hats to shield them from the heat. Simple blouses and calf-length loose pants are common for women, as are long wraparound or tube skirts.

The color black is associated with death in Thailand and should be avoided in ordinary dress.

When prices in small shops are not fixed, bargaining is expected, but should be done in good taste because the shopowners make very little profit.

# VIETNAM: HISTORICAL OVERVIEW

- For 1,000 years of Vietnam's long history, the country was under Chinese domination which ended in the 15th century.

- A succession of Vietnamese dynasties followed until France established colonial rule in the late 19th century.

- Japanese occupation during World War II interrupted French rule.

- At the end of World War II, Vietnam was divided into two zones. In the south, the British restored French rule; in the north, China ceded power to Vietnam's emperor, Boa Dai, who abdicated in favor of Ho Chi Minh. Ho Chi Minh declared Vietnam's independence in 1946 and subsequently led a revolt against the French and their southern allies. The French were defeated in 1954 at Dien Bien Phu.

- The Geneva Accords temporarily divided Vietnam into north and south regimes in preparation for national elections in 1956. The southern regime, led by President Ngo Dinh Diem opposed the Accords, refused to recognize them and did not hold elections. A civil war ensued between the north and south.

- The U.S., alarmed at the possibility of the spread of Communism, gave support to South Vietnam, including troops and supplies. The war spread to Cambodia and Laos.

- The war ended with the withdrawal of U.S. troops and the fall of Saigon (now Ho Chi Minh City) in April 1975. Vietnam, as well as Laos and Cambodia, came under Communist rule. Thousands of people fled the area. For those who remained, difficult years of repression, poverty and isolation followed.

- Vietnam was officially reunited in 1976 as the Socialist Republic of Vietnam. The U.S. refused to recognize the new government and did not establish diplomatic ties. This kept Vietnam relatively isolated from Western nations.

- In 1978, Vietnam invaded Cambodia deposing the Pol Pot regime and installing a government loyal to Hanoi. In 1989, Vietnam withdrew from Cambodia. During the same period, Vietnam fought off a Chinese invasion.

- The Communist leaders of Vietnam introduced market reforms in 1986 and stepped up its efforts to improve relations with their non-communist neighbors as well as with the West.

- The peace treaty with Cambodia led the U.S. to renew relations with Vietnam. The U.S. opened a diplomatic office in Hanoi in 1991 to coordinate the search for American MIAs and to pave the way to better relations. Economic sanctions were lifted on February 4, 1994 and full diplomatic relations were announced in July 1995.

- The Communist Party still runs Vietnam, but a new constitution and a National Assembly point to a changing political apparatus. Currently, the economy is currently booming and new governmental structures and functions are needed to organize this increasingly dynamic society.

# VIETNAM

## INTRODUCTIONS

Introductions are usually facilitated by a third party. It is best not to directly approach someone whom you want to meet. Rather, it is appropriate to find someone to introduce you.

Vietnamese people generally shake hands when greeting and saying "Good-bye." The use of both hands shows respect for the individual. Bowing the head slightly while shaking hands also indicates respect.

Women usually bow their head slightly instead of shaking hands.

The Vietnamese address each other by their given names, but add a title signifying their relationship to the other person. The younger of two colleagues might combine the given name with the title of *"Ahn"* ("Older brother").

*"Xin chao"* (seen-chow) is a basic greeting. Because Vietnamese is a tonal language, this phrase could have several different meanings depending on how it is pronounced.

In formal meetings, people may exchange business cards while greeting each other.

Vietnamese names begin with the family name and are then followed by the given name.

## SOCIAL TIPS AND CONVENTIONS

It is inappropriate to visit a home without being invited. Vietnamese people have a great sense of hospitality and feel embarrassed if they cannot show their guest full respect with proper preparation.

Everyday attire for both men and women is generally slacks worn with a casual cotton or knit blouse or sport shirt.

For special occasions, women wear the traditional *ao dai* (a long dress with front and back panels worn over satin trousers).

Use both hands to pass an object to another person.

## CUSTOMARY BUSINESS PRACTICES

The average workweek is six days, Monday through Saturday.

An initial business meeting may begin with light conversation over tea or coffee and fruit or sweets.

Business clothing should be conservative, but casual.

Vietnamese appreciate punctuality.

# VIETNAM (Cont'd)

## CUSTOMARY BUSINESS PRACTICES (Cont'd)

The typical workday is from 7:00 a.m. to noon and from 2:00 p.m. to 4:30 p.m. The Vietnamese people have a strong work ethic and many people hold two or three jobs.

Punctuality is valued in the Vietnamese culture.

It is best to err on the formal side in attire. The north, which is cooler, tends to be more formal. Men should wear suits and women should cover their shoulders and knees.

Important meetings should be scheduled in the morning as the afternoon is usually reserved for running and supervising operations.

Personal contacts are crucial and the establishment of trust and friendship precedes doing business. Discuss business only when your host is ready.

If using a translator, focus your eyes and attention on the person with whom you are meeting, not the translator.

Start with the basics when discussing business in Vietnam. Do not assume that your counterpart will fill in any missing information.

## BUSINESS ENTERTAINING

Gifts are not required, but are appreciated. Flowers, incense or tea may be appropriate gifts for the host. A small gift for the children of the host or his/her elderly parents is appreciated.

Business dinners will usually not occur until a partnership has developed.

It is important to make formal, courteous toasts before a meal. Once the party is underway, alcohol usually flows freely and things can get quite rowdy. Men are expected to participate for a couple drinks, while women can easily refuse drinking if they prefer.

## DINING OUT

Rice is the staple of Vietnam. Vietnamese people use chopsticks and rice bowls at most meals. The rice bowl is held in the hand; it is considered lazy to eat from a rice bowl that is on the table. Food is placed on dishes in the center of the table and each person helps himself or herself. The host might serve guests, but usually simply invites them to help themselves.

*Nuoc mam* (a fermented fish sauce) is the main seasoning used to flavor dishes. Special foods are also dipped in the sauce.

The most common beverages served are hot tea, coffee and beer. Often beverages are not served until the meal is finished.

Tips are not expected in restaurants.

# VIETNAM (Cont'd)

## DINING OUT (Cont'd)

The Vietnamese have a keen sense of humor and will often order or serve exotic dishes, such as snake blood, to a foreign guest, whose reaction rarely fails to entertain.

When eating in someone's home, the oldest man typically sits near the door. You will, most probably, be shown where to sit.

Leaving rice in one's bowl is considered wasteful.

It is polite to rest one's chopsticks on top of, rather than in, one's bowl.

The Vietnamese are noisy eaters.

## PUBLIC CUSTOMS

Do not touch the head of a young child as it is considered a sensitive spiritual area.

It is considered rude to summon someone with the index finger. Instead, wave all four fingers with the palm facing down.

Men and women generally do not show affection in public.

Members of the same sex often hold hands when walking together in public.

Shorts are not worn in public except at the beach.

Most Vietnamese families have an altar for ancestor worship. Fruit and/or flowers are placed there twice in each lunar month. Incense is burned and prayers are made to ancestors for support in overcoming misfortune and for achieving good luck and good health.

Vietnamese people enjoy team sports such as volleyball and soccer. In urban areas, it is common to see people out early in the morning for various exercises like jogging, *tai chi*, yoga or group calisthenics.

Showing anger or frustration is not advised, even as a tactic. Courtesy is important and one should not cause someone to lose face in front of his/her peers.

# EUROPE

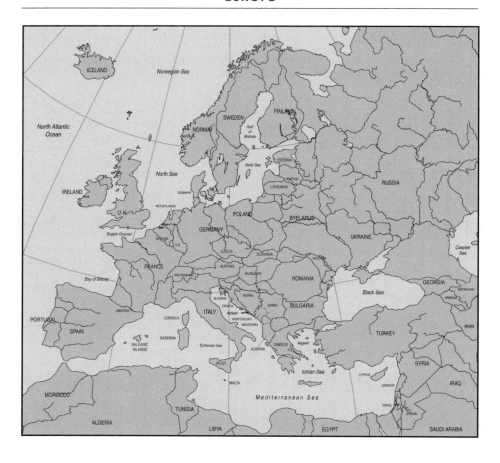

# AUSTRIA: HISTORICAL OVERVIEW

- Present-day Austria was once part of both the Roman and Charlemagne's empires. When the Roman Empire began to crumble, the area that is now Austria became vulnerable to invasions by Germanic, Hun and other tribes. The ensuing conflicts caused much destruction to the area between the fifth and eighth centuries. The area only became stable when Charlemagne took a larger role in the area in 799.

- Otto I, who later became emperor of the Holy Roman Empire, began his rule of Austria in 955 and is often considered to be the real founder of the country because of the borders he established. In 962, Austria became a part of the Holy Roman Empire.

- Austria became an autonomous territory under the control of an aristocratic family, the Babenburgs in 1156. Vienna was its capital. In 1273, the Hapsburg dynasty came to power and for 600 years, the Hapsburgs gradually expanded the Austro-Hungarian empire. They reached the height of their power in the 19th century when they helped defeat Napoleon. In 1914, the empire covered present-day Austria, Hungary, the Czech Republic, Slovakia, Slovenia, Croatia, Bosnia-Herzegovina and parts of Poland and Romania.

- In 1914, Archduke Franz Ferdinand of Austria was assassinated by a Serbian revolting against Austrian rule. This event quickly developed into World War I as the European powers became involved. The war led to the dissolution of the Austro-Hungarian empire, as the new countries of Yugoslavia and Czechoslovakia (which have since further divided) were created from parts of the old empire.

- The first Austrian republic lasted from 1918 to 1938 until it was absorbed by Hitler's Germany just before World War II. After the war from 1945 until 1955, Austria was divided into four zones, which were each governed by one of the four allied powers (Great Britain, France, the U.S. and the Soviet Union).

- Finally in 1955, Austria became an independent democratic republic when the allied forces signed a treaty ending the occupation. Subsequently, the country declared itself to be permanently neutral. Since 1955, the country has maintained close ties to Western Europe and has been marked by political, economic and social stability. In addition, Vienna has become a key United Nations city where other nations meet to discuss problems or negotiate treaties.

- In 1989, Hungary tore down the barbed wire fence along the Austrian-Hungarian border, in part because of the economic ties between the two countries. This act has been recognized as a significant event which encouraged the 1990 political reforms in Eastern Europe.

# AUSTRIA

## INTRODUCTIONS

Austrians shake hands when greeting and parting. Even children shake hands with adults when greeting, as this is an important social courtesy.

In Vienna, a man may kiss the hand of a woman when introduced to her.

Common greetings include *"Grüß Gott"* ("May God greet you"), *"Guten Morgen"* ("Good morning"), *"Guten Tag"* ("Good day") and *"Guten Abend"* ("Good evening"). Proper casual greetings include *"Servus"* (used as "Hi") and *"Grüß Dich!"* ("Greetings to you").

Austrians do not ask *"Wie geht es Ihnen?"* ("How are you?") unless they wish to hear a detailed account.

Professional titles are important among the adult population and are used whenever known. Otherwise, titles such as *"Herr"* ("Mr."), *"Fraülein"* ("Miss") and *"Frau"* ("Mrs." or "Ms."), are combined with family names when addressing acquaintances and strangers. Close friends and the young people use first names.

## SOCIAL TIPS AND CONVENTIONS

The official language is High German, but each area has its own dialect.

English is a required language in high schools and is spoken by many people.

Austrians are known for their *Gemütlichkeit*, a relaxed and happy approach to life. A good-natured sense of frustration and bittersweet attitude toward reality are considered unique national traits.

Austrians are not Germans and should not be referred to as such; it can be considered an insult. While the two peoples speak the same basic language (with important differences in dialect), Austrians and Germans have a different historical and political heritage; they also differ in some customs, values and attitudes.

Austrians are generally more religious than people in many other western European countries.

## CUSTOMARY BUSINESS PRACTICES

Large stores are open from 8:00 a.m. to 6:00 p.m. on weekdays and from 8:00 a.m. to noon on Saturdays. Large chain stores remain open on Saturdays until evening. An increasing number of stores are open on Sunday.

Small, private shops might still close for the traditional *Mittagspause* (midday break), which was once universal as the two- or three-hour break for the main meal.

Banks close at 4:30 p.m.

# AUSTRIA (Cont'd)

## BUSINESS ENTERTAINING

Although Austrians enjoy entertaining in their home and having guests, it is impolite to drop by unannounced. It is better to make arrangements in advance or telephone ahead of an impromptu visit.

Invited guests should arrive on time. Punctuality is important. Guests remain standing until told where to sit. Hosts customarily offer the best seats to their guests.

If the host must leave the room for a moment, the guest is offered something to read or do to occupy the time until the host returns.

Men stand when a woman enters the room or when talking to a woman who is standing.

A drink is usually offered to guests, while further refreshments depend on the hosts.

Invited guests bring flowers, candy or a small gift (such as a handcrafted item or something appropriate for the occasion).

Gifts are given to the wife, or perhaps the children, but not the husband – even if the gift is for the family.

Flowers are given only in odd numbers (even numbers are bad luck), and they are un-wrapped in the presence of the hostess. Red roses are only given as a sign of romantic love. Giving purchased flowers is more polite than flowers from one's own garden.

To show courtesy to the hosts, guests should not ask to use the telephone (all calls are billed, even local ones and the cost is high). They offer to help make preparations only if they are well acquainted with the hosts or if the hostess seems not to have everything under control.

When guests are present, the hostess will nearly always offer second helpings, but a polite *"Danke, nein."* ("Thank you, no.") is gracefully accepted.

Most Austrians prefer to entertain in the home; however, they also socialize in restaurants and other public places.

For many people, especially those residing in small villages, it is a custom on Sunday after church services (usually Catholic) services for the women to go home and fix dinner and the men to go to a *Gasthaus* (pub) to do business, exchange ideas and drink. This socializing is less about drinking and much more about networking and socializing with male friends.

Keep hands above the table during the meal.

Do not gesture with utensils.

Do not put your elbows on the table while eating.

# AUSTRIA (Cont'd)

## BUSINESS ENTERTAINING (Cont'd)

Austrians eat in the continental style, with the fork in the left hand and the knife remaining in the right.

In restaurants, tap water is not served, but mineral water is available. Tap water is generally only consumed in the home.

The bill is paid at the table to the server and a service charge is usually included.

Most people round the bill up to the nearest *Schilling* as a tip.

## DINING OUT

Austrians love good food and have a rich and varied cuisine drawn from the various cultures that once comprised the Austro-Hungarian Empire.

Specialities vary by region, but include such favorites as *Wienerschnitzel* (breaded veal cutlet), *Sachertorte* (a rich chocolate cake with apricot jam and chocolate icing), *Knödel* (moist potato dumplings) and goulash.

A typical day begins early with a light breakfast of coffee or hot chocolate, rolls, bread and jam or marmalade. Later in the morning, some eat a second, heartier breakfast including goulash or hot sausages.

The main meal, whether at midday or in the evening, may include soup, meat (often pork) with potatoes or pasta, vegetables, a salad and often dessert (such as a homemade pastry).

*Jause* (afternoon tea) may include sandwiches, pastries and coffee.

If the main meal is eaten at midday, it generally includes cold cuts, eggs, cheese, rye bread and other breads, and a salad. In this instance, families have *Abendbrot* (evening bread) in the evening.

After a visit to the theater or other evening activity, a light supper might end the day.

Austrians enjoy beer, wine, herbal teas, apple juice with sparkling mineral water, fruit juices and soft drinks.

# AUSTRIA (Cont'd)

## PUBLIC CUSTOMS

It is important to dress properly for all events.

Hand gestures are used conservatively in polite company, as verbal communication is preferred.

It is impolite for adults to chew gum in public.

Motioning with the entire hand is more polite than using the index finger.

Touching the index finger to one's forehead or temple is an insult.

Yawns and coughs are covered when they cannot be avoided.

Cultural arts play a key role in Austrian society.

Austrians celebrate New Year's Day, *Heilige Drei Könige* (Three Kings, January 6), Easter (Saturday – Monday), Labor Day (May 1), Flag Day (October 26; this is the national holiday), All Saints Day (November 1) and Christmas (December 25-26), as well as various religious holidays throughout the year.

Most family vacations are taken in August. Small family-owned shops might be closed the entire month while the family is away.

Austrians love the outdoors. *Ein Spaziergang* (taking a walk) is a national pastime.

Most families own at least one car and private cars are important for daily transportation. The public system of trains, buses and streetcars is also heavily used, especially in large urban areas. Buses reach even the most remote areas and a good system of trains crisscross the country.

On the expressway, there is a speed limit of 80 miles per hour (120 km per hour). Seat belt laws are strictly enforced. Children under age 12 must ride in the back seat.

Customarily, guests remove their shoes when entering a home. This tradition is not practiced in many homes today, however, and guests who reach for their shoes might be told by the hostess that it is all right to leave them on. In homes where the hosts expect guests to remove shoes, guest slippers are usually visible near the door.

# BELGIUM: HISTORICAL OVERVIEW

- Because of its geographical location and topography, Belgium's territory has been coveted, invaded and conquered by the Romans, the Germanic Franks, France, the Netherlands, Austria, Germany, Napoleon and Spain.

- The name "Belgium" comes from the name of a tribe, the Belgae, that lived in the region when Julius Caesar conquered it more than 2000 years ago. In the late 700s, Charlemagne established himself as the ruler of the region. After his death, his empire broke up and a number of nobles took over the six regions that covered the area now known as Belgium.

- Toward the end of the 14th century, the French dukes of Burgundy began to consolidate territory and eventually gained all of what is now Belgium. During this time, the area prospered.

- Belgians were the first to arrive on the island of Manhattan in 1623. They later founded New York at Albany, calling it *Novum Belgii*. A Belgian named Minuit purchased Manhattan Island from the local indigenous peoples for goods worth only 24 dollars.

- In the 1830s, the territories of Belgium gained independence from the Netherlands and became a constitutional monarchy. Although the territories were politically united, they were divided based on language and culture. Historically, what later became French was spoken by Celtic tribes in the south and low German (similar to Dutch) was spoken in the north by Germanic Franks.

- Despite its neutrality in both World Wars, Belgium was taken over by German armies in 1914 and in 1940. Famous battles, such as World War I's battles in Flanders and World War II's "Battle of the Bulge," were fought on Belgian territory.

- Since the 1940s, Belgium has had a strong inclination toward European cooperation and integration. It was a founding member of the North Atlantic Treaty Organization (NATO), and Brussels serves as that alliance's headquarters. Brussels is also home of the European Union headquarters and is an important business and diplomatic center both within Europe and in a global context.

- Belgium has been very progressive in dealing with internal cultural conflicts. In 1960, it granted independence to its African colony, which was called the Belgian Congo and is now called Zaire. Also, it has created a system to meet the needs of both the major linguistic groups and the various minorities within its borders. After the last constitutional reform (1988), Belgium was subdivided into three regions and three communities. Sovereignty was divided between the central state, the regions (Flanders, Wallonia and Brussels) and the communities (Flemish, French-speaking and German-speaking). The further division of the country into four language regions (Dutch, German, French and bilingual regions) also helps divide the territorial scope of the acts of the communities and regions.

# BELGIUM

*Belgium has three official languages: French, Dutch and German. The different linguistic areas are divided by legal lines. According to a new federal structure, policy-making is divided between authorities – the central state, the regions (Flanders, Wallonia and Brussels) and local communities. The majority of Belgian people are Flemings. Most Flemish live in Flanders (the northern part of Belgium) and speak a dialect similar to Dutch. A sizeable minority, the Walloons, speak French and most live in Wallonia (the southern part of Belgium). A small German-speaking community lives in the far eastern part of Belgium. French and Flemish dominate the capital, Brussels. Most Belgians speak three languages as well as English. Specific social and eating customs vary among the different regions.*

## INTRODUCTIONS

Belgians greet each other with a quick, light handshake. Firmer handshakes are given in some areas. When you shake hands, you should repeat your name.

If you have not been introduced to someone in the group, you should introduce yourself and shake hands.

Close friends or young people greet each other with three light kisses on the cheeks (alternating). Men who know each other well may embrace.

The phrases used for greeting depend on the region. English greetings are quite common in Brussels and some other big cities.

Last names should always be used following the title "Mr.," "Mrs." or "Miss." Only friends and relatives are greeted using first names. Professional titles are not necessary.

When leaving, Belgians usually shake hands and bid farewell to each person in the group.

## SOCIAL TIPS AND CONVENTIONS

An appreciation of culture is important to Belgians. They tend to maintain tight ties to family, their native region and its traditions. At the same time, due to Belgium's geographical position in Europe, the people are very cosmopolitan and open to outside interaction.

The Walloons and the Flemish can be distinguished by their manner in personal relations. The Flemish are more reserved, while the Walloons exhibit great personal warmth. However, both have a love for life and live it to the fullest, enjoying both hard work and good entertainment.

Belgians tend to be quite cautious toward new people. However, once you become acquainted, you will be treated with genuine warmth.

Personal privacy is important. Discussions about personal matters or the linguistic divisions in Belgium should be avoided. You may also want to avoid discussing issues relating to religion or to immigrants in Belgium. Due to some recent problems in integrating immigrants into society, the issue is quite volatile.

You should avoid confusing Belgians with the French or discussing French-Flemish rivalries.

# BELGIUM (Cont'd)

## SOCIAL TIPS AND CONVENTIONS (Cont'd)

A good topic of discussion is the Belgian cultural heritage (including art and architecture, and the area in which you are visiting). Belgians are extremely proud of their rich heritage. World-renowned masters such as Brueghel, Van Eyck and Rubens came from Belgium. Also, Van Gogh lived in Belgium for 20 years. While Flemish architecture reflects a clear Germanic influence, Wallonian architecture maintains a French flavor.

Other good conversation topics include movies, recent and popular books, theater and sports. Cycling, football (soccer) and game sports are popular (Belgium's national soccer team competed in the 1994 World Cup). It is acceptable to discuss political topics, but you may want to avoid taking sides.

Belgians appreciate your knowledge of and curiosity about the region that you are visiting.

Luxembourgers, like Belgians, value privacy, education, humor and friendship. Loud behavior is not appreciated.

The people of Luxembourg are descendants of different nationalities and speak several different languages. Luxembourgish, which comes from a Franco-Moselle dialect mixed with many German and French words, is the mother tongue in Luxembourg. French and German also have official status. Luxembourgers have been influenced by Belgium, Germany and France. However, they maintain a strong feeling of national pride and consider their independence and separate identity in Europe important.

## CUSTOMARY BUSINESS PRACTICES

Appointments are necessary. When you write or phone to make an appointment, the Belgian firm will usually set the time. If the appointment is scheduled for 11:30 a.m., you should presume that you will be invited to lunch. You should try not to schedule afternoon appointments before 2:30 p.m.

When you arrive at an office or a business meeting, you should shake hands with everyone there including the secretaries. You should do the same when you leave.

Punctuality is expected and observed.

You should be aware that the first meeting with a Belgian businessperson is primarily used for introductions as well as for getting acquainted. You should exchange business cards and answer questions about yourself.

Belgians must trust you before they will have confidence in your company. You will come across as pushy if you try to do business immediately.

You should avoid using the same business contact in both French and Flemish Belgium.

A strong work ethic is important to Belgians.

Suits are standard for both men and women in office settings. It is also common for women to wear dresses or skirts with blouses.

# BELGIUM (Cont'd)

## CUSTOMARY BUSINESS PRACTICES (Cont'd)

You should bring plenty of business cards since they are widely used.

Businesses are generally open from 9:00 a.m. to 6:00 p.m. with a one- or two-hour lunch break. Once a week (usually Friday), most businesses remain open until 9:00 p.m.

## BUSINESS ENTERTAINING

Belgian businesspeople enjoy spending the evening at home with their families. Lunch dates are preferred when entertaining a Belgian businessperson. The typical business lunch lasts from 1:00 to 3:00 p.m. If you do invite a businessperson to dinner, you should be sure to include the spouse in the invitation.

If you entertain Belgian colleagues in a restaurant, a French wine is appropriate.

Business entertaining at home has become increasingly popular in Belgium, but it is still not very common. If you are invited to a home, a small gift (flowers, candy, etc.) is appreciated. If you bring flowers, you should avoid chrysanthemums because they are associated with funerals.

When U.S. businesswomen entertain Belgian businessmen, they should make arrangements to pay in advance or they should indicate that their company is paying. Under any other conditions, a Belgian businessman won't allow a woman to pay.

Punctuality is important for social events. Arriving more than 30 minutes late is considered rude.

At a large party, you should rely on the host or hostess to introduce you to the entire group. It is not necessary to shake hands with each person.

In restaurants, cafes and bistros, one pays at the table. Usually, the tip is included in the bill. If the service is especially good, you may leave an extra 3-5%. If the tip is not included, you should leave a tip of about 15%. In an elegant restaurant, you should tip the *somelier* (wine steward) 10% of the wine bill if he assists you in selecting a wine.

## DINING OUT

Meals are social as well as cultural events and they are usually quite lengthy.

The continental style of eating, with the knife in the right hand and the fork in the left, is most common.

Belgians do not approve of waste and it is considered rude not to finish one's food.

Breakfast is light. It usually consists of a hot drink with rolls or bread with jam. Sometimes it is accompanied by cold cuts or cheeses. A larger meal is eaten at midday. Dinner is usually at 7:00 or 8:00 p.m.

Belgians eat a rich variety of foods, including pork, game birds, fish, cheeses, fruits, vegetables, breads and soups. Belgium is famous for mussels, chocolates, 300 varieties of beer, waffles and french fries (which Belgians claim to have invented). French fries are served with mayonnaise, rather than with ketchup.

# BELGIUM (Cont'd)

## DINING OUT (Cont'd)

Belgians take great pride in the quality of their food as well as the variety of cuisine available. This includes both domestically developed dishes and those adapted from other cultures. Restaurants offer a wide variety of international dishes.

Wine, beer or mineral water is often served with meals. While the water is generally safe, Belgians do not drink water from the tap. Bottled water is preferred.

If your host offers a before-dinner drink, wait for him/her to name the selection and don't ask for something other than what is offered. Aperitifs, such as vermouth or Cinzano, are usually offered rather than mixed drinks.

At a dinner in a home, the host and hostess will seat everyone. Husbands and wives are never seated together. The host and hostess usually sit at either end of the table, with the male guest of honor to the right of the hostess and the female guest of honor to the right of the host.

Wrists should be kept on the table during the meal. You should not put your hands on your lap.

When dining out, never order tea or coffee during a meal. Rather, wait until the meal has ended.

When finished eating, place your fork and knife horizontally across the top of the plate, with the tines of the fork and the point of the knife facing left. It is impolite to cross your knife and fork.

Very dark, strong coffee and liqueurs are often served at the table after an informal dinner. In contrast, they are served in the living room after a formal meal. Cigars may also be smoked. It is recommended that you stay between a half-hour to an hour once the meal has concluded.

## PUBLIC CUSTOMS

Belgians follow European fashion and tend to dress well in public. Tattered or extremely casual attire is usually not worn outside of the home. Men who wear hats remove them when entering a building. On Sundays, Belgians tend to dress more formally, wearing their best clothes to go walking or visiting.

It is considered rude to talk with something in your mouth (food, toothpick, gum) or with one's hands in one's pockets.

Good posture is important, and people do not put their feet up on tables or chairs.

Snapping fingers, pointing with the index finger, blowing one's nose, scratching, yawning or using a toothpick in public are all avoided.

Men usually allow women to be seated first, enter rooms first, etc. Men usually stand when a woman enters a room.

# BULGARIA: HISTORICAL OVERVIEW

- The oldest known inhabitants of the region, which is now known as Bulgaria, were Thracians. In the fifth century B.C., they founded the Odrisaw kingdom in that area. A few hundred years later, Slavic tribes began to migrate to the region.

- In the seventh century, a central Asian people called Bulgars migrated to the area. The three ethnic groups in the area (Bulgars, Thracians and Slavs) mixed. In 681, a Bulgarian state was recognized by the Byzantine empire.

- Three Bulgarian kingdoms had existed before the area was conquered by the Turks in 1396. The Ottoman empire then ruled until 1878. This period of Turkish rule is known in Bulgaria as the "Turkish yoke." The struggle for political and religious freedom during this period gave rise to a cultural renaissance at the end of the 18th century.

- In 1878, Bulgaria became independent as a result of the Russian-Turkish War.

- Following independence, Bulgaria was briefly divided into the Kingdom of Bulgaria (the northern region) and Eastern Romelia (the southern region). Eastern Romelia remained part of the Ottoman empire until it was reunited with the northern part of Bulgaria in 1886.

- In the 20th century during both World Wars, Bulgaria was allied with Germany and was, therefore, defeated with Germany.

- In 1944, Soviet troops marched into Bulgaria and seized control. A nationalist hero against the Nazis in World War II, Georgi Dimitrov, became the Communist leader of Bulgaria. The 1947 Bulgarian constitution was named after him. He died shortly thereafter, in 1949.

- Todor Zhikov held power from 1954 until 1989, when he was removed by a palace coup. Bulgaria was caught in the wave of reforms which swept through Eastern Europe at that time. After the coup, Petar Mladenov was named the new leader of the Communist party and the head of state by the National Assembly. The government began to consider constitutional reform and the Communists renamed their party the Socialists prior to the free elections in 1990.

- While the new Socialists succeeded in passing reforms, they could not maintain a stable government and Mladenov and his Prime Minister soon resigned. A coalition government was then formed. Dimitar Popov was the Prime Minister and Zhelyu Zhelev was the President leading this coalition.

- In 1991, a new constitution was approved and a nonsocialist, multiparty parliament was formed. In 1992, Zhelev (who was a popular former dissident) was reelected president. Since that election, his government instituted measures to privatize the economy, to eliminate collective farms and to return property that was confiscated by Communist authorities in 1948 to its rightful owners or heirs.

# BULGARIA

## INTRODUCTIONS

Bulgarians usually shake hands when meeting someone. The handshake might be accompanied in formal situations by *"Kat ste?"* ("How are you?") or *"Zdraveite"* ("Hello"). The informal terms for these greetings, *"Kak si?"* and *"Zdrasti"* or *"Zdrave,"* are used among friends, relatives and colleagues.

Close female friends might kiss each other on the cheek.

Handshakes are not used when saying *"Dobro utro"* ("Good morning"), *"Dober den"* ("Good day"), *"Dober vetcher"* ("Good evening") or *"Leka nosht"* ("Good night").

First names are used in informal settings. Otherwise, titles and family names are used to address people. *"Gospodin"* ("Mr."), *"Gospozha"* ("Mrs.") or *"Gospozhitsa"* ("Miss") are common titles. Professional titles are also used.

It is polite to greet each person individually, beginning with the eldest, at a small gathering.

In rural areas, it is considered polite to greet strangers on the street, but this is uncommon in urban areas.

## SOCIAL TIPS AND CONVENTIONS

Socializing is an important part of life and friends and neighbors commonly drop by unexpectedly. Beyond close friends and relations, it is more typical for an invitation to be extended first.

Bulgarians generally respect those who are open, strong, capable, good-humored and are loyal to family and friends.

Bulgarians take pride in their heritage and culture, which have been preserved despite centuries of foreign domination.

Women usually enter a home before men.

Evening visits usually start after 8:00 p.m. and may last until after midnight (3:00 a.m. for special occasions). It is considered rude to leave early.

Be aware that toilet paper is not always available in public restrooms.

## CUSTOMARY BUSINESS PRACTICES

Professional women usually wear a skirt, blouse or sweater, and high heels to work.

Professional men wear suits and ties to work, although older men prefer trousers and sweaters.

Offices are open from 9:00 a.m. to 6:00 p.m. in most cases. Private shops often have additional hours.

# BULGARIA (Cont'd)

## CUSTOMARY BUSINESS PRACTICES (Cont'd)

The official language is Bulgarian, and nearly all inhabitants speak it. About half of the Turkish population (which makes up 8.5% if the population) speak Turkish and Bulgarian.

Some businesses close for the midday meal.

Many businesses close by noon on Saturday, and most are closed all day Sunday.

## BUSINESS ENTERTAINING

At a home, guests are usually offered refreshments, even if not invited for a meal.

Invited guests often bring flowers for the hostess, a bottle of alcohol for the host and candy for the children. An odd number of flowers are appropriate, as even numbers are reserved for funerals.

Many professional organizations, schools and local governments own lodges in the mountains where their members can stay for minimal cost.

Bills are paid at the table. Diners round the bill up to the next *lev* (Bulgarian currency) as a tip.

## DINING OUT

The continental style of eating is most common, with the fork in the left hand and the knife in the right. It is polite for guests to accept second helpings. An empty plate or glass will usually be refilled.

A small amount of food left on the plate (usually after second helpings) indicates that one is full.

Bulgarians eat pork, fish or lamb with most main dishes.

Popular main meals include *moussaka* (pork or lamb casserole with potatoes, tomatoes and yogurt) and *nadenitsa* (stuffed pork sausage). Other common dishes include *kfteta* (a fried meat patty), *sarmi* (a pepper or cabbage stuffed with pork and rice), *shopska* (a salad made with Bulgarian cheese, cucumbers and tomatoes), and *baklava* (a thin, layered pastry with a syrup and nut filling). Espresso or Turkish style coffees are usually served.

## PUBLIC CUSTOMS

European and U.S. fashions are popular.

In rural areas, guests remove their shoes upon entering a home. This courtesy is also practiced in many urban homes. Slippers are sometimes offered to guests.

"Yes" is indicated by shaking the head from side to side and "No" is expressed with one or two nods of the head.

One might shake the index finger back and forth to emphasize the "No" and even add a "tsk" sound to express displeasure.

# BULGARIA (Cont'd)

## PUBLIC CUSTOMS (Cont'd)

Hands are not generally used to replace or emphasize verbal communication.

It is impolite to point with the index finger.

It is impolite for men to cross an ankle over the knee.

In a line or crowd, it is not impolite or uncommon for one to touch or press against another person.

Bulgarians often touch while conversing. Female friends might walk arm in arm down the street.

Public holidays include New Year's Day, National Day of Freedom and Independence (March 3), Labor Day (May 1-2), the Day of Bulgarian Culture and Science (May 24) and Christmas Day (December 25). Religious holidays such as Easter are popular, but they are not public holidays.

# COMMONWEALTH OF INDEPENDENT STATES: HISTORICAL OVERVIEW

- During the Christian era, Slavic people first settled in the region of Eastern Europe. Prince Vladimir converted them to Christianity in 988. The region was then conquered by the Mongols in the early 13th century. They dominated the Slavs for 240 years. In 1480, the Slavs defeated the Mongols and regained their territory. In 1547, Ivan the Terrible, was crowned Czar of Russia.

- Subsequent rulers of Russia, Peter the Great and Catherine the Great, continued to expand Russia's territory. By the 19th century, the Russian empire reached from Warsaw to Vladivostok (on the Sea of Japan). Russia became a world power after defeating Napoleon in 1812.

- During World War I, Czar Nicholas II abdicated his throne because of popular unrest. Vladimir Lenin, head of the *Bolshevik Party*, led a revolt in 1917 which dissolved the provisional government and put the Communists in power.

- A civil war between Lenin's Red Army and the White Army lasted until 1921, when Lenin emerged victorious. Following victory, the Bolsheviks formed the Union of Soviet Socialist Republics (USSR). In 1922, the countries of Armenia, Azerbaijan, Georgia, Ukraine and Belarus were incorporated into the union.

- Lenin died in 1924 and was replaced by Joseph Stalin, a dictator who implemented forced industrialization and collective agriculture. Millions of people died during Stalin's reign. Stalin signed a nonaggression pact with Hitler at the beginning of World War II. Nevertheless, Hitler invaded the Soviet Union in 1941, and the war took more than 25 million Soviet lives.

- After Stalin died in 1953, Nikita Khruschev took his place. His reforms were opposed by hard liners, and he was replaced by Leonid Brezhnev in 1964. Brezhnev sought to expand Soviet influence in the developing world. He died in 1982 and was followed by two short-lived leaders, Yuri Andropov and Konstantin Chernenko.

- In 1986, Mikhail Gorbachev emerged as the new leader. He implemented *perestroika* (restructuring) and *glasnost* (openness). These measures brought about the development of political and individual freedoms, free enterprise and privatization. However, many reforms failed.

- An unsuccessful coup in 1991 exposed inherent weaknesses of the Soviet system and the country quickly unraveled. Russia, led by its elected president Boris Yeltsin, became an independent country and moved to introduce democratic and free-market reforms. The former Soviet Union was dissolved and Belarus, Ukraine and Russia founded the C.I.S.

- In 1993, there was a crisis when Yeltsin attempted to dissolve Parliament and, in response, it voted to impeach him. Even with that crisis over, Yeltsin continued to face challenges from ultranationalist leaders in 1994.

# COMMONWEALTH OF INDEPENDENT STATES

*The Commonwealth of Independent States (C.I.S.) is a mix of more than one hundred different languages and a great variety of cultures. It would be impossible to cover all cultural variations. This section is an attempt to provide an overview of the business and social customs of ethnic Russians, Belorussians, Ukrainians and the Russian Federation. These customs have played an important role in the culture and traditions of all parts of the C.I.S. While there are significant variations between the different regions (Ukraine, Belarus and the Russian Federation), the similarities are greater than the differences. The Russian/Ukrainian customs dominate the large, urban business centers (Moscow, Kiev, Minsk and Leningrad) and the Russian language is spoken throughout the C.I.S. (even if only as a second language).*

*There are separate entries in this book for Central European countries and one of the Baltic countries. These entries include Bulgaria, the Czech Republic and Slovakia, Hungary, Lithuania, Poland and Romania. While these countries have been influenced by Russian customs, they have quite distinct cultures. There are also separate entries for Azerbaijan, Kyrgyzstan and Tajikistan. While the Southwestern republics (Armenia, Azerbaijan, Georgia, Kazakhstan, Kyrgyzstan, Tajikistan, Turkmenistan and Uzbekistan) are influenced by Russian culture, they are strongly influenced by Middle-Eastern and Asian cultures as well. You may find it helpful to look at the Azerbaijan, Kyrgyzstan and Tajikistan entries, as well as the entries for some Middle-Eastern countries to get a sense of the customs practiced in these Southwestern areas.*

## INTRODUCTIONS

When meeting strangers, the people of the C.I.S. offer to shake hands and then state their names. The handshake is the most commonly accepted greeting. A person of the C.I.S. usually prefers to be direct and informal.

A person from the C.I.S. usually shakes hands with an acquaintance every time they meet. Good friends (male or female) kiss each other on the cheek three times in greeting. Men and women do not kiss each other in public unless they are relatives or are romantically involved.

Forms of address may be confusing to a foreigner. After 1917, the Russian words for "Mr.," "Mrs." or "Miss" were abolished. However, the use of the word *"tovarisch"* ("comrade") is not used as commonly as some Westerners may believe. It is usually only used at political meetings. Strangers in the street will address each other as *"grazhdanin"* or *"grazhdanka"* ("citizen" for men and women respectively). Specific greetings and titles may vary according to local language and custom.

The patronymic is formed by adding *"-vitch"* (male ending) or *"-ovna"* (female ending) to the person's father's name. For example, if someone is the "son of Ivan" then his patronymic is "Ivanovitch" and if someone is the "daughter of Ivan" then her patronymic is "Ivanovna." The people of the C.I.S. treat their foreign acquaintances in much the same manner. No matter how clumsy a foreign patronymic might sound in Russian, they will be offended if it is not accepted as a token admission of familiarity.

People from the C.I.S. will usually introduce themselves by stating their *imya* (first name), *ochestvo* (patrynomic) and *familia* (family name). Do not be surprised if a husband and wife have different last names. In the C.I.S. it is common for a woman to retain her own last name when she gets married. The standard way of addressing someone is by using his/her name and patronymic only without the last name.

## COMMONWEALTH OF INDEPENDENT STATES (Cont'd)

### INTRODUCTIONS (Cont'd)

First names are reserved for close friends and family.

If asked by a friend, "How are you?" a person will answer modestly, saying "okay" or "not bad" rather than "fine" or "good." Even if things are going well, one generally does not say so. This is so as not to appear ahead of others, which is not appreciated by the people of the C.I.S.

### SOCIAL TIPS AND CONVENTIONS

Life in the C.I.S. has become more free, and many people will discuss politics and living conditions. However, political discussions are still generally taboo. For conversation, stick to common interests: the arts, sports, architecture and other neutral topics.

People of the C.I.S. generally dislike comparisons with the West, unless it is in their favor. They are very proud of their accomplishments, so you should praise what you genuinely admire. If they criticize their country, do not join them in criticism.

To the uninitiated observer, some people in the C.I.S. may appear still and lifeless. Gestures are usually kept to a minimum. Expressions may seem blank and uninterested. Smiles are rare, except between people who are very close.

### CUSTOMARY BUSINESS PRACTICES

Most C.I.S. executives are serious about business and follow conservative business protocol and courtesies. They love to do business over a glass of vodka and a hearty plate of meat and potatoes. They have a good sense of humor.

English is widely used in commercial and government transactions, and interpreters are plentiful. English is the most common foreign language spoken by C.I.S. foreign trade officials. Nevertheless, avoid slang and idiomatic expressions. Many officials also speak German.

Business appointments are often arranged in advance through C.I.S. representatives abroad. The best time to contact businesspeople in the C.I.S. is between 9:00 and 10:00 a.m. Appointments can usually be arranged from 9:00 a.m. to 6:00 p.m., Monday to Friday. Take along written confirmation of dates, and be punctual for appointments.

It is helpful to send letters of introduction with the resumes of the visiting businesspeople two weeks before departure to the C.I.S. Preferably, the letters and resumes should be in the local language. Bilingual business cards are appreciated.

It is considered polite to bring a small gift for your colleague. A cigarette lighter, chocolates or a bottle of French cognac or Western whiskey would be appreciated by men. Women might enjoy a scarf, some make-up or costume jewelry.

It is a good idea to have on hand a large supply of business cards. The university degree of the business visitor should be included on the card and it should be printed in *Cyrillic* (the Russian alphabet). At negotiations involving many C.I.S. officials, be sure to give a card to everyone present, in order not to overlook someone who might turn out to be important.

# COMMONWEALTH OF INDEPENDENT STATES (Cont'd)

## CUSTOMARY BUSINESS PRACTICES (Cont'd)

Most importantly, you will need a good deal of patience, flexibility and understanding in the C.I.S. Doing business there has changed over the last 10 years, mainly due to governmental reforms. On one hand, these reforms have made joint ventures easier, and while encouraging more private ownership, they have also increased control of privately-owned firms in foreign trade and capital management. On the other hand, these changes require structural and behavioral adjustments. A good number of businesses are still owned and operated by the government. You may often be dealing with bureaucratic and business practices that remain as a legacy from the Soviet era, despite recent broad reforms.

Trying to meet with businesspeople can be a time-consuming process. You may have to go through several ministries and agencies, and approval from one does not guarantee approval from the others. You may have to devote a lot of senior executive time, since broad segments of bureaucracy can be involved. At the same time, you may encounter a simplified process since many segments of this bureaucracy are gradually becoming obsolete and are being phased out, as the former Soviet Union is making the transition to a market-style economy. Generally, you should be aware of and prepared for possible bureaucratic obstacles within your field of business.

C.I.S. executives dislike a quick tempo of business and the U.S. attitude that time is money. They are able to devote far more time and manpower to negotiations than Westerners ordinarily do and will use the slower tempo to good advantage. One proverb states, "If you travel for a day, take bread for a week," and another, "Patience and work, and everything will work out."

Continuity is an important factor. One person should be identified as the project manager throughout all negotiations.

C.I.S. businesspeople will enter all negotiations well prepared and having conducted thorough research. It is advisable to be accompanied by at least one colleague with technical expertise.

Problems of protocol can arise when doing business in the C.I.S. Deference must be given to top officials in such matters as seating arrangements and invitations. The protocol department of each ministry can assist in preparing a list of top officials. It is sometimes difficult to quickly identify high officials, so make sure not to overlook anyone in your initial contacts. He/she may well turn out to be the head of the team. Allow ample time for this process.

C.I.S. officials expect to do business with only the highest-ranking executives.

Any person representing an international company in the C.I.S. should be at least a Regional or East European manager. Executives there are not impressed with "representatives." Final negotiations on larger deals should be handled by a top executive. This demonstrates to the C.I.S. executives the importance the firm is placing on this business. The chairman or deputy chairman might even consider entering the negotiations at some key stage.

Conservative business suits or dresses are appropriate for all meetings.

# COMMONWEALTH OF INDEPENDENT STATES (Cont'd)

## BUSINESS ENTERTAINING

The people of the C.I.S. are, by nature, very friendly and welcoming. They enjoy business entertaining. In fact, within the C.I.S., it is sometimes said that the notion of hospitality is a Russian invention.

It is quite common for hospitality to include an invitation to visit one's home. However, you should not be offended if an invitation of this sort is not extended.

As in many European countries, it is common (but not required) for guests to bring flowers or liquor for their hosts. If you bring flowers, you should be sure to bring an odd number. An even number of flowers is reserved for funerals only and will offend the host. You should also avoid white flowers, which are also reserved for funerals.

Gift-giving is popular among the people of the C.I.S. It is important to give presents to the people you meet, or if you go visiting. Although gifts may be very simple, what counts is the friendship expressed in giving them. Gifts from international visitors should include items, which are difficult to obtain in the C.I.S. These include chewing gum for the children, jeans, books, perfume and certain food items.

The people of the C.I.S. enjoy food and entertaining. Meals are long and elaborate, and toasts are frequently and generously made to good business.

## DINING OUT

Entertaining C.I.S. colleagues by hosting a meal or a reception can be arranged at a number of hotels or restaurants. Some restaurants and bars accept foreign currency.

Good food can be obtained for low prices in a variety of restaurants. Specialty restaurants offering traditional Georgian or Armenian foods (chicken dishes and kebabs) are quite common. There are also some very good Indian restaurants in the main cities.

Be aware that service in restaurants may be very slow.

Traditional foods that you may want to try include *chicken Kiev* (a piece of breaded chicken rolled up and stuffed with herbed butter), *beef stroganoff* (beef stew with cream), stuffed cabbage leaves, *borscht* (beet soup) or cabbage soup, *pirogi* (meat, cheese or fruit pies), *vareniki* (small, boiled pastry-wrapped cheese, meat or fruit) and a variety of salads. *Kebabi* (meat and vegetable kebabs) are popular in the Southwestern areas.

Ice-cream cafés are very popular for quick snacks. These cafés offer a variety of flavors of a delicious, special kind of soft ice cream. Some of these cafés may also sell champagne by the glass. There are also a number of fast-food restaurants and pizzerias in the big cities.

It may be difficult to obtain spirits or wine in the C.I.S., due to periodic active government campaigns against alcohol. However, vodka remains popular. Russian champagne and Georgian wine are also enjoyed.

# COMMONWEALTH OF INDEPENDENT STATES (Cont'd)

## DINING OUT (Cont'd)

You may want to try a local, unique alcoholic beverage, called *kvass* (a slightly alcoholic, refreshing beverage made from black bread). Beware of drinking another local specialty, called *samogon* (a very strong, homemade beverage).

The main meal usually begins with *zakuski* (hors d'oeuvres made from salads, sausages, pies, pieces of fish, etc.), served with vodka. Vodka is served in tiny glasses and you should drink it down all at once. Do not sip it. Typically, there will be a series of toasts and speeches. After each proposed toast, everyone at the table will drink their vodka and then eat something.

After the meal, liqueurs (such as cherry, Armenian or Georgian brandy or fruit-flavored vodka) are often served. Finally, at the end of the meal, tea and coffee accompanied by an elaborately prepared *torte* (cake) are usually served. People generally remain seated around the table, talking until late in the evening.

## PUBLIC CUSTOMS

Friendship is very openly expressed. It is common to see men walking hand in hand with other men. It is also common for women to walk arm in arm.

In the big cities, the streets can be wide and difficult to cross. Jaywalking is strictly prohibited, and the streets are often monitored for jaywalking by police officers. It is not unusual for locals and foreigners to be fined for this offense.

While in the C.I.S., you should take special care not to litter. People of the C.I.S. are very proud of their cities and the *Metro* transit system. They are both very clean and free of graffiti. If you inadvertently drop something, do not be surprised if you are asked by someone to pick it up.

It is customary to leave your boots and jacket or coat in a cloakroom, when you go into a public place (e.g., library, theater, restaurant), especially in the winter.

Shopping in the C.I.S. can be cumbersome and time-consuming. Large supermarkets have now opened where people walk around the store and put food into shopping carts. In large cities, special hard-currency shops, called *beriozki*, are available to foreigners. A wide variety of items can be purchased here at low prices. However, it is much more common for smaller stores to have an old-fashioned, lining-up process: First you line up to choose the item that you want; second, you are told the cost of the item; third, you line up to pay the cashier for the item; finally, you take the receipt back to the desk to pick up the item.

# CZECH REPUBLIC AND SLOVAKIA: HISTORICAL OVERVIEW

- Slavic tribes began settling in the region in the fifth century, and, by the middle of the ninth century, they lived in a loose confederation known as the great Moravian Empire. However, as early as 907, the invasion of the Magyars (ancestors of today's Hungarians) brought an end to the Moravian Empire. The Slovak region was controlled by Hungarian rule, while Czechs developed the Bohemian Empire centered in Prague.

- In the 14th and 15th centuries, under the leadership of Charles IV, Prague became a cultural and political capital, and Bohemia was a center of the Protestant Reformation led by Jan Hus. Civil war in Bohemia and events elsewhere in Europe during the 15th century led Czechoslovakia (as well as Hungarians and Slovakians) to become part of the Austro-Hungarian Empire in 1526.

- When the Austro-Hungarian Empire collapsed upon being defeated in World War I, Czech and Slovak lands were united to form a new Czecho-Slovak state (The hyphen in the name was dropped in 1920.). Democracy and the economy of the new state flourished.

- In 1938, Hitler annexed the Sudetenland, a Czech area of German-speaking people. By 1939, Germany took over all of the Czech regions. Czech society was deeply affected by World War II and more than 350,000 citizens (250,000 Jews) lost their lives. After the war, three million Germans were forced out of the country.

- At the end of World War II, Czechoslovakia was liberated by Allied Forces. It held elections in 1946 under Soviet auspices. Left-wing parties performed well in the elections, and by 1948, the Communists seized total control. Rapid industrialization was promoted during the 1950s. In the 1960s, due to a decline in the quality of life, the government began to liberalize, and there were discussions about easing political restrictions. However, leaders in other East-bloc countries and the Soviet Union as well as top Communists in Czechoslovakia activated Warsaw Pact troops to crush the movement. Reforms were abolished, and the *Czech Communist Party* was purged of liberals.

- Many dissident groups organized against the regime in the 1970s. In 1989, many people took part in peaceful demonstrations which became known as the "Velvet Revolution." A crackdown on a student protest in 1989 led to a general strike that prompted General Secretary Milos Jakes to resign. Reform-minded Alexander Dubcek, a Slovak, was elected leader of parliament and Vaclav Havel, a dissident playwright, became president in 1990.

- Full multiparty elections were held in 1992, and Havel remained president, Vaclav Klaus became prime minister of the Czech national government and Vladimir Meciar became prime minister of the Slovak national government. Disagreements between the Slovak and Czech leaders regarding economic policies led the two national governments to agree to split the country into two sovereign states in 1993. Havel resigned, refusing to oversee the dissolution of the country, but he was reelected president of the Czech Republic after the split. The breakup was peaceful, and ties between the two nations remain strong. Klaus launched an impressive program of economic reform in the Czech Republic.

# CZECH REPUBLIC AND SLOVAKIA

*On January 1, 1993, the Czech Republic and Slovakia split apart peacefully. While the countries are now separate, the languages and customs remain very similar. For this reason, they have been combined under one heading. Any differences in customs between the two countries will be mentioned.*

## INTRODUCTIONS

Upon introduction, people shake hands firmly and say their last names, followed by a verbal greeting, such as *"Tesi mne"* ("Pleased to meet you") or *"Dobry den"* ("Good day"). Women and older people extend their hands first when greeting others.

It is customary to shake hands with everyone present upon arrival and upon departure at both social and business occasions.

To show respect, it is important to address both men and women by their professional titles ("Engineer," "Doctor," "Professor"), followed by the last name. If the people you are meeting are not professionals, you may use the titles *"Pán"* (pronounced "Pahn") which means "Mr.," *"Pani"* (pronounced "PAH-nee"), which means "Mrs." or *"Slecna"* (pronounced "SLEH-chnah" ) which means "Miss."

It is also common to precede a professional title with *"Pán"* or *"Pani,"* when greeting someone. For example, you can say, *"Dobr den, Pani Doktorko Cekan"* ("Good day, Mr. Dr. Cekan").

Normally, first names are only used among relatives, good friends and young people who also sometimes hug each other in greeting.

To say good-bye, the formal *"Na chledanou"* or the informal *"Ciao"* are used. *"Ahoj"* can be used as an informal "Hi" and "Bye."

## SOCIAL TIPS AND CONVENTIONS

Both Czech and Slovak are Slavic languages, related to Polish, Croatian and Russian. Both languages use a Latin alphabet. Czechs and Slovaks also often speak German, Russian or English, depending on their generation. German is the most commonly spoken foreign language.

Czechs value cleverness, humor and wit, especially dry or ironic humor. Jokes and anecdotes are used often in conversation. They value education and social standing as well. While professionals (doctors, lawyers, engineers, etc.) are admired, so are skilled manual workers.

Czech society emphasizes conformity and cooperation over individuality. Community leaders are held in high esteem, and the youth are encouraged to participate in community and sports clubs. Czechs can also be individualistic in stating their opinions or in being stubborn about individual beliefs or wishes.

While 81% of the population of the Czech Republic are ethnic Czechs, there are a number of ethnic minorities who speak their own language. Some of these groups may exhibit particular character traits, customs and values. Moravians (about 13% of the population) and Slovaks (about 3%) are known to be more lighthearted and jovial than Czechs.

# CZECH REPUBLIC AND SLOVAKIA (Cont'd)

## SOCIAL TIPS AND CONVENTIONS (Cont'd)

In Slovakia, Slovaks (who constitute about 81% of the population) are outgoing and value good humor. They are generous and will go out of their way to make a guest feel comfortable. Like Czechs, they value education, modesty and honesty.

Due to the difficult transition period to Slovakian statehood, some people are extremely sensitive about topics related to independence. They are particularly interested in the way foreigners view them and are eager to project a positive image.

Sports, especially soccer, tennis and ice hockey, make good conversation topics. The countryside and area you are in also make good conversation topics since Czechs and Slovaks have a love for nature and enjoy a number of outdoor activities. Music (including Czech composers Dvorak and Janacek) and other arts also make good topics of conversation. Traditional arts, such as the theater, are close to the hearts of many Slovaks.

Do not discuss politics, especially socialism and the former Soviet Union. If your host brings up political matters, feel free to participate, but avoid criticizing the government.

It is perfectly acceptable to ask personal questions about someone's job or family, even if you have just met the person.

Eye contact is very important in conversation. Also, gesturing is used extensively for emphasis in conversation.

Speaking loudly is considered impolite.

Czechs will commonly look at or even stare at people in public. However, usually this has no ill intentions.

## CUSTOMARY BUSINESS PRACTICES

When doing business in the Czech Republic, be aware that the country has just made the transition from a planned economy to a free market. Both small and large private companies are opening and developing. Additionally, people are generally eager to do business and to encourage foreign investment. However, you should not be surprised if your Czech colleagues seem very cautious since new business laws and customs are being introduced and developed. In fact, it is advisable to hire a Czech business lawyer since radical changes in business law have created considerable complexity in doing business.

You should avoid planning business trips for July or August, as most people take vacations during the summer months.

Make appointments well in advance (at least 10 days).

It may take some time for first introductions. If you are sending a letter from abroad, you should send it at least a month in advance. When writing a letter to a Czech or Slovak company, you should address the letter to the firm, not to an individual.

## CZECH REPUBLIC AND SLOVAKIA (Cont'd)

### CUSTOMARY BUSINESS PRACTICES (Cont'd)

Czechs and Slovaks typically converse before conducting business. Drinks and coffee are often offered at business meetings. It is polite to accept these refreshments. If a toast is made, it is polite to return it.

Expect decisions to be made much more slowly than in the U.S. Many Czechs have adopted the German style of conducting business, which involves slow, methodical planning.

Business dress is conservative. Businessmen wear dark suits, ties and white shirts; business-women wear dark suits with white blouses or dresses. Follow the lead of your colleagues in regard to removing ties or jackets.

Have business letters sent in English as well as the local language (Czech or Slovak) to make an extremely good impression.

Keep in mind that English is not widely spoken; therefore, an interpreter may be needed.

Bring plenty of business cards, as they are used abundantly. It is appreciated if your card is printed both in English and in the local language (Czech or Slovak). Czechs and Slovaks respect education; therefore, you should be sure to include any degree above a bachelor's level on your card.

Business hours are usually from 8:00 a.m. until between 3:00 and 5:00 p.m during the week.

### BUSINESS ENTERTAINING

Entertaining rarely takes place in the home, since Czechs and Slovaks consider the home to be strictly private. Normally, people socialize in pubs, coffee houses and wine bars, and dinners take place in restaurants. If you are invited to a home, even for a drink or coffee, you should consider this an honor.

Do not expect to have much contact with your business associates outside of the office. While Czechs and Slovaks are very hospitable, it may take a lot of time to establish a close business relationship. Historically, business meetings have been confined to offices. However, Czechs are becoming more accustomed to Western customs, including the business lunch.

Meal reservations should be made in advance since there are only a few good restaurants for business entertaining, and they are very busy.

Business is generally discussed before and after, but not during, a meal.

It is appropriate, but not necessary, to include spouses in invitations.

Czechs remove their shoes and leave them in the entryway when entering a home.

When entertaining, Czechs and Slovaks tend to be very formal, but at the same time very warm. Guests are usually offered drinks or, before meals, hors d'oeuvres.

# CZECH REPUBLIC AND SLOVAKIA (Cont'd)

## BUSINESS ENTERTAINING (Cont'd)

If you are invited to a home, it is polite to bring flowers. Bring an odd number of flowers (but not 13) to the host, since an even number of flowers is associated with a funeral. Avoid chrysanthemums or cala lilies (which are associated with funerals) and red roses (which are associated with romance). Unwrap the flowers before giving them. Liquor (wine, whiskey or cognac), chocolates or gifts for the children are also appreciated.

Generally, businesspeople do not give or expect to receive expensive gifts. Acceptable business gifts include good quality pens, pocket calculators, cigarette lighters or imported wine or liquor.

At formal parties, your host should introduce you to the other guests. In fact, at formal parties it is impolite to speak to someone unless you have been introduced. However, at informal parties, it is acceptable to introduce yourself if your host has not introduced you.

Wait until everyone has been served a drink before picking up your glass. Toasting is common both for formal and informal events. If it is a special occasion, toasts will probably be proposed. As a guest, you should feel free to offer a toast in honor of the celebration.

When dining in a home or in a restaurant, men should wear casual slacks, a shirt and a sweater (optional); while women should wear dresses or skirts and blouses. In more formal restaurants, men should wear suits and ties.

## DINING OUT

If the tip is included in the bill, it is common to leave extra change on the table. If service is not included, a 5-10% tip should be left at the table.

Czechs and Slovaks generally eat three meals a day as well as a mid-morning snack. For most people, lunch is the main meal with breakfast and dinner being lighter.

Breakfast, which is served early, usually consists of rolls, coffee cake, butter, jam and coffee. Lunch usually begins with a hearty soup, followed by a main dish of meat and potato or bread dumplings. A common dish is *vepro-knedlo-zelo* (pork roast, dumplings and sauerkraut). Ham on bread and sausages in buns are popular snack foods that can even be purchased from sidewalk vendors. Puddings and desserts made from fruit are popular. Common drinks are juice, beer, mineral water and soda.

The mid-morning snack, eaten at about 10:00 a.m., usually consists of sandwiches or hot sausages and yogurt. At 4:00 p.m., there is often a break for sandwiches and Turkish coffee.

Supper is usually served between 5:30 and 6:30 p.m. If lunch was a full meal, supper will be lighter, often just cheese or meat sandwiches and milk. The meal will be heavier at a dinner party. *Slivovitz* (plum brandy) or *becherovka* (herb brandy) may be served before the meal. Dinner usually begins with soup followed by a main course such as roast pork, sauerkraut and dumplings. Turkish coffee generally follows the meal. Dessert is often apple strudel, fruit cake or cookies.

## CZECH REPUBLIC AND SLOVAKIA (Cont'd)

### DINING OUT (Cont'd)

Traditional Czech and Slovak food is heavy and difficult to prepare. In the past few years, a healthier diet (with fewer heavy sauces, leaner meat, more vegetables and easier to prepare food) has become more popular as the pace of life has accelerated, and people have become more conscious regarding their health. Still, Czechs and Slovaks usually prefer a hot meal to a cold one, even in hot weather. Popular dishes include *franecek* (herring), *sardinky* (sardines), *husa* (roast goose) and *svickova na smetane* (filet of beef with sour cream). The Slovak national dish is *bryndzove halusky* (potato pancakes).

Plates are usually prepared in the kitchen and are carried to the table. At a dinner, guests are usually served first, although the oldest woman at the table is sometimes served first.

People eat in the continental style, with the fork in the left hand and the knife remaining in the right. You should not put your knife and fork down between bites.

Hands, but not elbows, should be kept above the table during meals (even once the meal has been finished and people are talking).

Conversation is not abundant during meals and usually is only encouraged if guests are present or if the head of the household speaks first. After the meal, people will stay at the table and talk.

Normally, second or third servings are offered. It is not impolite to decline the food graciously. However, on a first offer for a second serving, it is polite to accept a little food after initially refusing.

To indicate that you have finished, you should place utensils together at one side of the plate. If you want to signal that you are just taking a break, you should cross your utensils on the plate.

### PUBLIC CUSTOMS

Avoid taking pictures in museums or galleries or photographing policemen, military installations, airports and railroad stations.

European fashions are commonly worn in the Czech Republic. Younger people, in particular, wear the latest styles. Casual wear, including jeans and t-shirts, is popular. Adults do not

normally wear shorts on city streets (only in parks). Also, members of the older generation may dress more formally. For example, older women do not wear slacks, and older people wear hats more often than members of the younger generation.

It is acceptable to beckon others and point using the index finger. To gain someone's attention, raise your hand, palm facing out, with only the index finger extended. You should avoid waving.

When sitting, you should cross one knee over the other, rather than resting your ankle on the other knee. You should not prop your feet up on furniture.

It is impolite to converse with your hands in your pockets or while chewing gum.

To wish someone good luck, Slovaks cross their thumbs (they fold the thumb and close the fingers on it).

Bargaining is not acceptable anywhere in the Czech Republic.

# DENMARK: HISTORICAL OVERVIEW

- As long as 100,000 years ago, people lived in the region that is now known as Denmark. As the climate changed, the region became uninhabitable for humans. However, after the climate began to get warmer about 14,000 years ago, continuous settlement began. Eventually, at the turn of the millennium, trade by sea brought people in the area of Denmark into contact with other civilizations. During this period of contact, Denmark came under the control of Vikings. People lived in small communities governed by local chieftains.

- During the rule of the Vikings (c. 750-1060), Denmark was a great power. However, the exact dates and names of the different rulers during the first decades of that time period are not known exactly. The first known king was Gorm the Old, who ruled in the early 900s. His son, Harald Bluetooth first united all of Denmark under Christianity and ruled in the latter half of the 900s. Canute the Great commanded a vast empire that included England until 1035. During this period of Viking rule, Danish seamen raided European coastal towns and spread terror through much of Western Europe. Queen Margrethe I became ruler in 1375 and united Denmark, Norway and Sweden in the Union of Kalmar, with the power centered in Denmark in 1397.

- Between the 16th and 18th centuries, Denmark engaged in costly wars, particularly against Sweden. Sweden left the Kalmar Union in 1523, and in the Danish-Swedish War, from 1657 to 1660, Denmark lost its Swedish provinces. In 1814, Denmark lost Norway to Sweden. In 1864, some additional territory was lost to Prussia (Germany). Despite this series of territorial losses, Denmark regained stability. Finally in 1849, King Frederik VII signed a liberal constitution, making the country a constitutional monarchy rather than an autocracy.

- Denmark was neutral during World War I. Although it declared neutrality in World War II, Nazi Germany occupied it. After the war, in 1949, Denmark joined the North Atlantic Treaty Organization (NATO) and joined the European Union (EU) in 1973.

- During the 1970s and 1980s, government policies focused on increasing the standard of living and maintaining the social welfare system. During the 1980s, Denmark passed some of the most severe environmental legislation in the world as it became interested in environmental protection.

- In the 1990s, Denmark has been gradually moving toward greater integration with its European Union partners. In 1992, the Danish rejected the Maastricht Treaty, later accepting a modified version in 1993. This version exempts Denmark from certain aspects of union and allows the country greater flexibility in its interactions with other EU nations. Many provisions of this treaty will take effect at the end of the decade. Until recently, Denmark was the only Scandinavian country to have full membership in the European Union.

- The current Queen of Denmark, Margrethe II, is the first queen since Margrethe I ruled in the 14th century. Denmark has had 53 kings, but only two queens, both named Margrethe. 1997 marks the 25th anniversary of the reign of Margrethe II.

# DENMARK

## INTRODUCTIONS

When you are introduced, you should rise and shake hands, whether the occasion is business or social. You should make eye contact, nod and say "Hello" or "Good Day." Feel free to introduce yourself if necessary.

You should shake hands heartily when you meet someone you know as well as when you leave.

Generally, you should use last names following a title (e.g., "Mr.," "Mrs." or "Miss"). However, if your Danish colleague switches to first names in conversation, you should feel free to do the same.

If you wish to be very polite, use professional titles (e.g., "Doctor," "Professor," etc.), especially with older people.

Young people and close acquaintances may nod and wave and say, *"Dav"* or *"Davs"* (pronounced "Dow"), which is like saying "Hello." The youth often also say *"Hej"* (pronounced "Hi") when greeting or parting. The term for "Good Day" is *"Goddag."*

## SOCIAL TIPS AND CONVENTIONS

Danish is the official language of the country and German is spoken in small communities along the border of Germany. English is widely studied, understood and spoken, although less so in rural areas and by older people.

Eye contact is important in conversation.

Danes are quite reserved but are very friendly and informal. They do not generally show their emotions in public or use hand gestures in conversation.

Danes are very progressive. One way this is reflected is in Denmark's high standard of living. They are known for their tolerance of other people and diverse points of view. They are proud to take responsibility for their nation's social welfare, despite the heavy taxes imposed on individuals.

Good topics of conversation include food, Danish culture, your own hometown or area, the area in which you are staying and in current events. Danes also enjoy discussing scientific or cultural topics. They are well-educated and respected for their accomplishments in science, art, literature and architecture. Recent and popular books and sports are also good conversation topics. Soccer is particularly popular.

Avoid discussing income, religion, divorce or any other personal subject. Commenting on someone's clothes, even if you are making a compliment is considered odd.

The Danes do not like to be confused with Norwegians or Swedes.

# DENMARK (Cont'd)

## CUSTOMARY BUSINESS PRACTICES

You should avoid scheduling business trips between June 20 and August 15 (summer vacation) as well as around Easter, April 16 (birthday of the Queen), June 5 (Constitution Day) and Christmas.

Appointments are necessary. Try not to schedule an appointment on a weekend.

The Danish people respect tradition, so it is useful to mention the age and history of your firm (if it is well established).

Punctuality for business appointments is practiced and expected.

For business, men should wear suits or sports jackets and ties. Pants should be neatly pressed and shoes should be polished. Women should wear skirt suits or dresses.

Businesses are usually open from 8:00 or 9:00 a.m. to 5:00 p.m., Monday through Friday.

## BUSINESS ENTERTAINING

Danes enjoy entertaining visitors in their homes and making guests feel welcome. Refreshments are almost always served.

Proper etiquette is important when visiting in Denmark. You should not enter a home until invited to do so. The host will suggest where one should sit. When visiting, conversation about one's personal life is avoided.

If you are invited to a Danish home for the evening, do not assume that dinner will be served, unless your host specified this in your invitation.

If you are invited to a dinner in a home, you should be punctual. There is no pre-dinner cocktail hour and you may be seated in the dining room immediately.

Appropriate gifts include liquor (particularly appreciated since taxes on alcoholic products are very high in Denmark), wrapped flowers (tiny roses, anemones or flowers of the season), a product typical of your hometown, a book describing your home area, etc. U.S. cigarettes are not a good gift since Danes do not like them. If you know a family well, you can bring records, blue jeans, t-shirts or even makeup (which is very expensive in Denmark).

Alcohol may be ordered in a bar or restaurant 24 hours a day, unlike in other Scandinavian countries.

If you are invited to a casual dinner, it is acceptable to wear clean jeans. At a more formal dinner, men usually wear jackets and ties; women wear dresses, blouses and skirts or dressy pants. It is advisable for businesspeople to pack formal wear since senior businessmen in Denmark host black-tie dinners more often than in other countries.

# DENMARK (Cont'd)

## BUSINESS ENTERTAINING (Cont'd)

In restaurants, men customarily handle all affairs. A waiter can be summoned by raising the hand and index finger.

It is not necessary to leave a tip, as a service charge is included in the bill. However, some people also leave a small additional gratuity.

## DINING OUT

Dinners are usually long and slow with a lot of conversation. People will stay at the table talking long after the meal is finished.

Breakfast (served about 8:00 a.m.) is a light meal consisting of cereal, *ymer* (a type of yogurt) or soft-boiled eggs, bread or hard rolls, cheese and a hot drink or milk. A midday meal, consisting of open-faced sandwiches with beer or soft drinks and coffee, is eaten between noon and 2:00 p.m. Dinner is served between 6:00 and 8:00 p.m.

Usually Danes take a coffee break at 9:00 or 10:00 a.m., a tea break at 3:00 p.m. and, often, an evening snack of pastries and fruit around 9:00 or 10:00 p.m.

A formal dinner begins with soup, followed by a fish dish, then meat, potatoes and cooked vegetables. If there is a salad at dinner, it is served after the meat course. The meal ends with cheese and fruit, followed by dessert and coffee. Sometimes, brandy and cognac are served. After-dinner drinks (such as Scotch and soda or gin and tonic) are then offered.

A less formal dinner may start with sandwiches and beer, or it may consist only of a main course and dessert. Sometimes *akvavit* (an alcohol made from potatoes and served ice cold with a beer chaser) accompanies the sandwiches.

Usually, the host and hostess sit at either end of the table with the guest of honor being seated beside the host. Everyone is seated and served before anyone starts eating.

Toasting in Denmark involves quite formal etiquette. You should not taste the wine until the host makes the first toast. Before you take your first sip of wine, lift your glass and look around at everyone. After you have tasted the wine, look around at everyone again. The guest may propose subsequent toasts. However, a guest should never toast the host or a person senior in age until that person toasts him/her first. If you are the guest of honor, you may propose a toast by tapping your glass with a spoon. An appropriate toast would be to say, "Thank you for having this dinner in my honor." During dessert, the person seated to the left of the host should propose a toast. The person seated on the right should make a brief speech of appreciation.

The Danish eat continental style, holding the fork in the left hand and the knife in the right.

At a dinner, the food will usually be passed around several times on platters. You may want to take small portions the first time, since it is considered insulting not to take a second helping of at least some dishes.

# DENMARK (Cont'd)

## DINING OUT (Cont'd)

It is considered impolite to leave food on your plate. However, if you did not like a particular dish, do not feel obliged to take a second helping of it.

To show that you have finished eating, you should place the knife and fork, tines up, side by side vertically on the plate. Placing the fork with its tines down indicates that you would like more food.

Do not get up from the table until the hostess has done so. It is proper to thank her for the meal before leaving the table. Very often, the dinner party will move to the living room for after-dinner cocktails. Guests often stay as late as 1:00 a.m. after dining. The host may serve coffee, soup or sandwiches between 11:00 p.m. and 1:00 a.m.

Danish specialties include: *bøf tartare* (raw ground sirloin on white bread with a raw onion ring and raw egg yolk on top of it), *flæskesteg* (roast pork served with red cabbage), *frikadeller* (meatballs), *øllebrød* (rye bread mixed with black beer, sugar and lemon, with a soup-like texture), *rødspætter* (sole), *sild* (herring), *lagkage* (layers of sponge cake with custard, strawberries and whipped cream) and *rødgrød* (fruit compote).

The staples include pork roast, fish, beans, brussels sprouts, potatoes, various fresh vegetables and breads such as wheat, rye and pumpernickel. The *frokostbord*, a cold buffet of many different foods, is very popular in Denmark. This kind of meal can last several hours.

## PUBLIC CUSTOMS

Danes follow general European fashion trends. Due to the climate, which is cool and rainy, coats and woolen clothes are essential. Casual dress is generally appropriate and fashionable. Both men and women often wear slacks and sports shirts or sweaters. Sloppy clothes are inappropriate, as neatness and cleanliness are valued.

Touching others is considered inappropriate.

Men usually allow a woman to be seated first, enter a doorway first, etc. Men usually stand when a woman enters the room. Going *up* stairways, men should go first; going *down* stairways, women should go first.

It is common for women to wear topless bathing suits at the beach.

# ESTONIA: HISTORICAL OVERVIEW

- Present-day Estonians are descendants of an ancient Finno-Ugric tribe that inhabited the region for thousands of years. Before the 13th century, predominantly rural Estonians generally lived in free association without an aristocracy of any kind.

- In the 1200s, German and Danish crusaders invaded the region and eventually dominated it. This invasion introduced aristocracy in the region. Baltic Germans remained the ruling class until well into the 20th century.

- In 1561, Estonia came under Swedish control. The country then fell under Russian influence beginning in 1710.

- In 1917, Estonia took advantage of the chaos created by Russia's Bolshevik Revolution and declared its independence. Although the Red Army invaded at this time, it was defeated in the Battle of Vonnu.

- Estonia maintained its independence for 22 years. Then, under the secret Molotov-Ribbentrop pact between Germany's Hitler and Russia's Stalin, Estonia was invaded by the Soviet Union in 1940. Then, Germany occupied the territory of Estonia from 1941 until 1944.

- At the end of World War II, the Russians reestablished their power and reincorporated Estonia into the Soviet Union. Under Soviet control, Estonia was Russianized and communized. Soviet policies also contributed to substantial environmental degradation.

- When Soviet leader Mikhail Gorbachev instituted reforms in the mid-1980s that affectively relaxed the Eastern-bloc political climate, Estonia's desire for independence became more visible internationally. A number of large demonstrations took place throughout Estonia during the 1980s.

- When the Soviet Union finally collapsed in 1991, Russian President Boris Yeltsin accepted Estonia's declaration of restored independence.

- Since the country regained independence, it has moved toward reestablishing its sovereign and democratic government, improving the economy and standard of living and opening itself up to the West. It has issued its own currency and has established border as well as immigration and customs controls. At the same time, the country has been reasserting its cultural and national identity. The population is 63% ethnic Estonian, while the rest are Russians, Ukrainians and Belarussians.

- In 1993, the Baltic republics – Latvia, Lithuania and Estonia – established a free trade zone and agreed to coordinate their trade and defense policies. In contrast to most other republics of the former Soviet Union, there is political and economic stability in Estonia as well as in the other Baltic republics.

# ESTONIA

## INTRODUCTIONS

When beginning a conversation, Estonians commonly say *"Kuidas käsi käib?"* ("How are you?"), or *"Kuidas läheb?"* ("How is it going?"). Another popular greeting is to say *"Tere"* ("Hello") and shake hands.

Among friends and relatives, the informal *"Sina"* ("you") is used, but when greeting someone for the first time, the formal *"Teie"* ("you") is used as a courtesy.

The elderly are greeted first and a conversation usually begins with *"Tere hommikust?"* ("Good morning") or *"Tere Õhtust"* ("Good evening").

It is polite to greet people while standing, and you should maintain eye contact during the greeting. It is also polite to offer a greeting when passing someone on the street.

Gentlemen tip their hats upon meeting someone.

## SOCIAL TIPS AND CONVENTIONS

Estonians are reserved in manner; however, they tend to speak quite frankly. They are strongly individualistic, and have a great love of solitude. At the same time, Estonians are friendly and helpful.

Estonians speak Finnish, English and Russian. English is very popular among young people and is taught in school.

The Russian language was imposed on the Estonian people during the Soviet era. Estonian, however, became the official language in 1991, after the country's independence.

Even though many ethnic Russians do not speak Estonian, they are now required to pass a language test for citizenship.

Estonians are ordinarily secular, following many years of the Soviet communist era. Christian denominations are active, but most people are Lutheran, which is the dominant Christian faith in Estonia.

Religious freedom is guaranteed, and the government is not tied to a particular religion; however, prayers are sometimes offered at official functions.

Every city has a theater or community playhouse. Western plays and local plays are often performed.

Many families own cars; however, trains and buses run between cities. In urban areas, public transportation such as buses, street cars and private cars are used.

Electric trains are used in suburban areas, and train service is available between Estonia, Finland, Sweden and Germany. Elderly Estonians ride free on public transportation.

Estonians identify with the Scandinavian value system and way of life; they are patriotic and proud, and they cherish freedom as well as their traditional culture.

# ESTONIA (Cont'd)

## SOCIAL TIPS AND CONVENTIONS (Cont'd)

Estonia is proud of it's representation in the Olympics and has produced a number of Olympic champions.

Several types of music, sports and recreation are enjoyed by Estonians.

Among the most popular sports are soccer, basketball, volleyball, sailing, cycling, cross country skiing, swimming, ice skating and ice boating. The favorite summer pastime activity is picking wild berries and mushrooms in the forest.

## CUSTOMARY BUSINESS PRACTICES

Business offices are open from 8:00 or 9:00 a.m. to 5:00 p.m. Offices close for lunch, but shops and restaurants remain open.

On weekdays and weekends, food stores are open until 9:00 p.m. Some stores open on Saturdays, but close by noon.

Contracts may be verbal. Expect to be held to your word if you make a verbal agreement.

Remain formal in your manners and posture, even if you are using first names.

Many businesspeople speak English, but do not take this for granted. Always check to see if a translator is necessary.

Presentations should be precise, logical and straightforward.

## BUSINESS ENTERTAINING

People eat breakfast before work, have a light lunch during the day, and eat the main meal after work.

Punctuality is expected.  People usually bring flowers when visiting someone for the first time.

Many Estonians enjoy having friends to their homes and will usually offer tea or coffee to guests.

A host gives departing guests a bouquet of flowers as a token of friendship, and guests thank the host for his/her hospitality.

## DINING OUT

Hands are kept above the table during meals, and no one leaves the table until everyone is finished. A request for a second helping is considered a polite gesture.

Alcohol is consumed with gusto. Someone will always be there to fill your glass, but you may opt out of drinking after a couple of rounds.

Dinner is eaten after 6:00 p.m., and usually consists of soup (bouillon, cabbage or pea) or stew, and a main dish of meat or fish and potatoes.

# ESTONIA (Cont'd)

## DINING OUT (Cont'd)

Dessert consists of cake, ice cream, fruit or preserves. The most commonly served fruits are apples, cherries, pears and wild berries.

Vodka is popular as are *rosolje* (a Russian dish), *verivorst* (blood sausage), *pirukas* (a pastry of meat and vegetables) and *sült* (head cheese).

## PUBLIC CUSTOMS

Hand gestures are not common among Estonians; however, they do use the "thumbs up" gesture to indicate that things are going well. Pointing the index finger as well as talking with one's hands in one's pockets is considered impolite.

Men dress well in public and very formally when going out to eat, to the theater or to visit friends.

Women prefer dresses over slacks; however, young women are now wearing slacks more frequently. In general, young people prefer European fashions.

In rural areas people dress in a more relaxed manner than in cities.

Traditional clothing is worn for special occasions, holidays, weddings and festivals.

Estonians celebrate New Year's Day (January 1), *Vastlapäev* (February 15), Independence Day (February 24), Fools Day (April 1),  the day which honors when Stalin deported Estonians in 1949 (June 14), Victory at *Võnnu* Day (June 23), *Jaanipäev* (Midsummer's Day – June 24), *Kadri* Day (October 25), All Souls Day (November 2),  *Mardi* Day (November 10) and Christmas (December 24-26).

# FINLAND: HISTORICAL OVERVIEW

- Finnish people have lived in the area known as Finland since about 3000 B.C. Germanic peoples and other tribes, including the Tavasts, the Same (Lapps) and Karelians, inhabited the area thousands of years ago. Nomadic Lapps, known as *Fenni*, lived in "Fenn-land" ("Land of fens and marshes") during the Stone Age. Gradually, the ancient Finno-Urgic tribe, which crossed the Gulf of Finland each year to hunt and fish, settled in the southwestern corner of Finland, pushed the Lapps northward and eventually became dominant.

- In 1155, Swedish crusaders invaded the region, bringing Catholicism to the area. Finland was part of the Swedish kingdom for the next several hundred years. During this period, it was only considered to be a group of provinces rather than a unified entity. Catholicism was replaced by Protestantism during the Reformation.

- During the Napoleonic Wars, Sweden lost a war to Russia in 1809, and it ceded Finland to the Russians. Russian Czar Alexander I granted Finland extensive autonomy, and the region became a unified entity. It became a Grand Duchy (area under the control of a duke) of the Russian Empire. Under Russian control, a Finnish national movement led to a switch from Swedish to Finnish as the national language (in 1863) and supported a semi-autonomous legislature that administered local affairs.

- In 1899, "Russification" policies were imposed in an attempt to integrate Finland more fully into Russia. These policies were resisted in Finland, and it was likely that they would have led to armed rebellion. However, before violent rebellion developed, Russia's Bolshevik Revolution broke out. Finland took advantage of the chaotic situation and declared its independence in 1917. After a brief civil war, the Finns adopted a republican constitution in 1919.

- During World War II, Finland fought the Soviet Union twice – in the 1939-1940 Winter War and then in the Continuation War until 1944. As a result, Finland was forced to cede one-tenth of its territory to the Soviets (the province of Karelia and a strip of Lapland). Nevertheless, Finland avoided Soviet occupation and preserved its independence. Since World War II, the country has maintained its neutrality.

- In 1948, Finland signed a treaty with the Soviet Union, according to which it promised to repel any attack on the Soviet Union that involved Finnish territory. This treaty created a situation according to which the Soviet Union could influence Finnish foreign policy.

- In 1989, Soviet President Mikhail Gorbachev officially recognized Finnish neutrality and, in 1992, Russian President Boris Yeltsin signed a treaty with Finland's President to void the 1948 agreement. The new treaty recognizes Russia's and Finland's equality, sovereignty and positive economic relations.

- In 1992, Finland decided to more fully integrate with Europe by applying for membership in the European Union (EU).

- Though unemployment in 1996 was high, Finland had one of the fastest growing economies and one of the highest levels of prosperity in the world.

# FINLAND

## INTRODUCTIONS

Both men and women shake hands firmly when greeting. You should shake hands when introduced, when greeting someone you know and when parting. Sometimes both hands will be offered to shake simultaneously.

When introduced, people state their full name or a title and last name. Traditionally it was not appropriate to use first names until invited to do so. However, it is now quite common to use a first name even on a first meeting, especially among young people. You may want to wait until your Finnish colleague uses your first name or invites you to use his/her first name so as not to offend anyone.

Finns kiss and hug only very close relatives and friends whom they have not seen in a long time.

The titles "Mr.," "Mrs." or "Miss" may be used. However, most businesspeople prefer to use their occupational title with the last name. If you are not sure of someone's title, you can use *"Johtaja,"* which means "Director."

The general term for greeting is *"Hyvåå påivåå"* ("Good morning/afternoon") or simply *"Påivåå."* Another expression for "Good morning" is *"Hyvåå huomenta."*

## SOCIAL TIPS AND CONVENTIONS

More than 93% of the population speaks Finnish. Swedish is also officially recognized. Finland has two small minorities, who respectively speak Sami and Russian. English is a popular second language, especially among the young people, the educated and businesspeople.

In many ways, Finland is very different from the other countries commonly grouped together as "Scandinavia." While Finns reflect Scandinavia in customs and lifestyle, they are linguistically and racially different from Scandinavians.

Finnish people are quite reserved and appreciate general courtesy. They avoid showing emotions in public and are quiet.

Eye contact is very important during conversation, although touching and gesturing are uncommon. Folding one's arms while talking is interpreted as arrogant and prideful.

Finnish people are very proud of their heritage and national identity. Despite the country's small size, it has been a leader in peace conferences and initiatives. It also has the cleanest environment in the world. Finland is also a leader in women's rights. In fact, there is no such thing as "feminism," since women's involvement in all spheres of life has become a way of life. The Finns stress and appreciate the values that maintain these elements of life.

Because Finland has survived centuries of domination by other powers, Finns are not only proud of their national identity, but they have developed a wry humor and a cheerful sense of fatalism.

# FINLAND (Cont'd)

## SOCIAL TIPS AND CONVENTIONS (Cont'd)

Conversation can cover a wide range of topics. Religion or politics is not avoided, but you may want to be cautious in taking sides. You may want to avoid discussing socialism or Finnish neutrality as well as asking personal questions of your host (i.e., questions about someone's family or job, religion, etc.).

Sports and hobbies make good conversation topics, since recreation and general fitness are important to the Finns. Favorite hobbies include fishing, hunting, camping, skiing, soccer, *Pesåpallo* (Finnish baseball), ice hockey, cycling and boating. Finns also enjoy picking wild berries and mushrooms and taking vacations in the woods. The sauna is a traditional and popular way to relax. In fact, *sauna* is a Finnish word that has been adopted by English and other languages.

Good topics of conversation also include the history, sights and architecture of the area you are visiting.

## CUSTOMARY BUSINESS PRACTICES

Avoid planning a business trip during July or August since most people take vacations at that time.

Appointments are necessary. Try to make the appointments with the managing directors of firms, since they are the decision makers.

Punctuality is very important.

Finns maintain high ideals of loyalty and reliability. They take promises and agreements seriously.

Women wear dresses or suits for business, while men wear suits and ties.

Businesses are open from 8:00 or 8:30 a.m. to 4:00 or 4:30 p.m., Monday through Friday.

## BUSINESS ENTERTAINING

Finns enjoy entertaining. Most visits involve informal relaxing and socializing. Refreshments, usually coffee and cakes or biscuits, are almost always served.

The most popular way of entertaining is to invite people to a "coffee table" in the afternoon or evening. Cookies and cake are served with coffee. You should taste each of the pastries so that your host will not be insulted.

Finns are more likely to entertain foreign visitors in restaurants than in their homes.

Spouses should be included in invitations to business dinners.

If you are invited to a meal, it is appropriate to bring cut flowers (as opposed to a potted plant) as a gift for the host. The bouquet should not be large, as this would be considered ostentatious. A bottle of wine or a box of chocolates is also appropriate. A gift may also be sent afterwards to thank the host.

# FINLAND (Cont'd)

## BUSINESS ENTERTAINING (Cont'd)

You should wait until the host has taken a first sip before you drink, even if you are simply having refreshments (not seated for a full meal).

At a small party, the host will introduce the guests to each other. However, at a large party, you should introduce yourself.

Do not be surprised if you are asked to spend some time in the sauna with your host. Spending time in the sauna is a national pastime. However, an invitation to a sauna is less likely if you are a businesswoman dealing with businessmen. (There are usually separate saunas for the different sexes.) Business discussions may even take place in the sauna. In fact, after a business deal is concluded, there is usually a long lunch, often followed by a sauna.

While it is common for Finns to take their saunas naked, they will not feel uncomfortable if you do not do the same. Bathing suits or a towel wrap may be worn. Snacks are often served after a sauna. A beverage called *Kalja* (similar to beer, but non-alcoholic) may be served.

Dress is conservative in restaurants, but it ranges from casual to formal, depending on the restaurant. Better restaurants usually require men to wear jackets and ties. At dinner in someone's home, women should wear dresses and men should wear suits and ties.

The restaurant check is presented upon request and is paid for at the table. A 15% service charge is usually included in the bill, although most people also leave an additional gratuity on the table. If the service charge is not included, you should leave a 10-15% tip. Porters, doormen and coat checkers should also receive moderate tips. The check is never split in Finland. Therefore, if you invite someone to a restaurant, you should pick up the check.

## DINING OUT

Guests are seated by the host when invited to a dinner at someone's house.

At a dinner party, the host and the hostess usually sit at opposite ends of the table and guests sit on the sides. Often women sit on one side and men on the other.

The Finns eat in the continental style, with the fork in the left hand and the knife in the right. Do not eat anything with your hands. Even fruit should be peeled and sliced using a fork and knife.

Guests begin eating after the host does and they also leave the table after he/she has. Guests should refrain from drinking until the host proposes a toast. It is inappropriate for guests to toast the host(s).

It is rude to leave food on your plate, so you may want to take small portions at first.

You do not need to leave your utensils on the plate in any particular position to indicate that you are finished. At the end of the meal, you should approach your host and thank him/her. However, this does not signal the end of the evening. Guests stay about one-and-a-half to two hours after the meal.

When passing the salt during dinner, it is considered bad luck to pass it hand to hand. Instead, put the salt shaker down on the table and let the next person pick it up.

# FINLAND (Cont'd)

## DINING OUT (Cont'd)

Finnish cuisine has been influenced by many cultures, from French to Russian. It includes a number of Finnish specialties using seafood, wild game and vegetables. Reindeer steak and salmon are traditional specialties. Wild berries (including blueberries, cloudberries, strawberries and raspberries) are popular in desserts and liqueurs. Potatoes, rye bread and cheeses are popular, and open-faced sandwiches are commonly eaten for snacks, lunch and breakfast. The *smørgåsbord*, a Finnish buffet, is also very popular. Coffee and milk are the most common beverages.

For breakfast, which is served between 7:30 and 9:00 a.m., people eat hot cereal, *pulla* (yeast bread) and either open-faced sandwiches or yogurt and fruit with coffee. Lunch, between noon and 1:00 p.m., is a light meal consisting of soup, sandwiches, salad and milk or buttermilk. Coffee breaks are normally taken at 10:00 a.m. and 2:00 p.m. Dinner is served at 6:00 or at 7:00 p.m. for a dinner party. An informal dinner will consist of meat, potatoes, vegetables or salad and pudding with milk.

At a dinner party, drinks (commonly beer, straight vodka or whiskey, gin and tonic or martinis) usually precede the meal. The meal usually begins with soup, sometimes followed by a fish dish (smoked or salted salmon) or herring salad. The main course is meat, often a roast or stew, with potatoes and vegetables. Bread, usually a heavy dark rye, often accompanies the meal. Beer or wine is usually served with the meal, although fruit juice or mineral water can be requested. Cheese and a sweet dessert usually end the meal. Coffee is served later in the evening rather than right after the meal.

You should be aware that large quantities and, often, a great variety of alcoholic beverages are consumed during dinners in Finland.

## PUBLIC CUSTOMS

Finnish fashion standards are very high and internationally recognized. People may dress quite formally and follow European fashion trends closely. Also, a variety of native costumes are worn at festivals, weddings or graduation balls.

Hats are very often worn by men in the winter. All men in Finland, even teenagers, wear ties and hats when they dress up. Men remove their hats when they enter a building or elevator or when they are speaking with another person. Men may also raise their hats to greet people from a distance.

It is considered impolite to talk with one's hands in one's pockets or with something in one's mouth (toothpick, food, gum, etc.). Also, if a yawn cannot be suppressed, cover your mouth.

Finns will wave in greeting if they see someone they know at a distance.

It is preferable to cross your legs with one knee over the other, as placing one ankle over the other knee is inappropriate.

Loud talking and noise are avoided in public places. Also, it is inappropriate to eat food (except for ice cream) while walking down the street.

# FRANCE: HISTORICAL OVERVIEW

- Around 1200 B.C. the Gauls established themselves in what is now France. Julius Caesar conquered Gaul around 58-52 B.C. and began Roman colonization, which ended with the end of the Roman Empire and barbarian invasions. The Franks, from whom France gets its name, established themselves around 600 A.D.

- Charlemagne was named Emperor of the West and attempted to recreate the Roman Empire (around 800 A.D.). He absorbed what is now France into a huge political unit encompassing much of present Europe. This Empire did not survive his death.

- The Capetians chose what is now the city of Paris as their capital around 1000 A.D.

- During the 14th to 15th centuries, French-English rivalries culminated in the Hundred Years' War. During the late 16th century, wars of religion raged between Catholics and Protestants. The absolute monarchy of Louis XIV (The Sun King), 1661-1715, saw royal authority reach its zenith. The 18th century saw the Age of Enlightenment, absolutism questioned and the French Revolution starting in 1789. Napoleon was named Emperor in 1804, followed in 1815 by the restoration of the monarchy.

- The 19th century was marked by a number of revolts and the establishment of the Second Empire under Napoleon III. The Third Republic was established in 1875, which lasted until 1940. The Alsace and Lorraine regions were lost to Germany (Prussia) following military defeat in 1871. They were regained by France after World War I.

- France was occupied by Germany during World War II.

- War in Vietnam (Indochina), a French colony, broke out when France tried to reestablish its authority after Vietnam was liberated from Japanese occupation following World War II. A rebellion in Algeria, considered part of France rather than a colony, lasted from 1954 to 1962.

- Charles de Gaulle became president in 1958. De Gaulle expanded educational opportunities, stabilized the currency, helped bring about a rise in real wages and expanded the social security net. His real interest, however, was foreign policy, and he set out to create an independent foreign policy for France and to diminish Soviet and U.S. influence in Europe. In 1969, de Gaulle resigned and was succeeded by Georges Pompidou, who continued with similar policies. Pompidou died in 1974, and Valery Giscard d'Estaing won the presidency in a narrow victory over Socialist leader François Mitterand. Giscard reorganized industrial priorities and introduced modest social reform, but voters upset with high inflation put Mitterand into office in 1981. His two major reforms were the nationalization of certain industries and the decentralization of the French political system.

- Public sentiment shifted to the right in the late 1980s, and Prime Minister Jacques Chirac fought President Mitterand on a number of privatization versus nationalization issues. In 1995, Chirac won the presidency on the promise of "profound change." Once in office and faced with harsh realities, he turned from the mission of job creation to economic austerity, which led to the worst demonstrations since 1968.

# FRANCE

## INTRODUCTIONS

Upon introduction, it is customary to shake hands with a single, quick shake and light pressure, rather than the firm U.S. pumping handshake, which is considered boorish. It is also customary to shake hands with all those to whom you were introduced upon leaving.

It is best to address everyone as either *"Monsieur"* ("Mr."), *"Madame"* ("Mrs.") or *"Mademoiselle"* ("Miss"), without adding the surname. In business circles, first names are rarely used, even among colleagues, unless they are close friends. Use of first names can be initiated by the eldest person present or the one with superior rank.

Women who know each other very well kiss each other on both cheeks. Men will also do this with relatives. Rather than an actual kiss, it is more like touching cheeks and kissing the air.

Always carry business cards as they are exchanged often.

## SOCIAL TIPS AND CONVENTIONS

Follow the same advice about conversation topics that would apply in the United States. Sports (especially soccer), local history and culture are generally safer topics than politics, money or personal matters.

The French are very proud of their history and their culture and will be delighted if you are knowledgeable in this subject.

The French are very private people. Questions about their families are considered too personal for business conversation.

The French are modest when given a compliment. They will often respond with a self-deprecating remark instead of "Thank You."

The majority of French people are Roman Catholic (around 90%).

## CUSTOMARY BUSINESS PRACTICES

Dress in France is more formal than in the U.S., even casual dress. They take care to dress well and fashionably in every situation.

Men should wear conservative business suits, with colored, striped or white shirts and a tie. Women should wear business suits or conservative dresses.

Business appointments are necessary. Mid-morning and mid-afternoon are preferred times.

Always be punctual for your business appointments. Give your business card to the secretary or receptionist when you arrive.

# FRANCE (Cont'd)

## CUSTOMARY BUSINESS PRACTICES (Cont'd)

General conversation often comes before business discussion.

Business presentations should be formal, rational and subdued.

Business negotiations in France tend to take longer than those in the U.S. The French apply reason and logic to negotiations, and they tend to be argumentative. At times, they may seem to disagree for the sake of discussion.

Decisions often follow lengthy deliberations, so be patient. Trying the U.S.-style "hard sell" could cause you to lose a customer. An agreement may be reached orally; however, written contracts may follow after approval by top management.

It is advisable to have a local agent or representative to conduct business. It may be necessary to create joint ventures, branch offices or even a network of distributors through-out France to ensure your success.

If you need to give a business gift, items that appeal to the intellect or aesthetics are particularly prized, such as recordings, art prints and books.

## BUSINESS ENTERTAINING

Business entertaining is usually conducted in restaurants. You will probably be invited to someone's home only after you become friends as well as business associates.

If you are invited to someone's home, you will probably not get a tour of the entire house. You will probably be entertained in the living room and will not be encouraged to enter other rooms.

Bring a gift with you when invited to a French home for dinner, such as a box of candy, cookies or flowers. If you bring flowers, avoid chrysanthemums or red roses and always bring an odd number of flowers. Only bring wine to a very good friend and then make sure it is a very high quality wine.

Whether you are entertained at home or in a restaurant, your host would appreciate receiving a telephone call or brief note the following day expressing your thanks.

French restaurants are frequently very expensive. You should refrain from ordering the most expensive items on the menu, as this might embarrass your host. Also, avoid the temptation to overeat – or worse – overdrink.

Wine usually accompanies lunch and dinner. You may choose to drink mineral water instead of, or in addition to, the wine. Do not drink until your host has poured wine for everyone and has proposed a toast.

Spouses are seldom included at business meals. As a rule, your spouse should only be invited when you have already met your colleague's spouse.

# FRANCE (Cont'd)

## DINING OUT

In France, cultured dinner conversation is valued as highly as the delectable food. When attending a business meal, avoid discussing business until your host indicates that it is appropriate to do so. Dinner conversation is very important. The French enjoy sitting and talking for hours at the table.

In many French restaurants, it is customary to use the same cutlery throughout the meal. If this is intended, a little glass or china rod is provided for resting the knife and fork between courses. Tables may be set with the fork and spoon facing down.

The French eat in the continental style, with the fork in the left hand and the knife in the right.

Since it is considered impolite to point with the hand and the fingers, beckon a waiter by tipping the head back slightly and saying *"Garçon"* ("Waiter").

Smoking between courses is frowned upon. Always ask permission before you smoke.

Keep both hands on the table. It is considered impolite to keep your hands in your lap, even when you are not eating.

Breakfast is customarily *café au lait* (coffee with milk) or *chocolat chaud* (hot chocolate), bread or croissants, butter and jam. This is the only meal where butter is served with bread.

Lunch has traditionally been the main meal of the day. It was common for a businessperson to go home for a long lunch rather than dine at a restaurant. However, this is becoming less common as more women work outside the home. *Demi-tasse* coffee (strong, black coffee in small cups) is served after the meal.

Dinner traditionally has been simpler, perhaps soup, a casserole and bread. If it is a social occasion, however, it will be more elaborate, similar to lunch.

Break your bread with your hands; do not cut it with a knife. If there is no separate bread plate it is appropriate to put the bread directly on the tablecloth.

It is considered rude and wasteful not to finish everything on your plate.

Cheese and fruit are frequently served at the end of a meal. Help yourself to the cheese only once. Peel the fruit with a knife and eat it with a fork.

The specialties of each region differ. In Alsace and Lorraine try *choucroute garnie* (sauerkraut with sausage and pork), *pâté de foie gras* (goose liver paste) and *quiche Lorraine* (pastry filled with bacon, cheese, eggs and cream). In Brittany, *crepes* (with jam or Grand Marnier and sugar) are a specialty. *Boeuf bourguinonne* (beef stew with wine, carrots, onion and mushrooms) is a specialty of the Burgundy region. In Provence, near the Mediterranean, try *bouillabaisse* (seafood soup) and *ratatouille* (a mixture of zucchini, tomatoes, eggplant, onions and peppers).

# FRANCE (Cont'd)

## PUBLIC CUSTOMS

Keep in mind the French motto *"Toujours la politesse"* ("Always be polite"). Courtesy is valued.

It is not considered polite to chew gum or speak or laugh loudly in public. If you need to blow your nose, do it discreetly and always use a handkerchief or tissue. In addition, yawning in public is avoided.

Don't keep your hands in your pockets when speaking.

The U.S. "okay" sign (rounded index finger and rounded thumb touching at the fingertips) means "zero" in France. The French use the "thumbs up" sign for "okay."

Sit straight in a chair with knees together or with legs crossed at the knees. Never place your feet on tables or chairs.

Do not be surprised to see nude or topless bathers at public beaches and swimming pools, especially near the Mediterranean as this is very common.

Many stores, restaurants, theaters and businesses close during August for vacation.

# GERMANY: HISTORICAL OVERVIEW

- Parts of present-day Germany were first occupied by the ancient Romans, starting with Julius Caesar in 58 B.C. After the fall of Rome, a vast empire was established over much of northern Europe, which reached its peak under Charlemagne, who ascended the throne in 768 A.D. After his death, his empire was divided, the borders of which correspond greatly to the present border between France and Germany.

- The eastern realm was a multitude of local states and independent cities that eventually claimed the title of "Holy Roman Empire." The Emperor depended on alliances with the various dukes and archbishops who ruled the cities and provinces.

- The absence of any strong, centralizing power in Germany prevented the development of a unified German nation for six centuries. The fragmentation of Germany became acute after the Thirty Years War, which ended in 1648. Until becoming a nation-state in 1871 under Prussian leader Otto von Bismarck, Germany remained a patchwork of separate principalities.

- Germany was allied with Austria and Turkey in World War I. After its defeat in 1918, Germany was required to pay reparations and cede some of its territory. The Weimar Republic, a democratic government, was established in 1918.

- Adolf Hitler was named Chancellor in 1933. Hitler declared himself Führer (leader) of the Third Reich in 1934. Hitler's actions soon led to World War II. The Nazis occupied much of Europe, killing millions in concentration camps. Germany was defeated by Allied forces in 1945.

- After World War II, Germany was split into occupation zones, which led to the country being divided into essentially two countries. The western portion became the democratic nation of the Federal Republic of Germany (FRG). The eastern portion became the communist nation of the German Democratic Republic (GDR). The two countries were more commonly known as West Germany and East Germany. The city of Berlin, which was in the GDR, was divided into East (communist) and West (democratic) Berlin.

- With thousands of people fleeing the east, the GDR built the Berlin Wall in 1961 to close off access to West Berlin. The wall remained in place until late 1989 when it was opened to traffic on both sides. It was eventually torn down.

- The two nations became reunited as the Federal Republic of Germany in October 1990.

- Chancellor Helmut Kohl was successful in leading Germany through its dramatic reunificiaction. He placated Germany's understandably nervous neighbors by stating that the FRG was only interested in peace.

- The huge challenge facing the Bonn government was to transform the unproductive, socialist economy of the East into the highly dynamic and complex capitalist economy of the West. Change was slow and required raising taxes in the West to pay for subsidies. The deficit grew and foreign trade problems developed. On the bright side, demand in the East rose.

# GERMANY

## INTRODUCTIONS

While customs vary in different regions of Germany, the general rule is to shake hands both upon meeting and upon departing.

Always shake hands, firmly but briefly, when introduced to a German man. When introduced to a woman, wait to see if she extends her hand first before offering to shake.

In formal social situations, older German men may kiss the hand of a woman in greeting. However, this is rare, and foreigners are not expected to kiss hands.

When several people are being introduced, take turns shaking hands. It is impolite to reach over someone else's handshake.

Never keep your left hand in your pocket while shaking hands with your right.

Traditionally, only family members and close friends address each other by their first names. You may never establish a close enough relationship with a German to be on a first name basis.

It is very important to use professional titles. Attorneys, engineers, pastors and other professionals will expect you to address them as *"Herr"* ("Mr.") or *"Frau"* ("Mrs.") plus their title. This goes for anyone with a Ph.D. as well, e.g., *"Herr* (or *Frau*) *Doctor Professor."* Make sure you know the correct professional title.

When speaking to people who do not have professional titles, use "Mr.," "Mrs." or "Miss," plus the surname. In German, these titles are *"Herr"* ("Mr."), *"Frau"* ("Mrs." or "Ms.") and *"Fräulein"* ("Miss"). *"Fräulein"* is nowadays used only for very young women (under the age of 18). Any businesswoman you meet should be addressed as *"Frau"* (plus surname), whether or not she is married.

The order of names in Germany is the same as in other Western countries (the first name followed by the surname).

In accordance with German formality, it is better to be introduced by a third person than to introduce yourself. However, if no one is available, it is acceptable to introduce yourself.

When you are the third person making an introduction between two parties, give the name of the younger (or lower-ranking) person first.

Never use first names unless you are invited to do so. Greetings are done in a formal manner.

## SOCIAL TIPS AND CONVENTIONS

In most regions of Germany, men stand when women enter a room. Women need not rise. As long as a woman remains standing, any man talking to her will probably remain standing as well (unless the man is elderly or of much higher social rank).

Germany makes some of the finest beer in the world. A German beer drinker will be happy to discuss the local brews, especially the seasonal beers and the specialty brews like *Berliner Weiße*, a Berlin beer made from wheat.

# GERMANY (Cont'd)

## SOCIAL TIPS AND CONVENTIONS (Cont'd)

Sports are a good topic for conversation. Many Germans are passionate *Fußball* (soccer) fans. Skiing, hiking, cycling and tennis are also popular. However, the collapse of the state-run East German Olympic sports program may be an uncomfortable subject.

Embarrassing political comments should be avoided. Keep in mind that politics and the Second World War may be sensitive topic areas. Open-ended questions or asking for explanations are appreciated.

Germans tend to be well-informed about politics and to have firm political opinions. They are also honest and may tell you their opinions about your country (or its actions), even if these opinions are negative.

Expect to be hushed if you so much as cough while attending an opera, play or concert. German audiences remain extraordinarily silent, rarely even shifting in their seats.

Be aware that Germans have a strong sense of privacy. Their personal space tends to be slightly greater in size than that of people in the U.S.

As a rule, Germans answer the phone by giving their name.

## CUSTOMARY BUSINESS PRACTICES

Business is conducted with great attention to detail, order and planning. Discipline and restraint are encouraged and duty, obedience and loyalty are highly valued.

Germans make a point of laying a proper foundation prior to explaining something. Consequently, explanations tend to be lengthy and somewhat complicated.

Business negotiations in Germany are done in a technical and factual manner. You should be aware that it is best to avoid humor, little anecdotes, surprises and the "hard sell" approach.

Top management dresses more conservatively than middle management and nonprofessionals.

German managers tend to keep office doors closed for privacy. You may enter an office, but never open a door without first knocking.

Punctuality is of the utmost importance. It is acceptable to leave work on time, but it is customary to work beyond official hours.

Business appointments should be made far in advance, and everything must be planned. The best time to schedule an appointment is between 9:00 a.m. and 1:00 p.m. as well as between 3:00 and 5:00 p.m. Friday afternoons should be avoided.

Humor is used only in certain settings and does not include the workplace. As a rule, the more formal the occasion, the less humor is acceptable. Germans may feel uncomfortable joking among strangers or new acquaintances. In some countries, people feel they can relax more as they gain seniority; however, in Germany, the opposite is the case. At the same time, among close colleagues, in private, there is banter and joking.

# GERMANY (Cont'd)

## CUSTOMARY BUSINESS PRACTICES (Cont'd)

Conservative business wear is appropriate for most formal social events such as parties, dinners and the theater. Remember that one is obliged to check one's coat in German theaters; therefore, if you tend to be cold, bring a sweater. On the opening night of an opera, concert or play, men are expected to wear their best dark suit or tuxedo, and women a long evening gown.

Casual wear is essentially the same as in the U.S. Jeans are quite common, but they should not show signs of wear.

On correspondence and other dated papers, remember that Germans, as well as many other Europeans write the day first, then the month, then the year (e.g., December 3, 1999, is written 3.12.99). Before writing the date, Germans will also write the place from which the correspondence is originating (Munich, den 3. December, 1999).

Everyone in Germany takes at least four weeks of vacation per year. Many people take long vacations during July, August or December, so check first to see if your counterpart will be available. Also be aware that little work gets done during regional festivals, such as the *Oktoberfest* or the three-day Carnival before Lent.

Business hours are 8:00 or 9:00 a.m. to 4:00 or 5:00 p.m., Monday through Friday, except for *Long Thursday* when business hours extend until 8:30 or 9:00 p.m.

Store hours are 8:00 or 9:00 a.m. to 5:00 or 6:30 p.m., Monday through Friday. On Saturday, most shops close by 1:00 p.m., except for one Saturday per month, when they remain open until 4:00 p.m. Legally, store hours have been extended to 9:00 p.m. Monday through Friday, however, most stores outside of urban areas still maintain the earlier store hours.

When entering or leaving a shop, it is considered polite to say "Hello" and "Good-bye" to the sales clerk.

## BUSINESS ENTERTAINING

If you are invited out to lunch, you may offer to pay, but expect your host to decline your offer. Insist on paying only when you have made the invitation.

Be on time for social events. Drinks are served before the meal, usually with a few appetizers. The meal itself will start soon after.

Any gift should be of good quality but not of exorbitant cost. Appropriate gifts include good quality pens or imported liquor.

At everyday restaurants, people find their own seats. There is no host to seat customers. Do not be surprised if someone you do not know joins your table if there is an empty seat. Additionally, you have to get the waiter's attention since the bill will not be brought to you automatically at the end of the meal.

The only article of clothing considered an appropriate gift is a scarf. Other clothing, or for example, perfume **or** soap, are considered too personal.

# GERMANY (Cont'd)

## BUSINESS ENTERTAINING (Cont'd)

When invited to dinner at a German home, always bring a bouquet of unwrapped flowers (removing the wrapping before entering the house) for your host. The bouquet should not be showy and overly large and should have an uneven number of flowers (but not 13). Red roses are reserved for courting, and calla lilies are for funerals. Also do not bring carnations as they are considered to be cheap. Remember that heather should never be included in a bouquet in Northern Germany (because of its hardy nature, heather is often planted on graves, and deemed bad luck to bring into a house).

A gift of a locally available wine can be interpreted as saying that your host's wine cellar is inadequate. However, a good wine brought from your home country (one not sold in Germany) or a top-quality imported red wine will be appreciated. Since Germans make some of the finest beers in the world, it is unlikely that you could bring a foreign beer of interest to them.

Consider it an honor to be invited to a home. However, do not expect to be given a tour of the house.

If you smoke, always offer cigarettes before lighting up.

## DINING OUT

A German meal customarily begins with saying *"Guten Appetit"* to each other before eating. Drinking is preceded by the host's toasting the guests with *"Prosit,"* or *"zum Wohle."* If someone raises a glass to you personally, you should reciprocate sometime during the meal.

When dining out in Germany, keep your hands on the table throughout the meal.

When eating, always use utensils. Very few items are eaten with the hands. Place your utensils vertically side by side on the plate when you are finished.

At all meals except breakfast, bread or rolls should be broken with your hands rather than cut with a knife. Potatoes are eaten with a fork only, and not cut with a knife.

It is considered wasteful to leave food on your plate.

Smoking should be saved until the end of the meal, after the last person has finished eating and coffee or brandy is served. Always ask permission to smoke.

Breakfast usually consists of rye bread, rolls, butter and jam served with coffee with milk.

Lunch is usually a large meal. Soup, a main dish featuring meat, potatoes and vegetables, and a salad may be included. Rye bread (without butter) and beer usually accompany the meal. Coffee and pastry are generally consumed at a late afternoon break, rather than at the end of the lunch meal.

The evening meal is generally simple, except on special occasions and at parties. It will often consist of open-faced sandwiches.

# GERMANY (Cont'd)

## DINING OUT (Cont'd)

The Germans keep the fork in the left hand and the knife in the right hand. Use the knife to push food onto the fork. Hold onto the knife even when you're not using it.

Never eat with your fingers. Even sandwiches are eaten with a knife and fork.

Some German food specialties include: *Wurst* (sausages), *Wienerschnitzel* (a veal dish), *Sauerbraten* (marinated beef pot roast cooked with raisins and crumbled gingersnaps) and *Spätzle* (noodle dumplings).

German pastries abound. One specialty is *Schwarzwalder Kirschtorte* (Black Forest cake) made with chocolate and cherries.

## PUBLIC CUSTOMS

While Germans are open and generous with close friends, they tend to be formal and reserved in public. You will not see many smiles or displays of affection on German streets.

The avoidance of public spectacles is reflected in the way Germans will wait until they get quite close to each other before they will offer a greeting. Only young or impolite people will wave or shout at each other from a distance.

To get someone's attention, raise your hand, palm facing out, with only the index finger extended. Don't wave or beckon, as it is considered rude.

The eldest or highest-ranking person enters a room first. If their age and status are the same, men enter before women.

When speaking with someone, do not keep your hands in your pockets or chew gum.

When a man and a woman walk down a street, the man walks closest to the curb.

Germans will look you directly in the eye; however, they do not like to touch. Also, they do not smile readily, and their gestures are often restrained.

There are often no lines in places such as banks and post offices. Usually it is the boldest person who goes to the counter that is helped next.

# GREECE: HISTORICAL OVERVIEW

- The history of ancient Greece began around 3000 B.C. From 2000 until 1100 B.C., during the Bronze Age on the mainland, the Minoan civilization rose and fell on Crete. Athens took shape in 1300 B.C. and city states began to form about 1000 B.C. As city states began to form, Greek culture began to flourish, and the first Olympics were held in 776 B.C. The influence and culture of ancient Greece peaked around 400 B.C. with Athens as the center of a vast overseas empire. The country's rich heritage of architecture, sculpture, science, drama, poetry and government established the foundation of Western civilization.

- Under the rule of Alexander the Great, ancient Greece developed an empire that covered much of what is now the Middle East. However, after Alexander's death in 323 B.C., the empire began to decline, and, by 146 B.C., it became part of the Roman Empire.

- Centuries later, along with Constantinople (now Istanbul, Turkey), Greece was the center of the Byzantine Empire (which fell in 1453). In 1460, Greece became a province of the Ottoman Empire.

- After four centuries of Turkish rule, the Greeks began a war of independence, supported by Great Britain, France and Russia. In 1832, Prince Otto of Bavaria was made king of Greece.

- During World War II, the country was occupied by German and Italian forces and lost one-eighth of its population due to the war. After the war ended and Greece was liberated, a civil war between the government and communist guerillas cost another 120,000 lives. With aid from the U.S., the Greek government was victorious in 1949.

- In 1965, a political crisis between Prime Minister George Papandreou and King Constantine II resulted in the dismissal of Papandreou. Then, in 1967, a group of military colonels staged a coup and, as a result, the royal family fled. Until 1974, the colonels ruled as repressive dictators.

- After the military dictatorship fell, general elections took place and a republic was formed since voters rejected a return to monarchy. Andreas Papandreou's socialist party was democratically elected for two terms and, therefore, was at the head of government from 1981 until 1989. After that, the party lost the majority vote due to various financial and political scandals.

- In 1981, Greece joined the European Economic Community (EEC).

- Konstantinos Mitsotakis' *New Democracy* party finally received enough votes to form a government in 1990, after running in the two previous elections. Under this party, government policies aimed to privatize state enterprises, cut government spending and prepare Greece for greater integration within Europe. The austerity measures that supported these policies led to voter discontent. As a result of this discontent, the *Socialist Party* regained parliamentary leadership in the 1993 elections. Andreas Papandreou returned to office as Prime Minister and began to reverse privatization and other economic measures.

# GREECE

## INTRODUCTIONS

When being introduced to either men or women, it is customary to shake hands. One may also receive an embrace and a kiss on both cheeks. A common, more informal way of greeting is by slapping a friend's hand at shoulder level.

In Greece, everyone shakes hands almost every time they meet and a firm handshake is considered a sign of good character.

Carry a large stock of business cards and distribute them generously.

Wait for your Greek colleague to use first names before you do.

## SOCIAL TIPS AND CONVENTIONS

While women have gained greater prominence and rights, Greek society is still dominated by men.

Greeks are influenced by European fashion trends. Traditional costumes are worn at folk festivals and on other special occasions. Women wear dresses more often than their North American counterparts.

Men consider it a matter of personal honor to fulfill obligations to their families and others. They may attribute their failures to external circumstances rather than to personal inadequacies.

When eating at a person's home, the host will offer several helpings of each dish. As a general rule, the more one eats, the greater the indication of approval.

A man may praise the food served in his home as especially good, or he may be the hero of his own tales. Such self praise is not considered bragging.

One should use verbal terms for "Yes" and "No," rather than gestures. A slight upward nod of the head can mean "No" rather than "Yes" and tilting (not shaking) the head to either side means "Yes" or "Of course." This is not always the case, as Greek society is using North American gestures more often, but the fact that both systems are used can lead to confusion.

The family unit is very strong in Greece. The elderly are respected, addressed by courteous titles, served first and have much authority. Most Greeks care for their elderly parents.

## CUSTOMARY BUSINESS PRACTICES

Greeks like to "pass" time, not "use" time. They may not be prompt in keeping appointments and consider it foolish to set a specific length of time for a meeting. Foreigners are expected to arrive on time, but don't be surprised if a Greek is a half-hour or more late. This may partly be due to their temperament and the horrendous Athenian traffic and parking conditions.

Men should wear suits and ties in the winter. In the summer, Greeks dress more casually; however, wearing a suit will make a good impression. Women should wear dresses or suits and heels.

Work and business hours vary, depending on the season and the type of business. In general, most Greeks work from 8:00 a.m. to 1:30 p.m. and from 5:00 to 8:00 p.m. Some government offices may close as early as 2:30 p.m. Also, many businesses close early on Wednesday afternoons.

# GREECE (Cont'd)

## CUSTOMARY BUSINESS PRACTICES (Cont'd)

The *siesta* (a rest after the midday meal) hour is taken seriously. Don't try to make appointments or call people at home during afternoon closing hours.

Avoid business trips during the summer (June through August) and the weeks before and after Christmas and Greek Orthodox Easter.

Do not be offended if Greeks ask you pointedly personal questions, such as how much you earn. If you prefer not to answer, try to make your evasions tactful.

## BUSINESS ENTERTAINING

Greeks have a tradition of hospitality that goes back to ancient times. Ancient Greeks believed a stranger might be a god in disguise and were therefore kind to all strangers.

Greeks expect personal contact in business relationships and may accompany you for meals, take you out in the evening or even pick you up at the airport.

Business associates will invariably offer sweet Greek (never "Turkish") coffee accompanied by a glass of cold water.

Drinking and dancing the night away is often considered an inherent part of doing business in Greece.

At home, men traditionally stay with their guests while the women prepare food or serve drinks.

Hosts appreciate compliments about their homes, but one should avoid praising a specific object to excess as the host might insist on giving it to the guest.

A guest may praise the host's children, and, if the parents approve, give them a small gift.

If a Greek host continues to insist about anything (that a guest stay longer or eat more, for example), they mean it and the guest should try to be accommodating.

Tip a hotel concierge if he performs a special service, such as obtaining hard-to-get theater tickets.

## DINING OUT

Greeks often eat dinner (a small meal) as late as 8:00 or 9:00 p.m. The main meal of the day is lunch, served between noon and 2:00 p.m.

Mealtime in Greece is a social occasion.

At restaurants, a group will often order a number of different dishes for everyone to share. Sometimes Greeks will go into the kitchen of a restaurant and choose their dinner by looking into the pots.

## DINING OUT (Cont'd)

While tastes vary between urban and rural residents, certain foods are common to all Greeks. These include lamb, seafood, olives and cheese. They also eat potatoes, rice, beans, breads, chicken, fruit and vegetables. Olive oil is used in cooking. Garlic, onions and spices are also popular. Salads are often eaten with the main meal. Meats and vegetables are grilled or fried in their own juices or with lemon and garlic. *Souvlaki* is a shish kebab with cubes of meat (often lamb), mushrooms and other vegetables. Yogurt is often used in sauces with cucumber, dill, mint and garlic.

Greeks often make a meal out of *mezedes* (hot and cold appetizers) such as *melitzanosalata* (mashed eggplant), *dolmadakia* (meat or rice rolled in grape leaves), *taramoslata* (caviar spread), stuffed peppers and other dishes.

Greece produces a number of wines, the best-known of which is *retsina*.

The favorite local alcoholic beverages are *metaxa* and *ouzo*.

A guest may courteously insist on sharing the bill.

A 15% service charge is usually added to restaurant and bar bills. If not, leave the waiter 12-20% on the plate and loose change (5%) for the bus boy on the table.

## PUBLIC CUSTOMS

Coffee houses are favorite leisure spots for men.

Folk dancing is common, and visitors may be invited to join in. Accepting the invitation is considered a gesture of friendliness and appreciation to the Greek people.

The U.S. "okay" sign (with the thumb and forefinger forming a circle) is an obscene gesture in Greece. Waving the whole hand, called the *moutza*, is a threatening gesture – particularly when the hand is close to another person's face.

Greece is a male-oriented Mediterranean society where women visitors may need to take special precautions. To avoid harassment by men, women dining alone should choose one of the more elegant restaurants. For similar reasons, women should take taxis at night unless they know the area they are in very well.

When visiting a church or monastery, women should wear skirts (never pants) and have their arms covered. Women are not allowed behind the altar in a Greek Orthodox church.

# HUNGARY: HISTORICAL OVERVIEW

- The region now known as Hungary became part of the Roman Empire in 14 B.C. as the province of Pannonia. However, the region to the east remained under the control of Germanic and other tribes. In the fifth century, the Magyars, led by Arpád, began migrating from the east and conquered the resident Moravians. They began permanent settlement by the end of the ninth century.

- Arpád's grandson, Géza, introduced Christianity in the late 10th century. When Géza's son, Stephen, became Hungary's first king in 1000 A.D., he converted the people to Christianity. The dynasty lasted until the 14th century, after which other powers controlled the area.

- The country was conquered by the Ottoman Turks in the 15th century and was then taken under the crown of the Austrian Hapsburgs during their rise to world prominence between the 16th and 18th centuries.

- In 1848, the Hungarians rose in a rebellion, but they were defeated after two years. In 1867, a sharing of power between the Austrians and Hungarians in Central Europe, known as the Dual Monarchy, was established. However, internal ethnic conflicts, due to the increasing desire for self-rule among the Slavic minorities of the empire, contributed to the beginning of World War I. This led to the dissolution of the Austro-Hungarian Empire.

- Following World War I, according to treaty settlements, Hungary became an independent republic but lost much of its territory to neighboring countries.

- After Germany invaded Hungary in 1944, the country fought as a German ally in World War II. After the war, the Soviets briefly occupied the territory. Following an armistice, free elections reestablished a republic in 1945.

- After the war, the Communist party, supported by the Soviets, seized control of the country by 1947 and declared Hungary a socialist state called the People's Republic of Hungary in 1949. Communist reformer Imre Nagy tried to bring about systemic changes; he withdrew Hungary from the Warsaw Pact and declared the country neutral in 1956. In response, the Soviets attacked Hungary, repressed the movement and executed Nagy.

- After Nagy's death, Janos Kadar was the leader of the communist government until he was forced to resign, under pressure for reform in 1988. By 1989, the Communist monopoly of the government was abolished, the country was renamed the Republic of Hungary, and Nagy was reburied as a national hero.

- In 1990, free elections were held and Jozsef Antall became the new prime minister. Antall died in 1993 and was briefly replaced by Peter Boross. Antall's and Boross's party, the Hungarian Democratic Forum, that had defeated the Communists in 1990, lost the May 1994 election due to popular disillusionment with economic reforms. The Socialists (who were former Communists) gained the parliamentary majority, and Gyula Horn became Prime Minister.

# HUNGARY

## INTRODUCTIONS

It is customary to shake hands when first being introduced. People shake hands upon meeting and departing. A man should wait for a woman to extend her hand.

Hungarians address each other using their appropriate titles followed by "Mr." or "Ms." The surname should *not* be used. An example would be "Mr. Engineer." If someone does not have a title or you are uncertain, address that person by "Mr.," "Mrs." or "Miss" followed by his/her last name.

It is common for two men who are close friends and who have not seen each other for some time to shake hands and embrace, making cheek-to-cheek contact, first the left and then the right. Close women friends embrace.

In business settings or at formal parties, you should wait to be introduced by your host. In more informal settings, it is acceptable to introduce yourself.

First names should only be used after being invited to do so by your Hungarian colleague.

## SOCIAL TIPS AND CONVENTIONS

It is common during conversation for the subject to be changed rather abruptly. Hungarians often have an "official" opinion and also a very private opinion. Changing the subject could either indicate that you have said too much or that you have touched too closely on an unacceptable political topic.

Hungarians can be very modest and self-effacing. If you pay them a compliment, it is not unusual for them to belittle their achievement.

Hungarians enjoy hearing visitors describe what they have seen in other parts of the world, since their travel has been restricted. They have a strong sense of both personal and national pride, and relish discussing what you like about Hungary as well as other topics such as food and wine.

When answering the phone, the usual greeting is *"Hello."*

## CUSTOMARY BUSINESS PRACTICES

Unless you are fluent in Hungarian, it is best to write all business letters in English. Businesses expect to translate letters written in different languages.

Business cards should be distributed liberally.

Consider hiring an interpreter if you do not speak Hungarian or German well enough to conduct business. If the business you are visiting is in an outlying area, you will almost certainly need an interpreter.

Business appointments should not be scheduled for July or August because of the summer vacation, or from mid-December to mid-January because of the Christmas holiday.

# HUNGARY (Cont'd)

## CUSTOMARY BUSINESS PRACTICES (Cont'd)

For business meetings, men wear suits, white shirts and ties. Women can wear suits or dresses.

## BUSINESS ENTERTAINING

If your business dealings are successful, consider hosting a cocktail party for your Hungarian colleagues. Guests should be greeted at the door, and you should be prepared to give a short speech.

If you want to have a meal with business associates, you can suggest meeting them for lunch.

After you have developed a personal relationship with a business colleague, you can entertain at a dinner and include spouses.

Most business entertaining is conducted at restaurants because homes are often too small to accommodate entertaining.

## DINING OUT

If you are invited to dinner at someone's home, Western liquor or wrapped flowers are appropriate gifts. Avoid bringing chrysanthemums.

The host and hostess sit opposite one another, with the guest of honor seated to the hostess's right.

Before starting to eat, it is customary to wish everyone a good appetite. Hungarians say *"Jóèt vagyat"* ("Enjoy the meal").

After each course is served, it is polite to wait until your hostess begins to eat before you start.

If wine is served, it is a Hungarian custom for the guest to propose a toast, saying "To your health."

Hungarians eat Continental style, with the fork in the left hand and the knife in the right. Push food onto the back of your fork with your knife.

When eating fish, use only a fork or the hostess will think the fish is not tender enough.

It would be wise to taste the food before adding seasoning, or you could insult the hostess. Begin by eating small portions of various dishes. The food tends to be very rich and you are expected to finish everything on your plate. If you must leave something, apologize to your hostess.

When complementing the hostess on the meal, expect her to make light of her efforts.

Breakfast usually consists of bread with butter and jam. Espresso will be served with hot milk.

Lunch is the main meal of the day. It may include soup (a cold fruit soup in the summer), a main course and salad. Dessert will follow with espresso served last.

### DINING OUT (Cont'd)

Popular main dishes include *pörkölt* (pork stew with paprika), *töltött káposzta* (stuffed cabbage) and *fátanyéros* (mixed grill of meats and sausages served on a wooden platter). *Palacsinta* (crepe-like pancakes) are used with various courses. They can be part of a main dish or a dessert.

Desserts can be elaborate, such as *dobos torta*, a 12-layer cake with chocolate filling. Other popular items are marzipan balls dipped in chocolate and glacéed chestnuts.

Hungary is famous for its sweet dessert wine, *Tokay*.

The evening meal is usually light, consisting of open-faced sandwiches or salad and cold cuts. Dessert is generally served after the evening meal. A dinner party, however, will be more like the midday meal.

### PUBLIC CUSTOMS

It is customary for a man to walk to the left of a woman or an honored guest of either sex.

Do not wear shorts except on country outings or at the beach.

# IRELAND: HISTORICAL OVERVIEW

- Ireland's modern history began when the Celts conquered the region in the fourth century B.C. Saint Patrick came to the region in 432 A.D., bringing Christianity to the people. In 795, Vikings invaded Ireland destroying the monasteries, libraries and settlements, and establishing a number of seaports along the coasts. They were eventually defeated in 1014. In the 12th century, the English began invading. In 1171, King Henry II forced Irish nobles to recognize his supreme rule.

- In 1603, England established control over all of Ireland after defeating the last of the major Gaelic leaders. Irish Anglicans, supported by England, excluded Catholics from controlling land and from playing a role in politics. Adding to frictions, in 1609 King James I seized Irish land to give to settlers who were loyal to England. These loyalists were mostly Protestants in the Northern section of the country. In 1801, the United Kingdom of Great Britain and Ireland was established by the Act of Union, to the dismay of Irish Catholics.

- In the 1840s, the country was devastated by the great potato famine, during which at least one million people died in five years and another two million emigrated to other countries, especially to the U.S. Political conflict and agitation for independence intensified after the famine.

- The Irish independence movement peaked in 1921 with the signing of the Anglo-Irish Treaty. The treaty established the Irish Free State as a British dominion and allowed six northern counties, with a Protestant majority, to remain in the United Kingdom as Northern Ireland.

- In 1937, a new constitution changed the country's name to *Éire* (Ireland) and the country began to decrease its association with the British Commonwealth. Finally, in 1949, Ireland formally withdrew from the Commonwealth and declared its independence.

- Since independence, talks have taken place between England and Ireland about returning Northern Ireland to Irish sovereignty. A 1985 agreement established a consultative role for the republic in the affairs of Northern Ireland. Talks were revived again in 1991 and 1992, but failed both times. Talks about sovereignty, about ending violence in Northern Ireland and about ending terrorism by the Irish Republican Army, an outlawed group in Great Britain, continued.

- Ireland's coalition government collapsed in 1992, due to a poor economy and various political issues. After a parliamentary no-confidence vote, the Parliament was dissolved and elections were held in November 1992. While Prime Minister Albert Reynolds retained his position, he was forced to enter his party, *Fianna Fail*, into a coalition with the *Labour Party*.

- When a cease-fire was honored in 1994, it seemed that progress was made in talks to eliminate violence. However, stability was difficult to maintain, and violence soon erupted again. Aside from the issue of violence, the question of sovereignty remains sensitive since most Protestants in Northern Ireland want to remain part of the United Kingdom.

# IRELAND

## INTRODUCTIONS

The Irish are somewhat reserved when greeting people, although they are very friendly. A firm handshake is appropriate for both men and women. You should wait for a woman to extend her hand first.

The traditional Irish greeting *"Céad míle fáilte"* (which means "One thousand welcomes") is used to greet visitors. Otherwise, usual English greetings, such as "Hello" or "How are you?" are used.

Last names are used, following the title "Mr.," "Mrs." or "Miss," as an appropriate form of address. The only occupational titles commonly used are "Doctor" and "Professor."

First names should only be used if you are invited to do so or if your colleague uses your first name. It is common to use first names after even a short acquaintance. However, you should use last names whenever your Irish colleagues address you using your last name.

At a large party, you should introduce yourself, while you should allow your host to introduce you at small parties.

## SOCIAL TIPS AND CONVENTIONS

The Irish can be quite reserved. Personal space is valued and hands are not used excessively during conversation.

Although Irish (called Gaelic) is the first officially recognized language, it is only spoken in small areas of the Western seaboard. English, recognized as Ireland's second language, is spoken and used everywhere (with accents varying as you move through the country).

The Irish are easygoing, lighthearted, good-humored and cheerful. They are also quick-witted, appreciate a sense of humor and they enjoy lively conversation. They particularly enjoy telling British jokes (just as the British enjoy telling Irish jokes).

The Catholic faith has a strong influence on the values of the Irish people. Traditions are important and material goods do not have the same priority as they do in other countries.

Both the Republic of Ireland and Northern Ireland have similar cultural roots and similar customs and values. The main differences are religious and political. The majority in the Republic of Ireland are Catholic and very nationalistic. The majority in Northern Ireland are Anglican and consider themselves to be part of Great Britain, not Ireland.

Good topics of conversation include the beauty of the country, Gaelic culture, Irish handicrafts and the weather. You should avoid discussing the division of the country, Ireland's relationship to the U.K., religion, politics and feminism. Also, avoid making pro-British comments or being unkind, which will offend the Irish. Visitors should also be aware that the Irish have strong emotional ties to the U.S. Contrasts between Ireland and the U.S. should be avoided.

# IRELAND (Cont'd)

## SOCIAL TIPS AND CONVENTIONS (Cont'd)

Another good topic of conversation is sports, as the Irish are very sports-oriented. Gaelic football (a cross between soccer and basketball) and hurling (played on a soccer-type field with wooden sticks and a small leather ball) are two national pastimes. Soccer, rugby, fishing, sailing and horse racing are also favorite activities.

## CUSTOMARY BUSINESS PRACTICES

English is always used in business transactions. There is no need to make arrangements for an interpreter to translate discussions to Gaelic.

You should avoid making business trips to Ireland during the first week in May (when most people are busy with trade fairs), in July and August and during the Christmas and New Year periods, when people are on vacation.

Business appointments should be made by letter or by phone.

You should be punctual for business appointments. However, the Irish are not very time-conscious and may not be punctual for an appointment. This may require some patience. Someone who offers to meet you in five minutes is more likely to appear in a half hour.

Avoid being demonstrative when you are making presentations. While the Irish have a reputation for being friendly and hearty, they are not very demonstrative and are not comfortable with people who are overly vehement.

Business attire is very conservative in Ireland. Men should wear suits and ties or tweed sports jackets. Women usually wear suits or wool blazers and wool skirts. Both men and women wear subdued colors.

Business cards are not as commonly used in Ireland as in other countries. However, it is a good idea to bring some with you so that you can leave a card with a secretary if the person you want to see is unavailable.

Business hours are usually 9:00 a.m. to 5:00 p.m., Monday through Friday, with an hour break for lunch in all but the major cities.

## BUSINESS ENTERTAINING

The Irish are a warm and hospitable people. However, it is not very common to invite foreigners to one's home for dinner.

There are no set rules about including spouses in dinner invitations. If you intend to include the spouse of an Irish colleague in an invitation to a dinner party, you should be specific. Similarly, if you are invited to a dinner, you should take note as to whether spouses are included in the invitation, or you may ask the host specifically.

Irish people like to have conversations in "pubs" (public houses). Some say that conversation is the national pastime. Many "pubs" feature folk music as entertainment. Pubs usually have two sections, the bar and the lounge. Women usually frequent the lounge, although the drinks are more expensive there.

# IRELAND (Cont'd)

## BUSINESS ENTERTAINING (Cont'd)

Gift-giving is not common when conducting business in Ireland. In fact, because visiting is infrequent outside of holiday periods, it is not customary to bring a gift, even when invited to someone's home. However, if you are invited to a dinner, a gift of flowers, chocolates, wine or cheese is usually appreciated.

You should be aware that refusing a drink is a serious insult in Ireland. If you really don't care to drink, explain that you don't drink for health reasons. If you accept a drink, you should raise the glass before you take a sip and say "Cheers."

Drinks are not served with ice. However, it is perfectly acceptable to request ice if you prefer beverages chilled.

Pub drinks include Irish whiskey, Scotch whiskey, shandy (beer and lemonade), gin and tonic and Guiness stout. Normally, Irish beer is served at room temperature. If you order lager served cold, you will get the equivalent of U.S. beer.

There are customs associated with the size of the drink you order. Women are expected to order half-pints (10 ounces) of beer or stout. In fact, some pubs will not even serve full pints to women. On the other hand, if a man orders a half-pint, his virility may be called into question.

If you are with a group, you are expected to buy a round of drinks. However, women are never allowed to buy a round.

## DINING OUT

In restaurants, a service charge is usually included in the check. You may also want to leave some extra change for exemplary service. If a service charge is not included, you should leave a 10-15% tip on the table.

Traditional Irish dishes are hearty and simple. Fresh dairy products, breads, seafood and vegetables are widely available since Ireland is an agricultural country. Potatoes are a staple. Smoked salmon is considered an Irish specialty. The main meats eaten for dinner include chicken, pork, beef and mutton. Tea is the most popular drink.

Some Irish specialties include *colcannon* (a mix of potato and cabbage), fish and chips, Galway oysters, *grouse*, *mixed coddle* (boiled bacon and sausages), pheasant, smoked and fresh salmon, steak and kidney pie, trout, *black pudding* (blood pudding') and *rognons* (kidneys).

European dishes are also popular in Ireland. Many types of restaurants, including U.S. fast food chains, are found throughout Ireland. "Farmhouse" restaurants serve traditional Irish dishes. Tea kitchens serve hot drinks as well as homemade cakes and pastries in the afternoon.

Breakfasts are usually large, often including bacon and eggs. Lunch, served between 1:00 and 2:00 p.m., usually consists of hot dishes, such as steak and kidney pie or boiled bacon and cabbage. It may also consist of a cold meal, such as a ham and cheese salad (ham and cheese slices with lettuce and tomato). The type of dinner, between 5:00 and 8:00 p.m., depends on the size of the midday meal. A light dinner, sometimes called "tea," may consist of cold cuts and salads or a "fry-up" (eggs, grilled sausage, bacon, tomatoes and *black pudding* cut up and grilled).

# IRELAND (Cont'd)

## DINING OUT (Cont'd)

A more formal meal is usually served later in the evening. A heavier dinner, which is served at a dinner party, usually starts with drinks (usually vermouth, sherry, wine, whiskey or brandy). The meal begins with soup, followed by meat (usually a roast) with potatoes and vegetables. Wine is usually served with the meal. The main dish is followed by cheese and crackers, then dessert with coffee or tea and port or other spirits.

Dining etiquette is neither formal nor strictly adhered to in Ireland. The Irish eat in the continental style, with the fork in the left hand and the knife remaining in the right.

When you eat at someone's home, it is common for your plate to be brought to you with food already on it. Even though you do not have much choice of portion size or type of food, you should try to eat everything on the plate.

If there is a small plate next to your dinner plate, be aware that it is not for bread. Rather it is for the peelings, which should be removed from boiled potatoes (you should not eat them). Bread is usually not served with dinner.

Be aware that huge portions are served in restaurants, even those offering gourmet dishes.

## PUBLIC CUSTOMS

The Irish wear tailored clothes, especially tweeds and woolens in dark colors (even for casual wear). Shorts are only worn at the beach.

General courtesy and politeness are valued. However, the Irish are very easygoing and informal, and it is difficult to offend anyone by using the wrong fork or shaking hands at the wrong time.

You should avoid handing money to a store clerk before he/she is finished packing your purchase.

Long lines are common and expected. Pushing and shoving when waiting in line for buses, theaters and in shops or barging into line is unacceptable and considered extremely rude.

Most gestures used in Ireland are the same as those used in the United States. However, gestures that specifically use the fingers (i.e., pointing or summoning with the index finger, etc.) are not as common and should be avoided. You should be aware that the reverse "V for victory" sign is especially offensive.

In the North, women are generally seated first.

# ITALY: HISTORICAL OVERVIEW

- One of the first civilizations to flourish in Italy was that of the Etruscans between the eighth and second centuries B.C. They mostly influenced central Italy and later, the entire Roman Empire. Greek civilization had dominated southern Italy before the Romans became prominent. In fact, Rome adopted a number of elements of Greek culture after it conquered the Greek Empire.

- After 400 B.C., Rome became a major power that flourished and expanded throughout the Mediterranean region. The Roman civilization has had a strong impact on modern legal, social, political and military structures throughout Western nations. However, by the fifth century A.D., the Roman Empire fell to a number of invasions, and the peninsula was then divided into several separate political regions. In addition to local rulers, parts of Italy were ruled by the French, Spanish and Austrians at different times. At the same time, the Italian peninsula was the center of many artistic, cultural and architectural revolutions, including the great Renaissance of the 15th and 16th centuries.

- In the 1800s, *Risorgimento*, the Italian unification movement, began and in 1861, national unification was declared by the first Italian parliament in Turin. A king (Victor Emmanuel) was named, and unification was completed in 1870 when Rome was unified with the rest of the area.

- From 1922 to 1943, Italy had a fascist dictatorship under Benito Mussolini, and the country initially helped Hitler in World War II. However, after the fascists were overthrown in 1943, Italy supported the allies. After the war, a republic was established through elections in 1946, and the monarchy was officially abolished. Political violence and terrorism marked the 1970s, and the 1980s were marked by frequent collapses of the government. As the 1990s approached, voting patterns began shifting to favor non-Communist parties, such as the *Social Democrats*.

- The elections of 1992 hurt the ruling coalition and failed to bring a strong government to power. Many people blamed the proportional system of voting, which was originally designed to prevent totalitarianism, for the weakness of government. Oscar Luigi Scalfaro was elected as President by Parliament in 1992, but political stability was still not achieved. A number of political scandals emerged, top officials (including the Prime Minister) resigned, and by 1994, 6000 individuals were under investigation for corruption. Finally, the Parliament was dissolved. In a 1993 referendum, 80% of voters supported a switch from a proportional to a majority system as well as other reforms. At the beginning of 1994, early elections were held and Silvio Berlusconi's *Forza Italia* party won on promises of running a government without corruption and stimulating the economy. However, with the party's ties to neo-fascists and the separatist *Northern League*, it was difficult for Berlusconi to form a government. However, in May 1994, the last obstacles were cleared and Berlusconi officially became Prime Minister, disavowing neo-fascist views and promising true democracy.

- Since 1994, many prominent politicians have been brought to trial for corrupt activities, including Berlusconi, for bribery charges. He was blocked out of power by opposition parties, and a non-party government was temporarily implemented. In April 1996, a national election brought Italy closer to stability. The center-left *Olive Tree Alliance* won a near majority of seats and was able to do so without corruption.

# ITALY

## INTRODUCTIONS

The Italian custom is to shake hands when meeting or departing. Italians tend to show more physical contact than many other Europeans, so don't be surprised if a colleague or a client greets you with a hug after you have become familiar.

Italian businesspeople usually address each other by surnames. Do not use first names until you are asked to do so. Use *"dottore"* or *"dottoressa"* plus the last name if a person has a college degree.

When addressing a woman who is a professional, use *Signora* ("Mrs.") or *"Signorina"* ("Miss") plus her title; i.e., *"Signorina Avocatessa"* ("Miss Lawyer"). *"Dottoressa"* can be used if you are uncertain of her marital status regardless of her profession.

Bring business cards with you and exchange them when first introduced to new people, after shaking hands and sitting down.

If no formal introductions are made (for instance, at a party), introduce yourself by saying your name and shaking hands.

People who know each other well, greet each other with a kiss on each cheek, which is really "kissing the air."

## SOCIAL TIPS AND CONVENTIONS

Italians dress elegantly for both business and social occasions. Dark suits with ties for men and classic dresses or suits for women are recommended.

Italians always appreciate when a foreigner speaks a few words in Italian.

Italians are very family-oriented, and they appreciate discussing each other's families.

Food, wine and restaurants are savored, and the people enjoy conversing about them. Other good conversation topics include sports, especially soccer and bicycling.

Italians tend to be demonstrative and use frequent hand gestures.

Nearly all Italians are Roman Catholic.

In adherence to Italian custom, always stand when an older person enters or departs from the room.

## CUSTOMARY BUSINESS PRACTICES

Northern Italians tend to respect punctuality, while people in the south have a more relaxed attitude about time. Since meetings may be cancelled on short notice, always confirm an appointment by telephone just prior to the meeting.

# ITALY (Cont'd)

## CUSTOMARY BUSINESS PRACTICES (Cont'd)

Good times for business appointments are between 10:00 and 11:00 a.m. or after 3:00 p.m.

In Italy, there is a clear distinction between business and pleasure. At business meetings, the focus is on business. You should not spend much time making light conversation, and jokes are considered out of place. At your first meeting, however, it is appropriate to take time to get to know each other before transacting any business.

The time for lighter conversation is during drinks or dinner, where you can safely discuss a wide range of subjects.

Work is not usually discussed at social functions. Therefore, only after you get to know your client well should you meet for lunch to discuss business.

Italians prefer not to take work home.

Your client will expect you to be very knowledgeable about your product/service and how it is used worldwide.

Your client may not indicate his/her disinterest in your product or service with a definitive "no," but instead may be somewhat tactful in rejecting a proposal or business plan, etc.

The formal meeting is not usually utilized to decide significant matters, but rather to ratify them and to communicate them to other levels of management. Major decisions are made somewhat more privately.

The person presiding over the meeting may or may not be the most senior person. He/She may be the second in rank so that the proceedings will not be disrupted should the senior person be called away.

When negotiating in Italy, do not display any urgency, as it will weaken your bargaining position. Also, when an agreement seems near, be aware that Italians sometimes bring in a large number of new demands.

As in most of Europe, many businesses are closed for vacation in August.

The custom of giving business gifts is very common. Give a small gift to any staff members who were especially helpful to you.

## BUSINESS ENTERTAINING

Most business entertaining is done in restaurants. It is unusual to be invited to a private home.

If you have a lot of business to conduct with one person, invite him/her to dinner and possibly to a club after the meal. You should treat this as a strictly social occasion and include spouses.

# ITALY (Cont'd)

## BUSINESS ENTERTAINING (Cont'd)

Sometime during the course of a business relationship you may be invited to a sporting event, but the usual invitation is to a restaurant for dinner. It is considered important to reciprocate.

If you are invited to a colleague's home, a gift of chocolates, individual pastries or flowers would be appreciated. If you bring flowers, buy an odd number and never purchase chrysanthemums. Italians often appreciate gifts from your home state or region.

## DINING OUT

At an Italian meal, the host is always the first to begin eating. Wait until the host indicates this before you start. Wait to see if you should pass food around the table or if the hostess will serve everyone.

It is considered impolite to smoke between courses because Italians believe that it ruins the taste of the food.

The Italians eat in the continental manner, keeping the fork in the left hand and the knife in the right. Pasta should be eaten by twisting it around your fork using the sides of the pasta plate, not by twirling it around your fork with a spoon.

Keep your hands above the table during a meal.

You may not have a separate bread plate. Italians break rolls next to the main plate.

Allow the host to pour the wine. If you do not want more, keep your glass almost full by taking small sips. Take care not to get drunk, as it is considered very offensive.

The host and hostess generally sit opposite one another at the table. The most important male guest is seated to the left of the hostess and the second most important male guest to her right. Female guests are seated similarly next to the host.

It is considered polite to refuse a second helping when it is first offered. If your hostess insists, then it is polite to accept. If you really don't want more, say that you really can't eat any more.

Indicate that you are finished by placing the knife and fork parallel on the plate, with the fork tines facing down.

To beckon a waiter or waitress, raise your hand slightly and say *"Camariere"* or *"Signorina."*

Expect that the person who invites someone to a meal will pay for it. The guest should try to reciprocate within a few days. When inviting an Italian to a meal, ask him/her to recommend a restaurant.

# ITALY (Cont'd)

## DINING OUT (Cont'd)

Breakfast usually consists of bread and butter, served with *cappucino* (strong coffee with hot foamy milk) or hot chocolate. Lunch is traditionally the main meal of the day, although less so now than in the past. It usually begins with a pasta course, followed by a meat course (frequently veal). Bread is served with the meal and salad follows. The beverages usually served are wine and water. Italians will end the meal with cheese and fruit, followed by *espresso* (strong black coffee served in very small cups). *Espresso* is not lingered over; it is consumed rapidly.

If it is a special occasion, or if the family is having company, there may also be an *antipasto* course, such as *prosciutto* (paper-thin slices of ham) and melon, before the pasta. Pastries will be included after the cheese and before the fruit. In addition to the *espresso*, a digestive drink may follow (a bitter, after-dinner liqueur).

The evening meal is usually lighter than the midday meal. There might be soup, cold cuts, salad and fruit. If it is a dinner party, however, the meal will be more elaborate, similar to lunch.

Fruit is eaten with a knife and fork, except for grapes and cherries, which you may eat by hand.

Some regional specialties include: in Bologna, *tortellini* (small loop-shaped filled pasta); in Florence and Tuscany, *bistecca alla Fiorentina* (grilled beefsteak); in Genoa, *gnocchi* (potato dumplings) or *pesto* sauce (basil and pine nut sauce served with pasta); in Milan and Lombardy, *osso buco* (lamb shanks); in Rome, *cannelloni* (tube-shaped pasta filled with meat or cheese); in Sicily, *caponata* (eggplant, tomatoes, green pepper and olives); and in Venice, *risi e bisi* (rice and peas).

## PUBLIC CUSTOMS

Do not wear shorts or old jeans in cities, especially when visiting churches.

In Italy, men often walk arm-in-arm with other men, as in Latin America.

Always ask permission before photographing someone. Italians are usually pleased to cooperate.

# LATVIA: HISTORICAL OVERVIEW

- The people living along the southern shores of the Baltic have occupied the area containing present-day Latvia for more than 2000 years. In the ninth century, the Vikings established control in the region.

- The Baltic people continued their pagan religion for many centuries. A Christianizing effort by German missionaries in the 13th century was followed by an invasion of crusading knights. The most significant being the invasion of the Teutonic Knights, who conquered the area of present-day Latvia in 1225.

- The spread of the Protestant Reformation in the 16th century led to the dissolution of the Teutonic Knights and the conversion of Latvian serfs to Lutheranism. Soon thereafter the Russians became interested in the region.

- Peter the Great defeated the Swedes in the early 18th century and gained control of the region. The Russians industrialized the region and fostered the spread of the Orthodox Church.

- By 1905, illegal nationalist political parties operated in Latvia. When World War I broke out, these parties at first supported the war effort, but then became dissatisfied and began pressing for their own governments. The Bolshevik Revolution further alienated the Baltic peoples. However, they were able to withstand both the Bolshevik threat as well as the threat of German annexation. In August 1920, the Bolsheviks signed a treaty recognizing Latvia's independence. Latvia moved toward authoritarianism in the 1920s as the economic situation worsened and the Premier, Karlis Ulmanis, argued convincingly that he needed additional powers to defend Latvian democracy.

- Latvia was weakened by the authoritarian direction, and in 1939, the Nazi-Soviet non-aggression pact stipulated that Latvia would fall under Soviet rule. Noncommunist parties were outlawed, and a program of agricultural collectivism began. Over the next 35 years, the Soviets tried to integrate Latvia into the union. Branch factories were located in the area, education was restructured to include Soviet indoctrination and non-Baltic nationals were relocated to Latvia.

- Latvians were among the earliest supporters of *glasnost* (a term describing Gorbachev's attempts to get his supporters to speak out and make their opinions known). The *Popular Front of Latvia (PFL)* won 75% of Latvia's 1989 elections to the USSR Congress of People's Deputies. The move toward independence was at first resisted by Gorbachev, but negative international reaction, coupled with the mounting pressure from all the Baltic Republics, led to the recognition of Latvian independence in 1991. A major concern since that time has been the continuing presence of ex-Soviet troops in the Republic. Another concern is the issue of ethnicity, since there are many Latvian nationalists but also a huge non-Latvian population.

- Parliamentary elections in 1995 produced a heavily fragmented assembly with nine political blocs. Although the political scene was unstable, Latvia made significant progress in moving toward a market economy. In the area of privatization, this new nation lagged somewhat, but to its advantage, its work force was well educated, and its populace disciplined.

# LATVIA

## INTRODUCTIONS

The word used for greeting in Latvia on formal and informal occasions is *"Sveicinati"* ("Hello"). The Italian word, *"Ciao,"* (also meaning "Hello") is used quite often, though only among good friends and on informal occasions.

Handshaking is a customary greeting practice in Latvia.

Latvians love flowers and they are typically given during the first welcome meeting at the airport. They are also regarded as an essential part of a present on important occasions and celebrations.

## SOCIAL TIPS AND CONVENTIONS

Latvians are somewhat reserved at first but are generally very hospitable people. It is important to know that Latvians do not smile often, and so one should not misinterpret a serious expression as indicating dissatisfaction.

The official language is Latvian, though most speak Russian as a first or second language. Ethnic Latvians make up 53% of the population, which has a large component of resident Slavs.

Cultural heritage, especially folklore, is a source of tremendous pride to Latvians. There are amateur artists everywhere. One form of folk art is *daina*, a four-line song form which reflects the morals and lifestyle of Latvia's past. The Song Festival, held each year since 1873, features much choral singing and dancing and is an important symbol of Latvian nationalism.

During the existence of the Soviet Union, Latvians were the most frequent visitors to theaters, concerts and museums. Presently, due to economic difficulties, cultural life has decreased.

Extended families are found mostly in rural areas. One-third of marriages are ethnically mixed and the divorce rate is very high – at about 50%.

Most Latvians consider themselves Nordic, though Eastern Latvians retain Polish and Russian cultural and linguistic influences.

Latvians are the most entrepreneurial of the Baltic peoples and most at ease with foreigners.

Riga is home to one-third of the Latvian population. It is a very diverse city, including large numbers of Russians, Ukrainians and Belarussians. Riga is quite impressive architecturally and archeologically. The heart of the city is the Freedom Monument, built during the the 1920s and widely used today as a site for official occasions.

Evangelical Lutheranism and Roman Catholicism are the most practiced religions. There are also sizable minorities of Russian Orthodox and Baptists.

The society is highly literate, with free and compulsory education until the age of eighteen.

Taxis in the capital of Riga are cheap, but fares are on the rise due to increasing gas prices. It is advisable to bargain over the price for private taxis. All parts of Riga are accessible by public transportation.

# LATVIA (Cont'd)

## SOCIAL TIPS AND CONVENTIONS (Cont'd)

A good rail and bus network connects the capital city with major towns and points of interest within the country.

Taxi drivers, room service personnel and others should be tipped according to the quality of service.

Credit cards, travelers' checks and other non-cash payments are not widely accepted. Major credit cards (Visa Card, Mastercard, American Express, etc.) are accepted at the big stores in downtown Riga.

In Vecriga, the oldest part of Riga, there are many small shops selling Latvian jewelry, which typically is made with silver and amber according to the patterns of ancient Latvian jewelry-makers. The most popular piece is a ring called *Nameis*, which serves as a sort of identification for Latvians at home and among Latvians abroad. It is popular with men and women who are proud of their nationality.

To make phone calls from the public phones, you have to purchase a pre-paid calling card which is available at newsstands and other stores.

## CUSTOMARY BUSINESS PRACTICES

To tell time, Latvians use the same system as our military. Thus, 6:00 p.m. is 18:00, midnight is 24:00, etc. Using a.m. and p.m. may be confusing for Latvians.

Presentations should be precise, logical and straightforward. Efforts to be diplomatic may be misunderstood as hesitation or dissatisfaction with negotiations.

Contracts can be verbal, especially if the matter is relatively minor. Expect to be held to your word if you have assented verbally.

Many Latvians in business speak English or German. These languages are considered appropriate for official business, so do not hesitate to use them.

Latvian businesspeople usually have business cards printed in Latvian on one side and English on the other.

Negotiations usually begin immediately, without introductory social conversation. Conversations about family, culture, country, etc. should be left for after the working day.

If you are not very familiar with your Latvian business partner, it is wise to avoid conversations or correspondence in Russian. This may be construed as a lack of respect for Latvia's own culture and an offensive reminder of the Soviet Union's occupation of the country. Latvians usually prefer to talk about their future rather than the past.

Before World War II, Latvia had a well-established European business culture. Now that the Soviet Union has dissolved and Latvia has been liberated, it is going through a re-integration process into the European Community. As a result, the business culture is European with a strong influence from the Soviet Era.

# LATVIA (Cont'd)

## CUSTOMARY BUSINESS PRACTICES (Cont'd)

Appointments should be made in advance.

There is a daily business newspaper, *"Dienas Bizness,"* issued in English and Latvian. In style and content it is similar to the "Financial Times."

Office hours are typically 9:00 a.m. to 6:00 p.m., Monday through Friday. Many shops are open late, some until 11:00 p.m. There are quite a few 24-hour convenience stores.

## BUSINESS ENTERTAINING

Depending on the situation, lunch may or may not include alcohol. It is polite to take a taste but not necessary to finish your glass.

Often, the Latvian business partner acting as host will pay for your accommodations, evening entertainment, etc. This should be regarded as hospitality. Keep in mind that Latvian businessmen visiting your country may expect similar treatment.

Restaurants begin serving lunch at about noon, and dinner is served after 6:00 p.m.

For US $10-$15, you can get you a good meal in Latvia. Service charges are usually included. Keep in mind that men's bathrooms are marked by a triangle pointing downwards and women's bathrooms by a triangle pointing upwards.

Latvians eat continental style, with the knife kept in the right hand and the fork in the left.

## DINING OUT

Meals are rather high in fat and calories. Local specialties include cabbage soup, grilled pork ribs, smoked fish and grey peas with fat.

Water is not customarily served with meals; it will be brought if requested.

A popular liquor is Riga's *Black Balsam*, an herb concoction which can be consumed with small sips or used to make cocktails. Latvians are very proud of their brewing traditions. Local beers include *Aldaris, Cesu Alus* and *Rigas Alus.*

## PUBLIC CUSTOMS

There are two types of celebratory days in Latvia: holidays and commemorative days. Holidays are usually observed by all Latvians and are official days off. Commemorative days acknowledge important events in history, but there is no holiday from work.

The following days are official holidays: January 1 (New Year's Day), Good Friday, Easter, May 1 (Labor Day; anniversary of the Constitutional Convention of 1922), June 23-24 (Midsummer's Eve celebration), November 18 (Independence Day) December 25-26 (Christmas), December 31 (New Year's Eve).

## LATVIA (Cont'd)

### PUBLIC CUSTOMS (Cont'd)

The following are commemorative days: March 25 (commemorative day for victims of Communist terror), May 8 (commemorative day for victims of WWII), 2nd Sunday in May (Mother's Day), June 14 (commemorative day for victims of 1941 Soviet deportations), July 4 (commemorative day for victims of anti-Semitic genocide), November 11 (*Lacplesis* Day (Veterans' Day).

# LITHUANIA: HISTORICAL OVERVIEW

- In 1236, Duke Minaugas first united the lands then inhabited by the Lithuanians, the Yatwingians and the Couronians to form the Grand Duchy of Lithuania. In the 14th century, the state was ruled by strong monarchs who annexed neighboring lands. In 1323, Vilnius became the capital. In 1386, in response to a serious threat from Germanic invaders, the Grand Duke of Lithuania married the Polish crown princess, uniting Lithuania and Poland. This allowed the two nations to defeat the German (Teutonic) invaders in 1410. At the same time because of the union, the Lithuanians adopted Roman Catholicism and began to adopt Western culture. The association between Poland and Lithuania was solidified in 1569 with the Lublin Union.

- After a gradual partition of the Polish-Lithuanian state (in 1772, 1793 and 1795) by its neighbors, Lithuania came under the control of the Russian Empire. A number of attempts to gain independence in the 19th century proved unsuccessful.

- Germany occupied Lithuania in World War I. But in 1917 after the Russian Revolution, the Germans allowed Lithuania to elect its own officials. These officials declared Lithuania an independent state in 1918. However, the Bolsheviks soon invaded from Russia.

- By 1919 determined to regain sovereignty, the Lithuanians drove the Soviets out of most of their country. Simultaneously, Poland sought to regain the territory it had claimed before 1795, including Lithuania, and was fighting the Soviets. In response to the Polish threat, Lithuania signed a peace treaty with the Soviets that recognized Vilnius as belonging to Lithuania. The same treaty was later signed with Poland, which was to give up its claim to the region. Nevertheless, the Polish army seized Vilnius, and Kaunas became the capital of Lithuania.

- Between the wars, from about 1920 to 1940 Lithuania was independent and flourished under a free market economy. However, Lithuania was forced to accept Soviet military bases on its territory after a joint German-Soviet attack on Poland in 1939. As compensation, the Soviets returned Vilnius to Lithuanian sovereignty. However, the Soviets also soon dismissed the Lithuanian government and officially occupied the entire nation by 1940. Armed partisan fighters, called "Forest Brothers," fought unsuccessfully for independence between 1940 and 1954. Lithuania suffered mass deportations and other problems under Stalin. Even when relations relaxed in the 1960s, Lithuania continued to seek independence.

- In 1990, the freely elected legislature declared independence, and after the Soviet Union collapsed, Russia officially recognized Lithuania's independence. The government, led by members of the *Sajudis* political movement, implemented aggressive economic and political reforms. Due to widespread disappointment in the slow and painful transition, in 1992 voters rejected the *Sajudis* in favor of former Communists. The new government remained committed to democracy, but slowed privatization and other reform measures. In late 1993, the leaders were able to effect a full withdrawal of Russian troops from the country.

- President Algirdas Brazauskas, of the *Democratic Labor Party*, was a nationalist who maintained, but slowed down, the transition to a market economy.

# LITHUANIA

## INTRODUCTIONS

It is customary to shake hands with men and, to some extent in business settings, with women when greeting. Men sometimes kiss the extended hand of women in greeting. Good friends of both sexes may kiss cheeks.

A handshake is almost always used with professional contacts.

When introducing a man, use the term *"Ponas"* ("Mr.") before the last name. For a women use the term *"Ponia"* ("Mrs.") or *"Panele"* ("Miss"). When applicable, also use the professional title before the last name.

First names are not used among adults until one is invited to do so.

Men raise their hats or nod to greet someone at a distance.

The most common phrases for greeting are *"Laba diena"* ("Good day"), *"Labas rytas"* ("Good morning"), *"Labas vakaras"* ("Good evening"), *"Labas"* ("Hello") and *"Sveikas"* or *"Sveiki"* ("How do you do?").

## SOCIAL TIPS AND CONVENTIONS

Lithuanian is the country's official language. Most Lithuanians also speak Russian and English is becoming popular.

Lithuanians are proud of their heritage, except for the period under the Soviet Union. Lithuania only completed its transition from communism in October 1992. Many people are frustrated with the current transition and uncertain about the future.

Lithuanians are somewhat reserved although they are sincere and full of emotion. They mask their feelings to maintain privacy. Lithuanians are often openly critical of public institutions. They are also very self-critical. However, they are generally optimistic, patient and hard-working.

Lithuanians appreciate skill, intelligence and punctuality. They value education, family and loyalty to one's nationality.

Spontaneous visits are not common, even between friends and neighbors. However, unannounced guests will be welcomed.

Visiting, gardening, watching television and cultural events are the most common leisure activities.

Lithuanians place importance on neat dressing. Clothing styles are taken mainly from Europe and from the U.S. Hats are commonly worn in winter. Handmade clothes are often worn, especially in rural areas. Older rural women wear scarves on their heads.

# LITHUANIA (Cont'd)

## CUSTOMARY BUSINESS PRACTICES

Punctuality is expected for both business and social visits.

Business is usually kept separate from socializing.

Keep in mind that business generally operates along free market lines with state coordination only in key areas since the Lithuanian transition from communism in 1992.

Businesses are open from 9:00 a.m. to 6:00 p.m. with an hour break for lunch at 1:00 p.m. Banks are open from 9:00 a.m. to noon.

## BUSINESS ENTERTAINING

Visiting in Lithuanian homes is popular due to limited outside social opportunities.

For even a brief visit, one should bring an odd number of flowers. Your host will be offended if you bring an even number of flowers (appropriate only when there is a death in the family). Even if you bring a large number of flowers, they will be counted by the host. Also, be aware that carnations are associated with mourning.

Dinner guests often bring flowers and wine as gifts to the host. Unwrap the flowers before presenting them. White flowers are usually reserved for brides.

Guests are always offered refreshments, which may be coffee or tea and cake or cookies.

In formal situations, guests wait to sit down until they are invited to do so or until the host sits.

The length of an evening visit will depend upon the occasion. The host may accompany a guest outside when he/she leaves if the hour is late.

It is considered impolite to leave food on your plate – it implies that the food was not good.

In restaurants, you must request the bill from the waiter and pay it at the table.

Tipping has not been customary, but is becoming more common.

## DINING OUT

The continental style of eating is used, with the knife kept in the right hand and the fork in the left.

The midday meal (dinner) is the main meal of the day. Most businesses close for the meal; people either go home or eat at work site canteens.

Toasting is common for dinner and supper, whether or not guests are present.

Lithuanian specialties include smoked sausage and *cepelinai* (meat cooked inside a ball of potato dough, served with a special sauce). Soup and local fruits and vegetables often accompany meals. Rye bread and dairy products are eaten regularly.

# LITHUANIA (Cont'd)

## PUBLIC CUSTOMS

It is impolite to talk with your hands in your pockets.

Using the hands a great deal during conversation or using hand gestures instead of speech is generally inappropriate.

Eye contact is important during conversation.

Adults should not chew gum in public.

Favorite sports in Lithuania include basketball and soccer.

# LUXEMBOURG: HISTORICAL OVERVIEW

- Before Luxembourg became independent, the area was ruled by many powers including the Roman Empire and Charlemagne's kingdom. In 963, Count Siegfried of the Ardennes built a castle in present-day Luxembourg and founded the Luxembourg dynasty. He built an impregnable fortress which some called the "Gibraltar of the North." In fact, the word "Luxembourg" means "little fortress."

- Members of the Luxembourg family became monarchs in other countries during the Middle Ages. Charles Luxembourg, for example, became the king of Bohemia in the 14th century and strove to make Prague (now in the Czech Republic) as beautiful as Paris. In the same century, Luxembourg's duke, Henry VII, was crowned Holy Roman Emperor.

- In 1443, the region was conquered by the Duke of Burgundy and, subsequently, the country would be ruled by foreign powers for more than four centuries. In the 17th and 18th centuries, the powerful Austrian aristocratic Hapsburg family ruled Luxembourg. The Netherlands then took control and in 1815, the Congress of Vienna made Luxembourg a Grand Duchy in the Dutch kingdom.

- As early as 1830, the Luxembourgers, following the example of the Belgians, revolted against Dutch control. After the revolt, Luxembourg was divided between Belgium and the Netherlands.

- In 1867, the Treaty of London declared Luxembourg (the part that had come under the control of the Netherlands) an independent neutral state. Under the international agreement, according to which Luxembourg was to remain neutral and unarmed, the powerful battlements that Count Siegfried had built into the cliffs where Luxembourg's present capital city is located were destroyed.

- After independence, the country continued to maintain close ties with the Netherlands. However, a personal union between the monarchs of the two countries ended in 1890 when both died. In Luxembourg, the crown was passed to the House of Nassau until a new monarch could be found. In the Netherlands, the king was succeeded by his daughter, Wilhelmina. However, Luxembourg broke away because, at that time, its laws did not permit a female ruler.

- Although it maintained its neutrality, Luxembourg was invaded by Germany in both World Wars. A number of important battles were fought on Luxembourg's territory, including the "Battle of the Bulge." After its liberation, Luxembourg ended its neutrality in 1949 and joined the Western European alliances, including NATO.

- In 1958, Luxembourg was one of the six founders of the European Economic Community (EEC).

- In 1964, the Grand Duchess Charlotte abdicated, allowing her son, Grand Duke Jean to become the country's ruler. Since that time, Luxembourg has enjoyed peace, economic growth and beneficial relations with other European nations.

# LUXEMBOURG

## INTRODUCTIONS

A gentle handshake is appropriate when greeting acquaintances or meeting someone for the first time.

Close female friends will sometimes hug each other three times as well as kiss each other on the cheek three times.

Common greetings include *"Moien"* ("Morning), *"Gudden Owend"* ("Good evening") and *"Wéi geet et?"* ("How are you?"). The French *"Bonjour "*("Good day") is also used.

Luxembourgers tend to be reserved with strangers but are loyal and affectionate with their friends. Acquaintances use titles and surnames while friends and relatives use given names or nicknames. High-ranking persons may be greeted by more than one title such as *"Här Minister"* ("Mr. Minister").

## SOCIAL TIPS AND CONVENTIONS

The native language is Luxembourgish, descended from a Franco-Moselle dialect and mixed with many German and French words. Other languages used are German and French. German is often used for newspapers and French is the official language of the civil service, law and Parliament. English is also widely understood.

Luxembourgers, an ethnic mix of French and German origins, account for about 75% of the population. The rest consists of guest and worker residents, primarily from Portugal, France and Italy.

Over 90% of the population belong to the Roman Catholic Church. Most do not attend church on a regular basis and the society is basically secular.

Although Luxembourgers descend from various nationalities, they have a strong feeling of national pride which is reflected in their national motto, *"Mir wëlle bleiwe wat mer sin!"* ("We want to remain what we are!").

Through invasion and peaceful exchange, Belgium, France and Germany have influenced the customs of Luxembourg. There are ways in which Luxembourg is distinct from its neighbors. For example, the pace of life is not as hurried as its European neighbors. Still, Luxembourgers are hard-working and productive.

Family ties are strong. Parents are legally required to pay for their children's education and adult children must meet certain financial obligations of their parents if in need.

Nightlife is modest, even on weekends. There are a few well-patronized pubs in the capital and the neighborhood café is often a hub for social activity.

# LUXEMBOURG (Cont'd)

## CUSTOMARY BUSINESS PRACTICES

Customary business hours are from 8:30 a.m. to 5:30 p.m., Monday through Friday. Some shops and recreational facilities are open longer.

The business climate is healthy, with few labor disputes. All workers receive 25 vacation days a year and women receive four to six months' maternity leave.

## BUSINESS ENTERTAINING

When dining in a restaurant, service is normally included in the bill. An extra tip is not necessary but is appreciated. If service is not included, then it is customary to leave a 10-15% tip. Typical restaurant hours are from noon-2:30 p.m. for lunch and 7:00-10:00 p.m. for dinner.

Most restaurants serve German-style food. Menus are usually written in French and German.

Luxembourgers often visit friends and relatives at home, but rarely without notice. Dinner guests bring flowers, chocolates or a bottle of wine to their hosts. Among younger people, it is common for the guests to bring dessert.

Hosts expect guests to ask for second helpings and some cooks believe that the food has not been enjoyed if guests do not ask for seconds.

Traditionally, the main meal of the day is lunch, but dinner has become the main meal for those whose work does not allow them to return home to take a long lunch.

Guests are not usually invited to the home to discuss business. This is done in public places such as restaurants, cafés and offices.

## DINING OUT

Popular dishes are *Judd mat Gaardebounen* (smoked collar of pork with broad beans), *Bouneschlupp* (bean soup), *Kachkéis* (a soft cheese), *Quetschentaart* (plum tart), *Fritten, Ham an Zalot* (french fries, ham and salad), *Träipen* (black pudding) and freshwater fish (usually trout). Sausages, potatoes and sauerkraut are important parts of the diet.

The continental style of eating is used, with the fork in the left hand and the knife remaining in the right hand. It is impolite to rest one's hands in the lap during a meal. Burping at the table is also unacceptable.

## PUBLIC CUSTOMS

Luxembourgers are reserved in public; it is impolite to yawn, shout or use offensive language. Luxembourgers are attentive to neatness and cleanliness in their dress and overall appearance.

The education system is well-developed and literacy is 99%.

National holidays include New Year's Day, Labor Day (May 1), the Grand Duke's Birthday – also called National Day (June 23) and Fair Day (early September). Fair Day occurs in an ancient shepherds' market and focuses on shepherding. Religious holidays include Shrove Tuesday (February), Easter (including Monday), Ascension, Whitmonday, Assumption (August 15), All Saints' Day (November 1), All Souls' Day (November 2) and Christmas (December 24-26).

# THE NETHERLANDS: HISTORICAL OVERVIEW

- In the Middle Ages, the area now known as the Netherlands (or, as some call it, Holland) was a group of autonomous counties and duchies (territories ruled by a duke instead of by a count). In the 1300s and 1400s, the French dukes of Burgundy united the Netherlands. In the 1500s, the Netherlands, Belgium and Luxembourg were known as the "Low Countries" and were ruled by a Spanish monarch.

- In 1568, Prince William of Orange, also known as William the Silent, rebelled against the Spanish crown and began an 80-year war for independence. In 1579, Protestant leaders in the north signed the Declaration of Utrecht, swearing to defend liberty and religious freedom. The Catholic Spanish king was unwilling to accept such freedom, so in 1581, the northern provinces declared their independence from Spain. William of Orange became the first head of the new republic and was soon assassinated by order of the Spanish King. However, the Republic was able to resist Spanish efforts to regain control and in 1648, the Netherlands became independent.

- Following independence control, the Netherlands built a vast overseas empire and became the world's leading maritime and commercial power for a short time. During this time it discovered new lands and amassed great wealth. In 1602, the Dutch East India company was formed to strengthen and protect trade and to prevent competition between Dutch companies. By 1650, the Dutch navy was twice the size of the English and French fleets combined. However, numerous wars against England and France drained the Netherland's resources. In 1795, French forces began to move into the Netherlands and in 1810, Napoleon completely annexed the territory. Napoleon's brother, Louis, was made king and he gave the country the name of Holland.

- The Congress of Vienna ended the French occupation and the United Kingdom of the Netherlands was created in 1815. At this time, the kingdom included the area now known as Belgium.

- During World War I, the Netherlands remained neutral; however, the country was invaded by Germany in World War II. The Netherlands had a long history of liberalism and religious tolerance. Many German Jews found refuge in the Netherlands during the 1930s until the Nazi invasion, and many Dutch risked their own lives to protect them.

- After the war, the Netherlands played an important role in European economic development. In 1958, the Netherlands was one of the six founders of the European Economic Community.

- In 1980, Queen Beatrix took power after her mother, Queen Juliana, abdicated the throne. She continues as the head of state today. If the heir to the throne, Beatrix' son Crown Prince Willem Alexander, ascends to the throne, he will be the first male monarch since 1890.

- During the 1980s, the Dutch rapidly used up much of their natural gas reserves and this means that economic problems are ahead, which in turn means that the Dutch will no longer enjoy the near automatic balance of payment surpluses and an easily financed social welfare system.

- The *Labor Party* won the 1994 parliamentary elections, thereby putting an end to the domination of the *Christian Democrats*.

# THE NETHERLANDS

## INTRODUCTIONS

When introduced in the Netherlands, it is customary to repeat your last name while shaking hands. If you are not introduced at a business or social gathering, it is acceptable to introduce yourself and shake hands with each person you meet.

The preferred greeting is "Pleased to meet you."

A handshake is the appropriate greeting for both men and women when meeting or departing. Adults also shake hands with young children.

Close friends often kiss three times (alternating cheeks) and embrace when they meet.

Generally, titles followed by last names are used when addressing people. First names can be used after your Dutch business colleagues feel comfortable enough to do so.

A common greeting is *"Hoe gaat het?"* ("How are you?")

## SOCIAL TIPS AND CONVENTIONS

The correct name of the country is the Kingdom of the Netherlands. The Netherlands received its nickname "Holland" from two of its provinces: North Holland and South Holland. People from other provinces may object to this name. Therefore, you should refer to people as "Netherlanders" or "Dutch."

The Caribbean islands of Aruba and the Netherlands Antilles, which have unique cultural aspects, are part of the Kingdom of the Netherlands.

The official language is Dutch. However, French, English and German are commonly understood, spoken and are taught in secondary schools.

It is acceptable to discuss Dutch or European politics in the Netherlands. Other good topics of conversation include social trends, sports and travel and vacations.

Avoid discussing money or prices. Also, do not probe excessively into someone's profession or family – the Dutch value their privacy.

As a small dependent nation, the Dutch are very internationally-minded. However, note that the Dutch also take great pride in land reclamation, their art and history and the nation's strong history of liberalism.

Jokes about the Dutch Queen or Royal family are considered to be in poor taste and are not acceptable.

When answering the telephone, it is customary for both the caller and the receiver to state their names rather than "Hello."

# THE NETHERLANDS (Cont'd)

## CUSTOMARY BUSINESS PRACTICES

English is widely spoken in the Netherlands and the Dutch readily accommodate their English-speaking guests by switching to English for meetings and for formal presentations.

Correct titles should be used when conducting business, especially when writing business correspondence.

The Dutch are extremely experienced in business as their small nation is very reliant on foreign trade. As a result, they are efficient, open to new ideas and welcome foreigners and efficient.

Negotiations proceed quickly, because the Dutch do not like haggling. A good proposal will make a better impression than concessions will.

In the Netherlands, being organized and attentive will create a sense of trust. It is important to plan business appointments well in advance, including business entertaining. Also, punctuality is very important.

Exaggeration and fluff are not appreciated in business proposals. Presentations should be factual and full of figures.

The summer months and the Christmas and New Year's holiday times are for family get-togethers and travel, so it is best to avoid scheduling business during those times (unless you are encouraged to do so by your Dutch colleague).

Business hours are from 8:30 or 9:00 a.m. to 5:00 or 5:30 p.m., Monday through Friday.

## BUSINESS ENTERTAINING

Dutch businesspeople enjoy entertaining and being entertained. An offer to pay for a meal will usually encounter little resistance.

Usually the tip is included in the bill. If not, it is appropriate to leave a 15% gratuity on the table.

It is not uncommon to include spouses in business entertaining. If you are being entertained, you should ask your host whether spouses are included in the invitation.

Punctuality is considered to be extremely important. Normally you should stay about an hour-and-a-half after the meal is finished. However, meals can last quite a long time.

In the Netherlands, the toast is given just before as well as just after the first sip.

It is considered a real sign of friendship to be invited to someone's home. Sending a thank-you note several days after visiting a home is appreciated.

# THE NETHERLANDS (Cont'd)

## BUSINESS ENTERTAINING (Cont'd)

When invited to someone's home for dinner, flowers or chocolates are an appropriate gift. Gifts should be wrapped. However, flowers should be unwrapped before presenting them to your host.

If you are invited to a businessperson's home, your host will appreciate compliments on his/ her home, furniture, artwork, carpeting, etc.

## DINING OUT

The Dutch use the continental style of eating, with the knife held in the right hand and the fork in the left. The dessert spoon may be placed above the dinner plate.

It is proper to eat many types of food, including sandwiches and fruit, with a knife and fork. Dessert is eaten with a spoon.

When dining out, both hands should be kept above the table at all times. However, you should not rest your elbows on the table.

Make it a point to utilize restrooms either before or after the meal as leaving the table for personal purposes is considered rude.

It is impolite to begin eating before others at the table. Expect your host to indicate when to begin eating. It is even common for your host to serve you. It is also impolite to drink before the toast.

Guests generally do not leave directly after the meal when visiting someone at home. A dinner party may last until well after midnight.

Take small portions of food and try to taste every dish offered. It is considered impolite not to eat everything on your plate.

*Genevre*, the local, unique Dutch white alcoholic beverage, is similar in taste to gin or vodka, but it has a distinct (and acquired) taste.

## PUBLIC CUSTOMS

The Dutch are not physically demonstrative and generally refrain from touching. Instead, they rely on eye contact and facial expressions.

There is a noticeable difference between the general attitude of people in the southern and in the northern provinces. By reputation, the people in the south are more gregarious than those in the north.

It is best to suppress signs of boredom or irritation.

When entering a shop or train compartment, greet each person present.

# THE NETHERLANDS (Cont'd)

## PUBLIC CUSTOMS (Cont'd)

It is proper etiquette for the man to walk on the side of the pavement nearest the street when accompanying a woman. Men should stand when a woman enters the room.

People may wave in greeting from a distance, as it is considered impolite to shout.

Shaking the finger while speaking emphasizes a point.

In the Netherlands, a circular motion of the finger around the ear means that someone has a phone call. (In many other cultures, this might be interpreted as "crazy.")

In the Netherlands, tapping the elbow in reference to an individual signifies that person is unreliable.

If a Dutch person taps the thumbnails together (as if applauding), it is a signal that the person does not appreciate what has just transpired (e.g., a joke or comment).

It is considered impolite to chew gum or stand with your hands in your pockets in public.

# NORWAY: HISTORICAL OVERVIEW

- The Age of the Vikings lasted from 800 to 1050. During this time the Vikings conquered many areas in Scandinavia, Europe and even North America. Simultaneously, in the ninth century, many smaller Norwegian communities were organized into large regions. Viking leader Harald the Fairhead united the region of Norway and became the first supreme ruler of the unified kingdom of Norway around 872.

- The Norwegian Vikings were great sailors and explorers and settled in France, England, Ireland and Iceland during the Middle Ages. However, the Vikings declined as the Christian Church grew in power, foreign trade expanded and political confusion and struggles for power ensued. By 1030, Christianity had spread through the region. The country came under Danish control from about 1380 until 1814.

- In 1814, Norway was given to Sweden as a peace treaty provision to punish Denmark's alliance with Napoleon during the Napoleonic Wars. In reaction to being given to Sweden, Norway declared its independence and drafted a constitution. Nevertheless, the Swedish king was accepted as the country's leader and the two countries remained unified.

- In 1905, the union with Sweden was dissolved peacefully by referendum and the Danish Prince Carl was chosen to be the constitutional monarch of the independent Kingdom of Norway. When he became king, he took the name Haakon VII.

- Norway remained neutral in World War I. However, in 1940 during World War II, Germany attacked and held the country until it was liberated in May 1945. During this period of occupation, the monarchy was out of the country supporting the allied effort against the Germans.

- After the war, Norway became a member of the North Atlantic Treaty Organization (NATO) and later became a member of the European Free Trade Area. The postwar period has been marked by political stability, economic development and positive foreign relations.

- The son of Haakon VII, Olav V, was king of Norway from 1957 to 1991. When he died, his son, Harald V, ascended the throne.

- Norway recently applied for membership in the European Union (EU) and is working to be part of the European Economic Area (EEA). The issue of joining the EU has been very sensitive in Norway. In 1990, this issue led to the resignation of Prime Minister Jan Syse, who was replaced by the opposition leader, Gro Harlem Brundtland. In the 1993 elections she was reelected Prime Minister for another four-year term.

- In a 1994 referendum, Norwegian voters chose by a slim margin to remain outside the EU, and thereby protect the sovereignty and independence of this young country.

- The main problem ahead for the people of Norway is how to find a balance between the North Sea economy and that of the mainland. They would like to protect the traditional industries and the environment, while, at the same time, provide a stable base for the elevation of the standard of living as well as maintenance of the social security net.

# NORWAY

## INTRODUCTIONS

Always remember to shake hands when introduced, when greeting someone and when you are leaving.

In Norway it is very common for men to be addressed by their last name only (i.e., "Good morning, Jones"). This is perfectly acceptable and is not considered rude.

When you are first introduced to someone, use the person's first and last name when addressing him/her.

The Norwegians are quite restrictive about using first names only.

Use a person's occupational title before the last name when you are addressing a professor, doctor or engineer. However, you should not use a title when addressing a lawyer and a clergyman.

At a small party, wait for your host to introduce you. At a larger party, it is best to introduce yourself. If you are seated, always stand when you are introduced.

## SOCIAL TIPS AND CONVENTIONS

Norwegians admire self-reliance and the ability to put aside personal interests for the common good. They take great pride in individual and national independence. Tolerance, human kindness and personal independence are also admired. Do not offer any criticism of the people or their customs.

Good topics of conversation include interests or hobbies, politics or sports (especially soccer, skiing, hiking or sailing). Also, Norwegians are very proud of their history, culture and Viking heritage.

Norwegians are usually reserved about themselves. It takes time to get to know people personally. Avoid talking about aspects of personal life. For example, avoid questions such as, "What do you do?" or "Are you married?," etc. You should also avoid talking about employment, salary or social status.

Answer the telephone by giving your last name or phone number.

## CUSTOMARY BUSINESS PRACTICES

Most Norwegian businesspeople are fluent in English and are very familiar with U.S. business and trade practices.

It is recommended that appointments be set at least a week in advance and scheduled between 10:00 a.m. and noon or between 2:00 and 4:00 p.m.

Avoid scheduling business trips during July and August, since Norwegians often take holidays during these months.

Punctuality is considered to be very important. If you are going to be late, it is best to telephone to explain your tardiness. Also telephone to cancel or postpone the appointment.

# NORWAY (Cont'd)

## CUSTOMARY BUSINESS PRACTICES (Cont'd)

At business meetings, avoid becoming too familiar. It is not common to have casual conversations or make jokes at meetings. Presentations should be very clear; they should emphasize hard facts, since Norwegians value precision.

In Norway, business dress is fairly casual. Men can wear sports jackets, but should always wear ties. Women can wear suits, dresses or dress pants.

## BUSINESS ENTERTAINING

If you invite your host to a meal, expect different kinds of food to be served in different eating places. In addition to restaurants, which serve full meals, there are a number of options for light snacks, coffee or drinks such as *bistros* (offers sandwiches, beer, wine and soft drinks), *kafes* (offers sandwiches, coffee, tea and sometimes beer and wine), *kaffestovas* (self-serving cafeterias where you can get simple hot foods) and *Kondittori* (offers open-faced sandwiches, pastries and coffee).

In Norway, businesspeople usually eat lunch at their desks. Lunch is normally the lightest meal of the day. However, if you invite someone to lunch, expect the offer to be accepted.

It is very common for a Norwegian businessman to invite colleagues home for a meal.

If invited to dinner in a home, men should wear suits and women should wear dresses, skirts or dress pants and blouses. If invited to a restaurant, a man should wear a jacket and tie. (However, a jacket and tie is not necessary in smaller or neighborhood restaurants.)

Be punctual if invited for a meal. Even in a home, it is common for people to go immediately to the table. If there is time for cocktails, it is usually very brief.

If you are invited for a cup of coffee, it is appropriate to bring pastries or chocolates. When invited for a meal, bring wine, chocolates, pastries or flowers.

Liquor is always a welcome gift since it is very expensive in Norway. If you bring flowers, avoid bringing wreaths, carnations or any kind of white flowers, since these are reserved for funerals.

Spouses are usually not included in business meals at restaurants.

Avoid ordering wine or beer before 11:00 a.m. In Norway, hard liquor is usually not ordered between 3:00 and 11:45 p.m. Also, be aware that there is often an extra charge for soda water when you order a mixed drink.

Toasting is very common, using the expression *"Skoal."*

In order to get the attention of a waiter/waitress, raise your hand and extend the index finger. It is considered rude to snap your fingers to get someone's attention.

In restaurants, the tip is included in the bill. However, it is common to leave an extra three to five *kroner* (Norwegian currency) if the service was very good.

# NORWAY (Cont'd)

## DINING OUT

According to Norwegian eating style, the fork should be kept in the left hand and the knife in the right. The knife is used to push food onto the back of the fork.

Open-faced sandwiches, which are commonly served for lunch in Norway, should be eaten with a knife and fork and never be picked up with your hands.

At a dinner party, usually the host and hostess will sit at opposite ends of the table. The male guest of honor will be seated to the left of the hostess and the female guest of honor to the left of the host. Food is usually passed around the table on platters.

At first, take small portions of food since it is considered rude not to finish everything on your plate. It is also considered rude not to accept any food or drink that is offered to you. However, your host will not be offended if you do not want to eat something after tasting it.

You can indicate that you are finished eating by crossing your utensils in the middle of your plate.

If invited to dinner, you should plan to stay until about 10:00 or 11:00 p.m. It is common for the meal itself to last several hours. Dinner is commonly the largest meal of the day. In addition, when Norwegians entertain, there are usually numerous courses and dinner conversation is lively.

It is considered polite to thank the hostess at the end of the meal. However, this does not signal the end of the evening. In fact, it is impolite to leave immediately after the meal.

It is not unusual to have dancing after a dinner party, even in a home. Also, during the summer when it is light until about 11:00 p.m., it is not unusual for your host to suggest taking a walk after dinner. After the walk, it is common to return to the house for a liqueur.

In Norway, fresh fish is very common at meals. In addition, several common delicacies are *Fenalar* (cured and baked leg of mutton), *flatbrod* (crisp thin rye bread), *himmelsk lapskaus* (fruit salad with nuts, served with rum and egg sauce) and *rabarbragrot* (rhubarb compote). You may also want to be aware of several exotic foods that are served in Norway. These include *hval biff* (whale meat), *gjetost* (a cheese that tastes more like sweet fudge) and *sylte* (a fatty, gelatinous salami made of innards).

## PUBLIC CUSTOMS

Speaking in a loud voice and using demonstrative gestures (eg., slapping someone's back or putting your arm around someone's shoulder) should be avoided.

Courtesy and good behavior are important at all times. It is common for men to offer their seats to women or to the elderly.

# POLAND: HISTORICAL OVERVIEW

- The Poles are descendants of the Slavic people that settled in the region now known as Poland before the turn of the millennium. In 966 A.D., King Miesko I adopted the Roman Catholic faith for his family and the monarchy.

- In the late 14th century, during the reign of King Kasimir the Great, Polish life and culture flourished. In the late Middle Ages, Poland united with Lithuania, creating an empire that was a major power in Europe. Due to political fighting among the ruling nobles and other factors, the Polish monarchy declined until, in 1795, it was invaded and partitioned by Prussia, Austria and Russia. However, Polish identity and culture were preserved by the Polish Roman Catholic church.

- At the end of World War I, Poland became an independent nation again, but political life was neither stable nor strong. In 1939, in the midst of instability, the German army invaded. A Soviet invasion followed immediately from the East. Due to these invasions, Poland was again partitioned. When Germany was defeated at the end of the war, the Soviets were given administrative control of Poland. Although elections were held in Poland after the war, by 1948, a Communist government supported by the Soviets was in control, and the country's political system was generally patterned after that of the Soviet Union.

- In 1981, following the formation of the Solidarity Labor Union and a series of strikes, Polish leader General Wojciech Jaruzelski declared martial law. He outlawed the Solidarity group and jailed its members. Martial law was lifted in 1983 and Lech Walesa, the leader of the still-outlawed Solidarity union, received the Nobel Peace Prize in recognition for his efforts to win freedom for the Polish people. As a result of this recognition, Solidarity gained international support.

- In 1989, the Polish government legalized Solidarity and implemented changes in the government, including the creation of the office of president. Jaruzelski was elected President and stepped down from his leadership of the Communist party. Due to pressure for reform, the Polish parliament elected a top Solidarity official, Tadeusz Mazowiecki, as Prime Minister opening the way for Solidarity-led reforms.

- Due to the difficulties of economic transition, reform packages were rejected by Parliament in both 1992 and 1993. In the 1993 elections, the Democratic Left Alliance and the Polish Peasant Party won and they formed a coalition government. Since 1993, the government has slowed the pace of reform.

- The major news in Poland in 1995 was the presidential election. Incumbent Walesa, who had been President for the past six years, ran against Aleksander Kwasniewski. The latter stressed during the campaign that while he supported privatization and Polish membership in NATO, he thought that the reforms instituted after communism had been too hard on the poor and the elderly.

- Kwasniewski was victorious. The biggest problem that he faced was the problem of social costs, which accounted for 25% of the GDP. The Polish economy, however, was growing consistently from 1992 to 1996, foreign investment was up and inflation was down, thanks in large part to the 1995 move to make the *zloty* a hard currency.

# POLAND

## INTRODUCTIONS

People generally shake hands when meeting and when departing.

Use the term *"Pan"* before a man's last name when being introduced; use the term *"Pani"* for a woman. A professional person's title is used before his/her last name, but in formal conversation or business, use only the title.

First names are used by mutual consent between adult friends.

Men will often kiss the extended hand of a woman in greeting. Women greet close female friends with a kiss on both cheeks.

## SOCIAL TIPS AND CONVENTIONS

It is inappropriate for either friends or relatives to visit each other without first planning ahead. Poles do not appreciate people "dropping by" unannounced.

Poles are generally outgoing and outspoken. They are proud of their cultural heritage and enjoy conversing about their country and customs.

Except among very close friends, Poles do not generally touch each other in public. People generally stand about an arm's length from each other when conversing.

Loud behavior in public is considered rude.

Polish men have traditional views of women. For example, if a woman talks to a strange man, it is considered flirting.

## CUSTOMARY BUSINESS PRACTICES

A guest will usually be offered tea or coffee as a refreshment during business. Acceptance or rejection of this offer is immaterial and you may refuse if you wish.

Business dress is conservative. Men wear suits and ties while women wear suits or skirts and blouses.

European fashions are common in the major cities.

The majority of women work outside the home. They make up nearly half of the labor force.

Make appointments ahead of time and be punctual.

Good conversation topics include Polish national history and culture as well as one's family and its activities. Avoid any reference to World War II.

# POLAND (Cont'd)

## CUSTOMARY BUSINESS PRACTICES (Cont'd)

Poles have a strong work ethic.

It is to your advantage to have materials translated into Polish.

Poles generally are objective when making decisions. However, the legality of a certain action is often of secondary importance to how the action will affect relationships.

You should consider having local representatives assist you with handling business arrangements.

Direct communication is preferred.

## BUSINESS ENTERTAINING

Flowers are an appropriate gift, even if your visit will be brief. Always bring an odd number of flowers and avoid red roses, which give a romantic connotation. They should be given to the hostess unwrapped.

Consumption of hard liquor is widespread in Poland. Cognac and vodka are especially favored.

Toasting is often part of both formal and informal dinners. Let your host initiate a toast and then reciprocate later.

The main meal of the day is eaten after 3:00 p.m. A light supper is eaten at home after 6:00 p.m.

Dining in restaurants is expensive; therefore, entertaining at home is much more common.

Be aware that the guest of honor will often be seated at the head of the table.

When dining, keep your hands but not your elbows above the table.

Do not start eating until everyone has been served.

Because Poles start their day early, evening visits usually end by 11:00 p.m.

## DINING OUT

You may be entertained at a *kawiarna* (cafe) which serves fancy pastries. These visits may last a number of hours.

Poles follow the continental style of eating, with the fork in the left hand and the knife remaining in the right hand.

In restaurants, the bill must be requested from the waiter and is paid at the table. Tips are generally expected.

## POLAND (Cont'd)

### DINING OUT (Cont'd)

Some traditional foods include *pierogi* (dumplings filled with cheese and potatoes), *uszka* (a kind of ravioli), *bigos* (sausage, mushrooms and cabbage), poppy seed desserts and cheese-cake. Pork is more popular than beef.

Table manners and etiquette are similar to those used in the West. It is good manners when starting a meal to say *"Smacznego"* ("Bon Appetit"). When toasting, one says *"Na Zdrowie"* ("Cheers").

### PUBLIC CUSTOMS

When Poles sign their names, they sign their family name first and then their given name.

It is considered rude to chew gum when speaking to someone.

Soccer is very popular in Poland.

National holidays include Constitution Day (May 3), New Year's Day, Easter Monday, Christmas and December 26, All Soul's Day (November 1), Assumption Day (August 15) and Labor Day (May 1).

# PORTUGAL: HISTORICAL OVERVIEW

- Ancient Phoenicians, Carthagians and Greeks all built colonies on Portugal's coast. In 27 B.C., the Romans took control of the region, making it a province. Following the Romans, the Visigoths and then the Moors ruled the area. The Moors eventually governed Portugal from the 8th to the 12th century.

- Spanish Christians reconquered the peninsula by the early 12th century. Ruled by King Alfonso Henriques, Portugal became an independent nation in 1143. Portuguese influence grew in the 14th and 15th centuries as Portuguese explorers expanded its overseas holdings.

- In the 16th century, Phillip II of Spain ruled Portugal briefly as Phillip I, since Portugal's previous king had left no heirs. Eventually, Spanish control of the Portuguese monarchy was lost to the native nobility while Spain was involved in the Napoleonic Wars. However, after the 15th and 16th century period of grandeur, Portugal began to decline, in part due to the effects of the Spanish Inquisition and invasions by Spain, England and France.

- In 1910, Portugal's monarchy was overthrown, and a republic was established. However, political instability dominated the country, and a military coup overthrew the democracy in 1926. From 1928 to 1968, António de Oliviera Salazar led an authoritarian dictatorship which committed human rights violations.

- Portugal maintained its neutrality in World War II.

- In 1974, a socialist military coup, led by General Antonio de Spinola, took control of the government and vowed to restore democracy. In 1975, the *junta* held elections that led to the Third Republic. Under the new left-wing government, the economy was nationalized. The political situation remained somewhat unstable until 1985.

- In the 1985 elections, voting patterns were more concrete than in the past, and Mário Soares (a center-right candidate) won the election. Under his leadership and that of Prime Minister Aníbal Cavaco Silva, the government implemented privatization efforts and started other reforms. Portugal joined the European Union (EU) in 1986, and since the mid-1980s, the country has been a thriving democracy.

- Due to the popularity of his reforms, Cavaco, who was the first President to complete a full term since 1974, was reelected in 1991.

- An economic recession, excessive patronage and a 1994 scandal involving wiretapping of the attorney general's office put Cavaco Silva in trouble. The *Socialist Party* subsequently won the 1995 parliamentary election and the 1996 presidential election.

- The challenge for the current government is the reduction of the budget deficit from the current 5% to the 3% necessary for the European currency union.

- Despite these issues, since joining the EU in 1986, Portugal has experienced a huge economic boom, its democratic constitution has been reformed and strengthened, and the Portuguese have a renewed sense of national pride.

# PORTUGAL

## INTRODUCTIONS

A warm, firm handshake is the appropriate greeting for both men and women of all ages. Avoid very firm handshakes, since some Portuguese people may not grip very strongly. Gauge your handshake accordingly.

Relatives or close female friends will greet each other by appearing to kiss each other on both cheeks (actually "kissing the air"), starting with the right cheek. Close male friends will greet each other with a hug and a slap on the back rather than by shaking hands.

Men should stand when they are being introduced, but it is not necessary for women to do so. When you are introduced, shake hands with each person, even if you are meeting a large group of people.

First names are only used among friends, with children and with youth. Normally, a title such as "Mr.," "Mrs." or "Miss" should be used followed by a surname when addressing an adult. A person's professional title followed by a last name should be used when addressing a doctor, lawyer, professor or engineer. Sometimes the title is combined with a first name, depending on personal preference and the relationship between the people.

Common terms used for greeting are *"Bom dia"* ("Good day") and *"Boa noite"* ("Good evening").

## SOCIAL TIPS AND CONVENTIONS

Portuguese is the official language, but English, French and German are quite widely understood and are taught in school.

The Portuguese are very warm, friendly and hospitable to people of other nations. They value and cultivate strong and lasting friendships.

Be aware that, while Portugal is an open, liberal society, there is a greater emphasis on moral and religious values (especially Roman Catholic) than in other European countries. Therefore, avoid making remarks that might touch on moral or religious sensitivities.

Showing that you have some knowledge about the area in which you are staying or about the Portuguese culture is appreciated. The Portuguese are proud of their cultural heritage, sense of nationhood and economic progress. Even urban people have strong links to their home-towns or regions. In addition, political issues (not parties) are avidly discussed.

It is polite to converse about yourself and your host's family, positive aspects of Portugal, vacations, wines and personal interests and hobbies. However, inquisitive personal questions (especially about money issues, such as salaries and the cost of living) should be avoided. Popular participatory and spectator sports, including soccer, hockey, rollerskating, sailing and Portuguese bullfighting, are also good topics of conversation.

Both in public and in private, you should defer to older people. Always wait until an older person is finished speaking before saying anything. Make a point to walk to the left of an older person, especially when you are going down the street.

# PORTUGAL (Cont'd)

## CUSTOMARY BUSINESS PRACTICES

Avoid planning business trips during August when many Portuguese executives take vacations.

All correspondence, especially about making business arrangements, should be translated into Portuguese.

When doing business with a small Portuguese company, you may want to consider hiring an interpreter to ensure proper communication with your business counterparts.

The Portuguese consider people and relationships to be more important than time and formalities. As a result, punctuality is usually not stressed, but it is advisable that you be prompt since it will impress your colleagues. Expect other businesspeople, however, to arrive at a meeting 15 to 30 minutes late. Also, people living in the city tend to value punctuality more than rural dwellers.

When transacting business in Portugal, be aware that the Portuguese are quite conservative and traditional. Innovation or change is accepted, but only after careful consideration.

Since the Portuguese are quite reserved, avoid using a lot of demonstrative gestures when making presentations.

If you are offered refreshments by your colleagues at a business meeting, it is impolite to refuse.

Business cards are not as commonly used in Portugal as in other countries. Ask for someone's business card only if he/she is a senior member of a company.

Businessmen usually wear suits and ties, even when it is hot. Sports jackets and slacks are also popular. If your Portuguese colleagues remove their jackets, you may do the same. Businesswomen generally wear conservative skirt suits or dresses with high heels.

Business hours vary from place to place, but traditional business hours are from 9:00 a.m. to 1:00 p.m. and then from 3:00 to 7:00 p.m., Monday through Saturday.

## BUSINESS ENTERTAINING

Most socializing is done in the home, but it is also common for business associates to go to a restaurant or a cafe for conversation, sweets and tea or coffee.

When visiting a home, guests wait outside the door until asked inside. Similarly, guests allow the host to open the door when they are leaving.

Homes in Portugal are kept very clean and guests are expected to wipe their feet before entering. Dirty shoes should be removed entirely while still outside.

Punctuality by foreigners is appreciated, especially in urban areas.

Since the Portuguese people take great pride in their homes, they sincerely appreciate any compliments offered.

# PORTUGAL (Cont'd)

## BUSINESS ENTERTAINING (Cont'd)

When invited to a home, guests often bring a small gift to their host or they send a thank-you note after a dinner engagement. Nevertheless, don't feel obligated to bring a gift; you may simply reciprocate by inviting your host to a restaurant. Expensive chocolates are the most appropriate gift. Flowers are also acceptable, but never bring chrysanthemums (as they are associated with funerals) or inexpensive flowers. Also, wine does not make a good gift since it is inexpensive in Portugal and most people have good wine cellars.

If you have established contact with businesspeople in Portugal before traveling there, it is polite to ask them what gift they would like you to bring for them from your home country. People often like to receive technical books or computer programs, which are difficult to obtain in Portugal.

Refreshments are usually served when you visit someone's home and it is impolite to refuse.

If you are invited to a dinner, suits and ties are appropriate for men and dresses are appropriate for women. Even when attending the cinema, men wear jackets and ties and women wear skirts and blouses or dresses.

In restaurants, the waiter can be summoned with a raised hand. The service charge is usually not included in the bill and the customary tip is 15%. If a service charge is included in the bill, it is recommended that you leave an extra 50 *escudos* (Portuguese currency) on the table.

## DINING OUT

A small breakfast, which includes bread, butter and jam and coffee mixed with hot milk is eaten around 8:00 a.m. A large lunch is eaten between noon and 2:00 p.m. Dinner is usually served between 8:00 and 9:00 p.m. The main meal of the day usually consists of two main dishes (meat and fish), soup, vegetables and more than one dessert.

The staples in Portugal include fish, vegetables and fruits. One of the national dishes is *bacalhau* (dried cod), which is usually served with potatoes and green vegetables. It is served often and can be prepared in a variety of ways, such as *pasteis* (deep-fried with potatoes). Chicken is eaten throughout the country and is prepared in a variety of ways, such as *frango na pucara* (chicken in a pot) or *cabidela* (chicken with rice). Pork, partridge, quail and rabbit are also served frequently in Portugal. All parts of the pig are eaten when a meal highlighting pork is served. A popular dish is *cozido à Portuguesa*, which contains potatoes, many vegetables, rice and various meats.

Bread is almost always served with meals; corn bread is usually served in the north and wheat bread is generally served in the south. Olive oil is commonly used and garlic is the most popular seasoning. The traditional Portuguese salad includes dark green lettuce, tomatoes, onions, vinegar, olive oil and salt. Portugal has many pastry shops as sweets are very popular. The meal normally ends with fruit, dessert (a sweet or cheese and crackers) and coffee. Wine is inexpensive and it is consumed by people of all ages with their meals.

Dessert specialties include *flan* (caramel custard) and *figos recheados* (dried figs stuffed with chocolate and almonds and served with port wine). *Bica* (a strong espresso-type coffee) is often served after the meal. In some areas of the north, *bica* is called *cimbalino*.

# PORTUGAL (Cont'd)

## DINING OUT (Cont'd)

The Portuguese enjoy lengthy conversation during meals, especially dinner. In fact, to avoid seeming like they are in a hurry, diners all try to finish their meals at the same time. At dinner parties, guests usually stay after the meal until about 11:00 p.m. or midnight.

At a dinner party, before-dinner drinks are usually served. These include dry, white port or Scotch for men and Cinzano for women. Wine or beer are served with the meal. A fish course may be offered before the main or meat course. After the meal, *aguardente* (a very strong local brandy) may be served with the coffee.

The continental style of eating is used, with the fork held in the left hand and the knife in the right. A special knife and fork are used when eating fish. Never eat with your hands; even fruit should be eaten with a knife and fork.

When serving dishes are passed around the table, it is expected that you will help yourself first because you are the guest; then pass the serving platter to the other diners. At each course, do not begin eating until everyone has been served.

At a dinner party, the host may say a few words to the guests before the meal.

It is important to keep your hands above the table at all times. However, only your wrists should be on the table (never your elbows). The napkin should be on your lap and should never be tied around the neck. Also, it is considered impolite to stretch at the table. Stretching is taken to imply that you are tired or bored with the company.

You must cover your mouth when using a toothpick.

To indicate that you have finished eating, place your knife and fork with the tines up vertically on the plate. You should fold your napkin before leaving the table.

If you smoke, it is customary to do so after the meal, but not between courses. You should be sure to ask your host permission to smoke beforehand.

## PUBLIC CUSTOMS

The Portuguese generally dress conservatively. People are very careful to be dressed neatly and cleanly in public. Dirty or tattered clothing is considered improper. Leather dress shoes should be worn for most occasions; tennis shoes are only worn for sports activities. Even for casual occasions, the Portuguese tend to dress quite elegantly.

It is considered impolite for adults to eat while walking in public. Eating an ice cream cone is the only exception to this rule.

Pointing at someone with the index finger is considered rude. To beckon someone, all fingers are waved with the palm facing up.

# PORTUGAL (Cont'd)

## PUBLIC CUSTOMS (Cont'd)

There are a number of gestures that are commonly used in Portugal. Pinching the earlobe and shaking it gently while raising the eyebrows means something (e.g., a meal) is very good. Pulling down the skin just below the eye with the index finger can mean "You are perceptive" or "You are kidding me." Spreading the fingers with the palm down and rocking the hand means "more or less." Rubbing the thumb against the first two fingers with the palm facing up is a sign for money. Touching the tips of all fingers to the tip of the thumb with the palm facing up signifies fear or cowardice.

Keep in mind that it is a serious insult to make a "V" sign or to make "rabbit ears" behind someone's head because it connotes a lack of morals.

Bargaining is acceptable at markets; however, you should not bargain in shops or food markets.

Women may go into a cafe alone. However, going into a bar alone may bring unwelcome attention since it is not a common practice by local women. Also, women should avoid walking alone after 8:00 or 9:00 p.m. when there are not many people on the street.

# ROMANIA: HISTORICAL OVERVIEW

- Today's Romanians are descendants of the Geto-Dacians, an Indo-European people, who came to the area between the fourth and sixth centuries B.C. Around 100 A.D., the Romans conquered most of Dacia and made the area a province to supply grain, gold and cattle to the empire. The natives soon adopted the Roman language and culture. In fact, the name "Romania" means "Land of the Romans."

- Between 200 and 1100, various tribes invaded the region. In 1500 Moldavia (to the east) and Wallachia (in the south) fell under Turkish control. Several wars between European countries, in the 17th and 18th centuries, led to divisions of the country and exchanges of the territories among European powers. Although Romania was never a central part of the Ottoman Empire, complete freedom from Turkish rule did not take place until 1877, after Romania joined again with Moldavia and Wallachia.

- In World War I, Romania was part of the Allied alliance with France and England. As a result, when the war was over, Romania acquired Bessarabia from Russia and three provinces from the defeated Austro-Hungarian Empire. These acquisitions doubled the country's size.

- In 1940, during World War II, Romania was occupied by Nazi Germany. They joined the German army in attacking Russia in 1941. However, in 1944, Romania joined the Allies, and Russian troops occupied the country. Under Russian occupation, the Romanian monarchy was overthrown and a Communist regime was established.

- In 1965, under the leadership of Nicolae Ceausescu, the country broke away from the Soviet Union. The 1965 constitution recognized the primacy of the Communist Party in the country. Nevertheless, relations with the U.S.S.R. became strained.

- When democratic movements developed throughout Europe in 1989, large groups of demonstrators protested Ceausescu's regime and rioting broke out when security forces turned on the crowds. The army supported the people, and the government was toppled after only a few days of fighting. Ceausescu and his wife were executed and the National Salvation Front took control.

- The National Salvation Front organized elections and National Salvation Front leader, Ion Iliescu, won the 1990 election. While Iliescu's government restricted certain rights, some democratic reforms were implemented. A bicameral parliament was elected, which produced a new constitution in 1991. It also implemented economic reforms and scheduled national elections. Civil unrest led President Iliescu to form an interim government in 1991 that governed until the 1992 elections. In 1992, Iliescu was reelected President. Since then, the Romanian government has been working to improve the country's international image. The government has permitted considerable privatization in retail trade, though change has been slow in other areas. Transforming the inefficient industrial base will require tremendous capital, which Romania does not have. Another problem is that much of the country has been ecologically devastated.

- President Iliescu made an official visit to the U.S. in September 1995, arguing for membership in NATO and permanent access to the U.S. market. Romania gained "most favored nation" trading status, which should eventually lead to more foreign investment.

# ROMANIA

## INTRODUCTIONS

Adults commonly greet each other with a handshake, but a man usually waits for a woman to extend her hand first. In cities, some men might greet a woman by kissing her hand.

Greetings on a first-name basis are usually made only between close friends and relatives.

Use last names and titles when meeting people. Shake hands each time you see someone, and use a firm grip.

When applicable, it is most polite to use a person's title ("Doctor," "Professor") before the surname.

## SOCIAL TIPS AND CONVENTIONS

Romanians attach importance to their appearance and people generally dress conservatively in public.

When someone sneezes, one is wished *"Noroc"* ("Bless you") or *"Sanatate"* ("Good health"). *"Noroc"* is also used when toasting at parties to mean "Cheers."

On public transportation, men generally offer their seats to women.

Opinions are openly and freely expressed.

## CUSTOMARY BUSINESS PRACTICES

Conservative business suits are appropriate for men. Female office workers usually wear a skirt and a blouse with a scarf.

The usual workday begins at 7:00 a.m. for factory workers, but at 8:00 or 9:00 a.m. for office workers. The day ends between 3:00 and 5:00 p.m. depending on the institution.

Most factories are closed on Saturdays and Sundays; Friday is usually a shortened workday. With the exception of restaurants, coffee shops and some private shops, everything is closed on Sunday. Stores may be closed a few hours around lunchtime, but then remain open later in the evening. General department stores remain open all day.

Romanian businesspeople enjoy vacations of two to four weeks, depending on one's seniority.

The official language is Romanian which is a Latin-based language in the same family as Spanish, French, Italian and Portuguese.

The Romanian people have weak business management skills. Compounding the problem is the fact that there is widespread distrust of authority.

# ROMANIA (Cont'd)

## CUSTOMARY BUSINESS PRACTICES (Cont'd)

Letters should be sent in English, for these will be respected more than documents written in Romanian.

More educated Romanians are fairly objective when making decisions; however, emotions still play an important part in the process.

## BUSINESS ENTERTAINING

When invited to dinner, it is considered polite for the guest to bring an odd number of flowers (three or more) or a small gift for the host. Red roses are avoided for such an occasion, however, because they are a sign of romantic affection.

Romanians like to receive and pay visits. In the home, guests are usually offered refreshments – coffee, tea, brandy or wine.

The continental style of eating is used, with the fork in the left hand and the knife in the right.

Toasting is usually part of both formal and informal lunches and dinners.

Evening visits usually end before 11:00 p.m. because work begins early in the morning.

## DINING OUT

The host indicates when the meal will begin and when it will end.

Romanians generally consider it a great honor to entertain guests and visitors will usually be invited out as much as possible.

Popular Romanian food includes distinctive ethnic specialties such as *mititei* (grilled meatballs), *patricieni* (grilled sausage) and *mamaliga* (cornmeal mush).

Breakfast usually consists of eggs, cheese, rolls, breads and coffee.

Lunch is the main meal of the day and usually consists of soup, meat, potatoes, bread and vegetables.

Pastries are popular for dessert.

In the past, food shortages were common. Although food is generally now available, remember that people cannot easily afford much higher prices.

A small tip for good service is considered customary.

# ROMANIA (Cont'd)

## PUBLIC CUSTOMS

Both hands (not elbows) are kept above the table during a meal.

It is impolite to yawn or cough without covering the mouth.

Hats are removed by gentlemen before they enter buildings, except stores.

Romanians use many gestures when they speak, but visitors should not because gestures differ and they may be misinterpreted.

National holidays include New Year's Day (January 1-2), Easter Monday, Labor Day (May 1), National Day (December 1) and Christmas (December 25-26).

# SPAIN: HISTORICAL OVERVIEW

- The region now known as Spain, was populated by Iberians who migrated to the peninsula from North Africa, around 3000 B.C. Cádiz, which is believed to be the oldest city in Europe, was founded in 1130 B.C. Celtic invaders and Phoenician and Greek colonies came to the area around 1000 B.C. Around 218 B.C., Rome began to have influence in the area and it gained control of the entire area by the first century A.D. After the Roman Empire declined, the area was ruled by the Visigoths (Germanic tribes), followed by the Muslim Moors who invaded in 711.

- The people of the region, who were predominantly Christian, fought the Moors. When they finally defeated them in 1479, two dominant kingdoms emerged, and they united by 1492. During the 16th century, Spain flourished, becoming one of the most powerful empires in the world, holding numerous wealthy territories both in Europe and overseas. During this period, the Spanish King Phillip II strongly supported the Catholic Church and fought wars to destroy Protestantism.

- In the 18th and 19th centuries, Spain's power declined, as it was involved in numerous costly wars. Territories in Europe were lost during the War of the Spanish Succession (1701-1714). Spain was involved in the Napoleonic Wars (which ended in 1814) and the country lost most of its overseas possessions by 1850. In 1898, Spain lost another war to the U.S. and was forced to cede the Philippines.

- At the beginning of the 20th century, the Spanish people began to clamor for a republic, causing King Alfronso XIII to abdicate in 1931. In 1936, civil war broke out between the Nationalists, led by Francisco Franco, and the Republicans. In 1939, the Nationalists were victorious and Franco seized control and ruled as a dictator until 1975.

- When Franco died in 1975, the successor that he had earlier named, Juan Carlos de Borbón y Borbón, came to power. He established a constitutional monarchy, naming himself King and restoring democracy. In 1977, the *Union of the Democratic Center* won 34% of the vote and became part of the coalition government in 1990. The *Socialist Workers' Party*, however, won the 1982 and 1986 elections. Spain threatened to withdraw from the North Atlantic Treaty Organization (NATO) during the early 1980s, but relations with Europe and the United States improved late in the 1980s.

- As the Spanish celebrated the "Year of Spain" in 1992 (because of the Summer Olympics, the World's Fair and the 500th anniversary of Columbus' voyage to the Americas), it also faced internal economic and political problems. This caused Prime Minister Felipe Gonzáles to call elections a few months ahead of schedule. Gonzales was returned to office in 1993 elections.

- Political crises and corruption threatened to bring down the government in 1994. Some officials resigned, while others were arrested. Nevertheless, Gonzáles vowed to stay in office until the end of his term.

- In 1995, the conservative *People's Party* dominated the municipal elections and, in 1996, narrowly won both houses. Its leader, Prime Minister José Maria Aznar, faced the task of financial reform and deficit cutting. Another problem is the Basque separatists, who are expected to continue their acts of terrorism.

# SPAIN

## INTRODUCTIONS

When first introduced or when departing, both men and women shake hands.

The Spaniards are a particularly warm and affectionate people. Men who are close friends will embrace when they meet and women friends kiss each other on the cheek.

In Spanish, the last name is the surname followed by the mother's maiden name. When addressing people in conversation, it is polite to use only their surname (for example, when greeting Mr. Garcia-Lopez, you would call him "Mr. Garcia").

Among Spaniards, there is great respect for the elderly and for seniority. Even though someone older or of higher rank may address you by your first name, this informality is not an invitation for you to do likewise. You should still address that person as "Mr." or "Mrs." (*"Señor"* or *"Señora"*) and their last name. In some areas, *"Don"* and *"Doña"* are used, followed by the first name, to show special respect and to flatter the person you are greeting.

An unmarried woman is addressed as *"Señorita"* followed by her first name.

It is customary to address people by their surnames until you have become well acquainted.

## SOCIAL TIPS AND CONVENTIONS

Castilian Spanish is the official language, however, English is widely used in business and can be heard in business centers.

In both business and social circles, keep in mind that Spaniards are individualistic. This individualism translates into a strong sense of personal pride. Treat everyone with great respect and be careful not to cause them any embarrassment, as it offends their sense of honor.

Many Spaniards feel that appearance as well as the projection of affluence are of great importance. Style and quality of clothing are considered signs of social status and respectability.

Spaniards enjoy conversing and giving advice.

In Spain, it is acceptable to discuss politics; however, it is best to refrain from making political comparisons between Spain and your country. Other good conversation topics include sports, particularly soccer. It is also appreciated if you express an interest in Spain's history and culture.

Avoid discussing religion or asking too many personal questions about a person's family, job and interests until you are well acquainted. Also, never make negative comments about bullfighting.

In Spain, it is not considered rude to interrupt someone while conversing. Therefore, expect to be interrupted frequently during conversation.

In Spain, eye contact is very important. However, women should be wary of eye contact with strangers or acquaintances, as returning a gaze could be interpreted as indicating a romantic interest.

# SPAIN (Cont'd)

## SOCIAL TIPS AND CONVENTIONS (Cont'd)

In Spain, the family is considered very important. While it is inappropriate to ask Spaniards too many personal questions about their families, you may want to mention your family life. The importance you place on family life will be taken as a sign of your stability as a business partner.

## CUSTOMARY BUSINESS PRACTICES

Most businesses are open six days a week from 9:00 a.m. to 1:30 p.m. and then from 5:00 to 8:00 p.m. Between about 1:30 and 4:30 p.m., there is a break for the large midday meal and a *siesta* (a rest after the midday meal). The best time of day to schedule business appointments is early in the day between 10:00 a.m. and 12:30 p.m.

Appointments should be arranged well in advance, allowing at least ten days to two weeks if made by telephone. If appointments are being scheduled by mail, allow three weeks to a month.

Spaniards have a very relaxed attitude toward time. Business is conducted at a very slow pace and punctuality is not expected. It is a customary and an accepted practice to arrive 15 to 30 minutes late for a business meeting.

Business trips should not be scheduled between mid-July and the end of August as this is the time when most Spaniards take their vacation.

It is preferred that you write in English when corresponding with Spanish business firms. Most large firms conduct business in both languages. If you send an English letter that has been translated into Spanish, it may not seem as formal or descriptive as is the custom and may offend the recipient. Correspondence should be formal, even though you may have a casual relationship with your colleague after the first meeting.

Business cards should be printed in both English and Spanish.

It is useful to have a contact who can help you cultivate business relationships in Spain. Spaniards value personal influence and it is difficult to accomplish anything on your own.

Before beginning a first business meeting, there is a great deal of small talk. People like to get to know you as a person before they will conduct business with you. You may be asked questions about your background, education and interests. Serious discussions can begin after this is completed.

Spaniards have a strong sense of honor. Special care must be taken not to offend them, as in implying that they are not adequately prepared or by imposing decisions with orders.

Spaniards tend to dress formally and elegantly. Men wear jackets and ties for business even in warm weather. Jackets should be kept buttoned except when sitting. Appropriate business attire for women is a dress or a skirt with a blouse; pantsuits are not worn.

# SPAIN (Cont'd)

## BUSINESS ENTERTAINING

Business lunches and dinners are customary in Spain. The most substantial meal is lunch; therefore, if you are invited to a lunch, expect the meal to be quite long.

If you are invited to someone's home, it is polite to decline at first, since the invitation may be made simply as a courtesy. However, if the host insists, accept the invitation.

If you are entertained by several people, it is appropriate for you to reciprocate by inviting them all out to a meal together along with their spouses.

If you are a businesswoman entertaining a Spanish businessman, keep in mind that Spanish men always expect to pay for a meal. If you would like to pay for the meal however, speak to the maitre d' or waiter in advance and arrange to pay with cash or a credit card. In the event that this is impossible, you can discreetly leave the table at the end of the meal to take care of the bill.

Spaniards dress elegantly even for casual occasions. When entertained, men should wear jackets with ties and black shoes and women should wear dresses or skirts with blouses. Formal dress (tuxedos for men and long dresses for women) is only necessary for charity balls or official dinners.

## DINING OUT

In restaurants, a service charge is usually included in the bill. It is also customary to leave a small tip (about 5%) in addition to the service charge.

Breakfast is the lightest meal of the day consisting of a hot drink and bread with jam. The midday meal is generally served at about 2:00 p.m. and usually consists of soup, salad, a dish containing fish, a main dish and fresh fruit.

At about 5:00 or 6:00 p.m., Spaniards usually have a *merienda* (snack) which consists of a *bocadillo* (sandwich) or sweet bread or crackers with tea or hot milk.

Dinner is served very late about 9:00 or 10:00 p.m. In fact, most restaurants remain closed until 9:00 p.m. and do not really get busy until about 11:00 p.m. Dinner is smaller than the midday meal and will often include local specialties such as *paella* (rice with fish and seafood or meat), seafood, sausage, roasted meat or stew.

Adults usually drink wine with meals. However, there is no pressure to drink alcohol and you may request juice or a soft drink. Likewise, if you aren't hungry, you won't be pressed to eat. It is preferable to decline food than to leave any on your plate.

If you are invited for dinner at a colleague's home, it is customary to bring a gift of flowers, pastries, cookies or chocolates. Do not bring any other type of food. Avoid bringing dahlias or chrysanthemums as they are associated with funerals. If you are offered a gift, you should open it immediately.

If you are invited to a formal dinner, the host will indicate the seating arrangement. The guest of honor is usually seated to the right of the host and the hostess is seated opposite the host.

# SPAIN (Cont'd)

## DINING OUT (Cont'd)

Cutlery is arranged slightly differently in Spain than in most other European countries. The fruit knife and fork, or other dessert utensils, will be placed above the plate. Two glasses are provided, one for water and one for wine.

The continental style of eating is used with the fork held in the left hand and the knife in the right. Use the knife to push food onto the back of the fork. Neither fingers nor food should ever be used to push food onto the fork.

Wrists should be kept on the table when you are not eating.

When you have completed the meal, place your fork and your knife side by side on the plate. Leaving them on opposite sides of the plate indicates either that you haven't finished or that you weren't satisfied with your meal.

Spaniards tend to stay late and talk after dinner. Plan to stay until around midnight when you are invited to dinner especially if the conversation is lively.

## PUBLIC CUSTOMS

The U.S. "okay" sign, with thumb and index finger forming a circle, is considered a vulgar gesture in Spain.

It is common for Spanish men to call out expressions of admiration as women pass on the street. If they are not acknowledged with a reaction, the woman will not be bothered.

It is considered inappropriate for adults to eat while walking in public.

It is considered polite for men to wait until all women in the room are seated before taking their seats.

It is considered inappropriate for women to cross their legs. Spanish men usually cross their legs at the knees.

To beckon someone, you should wave your fingers or your whole hand with palm facing down.

It is considered rude to chew gum or place your hands in your pockets, especially when conversing with someone.

# SWEDEN: HISTORICAL OVERVIEW

- Sweden has been inhabited for almost 5000 years. It was one of the last countries in which the ice that covered most of Europe thousands of years ago melted. Nevertheless, hunters and fishermen settled on the southern tip very early and moved north as the climate warmed. Sweden was known to the Romans, since it was the home of the Gothic people who battled them.

- While the Norwegian and Danish Vikings sailed westward, the Swedish Vikings went eastward as far as the Black and Caspian seas. It is said that Rurik, a legendary Swedish Viking chief, founded Russia in the ninth century.

- By the 1000s, Sweden, Denmark and Norway had each become separate kingdoms. During the 13th and 14th centuries, struggles took place between the rulers of Sweden and the nobles. In trying to oppose German expansion, Queen Margrethe I of Denmark united Denmark, Norway and Sweden in the Denmark-based Union of Kalmar in 1397. However, Sweden remained autonomous and had its own parliament by 1435.

- In 1523, Sweden became an independent kingdom with Gustaf I Vasa as monarch. Sweden became one of the great powers of Europe and fought wars with its neighbors, including Denmark and Russia, to gain control of the lands surrounding the Baltic Sea.

- Sweden began to decline in the 19th century. There was an increase in population and a concurrent lack of jobs causing large numbers of people to leave the country to find work. In 1809, Sweden lost Finland to Russia. It acquired Norway in 1814 through the Napoleonic Wars. However, Sweden dissolved its union with Norway peacefully in 1905. A Frenchman, Jean Baptiste Bernadotte, was elected crown prince of Sweden and then became king in 1818 as Karl XIV Johan. His dynasty continues today.

- During the 20th century, Swedish foreign policy has focused on neutrality and non-alignment. The country maintained its neutrality in both World Wars, allowing it to develop its economy to become a prosperous welfare state. The *Social Democratic Party* has dominated politics throughout the 20th century, except when its leadership was interrupted between 1976 and 1982.

- The Swedish people, who pride themselves on their country's peace, egalitarianism and low crime rate, were shocked when Prime Minister Olof Palme was assassinated on the streets of Stockholm in 1986.

- Palme was succeeded by Ingvar Carlsson, who introduced austerity measures in 1990 to deal with the country's economic problems. However, when his austerity package was rejected, he resigned and formed a new minority government, which he led until the 1991 elections. After the 1991 elections, Carl Bildt of the right-center Moderate Party formed a coalition government. His administration focused on the economy and relations with Europe.

- In 1994, Swedes decided to join both the North Atlantic Treaty Organization's (NATO's) Partnership for Peace and the European Union (EU). On September 18, 1994, Swedes rejected Bildt's coalition and returned the Social Democrats to power who want a slower, more managed approach to reforming welfare.

# SWEDEN

## INTRODUCTIONS

Swedes commonly shake hands with each person in the room upon meeting and leaving. As a rule, you do not have to shake hands with friends and acquaintances on subsequent meetings. However, *always* shake hands with older people when greeting them and when leaving.

A person's last name preceded by "Mr.," "Mrs." or "Miss" is the appropriate form of address, unless you are a good friend or are invited to use a first name. Try to use professional titles (i.e., "Doctor," "Engineer," etc.), followed by a last name when appropriate. Using titles may not be necessary with younger people who consider this quite formal.

If there is nobody to introduce you, introduce yourself by shaking each person's hand.

More formal greetings include *"God dag"* ("Good day") or *"God morgon"* ("Good morning"). Most people are more casual and say *"Hej"* (pronounced "hey" and meaning "hi").

## SOCIAL TIPS AND CONVENTIONS

The Swedes speak Swedish, a Germanic language related to Danish, Norwegian and Icelandic. The Samis speak their own language (Same), and the Finnish minority speaks Finnish. Many people speak English which is taught at most schools.

While Swedes are very friendly, they are also quite reserved. They are more comfortable speaking with foreigners than talking to other Swedes. They value modesty and material security.

Sweden's economy, the high standard of living and the area in which you are staying are good conversation topics. Swedes are very proud of their nation and its accomplishments. They have managed to develop one of the most egalitarian societies in the world due to a generous social welfare system. Local patriotism is important. Therefore, be careful not to praise another area over the one being visited. Swedes are pleased if you know something about Swedish history and culture.

Swedes appreciate if a visitor demonstrates his/her knowledge of the cultural differences between Sweden, Norway, Denmark and Finland as well as an awareness that Swedes are more liberal politically and socially than the others.

An interesting topic of conversation is the Nobel prizes and prize winners. With the exception of the Nobel Peace Prize (sponsored by Norway), Sweden awards the Nobel prizes each year to significant contributors in the areas of chemistry, literature, medicine and physics. Alfred Bernhard Nobel (1833-96), the inventor of dynamite and a wealthy businessman, was born in Sweden.

Be aware that complimenting people you have just met is regarded as insincere.

Swedes are sports enthusiasts, which makes sports a good topic of conversation. Soccer, skiing, tennis, golf, swimming, ice hockey, *bandy* (related to ice hockey) and other winter sports are popular. The Swedes also love nature and participate in a lot of nature-related hobbies. Hiking, fishing and bird-watching are enjoyed. Cultural events, opera, ballet and recent books are other good conversation topics.

# SWEDEN (Cont'd)

## SOCIAL TIPS AND CONVENTIONS (Cont'd)

Avoid discussing costs, casual sexual attitudes, suicide rates, alcoholism or the country's neutrality during World War II while in Sweden. Comments about any of these topics may be interpreted as criticisms of Sweden, especially if the comment is made by a visitor from the U.S.

Traditionally, members of the upper classes refer to each other in the third person. They will avoid using the word "you." For example, in addressing a Mrs. Olson, they might say "How is Mrs. Doctor Olson today?" rather than "How are you today?" Although this tradition is changing, it is still appropriate to use this form when speaking to older people.

Eye contact is important during conversation. However, excessive hand gestures are avoided.

## CUSTOMARY BUSINESS PRACTICES

Avoid scheduling business trips during the vacation months of June, July and August. All Swedes take five weeks of vacation each year.

It is not necessary to send a letter of introduction in order to do business with a Swedish firm.

Always be punctual for any appointment.

Swedish businesspeople conduct business very seriously and may seem rigid when you first meet them. Since Swedes are quite reserved, it is best to keep gestures to a minimum when making presentations.

The pace of business in Sweden is somewhat relaxed. Swedes believe work breaks to be very important for their well-being. They also take very long lunch and coffee breaks. Remember that it is inappropriate to rush Swedish businesspeople since rushing is interpreted as pushiness.

For business, men wear suits and ties; women wear dresses or suits.

Businesses are usually open from 9:00 a.m. to 4:00 p.m., Monday through Friday. They are sometimes open from 9:00 a.m. to noon on Saturday as well.

## BUSINESS ENTERTAINING

Swedes enjoy visiting. Refreshments are almost always served and it is popular to invite friends over for an evening meal. Entertaining is most often done in the home although going out to restaurants is becoming more popular. Unlike their European counterparts, Swedes are more likely to invite new acquaintances for dinner. However, expect their behavior to be very formal.

Remember that punctuality is very important when invited to someone's home because the meal is served first. If drinks are offered before the meal, they will usually consist of Renat (vodka), Scotch, brandy or wine.

If you are invited to someone's home in the evening, do not presume that it is a dinner invitation unless the meal is specified.

# SWEDEN (Cont'd)

## BUSINESS ENTERTAINING (Cont'd)

Dress for dinner unless you are invited to a picnic. When the invitation specifies formal wear, men should wear tuxedos and women should wear short cocktail dresses in a color other than black.

When visiting the home of a Swedish business colleague, it is appropriate to bring an odd number of flowers or a box of chocolates for the host(s). Flowers should be unwrapped just before presenting them to the host. Liquor or wine is an appreciated gift since it is so expensive in Sweden. Candy, but no other kind of food, also makes a suitable gift.

If you choose not to bring a gift, then it is appropriate to send a thank-you card. Also, it is very important to make a point of calling the host the next day to thank him/her for the hospitality. The next time you see the person, it is also polite to express your appreciation for the meal once again.

Make reservations in advance for business lunches and dinners. Spouses should be included in dinner invitations, but not for business lunches. Formal restaurants, called *Kållare*, are a good choice for these occasions.

When you are in a restaurant, never snap your fingers or yell to a waiter/waitress to get attention. It is best to say "Sir/Madam" in English.

Be aware that because liquor is so expensive in restaurants, many people have a drink or two at home before going out to dinner.

It is not necessary to leave a tip since a service charge is included in the check. If you wish to leave an additional gratuity, it is advisable not to leave it on the table. Instead, give it to the head waiter.

## DINING OUT

Swedes eat a light breakfast around 7:00 a.m. and might have a coffee or tea break mid-morning. The main meal is traditionally eaten at midday. However, most urban residents have only a light lunch at noon and then eat the main meal in the evening around 6:00 p.m.

While the Swedish diet used to consist mainly of meat, fish and cheese, it now more often includes vegetables and fruits. This change is mainly due to health concerns in the same way that these concerns have affected eating habits in other parts of the world. Common foods include potatoes, cheeses, seafood and other fresh foods.

For breakfast, Swedes commonly eat *fil* (a kind of yogurt) and *knåckebrød* (crisp bread) with margarine. Also, cheese, rolls and herring are typical breakfast foods. *Smorgåsar* (open-faced sandwiches) are very popular for breakfast, lunch or snacks. Some favorite main dish specialties include reindeer meat, Swedish cloudberries, *Köttbullar med kokt potatis, brun sås och lingonsylt* (meatballs with boiled potatoes, brown sauce and lingonberry jam), *Stekt falukorv med senap och potatis* (fried slices of thick German sausage with mustard and boiled or fried potatoes) and *grillad lax med spenat, citron och potatis eller ris* (grilled slices of salmon with spinach, slices of lemon and potatoes or rice). Beer, mineral water or milk usually accompanies the meal.

# SWEDEN (Cont'd)

## DINING OUT (Cont'd)

The *smørgåsbord* is a lavish buffet eaten on special occasions or at parties. It includes warm and cold dishes such as meat and fish as well as a wide array of desserts.

A popular, local drink is called *aquavit*. It is an alcoholic beverage distilled from grain or potatoes and often flavored with caraway seed. It is served extremely cold.

A formal meal usually has four courses. The first may be smoked salmon, caviar canapés, marinated herring or fruit soup. The second course is usually meat (other than beef, since it is so expensive), potatoes and a vegetable. Salad follows. Finally, a dessert, such as ice cream and fruit or crepes and fruit, completes the meal. Wine usually accompanies a formal dinner. Coffee may be served after dessert along with brandy or cognac. Note that coffee is never served with the meal.

Swedes follow the continental style of eating, with the fork in the left hand and the knife in the right. Separate butter knives are usually provided and the dinner knife should not be used for spreading butter.

Hands, but not the elbows, should be kept above the table during meals.

The host usually seats all the guests at a dinner. The male guest of honor is seated to the left of the hostess and the female guest of honor is seated to the left of the host. Husbands and wives are not seated together.

On some occasions, the host makes a welcome speech at the beginning of the meal. After the speech, he will make a *skål* (toast) and then all the guests taste the wine. Guests should refrain from drinking before the toast is made. To make a toast in Sweden, look into the eyes of the person being toasted, say *"skål"* (pronounced "skoal"), bow your head slightly and

then consume the drink in one gulp. Before putting the glass back on the table, meet the other person's eyes again and nod. You should not toast the host or anyone senior to you in age, unless they toast you first.

Food is usually placed in serving dishes on the table. It is polite to try a little of everything. When guests are present, they usually wait for the host to offer second helpings. It is not impolite to decline food and it is perfectly acceptable to take more.

When you are finished eating, leave the utensils side by side on the plate. It is considered impolite to leave any food on the plate.

It is polite for the guest of honor to make a speech during dessert, elaborating on the meal and the charm of the hostess. Each guest personally thanks the host directly after the meal. Sometimes the thanks begin with the tapping of a knife on a glass. However, this does not signal the end of the evening.

Your host will expect you to stay after the meal has concluded for coffee and conversation, even until as late as 11:00 p.m. When leaving, guests should say "Good-bye" and step outside before putting on their coats.

# SWEDEN (Cont'd)

## PUBLIC CUSTOMS

European fashions are common in Sweden although warm clothing is worn more often due to the climate. Swedes generally dress conservatively on virtually all occasions. Even when they go out, they avoid glamorous clothing. It is important to be neat and clean when in public; even casual clothing is elegant, fashionable and high-quality.

It is considered impolite to chew gum, yawn or have one's hands in one's pockets when speaking with another person.

It used to be uncommon to see people touching, embracing or putting an arm around someone's shoulder in public. However, the population is becoming more casual and it is much more common to see displays of friendship. Despite changing attitudes, do not embrace or put your arm around anybody except a close friend.

From a distance, one may nod one's head or raise one's hand to greet someone. Men lift their hats when passing an acquaintance in the street. They also remove their hats when talking to a woman.

It is not uncommon for people to change into their bathing suits on the beach, with or without a towel as a shield.

When waiting for a bus, tickets, etc., lines are respected. Pushing and shoving or barging in line is unacceptable.

# SWITZERLAND: HISTORICAL OVERVIEW

- Since 4000 B.C., the region was settled by Celtic tribes. One tribe, called the Helvetians, tried to move into northern Italy and clashed with the armies of Julius Caesar. As a result, for five centuries, the area became part of the Roman Empire, serving as a buffer from Germanic tribes in the north. During this time, the Romans developed cities and the arts in the region, opening trade and military routes that would later be important to the development of Europe. By the fifth century A.D., northern tribes forced the Romans to withdraw. Burgundian tribes settled in the west of the region and Alemanians in the east. While both of these groups were Germanic, they developed along different lines. According to these lines, the region was separated into four language zones – German, French, Italian and Romansch (developed from Latin).

- In the eighth and ninth centuries, Charlemagne absorbed the area into his empire. During the Middle Ages, however, the region was part of the Holy Roman Empire. The region then came under the control of the Austrian Habsburg family. The three cantons of Uri, Schwyz and Unterwalden founded the Swiss Confederation when they began to revolt against Habsburg control by signing the Perpetual Covenant of 1291. By repelling Austrian and other armies, Swiss soldiers gained a reputation for their fighting prowess. Other cantons (Luzern, Zurich, Bern) joined the confederation, making it more powerful. After withstanding 16th- and early 17th-century wars, Switzerland received official recognition as a nation in the 1648 Treaty of Westphalia.

- In 1815, following Napoleonic invasions, the country became permanently neutral under the Congress of Vienna. The mountains of Switzerland and its well-trained army have helped the country maintain its neutrality. Early in the 19th century, Switzerland became a centralized nation-state. It adopted a constitution in 1848, making it a federal state. In 1874, direct democracy became part of the constitution.

- Switzerland remained neutral during the World Wars. Also as part of its neutrality, it is not a member of the United Nations (it only has observer status), the North Atlantic Treaty Organization (NATO) or the European Union (EU). Nevertheless, it maintains solid relations with many countries.

- For the Swiss people, membership in one of the 26 Swiss cantons, or communes, is more important than national identity. Switzerland has resisted the worldwide trend toward government centralization. In 1978, a proposal to create a federal police force was rejected. Swiss presidents are inconspicuous, to the point that most Swiss are unable to name their own president in any given year. Youth protests, particularly in Zurich and Basel, were a significant problem in the 1980s, but they have diminished significantly.

- The Swiss economy, one of the most efficient and prosperous, relies almost entirely on imports to meet its energy and food needs. To compensate, Switzerland has become highly industrialized and a great trading center. It has been one of world's major banking centers since the 16th century, though lately it is lagging behind New York, Tokyo and London. In the 1990s, Switzerland has endured such problems as political scandals, money laundering and rising drug use. While this has prompted some national intraspection, the economic future is bright, with industry being well equipped to handle the increasingly intense world trade competition. The political situation is also stable, the 1995 parliamentary elections produced no significant changes.

# SWITZERLAND

*Swiss society is tricultural and trilingual – French, Italian and German. Although there is a common Swiss culture, there are elements of French, Italian and German culture that can be detected in social and business etiquette. The specific situation, the region and the individuals with whom you are dealing define the appropriate variations in customs and etiquette.*

## INTRODUCTIONS

When the Swiss greet or are introduced to someone, they customarily stand and shake hands. Therefore, keep in mind to shake hands with each person present when either arriving or departing.

In the French region, women friends embrace and kiss twice (once on each cheek) according to French custom. In the Italian area, women friends embrace but don't kiss when they meet. In both the French and Italian regions, two male friends may embrace if they haven't seen each other for a long time.

The German region tends to be more reserved. Women may embrace or kiss only if they have been apart for a long time. Men in this area do not embrace when greeting.

When addressing people, remember to use last names. Using first names is considered very impolite unless you are invited to do so.

Verbal greetings vary according to the time of day and the region of the country. However, most Swiss people understand English greetings.

You can use *"Herr"* and *"Frau"* to address the German-speaking Swiss, *"Monsieur"* and *"Madame"* to address the French-speaking Swiss and *"Signor"* and *"Signora"* to address the Italian-speaking Swiss ("Mr." or "Mrs.," respectively).

Exchanging business cards is considered by businesspeople to be an important part of introductions.

## SOCIAL TIPS AND CONVENTIONS

Swiss/German, French and Italian are spoken in Switzerland. However, English is widely studied and spoken especially in business circles.

The Swiss take a very long time to establish a relationship, so don't expect people to be convivial and friendly immediately. Once you do make a Swiss friend, though, that person will be loyal for life.

Be polite, reserved and sensitive in personal relationships since the Swiss consider courtesy to be very important.

Good topics of conversation are participatory sports such as sailing, hiking and skiing; spectator sports such as soccer and bicycling; your impressions of Switzerland; and your travels in general. The Swiss are particularly proud of their independence and high standard of living.

# SWITZERLAND (Cont'd)

## SOCIAL TIPS AND CONVENTIONS (Cont'd)

The Swiss are quite conservative and reserved, and they dislike displays of wealth. It is best to avoid asking questions about someone's age, family, personal life or profession. Also refrain from comments regarding weight-watching or diets.

Be prepared for serious political discussions even at parties.

The Swiss are passionate in their opinions about military service. Discussions of this sort could lead to a major argument.

When answering the phone, you may hear a variety of responses. In the French region, people say "*Allo;*" in the Italian region, people say "*Pronto;*" and in the German region, people answer with their name.

## CUSTOMARY BUSINESS PRACTICES

When sending business mail to a specific person in Switzerland, it is best to address the envelope to the company, rather than to the individual. The letter itself, however, should be addressed to the individual. Envelopes addressed to an individual won't be opened if the person is away and may seriously delay your business.

It is best to avoid making appointments during July and August since they are the traditional vacation months.

The best time for scheduling business appointments is in the morning after 9:00 a.m.

Appointments can be scheduled by telephone or by mail. If you call, phone three or four days ahead. If you're writing, allow a minimum of two weeks to set up an appointment.

The Swiss respect punctuality and are insulted when people are late. It is expected that people be on time for all social and business engagements.

Bring plenty of business cards. If your company is very old, have the year of its founding printed on your card. It will impress the Swiss, who respect age.

Hand your business card to the receptionist, even if you've arranged an appointment in advance. Also give a card to the person with whom you're meeting.

At business meetings, Swiss people are direct, and they come right to the point without any initial small talk. Presentations should be thoroughly prepared, clear and should show attention to detail. Know your field very well so that meetings can run efficiently (especially in the German region).

In the French and Italian regions, business is generally conducted at a slower and more casual pace. Anticipate some opening small talk about your trip to Switzerland, where you are staying, etc.

# SWITZERLAND (Cont'd)

## CUSTOMARY BUSINESS PRACTICES (Cont'd)

It is important to realize that Swiss businesspeople are very conservative and value order. Be patient, as they proceed in a very deliberate manner to a decision. Avoid high pressure selling techniques. Once a decision has been made, the Swiss are extremely reliable.

In Switzerland, business is conducted in a very orderly manner and decision making is quite centralized. Cultivation of personal relationships will take place only after negotiations are completed.

The Swiss place a high value on cleanliness and neatness in dressing. Businesspeople dress conservatively. For business meetings, men wear suits and ties, and women wear dresses or suits. Women can wear slacks, if the slacks conform to business attire.

Business hours are usually from 8:00 a.m. to noon and then from 2:00 to 6:00 p.m., Monday through Friday.

## BUSINESS ENTERTAINING

The Swiss are very private and generally entertain visitors in restaurants rather than in their homes. If you are invited to dinner at someone's home, consider it a compliment.

When attending a party, wait for your host to make introductions.

When invited to dinner at someone's home, the dress is more casual – men should wear trousers, shirts and sweaters, and women should wear skirts or slacks with a blouse or sweater.

Formal clothes (tuxedos for men and long dresses for women) are worn to balls, openings of theater or opera, formal weddings or any other time the invitation specifies formal wear.

Impersonal gifts such as flowers or candy are popular in Switzerland, and your host would appreciate such a gift. Remember, however, that red roses and carnations are expressions of romantic love, and chrysanthemums and white asters are reserved for funerals. Three flowers, or a flowering branch are sufficient. It is not necessary to get a large bunch. If you don't have time to shop in advance, it is acceptable to send flowers the next day. A good bottle of whiskey or cognac is also considered an appropriate gift.

Business dinners are more common than business lunches. When lunching with a businessperson, it is common to be taken to the cafeteria at the work place.

Include spouses in dinner invitations, unless the sole purpose of the meal is to discuss business.

In restaurants, a service charge is always included in the bill.

# SWITZERLAND (Cont'd)

## DINING OUT

The largest meal of the day is the midday meal, which takes place around noon. This meal generally includes soup, a meat dish and fruit. Dinner, which takes place around 6:00 or 7:00 p.m., is a lighter meal. It usually consists of soup followed by salad or bread with cheese or salami.

A meal at a dinner party is often larger than a typical dinner. It consists of soup, a meat dish, vegetables, rice or potatoes and a green salad. The meal usually ends with fruit and cheese, cake or pudding. This may be followed by espresso or after-dinner drinks, such as *grappa* (brandy made from grape skins), cognac, kirsch or *pflümwasser* (plum brandy).

A wide variety of cuisines as well as regional specialties are available throughout Switzerland. Cheese dishes and liqueurs are common specialties.

Another popular Swiss dish is *fondue* – a dish containing melted cheese or gravy placed in the center of the table. Long forks are then used to dip pieces of bread into the cheese or gravy. *Raclettes bagnes* (cheese that has been grilled until it has melted and become crispy, served with cocktail onions and small potatoes) is another local delicacy.

If you are the guest of honor, you will be seated (or should seat yourself) in the middle of the side of the table.

When sitting at the table, never put either hand in your lap. Keep both wrists on the table when you're not eating.

Wait until the host has proposed a toast before drinking the wine. Then look the host in the eye and say "To your health," in the language appropriate to the region or in English. Clink glasses with everyone at the table.

Be aware that Swiss people rarely order drinks before the meal. If drinks are served, they may include beer, wine, Campari, *Cynar* (made from artichokes), *blanc-cassis* (white wine with a blackberry liqueur) or *Pastis* (anise liqueur).

Help yourself to hors d'oeuvres only when offered. Also, begin eating only after being prompted by your host.

Help yourself to the food passed around the table on serving platters. You are expected to finish everything you put on your plate, so if you're not sure whether you'll like something, take a very small portion.

Cutlery is arranged with the fork to the left of the plate and the knife and soup spoon to the right. The dessert spoon will be above the plate.

Eat as the Swiss do, with the fork in the left hand and the knife in the right. Use the knife to push the food onto the back of the fork.

# SWITZERLAND (Cont'd)

## DINING OUT (Cont'd)

Indicate that you're waiting for a second helping by crossing the fork over the knife. The fork should point diagonally to the right, and the knife to the left. To show that you have finished, place the knife and fork horizontally across the plate, with the handles to the right.

Break bread and rolls with your hands, rather than cutting them with a knife.

At a dinner party in a home, it is recommended that you stay until about midnight. You may take the lead from other guests in deciding when to leave, but you should not stay much past midnight. When leaving, shake hands with all family members (including children). It is appropriate to send a thank-you note the next day.

## PUBLIC CUSTOMS

When meeting an acquaintance on the street, stop and shake hands. It is also customary to shake hands when departing.

In the German region, men tip their hats when they see someone they know on the street.

In a restaurant, it is common practice for strangers to sit in any empty seats remaining at your table. However, it is not necessary to strike up a conversation with them.

Sit up straight in public as the Swiss consider sloppy posture rude.

Chewing gum or having your hands in your pockets is considered rude.

Legs should not be placed on a desk, chair or table. If you cross your legs, you should cross them at the knee.

The Swiss take pride in orderliness and cleanliness; littering is considered to be completely inappropriate behavior.

The elderly are treated with great respect in Switzerland. It is customary to help an elderly person getting on or off a bus or carrying heavy bags. Stand and give your seat to the elderly on public transportation as well.

Shorts and jeans can be worn for casual wear in the country, but avoid wearing shorts in the city.

Expect pushing and shoving when standing in a line.

# TURKEY: HISTORICAL OVERVIEW

- The oldest known site of human habitation is located in central Turkey at Chatalhuyuk (6500 B.C.). The great Hittite Empire, which dominated much of the Middle East from about 3000 until 2000 B.C., was centered east of Ankara. Alexander the Great conquered parts of the region in the fourth century B.C. In the first century B.C., the Romans conquered the area, establishing important cities as provincial capitals. The Roman Emperor Constantine founded the city of Constantinople. This city later became the center of the Byzantine Empire, which dominated eastern Europe for 1,000 years and is now known as Istanbul.

- The Muslim Seljuk Turks entered Asia Minor in the 11th century and began the long process of Islamization. In 1453, the Ottoman Turks, the successors of the Seljuks, captured Constantinople and created a vast empire that went beyond the bounds of the Byzantine Empire into the Balkans, the Middle East and North Africa. The Ottoman Empire survived until World War I during which it allied itself with the Central Powers and, therefore, was dissolved when the Central Powers were defeated. In 1923, after the Ottoman Empire was dissolved, a general in the Turkish army, Mustafa Kemal, formed the Republic of Turkey. Under Kemal, the nation was reformed from an Islamic empire to a secular state. The new country established ties with Europe and the U.S. It joined the North Atlantic Treaty Organization (NATO) in 1952 and provided land for a U.S. military base.

- The first three decades of the country's existence was marked by political turmoil. Then, in the late 1970s, serious economic and political problems contributed to domestic terrorism which paralyzed the government. The military seized control in 1980, restored stability and called for elections in 1983. While the military withdrew from power after the elections, the military commander, Kenan Evran, was elected President.

- In 1989, Evran's Prime Minister, Turgut Özal, was elected by parliament to the office of President for a seven-year term. While a wave of terrorism again erupted in 1990, the political structure was stable enough to handle the threat. Parliamentary elections in 1991 brought Özal's rival, Suleyman Demirel to power as Prime Minister. When Özal died suddenly in 1993, Demirel was elected by parliament to be the new President. Tansu Ciller was chosen to replace Demirel as Prime Minister until the 1996 elections, becoming Turkey's first female prime minister. Ciller's government was faced with economic challenges as well as the insurgency of Kurdish rebels. A cease-fire was declared in 1993, however, in 1994, it was broken and the violence worsened. Kurdish leaders offered to end the fighting in exchange for more rights for the Kurdish minority. While Ciller favored a peaceful end to the conflict, her critics disapproved of offering any concessions to the rebels.

- In 1995, the country passed constitutional reforms to clear the way to join the European Union, but the European Parliament has indicated that more work needs to be done with regard to terrorism and the Kurdish issue. Ciller formed a coalition in 1996, with Mesut Yilmaz of the *Motherland Party* agreeing to form a minority government that would rotate the premiership. But the coalition disintegrated in June, under intense criticism from the *Welfare Party*. The fact is that Turkey lacks a natural majority. The government is, therefore, weak and Turkey is unable to become an important regional power. The country had a strong economic recovery in 1995, but persistent economic problems remain, and Turkey failed to meet its budgetary goals.

# TURKEY

## INTRODUCTIONS

When greeting friends or strangers, one shakes hands and says *"Nasilsiniz"* ("How are you?") or *"Merhaba"* ("Hello"). To the first greeting, Turks generally reply *"Iyiyim, teshekur ederim"* ("Fine, thanks").

Long-standing friends and acquaintances may clasp hands and kiss both cheeks regardless of gender. To show respect for an elder, a Turk may kiss the elder's hand and touch it to his/her forehead.

Address Turks with "Mr." or "Mrs.," followed by the surname. An occupational title (e.g., *"Avokat"* for "Lawyer") should be used alone (i.e., not followed by a first or last name). For women, *"Bayam"* should be added to the occupational title (e.g., *"Avokat Bayam"*).

Turkish titles follow the first name which is normally used only among Turks. *"Hanim"* is used for women and *"Bay"* is used for men among friends or with younger people (e.g., *"Leyla Hanim"* or *"Ismail Bay"*). The modern form *"Bay"* (for men) and *"Bayam"* (for women), followed by the last name, is used the most in business and social contacts. With older people, *"Abla"* is used for women and *"Aabey"* is used for men, after the first name. (These terms mean "Sister" and "Brother"). If there is a great difference in age, *"Teyze"* ("Aunt") and *"Amca"* ("Uncle") are also used after the first name.

If you enter a room or an office, it is appropriate to say *"Günaydin"* ("Good morning") or *"Iyi günler"* ("Have a nice day").

If you enter a room in which there is a group, greet each person, beginning with the eldest, and shake hands. You need not shake hands with each person when you leave.

Show respect to elders by standing to greet them when they enter a room.

## SOCIAL TIPS AND CONVENTIONS

After years of interaction with both Europe and Asia, the Turkish people have incorporated features from both areas into their life-style, customs and thinking. Do not make the mistake of calling Turkey part of the Middle East since Turks consider themselves European. Similarly, do not make the mistake of referring to Turks as Arabs, which they are not.

Even though Turkey has been influenced by other cultures, the Turks are a very patriotic people and are proud of their successful modernization efforts as well as the role that they played in ancient history. Even though attempts have been made to westernize Turkish culture, many of the traditional Ottoman and folkloric elements still flourish in the arts, literature, music and everyday life.

It is best to avoid references to or criticisms of past or present political problems such as the Kurdish rebellion and terrorist violence. Turks often feel misunderstood by Western nations because of the publicity these issues have received. They consider their society to be progressive, modern, ethnically-diverse, tolerant and democratic.

# TURKEY (Cont'd)

## SOCIAL TIPS AND CONVENTIONS (Cont'd)

Avoid talking about politics, communism or the Cyprus-Greece conflict.

Honesty, cleverness and a sense of humor (which is considered a sign of intelligence) are very much admired by Turks. They also value a good education, social status and secure employment.

Family values are considered to be very important and, in fact, the primary social unit is the family. In rural areas, traditional values prevail, including the final authority of the father. An individual is loyal to and dependent upon the family. Turks particularly appreciate if you ask them questions about their son(s).

In Turkey, "No" can be expressed by shaking the head back and forth. However, shaking the head from side to side usually means, "I don't understand." "No" is commonly expressed by lifting the head up and back and raising the eyebrows or closing the eyes momentarily.

Inquiries about someone's health, family and work are appropriate particularly following a greeting. In fact, good topics of discussion include family, work or hobbies.

Cigarette smoking is a national passion. Don't insult your hosts by commenting on the habit.

Should you make a *faux pas*, a quick apology will be gladly accepted and will end the incident.

Try to pass objects with both hands; it is insulting to more traditional Turks if you use only your left hand.

Demonstrative gestures are used extensively by Turks during conversation to add emphasis or meaning. While gesturing is appropriate, speaking loudly is considered impolite.

Turkish women usually will not converse with a man unless they have been formally introduced.

## CUSTOMARY BUSINESS PRACTICES

While Turkish, Arabic and some Kurdish are predominantly spoken in Turkey, English is becoming increasingly popular as a second or third language. In particular, it is quite widely spoken in business circles. Many businesspeople also speak French or German.

Appointments are necessary for all commercial and government business. They should be made well in advance. A personal introduction or a letter of introduction from a Turk can be helpful in making a first contact with a Turkish firm.

Turkish businessmen appreciate and expect punctuality but, given Istanbul traffic, are sympathetic if you arrive late. However, government offices adhere to strict timetables. Also, you are expected to be on time for dinner invitations.

# TURKEY (Cont'd)

## CUSTOMARY BUSINESS PRACTICES (Cont'd)

You may want to avoid scheduling business appointments during the months of June, July and August, since these are the months most Turks take vacations.

Business meetings always begin with casual conversations over cups of strong Turkish coffee.

Turkish society is hierarchical with power flowing from top to bottom. Always try to transact business with the most important person in your field since lower personnel may not have the authority to make decisions.

In business, as in Turkish society, group orientation is valued over personal assertion or aggressiveness.

Never offer *baksheesh* (tips) in offices. If you recognize an obligation, exchange favors rather than cash.

Turkish names are not always easy to remember or pronounce. Carry plenty of business cards and after exchanging them, try to pronounce the name correctly. Feel free to ask for assistance to make sure you get it right. Remember to give a business card to the receptionist, to the person you are meeting and to anyone else that you meet in the course of your appointment.

Business dress is quite conservative. Western-style clothing is most common. European fashions are especially popular among the youth. Men should always wear a suit and tie for business meetings, and women should wear a business suit with high heels.

Businesses are generally open from 9:00 a.m. to 5:00 p.m., Monday through Friday. Some are also open for a half-day on Saturday. Business executives usually arrive around 10:00 a.m., leave for lunch at about noon, and return at about 2:30 p.m.

## BUSINESS ENTERTAINING

Hospitality is vital in Turkish culture. Visiting, even unexpectedly, is common. If you receive an invitation to "drop in," it is always sincere. Visits in homes usually begin around 9:00 p.m. Guests will almost always be invited for something to eat or to drink. It is impolite to decline the refreshments. In Turkey, it is appropriate to include a spouse in an invitation.

In private homes and offices, if you are a man, the host may offer you some cologne to refresh yourself. You should accept, pour a little on your hands and rub it on your face and hands.

Many restaurants in the major cities cater largely to a business clientele for lunch. You can expect to be invited for a leisurely working lunch. A Turkish businessman is more likely to invite you to a restaurant for a leisurely meal than to his home.

# TURKEY (Cont'd)

## BUSINESS ENTERTAINING (Cont'd)

In some restaurants, a service charge of 10-15% is automatically added to the bill. If 10% is included, leave about 5% more on the table for the waiter. If a service charge is not included, a tip of about 15% should be given.

Keep in mind that service in restaurants in Turkey is usually extremely fast. However, you should not feel "hurried" by the speed with which you are served.

While there are a number of international restaurants in Turkey, the most common type of eating place is the Turkish Kebab restaurant, called *Kebabei*. *Kahve hane* are coffee houses, which serve pastries, tea, coffee and liquor. *Pasta hane* are also coffee houses, but they do not offer liquor. Women may go into *kahve hane* and *pasta hane* only in large cities, and it is recommended that they not go in alone. A *restoran* or *lokanta* is a full-service restaurant.

If invited to a Turkish home, bring flowers, candy or pastries as a gift. Bring wine only if you know the family serves alcohol. Other appropriate gifts include books and records in English, which may be hard to find in Turkey. You should expect that, if the gift is wrapped, it will not be opened in front of you.

When you are a guest in a Turkish home, your hosts will work hard to make you feel comfortable. At the same time, visitors are expected to bring a pleasant presence into the home. Unpleasant news or problems should not be brought up, and it is best to avoid asking too many personal questions of your host. It is appreciated if you compliment the cook and the meal.

People often smoke between courses. However, generally, it is a good idea to ask permission and to conform to what others are doing. At the end of a meal, it is likely that you will be offered a toothpick. If you use a toothpick, be sure to cover your mouth while using it.

If you are visiting a family with children, bring them chocolates or small toys.

Many Turks remove their shoes when entering the home and replace them with slippers. Although hosts may tell foreign visitors that this is unnecessary, you should still insist on removing your shoes.

## DINING OUT

Breakfast (served about 7:00 a.m.) is usually light, consisting of tea, white cheese, bread, butter, eggplant or fig marmalade, honey and olives.

Lunch is a moderately-sized meal served about noon. Dinner is the main meal of the day and is served around 7:00 p.m. Meals can be lavish, and Turks are quite proud of their rich cuisine. Staples include lamb and rice. Seafood is popular along the coast. Yogurt is also used abundantly in Turkish cooking.

# TURKEY (Cont'd)

## DINING OUT (Cont'd)

Turkish cuisine is famous for many things, including *meze*, a tray or table of hors d'oeuvres, including stuffed grape leaves, salads, shrimp and many other items. *Shish kebab* (chunks of lamb on a skewer) are a favorite, as are vegetables prepared in olive oil. Rice *pilav* is common. Turkish desserts are famously sweet, including *baklava* (syrup-dipped pastry) and *muhallebi* (milk pudding).

The thick, sweet coffee called *kahve* is the most popular drink and is served with almost every meal. Another popular drink is *raki*, a drink made of fermented grapes (not a wine). Another popular non-alcoholic beverage is called *ayran*. This is a drink made from yogurt, water and salt.

Dining customs vary within the provinces. There are some places where it is quite common to eat with the fingers. However, in big cities and in most regions, avoid eating with your fingers. Turks use the continental style of eating, with the fork in the left hand and the knife remaining in the right.

Expect your hosts to urge you to eat a great deal.

If you are invited to a meal in a restaurant, you will not be allowed to pay any part of the check. Similarly, if you invite colleagues to a meal, you will be expected to pay the entire bill. In Turkey, it is not considered appropriate to "split" the bill.

## PUBLIC CUSTOMS

Avoid sitting with your legs crossed and, in general, when you are seated try to make sure that the sole of your shoe is not conspicuous. It is considered impolite to direct the sole of one's foot at anyone.

It is not polite to smoke or eat on the street.

Islamic cultures generally prohibit overt signs of affection (such as hugging and kissing) in public.

Holding the hand up, palm outward and slowly bringing the fingers into the thumb in a grasping motion is a gesture unique to Turkey signaling that "something is good."

Jerking the forearm up implies strength and has no insulting connotations.

The "thumbs up" signal means "okay." However, the circle made with the thumb and forefinger, which means "okay" in a number of other countries, means "homosexuality" in Turkey.

Men in Turkey may be seen holding and fingering loops of beads called "worry beads." These are used for relieving tension and have no religious significance.

# TURKEY (Cont'd)

## PUBLIC CUSTOMS (Cont'd)

It is considered rude to have your arms crossed in front of you or to have your hands in your pockets while conversing with someone.

To beckon someone, you should not use your finger. Rather, you should wave your hand up and down with your palm facing downwards.

Turkey is 98% Sunni Muslim. Due to the significant Muslim population, public prayer takes place five times a day in most parts of Turkey. In addition, one of the most important religious holidays is the fast period of *Ramadan*. The dates of *Ramadan* vary with the lunar calendar, but it is generally in the spring or early summer. During this period, most Turks refrain from eating or drinking during daylight hours. At the end of *Ramadan* is a three-day holiday called *Seker Bayrami* (Sugar Holiday) during which sweets are eaten to celebrate the end of the fast. Foreigners are not expected to adhere to the rules of *Ramadan*, but you may want to avoid eating in public during daylight hours at this time of year.

Expect to remove your shoes when visiting a mosque. In mosques, the doorkeeper will often ask for a small contribution toward maintenance. It is considered rude to refuse.

According to Muslim traditions, women in Turkey should dress modestly avoiding short skirts or low-cut blouses. When visiting mosques, they should cover their heads and wear long sleeves and pants or skirts. To avoid harassment, women should avoid traveling alone and should always walk purposefully, ignore catcalls and stay away from deserted streets after dark.

Before taking photographs, especially of individuals or a mosque, be sure to ask permission.

# UNITED KINGDOM: HISTORICAL OVERVIEW

- Roman leader Julius Caesar's forces reached Britain in 55 B.C., but the Romans did not invade until 43 A.D. The area was incorporated into the Roman Empire and the Romans stayed until 426, when they were driven out of Britain by the Angles and the Saxons (two Germanic tribes).

- In the ninth century, Vikings began invading the islands. Danish-led forces invaded in 865 as well, ushering in two centuries of Viking domination. Other groups also invaded, including the Norsemen. The last invasion took place in 1066, when William the Conqueror won the Battle of Hastings. This Norman conquest brought about great political and social change. One change was the signing of the Magna Carta in 1215 which established important principles of human rights and limits on the monarchy.

- Struggles between local dynasties continued but ended in the 15th century with the War of the Roses. Henry Tudor emerged with the crown and his son, Henry VIII, established the crown as the head of the Church of England. Henry VIII's daughter, Elizabeth I, reigned during a time of the expansion of the empire. As the empire spanned the globe, the saying that "the sun never sets on the British empire" emerged.

- As the empire gained power, Wales (1535) and Scotland (1707) joined England through acts of union and the expanded empire became known as the United Kingdom of Great Britain. Through an act of union in 1801, Ireland joined the empire and it then became known as the United Kingdom of Great Britain and Ireland. When most of Ireland became independent in 1921, the name changed to the United Kingdom of Great Britain and Northern Ireland.

- Britain had established itself as a great naval power, especially after it defeated the mighty Spanish Armada in 1588. During the Industrial Revolution, Britain became the most powerful economy in the world. The country's military and economic strength in addition to its colonial holdings, firmly established it as the greatest power in the world.

- Although the United Kingdom lost its U.S. colonies in 1776, new lands were acquired in the Mediterranean, the Caribbean, Africa and Asia. Also, Canada remained a British colony until 1867, when it became an autonomous part of the Commonwealth. After World War I, expansion halted and the empire began to shrink – some colonies had claimed independence even before the war.

- During World War II, under the leadership of Winston Churchill, Britain withstood severe Nazi bombings. After the war, most British colonies (almost 50) were granted their independence. Britain was a founding member of the North Atlantic Treaty Organization (NATO) in 1949 and it joined the European Union (EU) in 1973.

- Winston Churchill's *Labour Party* established the modern welfare state. However, in recent years, the conservative party governments of Margaret Thatcher and John Major have placed more emphasis on the private sector (while maintaining a broad welfare state). In 1996, Major's popularity was quite low, while the popularity of Labour leader Tony Blair rose exponentially. Major faces financial challenges as well as the continuing problem of the Northern Ireland peace process. The Tories have centralized power, weakening the system of checks and balances and many feel that constitutional changes are needed.

- After 18 years of Tory rule Tony Blair of the *Labour Party* was elected Prime Minister.

# UNITED KINGDOM

## INTRODUCTIONS

When introduced to people in the United Kingdom, it is customary for both parties to say "How do you do?" (However, this is a rhetorical question and an answer is not expected.) People also consider it polite to add an expression of pleasure about meeting each other.

Always address a person as "Mr.," "Mrs." or "Miss" until invited to use a first name. First names may be used after a short acquaintance, although you should take your cue on this formality from the English. Professional titles, such as "Doctor" or "Professor" may also be used. (However, a surgeon should be addressed as "Mister" rather than "Doctor.") Knights and baronets are called "Sir" along with their first names (for example, *Sir Francis Chichester* becomes "Sir Francis").

Men shake hands. Since a handshake is arbitrary for women, a man should wait for a woman to extend her hand first. Handshakes should be firm but not aggressive.

After people have already been introduced, verbal greetings without a handshake are appropriate upon subsequent meetings.

Among friends, both men and women kiss each other lightly on both cheeks.

## SOCIAL TIPS AND CONVENTIONS

When beginning a conversation with someone whom you may have just met, it is suggested that you start with the weather as a safe topic, even if you complain about the British climate. Other good conversation topics include British history, architecture, gardening, the city you are visiting and positive aspects of the British role in world affairs (past and present).

The British are somewhat sensitive about national politics so it is best to avoid a discussion on this topic. Also avoid making negative remarks or jokes about the Royal Family, the British affection for their dogs, the British work ethic, money and prices, religion, Northern Ireland and England's decline as a world power.

The British are very reserved and respectful of privacy. It is wise to avoid loud or demonstrative behavior as well as personal questions. Personal space is respected and if someone stands too close, an English person will interpret this as being intrusive and pushy. Touching is also avoided.

Conversations are conducted in a reserved and somewhat indirect manner. Project your voice to reach only your conversation partner. Gestures are used moderately. In arguments, the British will become cooler and cooler rather than openly angry.

Be aware that British humor tends to be satirical and sarcastic.

Keep in mind that the British tend to end sentences, which are really statements, with a question. An answer to the question is not expected. For example, a British person may say "The sun rises in the morning, doesn't it?" or "It's a beautiful day, isn't it?"

The British, especially members of the older generation, consider manners to be very important. Good manners are expected from visitors.

## SOCIAL TIPS AND CONVENTIONS (Cont'd)

Be aware that the Scots, Welsh and Irish each have their own cultural identity. They should not be referred to as "English."

## CUSTOMARY BUSINESS PRACTICES

Punctuality is highly respected throughout the U.K.

It is suggested that letters be addressed formally, beginning with "Dear Sir" or "Dear Madam" and ending with "Yours faithfully."

Business communication is conducted in an impersonal and detailed manner. Formal presentations should be understated, thorough and matter-of-fact.

It is wise to have a less aggressive business style with the British. Allow them time and ample opportunity to speak.

Most businesses are open from 9:00 a.m to 5:00 p.m., Monday to Friday. However, an increasing number of businesses are offering longer hours or are staying open on weekends.

Most businesspeople take a coffee break at about 10:30 a.m. and a tea break at about 3:00 p.m.

Businessmen should wear dark suits and ties; businesswomen should wear dressy suits.

## BUSINESS ENTERTAINING

During a business meeting, you are likely to be offered coffee or tea. However, keep in mind that refreshments are not always served to visitors. The U.K. is one of the few places in the world where declining a beverage is *not* an offense.

Throughout the U.K., visitors are entertained both in private homes and in restaurants. If spouses are not present, it is customary practice to discuss business during the meal.

The British enjoy socializing during "tea" at about 4:00 p.m. This is a snack of tea, buns (cupcakes) or biscuits (cookies). If a main meat dish is added, the meal then becomes "High Tea," which is considered a substitute for dinner.

In general, it is best to be conservative in both gift-giving and entertainment to avoid any suggestion of intentions to bribe. Appropriate gifts include chocolates, flowers or wine.

When invited to someone's home where you will be the only guest, a small gift (flowers or chocolates) is appropriate. It is proper to send a thank-you note the next day.

At a restaurant, a waiter/waitress is summoned by raising the hand. At the end of a meal, the bill is brought on a plate on which a 10-15% tip should be left.

Certain customary practices pertain to cutlery. Eating utensils are laid out in the order in which they will be used, starting from the outside. Hold a fork with the left hand. Soft foods, including omelettes, casseroles and potatoes are not cut with a knife. Instead, use a fork to separate portions.

# UNITED KINGDOM (Cont'd)

## BUSINESS ENTERTAINING (Cont'd)

Refrain from smoking until the end of the meal. It is also appropriate to ask permission from your host. If you smoke, you should offer a cigarette to everyone in your group before lighting up.

For a dinner at a restaurant or someone's house, men should wear a jacket and tie and women should wear a dress or a blouse and a skirt. If an invitation indicates that the event is formal, this term could mean a variety of things. It is suggested that you take the invitation to a formal wear shop; they will be able to tell you what would be appropriate attire.

## DINING OUT

A dinner party usually begins at about 7:00 or 8:00 p.m. The meal starts with cocktails (gin and tonic, sherry or whiskey) and small appetizers. The first course is often a soup or a prawn cocktail. Meat or fish with potatoes and vegetables are then served, accompanied by a salad. Dinner ends with cheese and crackers, dessert, coffee and liqueurs (port, cognac or Grand Marnier). Plan on leaving a dinner party between 11:30 p.m. and midnight.

Traditional English dishes include crumpets (similar to English muffins), Cornish pastries (turnovers filled with meat and potatoes), *bangers-and-mash* (sausage and mashed potatoes), *cock-a-leekie soup* (chicken and leek soup), *toad-in-the-hole* (sausages baked in pastry), roast beef, Yorkshire pudding (a baked batter usually served in a muffin form), steak or kidney pie and trifle (sponge cake soaked in sherry, topped with custard, fruit and cream). A traditional cooked breakfast may include grilled or fried tomatoes, fried mushrooms or bread. The British also eat a wide variety of ethnic and European food.

There are numerous Chinese, Indian and Italian restaurants in England. Fish-and-chips establishments and pubs are also popular eating places. Most pubs serve anything from snacks to full meals. Fast food is also becoming more prevalent.

When you have finished your meal, place your knife and fork on your plate vertically side by side.

## PUBLIC CUSTOMS

People in the U.K. tend to be polite and relatively unassertive. At a bus stop, ticket office or shop counter, take your place in line. Refrain from pushing and shoving. Older people should be treated with respect.

Usually men hold doors open for women and stand when a woman enters a room.

Staring at people, shouting or displaying affection in public is inappropriate.

If you see someone in the street whom you know and eye contact has been established, it is appropriate to say "Hello," "Good Morning," "Good Afternoon" or "Good Evening."

"God Save the Queen" is sometimes played at the end of movies or plays. It is recommended that you stand along with the rest of the audience when it is played.

# Additional Information For International Business

This section of the Resource Book leaves you with some helpful information when conducting business internationally. This information allows you to become familiar with the background and key provisions of the Foreign Corrupt Practices Acts (FCPA). It also offers some sound practical advice on the use of agents and intermediaries if you should require such services. General gift-giving guidelines are also explored and provide a handy reference when doing business with other cultures. We address pointers for working with interpreters, making yourself understood abroad, language insights for native English speakers and international business card exchange.

# FOREIGN CORRUPT PRACTICES ACT (FCPA)

## BACKGROUND

*Post Watergate Environment*

- Moral fiber of nation thought to be in jeopardy.

*Mid 1970s – SEC Investigation*

- U.S. companies using corporate funds to influence foreign officials in order to obtain or retain business overseas.
    - Some practices were legal under local law, others were not
    - Customary "grease" payments e.g., clearing a ship for off-loading
    - Bribes to government officials to influence official policy
    - Political contributions – some legal under local law, others not

- Use of special funds ("slush funds"), sales agents, foreign subsidiaries.
    - Extortion by foreign officials
    - U.S. initiatives

- Over 400 U.S. companies disclosed substantial bribery activities. 117 of the companies were on the Fortune 500 list.

- Revelations rocked governments of Japan and Netherlands.

*May 12, 1976 – SEC Report*

- Report on questionable and illegal corporate payments and practices submitted to Senate Committee on Banking, Housing and Urban Affairs. Recommended legislation to ensure accountability for disclosure of future payments of these kinds.

- 94th Congress (1976) approved legislation for a direct ban on overseas bribes.

- December 19, 1977 Foreign Corrupt Practices Act became law.

*1988 – Omnibus Trade and Competitive Act*

- Amendments made to remove ambiguities, facilitate prosecutions and increase penalties upon conviction.

*Foreign Policy*

- Questionable payment practices of private multinational corporations had created risks for U.S. political relations with important foreign countries, at times and places outside the control of United States governmental authorities.
    - Complications arose with governments of Japan, Italy, Korea and the Netherlands

# FOREIGN CORRUPT PRACTICES ACT (FCPA) (Cont'd)

## BACKGROUND (Cont'd)

*Economics*

- Was argued that bribery introduces inefficient, non-market distortions into sales considerations, raising the cost of transactions to the consumer.

*Ethics*

- Senate report stated, "...bribery is simply unethical. It is counter to the moral expectations and values of the American public, and it erodes public confidence in the integrity of the free market system."

## PROVISIONS

*Major provisions*

- Anti-Bribery

- Record-Keeping and Internal Control

*Anti-Bribery*

- It is a crime for a bribe to be made to:

    - A foreign official
    - A foreign political party
    - Party officials
    - Candidates for political office

    for the purpose of obtaining or retaining business, or directing business to another person.

- It is also a crime if the bribe is paid directly to a third-party agent, consultant or intermediary with the purpose of being passed on – in whole or in part – to a foreign official, foreign political party, party official or candidate for political office.

---

**NOTE:** A "bribe" is defined broadly. The definition is such that it makes it a crime for any public corporation, or any officer, director, employee, agent or stockholder acting on behalf of the company, to make use of the mails or any means or instrumentality of interstate commerce corruptly in furtherance of an offer, payment, promise to pay, or authorization of the payment of any money, or offer, gift, promise to give, or authorization of the giving of anything of value to foreign officials, political parties, party officials or candidates.

---

## FOREIGN CORRUPT PRACTICES ACT (FCPA) (Cont'd)

### PROVISIONS (Cont'd)

- Penalties are severe:

    - Companies which violate the Act can be fined up to $2,000,000.
    - Individuals may be fined up to $100,000 and imprisoned for up to 5 years.

> **NOTE:** Any willful violation by a corporate employee or agent is punishable as a felony, irrespective of the firms adjudicated guilt or lack thereof.

    - Individual fines cannot be paid by the company.

> **NOTE:** There is no threshold amount to trigger the statute. Any payment qualifies, if it is made with a corrupt purpose.

- Payments for routine governmental action by a foreign official, political party or party official are allowed. Such payments are known as "facilitating," "expediting" or "grease" payments. The Act specifies what type of action is considered routine:

    - Dispensing permits, licenses and other official documents needed to qualify to do business in a foreign country.

    - Processing visas, work orders and other governmental papers.

    - Providing police protection, mail service and scheduling inspections related to contract performance or transporting goods in a foreign country.

    - Providing utilities (phone, power and water), loading and unloading cargo and protecting perishables from deterioration.

> **NOTE:** Any decision made or encouraged by a foreign official with respect to whether or on what terms new businesses will be awarded, or business continued with a particular party, is definitely not routine governmental action.

### *Record Keeping and Internal Control*

- Every SEC-reporting company must make and keep books, records and accounts which accurately and fairly reflect both the transactions and resulting dispositions of the company's assets.

    - Quantitative and qualitative aspects of transactions must be recorded.

    - The parent company is responsible for the books and records of subsidiaries.

# FOREIGN CORRUPT PRACTICES ACT (FCPA) (Cont'd)

## PROVISIONS (Cont'd)

*Record Keeping and Internal Control (Cont'd)*

– Every SEC reporting company must devise and maintain a system of internal accounting controls that meets four objectives:

1. All transactions are executed in accordance with management directives (i.e., the schedule of authorizations).

2. The method of recording transactions will facilitate the preparation of financial statements according to generally accepted accounting principles (GAAP).

3. That access to corporate assets will be safeguarded by management.

4. That recorded and existing assets will be compared at reasonable intervals and discrepancies resolved.

---

**NOTE:** Only the anti-bribery provisions of the Act specify that violations are punishable as crimes; however, failure to observe the accounting requirements may also lead to criminal prosecutions.

Also note that falsification of financial records subjects you to criminal exposure. The willful violation of any rule or regulation under the Exchange Act of 1934 is a felony punishable by 5 years in prison and/or a fine of $10,000.

---

## SOME OPEN ISSUES/PROBLEM AREAS

- When does a facilitating payment become a bribe?

    **Guideline:** If the action you're paying for is routine and has no bearing on the obtaining or retaining of business, you're okay.

- Who – or who isn't – a foreign government official?

    **Guideline:** Don't assume! Find out!

- How successfully can it be determined when a corporation should have "reason to know" that funds are being used in a prohibited fashion, especially when intervening parties such as agents or dealers may be involved?

    **Guideline:** It's your responsibility to know. Ignorance is no defense.

- Determining whether or not extortion is a legitimate defense when it has been used to extract payment from a company.

    **Guideline:** If you give in to extortion, then you may have more problems than you bargained for.

# FOREIGN CORRUPT PRACTICES ACT (FCPA) (Cont'd)

## ETHICAL DECISION MAKING QUESTIONS

### Regarding the Foreign Corrupt Practices Act

- Does the questionable situation involve making payments to a foreign official, foreign political party, official of a foreign political party, candidate for foreign political office or any third-party who will forward the payment(s), in part or in whole, to any of the above categories of individuals?

- Does the situation in question involve giving anything of value (payments, offers, promises to pay, gifts, etc.) for the purpose of obtaining or retaining business or directing business to another person?

- If a situation involves making payments, would the payments be for routine governmental action (as defined in the Act) or for "facilitating" the decision-making process with respect to the awarding or retaining of business?

- Do you record both quantitative and qualitative aspects of transactions?

- Does your company – and the foreign subsidiaries of your company – use a system of internal accounting controls that fulfills the guidelines set forth in the FCPA?

- Do the records of your company – and the foreign subsidiaries of your company – accurately reflect both the transactions and resulting disposition of assets?

### Regarding Corporate Codes of Conduct

- Does the situation involve compromising the standards of conduct as outlined by your company?

- Does the dilemma involve using corporate funds or resources for the support of political parties or candidates?

- Does the situation in question involve accepting gifts of other than nominal value, loans, personal favors, services, special privileges or unusual hospitality?

- Would the activity in question create a conflict of interest?

- Would providing the gift or entertainment in question to a customer create unfair obligation on the part of the customer? Give the perception that favorable treatment was sought?

- If the dilemma under scrutiny involves a third-party consultant, representative or agent, is the third-party individual acting in any manner that is inconsistent with company policies?

# USING AGENTS AND INTERMEDIARIES

The following suggestions should guide you if you require the services of a business agent or intermediary while conducting business abroad.

1.  Ask your prospective agent, intermediary, consultant – even your prospective legal counsel or banker – for references; you are entitled to know if they have done this kind of work before and, if so, for whom.

2.  Get an estimate of the charges involved for each discrete aspect of the work to be done and make sure you receive an itemized bill.

3.  If you are considering engaging a business representative to act as a commission agent, be sure of the following:

    •   Be certain the agreement with the agent is made on the basis of a written contract; unwritten understandings, on the basis of which an enterprising representative will undertake discussions on your behalf, are an invitation to real trouble.

    •   Review the agent's list of clients or at least obtain a written assurance that it does not include any of your competitors.

    •   Your agent is presumably selling an ability to help you succeed, so try to fix compensation on the basis of success achieved – if possible, solely on the basis of a commission for sales actually made, or a project successfully undertaken. If a monthly retainer must be paid, try to keep it low, and as an advance against any future commissions payable.

    •   Every agent has expenses, and you will very likely be expected to cover money advanced for what your agent does for your company alone (e.g., travel and telecommunication expenses). Control these expenses by setting a ceiling on what expenses the agent can incur without first obtaining your approval.

    •   Most agents want exclusivity, that is they want to be your sole representative for a fixed period of time. If you are willing to agree to an exclusive arrangement, be certain it does not foreclose your company from seeking to make its own contacts in the given country.

    •   Provide terms for cancelling your agent's services with or without cause, at your sole discretion.

    •   Require activity reports, if not progress reports, to be sure that your agent hasn't gone to sleep on your project.

# GIFT GIVING GUIDELINES

## GENERAL GUIDELINES

Whether gifts are business or social, an understanding of cultural differences is the key to selecting a successful gift and avoiding embarrassment. Appreciation of cultural differences will also expand your ability to be effective in dealing with foreign businesspeople , both here and abroad, and help you avoid common gift giving mistakes.

Each country has its own seasons and symbols for giving. Be careful to study the specific country and/or culture you will be doing business in so that you can tailor your gift giving for maximum effect. Some factors which must be taken into account include such influences as:

- the local and national economy

- social customs

- religious customs and holidays

- political concerns

While gift giving may appear to be as complex a task as learning a foreign language, certain general characteristics apply everywhere. The following list of questions will help businesspeople from American companies in deciding an appropriate gift for international gift giving.

- Is the gift within the guidelines prescribed by your company's Code of Business Conduct?

- Is the gift made in the United States?

    In a study conducted by Dr. Kathleen Kelley Reardon (Dept. of Communication Sciences, University of Connecticut) on international gift-giving practices, investigators found that 95% of the executives surveyed felt that it was somewhat or very important that an international business gift be distinctly American. Famous brand names usually get a warm reception. Gifts that reflect some part of America or distinctly American culture (i.e., pictures of the Old West, American magazines, maple syrup, cowboy hats, U.S. coins, etc.) are also appreciated.

- Does the gift have conversational value?

    In the research study mentioned above, 84% of those surveyed said that it was some-what or very important that a business gift have conversational value (i.e., that the gift be unique or unavailable in the recipient's country).

- Is the gift practical or useful?

- Does the gift have an internationally respected designer name?

    With a name like Gucci, Tiffany, Hermès, etc. on the label, the thought is often as significant as the content. Designer-made products are universally appreciated.

# GIFT GIVING GUIDELINES (Cont'd)

## GENERAL GUIDELINES (Cont'd)

- Could your gift be considered an invasion of the recipient's private life? (i.e., a gift for your counterpart's wife or husband could be seen as an inappropriate intrusion of their private lives.)

- Is your gift appropriate to the status of the person who receives it?

- Does your gift show good taste and thoughtfulness for the intended recipient?

While following the above guidelines won't answer all of your questions, they do help serve as an overall framework for international gift giving.

## CULTURAL DIFFERENCES AND PERCEPTIONS

What American businesspeople consider a bribe is considered good will and custom in many other countries. For example, consider the following scenario told by guide and translator Niu Ching-Lu to writer Bart Jackson:

> "The Japanese will come to negotiate a $10 million deal with a Chinese firm. The corporate principal will personally present each Chinese committee member with a color television. Through the day the deal gets rougher, looks like it will fall through. The Japanese call for a lunch break. They return with a motorbike for each member of the committee. The deal goes through. The Americans, for the same deal, send a lawyer. He brings out just one matching pen and pencil – I have seen this – and gives it to the head committee man. The deal dies."

This scenario typifies cultural – and legal – differences between American businesspeople and their foreign colleagues. Whereas many Americans flatly refuse to receive or give any gift at all, most people in other cultures enjoy and expect gifts. Furthermore, they see gift giving as an important part in establishing long-term good will. For them, gift giving is not a means to personal profit, but rather is a polite ritual that serves as a platform for mutual, profitable, enduring business.

Western interest lies in doing business; non-Western, in forming bonds so that business can begin. Westerners seek to discharge obligations; non-Westerners, to create them. Americans focus on producing short-term profits; non-Westerners focus on generating favors.

Note that in Third World countries, western-trained and educated nationals are simultaneously drawn to both indigenous and Western ideals. This means that they may have internalized the Western norms of personal enrichment along with those of modern commerce, while simultaneously adhering to indigenous traditions by fulfilling communal obligations. Requests for payoffs may spring from both these ideals, and American corporate responses must be designed to satisfy them both.

What is of great importance is considering the request for a gift or money in its local context. In nations where gifts generate a sense of obligation, it may prove best to give them, thereby creating "inner debts" among key foreign colleagues in the belief that they will repay them over time.

# GIFT GIVING GUIDELINES (Cont'd)

### GIFT OR BRIBE?

This question has puzzled travelers for centuries, so if you're ever confronted with an outright bribe, you might as well know the terminology.

*Mordida* (mor-DEE-da) Spanish for bribe. Especially known in Mexico. Literally, "a little bite."

*Grease* (greese) Also "facilitating payments." Refers to legal and permitted payments of modest sums to foreign officials for speedy action of their normal duties. Used almost everywhere, including the U.S.

*Kumshaw* (KUM-shaw) Southeast Asian term for bribe.

In most cultures, gift giving is an established business custom that often yields tangible – sometimes extraordinary – results. However, no line exists dividing gifts from bribes. It seems that direct solicitation of gifts involves smaller amounts, while larger ones require go-betweens. Furthermore, while smaller gifts may signal a desire to work with the local business circles, a company that supplies larger sums could violate both local anti-payoff statutes and the Foreign Corrupt Practices Act.

With most business dealings, a happy middle path can be found which cuts successfully between rudeness and outright bribery, a path in which one can maintain personal and company ethics without rejecting other countries' cultural norms. In order to do so, you need to verify that:

- The gift giving wouldn't be in conflict with the law of the United States;

- Gift giving is a custom in your host country;

- Your gift is not a cash payment;

- Your company's gift giving is part of the overall strategy and is part of your company's budget.

*Sources: "Giving Abroad: Separating Gifts from Gaffes," Richard D. Smith, US 1, September 12, 1990; "Do's and Taboos Around the World," Parker Pen Co., John Wiley & Sons, 1985; "Beware the Purple Pigskin Clock," Dawn Bryan, Sales & Marketing Management, August 1990; "A Traveler's Guide to Gifts and Bribes," Jeffrey A. Fadiman, Harvard Business Review, July-August 1986.*

# WORKING WITH INTERPRETERS

1. Brief your interpreter in advance about the subject and your objectives.

2. Speak clearly, slowly and concisely.

3. Avoid little-known or difficult words.

4. Explain your major idea two or three different ways, as your point may be lost if expressed only once.

5. Do not talk more than a minute or two without breaking for interpretation.

6. Do not depend on your foreign counterpart's interpreter to effectively communicate your messages. If you need an interpreter, hire and brief one for yourself.

7. Allow time for the interpreter to clarify obscure points.

8. Never interrupt the interpreter.

9. Avoid long sentences, double negatives or negative wordings when a positive form could be used.

10. When speaking, always look at your foreign counterpart.

11. During meetings, write out the main points agreed upon so that both parties can check their understandings.

12. Ask the interpreter for advice if communication problems arise.

13. Allow your interpreter adequate rest periods.

14. Consider using two interpreters if interpreting is to last into the evening.

15. Be understanding if it develops that the interpreter has made a mistake.

*Adapted from "Managing Cultural Differences" by P. Harris and R. Moran, Gulf Publishing Co., 1987.*

# MAKING YOURSELF UNDERSTOOD ABROAD

**DO'S:**

- Speak plainly, clearly and slowly, but not loudly.

- Present only one point at a time.

- Paraphrase what has been said by asking, "Did I understand you to say that..."

- Confirm phone conversations by fax or telex.

- Use visual aids and printed matter wherever possible and follow up any meeting with a written summary.

- Learn the basics of your foreign associate's language (verbal and nonverbal) and use both languages, yours and theirs, when presenting material.

- Watch what others do and how they say things, and take your cues from them.

**DON'TS:**

- Do not use slang, jargon, colloquialisms, regional expressions or sports talk.

- Be wary of using American humor; it may not translate well.

- Do not use numerals unless you write them out.

- Do not rush negotiations or "push" the American way of doing things on your foreign associate.

- Do not interrupt a foreign associate when he or she is speaking.

- Never say "You're not making yourself clear."

# LANGUAGE INSIGHTS FOR NATIVE ENGLISH SPEAKERS

Most Americans are unable to conduct business in a language other than English. While it is desirable to speak in the language(s) of those from the country with which you are dealing, the following suggestions may help you communicate with non-native English speakers.

1. Practice using the most common 3,000 words in English; that is, those words typically learned by non-native speakers in their first two years of language study. Avoid uncommon or esoteric words and use simple words instead.

2. Restrict your use of English words to their most common meaning. Many words have multiple meanings, and non-native speakers are most likely to know the first or second most common meanings. For example, "to address" to mean "to send" (rather than "to consider") and "impact" to mean "the force of a collision" (rather than "effect").

3. Whenever possible, select an action-specific verb (e.g., "ride the bus"). Verbs to avoid include "do," "make," "get," "have," "be" and "go." For example, the verb "get" can have at least five meanings – buy, borrow, steal, rent, retrieve – as in, "I'll get a car and meet you in an hour."

4. In general, select a word with few alternate meanings (such as "accurate," which has one meaning) rather than a word with many alternate meanings (such as "right," which has 27 meanings).

5. Become aware of words whose primary meaning is restricted elsewhere. For example, outside of the United States, "check" most commonly means a financial instrument and is frequently spelled "cheque."

6. Become aware of alternate spellings of commonly used words and the regions where those spellings are used: for example, colour/color, organisation/organization, centre/center.

7. Resist changing a word's part of speech from its most common usage; for example, avoid saying "a warehousing operation" or "attachable assets."

8. Conform to basic grammar rules more strictly than is common in everyday conversation. Make sure that sentences express a complete thought, that pronouns and antecedents are used correctly, and that subordination is accurately expressed. For example, the sentence, "No security regulations shall be distributed to personnel that are out of date," needs to be rewritten as "Do not distribute out-of-date security regulations to personnel."

9. Clarify the meaning of modal auxiliaries; for example, be sure that the reader will understand whether "should" means moral obligation, expectation, social obligation or advice.

10. Avoid "word pictures," constructions that depend for their meaning on invoking a particular mental image (e.g., "run that by me," "wade through these figures," "slice of the free world pie"). A particular form of mental imagery likely to cause misunderstandings is the use of assumptions contrary to fact (e.g., "suppose you were me," "suppose there were no sales").

# LANGUAGE INSIGHTS FOR NATIVE ENGLISH SPEAKERS (Cont'd)

11. Avoid terms borrowed from sports (e.g., "struck out," "field that question," "touch-down," "can't get to first base," "ballpark figure") Also, avoid terms borrowed from literature (e.g., "catch-22") and the military (e.g., "run it up the flag pole," "run a tight ship").

12. When writing to someone you do not know well, use his or her last name and keep the tone formal while expressing personal interest or concern. Initial sentences can express appreciation (e.g., "We are extremely grateful to your branch...") or personal connection (e.g., "Mr. Ramos has suggested...") Closing phrases can express personal best wishes (e.g., "With warmest regards, I remain sincerely yours...").

13. Whenever the cultural background of your reader is known, try to adapt your tone to the manner in which such information – apology, suggestion, refusal, thanks, request, directive – is usually conveyed in his or her culture. For example, apologies may need to be sweeping and unconditional (e.g., "My deepest apologies for any problems..." ) Refusals may need to be indirect (e.g., "Your proposal contains some interesting points that we need to study further...").

14. If possible, determine and reflect the cultural values of your reader on such dimensions as espousing control versus adaptation to one's environment, emphasizing individual versus collective accomplishments, or focusing on quantitative versus qualitative changes. When in doubt, include a variety of value orientations: "I want to thank you [individual] and your department [collective]...."

15. When the cultural background of your reader is known, try to capture the flavor of his or her language. For example, communications to Spanish-speakers would be more flowery and lengthy than those to German-speakers.

16. Whenever possible, adopt the reasoning style of your reader or present information in more than one format. For example, the following sentence contains both a general position statement and inductive reasoning: "Trust among business partners is essential; and our data show that our most successful joint ventures are those in which we invested initial time building a personal trusting relationship."

*Adapted from "The Journal of Language for International Business," Spring 1985, D.I. Riddle and Z.D. Lanham. "International Written Business English."*

# INTERNATIONAL BUSINESS CARD EXCHANGE

- Overall, the tone of the business card exchange should be slow, deliberate and formal. Quick motions and speech can signify disrespect.

- Give your business card with one hand and receive business cards with both hands.

- After you have received a business card, study it carefully. Immediately pocketing the card would be considered an insult. Handle the card formally. Do not flip, stroke or put the card into your rear pants pocket.

- Make certain your own cards are in prime condition.

- It is appropriate to ask the giver how to pronounce his or her name. Card exchange is the proper time to inquire about pronunciation.

- It is not inappropriate for you to exchange cards with a person a second time if any information on your card has been changed.

- Make certain you have a sufficient supply of cards. Japanese businessmen, in particular, claim that Americans often say they've "just run out."

- Never inflate your job title.

- Consider having your card translated into the language of people you are visiting or hosting.

# Source Materials And Useful Resources

The potential list of useful cross-cultural materials is enormous. We have selected a sample that offers sound, practical advice for the business person.

You will learn best when you have a specific need, e.g., business trip or overseas assignment. Even on these occasions, however, you will learn more efficiently and effectively if you have maintained an on-going interest in cross-cultural business issues. Make your own additions to our list of resources; maintain a personal file of articles, reports, etc. *As the world gets smaller, your international files should be getting bigger.*

# SOURCE MATERIALS

**The following publications served as source material for the development of this program.**

Adler, N.J., *"Women in International Management: Where Are They?,"* California Management Review, vol. 26, no. 4, Summer 1984, pp. 78-89.

Adler, Nancy, *International Dimensions of Organizational Behavior,* Boston: Kent Publishing, 1986.

Adler, Nancy J., *"Pacific Basin Managers: A Gaijin, Not a Woman,"* Human Resource Management, vol. 26, Summer 1987, p. 169 (23).

Althen, G., *American Ways, A Guide for Foreigners in the United States,* Yarmouth, ME: Intercultural Press, 1988.

Axtell, R., *Do's and Taboos Around the World*, 3rd Edition, New York: John Wiley & Sons, 1993.

Axtell, R., *Do's and Taboos of Hosting International Visitors*, New York: John Wiley & Sons, 1989.

Barker, Joel Arthur, *Discovering the Future: The Business of Paradigms,* St. Paul, MN: ILI Press, 1989.

Bartlett, Christopher and Sumatra Ghoshal, *Managing Across Borders: The Transnational Solution,* Cambridge, MA: Harvard Business School Press, 1989.

Bartlett, Christopher and Sumatra Ghoshal, *"Matrix Management: Not a Structure, a Frame of Mind,"* Harvard Business Review, July-August 1990, pp. 138-45.

Bartlett, Christopher and Sumatra Ghoshal, *"Organizing for Worldwide Effectiveness: The Transnational Solution,"* California Management Review, vol. 31, no. 1 (1988).

Baskerville, Dawn M., et. al., *"21 Women of Power and Influence in Corporate America,"* Black Enterprise, vol. 22, no. 1, pp. 39-90, Aug. 1991.

Brake, Terence, Danielle Medina Walker, and Thomas D. Walker, *Doing Business Internationally: The Guide to Cross-Cultural Success,* Burr Ridge, IL: Irwin Professional Publishing, 1994.

Brake, Terence and Danielle Walker, *Doing Business Internationally: The Workbook to Cross-Cultural Success*, Princeton, NJ: Princeton Training Press, 1994.

Bridges, William, *The Character of Organizations* (a diagnostic testing instrument), Palo Alto, CA: Consulting Psychologists Press, 1992.

Broganti, Nancy L. and Elizabeth Devine, *The Traveler's Guide to European Customs & Manners,* Deephaven, MN: Meadowbrook, Inc., 1984.

Carney, Larry S. and Charlotte G. O'Kelly, *"Barriers and Constraints to the Recruitment and Mobility of Female Managers in the Japanese Labor Force,"* Human Resource Management, vol. 26, Summer 1987, p. 193 (24).

Central Intelligence Agency, *The World Factbook 1992*, Washington, DC: U.S. Government Printing Office, 1992.

## SOURCE MATERIALS (Cont'd)

Chesanow, Neil, *The World Class Executive: How to Do Business Like a Pro Around the World*, New York: Bantam Books, 1985.

Clutterbuck, D., *"Dow Makes the Most of Womanpower,"* International Management, vol. 31, no. 11, Nov. 1976, pp. 27-8.

Condon, J. C., *Good Neighbors: Communicating with Mexicans,* Yarmouth, ME: Intercultural Press, 1985.

Condon, J. C., *With Respect to the Japanese: A Guide for Americans,* Yarmouth, ME: Intercultural Press, 1984.

Copeland, Lennie and Lewis Griggs, *Going International: How to Make Friends and Deal Effectively in the International Marketplace,* New York: Random House, 1985.

Devine, Elizabeth and Nancy L. Broganti, *The Traveler's Guide to Latin American Customs & Manners*, New York: St. Martin's Press, 1988.

Doz, Yves, *Strategic Management in International Companies,* New York: Pergamon Press, 1986.

Drucker, Peter F., *Managing in Turbulent Times,* New York: Harper & Row, 1980.

Drucker, Peter F., *The Changing World of the Executive,* New York: Times Books, 1985.

Drucker, Peter F., *The New Realities,* New York: Harper & Row, 1989.

Elledge, Robin and Steven Phillips, *Teambuilding Sourcebook*, San Diego, CA: University Associates Press, 1989.

Engholm, Christopher, *When Business East Meets Business West: The Guide to Practice and Protocol in the Pacific Rim*, New York: John Wiley & Sons, 1991.

Evans, Paul, Yves Doz, and Andre Laurent, eds., *Human Resource Management in International Firms: Change, Globalization, Innovation,* New York: St. Martin's Press, 1990.

Feig, John Paul, *A Common Core: Thais and Americans,* Yarmouth, ME: Intercultural Press, 1989.

Ferguson, Henry, *Tomorrow's Global Executive,* Homewood, IL: Dow Jones-Irwin, 1988.

Fisher, Glen, *Mindsets: The Role of Culture and Perception in International Relations,* Yarmouth, ME: Intercultural Press, 1988.

Foster, Dean Allen, *Bargaining Across Borders: How to Negotiate Business Successfully Anywhere in the World*, New York: McGraw-Hill, 1992.

George III, Munchus, *"Discrimination Against Working Women in Japan,"* Women in Management Review, vol. 8, no. 1, pp. 9-14, 1993.

Ghadar, Fariborz, Phillip D. Grub, Robert T. Moran, and Marshall Geer, *Global Business Management in the 1990s,* Washington DC: Beacham Publishing, Inc., 1990.

# SOURCE MATERIALS (Cont'd)

Gibbs, Paul, *The Largest Market in the World*, Holbrook, MA: Bob Adams, Inc., 1990.

Gross, Thomas, Ernie Turner, and Lars Cederholm, *"Building Teams for Global Operations,"* Management Review, June 1987, pp. 32-36.

Hall, Edward T., *Beyond Culture,* Garden City, NY: Anchor/Doubleday, 1976.

Hall, Edward T., *The Hidden Dimension,* New York: Anchor Press, 1966.

Hall, Edward T., *The Silent Language,* New York: Doubleday & Company, 1959.

Hall, E.T. and M.R. Hall, *Hidden Differences: Doing Business with the Japanese*, New York: Doubleday, 1987.

Hall, E.T. and M.R. Hall, *Understanding Cultural Differences: Germans, French, and Americans,* Yarmouth, ME: Intercultural Press, 1990.

Harris, Phillip R. and Robert T. Moran, *Managing Cultural Differences* (Third Edition), Houston, TX: Gulf Publishing, 1991.

Harris, Philip and Robert Moran, *Managing Cultural Differences* (Second Edition), Houston, TX: Gulf Publishing, 1987.

Harris, Philip R., and Dorothy L. Harris, *"Women Managers and Professionals Abroad,"* Journal of Managerial Psychology, vol. 3, no. 4, pp. i-ii, 1988.

Heger, Kyle, *"A Tale of Two Lucys,"* Communication World, vol. 6, Jan. 1989, p. 32 (4).

Hoecklin, Lisa Adent, "Managing Cultural Differences for Competitive Advantage," Special Report No. P. 656, London: The Economist Intelligence Unit, 1993.

Hoffman, J., *The International Assignment: Is It For You?,* Foster City, CA: D.C.W. Research Associate Press, 1982.

Hofstede, Geert, *Culture's Consequences: International Differences in Work-Related Values,* Beverly Hills, CA: Sage Publishing, 1980.

Hofstede, Geert, *Cultures and Organizations: Software of the Mind,* London: McGraw-Hill, 1991.

Hendon, Donald W. and Rebecca Angeles Hendon, *World Class Negotiating: Deal Making in the Global Marketplace,* New York: John Wiley, 1990.

Hersey, Paul and Kenneth Blanchard, *The Management of Organizational Behavior* (Third Edition), Englewood Cliffs, NJ: Prentice Hall, 1976.

Imai, Masaaki, *Kaizen: The Key to Japan's Competitive Success,* New York: Random House, 1986.

Izraeli, D.N., et. al., *"Women Executives in MNC Subsidiaries,"* California Management Review, vol. 23, no. 1, Fall 1980, pp. 53-63, Bibliog. 41.

## SOURCE MATERIALS (Cont'd)

Keirsey, David and Marilyn Bates, *Please Understand Me: Character and Temperament Types,* Del Mar, CA: Prometheus Nemesis Book Company, 1984.

Kluckhohn, Florence and Frederick L. Strodtbeck, *Variations in Value Orientations,* Evanston, IL: Row, Peterson and Company, 1956.

Kohls, L. R., *Survival Kit for Overseas Living* (Second Edition), Yarmouth, ME: Intercultural Press, 1984.

Korn/Ferry International and Columbia School of Business, *21st Century Report: Reinventing the CEO,* New York: Korn/Ferry International, 1989.

Kras, E., *Management in Two Cultures: Bridging the Gap Between U.S. and Mexican Managers,* Yarmouth, ME: Intercultural Press, 1989.

Kupfer, Andre, *"How to be a Global Manager,"* Fortune, March 14, 1988, pp. 43-48.

Lanier, Alison R., *The Rising Sun on Main Street: Working With the Japanese*, Yardley, PA: International Information Associates, 1990.

Lansing, Paul, and Kathryn Ready, *"Hiring Women Managers in Japan: An Alternative for Foreign Employers,"* California Management Review, vol. 30, Spring, 1988, p. 112 (16).

Laurent, Andre, *"The Cross-Cultural Puzzle of Human Resource Management,"* Human Resource Management, vol. 25, no. 1, (Spring 1986), pp. 91-102.

Lee, S. K. Jean, and Tan Hwee Hoon, *"Rhetorical Vision of Men and Women Managers in Singapore,"* Human Relations, vol. 46, no. 4, pp. 527-42, April 1993.

Levitt, Theodore, *"The Globalization of Markets,"* Harvard Business Review, May-June 1983, pp. 92-102.

Lobel, Sharon A., *"Global Leadership Competencies: Managing to a Different Drumbeat,"* Human Resource Management, vol. 29, no. 1 (Spring 1990), pp. 39-47.

Maddock, Su, and Di Parkin, *"Gender Cultures: Women's Choices and Strategies at Work,"* Women in Management Review, vol. 8, no. 2, pp. 3-9, 1993.

Mead, Richard, *Cross-Cultural Management Communication,* New York: John Wiley, 1990.

Mole, John, *Mind Your Manners: Culture Clash in the Single European Market,* London: The Industrial Society, 1990.

Moran, Robert T. and William G. Stripp, *Dynamics of Successful International Business Negotiations,* Houston, TX: Gulf Publishing, 1991.

Nydell, Margaret K., *Understanding Arabs: A Guide for Westerners,* Yarmouth, ME: Intercultural Press, 1987.

Ohmae, Kenichi, *The Borderless World,* New York: Harper Business Press, 1990.

# SOURCE MATERIALS (Cont'd)

Ohmae, Kenichi, *"The Logic of Strategic Alliances,"* Harvard Business Review, March-April 1989, pp. 143-54.

*"Other Men's Shoes – Gill Lewis – A Toast to A Modern Marketing Success,"* The Director, vol. 30, no. 10, April 1978, p. 25.

Perlmutter, Howard V. and David A. Heenan, *"Cooperate to Compete Globally,"* Harvard Business Review, March-April 1986.

Peters, Thomas, *Thriving on Chaos: Handbook for a Management Revolution,* New York: Harper & Row, 1988.

Porter, Michael, ed., *Competition in Global Business,* Cambridge, MA: Harvard Business School Press, 1986.

Povall, M., *"Overcoming Barriers to Women's Advancement In European Organizations,"* City University, Personnel Review, vol. 13, no. 1, 1984, pp. 32-40.

Povall, M., et. al., *"Banking on Women Managers,"* Management Today, Feb. 1982, pp. 50-3, 108.

Prahalad, C.K. and Yves Doz, *The Multinational Mission: Balancing Local Demands and Global Vision,* New York: Free Press, 1987.

Quelch, John A. and Edward J. Hoff, *"Customizing Global Marketing,"* Harvard Business Review, May-June 1986, pp. 59-86.
Reich, Robert B., *"Who is Them?"* Harvard Business Review, March-April 1991, pp. 77-88.

Reich, Robert B., *"Who is Us?"* Harvard Business Review, January-February 1990, pp. 53-64.

Reier, S., *"The Feminine Mystique,"* Institutional Investor, vol. 18, no. 7, July 1984, pp. 223-4, 226.

Rhinesmith, Stephen H., *"Americans in the Global Learning Process,"* The Annals of the American Academy of Political and Social Science, vol. 442 (March 1979), pp. 98-108.

Rhinesmith, Stephen H., *A Manager's Guide to Globalization: Six Keys to Success in a Changing World,* Homewood, IL: Business One Irwin, 1993. (Co-published with the American Society for Training and Development, Alexandria, VA)

Rhinesmith, Stephen H., *"An Agenda for Globalization,"* Training and Development Journal, February 1991, pp. 22-29.

Rhinesmith, Stephen H., *Cultural-Organizational Analysis: The Interrelationship Between Value Orientations and Managerial Behavior,* Cambridge, MA: McBer and Company, 1971.

Rhinesmith, Stephen H., *"Going Global from the Inside Out,"* Training and Development Journal, November 1991, pp. 42-47.

Rhinesmith, Stephen H., John N. Williamson, David M. Ehlen, and Denise S. Maxwell, *"Developing Leaders for a Global Enterprise,"* Training and Development Journal, April 1989, pp. 24-34.

# SOURCE MATERIALS (Cont'd)

Ricks, D., et al., *International Business Blunders*, Washington, DC: Transemantics, 1974.

Rossman, Marlene, *The International Businesswoman of the 1990s*, New York: Praeger Publishers, 1990.

*SRI International Business Intelligence Program,* "Strategic Partnering: Keys to Success in the 1990s," D88-1255, 1988.

*SRI International Business Intelligence Program,* "More About Strategic Alliances," D88-1256, 1988.

Schein, Edgar H., *Organizational Culture and Leadership,* San Francisco: Jossey-Bass, 1989.

Shaeffer, Ruth G., *"Building Global Teamwork for Growth and Survival,"* The Conference Board Research Bulletin, no. 228, 1989.

Singer, Marshall R., *Intercultural Communication: A Perceptual Approach*, Englewood Cliffs, NJ: Prentice Hall (Simon & Schuster), 1987.

Skabelund, Grant Paul, (managing ed.), *Culturgrams* , Provo, UT: Brigham Young University, David M. Kennedy Center for Int'l Studies, 1993.

Steingraber, Fred G., *"Managing in the 1990s,"* Business Horizons, January-February 1990, pp. 49-61.

Stewart, E. C. and M.J. Bennett, *American Cultural Patterns: A Cross-Cultural Perspective* (Revised Edition), Yarmouth, ME: Intercultural Press, 1991.

Taylor, Lee, *"Developing an Organizational Strategy for Equal Opportunities: A Case Study From the Open University, UK,"* Women in Management Review, vol. 8, no. 2, pp. 24-8, 1993.

Taylor, William, *"The Logic of Global Business: An Interview with ABB's Percy Barnevik,"* Harvard Business Review, March-April 1991, pp. 91-105.

Tiglao, Rigaberto, "Far Eastern Economic Review," January 30, 1997, p. 17.

Terpstra, Vern and Kenneth David, *The Cultural Framework of International Business* (Second Edition), Pelham Manor, NY: South-Western Publishing, 1985.

Wolniansky, Natalia, *"International Training for Global Leadership,"* Management Review, May 1992.

Yoon, Julie, and Brian H. Kleiner, *What Companies Can Do For Women,* Equal Opportunities International, vol. 12, no. 1, 1993.

# SOURCE MATERIALS (Cont'd)

Copeland Griggs Productions: *Going International*

| | | |
|---|---|---|
| Part 1 | "Bridging the Culture Gap" | 28 minutes |
| Part 2 | "Managing the Overseas Assignment" | 29 minutes |
| Part 3 | "Beyond Culture Shock" | 28 minutes |
| Part 4 | "Welcome Home Stranger" | 14 minutes |
| Part 5 | "Working in the U.S.A." | 30 minutes |
| Part 6 | "Living in the U.S.A." | 30 minutes |
| Part 7 | "Going International Safely" | 30 minutes |

Copeland Griggs Productions: *Valuing Diversity*

| | | |
|---|---|---|
| Part 1 | "Managing Differences" | 30 minutes |
| Part 2 | "Diversity at Work" | 30 minutes |
| Part 3 | "Communicating Across Cultures" | 30 minutes |

Contact: Copeland Griggs Productions, 302 23rd Ave., San Francisco, CA 94121

Ernst & Young/MultiMedia, Inc.

*The Ernst & Young Guide to the European Single Market*

| | | |
|---|---|---|
| Tape 1 | | 21 minutes |
| | Introduction | |
| | Part One – Europe '92 | |
| | Part Two – Financial Issues | |

| | | |
|---|---|---|
| Tape 2 | | 14 minutes |
| | Part Three – Legal Issues | |
| | Part Four – External Trade | |
| | Part Five – Strategies | |

Contact: MultiMedia Inc., 15 N. Summit St., Tenafly, NJ 07670

## OTHER:

Economist Intelligence Unit: *How-to-Guides for International Managers*
Reports on business strategies from leading international companies

Contact: Business International Corp., 215 Park Avenue South, New York, NY 10003

Intercultural Press: *Current Intercultural Resources*
Listing of cross-cultural books, videos and other materials

Contact: Intercultural Press, 16 US Route One, P.O. Box 700, Yarmouth, Maine 04096

## Doing Business Internationally: The Resource Book to Business & Social Etiquette

*by Training Management Corporation*
(481 pages)    ISBN: 1-882390-07-5    $48.00 U.S.

***Doing Business Internationally: The Resource Book to Business and Social Etiquette*** is the capstone of the ***Doing Business Internationally*** series. This reference book provides information on protocol, business and social practices and communications in order to make life easier for both traveling and home-based personnel when dealing with different cultures. This Resource Book provides a simple frame of reference for profiling and understanding the major characteristics of cultures around the globe. Regional cultural profiles for every part of the world are provided along with business and social etiquette guidelines for over 90 specific countries. This book is an excellent frame of reference for anyone traveling or doing business in a culture other than their own. It will also benefit readers when they are thinking of expanding business overseas and want a quick overview of some of the challenges they may face.

## Doing Business Internationally: The Guide to Cross-Cultural Success

*by Terence Brake, Danielle Medina Walker, Thomas (Tim) Walker*
(284 pages)    ISBN: 0-7863-0117-1    $25.00 U.S.

***Doing Business Internationally: The Guide to Cross-Cultural Success*** provides executives and managers with the knowledge and skills they will need to compete in today's global marketplace. This is the ideal guide for executives and managers who are seeking to leverage culture and turn it into competitive advantage. The guide establishes the key principles of communication and negotiation across cultural lines and identifies the dynamics and scope of today's global workforce.

This hard cover book represents a rich composite of research, interviews and training guidelines based on the authors' 25 years of experience in the global business environment. Executives and managers with, or likely to have, international responsibilities, will need the information presented in this book in order to succeed.

## Doing Business Internationally: The Workbook to Cross-Cultural Success

*by Terence Brake, Danielle Medina Walker*
(269 pages)    ISBN: 1-882390-00-8    $49.50 U.S.

***Doing Business Internationally: The Workbook to Cross-Cultural Success*** is the companion, self-paced manual for TMC's popular international business seminar, ***Doing Business Internationally***. It was designed to compliment ***The Guide to Cross-Cultural Success***, although each one can be used independently of one another as a learning tool. It is intended for those who cannot fit a full seminar into their schedules and are looking for independent study. The book is organized into four modules:

- Global Business Thinking
- Communication
- Cross-Cultural Awareness
- Working and Managing

This workbook presents a program for building the knowledge and skills that will help executives and managers operate effectively in a variety of cultural settings and achieve cross-cultural success.

## Doing Business Internationally: Business Reports

*by Craighead Publications Inc.*          $29.95 U.S.

***Doing Business Internationally: Business Reports*** are designed to help the international business person succeed in today's global marketplace. These country-specific business reports provide a thorough and insightful review of information necessary to conduct business successfully with people from different cultures and countries. Topics include:

- General Country Orientation
- An Overview of Economic and Political Developments
- Business Etiquette and Protocol
- Business Meetings and Entertainment
- Business Networking and References
- Social Customs
- Holidays
- Gift Giving
- Financial Matters
- Communications
- Health and Safety Concerns
- Medical Care and Services
- Visas and Permits
- Airline and Airport Information
- Car Rental Details and Ground Transportation
- Hotels, Restaurants and Nightlife

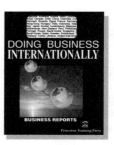

***Doing Business Internationally: Business Reports*** are available for over 50 different countries. Each guide is updated and revised annually.

---

## Business Reports Currently Available:

| | | |
|---|---|---|
| Argentina | Hong Kong | Portugal |
| Australia | Hungary | Russia |
| Austria | India | Saudi Arabia |
| Baltic Countries [1] | Indonesia | Singapore |
| Belgium | Ireland [2] | South Africa |
| Brazil | Israel | South Korea |
| Canada | Italy | Spain |
| Chile | Japan | Sweden |
| China | Kuwait | Switzerland |
| Colombia | Luxembourg | Taiwan |
| Czech & Slovak Republics | Malaysia | Thailand |
| Denmark | Mexico | Turkey |
| Ecuador | Netherlands | Ukraine |
| Egypt | New Zealand | United Arab Emirates |
| France | Peru | United Kingdom [3] |
| Germany | Philippines | Venezuela |
| Greece | Poland | Vietnam |

1   includes Estonia, Latvia and Lithuania
2   includes Northern Ireland
3   includes England, Scotland and Northern Ireland